HUBERT HUMPHREY

HUBERT HUMPHREY

The Conscience of the Country

Arnold A. Offner

Yale

UNIVERSITY

PRESS

New Haven & London

Yale University Press books may be purchased in quantity for educational, business, or promotional use. For information, please e-mail sales.press@yale.edu (US office) or sales@yaleup.co.uk (UK office).

Set in Electra and Trajan types by IDS Infotech Ltd. Printed in the United States of America.

Library of Congress Control Number: 2017963184
ISBN 978-0-300-22239-5 (hardcover : alk. paper)

A catalogue record for this book is available from the British Library.

This paper meets the requirements of ANSI/NISO Z39.48-1992 (Permanence of Paper).

10 9 8 7 6 5 4 3 2 1

For Ellen

CONTENTS

Preface   ix

Acknowledgments   xiii

Prologue   1

ONE   A New Star Is Born   9

TWO   The People's Mayor   24

THREE   The Next Senator from Minnesota   40

FOUR   Lonely, Bitter, and Broke in the Senate   59

FIVE   Confrontation and Cooperation   71

SIX   Prominence and Courtship   85

SEVEN   The Price of Leadership   101

EIGHT   Liberal without Apology   115

NINE   Candidate in Orbit, 1958–1960   134

TEN   The Insider as Outsider   152

ELEVEN   Tragedy and Triumph   170

TWELVE   The Best Man in America   193

THIRTEEN   LBJ versus HHH: The Great Society and Vietnam   210

FOURTEEN Humphrey's Vietnam Wars 230

FIFTEEN Northwest's Passage 249

SIXTEEN Last Man In 268

SEVENTEEN The Siege of Chicago 291

EIGHTEEN Battling the Torrents—and Johnson 315

NINETEEN Resurrection and Defeat 336

TWENTY A Time for Everything 364

Epilogue: The Conscience of the Country 391

Notes 395

Bibliography 453

Index 467

Illustrations follow page 222

PREFACE

This book, *Hubert Humphrey: The Conscience of the Country*, explores Humphrey's more than thirty-year mayoral and national career as the standard-bearer of American liberalism. Humphrey was elected twice as mayor of Minneapolis, five times as United States senator, and once as vice president, and he was his party's presidential nominee in 1968, when he lost a historically close election to Richard Nixon. In 1977, legendary Massachusetts Democratic Speaker of the House Thomas P. "Tip" O'Neill called Humphrey "the most genuine liberal the country has ever produced" and said he had "played a dramatic role in shaping every major legislative initiative that has become law in the past twenty-five years." In 1978, one thousand past and present congressional aides voted Humphrey the most effective legislator of the twentieth century.

Most significant, Kansas Republican senator Robert Dole said that although Humphrey had "overshot the Nation's highest office," he had become "one of the great world leaders—one of the major moral forces of our time or of any time." President Jimmy Carter, who believed that Humphrey deserved to be president, stated that from time to time the United States "is blessed by men and women who bear the mark of greatness and who help us see a better vision of what we are and what we might become," and Hubert Humphrey "was such a man." Vice President Walter Mondale called him "the country's conscience."

My prior scholarly research has focused on the history of American foreign relations from the era of Woodrow Wilson through Franklin Roosevelt and Harry Truman. But when I set out more than a decade ago to write a general history of the post–Second World War era, my research increasingly pointed to Humphrey as a major force for nearly every important liberal policy initiative, beginning with his bringing an urban New Deal to Minneapolis to his daring civil rights speech at the Democrats' convention in 1948 that urged his party "to get out of the shadow of states' rights and to walk forthrightly into the bright sunshine of human rights," putting civil rights on his party's and the nation's agenda for decades to come. As senator, he proposed legislation to effect national health insurance, foreign aid to poorer nations, immigration and income tax reform, a Jobs Corps, the Peace Corps, the Arms Control and Disarmament Agency, and the path-breaking 1963 Limited Test Ban Treaty, which opened the way to later nuclear nonproliferation and strategic arms reduction agreements. His masterful stewardship of the historic 1964 Civil Rights Act through the Senate led to the 1965 Voting Rights Act and 1968 Fair Housing Act. He became an advocate of global détente, "containment without isolation" of the People's Republic of China, and limits on the president's power to wage war without Congress's consent. Finally, his Full Employment and Balanced Growth Act sought to make a job a "right," but Congress eliminated this and made "full employment" a "goal" rather than a mandated target.

Significantly, both as a senator in 1964 and as vice president in early 1965, Humphrey, almost alone among senior officials, warned Johnson against expanding the Vietnam conflict. It could not be won by military means, he said, but only by winning hearts and minds through a lengthy reform process. Prolonged fighting would fracture the political coalition that made the Great Society possible. This brought the vice president painful exile from Johnson's White House, until he gave in to becoming the administration's spokesman for the war, which he said sought to defeat Communism and to bring Great Society programs to South Vietnam. But his backing of the war cost him support of his liberal constituency.

Humphrey finally proposed to wind down the war during his 1968 presidential campaign, and he swiftly regained his broad-based following. However, Johnson seriously undermined him because he believed Richard Nixon's position on the war to be closer to his, despite evidence that the Republican candidate and his aides were urging the governments of South and North Vietnam not to attend the Paris peace talks with a view to gaining a better settlement if he was elected president.

After trailing Nixon by about eighteen points, Humphrey lost the election by only the narrowest of margins. He might have won, or thrown the election into the Democratically controlled House of Representatives, but for Johnson's betrayal of him.

Humphrey's exceptional legislative and political achievements have been largely overlooked. Whereas he declared to his Senate colleagues in 1957, "I am a liberal without apology," the rise of conservatism in recent decades has led many Democrats to shy from identifying as liberals or with that political tradition, contributing to the lack of acknowledgment of his pioneering work shaping the liberal programs and traditions that buttress our modern order. Further, scholars of recent American history have preferred to focus on presidents and their accomplishments. Carl Solberg's early 1984 book *Hubert H. Humphrey: A Biography* is the only full study of him and is very brief on Humphrey's career after 1968. Solberg did not have benefit of access to the reorganized, extensive collection of Hubert H. Humphrey Papers at the Minnesota State Historical Society in St. Paul, the vast trove of personal papers and government records now available at the Lyndon Baines Johnson Presidential Library at the University of Texas, along with recently declassified US Department of State and National Security Council records, and the important scholarship of the past three decades about American history.

My biography assesses Humphrey's significant impact on American politics and his exceptional legislative achievements, his long and complex relationship with Lyndon Johnson, his shifting views on the Vietnam War, and the Minnesotan's post-1970 Senate career. During this latter period, he powerfully effected Democratic Party policy and its choice of national candidates, pressed major congressional domestic and foreign policy legislative initiatives, and became President Carter's chief ally in the Senate.

Humphrey's political record is of great relevance in the current era, when issues of civil rights, including voting and wages, as well as "jobs, jobs, jobs," national health care, US involvement in civil and regional crises, and negotiation of nuclear accords are high on the nation's political agenda and his maxim that "compromise is not a dirty word" seems to have been forgotten by too many politicians.

ACKNOWLEDGMENTS

Writing history is a collective enterprise; every researcher is dependent on the work of other scholars and the advice of colleagues and friends. Thus, I am greatly pleased to acknowledge the people whose scholarship, counsel, and commitment have enabled me to write this book.

Thomas G. Paterson, the late J. Garry Clifford, and Frank Costigliola have made their University of Connecticut Foreign Policy Seminar an extremely welcoming forum for my ideas and work for over three decades. Martin J. Sherwin of George Mason University has been a long-term extraordinarily knowledgeable critic, and he and his wife, Susan, have been steadfast advocates of my endeavors. Melvyn P. Leffler of the University of Virginia has been a highly valued analyst and supporter of my writings. The late Robert "Bo" A. Burt of Yale University Law School generously shared with me his profound knowledge of constitutional law and his experiences as a legislative aide to Maryland Senator Joseph D. Tydings during 1966–68. And Robert H. Ferrell of Indiana University, a prolific scholar and my mentor of many decades ago, set standards for research and writing to which I have always aspired.

Former Lafayette College president Arthur J. Rothkopf and his wife, Barbara, provided important encouragement of my scholarship and signal hospitality, and former Lafayette College president Daniel H. Weiss proved to be an intellectually and personally engaging academic leader. Provosts June Schlueter and Wendy L. Hill, scholars in their own right, provided friendship as well as support for my work. My Lafayette College History Department colleagues, including Paul Barclay, Andrew Fix, Rachel Goshgarian, Donald C. Jackson, Rebekah Pite, Deborah A. Rosen, Joshua Sanborn, and Robert I. Weiner, have been personally and professionally highly supportive of my teaching and scholarly endeavors.

I also wish to express my gratitude to the extremely generous Lafayette College benefactors the late Charley Hugel and his wife, Cornelia (Nina), who endowed a chair that made it possible for me to teach and do research there for twenty-one highly rewarding years.

My Lafayette College research assistants, EXCEL scholars Katerina Mantell and Douglas Michell, ferreted out more information than I ever imagined possible from microfilm records of government publications, magazines, and newspapers, and the Lafayette College Academic Research Committee helped to finance travel to distant archives. Librarians at the Minnesota Historical Society in St. Paul and the LBJ Presidential Library in Austin, Texas, were very helpful, and Mick Caouette, producer, South Hill Films in Stillwater, Minnesota, generously brought to bear his exceptional knowledge of Hubert Humphrey's life and times to provide and guide the selection of pictures in this book.

Most significantly, at a crucial time in my work, Irwin F. Gellman, distinguished scholar of US foreign relations and leading biographer of former president Richard M. Nixon, reached out to me in an extraordinary act of personal generosity and intellectual bipartisanship and offered to read chapters, proffer critical advice about important issues and sources, and urge my writing along. Then he graciously introduced me to his literary representative, Alexander Hoyt, an astute critic and highly supportive agent, who encouraged me to demonstrate Humphrey's historic importance and then brought this book to the attention of Yale University Press. There, William Frucht, executive editor for political science and law, recognized Hubert Humphrey's significant contributions to the American political tradition. Then he assigned this writer and his manuscript to Karen E. Olson, who brought to bear her exceptional skills as an author and editor—and her great patience—to help me put this book's story line and major points into sharper focus and make it more readable than its first version.

Last, I wish to express my immense gratitude and indebtedness to my family. My long-ago deceased parents, Samuel and Helen Offner, and my late elder brothers, Charles and Elliot, did their best to instill liberal, albeit critical, thinking in me and determination to see every endeavor to its completion. My daughter, Deborah Offner, son-in-law, Samuel Roth, and granddaughter Julia Roth, and my son, Mike Offner, daughter-in-law, Lonna Steinberg, and grandchildren Callie, Maddy, and Jason Offner have been the most deeply caring and loving supporters a scholar, father, or grandfather could hope for, and they brighten my world.

My wife, Ellen, whose idea it was that I write this biography, has been at the center of my life, family, and scholarly work for six decades. She has been a remarkably generous and perceptive (and sometimes necessarily unsparing) critic and editor, and a model by the standards she has set in her own profession, distant from academia. Above all, her love, devotion, and commitment have been inspiring.

HUBERT HUMPHREY

PROLOGUE

Hubert H. Humphrey's political stars were not favorably aligned in early 1948, although the thirty-seven-year-old mayor of Minneapolis had risen rapidly to political prominence.

A candidate for the US Senate, Humphrey faced a formidable opponent in incumbent Republican Joseph Ball, at odds with labor forces but an internationalist who had supported Franklin Roosevelt over Republican Thomas E. Dewey, the governor of New York, in the 1944 presidential election. Ball now had the backing of Minnesota's highly regarded progressive Republican governor, Luther W. Youngdahl, in a state where the GOP predominated. The Democratic National Committee (DNC) ignored Humphrey's pleas for funds despite his having spent $4,500 "of my own money . . . that I earned honestly" battling left-wing opponents in his own Democratic-Farmer-Labor Party (DFL).[1]

Humphrey had become prominently associated with a group of Democrats seeking a new standard-bearer to replace Harry S. Truman, who they believed would lose his presidential race against Dewey, the probable Republican nominee. This so-called Dump Truman movement failed, however, to entice either World War II icon General Dwight David Eisenhower or liberal Supreme Court Justice William O. Douglas to become their presidential candidate.

Humphrey, a delegate to the Democratic convention and a member of the platform committee and its small drafting group, arrived a few days early in Philadelphia amid sweltering July heat with a mission to impress upon Democrats that they needed to seize on a nationally significant and inspiring issue as a way to avert disaster in November. In his opinion, an advanced civil rights program was "one of those fortunate instances where the only realistic political alternative is the best moral alternative."[2]

1

The president's 1947 Committee on Civil Rights report, *To Secure These Rights*, called for a permanent Fair Employment Practices Committee (FEPC), equal voting rights, abolition of poll taxes, federal protection against lynching, desegregation of the military, and a civil rights division in the Justice Department. Truman endorsed this in an address to Congress in February 1948 but did no more to promote it. Humphrey's preconvention efforts made no headway, despite threatening a "minority report of one" against influential southerners' demand for a restatement of the vague 1944 plank that called for Congress to protect all citizens' constitutional rights. This meant little, however, given the limited reach of federal authority when states' rights denoted state control over rules for voting, school systems, public facilities, employment, and law enforcement.

Humphrey's lifetime commitment to civil rights was ignited during his graduate school days at Louisiana State University. Having had almost no prior contact with African Americans where he grew up in South Dakota or in Minnesota, he saw harsh racial segregation in Baton Rouge firsthand. "White" and "Colored" signs at every facility and pitiful African American housing near open sewage lines jarred his sensibilities, which intensified as he came to see that the North, too, was plagued by profound racial divisions.[3]

Humphrey labored long and hard with the platform group during the first two days and nights of the Democrats' meeting but made no progress despite his unusual threat to take his proposal to the convention floor for a vote. Finally, exhausted, he agreed to the drafting committee's restatement of the bland 1944 plank but, after conferring with political allies, demanded inclusion of his new "irreducible minimum": an amendment drawn by labor union official and former Wisconsin congressman Andrew Biemiller and Americans for Democratic Action (ADA) founder and prominent civil rights lawyer Joseph Rauh that restated the President's Committee on Civil Rights' call for equal employment opportunity, full political participation (voting rights), equal treatment in the military, and safety from lynching.

Humphrey told his southern colleagues that he was not trying to reform the social structure—promote "mixed marriages"—but that the United States could not fight the Cold War or "cry crocodile tears" over lack of freedom in Czechoslovakia or Bulgaria if people "who have ancestry in this country longer than 99% of the whites" were denied their rights. The platform committee, however, resoundingly rejected the Humphrey-Biemiller amendment and passed the restated 1944 plank—now the majority report—which Humphrey derided as a "sellout to states' rights over human rights."[4]

Humphrey and his ADA colleagues gathered at a nearby fraternity house at the University of Pennsylvania and vowed to fight for a strong civil rights plank.

They designated Humphrey to make their case to the full convention; they doubted that they would win but believed that it was their last best hope to block a major defection of liberal Democrats to former vice president Henry A. Wallace as the presidential candidate of the recently formed Progressive Party.

Humphrey stood at a critical political juncture. Taking the civil rights high road might bring instant national prominence, but he was already under fire from Truman's White House. David K. Niles, the president's trusted minority affairs adviser, warned Rauh that the minority plank would not get fifty votes "and all you'll do is ruin the chances of the No. 1 prospect for liberalism in the country." Democratic Senate minority leader Scott Lucas of Illinois, who called Humphrey a "pipsqueak," warned him that his action would "split the party wide open" and "kill any chance of Democratic victory in November," and Rhode Island senator J. Howard McGrath threatened, "This will be the end of you."[5]

Dispirited, exhausted, and inclined to back down, Humphrey returned to his room at the Bellevue-Stratford Hotel, crowded with friends and political allies who, courtesy of his elder brother Ralph, were drinking beer pulled from an ice-filled bathtub. Humphrey overheard Rauh say that he did not think they would get one-third of the votes needed to pass their resolution, and Orville Freeman, a decorated World War II marine veteran, a close friend from college days and a masterful DFL organizer, said he thought they would be "laughed out of the [convention] room," but both were willing to give it a try. Humphrey called his wife, Muriel, back in Minnesota tending to their four young children, and she encouraged him to finish what he had started regardless of cost. And his most important adviser in the room, his father, Hubert Horatio Humphrey Sr., who feared that "this may tear the party apart" and could promise only the eight votes of his South Dakota delegation, nonetheless told him, "You can't run away from your conscience, son."

The younger Humphrey still hesitated, but several supporters, including Biemiller and Freeman, pulled him into the room of Eugenie Anderson, an ally from Red Wing, Minnesota, who had helped him organize the DFL Party, and they raised his spirits. On returning to the larger group, he shouted, "Okay, I will do it!" He ordered his room cleared so that he could get some sleep—it was now 5:00 a.m.—and write his speech in the morning. Biemiller went to see the powerful convention chairman, House minority leader Sam Rayburn of Texas, who agreed to allow a vote on the civil rights resolution, with two states' rights provisos to be voted on first as amendments to it. But he limited debate to one hour and was certain that all three measures would be defeated.[6]

Humphrey got little sleep; he awoke early on July 14—the last day of the convention—to work on the speech with help from Milton Stewart, an ADA staff lawyer who had written much of the administration's Committee on Civil Rights report. He asked Humphrey to outline a draft text to be circulated, but the young Minnesotan was too impatient to focus more than ten or fifteen minutes and instead wrote nearly the entire speech himself, having made many of the exact arguments during the past couple of days. Humphrey held back in search of wording that would not offend Truman, until Anderson offered a solution: a statement preceding the resolution's four specific civil rights demands stating, "We highly commend President Harry Truman for his courageous stand on the issue of civil rights"—thus praising while coopting him.[7]

Later that afternoon, a tense Humphrey, who feared going from mayor to "oblivion," made his way into the sweltering convention hall and, joined by Biemiller, onto the rostrum. Bronx Democratic leader Edward (Ed) J. Flynn, keenly aware of the need to capture minority votes—"otherwise we are dead"— asked to see Humphrey's text and quickly said, "You kids are right. We should have done this a long time ago. We've got to do it. Go ahead, we'll back you." Flynn dispatched aides to bring on board the reluctant recent former mayor Ed Kelly of Chicago and political boss Jacob (Jake) Arvey; Pittsburgh mayor David Lawrence; and the powerful mayor of Jersey City, Frank Hague.[8]

Biemiller presented the liberals' civil rights amendment, after which southerners from Texas, Tennessee, and Mississippi put forward three amendments reaffirming the Democratic Party's "adherence to the fundamental principle of States' Rights" and denial of federal jurisdiction over state policies such as racial segregation and discrimination in private employment. Failure to respect states' rights, the Tennessee spokesman said, would mean "dissolution of the Democratic Party in the South."[9]

It was Humphrey's turn to speak. "No braver Daniel ever faced a more powerful Goliath," distinguished economist and Senate candidate Paul Douglas of Illinois recalled years later. Wearing a dark blue double-breasted suit and large yellow "TRUMAN" button in his right lapel, he stepped forward, still fearful but buoyed by word that senior senators Francis Myers of Pennsylvania, chairman of the platform committee, and Lucas were ready to vote his way. Humphrey, who always spoke rapid-fire and often digressed at length, now talked slowly, firmly, and faithfully to his text. He finished in just under ten minutes, perhaps his shortest speech ever.[10]

At first, he sought to assuage his diverse audience: he acknowledged that he was dealing with a "charged issue" and affirmed that he deeply respected the people whose views differed from his. His civil rights proposal was not aimed at any single class, racial, or religious group, he said, adding that all states have shared in our precious heritage of "American freedom," all states have at least some infringements of that freedom, and all people, white and black, have been the victims at times of "vicious discrimination."

Referencing Thomas Jefferson, founder of the Democratic Party, Humphrey said that Jefferson had declared "all men are equal" and equal in their right to "enjoy the blessings of free government." Moreover, the Democratic Party had done more than any other for civil rights, and America had made "great progress in every part of the country." But now it was time to realize a full program of civil rights for all, guided by the two great Democratic presidents, the "immortal" Franklin Roosevelt and Harry Truman, who had the courage to give the American people the "new emancipation proclamation," as Humphrey called the President's Committee on Civil Rights report.

Civil rights, however, were far more than a party matter. Every citizen had a stake in America's rise as a leader in the free world, which faced challenge from the "world of slavery," and for America to play its part effectively, "we must be in a morally sound position." American demands for democratic practices in other lands would be no more effective than "the guarantee of those practices in our own country." There could be "no hedging," "no watering down" of civil rights. Further, "To those who say we are rushing the issue of civil rights, I say to them that we are 172 years late. To those who say that this civil-rights program is an infringement on states' rights, I say this: The time has come in America for the Democratic Party to get out of the shadow of states' rights and to walk forthrightly into the bright sunshine of human rights. People—human beings—this is the issue of the 20th century."

Finally, he said, Americans could not turn from the path that had already led them through the "valleys of the shadow of death" and now was so plainly before them. Their land was "the last best hope on earth" for humanity, and the Democratic Party had to "march down the high road of progressive democracy" and courageously support "our President and leader Harry Truman in his great fight for civil rights in America."[11]

Humphrey's brilliant speech was successful beyond anything he might have imagined. "He was on fire, just like the Bible speaks of Moses," his face "shining with an inner incandescent light," Douglas recalled, and he labeled Humphrey "the orator of the dawn." Others likened the speech to William Jennings Bryan's historic "Cross of Gold" oration at the 1896 Democratic convention. Sixty million radio listeners heard the Minnesotan, and he was seen by about ten million viewers in the young television era.[12]

Humphrey had shrewdly linked civil rights to American heroes and epic themes: Jefferson and his concept of liberty and equality; the "immortal" FDR and the New Deal; America as the world's "last best hope" and leader of the free world; and the faith and courage of those who had risked their lives to defend freedom. Above all, he had waxed eloquent about the Democrats' need to advance human rights and linked Truman and "To Secure These Rights" to Abraham Lincoln and the Emancipation Proclamation.

Ironically, Truman dismissed Humphrey, Biemiller, and their civil rights proponents as "crackpots" who wished to cause the South to "bolt." But the convention audience repeatedly interrupted the speech with applause and erupted in thunderous cheers at the end. The Minnesota delegation was the first to rise to its feet, and Douglas implored the head of his delegation, Kelly, that if Illinois led a demonstration many others would follow, and the civil rights amendment would carry. Kelly, now in accord with the amendment, assented, but with his legs too weak to lead the way, he handed the state's standard to Douglas, a towering figure, who marched down the aisle followed by his compatriots, with the big California, New York, Michigan, and Pennsylvania delegations joining in. The demonstration lasted only eight minutes, but the political tide had turned.[13]

Voting began with the southern-sponsored amendments: a roll-call vote decisively defeated the first one, and two more went down overwhelmingly by voice votes. The Humphrey-Biemiller amendment came next. Freeman, sitting on the convention floor with a tally sheet, said he did not think it stood a chance. But after Alabama and Arizona voted "no," California offered encouragement, as did Illinois, Michigan, Minnesota, and New York, the largest delegation, with 98 votes. Suddenly, "we were rolling," Freeman said, and after Pennsylvania weighed in with its 74 votes, victory neared. Hubert Humphrey Sr. cast South Dakota's 8 votes in favor, and Wisconsin's positive votes brought narrow victory at 651½–582½ votes despite the entire South, including Truman's home state of Missouri, opposing the resolution. Convention chair Rayburn ignored the Alabama delegation's effort to declare that it was leaving the meeting and called for a voice vote to adopt the entire platform, after which Representative John W. McCormack of Massachusetts moved to recess for two hours.[14]

When the meeting reconvened that evening, Handy Ellis, chair of the Alabama delegation, announced, "We bid you goodbye," whereupon half of his delegation and all of Mississippi's walked out of the convention, intent to form a new party. But Humphrey's ally Anderson heard a newsman remark, "Can you beat that? The ADA has licked the South."[15]

Humphrey's daring speech had galvanized the convention to adopt the first civil rights platform in the Democratic Party's history, afforded an unprecedented victory for a minority plank in a presidential convention, and established a basis to garner African American votes in big cities crucial for Truman's stunning victory in November despite DNC and White House aides' efforts to derail the young Minnesotan's undertaking.

Most important, Humphrey had put civil rights on the nation's agenda for decades to come, and he would become the national leader in advancing the historic civil rights legislation of 1957, 1964, 1965, and 1968 that sought to assure all Americans their right to full and fair participation in every aspect of the nation's life. He would also become the leading voice of American liberalism, who, as President Jimmy Carter declared, "blessed our country" more than any other president in the modern era.[16]

A NEW STAR IS BORN

Hubert Horatio Humphrey Jr. was born in the windswept prairie hamlet of Wallace, South Dakota, population 210, on May 27, 1911. His family roots reached back to medieval Scandinavia, while more modern paternal ancestors came from England to the Massachusetts Bay Colony around 1648. Family members later moved to Ohio, Minnesota, and Oregon, where Hubert Horatio Humphrey Sr. was born in 1882, the fourth of five children of John Wadsworth and Addie Regester Humphrey.[1]

John and Addie Humphrey settled in Elk River, near Minneapolis, where John ran a successful dairy farm and Addie, formerly a Quaker schoolteacher, focused on their children's education. The two eldest boys, Harry Barker and John Wadsworth Jr., graduated from the University of Minnesota. Harry earned a PhD in plant sciences at Stanford University and became chief plant pathologist for the US Department of Agriculture. John invented the mechanical potato digger and chaired the economics department at the University of Kentucky. Hubert Horatio went to the Drew College of Pharmacy in Minneapolis. A fourth son, Robert Ford, an accomplished artist, died young from rheumatic fever. The lone daughter, Frances Estella, did not attend college but had a son who became a botanist.[2]

After graduating from pharmacy school, Hubert Horatio worked in a drugstore in the tiny town of Lily, South Dakota, where he met Christine Sannes, the daughter of a Norwegian former sea captain. They married in 1906 and moved to Granite Falls, Minnesota, where he went into partnership in an established drugstore. When the business faltered, the family moved to Wallace, South Dakota, in 1910. Christine gave birth to their first child, Ralph Wadsworth, in 1907, and in 1911, Hubert Horatio Jr. came into the world in the family apartment over his father's drugstore. Two sisters followed: Frances, born in 1914, and Fern, in 1917, two years after the Humphrey family had moved again, fifty miles southwest to Doland. Hubert Horatio Sr. thought the larger population of 550 would be better for business.[3]

Hubert Humphrey Jr.'s formative experiences in Doland shaped his worldview. Young Hubert was known as "Pinky" because his mother often dressed him in pink clothes. The family lived in one of Doland's best houses, a large, white frame structure with four bedrooms, a huge kitchen, two bathrooms, a screened porch, and a spacious lawn with trees. Hubert's father—or "HH," as everyone called him—ran a relatively successful drugstore on Main Street, where there were eleven other businesses. Humphrey would later recollect an idyllic childhood that included hay wagon rides, driving cattle from pasture to barn, Christmas celebrations, playing in open fields, and neighbors' houses with open doors. But as he reached adulthood, he found small town life too constraining and determined to build his career in a larger world, be it Minneapolis or Washington, DC.[4]

Young Humphrey greatly respected his mother, but they had markedly different dispositions. Christine Sannes, a superb cook who made prize-winning baked goods, was of stern Lutheran faith. Even though Hubert was baptized Lutheran, the family attended the Methodist church because there was no Lutheran church in Doland. Christine was intensely shy and had few friends, but when introducing her children to other people, she always emphasized, "This is Hubert." She disapproved of her husband's penchant for buying books (money was tight) and staying up late reading to his children, versing them in the liberal writings of Thomas Paine, Thomas Jefferson, and Woodrow Wilson. HH would tell her to go to sleep for all of them, saying that his two best friends were his books and his children.[5]

Christine disapproved when young Hubert, who sold newspapers, offered them to African American highway workers and accepted rides on their wagons. She preferred Republicans—including Warren Harding and Calvin Coolidge—to Democrats, which led HH to tell their children that their mother was "politically unreliable" but that they had to respect her. Moreover, although Christine prevailed on her eldest son, Ralph, to attend small, and relatively close by, religious-affiliated Dakota Wesleyan University, young Hubert insisted on going to the University of Minnesota, two hundred and fifty miles to the east, and ultimately chose politics instead of her preference for the ministry.[6]

Young Humphrey worshipped his father, a tall, extremely energetic, and garrulous man with "an undiminished appetite for life" and a passionate believer in democracy and social justice. HH had hoped to follow his older brothers to the University of Minnesota, but lack of family money forced him to work for a few years after high school before attending pharmacy school in Minneapolis. He brought his children, including young Hubert from age ten, into his drugstore business, where he worked from morning to night to support his family—but also because he sought to avoid going to bed, where most people died, he told his children.[7]

He had a strong intellectual bent. In his youth, he became an agnostic, influenced by writings of the prominent political and social orator Robert G. Ingersoll, who questioned religion and was an abolitionist and spokesman for women's rights. In 1922, at age forty, however, HH joined his sons, Ralph and young Hubert, in being baptized as a Methodist, and taught packed Sunday school classes, preaching a social gospel that said America contained enough wealth to allow its citizens to establish a heavenly kingdom on this earth. He subscribed to several major metropolitan newspapers, bought classical records, drove hundreds of miles to concerts in Minneapolis, and brought touring musical and theatrical groups to Doland, using his drugstore as a ticket office.[8]

He also made his drugstore a meetinghouse where leading townspeople gathered in the evenings to discuss local or national issues, which led young Hubert to stay up late listening to the talk he later equated with the best college or parliamentary debates he ever heard and to regard as a compliment the oft-expressed view that HH "never sells a pill without selling an idea." Hubert Jr. was also impressed by his father's generosity; when he brought a barefoot boy from a nearby shantytown into the drugstore, HH took money from the cash register to buy the boy socks and boots. And when depression years came to South Dakota, HH forgave his customers thousands of dollars in debts—money his family sorely needed—believing that this would win their business when better days returned.[9]

Politics coursed through the blood of HH, who began as a Republican but, after hearing William Jennings Bryan speak, became a Democrat and later strongly supported Woodrow Wilson, Al Smith (despite his "wetness" during the Prohibition era), and, especially, Franklin Roosevelt. Although HH was almost the lone Democrat in his community, he won election to the town council and later became mayor, vociferously if unsuccessfully arguing against the sale of Doland's public power plant to a private enterprise in 1923. He attended the Democratic national convention in Houston as a Smith delegate in 1928 and was elected to the South Dakota legislature in 1936, with a run for governor in the offing.[10]

Young Hubert immensely admired his father's political intensity and outspoken but always agreeable manner and unshakable conviction that the United States was a special nation where people could create the good society. Or as HH liked to say, "Before the fact is the dream." Young Hubert modeled himself after his father and recalled, "I was at my father's elbow constantly, watching him, listening to him, debating with him. It was the luckiest legacy he could have left me . . . working at the side of a wise and sensitive man for whom idealism was not a cold creed but a way of life."[11]

Young Hubert's intelligence and energy led to his earning A's in nearly every subject in high school, playing on the football and basketball teams, running track, playing the baritone horn in the school band, and graduating as valedictorian.[12]

He also learned how powerful, impersonal forces could adversely affect one's life. At age seven, he suffered a life-threatening bout with influenza during the national epidemic of 1918 that caused the death of half a million Americans. But HH drove six hundred miles through a snowstorm to Minneapolis and back to secure the medicine that restored his son to health.[13]

In 1927, sixteen-year-old Hubert returned from high school classes to find his parents and a stranger standing under a large tree on the front lawn, with his mother crying and his father fighting back tears. A banking credit crisis and the Great Depression had come early to South Dakota, and the Humphreys had to sell their home to meet their debts. That was the moment, Humphrey Jr. would recollect, when he began to have an adult's awareness of the possibilities for pain and tragedy in life.[14]

The resilient HH, however, rented a smaller home at the edge of town for his family, increased the variety of goods sold in his drugstore, and took a short course in veterinary medicine, enabling him to make money tending to farmers' sick animals and vaccinating them. Young Hubert often traveled with his father and learned how to keep the syringes sterile, vaccinate hogs, and talk to farmers, who later became a vital part of his political constituency.[15]

After graduating from high school in June 1929, Hubert Jr., encouraged by his father, set off for the University of Minnesota. HH drove him to Minneapolis, helped him find lodging in a rooming house, and told him that "from here on out, it's on you" to make good. HH also sent ten dollars monthly, more than adequate for expenses.[16]

Hubert felt overwhelmed by the "fantastically large" city and university and made no "great splash" academically. But he joined the debate team, and after his father had to cut off his expense money, wangled a stock-clerk job at a new drugstore. After returning to Doland for the summer, however, his father told him that he had to remain there to help in the store because his older brother, Ralph, who had sat out the school year to do this, wished to return to college. So a disconsolate Hubert remained in Doland, until his Uncle Harry sent him a fifty-dollar Christmas gift to pay tuition, and HH agreed that Doland held no future for his son.[17]

But shortly after Hubert returned to college in winter 1931, HH arrived with the "shocking" news that he had to move his drugstore to Huron, a growing town about forty-two miles to the south with a population five times that of Doland. HH secured merchandise and a line of credit from his longtime supplier, the Minneapolis Drug Company, and left the family to finish the school year while he rented a room in Huron and opened his new store. Hubert and his brother, Ralph, moved into the basement of the store, where they worked long hours for no salary. And in winter 1932, Hubert, convinced that this would be his vocation for the rest of his life, went off to the Capitol College of Pharmacy in Denver, where he crammed a two-year program into six months of coursework to earn his pharmacist's license.[18]

Huron's chamber of commerce assailed HH's lowering prices to gain business, and he added a small restaurant in the store, with Christine and their daughters, Frances and Fern, cooking and serving. HH and his sons also bartered goods and drugs for farmers' produce, continued their veterinary practices, and mixed and sold patent medicines. Ultimately, HH had to give way to Walgreens, which made his drugstore part of its chain, although he kept a "Humphrey and Sons" sign out front much larger than that of the new "Walgreen's Agency."[19]

Young Hubert was miserable in Huron. He endured a broken engagement and loss of his grandmother's diamond ring to a young woman from a nearby town and a failed relationship with another frequent companion. South Dakota dust storms and economic depression were unrelenting, and he suffered fainting spells and stomach upset and became almost emaciated. When in summer 1933 HH vetoed his plan to hitchhike to Chicago to see the "Century of Progress" World's Fair, he smashed glasses behind the counter and had a bitter shouting match with his father.[20]

Hubert became a scoutmaster for the Methodist church troop, coached their basketball team, and joined the Young Democrats. In 1934, he met Muriel Fay Buck, a sophomore at Huron College, when a friend of hers brought her to the drugstore to meet the relatively new boy in town. The Buck family ran a prosperous produce and dairy dealership and tended to look down on the Humphreys. But Hubert and Muriel soon began going to a weekly dance or for a drive in the countryside, and by summer 1935, they were weighing marriage, despite mother Christine's unexplained coolness toward Muriel.[21]

That August, Hubert took his boy scouts to tour Washington, DC, and stayed with Uncle Harry, who was also lodging younger sister Frances, a student at George Washington University. Hubert was enthralled to see the US Senate, where he heard Louisiana's fiery Huey (the "Kingfish") Long give a speech, and visited Washington's myriad monuments. He was also more enamored than ever of Roosevelt, "who is a super-man," he said, who baffled his Republican opponents. He promptly wrote Muriel ("Bucky") a self-defining letter: the trip had impressed upon him the need for more education and "clean living," and he hoped she would not laugh at him because he believed that if they worked for bigger things, they, too, could live in Washington and "probably be in government politics or service." He intended to aim for Congress. "Why haven't I a chance?" he said, "You'll help me, I know." But first, he said, he would prepare for his task "by reading and thinking always as a liberal."[22]

Washington became Hubert's Mecca; he longed to live and work there. The next year, in late August 1936, he and his father managed to climb aboard Roosevelt's campaign train and shake the president's hand when he visited Huron on a "drought inspection tour."[23]

Muriel encouraged her beau to return to college, although her mother's death and decline of the Buck family's business impelled her to move with her father during summers to the family's country home on Big Stone Lake—150 miles to the northeast—where they rented cabins to vacationers. Hubert hitch-hiked on Saturday nights to see Muriel, who threatened to move to California if they did not soon marry. They wed on September 3, 1936, in Huron's Presbyterian church, and, with HH's car and his gift of sixty-five dollars, took a five-day honeymoon in Minneapolis and Duluth on Lake Superior, although on their late-night drive home they hit and killed a cow, which cost them twenty-five dollars, plus a new car radiator.[24]

The newlyweds rented a tiny house in Huron; Muriel worked as a billing clerk for a local utility company, and Hubert continued to work in the drug-store, drawing a salary of fifteen dollars a week. But HH's election to the state legislature in Pierre in 1936 compelled his son to carry a larger share of the drugstore demands, which, combined with another year of depression and dust storms, wore the young couple down. Muriel said that they could not continue to live together in these circumstances, and in August 1937, Hubert told his father that he could no longer "peddle pills," which led to a family debate over whether to give priority to young Hubert's future education or HH's prospective run for governor.

Christine sided with her son, and Frances with her father, who offered Hubert full partnership in the drugstore, but to no avail. HH set aside his political ambitions, and the next month he and Christine drove Hubert and Muriel, with the six hundred dollars she had saved, to the University of Minnesota for the start of the fall term.[25]

The young couple took a garretlike apartment and moved frequently during the next two years. Hubert bartered janitorial services for reduced rent and worked part-time in a pharmacy, and Muriel got a bookkeeping job. He was uncertain of his academic direction but recognized that as an older, married student he needed to make up for lost time and persuaded a reluctant dean to allow him to take a significant overload.[26]

Hubert soon settled on a political science major and struck a close relationship—more peerlike than student and professor—with a young instructor, Evron Kirkpatrick, a University of Illinois graduate and recently minted PhD from Yale, who taught American constitutional development and emphasized applied politics. The two men frequently continued their discussions at Hubert's apartment, where they were often joined by, among others, Orville Freeman, from north Minneapolis, a year behind Hubert and an excellent debater and star football player who would later work closely with him in state and national politics; and Arthur Naftalin, a classmate from North Dakota, who would aid Hubert in local and state politics, become Minneapolis's first Jewish mayor, and build an academic career.[27]

Hubert found the university emancipating. He thrilled to a broad range of reading from Plato and Aristotle to contemporary authors, spoke constantly during class discussions, and took readily to public forums. He helped organize a debate among professors about socialist society, addressed a youth rally in 1938 favoring reelection of Farmer-Laborite governor Elmer Benson over rising Republican star Harold Stassen, and traveled to Big Ten campuses on the debate team. He compressed three years of work into two, with a nearly straight A record in political science. In spring 1939, he graduated Phi Beta Kappa and magna cum laude, winning the William Jennings Bryan Prize for best political science essay and the Forensic Medal for his debating skills. The Humphreys' first child, Nancy, had been born that February.[28]

Hubert now looked to earn a PhD and become a professor. But money remained short, and in spring 1939, Muriel's father suffered a heart attack, compelling her to leave her job to return with baby Nancy to South Dakota to care for him. Humphrey had acceptances at several midwestern universities but opted for Louisiana State University (LSU), where the chairman of the Political Science Department, Charles S. Hyneman, a friend of Kirkpatrick, took his recommendation of the aspiring graduate student as a basis to offer him a $450 fellowship. In summer 1939, Humphrey rode by train and bus to Baton Rouge and slept in dirt-cheap quarters until he found a small apartment fit for Muriel and Nancy to join him.[29]

Politics, race, and education in Baton Rouge proved challenging. This was the land of Huey Long, who waged an extreme populist campaign against Louisiana's powerful oil and utilities companies to become governor in 1928. He taxed the oil companies, utilities, and major corporations to pay for public programs: free textbooks for schoolchildren and unprecedented building of highways, bridges, hospitals, and educational institutions. But he also forged a dictatorial and corrupt political machine. Elected senator in 1932, Long initially supported Roosevelt, but in 1934 he formed the "Share Our Wealth" movement, which called for a minimum annual family income and limits on personal fortunes. He looked to run for president as a third-party candidate but was assassinated in August 1935.[30]

Hubert acknowledged Long's demagogic behavior but also believed that his public works programs had taken Louisiana's poor people "out of the mud, at least part way." He also found that campus politics reflected state politics, at least in terms of extravagant campaign pledges, such as that of Russell Long—Huey's son—who won the student government presidency by promising to provide cheap laundry facilities. Hubert took this style to be more amusing than threatening. He soon became friends with Long, who would be elected to the Senate at the same time as Humphrey in 1948 and would be one of the only southern Senators to reach out to the Minnesota firebrand at the start of his national career.[31]

Most significantly, Humphrey experienced race in Louisiana as never before. He had almost no previous contact with African Americans, except for the highway workers he had met as a boy in Doland and one serious conversation with an African American student during his college days in Minnesota, where just 0.5 percent of the state's population was black. By contrast, nearly half of the population was African American in strictly segregated Baton Rouge. Humphrey was appalled when he saw public facilities marked WHITE and COLORED and African Americans living in unpainted shacks near open sewage lines, while wealthy whites lived in stately mansions and middle-class citizens resided in neatly painted homes. He realized that the North was also plagued with bad race relations, but living amid severe southern segregation resulted in his "abstract" commitment to civil rights taking on "flesh and blood" meaning.[32]

Graduate student life resembled that of Minnesota days: Muriel typed papers for students and faculty and made peanut-butter-and-jelly and ham salad sandwiches for him to sell on campus. He borrowed money from Uncle Harry and earned an extra fifty dollars when Hyneman recommended him to speak to a women's club in New Orleans about state taxes. But the Humphreys had to sell their refrigerator to pay the rent.[33]

Hubert shone academically, especially as a teacher. His classes, one young professor noted, were marked by lucid, well-organized, and statistic-filled lectures, a literal "public performance." At Russell Long's request, Humphrey joined the LSU debate team to defeat a troupe from Oxford University, with the Minnesotan arguing, contrary to his personal view, against US aid to Great Britain in the war in Europe that had begun in September 1939.[34]

Hubert began writing his MA thesis on "The Political Philosophy of the New Deal," which would define his own beliefs as much as provide a rational critique. His initial adviser, Alex Daspit, a doctoral candidate at Harvard, challenged the work as insufficiently objective and insisted on major revision. But fortunately for Hubert, Daspit had to return to Harvard to complete his own graduate studies, allowing the MA candidate to defend his thesis in early summer 1940 in front of a more intellectually compatible committee that included Professor Hyneman.[35]

Humphrey sought to divine the philosophic roots of the New Deal largely in terms of John Dewey's early twentieth-century pragmatism, but his thesis also reflected the powerful impact on his thinking of the Great Depression and the start of European war. He noted that the world economic collapse had brought Adolf Hitler and Fascism or Nazism to power in Germany and dictatorships elsewhere but led to Roosevelt and the New Deal in the United States. He attributed this to Americans, unlike Germans and other Europeans, not venerating the state but viewing government as an instrument of the people that justified itself by the benefits conferred on its citizenry. The New Deal was neither revolutionary nor counterrevolutionary but a balanced and pragmatic system that "stops at the gateway of immediate fundamental change in either the political or economic order."[36]

Humphrey believed that the Constitution and capitalism were the bedrocks of the New Deal, but New Dealers, or liberal Democrats, differed from conservatives in viewing the Constitution as an instrument of power—not its negation—designed to meet the problems of the modern world. Hence, the New Deal's expansion of federal authority and programs was neither unconstitutional nor revolutionary but a series of bold, experimental readjustments intended to stabilize society, preserve capitalism, and achieve reasonable security for all.[37]

Humphrey judged Roosevelt to be the leading exponent of modern liberalism and praised him for his pre-1932 election insistence on the need for "bold, persistent experimentation" and citing Lincoln's view that the "legitimate object of government is to do for the people what needs to be done." Humphrey further applauded FDR and the New Deal for having fostered the "administrative liberal," who sought not only to make capitalism function smoothly but also to meet the demands of social justice and confront the power of the financial community.[38]

Humphrey equated FDR's effort in 1937 to enlarge—or "pack," as critics charged—the Supreme Court as akin to Congress's having increased the size of the House and Senate at various times and to Jefferson, Andrew Jackson, and Lincoln having strongly contested Court rulings. In short, he judged FDR and the New Deal as squarely within the American tradition, using "tested liberal" means to try to assure that every person had sufficient property (including income) and liberty to remain politically free and economically independent within a democratic society.[39]

Humphrey said nothing about the New Deal's failure to advance civil rights or race relations significantly but criticized its focus on independent national economic recovery before 1938 and the failure of leaders in Washington and other capitals to recognize sooner the extent to which the world was economically intertwined and the threat the Axis powers posed to the world order. Overall, Humphrey's thesis revealed his admiration for New Deal liberalism and an active chief executive who fostered its expansive federal programs and believed that the purpose of democratic government was to improve conditions for as many people as possible, especially those most in need.[40]

The examining committee unanimously approved Humphrey's thesis, although one member humorously proposed to flunk the candidate so that he would go where he was most needed—into politics. Humphrey was intent to continue graduate studies, however, preferably at Princeton University, which he viewed as a "shining educational heaven" and the home of Woodrow Wilson's ideas. But with a wife and child and virtually broke, not even Princeton's offer of a scholarship could overcome his fear of living so far from home again in an even more expensive region.

He returned to the University of Minnesota, where his mentors set aside a teaching assistantship at six hundred dollars a year and Kirkpatrick arranged a summer job at two hundred dollars per month working for the Works Progress Administration (WPA) in Duluth training unemployed teachers to run adult-education programs. It was an intense, lonely experience because in order to save money, Muriel and baby Nancy went to live in South Dakota until the fall term started. Later, Muriel expressed the belief that if her husband had gone to Princeton, the national press would have perceived him differently during his campaigns and he would have been elected president.[41]

In fall 1940, Humphrey threw himself into his graduate course work and assistantship. Impressed with his training of teachers, WPA officials offered him the directorship of their Twin Cities Worker Education program for $1,500 a year. This full-time job meant that writing a doctoral dissertation would be prolonged. His university friends urged him to stay on, but he felt too financially pressed to decline the WPA job. He borrowed $250 from Freeman to buy his first automobile, which he needed to travel around the state to meet teachers and set up new programs.[42]

Humphrey quickly took command of his new position, which became a launching pad for his political career. Years later, he said that the WPA teachers comprised three groups: ordinary folks and Stalinist and Trotskyite Communists who hated one another and did not meet their classes regularly. So he gave everyone about six weeks to establish a full schedule and fired several teachers who did not comply—withstanding their complaints to state and federal officials.[43]

Humphrey's travels also led him to see the grim working and living conditions of mineworkers on Minnesota's Iron Range, lumberjacks in the forests of the northern areas of the state, and laborers in the Twin Cities' manufacturing plants and slaughterhouses. He sought out union officials, including AFL (American Federation of Labor) and CIO (Congress of Industrial Organizations) leaders, and farm cooperative leaders to start new programs, and he provided his own signed course completion "certificate" to thousands of students, many of whom later would show them to him at political rallies when he was running for office. Humphrey enlisted eight university professors to teach night classes at his "Labor College" in Minneapolis, and by summer 1941, he was writing to Professor Hyneman at LSU that his programs were reaching eighteen to twenty thousand people a month.[44]

Humphrey was soon promoted to district director of education and then to director of workers' services, which included recreational and vocational programs, English courses, and public speaking training. He became divisional director for training and employment, which meant, ironically, liquidating the Worker Education programs because by 1943 the young people taking courses either had been drafted, or enlisted, into the military or had taken jobs in the burgeoning wartime industrial sector. Humphrey himself moved on in early 1943 to become assistant regional director for Minnesota of the War Manpower Commission, which was charged with resolving conflicting personnel demands between draft boards and local industry.[45]

Humphrey began to build his reputation as a dynamic public speaker. Initially, he joined a Congregationalist church in southeastern Minneapolis, where the Humphrey family lived and home to the university. A meeting with a minister from the city's leading Methodist church led Humphrey to start teaching on Sunday mornings in the church's "University of Life." He often talked about labor issues, including his contention that a job was a property right that needed to be protected, a view he would seek to write into legislation thirty years later.

Increasingly, however, his subject was foreign policy. In spring 1941, he wrote to William Allen White's Committee to Defend America by Aiding the Allies, offering to be at their service speaking about "our war." After Germany attacked the Soviet Union in June 1941, he took issue at a public forum with Herbert McClosky, an exceedingly bright new graduate student from a working-class background in New Jersey who would become a close friend, political adviser, and distinguished political scientist. McClosky opposed American intervention against Germany on grounds that the war was just one between competing capitalisms. But as he recalled, Humphrey "demolished" his arguments and, without being "pro-Soviet," spoke powerfully about the meaning of democracy and the threat Nazi armies posed to civilization. In early 1942, Humphrey wrote to Professor Hyneman that he had been raising hell all over the state with "Minnesota's isolationists."[46]

Humphrey enjoyed his government work and an increasing number of speaking engagements—with small but helpful fees—that brought him public notice. He also considered enlisting in the military, a matter that would arise later in his political career. He had registered for the initial draft in 1940 but was classified 3A because he was a father. The birth in June 1942 of a second child, Hubert Horatio Humphrey III, combined with Muriel's ailing father having joined the household, made it relatively easy for Humphrey to give priority to family finances over military service. He sought a federal position but declined to join the Budget Bureau because of the high cost of moving to Washington, DC, and despite his union ties, he failed to gain a position as a field examiner for the National Labor Relations Board.[47]

His university friends thought he belonged in politics, but in 1942, he declined to run in Minnesota's third congressional district, which included working-class northern Minneapolis, because the incumbent, Richard Pillsbury

Gale, was a moderate Republican and scion of the Minneapolis-based flour-milling family that had long been prominent in politics and public affairs. Moreover, the Republican Party, led by popular governor Harold E. Stassen, elected in 1938 and again in 1940, was predominant in the state.[48]

There was, however, the position of mayor of Minneapolis, a nonpartisan office (most often held by a Republican) with little real power, which resided in the city council. The incumbent, Republican Marvin L. Kline, was lackluster, had minimal support from labor and the business community, and showed no leadership in dealing with widespread crime and corruption in the city. The first person to suggest a mayoral run for Humphrey might have been Dr. Walter H. Judd, a former medical missionary for almost a decade in China who had returned to the United States in 1938—establishing his medical practice in Minneapolis—to urge American sanctions against Japan for its aggression in China.[49]

In 1942, Judd upset incumbent Oscar Youngdahl, an outspoken isolationist, in the Republican primary in the fifth congressional district, which included much of Minneapolis and several small cities to the west. Humphrey went to talk with Judd about his victory, and the two men apparently got along well, especially regarding foreign policy. Judd put him in touch with his campaign supporters, including Gideon Seymour, executive editor of the *Minneapolis Star-Journal,* and Ronald Welch, a senior executive at General Mills. They offered to provide Humphrey with the ten-dollar filing fee and an additional sixty-five dollars for campaign expenses.[50]

Kirkpatrick and McClosky also urged him to run for mayor, as did Vincent Day, a progressive and politically influential municipal judge. But Humphrey was uncertain; he needed to complete his dissertation, was neither versed in municipal politics nor well known, and was virtually broke.[51]

Humphrey also viewed Minneapolis as a city of light and darkness: by day, a vibrant center of finance, transportation, and milling dominated by New Englanders who had moved westward, were largely Republican in their politics, and lived in stately homes around the attractive lakes in the southwestern area of the city. By night, Minneapolis was akin to a frontier town with a long history of violent labor-management battles, major illegal gambling, prostitution, and liquor enterprises run by two rival groups known as the Syndicate and the Combination. There were numerous unsolved murders of underworld figures, and city government was filled with corruption.[52]

Still, after the 1942 congressional elections—in which Judd won the seat he would hold for ten terms—Humphrey discussed running for mayor with his friend and college classmate Arthur Naftalin and apparently expressed his concerns about crime (even worried he might get shot) and corruption in the city. Naftalin, who had worked the past few years as a reporter in Minneapolis and recently returned to study for his doctorate under Kirkpatrick, confirmed Humphrey's fears about the city's woeful condition, and soon the Republicans who had offered Humphrey their support withdrew it after they learned of his ties to labor unions.[53]

The mayoral issue lay dormant, although Judge Day continued to raise Humphrey's name with George Phillips, president of the Central Labor Union, and George E. Murk, president of the musicians' union. Humphrey happened on the two men while taking a morning walk downtown on a Sunday morning in April 1943, and they offered him AFL support if he ran. Suddenly, he grew inspired to make the race, hastened to check with Naftalin and Kirkpatrick, and after a few days of deliberation, paid his filing fee at city hall on April 17 — just nineteen days before the initial primary. There were ten other candidates, including Kline and T. A. Eide, a perennial who headed a dairy cooperative in the Twin Cities.[54]

Humphrey threw himself into the race with the zeal and endless energy that would mark his entire political career. He demanded the same of his friends, who now became his campaign staff. Naftalin, whom the Central Labor Committee put on their payroll, became chief publicist and speechwriter, and quickly put out an elections news broadside that proclaimed "A New Star Is Born." He also raised the money and wrote the scripts for four radio broadcasts that gained Humphrey needed name recognition. Kirkpatrick and McClosky served as a brain trust, developing strategy, writing speeches, accompanying Humphrey every place, and distributing campaign literature to all parts of the city late into the night.[55]

Humphrey went everywhere he could to speak. He criticized Kline's failure to deal effectively with crime and corruption and sought to establish his own credentials as a nonpartisan progressive who supported the Roosevelt administration's effort to build support for a United Nations, had an open mind with regard to the workingman's workplace grievances (though he eschewed ties to the left-leaning, Marxist leadership of the militant Teamsters union in Minneapolis), and emphasized the need to prepare the city for postwar expanded housing and economic development. The brief whirlwind campaign caught on and — to Humphrey's surprise — on May 10 he came in second with 16,088 votes (22 percent), while Kline led the field with 29,565 votes (40.5 percent). The city's leading newspaper, the *Minneapolis Star-Journal*, proclaimed Humphrey to be a "new leader" who had come from nowhere to claim the high honor of contesting Kline in the runoff.[56]

Humphrey continued to campaign at breakneck speed during the next six weeks. He attacked Kline for failing to deal with crime and corruption and ignoring the need to reform the police force (noted for taking graft and hostility to labor) and restructure the city charter to provide the mayor with real power. Humphrey also pushed his own ten-point postwar development program for attracting new industry, improving labor-management relations, expanding air and river transport, retraining workers, and expanding housing, including for returning veterans. At the end of the campaign, his aides developed and distributed a brochure that pictured him reading Wendell Willkie's new best seller, *One World,* which identified Humphrey both with the 1940 Republican presidential nominee's position in favor of postwar international cooperation and his outspoken views on the need for political, economic, and civil rights for African Americans.[57]

Despite running a dynamic and forward-looking campaign and raising $12,000, mainly from labor unions, Humphrey could not overcome the support Kline received from Republican governor Stassen's well-heeled organization and the major newspapers that backed his choice of candidate. Kline won reelection by a close margin—by 60,075 votes to Humphrey's 54,350 votes—but the aspiring "new leader" had proved to be an outstanding campaigner.[58]

Gideon Seymour of the *Star-Journal* invited Humphrey to visit him and proposed that he become a Republican. The executive editor indicated that this would bring significant financial backing—even help Humphrey acquire an expensive home on one of the city's lakes—and open the way to his becoming governor or a senator, given the Republican Party's recent political ascendancy in the state. Humphrey had to be tempted: he regarded Seymour as a liberal Republican who sought to make Minneapolis a better city and similarly viewed Stassen and Judd as respectable politicians. Moreover, Humphrey had emerged from the mayoral race with just $7 remaining in his bank account, and he owed $1,300 on an outstanding printing bill. He talked to his friends, especially McClosky, who recalled the deliberation as a " 'Faustian struggle,' " although Muriel later said that she thought "it would have been the end of us" had her husband gone Republican. Ultimately, Humphrey told Seymour that he intended to remain a Democrat and a liberal.[59]

2

THE PEOPLE'S MAYOR

After his first taste of elective politics in 1943, Humphrey was "hooked." Rather than complete his doctoral dissertation, he aimed to seek either the mayoralty again or a seat in Congress. But choosing principle over politics was costly. He had to find a way to earn a livelihood for his wife, Muriel, and two children, Nancy and Hubert Horatio III, and a third child was due in early 1944. The would-be politician also had to pay off his campaign debts. He accepted every speaking engagement he could at local picnics and social or civic clubs, earning five- or ten-dollar fees, and took on superintendent duties at the apartment house where he and his family lived. Humphrey also broadcast nightly news at local radio station WTCN and taught political science at Macalaster College in St. Paul, where army air corps officers who were stationed there for six-week courses of study chose him three times to be their commencement speaker. Macalaster required that he pledge not to engage openly in politics, but he joined Naftalin and Kirkpatrick in a small public relations firm that was largely a front for his plan to run again for mayor of Minneapolis.[1]

His growing reputation as an inspiring speaker gained him countless invitations and needed fees to address many business, labor, church, and fraternal groups, including the National Association for the Advancement of Colored People (NAACP) and the Minnesota Jewish Council. He built a strong reputation as an opponent of racial or religious discrimination and proponent of a federal Fair Employment Practices Committee. Above all, he insisted in this wartime era that the citizenry had to do more than "defend the American way of life." They needed to "dream new visions, chart new plans of social organization," and spread their belief in "democracy and the common man."[2]

Although the mayoralty was technically nonpartisan, Humphrey knew he could not win against a Republican-supported candidate unless Minnesota's weak and divided Democratic and Farmer-Labor Parties revitalized themselves and combined forces. The Farmer-Labor Party had begun as an economic protest movement during the post–World War I recession and included many left-wing farmers and militant laborers from Minneapolis, the port city of Duluth, and the Iron Range. The Farmer-Laborites had dominated Minnesota state politics during most of the 1930s until 1938, when Republican Harold Stassen won the governorship and the GOP gained every statewide office, control of the legislature, and eight of nine of the state's congressional seats.[3]

After Farmer-Laborite senator Ernest Lundeen died in August 1940, Governor Stassen named Joseph Ball, a conservative Republican journalist from St. Paul, to his seat. Ball, like Stassen, supported FDR's aid to allies in the European war, while Farmer-Labor senator Henrik Shipstead, critical of FDR's policies, quit his party and won reelection as a Republican in November 1940. Stassen also gained overwhelming reelection, and Republicans kept control of every state-wide office. President Roosevelt won a third term over Republican Wendell Willkie, but his Minnesota margin declined sharply from 350,000 votes in 1936 to just 48,000 votes.[4]

Republicans consolidated control in Minnesota in 1942 when Ball won a full Senate term, Stassen won a third term, and his party kept control of every state-wide office and eight of nine congressional seats. The Democrats again ran a poor third behind Farmer-Laborites, but leaders of both parties saw their need and opportunity to seek unity when the popular Stassen resigned in April 1943 to take a US Navy commission. Support for unity came from Earl Browder, head of the Communist Party USA (CPUSA); Sidney Hillman, longtime FDR ally, president of the Amalgamated Clothing Workers and head of the CIO's Political Action Committee; Robert Wishart, a Communist who headed the Hennepin County CIO and was business agent for United Electric Local 1145, the largest CIO union in Minnesota; and Democratic National Committee officials. All were mindful that Roosevelt's slim margin in 1940 in Minnesota made it a critical swing state in 1944.[5]

Nonetheless, when Humphrey and his friend and mentor Kirkpatrick sent a twelve-page, statistic-filled memorandum to Frank Walker, the current postmaster general and DNC chair, showing the necessity of Democratic and Farmer-Laborite unity, they drew only a perfunctory reply. Humphrey took the bulk of his family's savings, about seventy-seven dollars, and rode a bus to Washington, staying with his Uncle Harry and Aunt Olive. He camped out for five days at the DNC headquarters on Pennsylvania Avenue but failed to gain a meeting with Walker or anyone else. "It looks like a political operation on crutches," he wrote Muriel, and "they aren't very interested in listening to a young fellow like me." But en route to the bus depot to return home, he paused for a drink at a hotel on Pennsylvania Avenue and called W. W. Howes, a friend of his father from South Dakota who had once been an assistant postmaster general and was now in business in Washington. Howes listened to Humphrey and called Walker, who sent a limousine to bring the young Democrat to his office, heard him out, and agreed to send help to Minnesota.[6]

Oscar Ewing, vice chair of the DNC, met with a St. Paul delegation and then with Humphrey and a Minneapolis contingent. Elmer Benson, a former populist governor and head of the Farmer-Labor Party, was ready to move, but his Democratic counterpart, Edgar Kelm, a cautious small-town banker, would not act without assurance that Democrats would control the new party. Benson-Kelm negotiations proceeded tediously throughout 1943, with Humphrey acting as Kelm's chief assistant—and general publicist—and using his facility with words to smooth over disagreements. He proposed the composite Democratic-Farmer-Labor Party name to ensure Farmer-Laborite votes and agreed to organize a mass rally at the Minneapolis Armory in February 1944 and introduce the main speaker, Vice President Henry Wallace, whom he revered. Wallace was the Democrats' foremost progressive, a modern Jeremiah to many midwesterners whose widely distributed 1942 "Century of the Common Man" speech envisioned a postwar liberal era of global prosperity and peace.[7]

Humphrey introduced Wallace to a cheering crowd of ten thousand. The vice president called on Farmer-Laborites to join with Democrats to create a "people's peace" and liberal public policies that would include regional planning and development and government responsibility for feeding ten million impoverished American families. Afterward, Humphrey wrote Wallace that the "progressive forces look to you for leadership."[8]

Democratic and Farmer-Labor negotiators finally reached agreement in March 1944, with Kelm chairing the new party and Benson's Farmer-Laborites gaining a majority of executive committee seats. Both parties agreed to a joint convention in mid-April—with Humphrey as chairman—to reconstitute as the Democratic-Farmer-Labor Party, appoint party officials, select delegates to the national Democratic convention, and nominate candidates for state offices. Humphrey's concern for party unity was such that when Muriel's father died at this time, he left it to her—although she had given birth only a few weeks earlier to their third child, Robert—to take her father's body for burial in South Dakota.[9]

At the April convention, delegates voted to merge their parties and agreed on a constitution and delegates (including Humphrey) to the national Democratic convention. One delegate nominated Humphrey for governor, although he had made clear he intended to enlist in the navy. He and his father believed military service would be a critical credential for any office-seeker in the postwar period; Humphrey also thought that incumbent Republican Edward Thye, who as lieutenant governor had succeeded Stassen in 1943, was unbeatable. Nonetheless, after a series of rousing seconding speeches, the new DFL Party nominated Humphrey for governor, but he withdrew in favor of Barney Allen, a relative newcomer to Minnesota politics, who lost to Thye in 1944.[10]

After the DFL convention, Humphrey sought a naval reserve officer's commission but was rejected because he was color-blind and had calcification and scars on his lungs and a double hernia. He had the hernia repaired but gained only IA-Limited classification; the army was not seeking to support soldiers with a wife and three children. Humphrey was called for reclassification after the Battle of the Bulge in December 1944—and after he had announced his second mayoral run. His picture, with uniform in hand at the induction center in nearby Ft. Snelling soon appeared in newspapers. But discovery of a scrotal hernia that had been missed during prior examinations led to his being "a lousy IV-F," he wrote, despite his pleas to the commanding officer that he be spared the political embarrassment of rejection. Ultimately, lack of military service did not harm Humphrey politically, although opponents would raise the issue in 1960 when he sought the Democrats' presidential nomination.[11]

In summer 1944, the Humphreys managed to buy a house on the northern fringes of the University of Minnesota. He attended the Democratic convention in Chicago as part of the DFL delegation pledged to renominate Roosevelt and Wallace. The DFLers were outraged, however, when the DNC leaders dumped Wallace and chose Senator Harry S. Truman of Missouri. Humphrey, unimpressed with the little he knew of Truman, joined with DFL Popular Fronters to lead a passionate demonstration after Wallace was nominated and delivered a resounding seconding speech. He likened Wallace to the greatest Democratic leaders from Jefferson to Bryan to FDR, whose idealism, he said, lifted the nation to the heights of political morality and social responsibility. But this was to no avail.[12]

Humphrey chaired his state campaign for Roosevelt and Truman, made countless speeches in their behalf, and got to meet Democratic leaders, including the new DNC chair, Robert Hannegan. Humphrey's efforts helped Roosevelt and Truman win Minnesota over New York governor Thomas E. Dewey and Ohio governor John Bricker by 82,000 votes. The DFL elected its first two congressmen, Frank Starkey, a Farmer-Labor veteran, in the fourth district (St. Paul), and William Gallagher, a sixty-six-year-old long-term sanitation worker, upset incumbent Republican Richard Pillsbury Gale in the third district (suburban Minneapolis).[13]

In December, a disconsolate Humphrey wrote Wallace that "power politics" seemed to have returned in Britain, Russia, and "even America," and that this would undermine public support for the nascent United Nations. Further, conservative forces were coming to the fore in the Democratic Party, and his hope that Wallace would be named secretary of state went unfulfilled; the post went to prominent businessman and New Deal administrator Edward R. Stettinius Jr. But Humphrey looked forward to having Wallace as "our presidential standard bearer in 1948." Wallace replied that Humphrey typified more than anyone else he knew "the hope of an effective constructive liberal party in a position of national responsibility."[14]

On April 12, 1945, Humphrey again wrote Wallace to congratulate him on being confirmed as secretary of commerce and to remind him that "Minnesota is expecting you to be our Presidential candidate in 1948." Before mailing the letter, however, at 5:05 p.m. Humphrey heard—he added in a handwritten postscript—of the "death of our great President." He hardly knew what to say: "It is as if one of our own family had died." And even though he thought that Truman would rise to the heights of statesmanship, he told Wallace, "How I wish you were at the helm . . . we need you as you have never been needed before." Wallace answered that he shared Humphrey's faith in Truman, who he thought had gotten off to "an unusually fine start."[15]

Humphrey, too, had gotten off to an unusually fine start in his second campaign to become mayor of Minneapolis. He had strong backing at the outset from the United Labor Committee for Political Action (ULC), an AFL and CIO coalition begun in 1944 to support Roosevelt and led by George Phillips, head of the Minneapolis Railroad Brotherhoods, and the Hennepin CIO Council, led by Wishart (who also headed the Hennepin DFL Party). Phillips gained Wishart's support by backing his endeavors and those of his Popular Front allies in state and national politics. The ULC, which sought to play a major role in Minneapolis politics, began to support Humphrey for mayor in early 1945, provided a major share of his campaign funds, and recruited volunteers to distribute literature, put out the inevitable lawn signs, and undertake voter registration. The DNC, which did not involve itself in local races, gave

Humphrey some funds, but his single largest contribution, two hundred dollars, came from his father.[16]

Labor's support was critical, although Humphrey carefully courted the business (and Republican) community, especially John Cowles, owner and publisher of the three major Minneapolis papers, the *Star-Journal*, the *Morning Tribune*, and the *Times*. Humphrey assured him that he would not be any special interest group's mayor and that he was determined to rid Minneapolis of its Syndicate and Combination, who, along with Chicago gangsters, ran the city's flourishing gambling, prostitution, and illegal liquor sales operations and fed the culture of corruption in the police department.[17]

Cowles introduced Humphrey to other business leaders, including John Pillsbury, head of Pillsbury Flour Mills, and that company's general counsel, J. Bradshaw Mintener, who became a prominent supporter, and Lucien Sprague, president of the Minneapolis and St. Louis Railroad. A group of young "Businessmen for Humphrey" backed him, and he won minority support when in late March a group of Jewish youngsters were beaten up in northern Minneapolis. Mayor Marvin Kline, seeking reelection, called for action to prevent future incidents, but Humphrey labeled this response "superficial" and insisted that the city had to create a human rights council and an FEPC, modeled on FDR's 1941 temporary body, to ensure equal employment opportunity. African American and Jewish communities now rallied to him.[18]

Humphrey also had a well-run campaign organization, chaired by Ralph Dickman, a lawyer and member of the Hennepin Board of Commissioners and Minneapolis Planning Commission. Naftalin directed publicity and fed favorable stories to the newspapers, and Kirkpatrick was a key adviser. An important new backer was Fred Gates, the son of Lebanese immigrants from Chicago. He spoke ungrammatically and was overweight but owned a penny arcade with pinball and penny movie machines on Hennepin Avenue in the heart of downtown Minneapolis and was highly versed about the city's deep-seated culture of crime and corruption. Once Gates became convinced that Humphrey intended to play it straight regarding law and order, he became a vital intelligence bureau and key fund raiser who shielded him from potentially compromising contributors and contributions, and remained an intensely loyal friend for the next quarter-century who asked for nothing in return.[19]

Humphrey used as his slogan the words of the contemporary hit song, "Accentuate the Positive, Eliminate the Negative." He emphasized the need for government reform, law and order (ridding the city of the "leeches of crime, vice, and corruption"), and planning for postwar housing, schools, and urban development. Labor distrusted Mayor Kline, and he lacked business community support. Further, in January 1945, one of his sharpest critics, Arthur Kasherman, whose scandal sheet the *Public Press* accused him of running the most corrupt administration in memory, was gunned down gangland style, with no one ever arrested for the murder. Humphrey won the primary in May by more than a two-to-one margin, and also gained the endorsement of Cowles's newspapers. He won the final vote on June 11 by a resounding 61 percent margin, 86,377 votes to 54,893 votes, carrying every ward in the city but one.[20]

Humphrey promptly declared his victory to be a "broad endorsement of the entire Roosevelt program" and a clear sign the trend in the area was toward "progressive and liberal policies." But this belied the fact that so-called liberals held only a fourteen-to-twelve margin over conservatives on the city council, and real power, especially over the budget, resided in that body, not the office of the mayor, whose chief authority was to appoint the police commissioner, with council approval. Humphrey, at age thirty-four the youngest mayor in the history of Minneapolis, the sixteenth largest city in the United States, was set to govern from the moment he took office on July 2, 1945.[21]

Mayor Humphrey's first priority was to appoint a police chief who would act decisively against organized crime, enforce the law evenly, bring down the high rate of violent crime and juvenile delinquency, and reform the corruption-ridden police department. Even before the election Humphrey had named Mintener chair of a twelve-person (four each from business, labor, and the general public) Advisory Law Enforcement Committee to recommend a police chief, although the two men were predisposed to Edwin Ryan. He was the current head of the department's internal security division (and Humphrey's former neighbor) and had attended the Federal Bureau of Investigation's National Academy. The committee quickly settled on Ryan, but Wishart, head of the Hennepin County CIO, held out—Humphrey had asked for a unanimous choice—for an outsider because of the police department's long record of hostility toward unions.

This allowed numerous councillors, who wanted to embarrass the new mayor, to oppose Ryan. But Humphrey personally persuaded Wishart that Ryan would not engage in witch hunts, although giving in nearly cost the CIO leader his position. Humphrey took to the radio to mobilize public support for Ryan, who was confirmed by a 21–4 vote after only two weeks of delay. And when the head of the Syndicate, "Chickie" Berman, came to see Humphrey, he made it clear that he was not interested in any split of the mob's "take"—but intended to "break" them.[22]

During his first year, Humphrey focused on law enforcement, even riding after hours with police in their squad cars to learn about the dark side of urban night life. Ryan posted the new mayor's order—"we will enforce the law"—and sought to rid the department of police who took or demanded payoffs from local businessmen, raided gambling establishments and destroyed their gaming equipment, and prosecuted liquor sales to minors but, as Humphrey insisted, without resorting to entrapment. He also prevailed on the tavern owners to agree to higher liquor license charges to fund salary raises for the police who, presumably, would no longer seek payoffs. Humphrey also established a chain-of-command reporting system for the police, and Ryan introduced modern FBI-style record keeping. But they were able to add only eighty officers, half their goal, to the five-hundred-person officer force, which was far smaller than in comparable cities.[23]

Most notably, Humphrey and Ryan largely succeeded in denying multiple liquor licenses to organized crime groups and in closing down many of their illicit operations by requiring city council, not just police department, control of the licensing procedure, although the council never fully reformed the procedure to end all illicit activity. One night in February 1947, shots were fired at Humphrey as he neared his house that he concluded were intended to scare—not kill—the reform-oriented mayor.[24]

Ryan sought to curb mob violence, enlisting FBI help in February 1945 to track down the fleeing owner of a gambling club who fatally shot a Teamster official. Ryan, who left his job in May 1946 to run for a county office, and Humphrey struggled to bring down the number of violent crimes, and during 1946–49, homicides declined from ten to three per year, and aggravated assaults went from forty-six to twenty-three. Humphrey's administration helped Minneapolis to shed much of its reputation as a crime capital.[25]

Humphrey also was determined to act swiftly to ameliorate Minneapolis's postwar housing shortage, which was intensified by the return of veterans, many of whom had young families or were eager to start them. The city needed to add about nine thousand units to reach its requisite goal of eighty thousand units. Even before his election, Humphrey had visited with federal officials and studied housing programs in New York, Chicago, and Louisville. After taking office, he proffered a three-point program that included a door-to-door campaign to list all unused living quarters; action by federal, state, and local authorities and social agencies to obtain prefabricated or emergency-style housing units under wartime legislation; and urging private contractors to build new units, although they preferred to construct more expensive housing than veterans could buy. After Humphrey spotted 107 US government-owned surplus trailers in Lima, Ohio, he created a representative Mayor's Housing Committee, which established a nonprofit corporation, the Minneapolis Veterans' Trailer Housing,

Inc., that borrowed thirty thousand dollars from a Hennepin County chapter of the American Red Cross to pay for the trailers, and then repaid the debt from trailer rentals.[26]

His administration orchestrated a relatively elaborate "Shelter-a-Vet" advertising campaign to urge Minneapolis residents to open their homes. This gained quarters for about three thousand veterans and their families, about one-third of the number of places needed. Humphrey secured another four hundred trailers and other temporary housing units from the federal government for use by veterans attending the University of Minnesota. But the city council denied Humphrey's pleas for funds to survey for sites for portable housing or to search vacant buildings for space convertible to living quarters. He did gain city council approval of a public referendum to establish a municipal housing authority empowered to issue bonds for home construction, but Minneapolis's voters rejected this proposal in November 1946.

He pressed the city council to issue housing bonds, but that body approved only seventy-two housing starts and appropriated no funds. In short, Minneapolis did not begin to resolve its housing crisis until federal housing programs began in 1947, and—as was the case in many urban areas—the problem did not truly abate until more well-to-do residents migrated to the suburbs, but they also took their tax base with them. Nonetheless, Humphrey gained national attention for his creative endeavors.[27]

The young mayor proved highly adept at brokering labor-management relations in Minneapolis, which were marked by a long record of violent confrontations, with more expected when wartime "cost plus" contracts guaranteeing corporate profits ended in 1945. Humphrey, a member of the American Federation of Teachers, was perceived as an ally of labor, had gotten strong backing from the ULC, and was friends with CIO leader Wishart. Humphrey also knew of the police department's antilabor history, and he developed rules to be followed when strikes seemed imminent. He told Chief Ryan that police were not to be used "promiscuously"—that is, forcefully against strikers— because this would discourage responsible parties from settling. "Any dummy can break up a picket line with the police. It takes brains to enforce picketing laws without cracking skulls," Humphrey said, and during his tenure, the police never intervened in a strike.[28]

Humphrey skillfully helped contesting parties reach accord. In July 1945, when workers at the Honeywell Corporation's main plant in Minneapolis were near striking over retroactive pay for wartime work, he pressed union leaders to "forget" this claim and proposed a new idea: a bonus, or premium payment, that broke the negotiating logjam. Humphrey also believed that wages had not kept pace with postwar price increases; thus, he and his aides developed the so-called Minnesota Formula to avert deadlocks in negotiations. The mayor would appoint a balanced labor-management committee to eliminate inequities in work conditions and wage classifications, followed by an overall 10 percent to 15 percent wage increase, with the same cents-per-hour increase given to all workers so as to give the greater percentage increase to the lowest-paid workers.[29]

Humphrey interjected himself into negotiations when he thought imminent or actual strikes jeopardized public welfare. When a labor dispute threatened closure of the city's ten hospitals in May 1946, he announced to both sides—with pickets already assembled—that "these aren't beer parlors or candy factories. These are hospitals, where some of your neighbors are sick or dying," and anyone who thought that he would permit the hospitals to be shut down was "plain crazy." This brought a rapid settlement.

On the other hand, when in spring 1947 striking telephone workers engaged in illegal picketing, Humphrey refused to send in the police on the grounds that this would cause violent confrontations. But when Bell Telephone sought to get around the pickets by having its supervisors sleep in their offices, the mayor defeated this maneuver by insisting, "If you want to run a hotel, you will have to apply for a license." Despite Humphrey's bias favoring labor—especially the lowest-paid workers—the Minneapolis business community quickly recognized his creative capacities and desire to maintain a peaceful and productive order, and they largely supported him, as long as he sought no office higher than mayor.[30]

The issue that most moved Humphrey, however, was rooting out discrimination in Minneapolis. African Americans comprised just 1 percent (5,000) of the city's population, and Jews were 5 percent (25,000). But only a handful of African Americans owned their own businesses; the vast majority struggled to find jobs, usually the most menial. Unions generally excluded them, and major hotels and restaurants denied them their facilities and services. Jews fared little better. In winter 1946, journalist Carey McWilliams published a scathing indictment, "Minneapolis: The Curious Twin," which labeled the city the "capital of anti-Semitism in America," whose deep prejudice had been rekindled by the Great Depression and nativist and Republican political attacks on former governor Elmer Benson for having Jewish aides. Jews in Minneapolis chiefly had to look to their own businesses for employment and were excluded from major civic and private organizations into the 1960s and, in some cases, the 1970s.[31]

Soon after his election, Humphrey and DFL chair Edgar Kelm went to Chicago to talk with Mayor Ed Kelly about a Fair Employment Practices (FEP) ordinance he was weighing. Humphrey sent his own draft FEP bill to the city council subcommittee on ordinances and legislation, which voted it down by 3–2. Naftalin told him that he had erred seriously by not giving advance notice of the bill to the council, allowing it to choose a subcommittee to review it. Humphrey further stumbled at the outset by seeking to establish a human rights council composed of prominent citizens he wanted to appoint, whereas the established organizations, such as the Urban League, NAACP, and Round Table of Christians and Jews, preferred to name their own people.[32]

Humphrey did establish in early 1946 a large advisory panel composed of leaders from business, labor, and the professions and a smaller ten-person Mayor's Council on Human Relations. He named as its head the Reverend Reuben K. Youngdahl, a dynamic and progressive Lutheran pastor who had built a large congregation and whose brother, Luther W. Youngdahl, a federal judge and Republican, would be elected governor that November. Humphrey charged his council with investigating all "cases involving discrimination." That body organized a major self-survey, drawn by Fisk University sociologists, that enlisted six hundred volunteers who went across the city to business and labor union offices, churches, hospitals, schools, and homes to query people about racial attitudes and discriminatory practices. The mayor's council got the city council to endorse, in mid-1946, a measure urging real estate agents to eliminate restrictive covenants from housing deeds when seeking that body's approval for their developments and, in early 1947, a measure banning dissemination of hate literature. Humphrey also got the council to make the Mayor's Council on Human Relations an official organ of city government, although it lacked legal authority and had to raise its own funds to maintain its staff and programs.[33]

Humphrey gained his most significant breakthrough in January 1947 when the city council finally passed an FEP ordinance by a 21–3 margin that outlawed discriminatory practices in hiring, firing, promotion, and compensation and— distinct from laws in Chicago and Milwaukee, the only other cities with such legislation—called for fines of up to $1,000, or jail sentences up to ninety days, for violators. The bill also established a commission (FEPC) to administer it, to which Humphrey appointed a diverse membership. But the body had a small budget and staff, and lacked subpoena power, and most cases arose from refusal to hire African Americans and were either dismissed or deferred. Breakthroughs in hiring were fewer than twenty in the city's stores, and results were scarcely better than in neighboring St. Paul, which lacked an FEP ordinance.[34]

Finally, Humphrey sought to desegregate one of America's greatest after-work facilities, bowling alleys, first in Minneapolis and then nationwide. He succeeded in his own city, and as president of the National Committee on Fair Play in Bowling Alleys in 1947 pressed the American Bowling Congress (ABC) to encourage the owners of the nation's 75,000 bowling alleys to open up their lanes to all players. But the ABC refused to budge, and Humphrey had to settle in April 1948 for having the Minneapolis and St. Paul Committee on Fair Play in Bowling sponsor a nondiscriminatory "All American Bowling Tournament."[35]

Overall, Humphrey's mayoral efforts represented a new or expanded form of liberalism that signaled new emphasis on pluralism, namely the use of government to establish a broad consensus on public issues. Like most New Dealers, he accepted the need for legal sanctions and the use of government to improve conditions for the disadvantaged, but he also believed in the need to establish shared community goals and to persuade the majority population to attempt to live up to its professed ideals. Further, while his fight, for example, for the FEPC was meant to open up economic opportunity for African Americans, Jews, and other disadvantaged groups, he was also broadening the liberal agenda to include addressing the issue of race by confronting segregation and discrimination in public accommodations and in police behavior.[36]

Humphrey reveled at being mayor. Even before his swearing in, he told publisher John Cowles that the importance or strength of an office depended on the enthusiasm, initiative, and capacity of the occupant. He rode in police cars and seemed omnipresent at union picnics, teachers' meetings, and sessions at veterans' housing. He regarded almost every issue in the city to be within his purview, be it building a bridge over railroad tracks or chiding the president of Cargill, the world's largest grain firm, for having moved its fuel depot from the city to the suburbs or pressing Northwest Airlines' president, Croil Hunter, not to shift its company headquarters to Seattle. When Hunter rejoined that the Metropolitan Airports Association had told him there was insufficient space for Northwest to expand at the Minneapolis–St. Paul Wold-Chamberlain Field, Humphrey flew to Washington to see General Omar Bradley, famed World War II commander of US forces in Europe. Bradley now headed the Veterans Administration (VA), which was about to take over Ft. Snelling, adjoining the airport. Humphrey persuaded Bradley to cede a large parcel of Ft. Snelling's land for airport expansion, and the general proposed as well to build a large VA hospital on the remaining ground. Humphrey proclaimed these developments a "ten-strike" for Minneapolis.[37]

Humphrey was so committed to his job that when his former thesis adviser at LSU, Robert Harris, wrote in fall 1945 to say that there was a position open in his department, he replied that he was flattered by the offer but there was "one little immediate problem—I'm Mayor." And "I haven't been home for supper five times in three months," he added boastfully. A year after his inauguration, he wrote to the *Morning Tribune's* executive editor, in response to a favorable editorial, "I literally live for the job."

Success was costly, however. Frances Humphrey chided her brother that he was often physically, and perhaps emotionally, distant from the demands of family life. Humphrey conceded that this was "inexcusable" but held that it was his style to "put my work ahead of my family," a pattern he would continue during his long political life. Muriel Humphrey grew accustomed to taking their children—numbering four after the birth of son Douglas in April 1948—on summer vacations by herself and projecting the manner of a gracious, philosophical, and forbearing partner "cheerfully resigned" to having a husband for whom family life was limited largely to the breakfast table.[38]

Humphrey did take the time, however, to read the comics over the radio to children kept home from the city's closed schools in 1946 when Minneapolis was hit by an epidemic of poliomyelitis (infantile paralysis) that brought two thousand cases of the dread disease. He also appealed successfully to the White House for use of Ft. Snelling's army barracks to house stricken children, including many who had come to the city to be cared for under the auspices of Elizabeth "Sister" Kenny, the self-trained Australian bush nurse who had migrated to the United States in 1940.

Kenny soon established a center in Minneapolis for treating polio victims with her controversial hot packs and muscle-relaxing therapy, rather than traditional immobilizing plaster casts and iron braces. Humphrey managed to beg and borrow sufficient beds, nurses, and hospital attendants to manage the Ft. Snelling operation during the 1946 epidemic. He also knew how to handle the famous Sister Kenny, whose 1943 autobiography, *And They Shall Walk*, became a best-seller and basis for a Hollywood movie. When she threatened to remove her clinic from Minneapolis if her patients were not shuttled back and forth more frequently, Humphrey said that the city was running a hospital for patients, not a bus service, and that if she wished to leave, he would help with her exit plans. The dispute ended, and afterward Humphrey (who once sent Sister Kenny roses at the airport) got the city council and the labor unions to contribute fifty thousand dollars each to start the Minneapolis Polio Research Commission. And under his stewardship, the city became the first one in the nation to offer free chest X-rays.[39]

Mayor Humphrey's commitment to improving Minneapolis's quality of life rapidly won him a large and politically diverse following. During his first term, he made well over a thousand speeches and some four hundred radio appearances, and he turned down countless other invitations. The Junior Chamber of

Commerce voted him the city's Outstanding Young Man in 1945, with the leaked list of selection committee members revealing an array of older—and Republican—bank and business presidents. The next year, the press chose Humphrey as Minneapolis's Man of the Year. By early 1947, Humphrey was geared up for reelection. His volunteer campaign committee was composed not just of the usual friends, liberals, and labor officials but also of an impressive group of business leaders, including Mintener; Samuel G. Wells, vice president of General Mills; Fred Wilson, vice president of Minneapolis-Honeywell Company; the Dayton family, owners of the city's largest department store; and many other senior business executives. Minneapolis's three newspapers, the *Star-Journal*, the *Morning Tribune*, and the *Times*, all endorsed Humphrey.[40]

Opponents had difficulty finding a challenger, finally settling on a little-known Republican attorney, Frank Collins, who was unable to raise a significant campaign issue. Both candidates favored the central ballot issue, a proposed 1 percent levy on all earned income, intended to raise some $5 million for the school system. Humphrey made clear that he would seek to modernize the mayor's office and powers. He handily defeated Collins in the primary in May and in the general election in June, winning every ward in the general contest and carrying the city by the largest margin (66 percent) in its history, 102,696 votes to 52,257 votes. But the tax levy, which inspired the large voter turnout, was defeated resoundingly—102,279 votes to 50,346 votes—largely because many of Humphrey's supporters, especially labor, opposed the measure, which did not include a tax on the income of corporations headquartered in the city.[41]

Humphrey turned to the issue of reform of the city charter, with urban analysts long convinced that the mayor lacked real authority to govern. He did not have a voice or a vote in the deliberations of the city council, which controlled the budget and appointed all department heads except the police chief. Humphrey had compensated for his office's weakness by his forceful persona and by appointing public commissions to mirror city agencies as a shadow government. In fall 1945, he established a tax and finance commission to assess the city's administration and finance and a fifteen-person commission—headed by his business supporter Mintener—to rewrite the city charter, which dated to 1870 and had last been modified in 1920.[42]

Many people feared that a stronger mayor and more centralized control augured higher taxes and increased municipal spending, despite the city's housing, education, police, and social service needs. Ironically, Humphrey's strength as mayor undermined his proposal. Numerous city councillors had ties to organized labor, and much as they and union leaders appreciated his efforts in behalf of their constituents, they worried that a different mayor might use his augmented power to harm their constituents' interests. At the same time, the business community, which initially backed charter reform as means to more efficient government and perhaps lower taxes, feared that Humphrey's success might be his springboard to challenge Republican senator Ball in the November 1948 elections. Humphrey complained to Mintener that it now appeared that "some of our Republican friends" intended to sacrifice the charter on "the altar of partisanship."[43]

Humphrey was determined to contest Ball, although he postponed a formal announcement until April 1948 because, in addition to the charter vote scheduled for March 24, he had to deal with a strike by the city's teachers, who were members of Humphrey's own union, the American Federation of Teachers (AFT). Their work stoppage began in late February, after the board of education, facing a $2 million budget deficit, proposed to shorten the school year by two weeks in the fall and in the spring and to reduce teachers' salaries accordingly.

The AFT in turn called for raising annual minimum salaries from $2,000 to $3,000 and maximum pay from $4,200 to $6,000. The board rejected this, and the AFT struck, with support from nonunion teachers. Humphrey insisted that this debacle proved the need for a much stronger mayoralty to manage city finances and labor relations. He called for raises for the lowest-paid teachers and pressed both the board and the AFT to accept mediation quickly, a call that his CIO friend and leader Wishart said strained the mayor's relations with the unions. But after a district court judge ruled that the city's welfare required both sides to agree to conciliation, the board and the AFT agreed to a settlement that rescinded the proposed school year and salary reductions and instead raised teachers' minimum and maximum salaries for the next two years, with a temporary 1 percent levy on all city tax assessments providing the needed funds. This agreement also raised Humphrey's standing with teachers and unions.[44]

Meanwhile, a taxpayers' lawsuit led the Minnesota Supreme Court to rule that submission to the voters of a proposed new charter calling for approval by a four-sevenths (57.14 percent) majority violated state law, which required that the document had to be submitted to the old charter as eighty separate amendments, each of which needed a three-fifths (60 percent) majority. Consequently, need to redraft the charter delayed the vote from March to December 1948—by which time Humphrey was focused on his new national political career.[45]

First, however, he and his closest political allies in Minnesota would have to engage in a fierce battle to wrest control of the DFL Party away from the so-called left-wing faction, or Communists, who had predominated since the merger in 1944. Humphrey would also be a delegate at the Democratic National Convention in July and deeply involved in his historic call for his party to embrace human rights over states' rights—and segregation. Throughout fall 1948, he would campaign almost nonstop to realize his public pledge of April 23: to dedicate all of his time and ability "to remove from office the senior [Republican] Senator from Minnesota," Joseph Ball.

With Humphrey immersed in national politics, and Republicans in Minneapolis no longer part of his bipartisan coalition, opponents of charter reform easily defeated it in December 1948. By then, however, Humphrey had won a landslide victory, and the senator-elect was on his way to Washington, DC, where, he had told Muriel a decade earlier, he dreamed of playing a significant role in the nation's politics.[46]

3

THE NEXT SENATOR FROM MINNESOTA

Mayoral duties had left little time for DFL politics, and Humphrey was stunned in winter 1946 when the highly organized left-wing Popular Front won decisively in populous Hennepin (Minneapolis) County and Ramsey (St. Paul) County caucuses that chose delegates to the DFL Party convention. He even lost his own bid for a seat and had to attend the meeting as a delegate at large. Upon arrival on March 30 in St. Paul to deliver the keynote address, he was jeered as a "Fascist" and "war monger" and unable to finish his bland speech affirming New Deal liberalism.[1]

The Popular Fronters gained control of the party chair, executive committee, and almost every party position. Humphrey managed only by appealing to his Popular Front and CIO labor leader friend Robert Wishart to have his compatriot Orville Freeman named party treasurer (soon elevated to the critical role of secretary) and his liberal activist friend Eugenie Anderson named second vice chairman.[2]

Humphrey hoped to avert a political split but changed his mind after Anderson arranged for him to meet in August 1946 with James Loeb Jr., an early national director of the Union for Democratic Action (UDA), a left-leaning, anti-Fascist group founded in 1941 that supported both FDR's interventionist policies and major domestic reform. In May 1946, Loeb publicly called on liberals to be committed no less to "human freedom" than to economic security and urged ending wartime cooperation on progressive causes with Communists. After conferring with Loeb, Humphrey told his supporters, "We will never win a statewide election, nor will we deserve to win one, unless we clean up our act." This was the "historic occasion," Anderson recalled, that led Humphrey to determine to wage an anti-Communist fight for control of the DFL Party.[3]

Humphrey now told an American Federation of Labor audience there was no political liberty under Communist governments in Europe. His view hardened as Washington-Moscow tension increased over Soviet policies in Eastern Europe, pressure for an Iranian oil concession and joint control of the Turkish Straits, failed negotiations over international control of atomic resources, and the US call in September 1946 for economic reconstruction of western Germany.[4]

Humphrey also broke with his political idol, Secretary of Commerce Wallace, whose speech on September 12 called for an end to President Truman's "get tough" policy with Russia and his contention the United States had no more reason to intervene in Eastern European politics than Moscow had to interfere in Western European or Latin American politics. This led to Wallace's forced resignation.[5]

Humphrey was dismayed that his "very personal friend, courageous progressive" was out of the cabinet; he disagreed with only "one small paragraph" of Wallace's speech, but this was the critical "spheres of influence" issue. Humphrey believed that "this is one world," and "whatever happens in any part of the world finally concerns us." He viewed spheres of influence diplomacy as "the philosophy that motivated Chamberlain at Munich. That is what brought on the World War."[6]

Humphrey broke completely with Wallace when he came to speak in Minneapolis on October 30 and declined his host's request to say that he did not endorse American Communists, stating that current "left-wing" regimes in Eastern Europe were emphasizing "freedom from want" and clumsily trying to help the common man. The speech ignored Moscow's imposition of Communist governments in Poland and Romania.[7]

During the November 1946 elections, the only DFL Party candidate Humphrey supported was John Blatnik, a Farmer-Labor legislator who won his congressional district that covered Duluth and the Iron Range. Republicans won the other eight seats, every statewide office, and control of the legislature. On the national scene, Republicans charged that Democratic liberalism had brought economic distress and failed to halt Soviet Communism abroad. The GOP gained control of both houses of Congress for the first time since 1928 by margins of 246–188 in the House and 51–45 in the Senate.[8]

The Democratic defeats augured a sharp divide on the Left in American politics. Humphrey and his friends, readying for ideological battle, promptly established a state UDA chapter, with Art Naftalin, Humphrey's mayoral aide, as chair and Anderson as secretary. Initial membership was about thirty-five people, and the group, along with the national UDA, was soon challenged on its left by the Progressive Citizens of America (PCA), formed in December 1946 by the merger of two prominent left-oriented groups: the National Citizens Political Action Committee and the Independent Citizens Committee of the Arts, Sciences, and Professions, which included such public luminaries as Albert Einstein. The PCA looked for political leadership to Wallace, who called on the group to fight the "forces of reaction" globally, but without allegiance to another country.[9]

In early January 1947, Humphrey, Naftalin, and Anderson traveled to Washington to participate in transforming the national UDA into the Americans for Democratic Action, which aimed to rival the PCA. The ADA founders were politically active liberals and strong anti-Communists with close ties to the New Deal. They included Eleanor Roosevelt; labor leaders Walter Reuther of the United Auto Workers (UAW) and David Dubinsky of the International Ladies' Garment Workers' Union (ILGWU); noted economist John Kenneth Galbraith; distinguished civil liberties lawyer Joseph Rauh; and Pulitzer Prize–winning historian Arthur Schlesinger Jr.[10]

Loeb was named executive secretary of the ADA, whose leadership quickly recognized Humphrey as a dynamic leader and eloquent speaker and named him a vice chair. The ADA members aimed to promote a more advanced liberal agenda, particularly civil rights, through the Democratic Party. They denied membership to Communists and held that the United States was obligated to lead the postwar world and contain the Soviet Union.[11]

Humphrey played a key role in building a Minnesota ADA chapter, which by March 1947 had one hundred members and a strong recruitment program. His split with the Left was soon catalyzed in March when President Truman called for $400 million in military and economic aid to Greece and Turkey and support for "free people" everywhere resisting subjugation. The Truman Doctrine signified US intent to take over near-bankrupt Great Britain's role in Greece and the Middle East but ignored that the conflict in Greece was led by a broad Left coalition that included Communists, not then aided by Moscow, that opposed a reactionary regime in Athens.[12]

Humphrey grew angry at Wallace and the PCA for denouncing the Truman Doctrine as dividing the world into two camps, and he publicly assailed the Communists and their DFL sympathizers as "totalitarians of the Left," insisting that DFL political philosophy could not be "dictated from the Kremlin" and that one could be a liberal and a progressive without being a Communist or Communist sympathizer.[13]

Humphrey and the national ADA soon rallied around Secretary of State George C. Marshall's speech on June 5 proposing major US economic aid to all of Europe's needy nations, although the Marshall Plan's design led the Soviet Union to create its own Eastern Bloc trading system and establish the Communist Information Bureau (Cominform) to coordinate Communist nations' foreign policies. The PCA and Wallace charged that the Marshall Plan divided East from West and subordinated Europe's economy to American capitalism.[14]

Humphrey happily lent his name to the Committee for the Marshall Plan to Aid European Recovery, deemed reconstruction of the Western European democracies to be of "vital and transcendent importance," and wrote Republican congressman Walter Judd that Congress's proper funding of the Marshall Plan would determine mankind's fate for the next thousand years. The current "cold conflict" was between two faiths, and the United States had to demonstrate its "spiritual superiority." Humphrey became a strong public proponent of the Truman administration's policy of containment of the Soviet Union and Communism.[15]

Humphrey also determined to root Communists out of the DFL Party and transform it into a party of "honest progressives." He doubted that there were enough Communists in Minnesota to dominate any organization but thought that many groups had enough "innocent followers" to be influenced by people who blindly followed the "Commie party line" and *Daily Worker*.[16]

Humphrey and his allies chose their new ADA chapter as their vehicle to gain control of the DFL Party at its June convention. He served as president, Anderson became state chairman, and Eugene (Gene) McCarthy, an unknown instructor in sociology and economics at the College of St. Thomas in St. Paul, became state treasurer. Freeman, a masterful planner who handled veterans' affairs in Humphrey's mayoral office, took on the jobs of secretary and chief organizer, and also joined the recently formed American Veterans Committee, whose members were more liberal than their World War I counterparts who controlled the American Legion.

Freeman was joined in the American Veterans Committee by an able group of political activists and anti-Communists, who became Humphrey allies. These included Donald Fraser, who later became a multiterm congressman; Gerald Heaney, a rising labor lawyer in Duluth and later an influential federal judge; Douglas Kelm, son of the former head of the Democrats and first chair of the newly formed DFL Party; and Max Kampelman, a wartime conscientious objector, lawyer, and young political science instructor at the University of Minnesota who would become Humphrey's legislative counsel during his first Senate term.[17]

As historian Jennifer Delton has explained, the Minnesota ADA members were exceptionally disciplined and made no pretense at being a mass movement. Ironically, much like the Communists, whom they disdained, they selected their prospective party leaders and associates with extreme care, sifting through stationery headings and party lists to determine who was "okay" and who "commie-line." As Freeman wrote, it was necessary to draw lists of people in every county and to write every name on a separate card with the information kept "up to date and continually supplemented," and each person marked " 'O.K.' or 'B' (bad) in ink."[18]

By spring 1947, Humphrey and his relatively young counterparts—often disparaged by opponents as the "diaper brigade"—were ready to purge the "militant minority," that is, Communists, from the DFL Party. As Humphrey wrote in late 1947, "If anyone can show me how the Commies believe in democracy," he would be willing to learn.[19]

ADA ranks grew from 100 to 538 dues payers by late 1947. Humphrey used his ties to the Minneapolis Central Labor Union to recruit key Teamster and Boilermaker leaders, and the AFL and CIO encouraged union workers to join the ADA.[20]

At this time, Humphrey had an "exhilarating" five-and-a-half-hour meeting with CIO head Philip Murray, in which he stressed his need for strong union support for his Senate run in 1948 in order to unseat Republican Joseph Ball, a major proponent of the 1947 Taft-Hartley Labor Management Act, which allowed employers to contest unions in representation elections. Humphrey pledged not to accept DFL Party aid as long as the Popular Front remained in control. Murray, who feared that Popular Front criticism of Truman's Cold War policies might bring further Republican gains at labor's expense, agreed to send money and three people to align union workers in Minnesota with Humphrey, and UAW head Reuther paid for a full-time CIO staffer to focus on Twin Cities' union workers.[21]

After the left wing of the DFL Party decided to create a statewide Young Democratic-Farmer-Labor (YDFL) organization and hold a state convention, Humphrey's allies recruited college students who had joined the ADA's Students for Democratic Action (SDA) chapters to fight for control of the YDFL. Humphrey addressed a meeting of more than six hundred University of Minnesota students. McCarthy, at St. Thomas, and Walter Mondale—then an undergraduate at Macalester College in St. Paul—and other liberals at St. Olaf's and Carleton Colleges in Northfield recruited student activists, while Heaney in Duluth and Teamster official Jack Jorgenson in Minneapolis pulled in young workers. As Doug Kelm recalled, by the time of the YDFL convention on November 9, 1947, Humphrey's factions were able to "steamroller" passage of their resolutions to take control of the YDFL.[22]

Still, Humphrey sent an "S.O.S." message to DNC executive secretary Gael Sullivan and Postmaster General Robert Hannegan stating that although recent polls showed him running ahead of Ball and Governor Luther Youngdahl, he would not enter the Senate race unless he got more money. He claimed that the left-wingers had turned the DFL Party into a "Commie Front organization," that he and his ADA chapter were the only real opposition to the Communists, and that he alone was willing to speak for Truman.[23]

Humphrey's battle with the Left intensified after Wallace announced on December 29, 1947, that he would run for president in 1948 as the candidate of a new party and that the Popular Front faction of the DFL Party aimed to nominate him, forcing Truman to run in Minnesota as a third-party candidate. Ironically, Wallace's prospective candidacy and a tense European scene may have helped both Truman and Humphrey. The president, urged on by his special counsel Clark Clifford, turned to a liberal domestic agenda and a strong stand against the Soviet Union in the belief that the greater the sense of "crisis," the more Americans supported the president. Truman's January 1948 State of the Union address proffered a liberal economic agenda, and in February he sent major civil rights legislation to Congress based on the November 1947 report, *To Secure These Rights*, of the high-powered President's Committee on Civil Rights. Truman said he would desegregate the military and end discrimination in the civil service by executive orders but held back when his poll ratings, especially in the South, began to slide. This civil rights program—concerned with voting rights, nondiscrimination in employment, antilynching laws, and freedom of expression—would become the basis of Humphrey's powerful charge to Democrats at their coming national convention.[24]

A bitter political struggle in Czechoslovakia in February 1948 led to the freely elected non-Communist government having to cede control to Communist leaders. Many Americans and Europeans analogized the actions of the Communists and Soviet leader Joseph Stalin to those of the Czech Nazis and Adolf Hitler during the 1938 Munich crisis, and in ringing speeches on March 17, Truman for the first time publicly blamed the Soviet Union for having caused the Cold War and destroyed Czech democracy. In the current world battle between "tyranny and freedom," he did not want the support of "Henry Wallace and his Communists."[25]

Neither did Humphrey. From late 1947 he began to press DFL Party leaders who supported Wallace to resign and to pillory DFL members whom he suspected of being Communists or being too inclined to their viewpoint. He and his supporters also planned to take over the DFL Party. As Freeman later recalled, "There are still some people who resent how rough we were. I drew the line, very, very tough with some old friends. I said if you didn't go with us in this fight, you were on the other side and you were out, and that was too bad. We paid a price for it, but we wouldn't have won otherwise."[26]

Humphrey's contingent secured control of the DFL Party apparatus and drew up voter lists for the state's four thousand precincts, named and trained captains for each, and—especially in the cities—held meetings to instruct their supporters about procedures in the April caucuses that would choose delegates to the state convention in June. Freeman also established the DFL Volunteers for the state's most populous areas—Minneapolis, St. Paul, and Duluth and the Iron Range—and they put out recruiting and instruction pamphlets stating that voters faced a choice between the DFL Party becoming a clean and honest Progressive Party or a "Communist Front Organization" and charging that the Communist Party was the most dynamic element in Wallace's campaign.[27]

The Popular Front accused Humphrey and his backers of ties to the "unsavory" ADA, being too close to the Cowles press and General Mills in Minneapolis, and serving as "liberal window dressing" for the Wall Streeters and "militarists" who were allegedly driving Truman's foreign policy. In turn, Humphrey and his allies charged that their opponents had "aided and abetted" the Communist Party, which they said stood for "totalitarianism and suppression of individual freedom," and his secretary George Demetriou asked the liberal anti-Communist journalist James Wechsler, head of the *New York Post's* Washington bureau, for material with which to smear Henry Wallace.[28]

By mid-April 1948, Humphrey's camp grew concerned that the Popular Front might win in Hennepin County—including by forging credentials—and pick up enough votes in Ramsey and St. Louis Counties to control the state convention and make Wallace the party's presidential nominee and choose James Shields—a former National Labor Relations Board official and Freeman's father-in-law—over Humphrey for the Senate race. Naftalin urged abandoning their "namby-pamby" tactics and using their control of the party's steering committee to deny seats to Wallace supporters at the precinct caucuses on grounds that they were members of another party.[29]

After Humphrey and Freeman learned on April 16 that the left-wing DFL Association had mailed out fake credentials for the precinct caucuses, the Humphrey-controlled steering committee announced that supporters of Wallace's third-party movement violated the DFL Party constitution mandating its members to advance the interests of the national Democratic Party and to elect delegates to its national convention and that they would have to turn their convention seats over to loyal Democrats.[30]

Humphrey issued a "Message to DFL Liberals" on April 18 calling for a "new policy of imaginative common sense liberalism" at home, a foreign policy "posture of preparedness," economic aid, and a lasting vision that would "win the battle for men's minds and hearts." He derided Wallace's foreign policy as "appeasement."[31]

The next day, Humphrey charged that Wallace's third-party movement was part of Moscow's plan to cause Americans to fight one another, and in a radio address four days later, he assailed Popular Front leaders for remaining "strangely silent" about aggressive acts of Russian policy. "We too believe in the century of the common man," he said. "But we are not prepared to see the century of the common man become the century of the Comintern." ADA supporters believed in a "militant and democratic program of the middle" that would comprise a "program of freedom for ourselves and other people."[32]

Humphrey "gleefully" reported to the national ADA that his forces had won a "resounding" victory in the crucial precinct caucuses on April 30, winning a majority in eighty-three or eighty-four of the state's eighty-seven counties. Minnesota now had the basis of a truly liberal grass-roots political movement, he said, and he attributed this "dramatic coup" to the ADA, the only body willing to take on "the Commies." Key ADA people now controlled the three largest counties. Freeman, the campaign "watchdog and organizer," was DFL Party vice chairman in Hennepin Country; McCarthy was the party leader in Ramsey County; and Heaney and his labor allies were highly active in DFL Party affairs in St. Louis County.[33]

A triumphant Humphrey said that the fight had brought in thousands of new young members and AFL, CIO, and Railroad Union Brotherhood union people. Most important, the people battling to reform the DFL Party were "all Roosevelt New Dealers," and he was "proud . . . to carry the banner of liberalism." The Popular Front announced that it would hold a Progressive-Democratic-Farmer-Labor Party convention in Minneapolis in June, while Humphrey's DFL wing met in Brainerd.

But the DFL Party's credentials committee, composed largely of Humphrey supporters, awarded Ramsey and St. Louis County delegations to his following and referred the Hennepin County case, where there had been dual precinct caucuses, to the full convention, which voted unanimously to seat his entire delegation.[34]

Humphrey's wing quickly named his allies to key positions: Anderson became national Democratic committeewoman and Freeman, DFL Party state chairman. He appointed Humphrey loyalists to offices statewide to replace party officials who backed Wallace. Shortly, the Minnesota ADA disbanded, having taken over the DFL Party.[35]

Most important, the DFL Party nominated Humphrey by acclamation for the US Senate, and his acceptance speech affirmed the DFL as a "fighting party that is going to war with the Republican Party." The "eyes of the nation were upon Minnesota," he said, which had brought Populism and "a native American philosophy of liberalism that provided the inspiration for the New Deal." He made clear the need to elect a Democrat as president but did not mention Truman's name.[36]

Notably, he resisted a DFL Party endorsement of Truman for president and instead backed the national ADA's position favoring an "open" Democratic convention. He brokered a compromise motion commending Truman's "real courage" in vetoing the Taft-Hartley bill and supporting the Marshall Plan and resisting Communism and the Soviet Union—but twenty of the party's slate of twenty-six presidential delegates to the forthcoming Democratic convention remained uncommitted.[37]

The Progressive DFL Party people "reconvened" at their Minneapolis convention and nominated James Shields to contest Humphrey for the DFL Party Senate nomination in the September primary. They named candidates for Congress and state offices and a slate of presidential electors pledged to Wallace. They were first to file their choices with Minnesota's secretary of state and claimed exclusive right to use of the name "Democratic" on the state ballot. Thus, when Humphrey's DFL Party shortly filed its election certificate, a Republican secretary of state rejected it. Ultimately, however, a unanimous Minnesota Supreme Court held that this "factional" dispute was best settled by allowing both wings of the DFL Party to place their candidates on the September primary ballot, with the voters to determine the winners, whose names and party affiliation would appear on the November ballot. This was a victory for Humphrey's DFL Party, far better organized than its left-wing opponents, although they would labor hard to defeat him for the Senate nomination.[38]

Humphrey worried that Truman was not committed to a strong liberal domestic agenda and was likely to lead the Democrats to major defeat in November. Humphrey's concerns intensified in February 1948 when southern governors threatened to deny electoral votes to any Democratic candidate who supported the president's civil rights package, and he soon shelved the program. Humphrey wrote ADA chairman Leon Henderson in March 1948 that the tragedy of the liberal movement was that "we have everything except a dramatic and appealing symbol on the national level," and there was "no enthusiasm out here for

Truman"; "for the good of the country, for the good of the party, and for the good of the progressive movement," prominent leaders should ask him to step aside. Otherwise, "the whole social Democratic bloc" would be defeated in November.[39]

The *Minneapolis Star-Journal* and the *Minneapolis Times* named Humphrey as at the forefront of a "Dump Truman" movement and quoted him as saying that southerners had revolted against the administration not because of the president's civil rights program but because they were "convinced that Mr. Truman cannot win." At the same time, mayoral secretary George Demetriou wrote *New York Post* columnist Jimmy Wechsler that "like you and everyone else in the country we are burning the wires to find out how we can get rid of the present incumbent—and at the same time measuring ourselves for new uniforms." In April, Humphrey cabled Chester Bowles, an ardent New Dealer and former head of the Office of Price Administration, that "the re-election of the President is a political impossibility purely aside from the rightness or wrongness of backing him."[40]

Humphrey, his ADA colleagues, and many liberal Democrats were inclined toward World War II icon General Dwight Eisenhower, despite doubts about his liberalism; the Minnesotan also looked to the highly liberal Supreme Court Justice William O. Douglas but thought he would likely lose. Occasionally, a newspaper cited Humphrey as a possible presidential candidate, which he brushed off, although Demetriou requested a copy of a *Milwaukee Journal* editorial that mentioned the mayor. Humphrey did harbor thoughts about a possible vice presidential nomination, and in the spring he prevailed on three ADA friends, Loeb, Rauh, and Anderson, to travel to Hyde Park, New York, to ask Eleanor Roosevelt whether he might be Truman's running mate. She thought it would be a good way for him to become better known, and in late June ADA officials agreed to support a Humphrey movement at the Democratic convention if the Minnesota delegation requested this.[41]

Humphrey tried to stay on the DNC's better side by praising Truman's veto of the Taft-Hartley bill in 1947 and fostering of the Truman Doctrine and Marshall Plan. But his sentiment was evident when he and his DFL colleagues sent twenty of their twenty-six delegates uncommitted to the national Democratic convention. He was not optimistic about finding a new standard-bearer but believed that a strong civil rights plank would help him contest Senator Ball, perhaps minimize Henry Wallace's appeal to liberals, and bolster Democrats nationally against Republicans. As he wrote in April 1948 to New York City mayor William O'Dwyer, "This is one of those fortunate instances where the only realistic political alternative is also the best moral alternative."[42]

Nonetheless, before the convention began, Humphrey recognized, as his father told him, that Truman would be the nominee and that Hubert Jr. would be wise not to show his hand for someone else and stay in the administration's good graces. Further, Truman was a "fighter" who would "lick the bunch of Hi-jackers." As for the vice presidency, if Hubert Jr., as he said, wanted his father to second his nomination, he should write the speech, but he never did. Civil rights remained the key issue for Humphrey.[43]

Humphrey knew that he confronted a challenging political landscape in spring 1948. Minnesota was a Republican state. Moreover, although Humphrey's followers in Minneapolis were relatively young and issues-oriented, Democrats, especially in St. Paul, were viewed as traditional urban machine politicians and had little appeal to rural voters, which made up half of the electorate. A strong conservative GOP majority controlled the state legislature, and Republican governor Youngdahl was a highly popular social progressive who would desegregate the Minnesota National Guard in 1948 by executive order and favored state and federal FEPC laws. Both Republican senators Ball and Edward Thye were internationalists, although Ball lost some Republican backers after he supported Roosevelt's reelection in 1944 and labor disliked him for favoring the Taft-Hartley bill. Humphrey trailed him by a good margin in a March 1948 poll.[44]

There was also the specter of the popular former governor Harold Stassen, seeking the Republican presidential nomination, who had returned from service in the Pacific and was Roosevelt's delegate to the San Francisco conference marking the formation of the United Nations. He gained some surprising victories in early primaries and ran well ahead of Truman in presidential polls, but he fared poorly in a crucial debate in Oregon with New York governor Thomas E. Dewey by proposing to outlaw the Communist Party. Dewey soon won a third-ballot victory at the Republican convention in late June in Philadelphia and chose as his running mate Earl Warren, the popular and respected governor of California. The moderate Republican platform called for support for the United Nations, foreign aid, the new state of Israel, and many New Deal programs. The Republicans also challenged the Democrats on civil rights by calling for desegregating the military and federal legislation to enforce equal opportunity in the workplace and to end lynching and poll taxes.[45]

Humphrey wrote to Secretary of Defense James Forrestal strongly supporting Governor Youngdahl's intention to integrate the Minnesota National Guard by executive order as "completely right," insisting that there was no "moral, legal, or political reason" to withhold federal funds because of the US policy of segregation in the military. In the weeks before the Democratic convention,

Humphrey also urged prominent Democrats to promote a strong civil rights plank and not to let the South continue to set the agenda on the issue because this would strengthen "our reactionary Republican opponents" and Wallace's "Communist-dominated Third Party movement."[46]

Humphrey gained support from some prominent liberals and mayors of large cities, and Connecticut senator J. Howard McGrath, chair of the DNC, named him to the platform drafting committee led by Truman supporters Senators Francis Myers of Pennsylvania and Minority Leader Scott Lucas of Illinois. Humphrey met with the group in Philadelphia starting on July 7. But he and his liberal allies made no headway against southerners' demand for a states' rights plank, while McGrath, speaking for the White House, proposed a compromise that restated the vague 1944 platform vowing federal government protection of constitutional rights but leaving states in control of critical matters such as voting, employment, schools, and public facilities.[47]

The first nationally televised Democratic convention opened on Monday, July 12, with defeat in November in the air, although Kentucky senator Alben Barkley's rousing keynote address electrified the delegates as he recounted every Democratic achievement from Jefferson to FDR's New Deal. But he referred to civil rights only by noting that Jefferson's declaration that all men were equal meant "equality in the right to enjoy the blessings of free government in which they may participate and to which they have given their consent." His oration drew a lengthy ovation and a "spontaneous" Barkley for vice president demonstration.[48]

The president, watching on TV at the White House, was displeased that Barkley had mentioned his name only once casually and was also miffed that Justice Douglas, citing political inexperience, had just refused his running-mate offer. Thus Truman tendered the vice presidential nomination to "old man Barkley," as he called him—a congressman during 1912–26 and a senator since then—although he was not an ideal choice to balance the ticket: he was almost seventy-one years old, his home state bordered Missouri, and many voters might have viewed him as too liberal.[49]

Humphrey labored for the convention's first two days with Senator Myers's small drafting group to secure a meaningful civil rights plank, but the cautious platform committee voted to restate the 1944 plank. This led to Humphrey's long night of soul-searching and decision to address the convention on the third and final day, in which he dramatically and successfully implored his party to "walk forthrightly into the bright sunshine of human rights" and to adopt his proposed minority plank—based on the *To Secure These Rights* report—calling for every individual's right to full political participation, equal opportunity employment, security of person (against lynching), and equal treatment in military service.[50]

When the Democrats reconvened on the evening of July 14, half of the Alabama delegation and all of Mississippi's bolted from the meeting, intent to form a new party. Truman arrived at the convention site, where he and Barkley waited together through four hours of seconding speeches before the president won an expected first-ballot victory with 948 votes against 263 token votes for Senator Richard Russell of Georgia, a powerful conservative and implacable foe of civil rights legislation. There was no customary motion to make Truman's nomination unanimous, however, while Barkley was nominated by acclamation.[51]

Finally, at 1:45 a.m., Truman and Barkley mounted the podium. The vice presidential nominee spoke briefly about carrying the story of Democratic achievements across the nation, after which a surprisingly feisty Truman declared that he and Barkley would win in November and make the Republicans like it. He assailed them as the party of special privilege and cited their failure as leaders of the Eightieth Congress to pass his administration's education, health care, housing, and civil rights legislation. Truman also stunningly announced that he would call Congress back into special session on July 26 ("Turnip Day" in Missouri) to act on his proposals, including civil rights. He drew a standing ovation and inspired thought that the Democrats might win in November.[52]

Humphrey, however, was the convention hero. As a United Press (UP) report said, he was the man "most responsible for putting over the New Deal civil-rights plank," although he called the victory a matter of "conscience" and political realism, and gave signal credit to "Boss" Flynn, "who gave me the courage." The national Democratic Party now knew who young Humphrey was and were relying on him, even in a presumably Republican year, to defeat Ball in one of the "hottest senatorial races in the country." As UP writer George Marder noted, shortly after arriving at the convention Humphrey went to Democratic headquarters, and after he left, a sign—soon widely distributed—appeared: "HUMPRHEY WAS HERE."[53]

Two thousand supporters greeted Humphrey at the Minneapolis train station on his return and carried him high on their shoulders along with placards proclaiming, "Humphrey Champion of Human Rights," to an eighty-car procession to city hall. He retold his convention saga and generously credited Truman for passage of the civil rights plank.

Angry southern Democrats met in Birmingham on July 17 to nominate Governors J. Strom Thurmond of South Carolina and J. Fielding Wright of Mississippi to head their States' Rights Party. These "Dixiecrats" charged the federal government with "police state" tactics in interfering with the states' "domestic institutions," said that they stood for "the segregation of the races and the racial integrity of each race," and called on Democrats to replace Truman and Barkley on their ballots with Thurmond and Wright, but only Alabama, Louisiana, Mississippi, and South Carolina did this.[54]

Wallace's new party met in Philadelphia six days later, with many of its liberal, labor, and farm groups having returned to the Democrats. His backers took the Progressive Party name, nominated him for president, and chose for vice president first-term senator Glen Taylor of Idaho. Their platform called for expanded civil rights, national economic planning, and the United States and Soviet Union taking joint responsibility to end the Cold War.[55]

Truman issued executive orders mandating equal opportunity (desegregation) in the military and federal civil service and called Congress into special session on July 26. He proposed legislation to curb inflation and foster low-rent housing construction, measures he knew a Republican Congress would not pass in an election year, but this would permit him to assail a do-nothing Congress.[56]

Humphrey was ready for his first Senate race. He dismissed the States' Rights Party as "rebel noise," and said that the Democrats would not survive if they compromised with the opponents of progressive democracy. "The Democratic Party belongs to the liberal people," he wrote to his ADA compatriot Bowles, "and it is about time we justly claimed that it was ours."[57]

Humphrey felt little challenge in the DFL Senate primary from the largely politically unknown Shields, whose left-wing allies attacked him as "much talk and little action," as well as a tool of Wall Street who would turn against labor once elected. Humphrey's campaign denounced Shields as always following the Communist Party line, and on September 14 he won by almost eight to one, 200,050 votes to 26,925. He swept all eighty-seven counties, helping to defeat nearly all of the other Popular Front candidates. This ended that group's role in Minnesota politics, although it reorganized as a new Progressive Party and got Wallace on the state ballot as its candidate for president. But the former commerce secretary endorsed Humphrey over Ball for the Senate.[58]

Freeman ran Humphrey's campaign. He sent operatives into the rural districts, oversaw an outpouring of press releases and position papers, and pulled together a major coalition of national and state labor and farm groups.

Humphrey's first major press release on August 5 staked out advanced liberal positions on domestic issues: the federal government had to correct the "ups and downs of the economy," foster full employment, create a welfare state within a capitalist context, and advance "human and civil rights," especially equal rights for African Americans. He strongly favored Marshall Plan aid and said that freedom was under attack from "the left and the right" and that America had to choose "the middle course of democratic action."[59]

Humphrey faced a formidable candidate in Ball, an early frontrunner, but with serious political deficits. Minneapolis's major newspapers, owned by the Republican Cowles family, endorsed him, if only because they did not want to see their favorite Democratic mayor advance to wave his party's banner on the national scene. Ball was a leading internationalist, but this cut into his support among isolationist-inclined farmers in rural areas, and many Republicans were angry at him for having supported Roosevelt over Dewey in 1944. The still popular Stassen, now president of the University of Pennsylvania, added that he was also "keenly disappointed" that Ball had retreated from early support for the Marshall Plan to being one of only seventeen senators who voted against it in March 1948, claiming that it did not do enough to move Europe toward economic self-sufficiency. Further, Ball, once a strong Newspaper Guild member, had become a leading advocate of the Taft-Hartley bill, which inspired national and local unions to make his defeat a major priority.[60]

Humphrey kicked off his campaign on Labor Day with speeches in Faribault, a small town an hour south of the Twin Cities, then traveled farther southeast to Rochester, after which he drove 225 miles north to Duluth. He proved an indefatigable campaigner, driving all day and night to speak—from a flatbed truck, with microphone in hand—to countless gatherings at ethnic or nationality picnics or festivals. He shook every hand he could, ate hot dogs until they were "coming out of my ears," and shrugged off critics' charges that it was "not dignified to campaign for U.S. Senator that way." He said he was delighted to appear at carnivals, where the barkers would point him out as "my friend . . . who is going to be the new Senator from Minnesota."[61]

Humphrey did not seek to exploit nationality, ethnic, or religious hatreds; rather, as historian Jennifer Delton has pointed out, he played to "the innocuous comfort of ethnic pride." He likened campaigning to running a drugstore: it was necessary to show interest in people and "take them to the door." He traveled at least twice into each of the state's eighty-seven counties, drove more than 31,000 miles (equal to the total of Truman's national whistle-stop campaign), and gave some seven hundred speeches (almost twice the number the president did).[62]

National labor unions provided significant aid for Humphrey, who warned the Minnesota AFL convention in September that "the American Labor Movement is the target and on the firing line. . . . This election is the most important of your life." A CIO agent, Smaile Chatek, who had helped Humphrey reorganize the DFL, now rallied Iron Range miners and steel-workers—many of whom were Wallace supporters—to his side, and many CIO locals in Duluth withdrew from their CIO council, which inclined toward Wallace, and redirected their dues to a Humphrey political action committee. President Emile Rieve of the Textile Workers led rallies in the Twin Cities, and AFL president William Green addressed a massive labor rally in late October in Minneapolis, where he decried Ball as having double-crossed labor and proclaimed Humphrey as "the most brilliant and sincere exponent of liberalism in the country."[63]

Robert Wishart, the left-wing head of the powerful Central Labor Union who collaborated with Humphrey as mayor, broke a CLU council tie vote to affect his endorsement. He became honorary chairman of Humphrey's Minneapolis campaign, and the CLU paid for eight telephone lines and sixteen operators to register new voters and arranged for four hundred electrical workers to go door-to-door to get out the vote in working-class districts on Election Day. Similarly, farmers and their cooperatives, especially the powerful Farmers Union Grain Terminal Association of St. Paul, swung behind Humphrey, who stood with them to oppose a feared Republican proposal to impose a corporate tax rate on the excess of revenue over costs that cooperatives rebated to their members. Members of the Jewish community, who would long support Humphrey, also provided important financial help.[64]

Humphrey issued a broad statement of his views in early October in the small city of Bemidji, in the center of the state. He decried the nineteenth-century outlook of those who saw government as a "dead hand" that could not contest inexorable "supply and demand" forces, and he proffered instead a twentieth-century "warm heart" view that aimed to improve individual and community life, whether this meant ridding a city of criminal influence, promoting community relations, or regulating banks and railroads and building highways and providing social security. The purpose of government, he said, was to do for people what they could not do themselves, which included not only improved wages and working conditions and increased agricultural prices and farm supports, but "health care for all," an issue he would promote for the next thirty years.

He also said American democracy was in a battle with Fascism on the Right and Communism on the Left, "two sides of the same counterfeit coin," and that the Marshall Plan was the most significant application of American values against these twin evils. And those who, like Ball, voted against it were "the unthinking bedfellows of the Communist Party." Further, US foreign policy had to be an extension of domestic policy; Americans could not urge Europe to treat labor respectfully while imposing the "punitive" Taft-Hartley Act at home. Humphrey also sketched his longer-term hopes for international control of atomic energy and armaments, a stronger United Nations, and, ultimately, world government.[65]

President Truman campaigned in Minnesota, "this center of practical liberalism," on October 13, first in a whistle-stop in Duluth, and then in St. Paul, where he addressed an overflow audience of more than three thousand people at the Municipal Auditorium. He said he was "proud to salute a fighting liberal," the next senator from Minnesota, as well as the "liberal and progressive forces of the whole region." He assailed Ball for his "fanatic zeal" in pushing through the "shameful" Taft-Hartley Act, and reminded his audience that Republicans expelled their liberals, such as Theodore Roosevelt and Robert La Follette. Americans now had to choose between the "forces of liberalism" that had provided so many benefits as opposed to the "Wall Street way of life and politics" that would cut it all back and limit medical care and hospitals to "people who can afford them." He called on "liberals and progressives" to unite behind the great program of social advance the Democrats had pioneered since 1933.[66]

Humphrey, like Truman, was adept at responding to his opponents. When Ball sought to label him as a man of the extreme Left, Humphrey retorted that he believed private property was "so good that everybody should have some of it, not a few all of it." He also wished to break up monopolies, "the socialism of the big corporations." In a national radio broadcast on October 14 sponsored by the International Ladies' Garment Workers' Union, he implored Americans to protect themselves against "the bandits of big business" and "the corruption of our country by greedy corporations." It was time, Humphrey said, "somebody went to Congress who will raise his voice for the underprivileged and the oppressed," and he assailed the "enemies of labor" who wished to re-create 1930s conditions of "widespread unemployment, low wages, and long hours."[67]

By mid-October, *Time* noted, Ball was running behind the "glib and gregarious" Humphrey and seemed like a "tired messiah" uncomfortable with grassroots campaigning. Ball's seeming last chance to catch his opponent was their only debate on October 25 in St. Paul. But the senator's effort to insist that "government controls" had never worked in peacetime fell flat in the face of Humphrey's spirited advocacy of farm price supports and rural electrification as vital to the economy. Both men favored containment of the Soviet Union and Communism, but Humphrey pressed a greater US "political and diplomatic offensive" as opposed to Ball's unpopular vote against the Marshall Plan.

Years later, Ball recollected that he simply could not keep verbal pace with Humphrey, who "could talk a bird off a tree." But as *Time* noted in 1948, Humphrey had proven to be a "crack executive" who noticeably improved Minneapolis's civic life; he was a genuine friend of labor and a "staunch anti-communist liberal" who also won farmers' votes by campaigning in rural areas. And as Freeman would recall, Humphrey was the "guy with charisma . . . the leader" who knew how to inform a broad middle class of voters, laborers, farmers, and minorities where their interests lay and how he would champion them.[68]

Humphrey, his family, and friends gathered at his home on election night. When early returns indicated a major victory, he went downtown to campaign headquarters to celebrate with his supporters. He triumphed overwhelmingly, gaining 729,000 votes to Ball's 486,000 votes, winning eighty-five of eighty-seven counties, to become the first Democrat elected to the Senate in Minnesota by popular vote since the state adopted direct election in 1916.

Equally significant, Humphrey's heavy campaigning for young Gene McCarthy played a major role in his winning 59 percent of the vote in the fourth congressional district (St. Paul), and he greatly aided Fred Marshall, head of the state Farm Security Administration, to score a nationally noted upset in the sixth congressional district over thirty-two-year incumbent Republican Harold Knutson. John Blatnik, the only DFL congressman with his own strong following, won reelection in the eighth congressional district (Duluth). Republicans did retain five of the state's nine congressional seats, the highly popular Republican governor Youngdahl won easy reelection, and his party secured all the other statewide offices. But this was Minnesota Republicans' worst defeat in a decade, and with Humphrey at the DFL helm, his party's ascendancy was imminent.[69]

There was no certainty until the next morning, however, that Truman had won "the greatest personal triumph in the history of the country," as Humphrey wrote to him in a congratulatory note. Truman had achieved an historic upset, defeating Dewey by 24,180,000 votes to 21,190,000 votes, and winning the Electoral College by 303 to 189 votes. The presidential election was much closer than the results indicated: Truman won three crucial states, California, Ohio and Illinois, with a total of seventy-eight electors, by less than 1 percent of the ballots cast. Dewey won New York's forty-seven electoral votes by just 61,000 votes (out of 6 million), with Wallace denying Truman that state by winning

500,000 votes, nearly all in Democratic New York City. Wallace's vote also cost Truman Michigan's nineteen electors and Maryland's eight electors.[70]

Most significantly, Humphrey and other liberals critically affected the outcome of the presidential race. Early polls had overstated the firmness of Dewey's seemingly insurmountable lead, and most pollsters ended their canvassing by mid-October, thereby missing the late and heavy movement of "undecided" and "won't say" respondents to Truman and other Democrats. In Minnesota, for example, the *Minneapolis Morning Tribune*'s poll on October 26–28 showed Dewey and Truman even at 48.5 percent, with Humphrey leading Ball by 53 percent to 47 percent. But ultimately, Truman won by 58 percent to 40 percent, and Humphrey increased his margin to nearly 60 percent to 40 percent.

Unquestionably, Humphrey's relentless campaigning (and Truman's nationally) brought out a greatly increased urban Democratic vote and pulled in many new and vacillating rural supporters. Other strong winning liberals, who ran well ahead of Truman, helped him, including noted economist Paul Douglas, who managed a major upset in Illinois in trouncing incumbent Republican senator Wayland Brooks, and the liberal reform candidate, Adlai Stevenson, who won the state's governorship. Nationally, the Democrats regained control of Congress convincingly, going from a 6-seat deficit to a 54–42 majority in the Senate, and gaining 75 seats in the House for a 263–171 seat advantage. Democrats also went from a 24–24 split of governorships to a 29–19 lead.[71]

Domestic issues chiefly determined the election outcome. Humphrey's remarkable performance at the Democratic convention played a central role in putting a new national focus on civil rights, "progressive democracy," and "issues-oriented" politics and voting. As William Benton, a Minneapolis-born New Dealer, publisher of the *Encyclopaedia Britannica,* and an ADA colleague and contributor to Humphrey's campaign, wrote to him shortly after the 1948 election: "You are already one of the marked men in the Democratic Party. And the eyes of the country are upon you."[72]

4

LONELY, BITTER, AND BROKE
IN THE SENATE

Humphrey set out for Washington in December 1948 with his trusted mayoral aide William (Bill) Simms and loyal benefactor Fred Gates. The senator-elect settled on a comfortable four-bedroom home in a new but muddy development tract in nearby Chevy Chase, Maryland. He needed a loan from his father for a down payment: his new home cost almost twice the sum he received for his Minneapolis house. Muriel arrived shortly thereafter, driving a new Plymouth station wagon—courtesy of "generous" Minneapolis businessmen—with their four young children: Nancy, Hubert III ("Skip"), Bob, and ten-month old Doug, and the family's cocker spaniel.[1]

The senator-elect paid a courtesy call on President Truman, who remained friendly despite Humphrey's recent effort to deny him the presidential nomination. Humphrey also arranged a pre–New Year's visit to the White House for his mother, Christine, and father, Hubert Sr. The president graciously gave them a personal tour and assured them that their son would make a great senator. After Humphrey was sworn in on January 3, 1949, his father hinted that the presidency might be in his son's future. Hubert Sr. also indicated that his own health was failing and that Hubert Jr. needed to watch over his mother, older brother Ralph, and the family drugstore.[2]

Other signs of strain were soon evident. While the outgoing Eightieth Congress remained in special session in January, Humphrey was the only new senator not assigned a temporary office; he had to rely on downtown space provided by Paul Porter, a well-known Washington lawyer and Democrat. Humphrey diligently instructed his eight-person staff to reply to every letter and request (two thousand missives in a week, more than any other new senator) and to track actions taken, with highest priority given to prominent Minnesota citizens.[3]

His second slight came as he sat in the Senate gallery viewing each of his new peers being introduced by their state's senior senator. But Minnesota's two Republicans, Edward Thye and the defeated Joseph Ball, ignored him. Finally, moderate Democrat Lister Hill of Alabama escorted Humphrey to the Senate floor, a gesture he never forgot.[4]

There were few other encouraging signs. Newcomer liberal Democrats Paul Douglas of Illinois and Estes Kefauver of Tennessee and New Deal stalwart James Murray of Montana were welcoming. But Republicans and more conservative Democrats, especially the so-called Oligarchs from the one-party South who dominated the Senate, snubbed him. Humphrey was also "crushed" when he overheard the powerful Richard Russell of Georgia question how the people of Minnesota could send such a "damn fool" to represent them. Further, Democratic majority leader Scott Lucas of Illinois, who relied on southerners for support and had fought Humphrey's civil rights platform, blocked his desired appointment to the Agriculture Committee, important for Minnesota. Instead he was put on the little-known Government Operations and insignificant Post Office Committees and given the junior-most slot on Labor and Public Welfare, where the highly conservative Robert Taft of Ohio held sway.[5]

Humphrey was the first senator to hire an African American as a senior aide. Cyril E. King was from the Virgin Islands, where he would later be elected governor. But when Humphrey brought him to the Senators' Dining Room in 1949, the African American head waiter indicated that segregation was the rule. Humphrey exclaimed he "did not give a damn" whether his colleagues liked it, but his guest, who had dined in his home, would be served. The cash-strapped Humphrey also had to deal with countless invitations to expensive dinners and functions and was relieved to learn, after he asked, "When in hell do we get paid?" that the answer was "every two weeks," in cash.[6]

Muriel Humphrey, who had arrived in Washington with Emily Post's *Etiquette* under her arm, was distressed at having to spend her first Monday with Supreme Court justices' wives and the next day with wives of various congressmen. Soon fatigued, she went to a Baltimore hospital to learn that she was suffering stress from setting up a new home, caring for the schooling and recreational activities of four children, the demands of Washington social life, and her workaholic husband's absence from the house. At the end of the school year, she drove her four children twelve hundred miles to spend the summer in a cottage on Lake Leech, two hundred miles north of Minneapolis, but political demands on the new senator sharply limited his time to visit. On her return to Washington, Muriel hired daily household help.[7]

Humphrey was partly to blame for his early Senate difficulties. Before he arrived in Washington, he issued an offending public remonstrance that there were enough votes in Congress to pass a civil rights bill if the legislators were "honest and sincere" and that if they were not, "they may have trouble in the future." Further, owing perhaps to insecurity, Humphrey often tried to appear more in command of issues than was the case and tended to speak nonstop to others. This led one White House aide to say he was "all blather," while James (Jim) Rowe, a prominent attorney, former FDR assistant, and political strategist for Truman's 1948 campaign, concluded after a long luncheon that Humphrey was "just awful. He knew everything about everything." When Rowe noted that Arthur Krock, the conservative *New York Times* bureau chief whose columns took a hard line toward civil rights advocates, was seated nearby, Humphrey said he would "knock his block off."[8]

The new senator was self-critical. On the popular radio program *Meet the Press*, he admitted that he and the ADA had been "dead wrong" to try "to ditch" Truman in 1948. When panelist Lawrence Spivak asked what he intended to do about FEPC legislation, Humphrey said that as a newcomer and Minnesota's junior senator, "I have an awful lot to learn, and I know it," and that he planned to be "a cooperative member" of the Senate. He would support Truman if he proposed a civil rights program, but "I'm surely not foolish enough" to think "some young fellow from out here in Minnesota is going to come down and upset the Congress . . . nor do I have any intention of trying to do so."[9]

Humphrey's chief problem in the Senate in 1949 and later derived not from being a brash newcomer but from the era's growing conservatism. President Truman's State of the Union address had proposed a sweeping "fair deal" that would expand Social Security and achieve prepaid national health insurance, federal aid to primary and secondary schools, low-rent public housing and slum clearance, and an FEPC. But little came of it, with the civil rights issue revealing the power of conservative and southern politicians.[10]

Humphrey put civil rights at front and center almost immediately on the start of his Senate career. In early March 1949, his strong speech to students at all-black Howard University angered conservatives. He was far ahead of his time in tying the growing movement for civil rights legislation in America to "a restless world-wide search for liberation" that was manifest in Asian peoples' efforts to jettison colonial rule, as well as Yugoslavia's Marshal Joseph Tito raising his voice against "the bondage of Moscow." Always ready to reference his view of America's global responsibility—and to score a Cold War point—Humphrey insisted that "when the Negroes in Mississippi can freely go to the polls, the iron curtain in Europe is ripped" and Asian peoples take hope. Similarly, he said that the Emancipation Proclamation in 1863 had liberated both whites and blacks from slavery and that the efforts of a minority of senators to wage "a last desperate resistance" against the movement for civil rights for all Americans would fail because "history is against them, the people are against them, the times are against them, and the President of the United States is against them."

He urged the many students who would be heading southward to their homes to use their education and energy to "liberalize the South" and to "solve the American dilemma," a reference to Swedish sociologist Gunnar Myrdal's classic 1944 study of the discrepancy between the American belief in the equality and equal treatment of all people and the prejudice of white people that was chiefly responsible for African Americans living in deplorable conditions. The American people, Humphrey said, had voted to end the dilemma in November 1948.[11]

Democratic leaders knew that they could not pass a civil rights bill without first limiting southern Democrats' ability to filibuster it. This required changing Senate Standing Rule XXII, adopted in 1917, which required two-thirds of the senators present and voting to invoke cloture, or end debate. Southerners had blocked all six attempts to cut off filibusters on civil rights legislation since the 1930s, and in early 1949 southern Democrats and Republicans defeated Vice President Barkley's effort as the Senate's presiding officer to change Rule XXII by holding that each new Congress set its own rules and requiring only a majority vote to invoke cloture.[12]

In February, thirty-three Democrats and Republicans of diverse views put forward a resolution to make cloture the business of the Senate. But Senator Russell began to filibuster the motion to consider their resolution, arguing that a motion to consider a bill, as distinct from the bill itself, was exempt from Rule XXII and cloture. Humphrey dared to dispute Russell's view and proposed round-the-clock Senate sessions to dramatize the issue. But Majority Leader Lucas said that this would endanger the health of older senators, while Russell's filibuster of a motion to consider changing a Senate rule threatened to preclude the Senate from taking up any business.[13]

Consequently, the Democratic leadership struck a deal: Russell agreed to end his filibuster and allow applying Rule XXII to effect cloture to a motion to consider, but only in return for requiring a two-thirds vote of all ninety-six senators (a so-called constitutional majority), not just those present and voting, usually about eighty-four senators. This raised the number of votes required to end debate from about fifty-six to sixty-four, making it relatively easy for twenty-six southern and Border State senators to garner just eight more votes to block a vote to end a filibuster.[14]

This enraged Humphrey and Democratic liberals. Humphrey said he had accepted the initial resolution as a "sensible compromise" but held requiring the so-called constitutional majority (based on ninety-six senators) to be "unconstitutional." The Constitution was built on the concept of majority rule, he said, and all five exceptions, such as treaty approval and impeachment, called only for a two-thirds majority of those present and voting, not of all senators. He disputed the view of his friend from Louisiana days, Democratic senator Russell Long, that unlimited debate was the minority's only protection against the majority; no constitutional principle, Humphrey said, gave the minority an unrestrained right to obstruct the majority from their obligation to conduct the government's business. A "willful" minority had caused the Articles of Confederation to fail, and the United States was not a collection of "sovereign states" but "one Nation."

Humphrey insisted that he had taken an oath to the Constitution, not to Senate rules, and asked what America's young people, or people in totalitarian nations, would think when they heard senators scorn majority rule. Sometimes "we get so cozy, we become so secure when we get into our six-year terms," he said, "we forget that there may be some people out there . . . who are expecting things to be done."[15]

Conservative segregationist senator Willis Robertson of Virginia charged that Humphrey and other senators who sought majority rule to invoke cloture "breathe by night of a crusade for the Holy Grail, which is civil rights," and wished to "ram these unconstitutional measures down our throats." Humphrey responded that since 1946 both Democrats and Republicans had sought to change Rule XXII to apply to a motion to consider and that both parties espoused civil rights. He warned that twenty-two southern senators were not "so wise, so good, so omnipotent" as to cause the other seventy-four senators to "run for the bushes, capitulate, and collapse." Later, he persisted that no "unholy alliance" of southern Democrats and Republicans would diminish the Fair Deal, including civil rights, which meant assuring "16,000,000 American Negroes," as well as "Catholics, Protestants, and Jews who suffer from discrimination . . . that we are not going to forget the evils of our society, that we are going to do something about it."[16]

Humphrey was more right than his opponents about constitutional principles and civil rights, but the resolution, requiring two-thirds of all senators to invoke cloture, passed by a 63–23 margin. He deplored this "reprehensible sellout" and that summer, after further difficult exchanges with colleagues, wrote privately that the Senate had been seized by "a society of wolves."[17]

The bitter defeat on Rule XXII led Humphrey, liberal Democratic icon Robert Wagner of New York, and Republican Wayne Morse of Oregon to introduce a bill to make lynching a federal crime and to criminalize an officer's failing to protect a person in custody from mob violence or not seeking to arrest members of a lynch mob. Humphrey said that without safety from lynching, the United States could not provide world moral leadership, and he challenged Republicans to pass this bill. He also introduced legislation to establish a permanent federal Commission on Civil Rights to assist all federal agencies and state and local governments to act to prevent civil rights violations. The White House proposed to establish a permanent FEPC and create a civil rights commission and civil rights division within the Justice Department.[18]

But Humphrey and most liberals lacked the standing to impose their will on southern Democrats and conservative Republicans who were ready to support a Russell-led filibuster. Democratic leaders put civil rights on Congress's back burner in fall 1949. Humphrey could only lobby Washington owners of hotels, restaurants, and theaters and managers of public recreation facilities to open up to African Americans.[19]

✦ ✦ ✦

Humphrey had no more success with the Democratic commitment to repeal the Taft-Hartley bill. When the Labor and Public Welfare Committee held hearings early in 1949, no senior Democrat showed leadership. Humphrey tried to step in but made no headway when Senator Taft caught him up on some facts. Humphrey quickly became highly versed in labor history and law, and in June he assailed Taft-Harley as "profoundly reactionary" and intended to return labor to the "dark ages" of the pre-1935 Wagner Act era when corporations used yellow-dog contracts, Pinkerton guards, and armed goon squads to break strikes and unions.

Humphrey also believed that the Taft-Hartley Act involved government too heavily—through use of injunctions to halt strikes—in labor-management relations, and permitted state law, or so-called right-to-work laws, to override federal law by allowing workers to opt out of union membership despite their coworkers having voted for union representation under the Wagner Act. He questioned whether those who favored right-to-work laws would include in that rubric the right to a job, free from discrimination, as an FEPC would require. But neither he nor Truman, despite his campaign pledge, could muster support to repeal the Taft-Hartley Act in 1949.[20]

Humphrey thought that he and his party were progressing after Congress passed, with bipartisan support, the National Housing Act in late April. He spoke knowledgeably, based on his mayoral experience, about the postwar housing crisis, the need for low-income homes, and the necessity for urban renewal and commercial revival of downtown areas to increase the tax base (to support social services) of cities. The bill authorized financing for slum clearance related to urban renewal, construction of 810,000 low-income housing units over six years, and Federal Housing Authority insurance of home mortgages and financing for rural homeowners.

Humphrey was keenly aware that conservative opponents had set traps for the bill, including insisting that the government had to tear down one slum building for each new one built, thus requiring near double appropriations, and prohibiting segregation in federal housing, a ploy to turn southern Democrats against it. Humphrey said candidly that "to talk in terms of things that we could never realize" and to call for perfection "may mean the death of the measure." Better to move ahead, he said, with what was possible—as he would say in coming years—rather than strive for an unattainable "social panacea."[21]

The National Housing Act was the Truman administration's sole major achievement during the first session of the Eighty-First Congress, although it appropriated only enough money to construct about 61,000 housing units before Truman left office and only 350,000 by 1964. Further, spending caps for units, and a requirement not to compete with private real estate development, led to poorly constructed, unattractive high-rise buildings in unappealing locations that often became blighted and crime-ridden. Urban renewal also brought displacement of African Americans without enough new public housing being built for them, while real estate developers profited from constructing expensive private housing and nonresidential public works.[22]

Humphrey also pressed national health insurance, which had been considered with Social Security in 1935 but omitted from the legislation. In 1943, Senators Murray and Wagner proposed a national health insurance bill, but it gained little support. On April 25, 1949, Humphrey became the only new senator to cosponsor an omnibus bill introduced by Murray and Wagner and Representative John Dingell of Michigan in the House to establish national health insurance financed through payroll taxes, with employer-employee matches.

Humphrey further proposed a significant amendment to permit nonprofit or consumer cooperatives to contract with doctors for fixed sums to provide their members with prepaid medical coverage, a practice that medical societies lobbied many states to outlaw because doctors greatly preferred more lucrative fee-for-service medicine. He charged that medical societies' prohibitions were monopolistic, whereas consumer-sponsored voluntary plans sought to provide comprehensive and preventive medicine and adequate income to attract doctors to less populous areas to work in group practices. Humphrey also introduced the Cooperative Health Care Act to provide loans and grants over five years to help cooperatives and nonprofit associations build and equip health facilities for their members.[23]

The White House, however, did not designate the proposed 1949 legislation as administration bills, and the American Medical Association (AMA) led a bitter public attack on the bills, alleging that it would bring new, high taxes, a vast government bureaucracy, socialized medicine, and, ultimately, a socialized nation. Other opponents included the Chamber of Commerce; organized labor, which preferred to secure health care for its members through collective bargaining; and the American Hospital Association, which feared government rate-setting for services.[24]

The chief administration spokesman for the legislation was Oscar Ewing, a liberal attorney and former DNC official, who headed the Federal Security Agency, a large subcabinet body that handled federal health and welfare programs. But when Truman proposed a government reorganization plan that raised the FSA to a cabinet-level Department of Welfare, the AMA spearheaded an attack on Ewing and the reorganization plan as leading to socialized medicine, and conservative Republicans and southern Democrats charged that the new department portended too much federal expansion and taxing power and that Ewing would push to desegregate federal health care facilities.

Humphrey assailed the AMA for orchestrating "vicious" attacks on Ewing and mixing politics and medicine, but 23 southern Democrats and 37 Republicans voted against the reorganization plan by 60–32 in August 1949, and Democratic leaders delayed a vote on the health insurance bill until after the 1950 congressional elections. By then the Korean War and military expenditures were of chief concern, and Humphrey's proposals and national health insurance died in committee.[25]

Humphrey enthusiastically supported bipartisan legislation introduced by Taft and Democrats Hill and Elbert Thomas of Utah in spring 1949 to provide $270 million in grants to states for operating expenses of primary and secondary schools, and he proposed the Public School Construction Act which sought to authorize $500 million per year for six years to build primary and secondary schools. He believed that the chief defense of democracy was education, which he decried as in "deplorable" condition in America, with fewer people becoming teachers because of the low pay. The consequence is "the debris we harvest in juvenile delinquency, crime, sorrow, and in social degradation."

When Massachusetts Republican senator Henry Cabot Lodge Jr. proposed denying money to segregated schools, Humphrey called his amendment "hypocritical"; if he wanted desegregation, he and his allies should enact antipoll tax, antilynching, and FEPC laws. Lodge relented, and the Taft-Hill-Thomas bill passed the Senate by 58–15 in May 1949. But Graham Barden, a conservative Democrat from North Carolina in the House, added an amendment limiting federal aid solely to public schools, turning major Catholic constituents in the Democratic Party against the legislation, while many other proponents of school aid believed that the Constitution's separation of church and state prohibited funding parochial schools. This bill, and Humphrey's school construction legislation, died in committee.[26]

By summer 1949, Humphrey concluded that "monopolistic corporate business" had delayed or defeated all progressive legislation, "and we have taken quite a beating." He also became a political target when Rudolf Lee, a right-wing newspaper editor from southeastern Minnesota, published a compilation of figures—provided by archconservative Virginia Democrat Harry Byrd's Joint Committee on Reduction of Nonessential Federal Expenditures—alleging Humphrey had sponsored or voted for legislation proposing to spend $30 billion, as reported variously by the Minneapolis *Star-Journal*, right-wing radio newscaster Fulton Lewis Jr., and the *Baltimore Sun*.[27]

Humphrey, a member of the Government Operations Committee, opposed Republican and conservative Democratic committee members' efforts to cut Truman's proposed $42 billion budget by 5 percent to 10 percent, which he deemed impossible, given that fixed debt and military and foreign aid commitments were $24 billion. Minority Leader Kenneth S. Wherry of Nebraska, citing Lee's article, charged that Humphrey had introduced or endorsed legislation that would cost taxpayers $30 billion, and he asked to enter into the *Congressional Record* a *Baltimore Sun* exhibit showing that Humphrey's social welfare proposals would cost over "one trillion two hundred and fifty billion dollars."

Humphrey responded that the FBI and criminologists agreed that education lowered crime and poverty rates and that without aid for the handicapped "we shall lose all claim to human decency." He sharply contrasted 1920s Republican economic policies with FDR's New Deal and wartime programs, and he lambasted Republican charges of "socialism": Wherry's state of Nebraska had one of the nation's finest public power systems—and that was "really socialistic." He assured Wherry that he was a Democrat, "free enterpriser," and part owner of a small drugstore, not a "monopolist." The Wherry-backed resolution to pare Truman's budget failed, and Humphrey wrote a friend, "I don't want to brag, but I think I took his britches off."[28]

✦ ✦ ✦

After Congress adjourned in fall 1949, Humphrey and his family were about to board a train to New York to begin a European vacation when he learned his father had suffered a cerebral hemorrhage. He canceled the trip and returned to South Dakota, where his "father and friend"—who never feared to be "swimming against the tide"—died on November 25 at age sixty-seven. The senator had lost "the one man with whom I could have most freely counseled as I tried to understand what moved this new political world and who held the levers that powered its movements." Humphrey's father's death was a major blow; had the older man lived a little longer, he might have counseled greater caution as his son chose to battle a Senate leader in late February 1950, an offensive that almost derailed his career.[29]

Harry Byrd, a descendant of one of Virginia's founding families, entered the Senate in 1933 as a Roosevelt supporter and was repeatedly reelected but turned against New Deal spending. In 1941, he became chair of the new Joint Committee on Reduction of Nonessential Expenditures, which he used to rail against social welfare spending and to claim the role of protector of the public purse. The "Byrd Committee," as it was known, did not meet formally after 1947 but continued to issue reports about "nonessential" spending. Byrd was a senior Senate oligarch, and as Humphrey recalled, "people almost kissed his ring, so to speak," although the younger man viewed Byrd as a "phony," more interested in publicity and slashing New Deal–Fair Deal programs than in genuine tax reduction.[30]

On February 24, 1950, Humphrey criticized a recent Byrd Committee report as presenting a distorted picture of growth in federal employment and introduced a bill to abolish the joint committee, which he said was redundant because the Legislative Reorganization Act of 1946 had created the Committee on Expenditures in the Executive Departments (with Humphrey a member). More important, the joint committee was "the No. 1 example of waste and extravagance" whose "blanket charges" about federal employee rolls were undocumented, its calls for monthly reports from federal agencies were extremely costly, and the committee was used as a "publicity medium." It was time, Humphrey said, that certain elements in Congress abandoned their "prosecute and persecute" sport with the executive branch and abolished a committee "which has no right to exist."[31]

The criticisms were largely accurate, if unprecedented. There was no immediate response, however, because—Humphrey had not realized—Byrd was away from the Senate, and the protocol breach of attacking an absent senator was deemed more offensive than the remarks. But six days later, with the Senate chamber more packed than usual, Byrd charged that Humphrey had made nine mistakes in two thousand words, "an average of a mistake in less than every 250 words," and that he speaks "like the wind"—and " 'it is an ill wind that blows no good.' " Byrd disparaged Humphrey's claims as "superexaggeration," insisting that the joint committee's personnel and deficit reports were accurate and that its recommendations had brought over $2.5 billion in savings, and he denied that its members engaged in "prosecution and persecution." Further, the joint committee had spent far less money than alleged, and the chairman had offered several times to resign.[32]

Majority Leader Lucas sought to defuse a prospective clash by proposing that the experienced Byrd provide the Appropriations Committee with a breakdown of how to reduce the federal budget. But senior conservative Democrat Walter George of Georgia praised Byrd and alleged that it was the "height of reckless irresponsibility" for anyone to suggest otherwise. This was the signal for Byrd's friends to offer lengthy testimonials to him and label talk of eliminating the committee as "reckless."[33]

The testimonials—and rebukes to Humphrey—continued for several hours, with "hapless Hubert," as *Time* dubbed him, seated in the back row, taking notes, and unable to gain the floor from Byrd, who yielded only to his supporters' "questions." When Humphrey finally was recognized, Byrd and friends turned their backs to the Minnesotan and marched together from the chamber. Humphrey was left to speak to a nearly empty room.[34]

Rebuked but not cowed, Humphrey apologized for being unaware of Byrd's absence earlier, offered some praise for him, but discounted the testimonials. Too often few senators were around when serious issues needed to be addressed, he said, but the "reactionary coalition which operates in the Congress" was always quick to gather to criticize the administration. Humphrey persisted that the joint committee had no work to do and no reason to exist and that the World War II and Cold War costs were chief contributors to increased budgets. Last, he called for collegiality in Congress, although the senators' primary function was not to make friends—"Dale Carnegie tells us how to do that"—but to legislate and improve the machinery of government.[35]

Subdued, Humphrey left the Senate chamber. When leaving his office that evening, he met Byrd at the elevator. "I know when I've been licked," Humphrey said, extending his hand, but the Virginian offered only a limp response. The new senator believed that his speech had been one of his better ones in terms of "principles, sincerity, and integrity," but it had been viewed as if he had assailed "the basic tenets of Christianity," and the vehemence of the attacks surprised him. When an aide soon offered new material and proposed that he reopen the issue, Humphrey said that he had been "walloped, beaten, and worked over" and that new ammunition—mainly "blanks"—was nothing as against his opponents' howitzers. He had discovered, he said, where power resided in the Senate and what he might expect if he attacked it frontally.[36]

Humphrey immediately accepted an invitation from a liberal group in Richmond to debate Byrd, who refused. Truman wrote the young senator to say that he knew Byrd would not dare to debate him. Humphrey also wrote the *New York Times* on March 20 that the joint committee violated the Legislative Reorganization Act and was a "brazen example" of redundant legislative functions. But the ferocity of the attacks on him was "stunning"; he appreciated Truman's support but also thought that the president and "my liberal friends" should have done more. And in his memoirs he likened conservative Democrat Millard Tydings having put a figurative arm around him on the Senate floor as akin to a father caring for "a sickly, possibly dying child."[37]

Humphrey was far from dying, but he felt "lonely, broke, and bitter" during this first year in the Senate and envious of newcomers from the South who already had many friends and influence, where he had neither. Occasionally on the long drive home at night along Connecticut Avenue tears came to his eyes. But he was too resilient to quit on himself or his liberal aims, and he determined to demonstrate mastery of every subject he addressed and to learn how to deal with those who controlled the levers of power in the Senate.[38]

5

CONFRONTATION AND COOPERATION

"Compromise is not a dirty word," Humphrey wrote in reflecting on his twenty-five years in the Senate. The Constitution was a national compromise, and experience taught him that significant legislative goals were rarely reached in a democratic society unless opponents made concessions. In 1950, Humphrey held that his legislative opponents were more concerned about preserving advantages than compromising, especially when dealing with critical national issues such as civil rights, corporate power, taxation, anti-Communism, and national security, and he was not afraid to challenge and criticize them.

At a National Emergency Civil Rights Mobilization in Washington on January 15, he told four thousand listeners who had come to lobby for an FEPC bill that recent passage of the Senate resolution requiring a two-thirds vote of all senators to end a filibuster was a "sellout of human rights" and that "bigotry, hypocrisy, intolerance, and discrimination" thwarted the American way of life.

He deplored the "secret" Dixiecrat-Republican alliance, insisted that it took more courage to oppose "anti-democratic forces in the United States than to oppose communism outside of America," and argued that failure to enact civil rights undermined American foreign policy. At a "Roosevelt Day" celebration in Pittsburgh, he lambasted the "reactionaries," "racists," and "conservatives" who professed their love of freedom but failed to protect basic civil liberties.[1]

Humphrey publicly challenged the American Medical Association's claim that national health insurance meant "socialism" or a "welfare state"; the real "compulsory insurance" was the AMA's twenty-five-dollar tax on its members to pay lobbyists to oppose the legislation. The Constitution charged the government with responsibility for the "general welfare," Humphrey reminded a

Harvard Law School Forum and other audiences, and successive administrations had provided land grants for educational institutions, railroads, and homesteaders, supported banks and businesses through the Reconstruction Finance Corporation, and aided individuals through Social Security, federal housing, and slum clearance.[2]

In Senator Harry Byrd's Virginia, Humphrey charged Dixiecrats and Republicans with forging a "secret alliance" to thwart the government from doing for the people, in Lincoln's words, what they could not do so well for themselves. In a nationally broadcast debate with states' rights Democratic senator Spressard Holland of Florida, who said that most states had rejected FEPC legislation, Humphrey responded that state legislatures had not been reapportioned in decades and did not reflect the rise of newcomers and urban centers. Further, the South could not solve its problems on its own because race—or human rights—was not just a southern problem but a national and world issue.[3]

Humphrey also challenged colleagues such as right-wing Republican Homer Capehart of Indiana, who announced in February 1950 his intent to talk about the coming of "state socialism" to America and enter into the *Congressional Record* a list of congressmen who were ADA members, whom he assailed for supporting Britain's Labour Party and Europe's "democratic left" or "vital center."

Incensed, Humphrey charged that Capehart's "political ignorance" led to his equating democratic socialism with Communist totalitarianism and assailing Europe's "democratic left" that had fought Fascism and now opposed Communism. Humphrey noted that current ADA members included Senators Paul Douglas, Herbert Lehman of New York, Frank Graham of North Carolina, Brien McMahon of Connecticut, James Murray of Montana, and—to Capehart's shock—Democratic whip Francis Myers. Humphrey also challenged Capehart and Republicans to live up to their 1948 civil rights platform and to say how they would reduce the budget and fight the global Cold War.[4]

Humphrey's primary goal in 1950 was to gain a civil rights bill, but the Senate delayed until May to take up weak House legislation proposing a commission, without enforcement power, to investigate employment discrimination and recommend solutions. Senator Richard Russell declared the bill a Communist-inspired "legislative monstrosity" that would advantage African Americans over whites in the job market, and he threatened "unlimited debate." Humphrey proffered evidence that blacks had suffered far greater rises in unemployment than whites since 1945, and he termed "unlimited debate"—really filibuster— "an effort to delude the American people."

Conservative Democrat Thomas (Tom) Connally of Texas charged that Humphrey's use of the word "delude" had violated Senate Standing Rule XIX prohibiting imputing an unworthy motive to another senator; thus he should not be allowed to speak. The Minnesotan had to promise good behavior to escape being silenced.[5]

Humphrey held that FEPCs in major cities had significantly lessened discrimination against minorities and their unemployment, but Lucas and the White House could not muster the required sixty-four votes to end debate. Similarly defeated was Humphrey's bid to amend the 1948 Selective Service Act to make it a federal offense to cause or incite harm of anyone in the armed services who was in police custody.[6]

The start of the Korean War in June 1950 and growing charges about Communist subversion ended hope for a civil rights bill. Only wartime manpower needs impelled military branches to increase their pace to fulfill the president's July 1948 executive order calling for integration of the armed forces.[7]

Humphrey's commitment to civil rights was paramount, but as a part owner of a family drugstore and an avowed antimonopolist he also considered himself a spokesman for small businessmen, whom he believed large competitors were driving out by gaining discriminatory price advantages from manufacturers or distributors. He called for strict application of antitrust laws to halt "the growing concentration of economic power, the continued acceleration of mergers of business enterprises," and the threat of monopoly control of the country's basic industries. "The captains of monopolistic power" used to talk about "competitive enterprise," he said, but after revelations that competition no longer existed in many areas of industry, they began to sell Americans on "so-called private enterprise or free enterprise," better called "corporate enterprise."

Humphrey further upset conservative colleagues by referencing the works of economic theorists such as Thorstein Veblen, a caustic critic of laissez-faire economics and business leaders and who coined the catchphrase "conspicuous consumption" in his satirical 1899 study, *The Theory of the Leisure Class.* Similarly, Humphrey cited former New Deal officials Adolph A. Berle and Gardiner C. Means, whose seminal 1932 work, *The Modern Corporation and Private Property*, held that some two hundred corporations dominated the American economy and stifled competition, and also contended prices were not always determined by demand but were "administered."[8]

In May 1950, Humphrey joined with Senators Douglas (a distinguished economist), Kefauver, and Long to take on corporate monopoly control by opposing legislation intended to legalize the controversial basing point system, long used by producers in heavy industries such as steel and cement to enable them to charge identical prices for their goods to all purchasers in a city rather than offer competing prices. A major producer would establish the market price for its goods at a selected basing point city, for example, Pittsburgh, add a fixed shipping cost from Pittsburgh to the purchasing company's city, and offer only a composite delivered price that included, or absorbed, shipping costs. By contrast, the traditional freight on board, or FOB, system required quoting the price for the goods and actual shipping costs. Thus industry leaders such as U.S. Steel used the basing point system to gain monopolistic controls by establishing delivered prices for their goods, which other producers matched in order to avoid a costly price war. In 1948, however, the Supreme Court ruled against the cement industry's delivered price system.[9]

Leading corporations lobbied Congress, and the House soon passed legislation insulating the basing-point system from antitrust prosecution, and the Senate went along, allowing producers to act independently, but not to combine or conspire, to offer delivered prices.[10]

Humphrey fought back; he persisted that the nation's largest 113 corporations used the basing point system to prevent newer and smaller businesses from competing by price, whereas FOB prices reflected supply and demand and allowed purchasers to choose the mode of transport for goods and to negotiate with carriers. FOB pricing also increased geographical decentralization of manufacturing in a large number of smaller plants, but freight absorption led to centralized production in fewer, very large plants. Despite these arguments, the Senate passed the bill in spring 1951, but Truman vetoed it in June.[11]

Humphrey and his allies had won a partial victory. The basing point system was soon allowed to continue, but subject to antitrust law. Significantly, the young senator had enhanced his reputation as a knowledgeable and forceful advocate, and he would again challenge leading conservatives over taxation policy.[12]

The start of the Korean War in June 1950 had brought vastly increased military spending; the 1950 defense budget quadrupled to about $50 billion. In July the president asked Congress to raise taxes, bringing Senate debate of a pending Revenue Act that reduced previously planned cuts in income tax rates and slightly raised corporate taxes.[13]

Humphrey firmly backed Truman's call for increased military spending and higher taxes and was appalled by the number of tax loopholes the Revenue Act provided for interest groups. He decided, along with Douglas and Lehman, to challenge the Senate Finance Committee, bastion of Senate patriarchs who were steeped in tax law, including esteemed chairman Walter George of Georgia.[14]

Humphrey organized a series of tax seminars led by specialists such as his friend Walter Heller, a University of Minnesota economics professor who had served as a Treasury Department tax analyst and later would chair the Council of Economic Advisers. The senator and his compatriots met secretly at night away from Capitol Hill parsing arcane tax issues, with Humphrey "the quickest study I ever met," one economist recalled. They gave Humphrey the lead, with Douglas to assist on the Senate floor to prevent a "slaughter of the innocents." Humphrey, having learned from his surprise attack on the Byrd Committee, notified Senate leaders of his intent to amend the Revenue Act and modestly said that working with these issues and Finance Committee "giants" was a "new experience." He used his keen wit to draw laughter from his opponents and asked questions "in a spirit of humility."[15]

Humphrey ultimately proposed twelve amendments to the Revenue Act to eliminate or sharply reduce tax loopholes, including the highly politically protected 27.5 percent oil and gas depletion allowances that exempted about one-fourth of oil companies' net income. He made no headway during the first two weeks; few senators would agree to institute withholding of taxes on corporate dividends in order to prevent "coupon clippers" from underreporting their income or to end businessmen's dubious practice of including their "wives" and children as partners in family enterprises in order to divide income and lessen graduated tax liability unless the partners actually contributed services or capital. His query as to what "one-year-old Charlie" contributed to a business drew widespread bipartisan laughter.[16]

All of Humphrey's amendments were decisively defeated, except for keeping the required capital gains period at six months instead of reducing it to three, which would have spurred speculation. As Heller recounted, Humphrey, the David who took on the Senate's Goliaths, had lost, but respect for his knowledge, debating skill, and engaging manner greatly increased. Afterward, Senators George and Michigan Republican Eugene Milliken put their arms around him, a previously unimaginable bipartisan signal of acceptance. The endeavor may have contributed to Congress's passing a moderate excess profits tax on corporations intended to limit profit gained from increased Korean War government spending and higher prices. But Humphrey's and Douglas's attempts to close tax loopholes during debate over the Revenue Act of 1951 were rejected once again.[17]

✦ ✦ ✦

Humphrey also lost ground in battles over internal security. Since the Bolshevik Revolution in Russia in 1917, fear had grown in the United States that Communism or its adherents threatened America's security, although Communist Party (CPUSA) membership fluctuated between just ten thousand and seventy thousand. In 1938, Texas Democrat Martin Dies fostered the House Un-American Activities Committee, which indiscriminately published names of people alleged to be Communists or sympathetic to totalitarian ideas, and in 1940 Virginia Democrat Howard Smith sponsored the Alien Registration Act, or Smith Act, that made it a crime to "advocate, abet, advise, or teach" the forcible overthrow of government, the law used in 1948 to gain conviction of the eleven top CPUSA leaders.[18]

Truman's Executive Order 9835 in 1947 established the Federal Civilian Employee Loyalty Program, which denied employment to current or prospective workers based on "reasonable grounds" for belief that they were "disloyal"; the program brought relatively few dismissals but increased fear of questioning difficult foreign policy decisions.[19]

The Red Scare was soon in full swing after first-term Wisconsin senator Joseph R. McCarthy claimed on February 9, 1950, to have a list of 205 alleged spies who were shaping State Department policy and continued to step up baseless charges about espionage. Four months later, only six Republicans were willing to sign Maine Republican senator Margaret Chase Smith's "Declaration of Conscience" excoriating "certain elements of the Republican Party" for exploiting "fear, bigotry, ignorance, and intolerance" for political gain. Even after a committee reported in July 1950 that McCarthy had perpetrated a "fraud and a hoax" on the Senate, that body took no action. In the meantime, Julius and Ethel Rosenberg were charged, convicted, and later executed for having passed atomic secrets during World War II to the Russians.[20]

An internal security bill (spawned by the House Un-American Activities Committee) sponsored by Senate Judiciary Committee chair Pat McCarran of Nevada in 1950 required all Communist-action and Communist-front organizations to register with the attorney general and provide names of their members, who would be denied passports and government or defense-related employment. The bill also created a Subversive Activities Control Board (SACB) to determine whether any unregistered organization was Communist action or a Communist front.[21]

Humphrey's liberal's emphasis on individual and equal rights, elective government, and due process led him to deplore Communism, especially after the 1939 Nazi-Soviet Pact and his battles with former left-wing DFL opponents and many Progressive Party supporters. In the heat of debate, he would say that "I detest communism with my whole heart and my whole soul."[22]

Humphrey did tell the graduating class at Bennington College in 1949 not to give in to the recent hysteria aimed not just at the "communist menace," which he termed "relatively insignificant," but at "critical, nonconformist, creative thinking." Nor should they overemphasize the "disloyalty" problem. In February 1950, Humphrey charged McCarthy with "character assassination" and "promiscuously hunting with facts" after he erroneously charged that a young White House speechwriter and former ADA employee was a security risk. Humphrey also criticized the *Washington Post*'s call for an "unpartisan" National Security Commission to handle domestic and foreign threats to rid the nation of current "terror" as a throwback to the Alien and Sedition Acts era.[23]

When debate began on the McCarran Act, Humphrey and numerous liberals said that requiring Communist or Communist-front organizations to register and provide their members' names violated Fifth Amendment protection against self-incrimination—and would cause Communists to go underground. Better to have FBI director J. Edgar Hoover release the thousands of names of Communists he claimed to have. Moreover, to empower the SACB to determine if it was "reasonable to conclude" whether a person or organization was Communist based on their advocacy of positions also taken by Communist organizations or foreign governments might lead to loyalty questions even of leading conservatives who, like the Communist *Daily Worker*, opposed Marshall Plan aid, the North Atlantic Treaty Organization (NATO), and US action in Korea.[24]

However, Humphrey and his liberal colleagues did agree on the need for anti-Communist legislation and sought to protect their own anti-Communist reputations. They had West Virginia senator Harley Kilgore propose an internal security bill, resting on the precedent of US wartime removal of persons of Japanese descent on the West Coast to internment camps, to empower the president, in times of an emergency, to detain anyone who might be thought to engage in espionage or sabotage or conspire to do so.[25]

Even conservatives such as Republican Homer Ferguson of Michigan dubbed Kilgore's measure the "concentration camp bill," and others assumed that it was a ploy to kill the McCarran Act by attaching to it an overtly unconstitutional measure. Humphrey insisted that Communists' self-registration was not needed; officials would use FBI files to determine "those who are to be registered, the dangerous ones who would commit acts of sabotage." This would "strike a hammer blow in behalf of internal security" and lock up people based on their views rather than actions.[26]

The Kilgore measure was soundly defeated, but Majority Leader Lucas, in a tough reelection fight—with anti-Communism a key issue—proffered an identical version of it to replace the McCarran Act. Lucas's measure was also defeated, only to have McCarran's allies add it to their bill, which passed and consisted of Title I, "Subversive Activities Control Act," and Title II, "Emergency Detention Act." Humphrey and most liberals voted in favor.[27]

Humphrey was embarrassed to have reversed course; he later told Kefauver that he was "very proud of him" for having voted against the McCarran Act and told colleagues that his own vote for the McCarran Act had shaken his conscience and led him to question his judgment. But, he added, since anti-Communist legislation seemed necessary, "I swallowed my feelings of frustration and despair," although he had "never been more unhappy in my life."[28]

Truman provided brief relief for liberals by vetoing the McCarran Act, insisting that Communist registration features were impractical and likely to suppress only freedom of speech. His chief complaint, however, was that the bill did not suspend habeas corpus—the right to contest detention in court— which would allow detainees to delay resolving their cases by lengthy judicial appeals all the way to the Supreme Court.[29]

Humphrey agreed with Truman. The Communists would "drive our judiciary mad" by "trickery" in the appeals process, he said, and Lincoln had suspended habeas corpus to save the Union, although Humphrey ignored that the Supreme Court had quickly ruled that only Congress could do that. Humphrey said that he wanted to be able to "point out to all the little Humphreys that their daddy had voted to sustain the president's veto" and was "on the side of the angels." But the Senate and House decisively overrode Truman's veto to enact the McCarran Act, which reflected a Cold War mentality equating dissent or unorthodox views with treason.[30]

Humphrey's record in the McCarthy era was contradictory. He opposed requiring "subversives" to register, expressed concern about McCarthy's undocumented allegations, and held that "we cannot lick communism by applying police state methods or degrading ourselves to communist tactics and character assassination, smear, and rumor." But his support for the Detention Act and suspension of habeas corpus meant resorting to methods that had been refuted a century earlier, and his idea to use FBI files as a basis to incarcerate people was highly dangerous, especially given that Hoover—who Truman feared would turn the FBI into an "American Gestapo"—aimed to build incriminating files against nearly everyone, including Eleanor Roosevelt and Albert Einstein, whose ideas he did not like or understand. In 1950, Humphrey's anti-

Communism sometimes overwhelmed his judgment and infused his foreign policy views.[31]

Humphrey was a Wilsonian and Cold War realist. He had faith in American exceptionalism and hoped that the United Nations would lead to a form of world government. He believed that past European disunity, including the US failure to join the League of Nations, had opened the way to Hitler's assaults; the Nazi-Soviet Pact of 1939 increased his disdain for Communists and Communism, and he dubbed Communism Nazism's "twin brother." But "God had spared our nation" during World War II, he said in 1949, in order that it might lift up mankind afterward: "We have a destiny to fulfill."[32]

Humphrey supported Truman's major initiatives, from aid to Greece and Turkey in 1947 to the formation of NATO in 1950. But containment policy "is defensive," he said, and had to be transformed into a "diplomatic offensive of democratic, humanitarian emancipation" of people everywhere. Anything less meant allowing another nation a sphere of influence and accepting "two worlds," which negated the UN Charter and democracy.[33]

Humphrey called for the United States to recognize the aspirations of the colonial peoples of Southeast Asia in 1949 and "avoid aid to European nations now putting down revolts and attempts at self-government," or colonial peoples would not trust America. "The future lies across the Pacific."[34]

He spoke repeatedly about the US need to provide significant aid to recently independent India even though US officials resented Prime Minister Jawaharlal Nehru's foreign policy of nonalignment and worried that he might introduce noncapitalist principles to India's economy. Nehru disdained US support for European colonial powers, refused to bend policy to please benefactors, and, like so many of his compatriots, loathed US racial segregation, despite India's own caste system.[35]

Humphrey contended that India was "a bulwark of democracy" strategically located in terms of Near Eastern and Asian geopolitics and had significant industrial and raw material potential. He claimed to be hesitant as a first-year senator to prescribe a major program for India but proposed extensive scholarships for its students to study in the United States, direct financial assistance to India under the same terms given European nations, and extensive technical and scientific assistance under Point Four, the "bold new program" of aid for "undeveloped areas" the president had announced in January 1949.[36]

This program was not just altruism, Humphrey said. India stood on the front line militarily regarding the Soviet Union but had only 300,000 volunteer troops and one navy cruiser. He worried that the "near starvation" living standard for the nation's 300 million people could invite a turn to Communism. Point Four aid amounted to little, however, and US direct investment in India in the 1950s grew only from $38 million to $113 million.[37]

Humphrey refuted Republican charges that the Truman administration had "lost" China but opposed sending a fleet to Taiwan (Formosa) to prevent the People's Republic of China (PRC) from taking control of the island, which the wartime Allies had pledged to return to China but now was the refuge of its former Nationalist (Guomindang, or GMD) government. Humphrey believed that the GMD's failure to deal with China's poverty had opened the way to the Communists, and they treated the Taiwanese so badly that they "literally hate" that regime. "Rather than fleets for Formosa," he said, "let us have some food for India."[38]

However, Humphrey and other liberals adopted a more global cold warrior view after 100,000 North Korean troops attacked South Korea on June 25, 1950. Truman and his advisers blamed the Soviet Union, although the attack was chiefly the brainchild of North Korea's leader, Kim Il Sung, with Stalin providing the military machines and battle plans.

The Truman administration quickly secured UN Security Council support for member states to help repulse North Korea, and the president ordered the US Seventh Fleet to the Taiwan Straits (but only to preclude military action by either the PRC or Nationalists), authorized US air strikes on North Korean military targets, committed US ground forces, and sent General Douglas MacArthur, US Pacific commander, to Korea to assess needs. But Truman's exaggerated sense of his authority as commander-in-chief and fear of protracted Republican criticism kept him from seeking a congressional declaration of war.[39]

Humphrey likened North Korea's attack to Benito Mussolini's assault on Ethiopia and Hitler's Rhineland coup. He praised Truman's actions as averting mistakes of the 1930s and said that the president had acted properly under the UN Charter and consulted Congress soon enough. Despite Humphrey's earlier criticism of European colonialism, he now praised Truman's aiding the French-controlled regime of Emperor Bao Dai in Indochina against Communists.[40]

The Korean War was a "conflict between freedom and tyranny," Humphrey said. The Communists had successfully played on "colonial exploitation" and used false promises of land reform, food, and education to win support. He called for a "Marshall Plan of Ideas" to repulse Communism's "all-out offensive" and to win over Soviet satellites and strengthen American ties with India, Indonesia, and Thailand, and urged immediate expansion of Point Four aid. Words alone do not "touch hearts and win the minds" of others, he said; hungry men do not eat pamphlets, but they are susceptible to Communism. Failure to act would lead to more Koreas.[41]

Humphrey and Lyndon Johnson of Texas engaged in a Senate colloquy on July 12, comparing 1938 German and current US/NATO and Soviet military forces, with the Russians far ahead in every category. Anticipating Truman's action, they called for a big military buildup: Humphrey depicted the Soviet Union as a "great powerhouse" whose "masters" could unleash forces anytime and anywhere in the world. Johnson also charged that North Korea's attack was "directed and led by the Kremlin masters" and argued that the United States had to seek "immediate and decisive victory."[42]

Victory in Korea proved elusive. Truman appointed MacArthur to head the UN Command. His forces soon secured a foothold in South Korea and launched a major amphibious operation on the west coast at Inchon in September that quickly liberated the country. But the administration's decision to have MacArthur carry the war into North Korea to vanquish that state led to major PRC intervention in late November, a bloody retreat of UN troops, and bitter military stalemate from early 1951 to 1953.

Humphrey strongly backed the president's calls for vastly increased military spending, and in early 1951 he again criticized containment as a "negative program." He proposed that the United States should "breathe hope into the hearts and minds" of people behind the Iron Curtain by smuggling out key democratic leaders, train them to reestablish free rule in their countries, and provide supplies and money and underwrite counterespionage and guerrilla warfare to liberate Eastern Europe.[43]

Humphrey also backed both Truman's unsuccessful call for universal military training in March 1951 and his announced intention to send four divisions of troops to Europe to serve under General Eisenhower, now NATO commander. Senator Taft and other conservatives kicked off a "great debate" strongly disputing the president's right to send troops abroad without Congress's approval, while Truman held that as commander-in-chief he could send troops "anywhere in the world." Humphrey sought compromise; Congress should share in the decision, but this was not the time to "warm over old biscuits." American troops were urgently needed in Europe, he said, lest Stalin use his 175 Red Army divisions to strike a "deathblow." The president's power to act was inherent in his office's responsibility to provide for the nation's defense, and Congress had to "face the facts of life": the United States, as the world's leading nation, had to bear a heavy burden. Humphrey and his colleagues concurred with a sense-of-the-Senate resolution on April 5 approving Eisenhower's appointment and placing four divisions under his command but requiring Congress's approval for additional forces.[44]

A major political storm broke six days later when Truman, with his senior advisers in accord, dismissed MacArthur from his commands for "rank insubordination" because he ignored administration directives to seek a negotiated settlement and instead threatened to carry the war to China and even to use atomic weapons and Nationalist forces if the PRC's field commander did not surrender to him. But the president's decision to fire the near iconic general brought public shock and bitter criticism, with senior Republicans accusing him of appeasing the Soviet Union and its allies.

MacArthur returned to the United States, told a joint session of Congress on April 19 that he could not explain to his soldiers why they were not allowed to seek victory and exited theatrically, an "old soldier" who had "tried to do his duty as God gave him the light to see that duty." Truman left it to his senior advisers to explain to the Senate's Foreign Relations and Armed Services Committees the reasons for fighting a limited war in Korea rather than the wrong war, in the wrong place, with the wrong enemy in China.[45]

Humphrey firmly insisted that the Constitution demanded that the general follow his commander-in-chief's orders and strongly disputed Republican conservatives who accused Truman of appeasement or Munich-style politics. The president had resisted the Soviets and Communism from Western Europe to South Korea, he stated, but carrying the war to China made no sense. The "real source of power" was the Soviet Union, and those who proposed to bomb Manchuria had better be prepared to go to Moscow, where the supplies were.

Humphrey also chided senators who sought to enlist the Nationalists, who he said had all they could do to defend Taiwan. He rejected Republican criticism that American allies were not contributing to the war. The French, Humphrey said—revealing his heightened Cold War view—had 150,000 troops in Indochina who were waging "war against the same communism, against imperialism, aggressive communism," and the loss of Indochina and its tin, oil, and rubber would be as bad as the loss of Korea. And the British, despite recognizing the PRC in 1950, were fending off Communists in Malaya. One might wish that the Allies would contribute more, he said, but they were independent nations, not American satellites.[46]

Humphrey's defense of Truman's policy spilled over into a heated argument during a radio debate in late April in a studio in the Senate Office Building basement with archconservative Capehart. Humphrey charged that Republican leaders pressing for military action against the PRC were guilty of "political and military stupidity," and the combative Capehart called Humphrey a Communist sympathizer and PRC supporter. Humphrey called Capehart—or so the latter claimed—a "son-of-a-bitch." The Indiana senator virtually pushed Humphrey out of the studio, after which "Slugger Capehart" and Humphrey, "The Lip," as a newspaper dubbed the men, clawed at each other. No blows were struck, but the loss of senatorial decorum led Vice President Barkley, usually friendly to liberals, to remark, "That Minnesota is a great state. First they sent us their Ball, then they sent us their Thye, and now they've sent us their goddamn hind end."[47]

By 1951, the once easily scarred Humphrey was able to weather such criticism. His friend Long had encouraged him to have lunch in the senators' private dining room, where neither staff nor visitors were allowed and politics was adjourned for conversation about social life and sports. Humphrey began to find acceptance and camaraderie.[48]

He had also become adept at helping himself. He kept a watchful eye on his reelection prospects and worried that his 1954 opponent would be the highly popular and progressive three-term Republican governor Luther Youngdahl, who had rid Minnesota of slot machines and improved education, veterans' benefits, and treatment in state mental health hospitals. But by 1950, Youngdahl, formerly a state supreme court judge, sought to move to the federal judiciary, which Humphrey learned from Ray Ewald, a Republican mutual friend and wealthy Minneapolis dairy businessman who had supported his mayoral campaigns and policies and arranged a meeting at his home with the governor that confirmed his interest in a federal judgeship.[49]

So when Humphrey read in the *Washington Post* on July 1, 1951, that a District of Columbia circuit judge had died, he immediately got an appointment with Truman, who was favorably disposed toward Youngdahl, the only Republican governor to support his firing of MacArthur. The president had Humphrey fly Youngdahl to Washington on July 4 and, without a word to the Justice Department, briefly interviewed him next morning and had his nomination announced first to the Minneapolis press corps, alerted in advance by a smiling Humphrey.[50]

Republican leaders were stunned. *Time* noted, "Hubert Humphrey now has professional standing in the big leagues," and a happy Truman shortly wrote to Humphrey that "it looks as if our judgeship appointment was ten-strike." The senator agreed. Youngdahl, who went on to a distinguished liberal judicial career, later reflected that "Hubert was exuberant and happy . . . and undoubtedly he was somewhat relieved that I would not be around to run against him."[51]

Humphrey had established his "big leagues" reputation and was ready to enhance his reputation as a liberal legislative leader, serve as a liaison between northern and southern Democrats, and become a major national political figure.

6

PROMINENCE AND COURTSHIP

When Arthur Naftalin, Humphrey's friend from graduate school and mayoral days, joined the senator's staff in summer 1951, he found Humphrey acting "like a beaten man." His political agenda—civil rights, labor relations, health insurance, and reform of the tax code and the Senate's rules—had been rejected. Moreover, Humphrey had made few friends in the Senate and had suffered personal ridicule, which was extremely painful for someone who, Naftalin recalled, wanted to be seen not as a maverick but as a moderator, if not as part of the inner circle.[1]

Early in 1952, Humphrey sought ways to raise his political standing and demonstrate his anti-Communist credentials. He used his chairmanship of a Labor subcommittee to seek to purge union officials who might have signed Taft-Hartley affidavits falsely testifying to their non-Communist ties. In 1949, CIO president Philip Murray had undertaken to expel all unions with Communist leadership, but Humphrey's legislative director, Max Kampelman, wanted more to be done.

Born to Romanian Jewish immigrant parents in New York in 1920, Kampelman had graduated from New York University, where he became a pacifist, and attended NYU's law school at night until the United States entered the war in 1941. Registered as a conscientious objector, he relocated to take part in a War Department study of starvation's impact on people (in anticipation of postwar treatment of concentration camp survivors and prisoners of war) at the University of Minnesota. He finished his law degree and earned a PhD in political science, writing his dissertation on "The Communists and the CIO." Kampelman also became friendly with Mayor Humphrey, helped him organize his staff after his 1948 election to the Senate, and served as his legislative director until 1955, when he joined a Washington law firm. He remained Humphrey's close friend, personal lawyer, and political adviser for the next three decades.[2]

In March 1952, Kampelman, who had abandoned his pacifism, was convinced that there was "evil" in the world that had to be confronted. He encouraged Humphrey to announce the start of an investigation with "one preconception" that "there are certain Communist-dominated unions in the United States operating in defense industries, and we must face up to what this fact means for our national security." The AFL and CIO, fearful of punitive legislation, opposed Humphrey's undertaking, but with support from liberal Labor subcommittee colleagues Douglas and Oregon Republican Wayne Morse, he proceeded. Ten days of poorly attended hearings over the next four months, however, turned up no evidence of Communist conspiracies. Humphrey garnered little publicity but drew sharp criticism from the *Daily Worker* and from unions such as the United Electrical Workers in Minneapolis. He ended his probe quietly.[3]

Humphrey was one of the few Democrats to back President Truman when in April 1952 he ordered government seizure of the steel mills after the Wage Stabilization Board (WSB), mediating contract negotiations, proposed a pay raise of about 26 cents an hour for union workers but no increase in steel prices and the owners refused this offer without a significant price per ton increase. A strike loomed, and on April 8, Truman, claiming that the 1950 Selective Service Act authorized him to maintain steel production during the national emergency, ordered the Commerce Department to seize the steel mills and to continue production under current management-labor conditions.

Truman's action stunned the nation, although Chief Justice Fred Vinson, a confidant and his former treasury secretary, had told him privately (a questionable act) that the Court would approve the seizure. But many in Congress, including Democrats, and the public questioned the constitutionality of his action without explicit legislative authority, and there were calls for his impeachment.[4]

Humphrey was uncertain about the constitutionality of Truman's action but believed that the president had very broad "inherent powers" to defend the nation, especially in an emergency. Moreover, Humphrey's Labor subcommittee had prepared reports showing that the WSB-proposed wage increases were justified, that the steel companies' profits were higher than at any time since World War I, and that their alleged anticipated costs were "preposterous."[5]

Humphrey strongly sided with Democratic colleagues to turn back a Republican-sponsored proposal to limit the president's power by reducing appropriations for steel purchases. Once again he analogized Truman's action to Lincoln's suspending habeas corpus during the Civil War, and when conservative Republican senator William Knowland expressed surprise that a liberal such as Humphrey was not more concerned about the danger of allowing the president unlimited seizure power, he reiterated his view of presidential power in a national emergency. He was not "underwriting" Truman's action: the Supreme Court would render final judgment, he said, but he challenged opponents of the president's action to offer articles of impeachment.[6]

A federal district court issued an injunction against the seizure, and in June the Supreme Court, including liberal justices Hugo Black and William Douglas, declared that the president's action required authority from the Constitution or Congress. The companies were returned to private control, and the Steelworkers went on strike until a settlement about two months later provided wage and price increases approaching those that the WSB had proposed in March. Truman never quite forgave the "so-called Liberals" for "doing what that Court did to me" and for "ruling against what was best for the country." He had acted rashly, however, and had given Republicans an issue with which to assail Democrats in the November elections.[7]

Humphrey stood with Truman once again in spring 1952 in seeking to liberalize US immigration policy, including overhaul of the controversial 1924 legislation that established the national origins quota system limiting annual immigration to the United States to 2 percent of the number of nationals from each country who were living in America as of the 1890 census, when emigrants from eastern and southern Europe were few. Minimum national quotas were set at 100 persons, but the law also barred admission of aliens, including Chinese and Japanese, who were ineligible for citizenship as per 1790 and 1870 laws. In 1929, the United States switched to use of the 1920 census, to take account of the increased post-1890 immigration, but national origins quotas were set as a proportion of a maximum annual admission of 150,000 immigrants. This assured that 85 percent of the new immigrants would come from northern and Western Europe.[8]

In June 1950, the Senate Judiciary Committee, having weighed immigration policy for several years, reported strongly in favor of Congress's retaining a national origins system that preserved the nation's "racial composition" and gave highest priority to people deemed more assimilable by their political-cultural backgrounds. In early 1952, two Democrats, Representative Francis Walter of Pennsylvania, and longtime Judiciary Committee chair Pat McCarran of Nevada—both strongly anti-Communist and anti-immigrant—sponsored legislation designed to continue the national origins system and to permit exclusion and deportation of categories of "undesirable" persons.

The McCarran-Walter Immigration and Nationality Act also altered the national annual quota system to one-sixth of 1 percent of the number of people from each country resident in the United States as of the 1920 census (slightly raising the annual quota from 150,000 to 155,000 persons) and continued the minimum national quota of 100 and exemption of Western Hemisphere nations from any quota. The law also ended the 1917 Asiatic Barred Zone (all of Asia) but created a twenty-nation Asian Pacific Triangle—including China, Japan, Korea, the Philippines, Southeast Asia, and India—limited to an annual quota of only 2,000 emigrants.

The racial aspect of this provision was evident: all immigrants born outside the triangle of even one Asian parent were to be counted against the quota of their country of Asian Pacific ancestry, not their birthplace. The law also gave wide discretion to US officials at home and in consulates overseas to exclude aliens who had mental, physical, or moral defects, had ever been affiliated with subversive organizations, or had advocated subversive ideas. The attorney general was also authorized to deport both aliens and naturalized American citizens believed to be engaged in subversive activity.[9]

Humphrey took the lead, strongly supported by liberals such as Lehman, Douglas, Kefauver, Murray, and William Benton of Connecticut, to press their own substitute omnibus bill. Humphrey accepted a national origins quota system but proposed to use the 1950 census, which counted 157 million Americans as against 105 million in the 1920 census, thus increasing the annual quota by 60,000 persons; he also sought to pool unused quotas, adding another 50,000 to 70,000 persons annually. Humphrey dismissed the 1920 census as racist and discriminatory because it did not count people descended from slave immigrants, and he charged that the McCarran-Walter bill affronted "all colored races and peoples" by limiting emigrants from Jamaica, Trinidad, and other British West Indies colonies to just 100 per year, whereas previously they were able to use the large quotas of their mother country.

Most important, Humphrey proposed to eliminate the Asian Pacific Triangle designation and to grant proportional quotas for all Asians, including Indians and Chinese. He also sought to end what he called the "discriminatory test" of "nationality by origin" (of one's parents) instead of "by birth" (place of birth) for Asians. Humphrey accepted the McCarran-Walter concept of excluding "undesirable" (for ideological reasons) immigrants and deporting aliens engaged in subversive activity (including Communist Party membership). But he proposed to admit individuals previously associated with totalitarian or Communist movements who had broken with their past, asserting that they had the poten-tial to become "outstanding advocates of democracy." This would also allow the United States to accept political refugees from behind the Iron Curtain and improve America's world standing. Finally, Humphrey sought to kill the McCarran-Walter bill's invidious distinction between nationalized and native-born citizens that arose from allowing officials to order deportation of natural-ized citizens for engaging in subversive activity. Equal justice required that all citizens be subject to the same punishment.[10]

Humphrey and his liberal allies were running against the political tide. The House passed the McCarran-Walter bill by a wide margin; the Senate voted down Humphrey's substitute bill and promptly passed the McCarran-Walter bill by voice vote. After both houses quickly approved the conference committee bill, Truman delivered a ringing veto in June that echoed the arguments of Humphrey and his supporters: the national origins system insulted and discriminated against Eastern and southern Europeans (including NATO allies Greece and Turkey) and all Asians, and set the quota far too low. But the House and the Senate overrode Truman's veto. Afterward Humphrey said that there was no room for "discrimination and bigotry" in American immigra-tion laws, and he would continue to fight for better legislation for years to come.[11]

✦ ✦ ✦

Humphrey had become a Truman loyalist. In January 1952, he agreed to run as a favorite son in Minnesota's primary to preclude a challenge to the president, and he hoped to be the Democratic convention keynote speaker, and perhaps more. Truman was under fire, however, for the continuing Korean War, allega-tions about Communists in the State Department, and corruption in the Internal Revenue Service and Tax Division of the Justice Department. Ambivalent about another presidential race, he sought to lure his NATO commander, General Eisenhower, to run as a Democrat, but Eisenhower soon revealed his Republican proclivities.[12]

Truman entered the Democratic race but suffered a major defeat in the New Hampshire primary at the hands of Estes Kefauver, who had served in the Tennessee legislature for ten years, won a Senate seat in 1948, and was an economic populist and civil rights moderate, especially for a southerner, willing to accept an FEPC plank in the Democratic platform.[13]

Humphrey won the uncontested Minnesota primary and its twenty-six delegates. Intending to withdraw soon, he formed a "Fair Deal" voting bloc to seek northern supporters of a liberal nominee, while Truman left the race in late March.[14]

Kefauver won twelve of the fifteen Democratic primaries but lacked the votes to win a first ballot victory, while no other major candidate emerged. Truman and his White House aides turned to Illinois governor Adlai Stevenson, whose grandfather had been vice president under Grover Cleveland and whose father was highly active in state politics. Stevenson, a graduate of Princeton and Northwestern University Law School, worked in the War Department during World War II, won a landslide victory for governor in 1948 that carried the state for Truman, and had a successful reform-oriented first term. But he rebuffed the president's entreaties to run, although he did not rule out a draft.[15]

By July 1952, both parties were focused on their nominating conventions in Chicago. The GOP divided between Senator Taft, "Mr. Republican," and the politically opaque Eisenhower, who sought to be drafted. Taft charged Democrats with promoting socialistic programs and being soft on Communism, and he urged hemispheric defense and denigrated NATO-type alliances. "Draft Eisenhower" Republicans inclined to accept limited New Deal–Fair Deal programs and supported Truman's containment policy. They entered the general's name in the New Hampshire primary, which he won decisively, and Stassen won easily as his surrogate in Minnesota.[16]

Eisenhower also won the eastern primaries, but Taft victories in the greater Midwest, and strong support from party leaders in the nonprimary South, led the general to resign his NATO command in June to campaign in the United States, while his managers pressed a "Fair Play" resolution at the Republican convention in early July denying votes to contested delegates, who were mainly in southern states and might have given Taft the nomination. The Eisenhower team got first-term senator Richard Nixon to swing the California delegation behind "Fair Play," and as the general neared a first ballot victory, Senator Edward Thye, head of the Minnesota delegation, threw Stassen's votes to him to put him over the top. He took Nixon as a running mate: he had collaborated on "Fair Play" and would appeal to conservatives as a vigorous anti-Communist who had accused the Democrats of losing Eastern Europe and China. He was also young at thirty-eight and had defeated liberal Democrats in bitterly fought elections for the House in 1946 and 1948, and for the Senate in 1950.[17]

The extremist Republican platform assailed the Democrats as having pursued a "negative, futile, and immoral" policy of containment, surrendered fifteen countries to "Communist Russia," and plunged the nation into the Korean War without Congress's assent. The GOP also accused the Democrats of having illegally seized industries and acted duplicitously about civil rights, which needed enforcement—but states had to control their own institutions. Eisenhower's acceptance speech said only that he wished to lead "a crusade" and to seek progressive policies.[18]

The Democrats followed the Republicans into Chicago. Humphrey had been encouraged to run by Senators Brien McMahon of Connecticut and the venerated eighty-five-year-old Francis Green of Rhode Island, but Kefauver's success in midwestern primaries preempted that region as a base, and the Minnesotan knew that he was too new to the national scene. Still, his protégé, Congressman Gene McCarthy, now nominated him as "a true apostle of democracy," and his friend and DFL leader Orville Freeman (running for governor) said that he would "carry the message of democracy to the little people of the world." Humphrey enjoyed the next twenty minutes, the maximum allowable demonstration time, but released his delegates during the first ballot.[19]

More realistically, Humphrey had sought, with Truman's support, the prestige of delivering the keynote address, but southerners vetoed this. He opposed seating of anti-Truman Dixiecrats from Texas and Mississippi who, he said, had attacked Roosevelt and his family, but the credentials committee sided with the Dixiecrats. Humphrey and his liberal allies rammed through the convention by voice vote a "loyalty oath" requiring the delegates to pledge to support only convention-nominated candidates, but DNC chairman Frank McKinney and Alabama senator John Sparkman had this watered down to apply to southern delegates only if it did not cause them to violate state law or contravene state party orders. Humphrey assailed this "first dagger in the back of New Deal–Fair Deal" and, urged on by other liberals, readied for a 1948-style floor fight. But he drew back out of desire for party unity.[20]

Humphrey turned to civil rights in the platform, which otherwise reaffirmed New Deal–Fair Deal programs and global containment of Soviet Communism and imperialism. Negotiating with Sparkman and Congressman Brooks Hays of Arkansas—considered moderates on civil rights—Humphrey got accord on equal employment opportunity, full and equal participation in the electoral process, personal security, and enrollment in public higher education. This was a "major victory," he declared; "we got more than I expected"; it was also "tremendous personal vindication" for Humphrey, as Kampelman recalled. Unlike in 1948, however, there was no call for an FEPC or for Congress to enforce civil rights. Nor could Humphrey get a pledge to end the filibuster, only a vague commitment to majority rule and decision-making after "reasonable debate."[21]

Meanwhile, Stevenson delivered an urbane and witty welcoming address that cited his state of Illinois, whose only three prior Democratic governors were a Protestant immigrant, a Catholic, and a Jewish son of immigrants, as the "story of America." He mocked the Republicans for their "pompous phrases [that] marched across the landscape in search of an idea," and urged his party to provide a "demonstration of democracy" because "all the world is watching and listening."[22]

Humphrey was surprised at the extent to which the speech energized the draft Stevenson movement. He and his Minnesota delegation favored Kefauver, a "fighting liberal." But Humphrey quickly conceded that the Illinois governor, who had established a state FEPC and also had more strength than Kefauver among southerners, appeared better able to contest Eisenhower. Humphrey quashed a protest movement by liberals to oppose Stevenson's nomination and held that they should not allow the South to claim credit for nominating him.[23]

Humphrey proved right. Kefauver's first ballot lead of 340–273 was far from the 615½ votes needed to win. Stevenson cut the gap sharply on the next ballot and won on the third round, with Freeman moving the convention to a unanimous vote. Stevenson's choice of Sparkman for his running mate, however, drew strong protest from African American leaders and liberals, including the Minnesota delegation, which had believed that Kefauver would be selected. But once again Humphrey assuaged liberals, insisting that although Sparkman had gone Dixiecrat in 1948, now he had bravely ousted them from the Alabama delegation and cooperated on the civil rights plank. "It's important that the voice of liberalism in the South be given a chance to be heard," he said.[24]

Stevenson stirred liberals' hopes with his rousing acceptance speech, "Let's Talk Sense to the American People," urging Democrats to tell their constituents that they faced years of sacrifice and patience, there were "no gains without pains," and they were on the eve of "great decisions, not easy decisions," in a long and costly struggle against "war, poverty, and tyranny." And the "acid" test for a political party was "not winning the election" but "governing the nation."[25]

During the campaign, however, the Republicans capitalized on Eisenhower's heroic but genial image ("I Like Ike"), bitter public frustration over the costly Korean War, fear of Communism, and concern about Democratic control of the White House for two decades. The GOP encapsulated this in their "K1C2" formula, "Korea, Communism, and Corruption," and "Time for a Change" slogan. Republican advertisements also quoted Humphrey ("Thank God for Eisenhower," he had said in March 1952), as well as Stevenson and Sparkman as having publicly praised Eisenhower, usually for his NATO work, and cited Truman as having urged Eisenhower to run for president as a Democrat.[26]

Eisenhower ran a shrewd, and sometimes unprincipled, campaign. He publicly reconciled with Taft to win over his party's conservatives and perhaps southern Democrats, who also liked the general's support for state control of offshore oil deposits and his emphasis on reduced taxes and limited national government. When news stories in mid-September revealed that wealthy businessmen had maintained an eighteen-thousand-dollar slush fund for Nixon, Democrats and many Republicans called for him to resign from the ticket. But Eisenhower insisted that he be allowed to explain himself, and in a melodramatic, nationally televised speech on September 23, Nixon said he had spent all the money on political expenses to save taxpayer dollars, stressed his humble origins, and said he would not return the only gift he had gotten, a cocker spaniel named Checkers, that his young daughters loved. Eisenhower declared that many men make mistakes and move on, and soon met with Nixon and declared, "You're my boy," preserving his place on the ticket.[27]

Further, when Eisenhower campaigned with Senator McCarthy in Milwaukee, Wisconsin, for his reelection, the general omitted from his speech planned words of praise for his military mentor, General George Marshall, whom McCarthy had charged with heading a "conspiracy" against America. McCarthy won reelection. Eisenhower also declared that if elected "I shall go to Korea," but did not say what he would do there.[28]

Stevenson supported "mankind's war" in Korea, disdained McCarthy's "reckless charges," and campaigned for moderate expansion of New Deal–Fair Deal programs, federal control of offshore oil, and civil rights legislation, if always with reminders of progress in the South. But southern Democrats like Senator Harry Byrd of Virginia and Governors James Byrnes of South Carolina and Allen Shivers of Texas either refused to support Stevenson or openly backed Eisenhower."[29]

Humphrey traveled to eighteen states in Stevenson's behalf and accused Eisenhower of peddling a "bill of goods" by claiming to support Social Security and federal aid to education, which Republicans had long opposed. But Humphrey also perceived a critical flaw in Stevenson's campaign style. In late September, he wrote to his friend Senator Benton, "Politics is a strange admixture of mind and body, of ideas and guts," and while people know that Stevenson can think for them, they did not know if he could "feel" for them. "Adlai has been giving remarkable speeches," he wrote, "masterpieces," but people had little time for politics, and "unless the story is told in the most dramatic way—in bold strokes, even exaggerated form—it will not command attention." People can be aroused over good causes as well as bad ones, such as corruption, he continued, but "we Democrats have got to challenge our people, we have got to make them feel they are an integral part of a great crusade for human freedom."[30]

This was not to be. Eisenhower won overwhelmingly and captured thirty-nine states, including four in the more prosperous, urbanized "rim" South of Virginia, Tennessee, Florida, and Texas, the first Republican presidential candidate to win in the South since 1928. Stevenson won only nine states, all (including West Virginia) in the deeper one-party South. The Republicans, however, gained 2 Senate seats to win narrow 48–47–1 control of that body, and they added 22 House seats to hold a 221–213 majority. In Minnesota, Thye won reelection and Governor Elmo Anderson defeated Freeman.[31]

Humphrey was aggrieved at the election results. The Democrats were now the minority party, and the archconservative Taft would be the new and powerful majority leader. Humphrey's friend Benton lost his Connecticut seat to a Republican businessman, William A. Purtell, largely due to Eisenhower's landslide, but also frequent attacks by McCarthy. In a major upset, Majority Leader Ernest McFarland lost in heavily Democratic Arizona to businessman-turned-Republican politician Barry Goldwater, who ran a strong anti-New Deal–Fair Deal and antiunion campaign.[32]

Humphrey saw clearly the new administration would not foster civil rights laws or programs to aid his farmer or labor constituents. But a ray of light seemed to shine through the dark clouds of defeat. McFarland's loss required the Democrats to choose a new Senate leader. Humphrey wanted this role but recognized the southerners would not support a civil rights advocate. He would have to organize liberals, including Douglas and their ADA followers, behind someone else.

Lyndon Johnson saw his opportunity; he secured the support of Russell of Georgia, which provided the Texan nearly enough southern votes for a majority, and he got Stevenson to remain neutral. Meanwhile, Humphrey declared on national radio on December 15 that he had great respect for Johnson, but "it would be better to have someone that wasn't so clearly identified with a sectional group." The Democrats needed to be the "great national liberal party."[33]

Humphrey had reason to be concerned about Johnson, having seen him in operation when, in spring 1949, President Truman nominated Leland Olds, chairman of the Federal Power Commission (FPC), for a third five-year term. During the 1920s, Olds had been an idealistic socialist (and anti-Communist) who wrote highly critical articles that appeared in left-oriented publications, including the *Daily Worker*. At the end of the decade, Olds left journalism to study the electric power industry, came to favor public ownership, and served as an adviser to Governor Franklin Roosevelt, who named him to head the New York Power Authority in 1931 and then appointed him to head the FPC in 1939 and 1944.[34]

Olds's confirmation for a third term seemed certain until Johnson intervened. Born three years before Humphrey in 1908 in the Hill Country of South Central Texas, Johnson had served in the House during 1937–48, lost a close Democratic Senate primary election in 1941, and then won a bitter and long-disputed Democratic primary in 1948, assuring he would gain his first Senate term that November. He considered FDR to be his mentor but in 1949 decided to earn the favor of the powerful oil and gas interests in his state and the Southwest that were determined to be rid of the consumer and regulatory-oriented Olds.[35]

Johnson, who chaired the Commerce Committee's subcommittee weighing the nomination, packed it with opponents of Olds, delayed hearings until September in order to dredge up Olds's "radical" 1920 articles, and brought in hostile witnesses who accused him of being a virtual Communist. Many liberal supporters and newspapers deplored this smear campaign, as did Truman. But both the subcommittee and full committee voted overwhelmingly against Olds. The outrageous charges had hit not just an antiregulatory nerve but an anti-Communist one. Full Senate hearings came in late September.[36]

Only Humphrey and four other senators were willing to speak on Olds's behalf. Humphrey pointed out the majority of hostile witnesses represented natural gas owners or producers who sought to escape FPC regulation. He insisted that there was "not one iota of evidence" that Olds was a Communist, and he commended him for having had the courage in the 1920s to declare that the American enterprise system ignored human rights and exploited child labor and widows who were "putting their money into phony stocks." Olds should have been awarded a "crown of diamonds" for doing this, Humphrey said; he was a "liberal, not a radical," who had been loyal to his government, conscience, and the American people. If the Senate now voted to "crucify" him, Humphrey said, it would show that his colleagues had "gone off the deep end."[37]

Johnson immediately repeated all the charges against Olds, insisted that even if he was not a Communist, his beliefs were the same, and the issue was "shall we have a commissioner or a commissar?" Two days later the Senate, with numerous liberals having left the chamber, defeated Olds's nomination. Johnson had won a victory, gained the support of powerful gas and oil interests, and earned respect from conservatives such as Russell. Meanwhile, Olds was crushed, and Truman had suffered defeat by his own party—and Johnson.[38]

Now, early in 1953, Humphrey, forewarned about Johnson's willingness to be ruthless in his quest for power, would have to deal with the Texan's determination to lead his party in the Senate. At the same time, Johnson worried that although "Hubert can't win," he "didn't want him gumming up the works for me. If he fights to the bitter end, then I won't have a cut dog's chance to be an effective leader," and the Republicans would "eat our lunch and the sack it came in." The Texan sent Robert (Bobby) Baker, the politically shrewd twenty-six-year-old secretary to the Senate Democrats, to solicit Humphrey's support with strong hints that Johnson, as minority leader, would look to him as the spokesman for Senate liberals and his growing national constituency, and might even bring him into the Senate's "leadership circle."

Humphrey resisted, but Johnson called him that night at home to urge acceptance. Humphrey said that his group had decided to back the liberal's beloved elder statesman, seventy-seven-year-old James Murray of Montana. That was too bad, Johnson replied, especially because he weighed making Humphrey minority whip—an "exhilarating" thought, the Minnesotan later wrote—but he wondered if the Texan was "just playing me off."³⁹

The next day, Humphrey, Douglas, Lehman, and Lester Hunt of Wyoming went to Johnson's office to seek accord. The Texan listened only briefly before he "politely but curtly dismissed us," Humphrey remembered, although Johnson soon called to ask him to come back to his office alone. There, in a take-charge, no-nonsense manner, Humphrey recalled, Johnson told him that the votes he thought he had were not certain and asked for his count. Humphrey said it was thirteen to seventeen. Johnson said that spread was too wide and, worse, pointed to names—including Hunt—on the list who he said had privately committed to him.

Johnson admonished Humphrey to "quit playing around with people you can't depend on" and then, in a friendlier manner, said that he would regret his "foolish" decision to turn down the whip position, which would now go to Mike Mansfield of Montana, just elected to the Senate after ten years in the House. Still, Johnson said, Humphrey had talked "straight" and said that after the Texan became minority leader, he would work with him, but "you and only you from the bomb throwers."⁴⁰

The Democrats met on January 2, 1953, to choose a minority leader. Johnson had a clear majority on the initial canvass of votes, while Murray had only himself, Humphrey, Douglas, Kefauver, and a few others. Humphrey realized that Johnson had been "right as day" about what each senator would do and immediately moved for a unanimous vote to avoid embarrassing Murray over his low count. He knew, and feared, that Johnson "would keep book" on how each senator voted on a formal roll call and would not forget or forgive.[41]

Nonetheless, Humphrey found that dealing with Johnson paid dividends. Immediately after their caucus, the Democrats' new leader called him to his office to ask, "What do you liberals really want?" Humphrey said that their first concern was representation on the Policy Committee, and their choice was Murray. Johnson dismissed him as too old to be effective but would accept the liberals' choice. He also agreed to liberal representation on the Steering Committee and to put Lehman (consigned by southerners to Interior) on the Banking Committee, but he denied new assignments to Douglas and Kefauver because they had initially voted for Murray.[42]

Humphrey stood to be the biggest gainer among liberals, with some sacrifice. He aspired to the Foreign Relations Committee, which he believed would lend authority to his speeches and ideas. Johnson knew this and that Taft was moving from Labor to Foreign Relations and bringing old-guard Republicans, including China bloc spokesman William Knowland of California. Johnson feared Republican attacks on Roosevelt-Truman foreign policy. The Democrats' new leader wanted strong people on the committee such as Humphrey and Mansfield, who had taught Latin American and Far Eastern history at the University of Montana and won respect on the House Foreign Affairs Committee. As Johnson told other senators, "Mansfield out-knows Taft and Humphrey can out-talk him."[43]

Humphrey balked at having to leave both Labor and Agriculture. His DFL Party would still provide strong ties to labor groups, he said, but there was no one else from his region on Agriculture to care for his farmer constituents, who would "just not understand it"—and he faced reelection in two years. But when Johnson persisted, Humphrey yielded, after gaining assurance he would get the next available seat on Agriculture. Johnson further insisted that Humphrey and several other Democrats had to remain on Government Operations because the party needed "real fighters," or else McCarthy, about to become committee chair, would "run wild" denouncing the Democrats as "the Party of Treason."[44]

The deal was struck, as the first half of a larger bargain. Reverting to the recent caucus, Johnson told Humphrey that "since you had enough sense not to drive it to a vote down there and made it unanimous, I am perfectly willing to deal with you." But "I don't want you to bring in a lot of those other fellows. . . . When you've got something that your people want, *you* come see me."[45]

Humphrey had achieved more standing and influence than he could have imagined a year or two earlier. He believed that his relationship with Johnson derived from mutual need and utility, and he knew that he could not secure important legislation, and ultimately a presidential nomination, without Johnson's lining up the necessary votes, especially among southerners. Similarly, Johnson required Humphrey's support to garner liberal votes in order to prove that he could lead effectively, unify the party, and enable it to thwart Republican efforts to roll back New Deal–Fair Deal programs. He also needed support of Humphrey's northern liberal allies to gain a presidential nomination.

Still, the Minnesotan recognized, "I needed him more than he needed me," and "I had become his conduit and their [the liberals'] spokesman not by their election but by his appointment." He also knew that many liberals regarded this success as "tokenism," and "suspect" because it came from Johnson.

Nonetheless, Humphrey and Johnson had begun a long political journey together that would reach an unforeseeable bitter climax during the fateful 1968 presidential election.[46]

There were important similarities in their backgrounds that helped them bridge their political or ideological differences and operating styles. Like Humphrey, Johnson was born in a small house in a rural, frontierlike community, Stonewall, Texas, in 1908 to Sam and Rebekah Baines Johnson. Young Lyndon, like young Hubert, learned his politics from his father, a former teacher, rancher, and farmer who served in the state legislature and earned a reputation of absolute integrity, including by resisting pressure from special interests and publicly denouncing the Ku Klux Klan in 1921 despite death threats. Sam Johnson, like the elder Hubert Humphrey, also lost his ranch in 1922 because of indebtedness.[47]

A very bright young Lyndon graduated from high school at age fifteen and worked at a few jobs before enrolling in 1926 at Southwest Texas State Teachers College in San Marcos, where he earned a teaching certificate and taught grade school and high school for a couple of years before returning to San Marcos to finish his college degree in 1930. He served as secretary to a Texas congressman and made friends with influential politicians such as Texas's Sam Rayburn, who in 1935 helped him gain the position of director of the National Youth Administration in Texas. In 1937, Johnson won a special election to represent Texas's tenth congressional district (running from northwest Houston to west of Austin), a seat he held until his famously bitter and controversial Democratic primary run-off victory for the Senate nomination in 1948 against a former popular governor, Coke Stevenson, by just 87 votes, earning his "Landslide Lyndon" epithet. Johnson then defeated his Republican opponent, Jack Porter, by a two-to-one margin. Meanwhile he had married Claudia Alta "Lady Bird" Taylor of Karnack, Texas in 1934, and they had two daughters, Lynda Bird and Luci Baines. He also secured a commission in the navy in 1941 and served on General Douglas MacArthur's staff in Australia in 1942 before returning to Congress later that year.[48]

Thus Johnson, like Humphrey, came from limited circumstances, although the Texan earned great wealth while in politics, beginning with the purchase in 1943, in his wife's name, of radio station KTBC in Austin, and then other businesses and properties in that city, notwithstanding seeming conflicts of interest because of his standing as a public official. Both Humphrey and Johnson were teachers, were ardent supporters of FDR, and served as state heads of New Deal agencies. Neither man was enamored of Truman, although Humphrey became a strong supporter after the 1948 election, while Johnson aligned more closely with powerful southern Democrats. Last, both Humphrey and Johnson firmly supported FDR's prewar and wartime foreign policy and were firm anti-Communists who viewed the Soviet Union darkly and as responsible for most of the postwar conflict.[49]

Although the two men had little contact during their first years in the Senate, Johnson admired Humphrey's eloquence and after his 1950 debacle with Senator Byrd tried to inject humor into the matter by telling Humphrey that he would like to "cross-breed" him with Byrd in order to cool him down. Thus when Johnson and Humphrey met one day in 1951 en route to the Capitol, the Texan surprised his accompanying new staff member, journalist George Reedy, by declaring, "Hubert . . . there are so many ways that I envy you. You are articulate, you have such a broad range of knowledge, you can present it with such absolute logic." Then in a harsh and patronizing tone Johnson said: "But goddamn it Hubert, why can't you be something but a gramophone for the NAACP? Goddamn it, Hubert, why can't you make a speech about farmers? Goddamn it, Hubert, why can't you do something for all those people *and* the NAACP besides talking about them? You're spending so much time making speeches there is no time left to get anything done."

Reedy's recollection of the event was exaggerated, but not long after the encounter Johnson began to invite Humphrey to his office for a casual drink and conversation. And Russell, who was often present, perhaps to take Humphrey's measure, would soon tell Johnson, "I just don't understand how you got me to liking Hubert so much."[50]

After Johnson became minority leader in 1953, he would invite Humphrey to his Texas ranch, meet his commitment to the Minnesotan's claim to a seat on the Agriculture Committee in 1954, and compliment him for Democratic achievements and campaign for his reelection that year.[51]

Similarly, Humphrey greatly respected Johnson from the time they entered the Senate together, and he was also envious that the Texan's prior decade in the House had allowed him to become well acquainted with leaders in both chambers, many government officials, and Washington's "satellite world" of business lobbyists, farmer and labor leaders, and other special interest advocates. Humphrey appreciated Johnson's bringing him into social contact with conservative and southern Democrats, who had provided him with better insight into the issues they confronted with their constituents. Humphrey also judged Johnson to be a "marvelous conversationalist" and a "teacher," who knew which colleagues he could threaten and which ones needed to be "nourished along." He also respected Johnson's belief that they could make steady legislative progress "if we didn't bite off too much."[52]

Above all, Humphrey would praise Johnson as an excellent leader who quickly changed Senate practices by giving each newly elected senator a seat on a major committee and who mastered the intricacies of coaxing legislation through Congress. The two men did divide on some important issues: Humphrey wanted federal control of the tidelands oil, and Johnson was wedded to state control; Humphrey wanted to eliminate or sharply reduce oil and gas depletion allowances, and Johnson sought to preserve them; Humphrey long favored expanded civil rights and an FEPC; Johnson favored African American enfranchisement and equal access to government programs but claimed that antilynching, anti–poll tax, and FEPC legislation violated states' rights. He recognized, however, the need for change after World War II, or eventually "blood will run in the streets." In a few years he would urge the Democrats to enact a civil rights bill before the Republicans outflanked them politically and gained support of a major constituency.[53]

Last, Humphrey recognized that Johnson lived politics day and night and that to reply to his many calls to come to his office during evening hours by saying it was time to go home would only draw the blunt response that one had to choose between being a good father or a good senator. Humphrey also knew that his newfound political partner kept close tabs on all of his colleagues — "I used to say that he had his own FBI," he recalled — and knew exactly where they went and with whom in the evening to eat, to drink, and to dance. Humphrey was under no illusion about the dual difficulty he faced in meeting the demands of the new Democratic Senate leader, as well as becoming "the loyal opposition" who had to confront a Republican president and his policies.[54]

7

THE PRICE OF LEADERSHIP

When the Eighty-Third Congress assembled in January 1953, Humphrey continued to push for civil rights even though Majority Leader Robert Taft's Republican backers and southern Democrats crushed his proposal to revise the Rule XXII requirement of a two-thirds majority vote of all senators to end debate. Despite this, Humphrey introduced civil rights bills to make lynching a federal crime, eliminate poll taxes and segregation in interstate commerce, protect voting rights, and create a civil rights division in the Justice Department. The senators were unmoved; Humphrey could only ask if Attorney General Herbert Brownell's office might use executive action to achieve these civil rights. He did not care if Republicans got the credit: "I am tired of having civil rights remain a political football," he said. But his appeal was in vain.[1]

Humphrey had omitted an FEPC bill from his agenda in order "to offer the olive branch," he said. "It is better to go a foot than to fail to go a mile." He also hoped to make progress by having his Labor subcommittee publish its findings that by 1950–51 unemployment for blacks was 50 percent greater than for whites, black family income was only 54 percent that of white families, and blacks averaged three years less schooling than whites. But Senate opponents dismissed FEPC legislation in 1953 and 1954 as leading only to job "quotas."[2]

Humphrey lauded the Supreme Court's 1954 ruling in *Brown v. Board of Education of Topeka* as "another step in the forward march of democracy." The historic and unanimous ruling crafted by Chief Justice Earl Warren stated that school segregation violated the Fourteenth Amendment's assurance of equal protection of the laws and that "separate but equal" facilities were "inherently unequal." President Eisenhower was less certain, saying only that the Court "had spoken," and "I will obey." His southern and military background inclined him to go very slowly regarding integration and he also clumsily tried to influence Warren in early 1954 by saying that the segregationists' aim was to keep "little white girls" from having to sit next to "sexually advanced black boys."[3]

Most southern senators were intransigent: Mississippi's James Eastland said that "the South will never abide by nor obey" the ruling, and Georgia's Richard Russell assailed the Court's "flagrant abuse of judicial power." The first White Citizens' Council was founded in July 1954, and by the end of 1955 there were 268 southern councils claiming to have more than 200,000 dues-paying members committed to thwarting desegregation and African American access to the vote.[4]

Humphrey realized that there was no prospect for passing civil rights legislation. Even so, in January 1955, after the Democrats regained control of the Senate, he wanted to attack Rule XXII again. But Johnson, about to become majority leader, opposed this, as well as mild measures such as a constitutional amendment to outlaw the poll tax and bills to make lynching a federal crime and establish a civil rights commission.

Frustrated, Humphrey wrote to Kentucky senator Earle Clements that if the Democrats did not take some civil rights action, they might become a "minority" in the next Congress. But Johnson refused to challenge his southern colleagues, and Humphrey was unable to add even an amendment to a school construction bill to deny funds to any district that segregated students. The session ended without a civil rights or school construction bill.[5]

A deeply distraught civil rights community now questioned Humphrey. In spring 1955, Roy Wilkins, executive secretary of the NAACP, wrote publicly that "even an outstanding liberal like Hubert Humphrey is not as active in the civil rights field as he has been in previous years," and perhaps he was being "sacrificed on the altar of Democratic Party unity." The charge hurt; "it does not help," Humphrey retorted, to have a prominent leader "going around the country weakening my position or contesting my sincerity." He expressed his great displeasure in August that eleven civil rights bills he had introduced had been buried in committees and faulted his colleagues' "lack of sensitivity and lack of responsibility." But he knew that Congress would not weigh civil rights legislation until leaders of both parties concluded that they had to do this if only to secure the support of African Americans, whose continued movement from the South to major northern cities meant that now they could vote and choose between the two parties.[6]

✦ ✦ ✦

Despite defeats on civil rights bills, Humphrey deftly built support on issues that served his constituents' interests and those of other senators and raised his political standing before seeking reelection in 1954. Secure among labor groups, he now acted in behalf of, and built support from, the agricultural community. This included not only farmers but Minneapolis-based corporations such as General Mills, Pillsbury, and Cargill, and commodities traders like Dwayne Andreas (a Cargill vice president), whom he first met after receiving an unsolicited and "spectacularly large" $1,000 contribution to his 1948 Senate campaign.[7]

The wealthy Andreas became a major contributor and political counselor to Humphrey, and accommodated the senator and his family at his Lake Minnetonka home, near Minneapolis, and at a Miami hotel he owned. He introduced him to wealthy businessmen and managed the blind trust Humphrey established for his stock holdings when he ran for vice president in 1964. Humphrey, who promoted legislation intended to spur US government-backed export of "surplus" agricultural goods, took Andreas along on trips abroad to introduce him to foreign officials who might open their nations' markets to his companies' products.[8]

In 1953 Humphrey brought on to his staff Herbert Waters, a California newspaperman who had worked for Charles Brannan, Truman's secretary of agriculture. Waters had wide contacts with farm organizations and keen knowledge of the economics and politics of agriculture, including its use as a foreign policy instrument, which fit with Humphrey's commitment to high price supports (parity payments) and his desire to promote foreign aid and foreign trade.[9]

Humphrey viewed foreign aid, especially foodstuffs, as both humane and a Cold War "weapon." He supported Senator James Murray's 1953 proposal to establish a UN international food reserve and said that "so long as there are millions of empty stomachs in the world, we shall have to keep our cartridge belts full." He favored authorizing the president under the 1951 Mutual Security Act to trade agricultural surplus to stockpile materials vital to national defense and to sell surplus agricultural produce at "concessional" prices to needy nations, especially India. Following revolts in 1953 in Berlin, Poland, Czechoslovakia, and Hungary, he proposed to send "food and fiber" to the East Europeans who had the courage to "revolt against their Communist masters and tyrants." He viewed the Soviet "empire" as about to splinter, and he wanted the United States to foster the demise of this "monstrous conspiracy."[10]

Humphrey fought the Eisenhower administration's initial efforts to slash high price parity supports. He strengthened his hand when he rejoined the Agriculture Committee in May 1954, and in the end Eisenhower and Secretary

Ezra Taft Benson had to settle for a relatively small cut in parity payments from 90 percent to 82.5 percent.[11]

Work on agricultural issues helped Humphrey build rapport with a "strange coalition" that included conservative southern Democrats, who represented cotton growers, and Republicans like Clifford Hope of Kansas, who spoke for wheat growers. This enabled Humphrey to gain passage on July 7, 1954, of his landmark Public Law 480, the Agricultural Trade Development and Assistance Act, his "food for peace" program. Public Law 480 authorized the president to use the Agriculture Department's Commodity Credit Corporation to sell "surplus" farm goods, including cotton and wheat, to less developed, "friendly" nations on long-term, low-interest terms; to take repayment in local currency rather than expensive dollars; to make humanitarian donations to address food and nutrition problems; and to barter farm surplus for strategic materials.[12]

Humphrey achieved several goals with PL 480. He pleased Minnesota's farmers, the Minneapolis-based Pillsbury and General Mills corporations, and commodity traders like Andreas, who saw a growing market for his soybean business. Humphrey was so committed to aid to less-developed nations that his liberal Illinois colleague Paul Douglas called him "the Senator from India," the leading recipient of PL 480 aid. Humphrey also wanted the United States to steal a march on the Soviet Union, which he said would use aid, if it had the goods, to bring other nations into its orbit. He won support from southern, cotton state conservatives, notably Georgia's Walter George, who told him, "You are certainly entitled to great credit for initiating this program."[13]

During the first five years of PL 480, the government signed 180 agreements with thirty-eight nations and sent $3.7 billion in aid, equal to one-fourth of US agricultural exports, to nations such as India, Spain, Yugoslavia, Pakistan, and Turkey. American farmers got higher prices for their goods, improved the diets of hundreds of thousands of impoverished people in recipient nations, and helped to curb inflation there.[14]

After leaving the Agriculture Committee in 1959, Humphrey used his Foreign Relations Committee seat to wage a difficult but successful jurisdictional fight to transform the program mandate to include education, health care, and public welfare projects and to expand uses of accumulated foreign currencies. He also sought to name the program "Food for Peace," but Eisenhower blocked this. Ironically, in March 1960, Senator John Kennedy, while contesting Humphrey for the Democratic presidential nomination, would call for expanding the "famous Public Law 480" into a larger "Food for

Peace," program, which he established in 1961 as president. He also named Humphrey's protégé, South Dakota's George McGovern, as its first director.[15]

✦ ✦ ✦

Humphrey's idealism and practical politics motivated him to write PL 480. Yet a more cynical calculation and deeply held belief led to his sponsoring the Communist Control Act (CCA) in August 1954. The Senate was weighing a bill sponsored by Maryland Republican John Marshall Butler that proposed to amend the 1950 McCarran Internal Security Act (ISA), which created the Subversive Activities Control Board to permit the attorney general to petition the SACB to determine if a union was "Communist-infiltrated" and, if so, to deny that union 1935 Wagner Act collective bargaining rights. Republicans and many conservative Democrats strongly backed the Butler bill, which organized labor feared augured a union-busting campaign.

Humphrey and his chief legislative aide, Max Kampelman, met with CIO assistant general counsel Thomas Harris to draft a substitute measure. They believed, Harris recalled, that success hinged on claiming that their bill "struck a really effective blow against Communism." The strongly anti-Communist Kampelman drafted the legislation, which he and Humphrey took to the liberal Wayne Morse, formerly dean of the University of Oregon Law School, who made a few changes and signed on as a cosponsor.[16]

Humphrey's bill proposed criminalizing the Communist Party USA by declaring it to be an agent of a hostile foreign power and dedicated to overthrowing the government. The measure also stipulated that anyone convicted of knowingly and willfully belonging to the CPUSA would be subject to SACB penalties of imprisonment and/or a fine. Humphrey had a long list of liberal to conservative cosponsors.[17]

Humphrey sought to thwart the Republican attempt to seize the high political ground on anti-Communism by claiming his bill "got at the root of the evil" by outlawing the party. "I am tired of reading headlines about being 'soft' toward communism" and "about being a leftist and about others being leftists." His bill, he said, would force senators to "answer whether they are for the Communist Party, or against it. They cannot duck this one." Further, "I do not wish to be half a patriot. I will not be lukewarm. The issue is drawn."[18]

Butler suspected that Humphrey's bill also aimed to destroy both the 1940 Smith Act that resulted in the conviction in 1951 of the Communist Party leaders for conspiring to overthrow the government and Senator McCarran's ISA of 1950, which required CPUSA registration with the government. If CPUSA membership were criminalized, however, Communists might invoke their Fifth Amendment rights against self-incrimination to thwart the Smith Act and ISA prosecution.

Texas senator Price Daniel, although a sponsor of the bill, thought the Supreme Court would strike down a law that outlawed or criminalized a group without specifying which of its actions were illegal. Thus he moved to combine the Humphrey and Butler bills into one measure, which the Senate passed by 85–1. But moderate Republican John Sherman Cooper of Kentucky worried Humphrey's provisions outlawing Communist doctrine denied free speech and provided for guilt by membership rather than for commission of an illegal act. Humphrey persisted, however, that CPUSA membership itself was an "overt act" subject to penalty, and Cooper settled for adding a stipulation that the Communist Party represented "a clear, present, and continuing danger," language intended to meet the standard the Supreme Court had accepted in the conviction of the CPUSA leaders. The Senate unanimously reapproved the Humphrey-Butler bill.[19]

Republican leaders still worried that to criminalize the Communist Party would hinder enforcing the Smith Act and ISA; they drafted a substitute House measure eliminating penalties for CPUSA membership and instead stripped the party of its "rights, privileges, and immunities," a phrase of uncertain meaning. After the bill returned to the Senate, however, Humphrey prevailed on his colleagues to reinsert his penalty provisions; only Kefauver dissented: "We do not have to abdicate the Constitution to catch Communists." But when the House-Senate conference committee took up final revision, McCarran, author of the ISA, prevailed on the group to revert to the House formula: loss of the party's undefined "rights, privileges, and immunities."[20]

Kampelman later complained that Congress's eliminating of Humphrey's proposed penalties defeated his effort to expand civil liberties since criminalizing the Communist Party would assure anyone accused of being a Communist the right to courtroom procedures, including Fifth Amendment privileges and the right to confront their accusers. Nonetheless, Humphrey readily voted for the conference bill, which passed by 79–0; he persisted, however, that the Communist Party was not a political party but a conspiracy to overthrow the government. Congress was "striking a great blow for freedom," and "we have closed all of the doors," Humphrey claimed. "These rats will not get out of the trap."[21]

Humphrey's sponsorship of the CCA drew widespread criticism. Left-wing critics derided the legislation as a "low grade partisan maneuver" that would undermine the Constitution and "widen the witch hunt." Liberal anti-

Communist leaders, like ADA chairman and historian Arthur Schlesinger Jr. and eminent civil liberties lawyer Joseph Rauh Jr., disdained the bill as a "super political ploy," and the Democrats' moderate standard bearer Adlai Stevenson said that there was no reason "for suggesting punishment for what people might think." The American Civil Liberties Union lambasted the law as a "mockery" of the nation's "most basic constitutional guarantees."[22]

The CCA has been judged "the most direct statutory attack on internal communism ever taken by Congress." The law did not advance national security or the national interest but reinforced the era's anti-Communist hysteria and undermined Humphrey's standing with his liberal supporters. In 1954, he told his Senate colleagues that the "great mistake of the liberal movement in America is that some liberals, conscientious as they may be, have been unwilling to come to grips head-on with the menace of communism. This should be the essence of the liberal's platform — as it is mine."[23]

By the time the CCA passed in August 1954, however, McCarthy's reign of political terror was over. His baseless charges about Communist influence in government agencies and abuse of witnesses at hearings led his Senate colleagues first to censure him and then to "condemn" him in the fall. Humphrey was certain of reelection, and Congress had long ago criminalized actions alleged to be on the CPUSA agenda, such as spying, espionage, and taking up arms against the government. The law was almost never invoked and its constitutionality was never tested. Enactment of the CCA was a frivolous exercise, as *Time* said.[24]

Yet Humphrey often demonstrated a zealous anti-Communist attitude that led the intellectual left-liberal journalist Murray Kempton to say in 1955 that the ADA should "unfrock" Humphrey as its vice chairman because he continues to defend the "disgraceful" Communist Control Act. "To hell with liberals," Kempton held. "What good's a man if he votes unlimited funds to build school gymnasiums and shuts his mouth when teachers are bullied?" This was too caustic, but the issue would remain while Humphrey looked to higher office in coming years. It was not until 1964 that he finally admitted that the bill was "not one of the things I'm proudest of."[25]

In 1953, Johnson had placed Humphrey on the Foreign Relations Committee to rebut anticipated criticism of past Democratic policies by Republicans such as Secretary of State John Foster Dulles, author of his party's 1952 platform plank that branded containment a "futile, negative, and immoral" policy.

Humphrey proved a strong defender of his party's record and advocate of a Cold War posture that was thoughtful but also confrontational.[26]

After Stalin died in March 1953, Moscow's new leaders, the troika of Lavrenti Beria, Georgi Malenkov, and Nikita Khrushchev, immediately indicated that there were no Soviet-American issues "that cannot be resolved by peaceful means," and they hinted at prospects for a Korean armistice. While Eisenhower sought such an armistice, rather than explore the Soviet suggestion, he looked to cut military expenses and slow the arms race, graphically describing the cost of countless weapons systems as denying food to the hungry and clothes to the cold, and leaving "humanity hanging from a cross of iron." His proposal to unify the far more populous West Germany with East Germany by means of popular vote and his call for "independence" for East Europe's nations offered little to the Russians.[27]

Humphrey, in a strident tone on Minnesota radio, expressed skepticism about "anything emanating from the Soviet masters in the Kremlin," warned against disrupting progress toward unified defenses in Europe, and opposed reducing military expenditures. The Kremlin was "changing its strategy — not its intent."[28]

Following strong antigovernment protests in East Germany, Czechoslovakia, and Poland in June, Humphrey assailed the "tyrannical bosses" there, called for increasing Voice of America broadcasts, stepping up aid to West Germany, and amending the 1952 McCarran-Walter immigration law to admit 240,000 political refugees. He opposed reducing US armed forces or NATO defenses. "Now is the time to keep the pressure on," he said. The Soviet Union "understands only one thing: strength." Stalin's death did not alter the nation's political-economic-social forces underlying the Kremlin bosses' "ruthless, brutal policies," he said, but these were starting to backfire, and the United States should champion the people now seeking freedom.[29]

Humphrey viewed the Soviets as engaged in global aggression: they proposed trade concessions to Western Europe to lure it into its orbit; fostered war in Korea to bring the "hammer and sickle" into Southeast Asia; and set "target dates" when it would be "fully equipped and prepared to launch any kind of attack." He also likened Stalin's treatise *Economic Problems of Socialism*, which anticipated war between capitalist nations before conflict with the Soviet Union, as akin to Hitler's *Mein Kampf*.[30]

In summer 1954, he proposed an amendment of the Mutual Security Act to permit the president to trade surplus agricultural products for strategic materials to be stockpiled and reduce US tariffs to keep Western Europe from trading with Russia. He cautioned against rushing into a Korean armistice that he claimed Moscow wanted because it could not meet its commitments to the PRC. And rather than seek accord with Russia, the United States should take "the initiative with everything we have—propaganda, economic aid, military assistance, and food and fiber" to aid people who "had the courage to revolt against their masters."

Further, the only answer to the Soviet Union was "to pour it on" and build "a defense second to no other nation." Anyone who wished to cut defense spending, he said, had to show that the Soviets were no longer "vultures" but "doves." The "Communist bear may change its mind but never its objectives."[31]

Humphrey also expressed an expansive view of the chief executive's authority. During debate in January 1954 over ratifying a mutual security treaty with South Korea, he insisted that the president could meet an attack on that country without asking Congress to declare war, take any action he deemed necessary for US security, and choose how and where to retaliate. This echoed Dulles's recently declared "New Look" policy, which entailed meeting aggression "by means and at places of our choosing," a statement sharply criticized as signaling that the United States would respond to an attack in a peripheral area, such as Southeast Asia, with an atomic assault on the Soviet Union or the PRC.[32]

In spring 1954, Humphrey's Cold War rhetoric and US policy met reality in Indochina (Vietnam, Laos, and Cambodia) as the French faced defeat in their war against Ho Chi Minh's Communist and nationalist (Vietminh) forces. The Truman and Eisenhower administrations had provided significant economic and military aid to France, but now Vietminh forces surrounded twelve thousand French troops gathered in Vietnam's northwestern highlands at Dienbienphu. Eisenhower and Dulles weighed US military intervention, but vainly sought France's commitment to Indochinese independence.

Months earlier, Kennedy, who like Humphrey and other Senate liberals equated loss of Indochina with loss of Asia, challenged Dulles to explain how massive retaliation policy could work against guerrilla warfare and soon charged that no amount of military assistance could defeat a force that had "the sympathy and covert support of the people." A group of congressional leaders told Dulles that they wanted "no more Koreas where the U.S. provided 90% of the ground troops," and said that air strikes alone were insufficient because "once the flag is committed the use of ground troops would surely follow." Above all, the United States should not go to war to support colonialism. But on April 7, Eisenhower stated if Indochina fell, all of Southeast Asia would topple "like a row of dominoes."[33]

Humphrey was of divided view. He suspected that the Eisenhower administration was not truly consulting Congress but he believed that the "loss" of

Indochina would bring a Communist "pincer movement" that would lead to the "loss" of Asia, including India and Japan—"a calamity" for the "free world." Further, the French, despite their vast manpower and firepower advantage over the Vietminh, would not be able to defend Dienbienphu, even with US airlift help. But if the president determined that military action was required, Humphrey said, he would find "friendly consideration and support" from Congress.[34]

Congress resisted action, however, and Humphrey berated the French for failing to build Vietnamese civil and military leadership and dismissed their chosen chief of state, Emperor Bao Dai, as a "puppet." He called on the French to declare their intention to give Indochina its independence, and urged the Eisenhower administration to support this action publicly whether the Indochinese "are ready or not."[35]

After Vice President Richard Nixon hinted to newsmen that the United States might have to intervene militarily to halt Communist expansion, Humphrey said that the American people had been led to believe that US involvements in "localized peripheral struggles were over." Moreover, US intervention required answering two critical questions: What was the objective for which the native peoples were fighting? And, did they have the will and leadership to fight? He called again for France to pledge Indochina's independence but also insisted that it was "unthinkable" to lose it to the Communists. "It cannot happen. It will not happen."[36]

The "unthinkable" happened quickly, however. Vietminh forces pounded the French into surrender at Dienbienphu on May 7. The next day, sixteen nations, including France, Great Britain, the Soviet Union, the PRC, and the United States, met at Geneva—where the United States said it would not be bound by the results—and reached agreement on July 21 to partition Vietnam between North and South at the seventeenth parallel, with French forces to be withdrawn from the North and the Vietminh to evacuate the South, as well as Laos and Cambodia, which would become independent. National elections to unify Vietnam were scheduled for mid-1956.

Dulles conceded to the Senate Foreign Relations Committee in August that the United States would not sign the Geneva agreements and would block unifying elections as Ho Chi Minh would win 80 percent of the vote to lead the reunited nation. Instead, the United States intended to build an American-friendly, non-Communist state in South Vietnam under its new prime minister, Ngo Dinh Diem, a former Vietnamese bureaucrat who was Catholic, anti-Communist, and anti-French, and whom Eisenhower and Dulles viewed as serving American interests.[37]

Humphrey was of like mind. Despite his caution about US military intervention to support French colonialism, he insisted that "the Geneva Conference will go down as one of the greatest and most colossal failures in American history." He largely blamed Dulles for having allowed the "Red Chinese . . . [to] run off with half of Vietnam." Still, Humphrey reported to the Senate Foreign Relations Committee in October that despite threats of a military coup against the autocratic Diem, his regime stood for "decent and honest government," and an alternative to the Communist Vietminh. And when uprisings against Diem began anew in spring 1955, Humphrey held that if this "honorable" man's regime was overthrown, "only the Communists will gain." Thus he supported Eisenhower's policy of thwarting unifying elections and seeking to build an alternative, non-Communist state in South Vietnam.[38]

Humphrey grew concerned, however, about the Eisenhower administration's efforts to "contain" the PRC. He had applauded Eisenhower's pledge of "continuous cooperation" with Congress in his State of the Union address in 1953, but he noted that the president had not consulted Congress about his "new" policy that the Seventh Fleet stationed in the waters around Taiwan (Formosa) would no longer be employed ostensibly to shield the PRC or "to protect a nation fighting us in Korea." Fourteen months later Humphrey publicly reminded the president that despite his having "unleashed" the Nationalists, they and the Seventh Fleet remained in place.[39]

In September 1954, the Americans organized the Southeast Asia Treaty Organization, a mutual security pact consisting of the United States, Great Britain, Australia, New Zealand, Thailand, Pakistan, and the Philippines. Washington signed a mutual defense pact with the Nationalist government on Taiwan, which the PRC countered by bombing the offshore islands of Quemoy and Matsu, where the Nationalists had stationed troops.[40]

The following January, the Eisenhower administration pushed through the House a proposed joint resolution authorizing the president to secure and protect Taiwan, the Pescadores (Penghu) Islands, and other related territories in the area. Humphrey did not object to defending Taiwan and the Pescadores; he believed that the 1943 Cairo Declaration mandated their return to the former Nationalist-governed, mainland Republic of China (ROC). But he viewed Quemoy and Matsu as part of a PRC-ROC civil war, and he feared that involving US forces so close to the PRC could lead to war with it. Further, he warned that "propagandists" were perpetuating a "myth" that Jiang Jieshi's (Chiang Kai-shek's) forces on Taiwan were capable of retaking the mainland, which he said could be done only by expending "American manhood, American blood, and American armament."[41]

Humphrey sought to avoid this trap by proposing an amendment to limit US action to the "specific purpose" of protecting Taiwan and the Pescadores, but its defeat was certain. He agreed to vote for the original motion, sponsored by numerous liberals, which passed in January 1955 and gave the president unprecedented authority to take military action in a region without consulting Congress and to "secure" Quemoy and Matsu, wholly unimportant islands.[42]

Humphrey again resisted administration policy in March when Eisenhower and Dulles declared that in the event of a need to retaliate against PRC action in the Taiwan Straits area, use of atomic weapons would not be seen as different from conventional weapons. Humphrey publicly countered that threatening the use of atomic weapons might embolden rather than restrain the PRC and that to drop "one American atomic weapon on Red China would do more to turn all of Asia against us than all the propaganda the Communists have been able to contrive." Further, the Soviets wanted the United States to become "endlessly engaged" in Asia while they advanced in Europe. He proposed a conference to demilitarize and neutralize Quemoy and Matsu.[43]

PRC officials ended the crisis, however, by making clear at an Asian and African nation conference in April in Bandung, Indonesia, that they did not seek a military conflict, and the Eisenhower administration backed off its provocative atomic policy. But American threats spurred the PRC to begin to develop its own nuclear capacity, and Jiang Jieshi continued to claim Quemoy and Matsu.[44]

Humphrey remained adamant about averting US military engagement in Asia, but said in June 1955 that the Soviets had not given up on seeking world domination despite their signing the Austrian State Treaty ending its postwar occupation and accepting Vienna's Cold War neutrality. The United States should not allow the Russians to think that neutrality was suitable for Germany, he said; West Germany had to be rearmed and brought into NATO. And the United States had to increase its strength, because "freedom has no price tag."[45]

During his five and a half years in the Senate, Humphrey established himself as a leading Democrat whom the Republicans most wanted to defeat for reelection in 1954. But he had sidelined his most formidable opponent, former governor Luther Youngdahl, by securing a federal judgeship for him. Republican leaders in Washington now tried unsuccessfully to entice several well-known figures into the race, including the current popular governor, C. Elmer Anderson; the head of the famous medical clinic in Rochester, Minnesota,

Dr. Robert Mayo; and Minneapolis congressman Dr. Walter Judd. The nomination ended up going to the state auditor, Kristjan Valdimar (Val) Bjornson, a highly able and respected former journalist and editor for the *St. Paul Pioneer Press,* but who lacked Humphrey's newfound national stature.[46]

He had built a nearly impregnable record as a liberal spokesman for civil rights and aid to education, an ally of organized labor and foe of the Taft-Hartley Act, and a friend of the farmer who supported high parity payments, fought Benson's cuts, and sponsored PL 480, fostering sale abroad of surplus farm produce. He was also a Cold War anti-Communist who favored increased military spending, depicted the Soviet Union as a global threat, and deftly challenged Dulles's rhetoric—such as "unleashing Jiang Jieshi"—and warned against war, especially with the PRC.

Humphrey inspired a huge turnout in the September primaries, which for the first time in a decade drew more Democrats (319,000) than Republicans (237,000). This also helped position his DFL compatriot Orville Freeman in his quest to upset heavily favored Governor Anderson. Humphrey knew the big issue would be agriculture, and he determined to "raise a little hell" about Benson's efforts to cut parity payments below 85 percent. As newsmen said, Humphrey "never lets up on the farm issue."[47]

Nor did he let up on his relentless campaign pace and insistence on need to expand the economy to provide jobs for the "5,000,000 surplus people" without employment and to elect a Democratic Congress that would vote for federal aid to education but not confirm antilabor people to sit on the National Labor Relations Board. Humphrey gained support from new groups "Businessmen for Humphrey" and "Students for Humphrey." Walter George, the South's most influential conservative and Senate Banking Committee chair, endorsed him with a letter to the Minneapolis financial community proclaiming him "a credit to the Senate and to the country." And in late October, Johnson campaigned for Humphrey in Minnesota's more conservative western farmlands and raised funds in Minneapolis.[48]

Bjornson could say little other than Humphrey and Freeman had been "errand boys for Truman" and were "soft on communism and corruption," and call for electing a Republican who would support Eisenhower's policies. Anderson could add only that Humphrey's lengthy speeches took up almost 3,500 pages in the *Congressional Record* at a taxpayer cost of $200,000.[49]

Humphrey won overwhelmingly by 57 percent to 43 percent, with the large margin helping to carry Freeman to victory over Anderson. The DFL won every statewide office except auditor and gained a congressional seat to hold a 5–4 margin in the state delegation. It was "an earthquake," Bjornson said. *Time* labeled Humphrey "The Welder," who not only won labor and urban voters but cut deeply into Republican strength in the farm areas. He was the undisputed master of an "efficient, solidly constructed organization in a state long known for hodgepodge politics." More important, Humphrey, who "works at politics 365 days a year" and was an uncompromising New Dealer who had driven two southern states from the 1948 convention, was endorsed by George, "the dean of Senate Southerners." And Humphrey was urging fellow liberals to be more accommodating of people with differing views in order to increase prospects for Democratic success, a sure sign that he was primed to seek higher office.[50]

The Democrats gained 2 Senate seats to secure a narrow 48–47 margin, elevating Johnson to majority leader, and picked up 19 seats in the House to secure a 232–203 margin, with Texas's Sam Rayburn becoming the Speaker. This worked to Humphrey's advantage as the crucial liaison between liberals and party leaders.[51]

8

LIBERAL WITHOUT APOLOGY

Humphrey had a romantic, Jeffersonian view of farmers as dedicated to hard work, family, and democracy, and the New Dealer in him believed that the federal government should aid farmers just as it had subsidized railroad, steamship, and airline companies. But he also recognized that the number of farmers was rapidly declining as part of the labor force from more than 40 percent in 1900 to about 10 percent to 12 percent in 1955. Traditional small family farms were giving way to very large, highly mechanized farms with increased output owing to the scientific revolution in agriculture. The family farm was becoming part of the past, and he worried that America was becoming "all metropolitan."[1]

In 1956, the senator called for a "Farmer's Bill of Rights," which included improving the standard of rural living and preserving "family values." This meant 90 percent parity payments (the approximate government standard since World War II) for farmers who earned up to $5,000 annually and permitting large "set asides" of land for crop reduction or conservation, with the land serving as full collateral for nonrecourse government loans for which farmers would not be personally liable. At the same time Humphrey counted Minneapolis's food processing and agribusiness companies as vital constituents who provided him and his DFL Party with money and votes.[2]

However, the Eisenhower administration proposed legislation in 1956 to create a sliding scale of 52 percent to 75 percent of parity payments. To offset farmers' income losses and curb production, the administration also proposed to establish a two-part Soil Bank Program: an Acreage Reserve System that would pay farmers to take land out of production or turn under crops already planted and put land into a Conservation Reserve for up to ten years. Presumably, this would provide farmers with income for land taken from production, reduce surpluses and storage costs, and reassure foreign countries that the United States would not dump its surplus farm goods on them.[3]

Humphrey strongly opposed the legislation even as Majority Leader Johnson questioned his battle against the administration's bill. But the Minnesotan became the voice of his party and rallied Democrats, including key southerners, along with some midwestern Republicans, to win a 50–44 vote restoring high price supports for dairy and other products and creating new land set asides for wheat, corn, and cotton. He put his prestige on the line and won, as the national media noted.[4]

Eisenhower, with strong public support, vetoed the bill, and the Democrats failed by a wide margin to gain an override. Congress soon rewrote the legislation, which passed with the administration's specifications: parity payments for reducing acreage of wheat, corn, and cotton, for example, were set at about 65 percent of current market price, and for other farm produce at 75 percent to 85 percent, and land put into a Conservation Reserve soon soared to over 28 million acres. The president disliked a provision requiring the government to "dump" five million bales of cotton on the world market at about 20 percent less than it had paid to southern growers, but overall he had gained his way. Humphrey said that this was the "best bill" the Democrats could get, and he called attention to an expanded Food Stamp Program and Congress's commitment to study the parity issue.[5]

Johnson was pleased, too, and savored making Eisenhower's initial veto a November 1956 election issue. He thanked Humphrey "for all you have done for me in the past session," and said that "one of the things that will always stand out" with him would be "Hubert Humphrey leading the fight on the agriculture bill. Maybe we didn't get all of it," but they had pushed Eisenhower on parity and "made him take our soil bank." Notably, Johnson said that the last thing he remembered was Humphrey saying, "Come, let us reason together." Humphrey and Johnson seemed to have come to understand each other better, maybe because Humphrey was "shifting over to Lyndon Johnson's point of view," as the Texan pointed out. Johnson also said that he hoped Humphrey would take a day or two off from his campaign for vice president—at least "the Texas press tells me he is a candidate!"—in order to visit his ranch.[6]

Humphrey sought the Democratic nomination for vice president in 1956 despite his belief that Eisenhower would likely win reelection. The senator hoped that his own strong campaign would position him to gain his party's presidential nomination in 1960. He and Freeman prevailed on Adlai Stevenson to run in the Minnesota primary, assuring him of the backing of the DFL leadership and victory. The DFL Central Committee issued an unusually early endorsement of Stevenson, who announced his entry into the Minnesota primary in mid-January 1956. The DFL leaders and their cadres had to deliver the votes on March 20 to set the former Illinois governor en route to another presidential nomination and incline him to choose Humphrey as his running mate. The senator sought to raise his national stature by persuading Democratic leaders to select him to deliver the keynote address at the party's convention.[7]

More populist-oriented and independent DFLers balked at having a presidential nominee thrust upon them, however, and Hjalmar Peterson, a prominent old-line Farmer-Laborite, entered Tennessee senator Estes Kefauver's name in the Minnesota primary. Kefauver's populist style—in contrast to Stevenson's more sedate manner—drew large, enthusiastic crowds in the state's mining and agricultural regions. Humphrey sensed the gathering political storm but believed he had to remain in Washington to continue his fight over the agriculture bill rather than return to Minnesota to campaign for Stevenson.

Kefauver built momentum with an uncontested win in New Hampshire's primary in March and stunningly upset Stevenson in Minnesota. Humphrey sought to ascribe this to crossover voters in the heavily Republican Minneapolis suburb of Edina. But even Humphrey, Freeman, and Congressman Gene McCarthy failed to win delegate seats as Kefauver swept seven of the state's nine congressional districts and forty-eight of its sixty delegates to the Democratic convention. Humphrey was "heartsick"—and humiliated. "I'm walking around in ashes and sackcloth," he told Stevenson. Or as Gaylord Nelson, a Wisconsin state senator and later governor and US senator, would recall, "Old Humphrey had to go around for a whole year kissing asses."[8]

Stevenson was equally humiliated but promptly adopted a folksier campaign style, agreed to the first televised presidential debate in Florida's primary, and won narrowly in May, although this was due largely to his being perceived as more conservative on the race issue, while his supporters in the northwestern region (Tallahassee) branded Kefauver a "leftwing integrationist." In California, strong Democratic Party backing and financing benefitted Stevenson, who ran as a more liberal candidate, although he always said "gradually" when referring to desegregation. He won by a surprisingly large margin, and Kefauver soon suspended his campaign, virtually assuring Stevenson's nomination.[9]

Humphrey failed to secure the role of keynote speaker; southerners wanted no repeat of his 1948 convention oration. But his fortunes seemed to rise dramatically on July 20 when, after a Democratic leaders' dinner at the Mayflower Hotel in Washington, Stevenson invited Humphrey and his legislative counsel, Max

Kampelman, to his room and asked for names of prospective vice presidential candidates, saying that he did not want Kefauver.

Humphrey offered several names, including Senators Albert Gore of Tennessee, G. Mennen Williams of Michigan, Stuart Symington of Missouri, and John F. Kennedy of Massachusetts. Stevenson praised Humphrey's qualifications and asked him to consider himself, although he would need to gain southerners' assurances that he was an acceptable nominee.[10]

Humphrey and Kampelman left the hotel that night "with stars in the skies and in our eyes," Kampelman wrote, and an excited senator called his wife, Muriel, at 4:00 a.m. to break the seeming good news. But Humphrey's elation may have been premature. He and Kampelman believed that Stevenson had agreed to choose the senator if he gained southern backing, but later Humphrey conceded he might have "over interpreted" Stevenson's words and he had meant only that southern support would improve his prospects. At the time, however, Humphrey felt assured; Senator Walter George was on record as recommending his selection, and soon other southerners, including House Speaker Sam Rayburn of Texas, Representative Brooks Hays of Arkansas, Senators Lister Hill of Alabama, Richard Russell of Georgia, and Lyndon Johnson (who also wanted the nomination) indicated that they would help. Humphrey declared his candidacy for vice president—an unprecedented step—and had McCarthy travel across the country to garner support.[11]

Humphrey arrived at the Democratic convention on August 13 in Chicago overconfident and unprepared for a rapid turn of events. He assumed that he was Stevenson's choice for vice president and began to write his acceptance speech and plan his campaign. He pursued a safe political course by refusing to join a liberal group led by ADA chairman Joseph Rauh that sought to rewrite the party's civil rights plank that only mildly affirmed the 1954 *Brown* decision and desegregation and rejected "all proposals" for use of federal troops to enforce judicial rulings. Humphrey said that he would take it as a "personal insult" when Rauh announced that his group was going to have Robert Short, a prominent businessman and owner of the Minneapolis Lakers basketball team who headed the Minnesota delegation, speak to the convention in favor of a stronger resolution, which was voted down. This gave labor leaders such as Walter Reuther, the longtime UAW president who inclined toward Kefauver for vice president, reason not to support Humphrey.[12]

The field quickly grew crowded. After Kefauver withdrew from the presidential race, Johnson's backers opened campaign headquarters for him, but his "favorite son" approach gained little support. He sent word to Stevenson that he wanted the second slot or to be in the room when the choice was made.

Kennedy, who was thirty-nine years old and had been elected to the Senate only in 1952, also wanted the nomination, if only, like Humphrey, to prepare to run for president in 1960. And Kefauver soon surprised everyone by indicating his willingness to settle for second place.[13]

Stevenson never replied to Johnson and worried about having a Catholic, like Kennedy, on the national ticket, although he did think that Kennedy would increase his appeal to urban minorities. The senator had become an instant celebrity on the first convention night as narrator of a Hollywood-style film celebrating Democratic Party achievements from Roosevelt to Truman. Stevenson also gave Kennedy more national spotlight by having the young senator nominate him, and he won easily on the first ballot over New York governor Averell Harriman, with Johnson a distant third.[14]

Stevenson shocked party leaders by forgoing the nominee's usual prerogative to choose a running mate and instead put the choice to the convention delegates. Rayburn, the convention chair, feared a divisive political fight, as did Johnson, who said that this was "the goddamned stupidest move a politician could make." But Stevenson persisted that the people had a right to decide who would be next in line in the event that the president could not fulfill his term. He may have sought to inject excitement into his campaign or avoid offending any of the candidates by choosing from among them. Kampelman insisted that Stevenson had to know that allowing the convention to decide virtually assured Kefauver's selection; he had the most organized and committed delegates, and he could help in border or southern states.[15]

Humphrey was stunned; he learned of the decision only as he watched the convention on television. He and his aides grew furious and then frenzied. Humphrey had visited delegations but had not thought it necessary to ask for binding commitments, and he soon learned that much of his support was tenuous. He had presumed that Florida senator George Smathers, despite his conservatism and anti–civil rights record, backed him. But Smathers immediately supported his close friend Kennedy, who made a quick decision to enter the race despite opposition from liberals like Eleanor Roosevelt, who said that he had failed to stand up to Joseph McCarthy. Reuther and other labor leaders now openly backed Kefauver, and even Short told Humphrey that the Minnesota delegation would vote for him only on the first ballot, after which about half of the delegates would go to Kefauver.[16]

Humphrey stood no chance. Kefauver garnered 466 votes on the first ballot, Kennedy got 294 votes from New England and the South, and Humphrey ran a poor fifth with 134 votes, trailing both Gore and New York City mayor Robert Wagner Jr. As the second ballot neared, Johnson tried to switch Texas's support from Gore to Humphrey, but the delegates refused, and as the roll call proceeded, Johnson cast Texas's 56 votes for the "fighting sailor," with Kennedy soon surging to within 38 votes of victory. At that juncture, according to Humphrey, Kefauver pleaded with him for help from the Minnesota delegation, and he sent word to his state's delegation to switch to Kefauver despite having committed earlier to Kennedy. Humphrey later said that he saved Kefauver's nomination, although his breakthrough came late on the second ballot when Gore suddenly withdrew in his favor, allowing Tennessee, Missouri, and Oklahoma to switch to him and to spur his win over Kennedy, who dramatically moved to make the nomination unanimous before the voting ended.[17]

Humphrey was deeply hurt and angered. He believed that Stevenson had left him in the lurch, and he was cold and rejecting, but civil, when the presidential nominee called the next day, presumably to apologize. By contrast, when a few days later Humphrey told Kennedy that he had unpleasant dreams about his failure to deliver Minnesota, Kennedy said it was of no matter. Kennedy had garnered new national celebrity, the convention's only "hero," Stevenson said. Humphrey left Chicago feeling rejected and vowed never again to go to a convention so unprepared or to seek the vice presidency.[18]

Johnson sought to console him. He wrote Humphrey to acknowledge that he was having "a bad year and my heart goes out to you." But, the Texan said, he had long recognized Humphrey as "one of those bold spirits that is tempered rather than weakened by adversity" and had the energy and ability to rise in the future. Perhaps more important, Johnson said, in the past few years he had seen the rise of a liberal philosophy "which holds that words are more important than deeds." But as a liberal, "you have breasted that current and clung fast to the position that there is nothing incompatible with liberalism and achievement." Thus, even though the vice presidential race may have been personally costly in relations with some colleagues, Johnson said it gave Humphrey a "unique status" in the country and meant that "you will be on the scene as a national leader long after the others have been forgotten." It also "put you in my book on this special page I reserve for men of integrity, and men whom I am proud to call 'friend,' and nothing will ever affect your standing in my eyes."[19]

Stevenson had little chance against Eisenhower, who remained highly popular despite a curtailed work schedule due to a heart attack in 1955 and illness in 1956. Eisenhower's campaign benefited from relative peace and prosperity. His first postwar summit with Soviet leaders in July 1955 did not alter the Cold War standoff but produced "the spirit of Geneva." The president, who told his brother Edgar in 1954 that no political party could survive if it did away with basic New Deal programs, agreed to legislation raising the minimum wage and expanding Social Security to include self-employed and salaried professionals, servicemen, domestic and religious workers, and farmworkers. He fostered the St. Lawrence Seaway Project that opened the Great Lakes to oceangoing vessels—a boon to Humphrey's Minnesota—and the 1956 Federal Highway Act that delighted the oil, automobile, and construction industries by proposing to build 41,000 miles of interstate highways financed by taxes on gasoline, tires, and trucks. The administration did curtail parity payments, but the Soil Bank Program ameliorated farmers' losses.[20]

Stevenson laid out his vision of a "New America" that promoted moderate new education, health care, and natural resources programs in a fast-paced campaign in which he hoped to contrast himself with Eisenhower, who made only scripted television appearances and let Nixon do the barnstorming. But Stevenson's grueling pace soon made him appear tired and prone to error.[21]

Humphrey, vice chair of the Senate Democratic Campaign Committee, sought to rally his party. He traveled constantly and gave many speeches, especially in the Middle West, focusing on agricultural policy and blaming the Republicans for causing a 25 percent decline in farm income since 1952. In his native South Dakota, he persuaded young George McGovern, who had taught history at Dakota Wesleyan and was now executive secretary of the state Democratic Party, to run for a House seat. Humphrey also made numerous appearances in California. Finally, he sought to prepare the way for Stevenson's major foreign policy proposal by releasing his own Disarmament subcommittee's staff report stating that the United States needed to reach agreement with Moscow to halt hydrogen bomb tests as a first step to foster arms cuts.[22]

Stevenson had raised the idea of a nuclear test ban and replacement of the draft with trained military men in a speech to the American Legion in Los Angeles. The test ban accorded with growing scientific concern about deadly atomic fallout, and many Pentagon planners viewed the draft as inefficient. But Eisenhower, a former five-star general, curtly rejected the proposals as endangering national security.[23]

Following Humphrey's subcommittee release, however, Stevenson declared on October 15 that the United States should not have to choose between "appeasement and massive retaliation" but instead had to develop a more professional military and promote arms control and a ban on nuclear tests before other nations began to produce atomic weapons. Eisenhower again cited his commander-in-chief role and long record of military commands and insisted that America's need to negotiate from strength included the draft and nuclear bombs.[24]

Eisenhower's campaign was further strengthened in late October by the Suez Crisis and brief Hungarian uprising. Although American officials disdained Egypt's president Gamal Abdel Nasser, who saw himself as a spokesman for Pan-Arab nationalism, sponsored fedayeen (guerrilla) raids on Israel, and recognized Communist nations, the United States agreed to help finance the $1.3 billion Aswan Dam on the Nile to provide vital irrigation and electricity.[25]

But after Nasser bought weapons from Czechoslovakia in 1955 and recognized the PRC in 1956, the United States canceled the Aswan loan. The Egyptian leader then nationalized the Anglo-French–owned Suez Canal to gain its tolls and rejected a US plan to have a "Users Association" run it. The British, French, and Israelis undertook military action in late October, with Israeli forces striking in the Sinai Peninsula and heading toward the canal, while the British called for a halt but bombed Egyptian air fields and landed paratroopers. The Egyptians blocked the canal and blew up a major oil pipeline to Europe. Eisenhower, fearing that a major conflict with the Muslim world would bring Soviet intervention in the Middle East, pressured the British to halt their joint military action, which ended on Election Day.[26]

The weekend before the election, the Soviets sent 200,000 troops and four thousand tanks into Hungary to crush an uprising against its oppressive control there and then deposed recently appointed premier Imre Nagy, who sought to withdraw his country from the Warsaw Pact. The administration assailed the Soviet action, but Eisenhower rejected US intervention as infeasible, thus revealing that the Republican slogan of "liberation" was empty. But the Suez and Hungarian crises allowed the president to emerge as a man of peace and reassuring military leader in a dangerous era.[27]

Eisenhower won in a landslide, capturing 57 percent of the popular vote, forty-one of forty-eight states, and gaining 39 percent of African American voters, nearly twice his 1952 showing. The Democrats retained control of Congress, adding 1 Senate seat for a 49–47 margin and gaining 2 House seats for a 234–201 edge. The latter included Humphrey's new protégé, George McGovern, the first Democrat elected to national office from South Dakota since 1936. And despite Eisenhower's winning 54 percent of Minnesota's vote, Humphrey's friend Freeman narrowly gained reelection as governor, McCarthy won overwhelming reelection to the House, and the DFL preserved its 5–4 margin over Republicans in the state delegation.[28]

✦ ✦ ✦

Immediately after the election, Humphrey called on the Democrats to commit to a renewed "liberalism" to replace the "centrist" views of the party's congressional leadership. The Democrats could not win by running on economic "trouble" and were "digging their own graves" by failing to enact civil rights legislation. "We must design a new liberal program," he argued.[29]

A group of liberals on the Democratic Party's executive committee called for the formation of a twenty-member Democratic Advisory Council (DAC) to shape such a program. Humphrey joined the DAC, along with Stevenson, Truman, former secretary of state Dean Acheson, and Eleanor Roosevelt. But Johnson and Rayburn curtly rejected it as infringing on Congress's affairs, and when that body reconvened in January 1957, the majority leader angrily told Humphrey, "You broke faith with me." Humphrey denied this, telling Johnson that he could get more votes out of the Senate than anyone else. You are a "great, great leader, Lyndon. I was simply trying to make you an even better leader."[30]

Humphrey was fired up to fight for civil rights. "I am a liberal without apology," he told his Senate colleagues in January 1957. "Insofar as I am sorry for anything it is not because I am a liberal but because I am not more liberal." He also quoted the Belgian writer and Nobel laureate Maurice Maeterlinck, who said that a progressive on the road to the future would always find a thousand men seeking to preserve the past but that "even the most timid of us" were obligated not to add to nature's "immense deadweight."[31]

The Senate's barrier to the future remained Rule XXII's required two-thirds vote of all senators to end a filibuster. So on the first day of the new Congress, Humphrey, Douglas, and a group of liberals supported New Mexico Democrat Clinton Anderson's resolution to permit this "new" Senate to set its own rules. But Johnson moved to table the motion, and he and Russell warned Senate newcomers that they would get poor committee assignments if they did not support Rule XXII. Humphrey sought to evade a vote by securing a parliamentary ruling from Nixon, the Senate's presiding officer, but was told that this could be advisory only. Johnson's motion passed, and the liberals had to take consolation in having done better than their loss in 1953. "We actually gained more votes than we had a right to expect," Humphrey wrote to Reuther, "and surely more than the opposition had anticipated."[32]

The heating civil rights struggle could not be ignored. During the past two years, numerous African American groups had been pressing for school desegregation and voting rights and beginning to boycott segregated public transportation systems, while in March 1956 some 101 representatives and senators (but not Johnson, Kefauver, or Gore) signed a "Southern Manifesto" calling for repeal of the *Brown* decision. Growing numbers of southern White Citizens' Councils openly, and often violently, sought to block integration and intimidate its proponents. Nonetheless, Eisenhower's strong gains in the 1956 election among African Americans in northern cities, where he won about 35 percent of the vote in Harlem and Chicago's South Side, heightened Republican interest in civil rights legislation. Humphrey argued forcefully that the Democrats should not allow "the Eisenhower Republicans to put their trade-mark" on a civil rights bill.[33]

Humphrey quickly introduced in January 1957 eleven civil rights measures and a twelfth omnibus bill to protect voting rights, end the poll tax, make lynching a federal crime, provide equal employment opportunity, and establish a civil rights division in the Justice Department. He listed the right to vote first, he said, because this "is the key to the rest of our human rights objectives." But his measures were soon brushed aside to allow focus on the administration's civil rights bill, crafted by Attorney General Herbert Brownell, that proposed to: (1) create a Civil Rights Commission to investigate violations and a civil rights division in the Justice Department; (2) authorize the attorney general to seek federal court injunctions against local officials and private parties who infringed a wide range of civil rights protected by the Fourteenth Amendment; and (3) permit federal judges to impose civil or criminal contempt penalties on persons who violated voting rights.[34]

Humphrey was happy to have Republican support for civil rights, but southern senators remained adamantly opposed. Johnson, despite having been in the southern camp, recognized that the "civil rights controversy" could not be "called off," and as majority leader he had to act, especially if he wished to preserve his presidential ambitions. The issue became more pressing in June 1957 after Republicans in the House voted with liberal Democrats to pass the Brownell bill. A similar Senate coalition used a procedural maneuver to skirt hostile James Eastland's Judiciary Committee to put the measure on the docket, assuring that it would reach the floor.

Johnson and his biographer Robert Caro have claimed that the Texan enabled this breakthrough by secretly arranging for liberal-oriented western senators to pledge to vote only for a very moderate civil rights bill, with mollified southerners agreeing in turn to federal funding for a Hells Canyon Dam on the Snake River between Idaho and Oregon, which was never built. Historian Irwin F. Gellman has demonstrated, however, that no contemporary evidence supports this claim. Humphrey could not remember any details on the matter, and the House killed the Hells Canyon bill twenty days before the Senate would vote on the civil rights bill.[35]

Regardless, Russell led the attack on the bill, focusing first on Part III, granting the attorney general injunctive authority to protect a wide range of civil rights, including accommodations in public places. He charged that the provision allowed the attorney general to bring a civil rights suit even without the affected party's involvement and deftly noted that Part III incorporated an 1870 law, the so-called Force Act, which authorized the president to use federal troops to enforce judicial rulings. Russell claimed that this portended imposition by "bayonet" of a second and brutal Reconstruction era.

Eisenhower surprised his own staff by saying that he thought the bill limited the use of troops to voting rights issues, although he and Brownell knew that school desegregation was a burning issue. Further, after Johnson arranged a Russell-Eisenhower meeting, the president stated that he did not understand "certain phrases" in the bill—a remark he would long regret—and a week later he said that the attorney general should intervene in school desegregation cases only if local officials requested this, which seemed unlikely.[36]

Humphrey was appalled. "One day Ike is for the bill," he wrote, "the next day he doesn't know what is in it, and the third day he backs off of it. It is unbelievable." Humphrey dismissed his colleagues' complaints that the bill gave the attorney general too much power; he wished that they expressed the same sense of outrage over the denial of voting rights or jobs to African Americans. "All this fuss, all these histrionics," he said, "all the diversions about race riots and troops use and all the rest is for the birds."[37]

Still, Humphrey was willing "to conciliate, to calm, and to heal." He joined with Republican minority leader William Knowland to offer an amendment eliminating the bill's reference to the Force Act that passed 90–0. However, the real issue, Humphrey suspected, was southerners' determination to eliminate Part III completely because it implied federal support not just for voting rights but many civil rights, including school integration.[38]

Fearing a filibuster, Johnson persuaded Senator Clinton Anderson of New Mexico, a civil rights proponent, to join with liberal Republican George Aiken of Vermont to propose an amendment to eliminate Part III. The majority leader also told Eisenhower that he had the votes to kill the bill if Part III remained, but this implied defeat of other administration legislation. The president, without a word to his attorney general, made what Brownell called a "political decision" to give way.[39]

Humphrey fought the Anderson-Aiken amendment; he insisted that Part III merely extended court jurisdiction to allow individuals to sue for equitable relief for violation of their rights. Further, authorizing the attorney general to sue in their behalf was "not a new right," as southerners argued, but an additional remedy to buttress existing statutes that protected individual rights. But the Senate voted to eliminate Part III.[40]

The legislation now protected only the right to vote, but Russell and his allies, including Johnson, demanded that Part IV, which provided for judges to impose civil or criminal contempt penalties on individuals who violated court orders pertaining to voting rights, be amended to guarantee the right to a jury trial. The jury trial proposal seemed reasonable; labor unions had long favored this to protect against judges who often held their leaders in contempt for defying injunctions against strikes.

Humphrey found the jury trial issue "terribly difficult." His Populist background emphasized its importance, but he also knew that in the South it was almost impossible to get an all-white jury to convict a white person for having harmed an African American. Further, the oft-cited Sixth Amendment right to a jury trial applied to criminal prosecutions, not judicial contempt rulings and the power of courts to enforce them. He viewed the jury trial issue as a ruse to kill the bill.[41]

Humphrey was equally angry that so many southern senators attacked a bill that sought only to guarantee the right to vote. The bill was not about the right to vote only in the South, he said, but in the whole country, and the senators needed to decide whether this was one nation or forty-eight separate entities.[42]

Humphrey worked quietly toward a compromise based on a proposal from Carl Auerbach, a friend and University of Wisconsin law professor, who distinguished between civil and criminal contempt: civil contempt did not require a jury trial because an individual could free him- or herself from a penalty by carrying out the court's order, whereas criminal contempt required a jury trial because the offending person was subject to a lasting penalty. Auerbach's proposal would allow northern senators to claim that the bill had procedures to enforce voting rights, and southern senators could tell their constituents that in criminal contempt cases they would be assured of a trial by southern (white) peers.[43]

Humphrey invited Auerbach to Washington to put his proposal into legislative language but made clear that publicly he would oppose a jury trial to appease liberal groups. He consulted with Johnson, who enlisted help from various New Dealers as well as Acheson and his colleagues at the prominent Washington law firm of Covington and Burling. This group enlisted Kefauver and Senator Joseph C. O'Mahoney, a senior, independent liberal from Wyoming and proponent of a jury trial in criminal contempt cases. The two senators proposed an amendment that differentiated between civil and criminal contempt and assured a jury trial in the latter case.

Recently elected senator Frank Church of Idaho offered a key addendum: repeal of the section of the US Code that barred citizens from federal juries who did not meet their state's requirements for jury service (the usual southern state requirement of being registered to vote kept most African Americans off federal juries). Church proposed instead to extend the right to federal jury duty to any citizen who was over age twenty-one and competent. Thus liberals could claim that the civil rights bill would not only reinforce the right to vote but create a "new civil right," allowing African Americans to serve on juries.[44]

Humphrey and liberals like Douglas still opposed the jury trial compromise because southern registrars would be able to deny African Americans their voting rights and afterward have generally all-white juries find them innocent of criminal contempt. Eisenhower and Republican leaders also opposed the jury trial proviso but worried that Democrats would pass a weak civil rights bill and take credit for it in the 1958 elections. Organized labor, however, continued to favor the jury trial amendment, and numerous northern Democrats, including Kennedy, now saw the amendment as a compromise that would at least avert a filibuster, as did many southerners who thought that the jury trial proviso would allow them to accept a mild civil rights bill in lieu of fighting against a stricter measure later on.[45]

Johnson put the amendment to a vote on August 1, stating that it established "a new civil right for all citizens—the right to a jury trial in all criminal contempt cases," and it quickly passed. Humphrey became a leading advocate for the full bill, placing into the *Congressional Record* a summary of the legislation he had introduced in January under the title "Civil Rights: An Idea Whose Time Has Come."[46]

Humphrey insisted that America's "greatest national weakness" was the "gap between our pretensions and our performance" in civil rights. He pleaded with his colleagues not to bury the bill despite opposition from major liberal organizations, and insisted to NAACP head Roy Wilkins, "If there's one thing I've learned in politics, it's never to turn your back on a crumb." Wilkins called a leadership conference of sixteen major organizations, including the ADA, and as the Senate prepared to vote on August 7, they proffered their endorsement, which Humphrey immediately put before his colleagues. The bill passed 72–18, with 5 southern yea votes coming from Johnson and Ralph Yarborough of Texas and Gore, Kefauver, and Smathers.[47]

Humphrey and others lobbied successfully to have an informal committee reconcile the Senate and House bills. He feared Republicans would kill the bill over the jury trial amendment despite NAACP support for it. As House minority leader Joseph Martin of Massachusetts said, the NAACP did not speak for all African Americans; Humphrey rejoined that it spoke for more of them than any other group, and he and the NAACP persisted that the Senate bill was better than no bill.[48]

Democratic negotiators reached a compromise on the jury trial amendment: it would apply only when criminal contempt penalties exceeded three hundred dollars or forty-five days in jail. The House readily passed the reconciled bill, and only Senator Thurmond waged a twenty-four-hour filibuster—disdained by southern colleagues as grandstanding—before he gave way to fatigue. The Senate approved the final bill, and Eisenhower, despite viewing it as insufficient, signed it into law.[49]

The 1957 legislation marked passage of the first civil rights act in eighty-two years and made it illegal for anyone to interfere with voting rights in federal elections, permitted the attorney general to take preventive action, created a Civil Rights Commission (for three years, but later made permanent) to investigate the issue, and raised the Justice Department's civil rights section to a full division. The law recognized the need to protect voting rights at the national level, although it was greatly weakened by excising of Part III—which would call for the attorney general to intervene in a wide range of civil rights matters—and by the addition of the jury trial amendment. As Humphrey said to Wilkins, the bill was a "crumb," while Douglas, who reluctantly voted for it, likened it to "a soup made from the shadow of a crow which had starved to death."[50]

The bill was central to Humphrey's core beliefs, however, and one for which he had struggled for nearly a decade. He wrote constituents that he voted for it because he was a "realist," and this was the best bill he could get. As civil rights chronicler Robert Mann has stated, the legislation was a harbinger of things to come, including Martin Luther King's immediate enlistment of nearly one hundred ministers in his Southern Christian Leadership Conference to begin voter registration drives.[51]

Humphrey would continue to work tirelessly at legislation and scoop up every "crumb." He had accepted "less than I had hoped for," he wrote a friend, but the bill represented a "singular advance." Further, "I did not yield on principle," he told his longtime DFL compatriot Eugenie Anderson. "I fought the good fight," and surely made an impression on other senators. In fact, conservative John Stennis of Mississippi told him that he had made the "best and most powerful five minute speech by way of summary and challenge to the jury trial amendment that he had ever heard"—and he hoped that now Humphrey would devote his energies to other major issues. But in Humphrey's view, "This is not the end of civil rights legislation. It is only the beginning."[52]

Just as Eisenhower signed the bill, the nation confronted a major civil rights crisis in Little Rock, Arkansas, where the city's school board, in response to a federal judge's court order, had selected nine African American students to begin integration of the all-white Central High School. Democratic Governor Orval Faubus, seeking segregationist support for his reelection in 1958, stationed three hundred National Guardsmen outside the school to deny entry to the black students, although he claimed he wished to avert violence. When school opened on September 2, the troops blocked the students' entry and again after the federal judge reiterated his order, which led him to request Attorney General Brownell's intervention.[53]

Eisenhower thought that the Supreme Court's 1954 ruling in *Brown* was "wrong," and he was unwilling to press for integration. But he believed in the necessity of upholding federal court rulings and persuaded Faubus during a meeting in mid-September to change the National Guard's orders from preventing the African American students' entry to preserving the peace. However, he mistakenly took the governor's conceding that the Supreme Court's ruling was the "law of the land" to mean that he would respect the court order.[54]

Humphrey joined with other liberal Democrats to express "disappointment" at Eisenhower's failure to lead and said anything less than admission of the students to the high school would be a defeat for law and order and "the Constitution itself." He thought it "almost unbelievable" that Eisenhower would not act while segregationists defied the Supreme Court's ruling, and he called on the president to go to Little Rock and "personally take those colored children by the hand and lead them into the school."[55]

Faubus removed the troops following a federal court order on September 20. The "Little Rock Nine" entered the school under police escort on September 23, but threats from an armed and violent mob forced them to leave under escort. Eisenhower now determined that he could not permit "mob rule" to override a federal court decision, and the next day he sent in one thousand paratroopers and federalized the Arkansas National Guard. The students reentered the school and remained there all year.

Eisenhower's use of troops in the South to enforce court orders—the first time this had occurred since Reconstruction—led to increasingly vitriolic resistance to integration by many southern leaders, who turned demagogic and alleged that the armed forces were being used to "mix the races" and were behaving like "Hitler's storm troopers," charges the president strongly denied.[56]

Humphrey was convinced, however, that Eisenhower's failure to lead had allowed the conflict to escalate and the Soviets to "[make] hay while the sun shines." He was alarmed by what he saw as growing tyranny in the South that silenced those who supported integration, whose views, he worried, were also hardening. He feared a domestic "cold war" that would diminish respect for the law and the process of persuasion. If whites, blacks, and the federal government did not find "common ground," the white South would ultimately be won over "not by persuasion but by force."[57]

Thus, at the start of 1958, Humphrey immediately introduced legislation to strengthen the 1957 Civil Rights Act by making the Civil Rights Commission permanent, enacting an FEPC and a modified version of the previously excised Title III that allowed the attorney general broad discretion to intervene in civil rights matters, and increasing the number of FBI personnel trained to investigate in civil rights cases. But these measures remained buried in committees, and an effort to amend Rule XXII also failed.[58]

Republican conservatives William Jenner of Indiana and John Marshall Butler of Maryland pushed legislation to reverse prior Supreme Court rulings bearing on admission to state bar associations and contempt of Congress rulings, which civil rights advocates feared would allow southern bar associations to disbar lawyers who accepted civil rights cases and weaken the Court's independence. Johnson seemed willing to let conservatives voice opinions and have their bill come to a vote in August 1958, confident that it would lose. But Humphrey and Douglas and several other liberal senators had to argue vigorously that the measure would impede desegregation and managed to table the bill by only a narrow 49–41 vote.[59]

This emboldened Douglas, with Humphrey's support, to introduce a measure affirming the Senate's "full support and approval" of the Supreme Court's ruling that racial segregation in schools and on public transportation was unlawful. But Johnson, fearful of southerners' wrath, angrily beat this back by threatening to tie it to various "anti-subversive" measures that liberals opposed. Senate conservatives, however, now pressed their second measure (HR 3), which passed in the House in July and proposed that no court could rule that a federal statute preempted state law unless Congress had specified this or there was a "direct and positive conflict" between federal and state law.[60]

Humphrey and Senator Thomas Hennings of Missouri, chair of the Civil Rights subcommittee, assured Johnson that they had the votes to defeat the bill. But Senate conservatives attached it as an amendment to another measure and shocked liberals by defeating their motion to table it. Neither Humphrey and his allies nor Johnson seemed able to forestall a favorable vote, but they were saved, ironically, by Russell, who grasped that the proposed new law would create havoc regarding federal legislation and federal authority. The Georgian prodded Johnson to exercise his majority leader's prerogative to call for adjournment to gain time to rally opposition to the bill.[61]

Johnson berated Humphrey in the Senate chamber: "I thought you had them beat. You boys screwed up. I don't know what you did wrong. You screwed up. You told me wrong." The majority leader continued his verbal assault in his office, having invited in *New York Times*'s Supreme Court reporter Anthony Lewis and the director of the Democrats' policy committee, George Reedy. Johnson implored Humphrey to stop inciting Senate conservatives by attacking the filibuster or promoting a civil rights bill and not to worry that liberals would attack him for having abandoned his principles.

Humphrey did not reply to Johnson, whose purpose may have been to impress his listeners that he was on the right side of the issues and gain credit for having defeated HR 3. Johnson soon prevailed on numerous friendly conservative Republicans and Democrats who favored the bill to vote instead to recommit it to the Judiciary Committee, which they did by a razor-thin 41–40 margin in August. Humphrey told Johnson he was "a great American" and "FDR would have been proud of you," while Lewis soon wrote of his great mastery of the legislative process but said nothing about his tirade at Humphrey.[62]

Congress adjourned, with elections looming. Despite Eisenhower's two sweeping victories, the Democrats had held a one- or two-vote majority in the Senate and a larger lead in the House since 1954. Their electoral prospects now improved due to the sharp 1957–58 recession that brought 7.5 percent unemployment, while unions were angry that seventeen states (mainly in the South) had passed so-called right-to-work laws authorized under the hated Taft-Hartley Act, and farmers were distressed at declining prices for their goods and reduced parity payments. Further, the Soviet Union's launching of *Sputnik*, the first artificial satellite, in October 1957 sharply undermined Americans' belief in their scientific superiority, and the next month the commission chaired by H. Rowan Gaither Jr., head of the Ford Foundation, reported that Moscow was ahead of the United States in missile development and that American defenses were too weak to protect against a devastating Soviet ICBM first strike.[63]

The administration was also plagued by House charges that the president's chief of staff, Sherman Adams, had improperly accepted gifts from a friendly New Hampshire manufacturer in exchange for helping him deal with the Federal Trade Commission. All of this caused Eisenhower's popularity to decline, and as usual, he did little to aid his party in the elections except to attack the Democrats, especially Humphrey, as "Gloomdogglers."[64]

In November 1958, the Democrats gained 14 Senate seats to raise their slim margin to 65–35 and added 48 House seats to increase their lead to 282–154, the greatest Democratic congressional margins since the New Deal era. Humphrey was quick to congratulate Johnson: "The election is a great victory for you, the Democratic Party &, I believe, the country. Responsible performance by the Democrats in Congress . . . under your leadership has paid off."[65]

Humphrey personally benefitted from the election. Initially he supported Eugenie Anderson, his longtime DFL ally and former ambassador to Denmark, for his party's Senate nomination. But he also encouraged McCarthy, who had grown restless after a decade in the House, to "give it all you got" and enter the Senate race. McCarthy defeated Anderson in a hard-fought primary and then toppled two-term incumbent Republican Edward Thye. Humphrey campaigned for McCarthy, loaned him staff, and facilitated generous funding from the Senate Democratic Campaign Finance Committee. McCarthy also profited from strong union support and an unusually high statewide DFL turnout. Governor Freeman easily won reelection.[66]

McCarthy's win marked the first time in fifty-seven years that Minnesota Democrats controlled the seat McCarthy won, giving Humphrey a new home-state ally. Even more important, as his political aide William Connell would say, the Senate had been transformed into "a liberal institution" that was more issues-oriented than before and less willing to compromise on principle. Most significantly, many senators now turned to Humphrey as well as to Johnson. The two men may not have become "equal partners," but Humphrey had become more important than ever to the majority leader.[67]

At the same time, Humphrey was also building a new, permanent home for his family. During the summers of 1952 and 1953, he had rented the vacation house owned by Ray Ewald, the wealthy Minneapolis dairyman who had befriended him during his mayoral tenure. The Humphrey family was so content in Ewald's house in Waverly, a small town with a large lake, thirty-five miles west of Minneapolis, that the senator purchased two adjacent lakeside lots from his friend for the "giveaway" price of two hundred dollars. In 1957 Humphrey, always short of funds, scraped together enough money, aided by a Waverly bank mortgage and loans from Minneapolis friends and supporters, to build an attractive one-story home modeled from plans for Lyndon Johnson's Texas ranch guesthouse. The new home included oak, cherry, walnut, and butternut wood-paneled rooms, a central fireplace that divided a modern kitchen from a big, beamed-ceiling living room with a large picture window facing south to the lake, a library, and four bedrooms, including a loft dormitory-style room. The Humphrey family also purchased a fourteen-foot motorboat, with the children working off the cost by doing chores instead of hiring household help.[68]

The financial assistance wealthy friends provided, in an era when ties between politicians and businessmen were not scrutinized, was indicative of Humphrey's longer-term dependence on such people. His three sons, Hubert III, Robert, and Douglas, attended Shattuck Military Academy in Faribault, Minnesota, courtesy of scholarships provided to the school by Minneapolis-born William Benton, who had made a fortune in advertising before becoming Humphrey's Senate colleague from Connecticut during 1950–52. Benton was a Shattuck alumnus and former board member. Eventually, Ewald also helped.

Later, when Humphrey became vice president, he would turn over his modest stock holdings to Dwayne Andreas, the multimillionaire agribusinessman who transformed the Archer-Daniels-Midland (ADM) Company into a multinational powerhouse, to be put into a blind trust. Andreas commingled Humphrey's funds with his own in his mutual income fund that invested heavily in ADM stock. Andreas never mentioned this arrangement to Humphrey, who never inquired. By the time of his death in 1978, Humphrey's share of the mutual income fund was about half a million dollars, a significant sum in that era, especially after he had withdrawn several hundreds of thousands of dollars to establish trust funds for his children.

Humphrey had little interest in wealth, however, although he knew that to support his family comfortably he needed more money than he earned from his Senate salary of $22,500 and the $30,000 per year he averaged in speaking engagements, the highest in the Senate, although that amount was sharply reduced after he decided to seek the presidency. Humphrey felt disadvantaged because his major Democratic allies and rivals for leadership, such as Johnson, who grew wealthy from Texas dealings, and Kennedy, whose father was a multimillionaire, were able to spend significant sums for personal and political undertakings. As 1958 drew to a close, however, Humphrey's eye was not on money but on travel abroad to establish himself as a foreign policy expert and the Democrats' 1960 presidential nominee.[69]

9

CANDIDATE IN ORBIT, 1958–1960

Having established his reputation as a leading liberal domestic policy spokesman, now Humphrey sought to burnish his foreign policy credentials. He hoped to tamp down the American-Soviet Cold War, especially the nuclear arms race, and help broker peace in the Middle East—and establish his credibility as a presidential candidate in 1960.

Humphrey felt that arms control should be "at the heart" of US foreign policy and the key to national and world security. In a press statement and a *New York Times Magazine* article in January 1958, he charged that the Eisenhower administration was acting as if military pacts were the "be-all and end-all" of diplomacy and labeled the United States and Soviet spread of weapons "a mutual suicide pact."[1]

As far as the Soviet Union was concerned, Humphrey viewed it from a liberal cold warrior's perspective. After Soviet premier Nikita Khrushchev's historic February 1956 speech denouncing Joseph Stalin's crimes, *New York Times* Soviet expert Harry Schwartz reported that current Soviet policy was no different, only subtler, than under Stalin, and the country was bolstered by a hydrogen bomb and growing economic power. When the Soviets put *Sputnik* into orbit in October 1957, Humphrey warned that the Soviet Union's increasing edge in producing scientists and engineers would lead to a "nonviolent defeat" for the United States. He readily voted for the National Defense Education Act (NDEA) to increase federal funding for secondary school and university education in science, engineering, math, and foreign languages and strongly supported Johnson's Senate Preparedness Committee's proposal for accelerated missile production and development of an antimissile system. He also criticized the Eisenhower administration for requesting only $3.9 billion for mutual security, which he said was $1 billion less than proposed the previous year and wholly inadequate in light of *Sputnik*, "a great scientific breakthrough."[2]

Humphrey strongly criticized Secretary of State Dulles's view in 1956 that neutralism was "immoral." He cited Eisenhower's acknowledgment that the United States remained neutral for its first 150 years and Vice President Nixon's recent statement that uncommitted nations would not be "frightened" into alliances by military weapons. Newborn nations were "not pro-Communist; they are pro themselves," Humphrey said, and the United States needed to switch its focus from mutual security programs composed almost entirely of military aid to promoting agricultural reform, the rights of labor, and respect for nationalism.[3]

Humphrey also said that America's complex disarmament proposals seemed designed for rejection, and he expressed concern that Harold Stassen's departure as special assistant to the president for disarmament implied the triumph of Dulles's views, with Moscow's basic disarmament calls gaining a decided propaganda edge.[4]

Further, after Soviet premier Nikolai Bulganin called for a moratorium on nuclear testing in January 1957, Eisenhower proposed a foreign minister's meeting on disarmament. Humphrey urged an immediate halt in nuclear testing as put forward by the recently formed National Committee for a Sane Nuclear Policy (SANE). With Johnson's accord and a signal to the White House, Humphrey delivered a major speech on February 4, insisting that the United States must negotiate a nuclear test ban and an inspection system: the test ban would slow the spread of nuclear weapons and help to prevent a Soviet-American collision, and an inspection system in the Soviet Union would constitute a "spectacular" breakthrough that would allow focus on ending production of fissionable materials.[5]

Humphrey's address gained support for a test ban. But despite experts' agreement that atmospheric and underwater tests were detectable, the Atomic Energy Commission (AEC) insisted that underground tests were hard to detect from beyond 250 miles, which would allow Soviets to cheat before inspection systems were placed on their soil. Humphrey warned the administration against allowing the Soviets to score a major propaganda victory with a unilateral announcement of a test ban. He soon found reinforcement for his proposal when Betty Goetz, whom he had appointed as his Disarmament subcommittee's staff director, learned from the US Geodetic Survey in the Commerce Department that a Soviet underground test in the northern Urals on March 23 had been detected by seismic stations one thousand to five thousand miles away in Alaska, Montana, and Nevada, as well as in Kiruna and Uppsala, Sweden.[6]

Humphrey immediately called Disarmament subcommittee hearings and took testimony from leading scientists such as Nobel laureate Hans Bethe of Cornell University about feasibility of detecting nuclear tests. In late May, Eisenhower reached an accord with Khrushchev at a major disarmament conference in October. The president announced on October 31 the indefinite halt of US nuclear tests. "Young Lochinvar," as syndicated columnist William V. Shannon dubbed Humphrey, had broken the logjam on disarmament talks and opened the way toward the first nuclear test ban agreement, still five years away.[7]

Humphrey was highly critical of the Eisenhower administration's Middle East policy. In February 1956, he objected to its sale of eighteen tanks to Saudi Arabia while refusing to sell $50 million in arms to Israel—a state he greatly admired—even as Arab states blacklisted all ships that stopped in Israeli waters. He openly suspected that oil and the US air base at Dhahran in Saudi Arabia influenced that decision. After the Suez Crisis that fall, he urged the administration to press the Arab states and Israel to reach a settlement, but the Arab nations also had to recognize Israel and Egypt had to open the canal to its shipping and halt its persecution of Jews. Even so, he cautioned that American ability to control events in the Middle East was "sharply limited."[8]

Humphrey balked at Eisenhower's January 1957 proposal to authorize the president to use funds appropriated under the 1954 Mutual Security Act, plus another $200 million in 1957 and each of the next two years, to provide military and economic aid and employ US forces to help any Middle Eastern country combat aggression from any nation "controlled by international communism." Humphrey viewed this new Eisenhower Doctrine as an open-ended military commitment, and he chided Dulles that the administration was requesting a "predated declaration of war." Further, the doctrine infringed Congress's authority to declare war and did not address the critical Middle Eastern issue of oil-rich monarchies and poverty-stricken people.[9]

He further charged that Eisenhower Doctrine aid was slated to go to the "most feudal and reactionary" regimes in the region, which sought to destroy Israel—"the only democracy in the area"—while the United States showed no intent to aid that state. He questioned the president's public threat in February 1957 to impose sanctions on Israel if it did not comply with a UN resolution calling for withdrawal of its troops from all of the territory—the Gaza Strip and Sharm el-Sheikh, the port near the Gulf of Aqaba—that it had occupied during the 1956 Suez conflict. The United States had not acted to insure Israel against attacks on its borders that prompted the conflict, Humphrey said. He proposed that the United States commit forces to the Middle East only under UN auspices, that it work through that body to guarantee the 1949 armistice and the borders between Israel and the Arab states, and assure the right of Israel's ships to pass through the Suez Canal and Gulf of Aqaba. The historic American demand for freedom of the seas, he said, was meant to apply to all nations.

The Senate Democratic Policy Committee supported Humphrey's opposition to sanctions against Israel, but party leaders sought to avert charges of denying the president money and arms to prevent Soviet advances in the Middle East. The senators modified the Eisenhower Doctrine to stipulate that if the president deemed it necessary, the United States was prepared to use force to resist Communist aggression in the Middle East. Humphrey voted with Senate and House colleagues to approve the joint resolution in March. The United States affirmed the right of Israel's ships to traverse the gulf, and Israel withdrew its forces and returned control of the Gaza Strip and Sharm el-Sheikh to Egypt.[10]

Humphrey was concerned that 90 percent of US Middle East foreign aid was for military support: "That is not economic policy, that is a military policy," he said. In April 1957, he proposed creation of a Middle East Development Association (MEDA), a hybrid of the World Bank and Tennessee Valley Authority, to undertake regional development projects to bring stability to the region and a higher standard of living for its peoples, notably the approximately 750,000 refugees who had left or were driven from Israel during the 1948–49 war and were living in nearby Arab states or the Gaza region. MEDA projects would lessen the danger to Israel, which was "an island of wealth in a sea of poverty."[11]

In April Humphrey traveled to the Middle East and southern Europe, winning plaudits from US diplomats for his articulation of American policy. He sought Arab-Israeli détente by means of his MEDA concept and PL 480 programs. But a lengthy talk with Nasser led him to conclude that Egypt's leader was too focused on past colonial domination, viewed the United States as having replaced the British in the Middle East, and sought leadership of the Arab world at the expense of reform and progress in Egypt, whose poverty was "appalling." Still, Humphrey said he could understand Egyptian resentment toward the United States after it canceled the Aswan Dam loan in 1956, and he urged the administration to release Egypt's frozen assets, provide its people with more foodstuffs and technical assistance, and show greater "patience and humility" in dealing with Cairo.[12]

Humphrey's brief stop in Beirut to visit two Palestinian refugee camps shocked him. He believed that the frightful plight of the people there should weigh on the conscience of the world and described the situation as "ready made for Communist propaganda and agitation." He immediately called for the "right of repatriation" for Arab refugees to Israel and to Arab countries and compensation for lost property. Realizing that he had touched a delicate diplomatic-political nerve, he followed up that he meant the right of repatriation only as a matter of principle and that Israel could repatriate only a limited number of refugees. He said it would be "suicidal" for Israel to accept large numbers of refugees who, he claimed, had been educated over the past decade to "hate" that state and would likely form a dangerous fifth column. The world had to deal with the "rootlessness, joblessness, and disillusion" of the Palestinian refugees, who he believed would best be settled in countries such as Iraq and Syria.[13]

Humphrey viewed the leadership of Israeli prime minister David Ben Gurion and foreign minister Golda Meir as strong and forward looking, and he lauded the nation's democratic processes and development, especially in agriculture and water supply. "The new Israeli state is a striking contrast to the ruin of older civilizations one sees on every side," he said. Israel had used American economic aid to "utmost advantage" and was a "showcase of what can be done in this dry, poverty-stricken area of the world." Israel was anti-Communist, "a pilot plant for democracy in the Middle East," and "a brave ally" without a treaty of alliance.[14]

On Humphrey's return to the United States, Dulles invited him to debrief at the secretary's home and publicly "heaped laurels" on him for his representation of the United States. Cables from abroad "were buzzing with well-dones," and newsmen referred to him as perhaps the Senate's "new voice of foreign policy." He played a key role in June in helping the administration push through its $3.8 billion foreign aid bill, with a sizable economic development fund of indefinite duration.[15]

Humphrey was the first politician to launch his presidential campaign from the steps of the Kremlin, *New York Times* columnist Arthur Krock wrote.[16]

Humphrey was in Berlin in late November 1958, planning to visit Moscow, when Khrushchev sent an ultimatum to the United States, Great Britain, and France demanding that they transform the post-1945 Four Power militarily occupied city into a demilitarized "free" city and either sign a peace treaty with a united Germany or, failing that, sign separate accords with the Federal Republic of Germany (FRG) and the German Democratic Republic (GDR). He also warned that the GDR would be less flexible than Moscow in allowing access to Berlin.[17]

Eisenhower was prepared, "if necessary," to put his "whole stack" of chips in the pot. Both sides viewed war as unthinkable, however, and Khrushchev's main goal was to gain the GDR diplomatic recognition and end its crippling "brain drain." Humphrey rushed to see West Berlin's mayor, Social Democrat Willy Brandt, to declare that "we cannot and must not back down," and the two men went to the Brandenburg Gate to be photographed together.[18]

Humphrey had told Soviet ambassador Mikhail "Smiling Mike" Menshikov before he left the United States for Europe that he would like to meet with Khrushchev, a request the senator repeated to Valery Kuznetsov, head of the Soviet delegation in Geneva. When Humphrey arrived in Moscow, he was irked because no one from the US embassy—only an Intourist guide—greeted him at the airport. He repeated his request to his hosts to meet with Khrushchev but during the next several days saw only various health and agriculture officials, appeared briefly on Russian TV, toured the Kremlin, and was taken to a symphony and the Bolshoi Ballet. He also wrote a signed article for *Izvestia* pointing to the material advantages of American life over that in the Soviet world; it went unpublished there but was widely circulated in the United States and Europe. After three days, however, there was still no word from the Kremlin—"it was a total Iron Curtain," Julius Cahn, one of his entourage, said.[19]

But just as Humphrey was about to meet with a cultural relations committee at 2:30 p.m. on December 1, his guide said that Khrushchev would see him at 3:00 p.m.—leaving no time to gather his wife, Muriel, or an aide. Twenty-seven minutes later, the senator was at the Kremlin, walking down two long, carpeted corridors, into an outer office and then into that of the premier, who was wearing a cuff-linked shirt and two Order of Lenin medals in the left lapel of his dark blue suit jacket. Khrushchev stood behind a large wooden desk, with a board room-style table nearby, and stepped forward to shake hands while photographers took pictures. Then he cleared the room, except for his translator, Oleg Troyanowsky.[20]

Khrushchev told Humphrey he was up to date on American politics—he had given interviews to Adlai Stevenson, business leader and special emissary Walter Johnston, and journalist Walter Lippmann—and he knew that Humphrey was on the Foreign Relations Committee and would likely be an important voice in the Democrats' foreign policy stance.[21]

The senator did most of the talking for the next hour and a half as the two men discussed their backgrounds, medical and scientific developments, cultural exchange, and foreign trade. Khrushchev agreed that Eisenhower was a man of peace but labeled Dulles "war-like" and an "imperialist." The Soviet leader also dismissed US proposals for a one-year test ban; it would take that long to put in inspection systems. He said he had two secrets for Humphrey to convey to Washington. First, the Soviets had exploded a five-thousand-kiloton hydrogen bomb with far less fissionable material than previously needed. Humphrey understood this to mean that a small warhead could carry it but gave no indication of being overly impressed. Second, Khrushchev said that the Russians had a missile with an 8,700-mile range, although he wryly jested that he would never bomb the senator's hometown.[22]

When Khrushchev indicated he wanted to talk about Berlin, Humphrey said he spoke only informally, not for his government. The Soviet leader held sway: Berlin was a "thorn" in East-West relations, and "it is a bone in my throat." He took credit for having thought up the demilitarized free city idea, despite his belief that Berlin belonged to the GDR, and he likened this "real compromise" to his having overruled other Soviet leaders to press for Four Power troop withdrawal from Austria, whose neutrality since 1955 lessened Cold War tension. But the FRG and GDR had to negotiate reunification directly, he said, not effect it by means of the all-German election the West wanted.

He spoke firmly about recent "stupid statements" of US military men who proposed to use tanks to break any future blockade. The Soviets also had tanks and missiles, "so don't threaten me." When Humphrey asked how the Russians would guarantee a free city, Khrushchev said he was prepared to sign a treaty to assure access to Berlin that would be registered at, and monitored by, the United Nations. He wished to "cut this knot" that spoiled East-West relations. He welcomed American proposals, but "don't threaten me." Finally, he was happy to have Humphrey report this conversation to Eisenhower: "We want no evil to the U.S."[23]

After almost four hours of conversation, Khrushchev proposed a bathroom break, after which Humphrey found that his host had ordered snacks, an elaborate meal, and vodka, wine, and brandy. He also summoned his "Armenian rug dealer," as he called Deputy Premier Anastas Mikoyan, to talk about trade and—on command—down shots of brandy. Khrushchev said he would like to visit America, as Mikoyan had. Humphrey put a last question to the premier about his recent trip to China, but Khrushchev refused to discuss "ally" business, noting only that the PRC's new agricultural communes were "reactionary" and would not work because there were no incentives. This sounded "rather capitalistic," Humphrey said. "Call it what you will. It works," Khrushchev retorted. Finally, after eight hours of talk, Humphrey, a little heady from his experience, returned to his hotel at midnight.[24]

The next day at the US embassy, Humphrey dictated a long memorandum for the State Department focusing on Khrushchev's contentions about Berlin and his stated willingness to guarantee equal access to a "free Berlin." The senator spent the next several weeks dealing with the newfound celebrity his Kremlin meeting had brought. En route to the United States, there were airport interviews in Oslo, London, New York, and Washington, where two hundred reporters were waiting. Initially, he said only that Khrushchev was "smart, strong, and tough" and that the Russians were tough competitors and "out to win." He insisted that he disliked the idea of Berlin as a "free city" and that the West should stand firm behind Eisenhower's position, but it was time for a "new approach" to the Cold War. Khrushchev was not likely to back down, but he had left "a loophole or two"; war was unlikely but "not impossible."[25]

In Washington, Humphrey met first with Undersecretary of State Christian Herter (Dulles was hospitalized), Director of Central Intelligence Allen Dulles, and AEC chairman John McCone. The senator emphasized his perception that Khrushchev strongly desired a summit meeting and an invitation to the United States and thought Eisenhower could do business with him. All three officials asked Humphrey to repeat his briefing to second-echelon employees, especially on techniques of "informal diplomacy."[26]

The next morning Humphrey reported to Eisenhower about Khrushchev's "secret" missiles and hydrogen bomb. The president said that he already knew about them, and the two men agreed that Khrushchev's Berlin proposals were neither new nor acceptable. Humphrey told the assembled White House press corps that he did not expect political progress with the Russians for a long time, and on *Meet the Press* on December 14 he reiterated his call for standing firm on Berlin but again doubted that force would be required. The Humphrey-Khrushchev exchange did little to resolve the Berlin crisis, but it contributed to the idea that Khrushchev wanted to deal on the basis of equality and sought an invitation to visit the United States.[27]

Humphrey's "informal diplomacy" also won him international press coverage. His full-color picture, wearing a Russian fur hat, graced the cover of *Life* on January 12, 1959; the magazine also carried his lengthy report, "My Marathon Talk with Russia's Boss," and another picture of him with Mayor Brandt at the Brandenburg Gate. Next month, however, Khrushchev told the Twenty-First Party Congress that Humphrey's remarks were "fairy tales"—especially the comments about the Chinese communes; he responded that the Soviet leader was protesting too much, probably due to pressure from his comrades and the PRC.[28]

Meanwhile Humphrey continued to urge the administration to stand firm in Berlin—but also to negotiate, which "is not to appease." Eisenhower ignored calls for dramatic action, and senior government officials, with views akin to that of Humphrey, concluded that the Soviet leader's real interest was to come to the United States and to negotiate on equal footing. American, British, and Soviet proposals on Berlin made no progress in 1959, but Eisenhower's inviting Khrushchev to the United States in September put the Berlin crisis on hold.[29]

Humphrey garnered more publicity in eight hours of debate with Khrushchev than Abraham Lincoln did in seven weeks of debating Senator Stephen Douglas a century earlier.

Liberal icon Eleanor Roosevelt, still supporting Adlai Stevenson, said on national television that Humphrey came closest of all the candidates to possessing that "requisite spark of genius" the next president would need, and syndicated columnist Roscoe Drummond lauded Humphrey for not allowing Khrushchev to use him.

Journalist Russell Baker's "Humphrey: Thunder! . . . And Lightning?" in the *New York Times Magazine* in January 1959 hailed the former "young pipsqueak from the windy prairie" as having become one of the "small coterie of men who dominate the Senate," as well as "liberalism's most effective champion" and a "leading contender" for his party's presidential nomination. Significantly, Muriel Humphrey, often unhappy about her husband's prolonged time away from home, wrote a political ally that "whether we seek it or not, we are in the race for 1960. I am no longer pulling back." And when a Humphrey aide said that *Sputnik* went into orbit in 1957 and that the senator did in 1958, he retorted that he hoped to stay in orbit longer than the Soviet satellite, which crashed to earth three months after its launching.[30]

Humphrey was no longer the "damn the consequences" liberal of 1948 but one who now insisted that America did not want a "radical" movement so much as a vigorous "progressive" and "international" party.

In January 1959, a greatly buoyed Humphrey hired a campaign manager, the well-known Washington lawyer James H. Rowe Jr., who had worked in Roosevelt's White House and was close to alleged noncandidate Johnson. Humphrey also hired Ernest Lafever, head of the Library of Congress's foreign affairs research division and a protégé of national security expert Paul Nitze, who had chaired the State Department's Policy Planning Staff under President Truman. To Humphrey's delight, his longtime DFL ally Governor Freeman agreed to a major campaign role and to prevent any DFL intraparty challenge to Humphrey's Senate reelection until the presidential issue was settled.[31]

Rowe's twenty-five-page campaign strategy memorandum in June 1959 stated that although primaries were politically risky, exorbitantly expensive, and physically exhausting, this "stern and bloody" path was Humphrey's sole chance to gain vital prolonged national exposure and to show that he was a "winner" by overtaking the front-running senator John Kennedy. Humphrey could use the two hundred or more delegates he would win to compel the more conservative "power brokers" in key large states (New York, Pennsylvania, Illinois, Michigan, Texas) to direct their delegates to him. Rowe advised entering contests in the District of Columbia, which had a large African American population, and in Oregon and Wisconsin, where the political climate resembled Minnesota's. Further, the early primary in Wisconsin, where Humphrey was known as the state's "third senator" because of his support for farm price supports, might allow him to set a winning trend. Another target was West Virginia, a poor state with a strong union tradition that was also 95 percent Protestant and unlikely to back Kennedy. On June 13, Senator Gene McCarthy and Governor Freeman announced their cochairmanship (with Lieutenant Governor Karl Rolvaag to run daily operations) of a Humphrey for President committee.[32]

The fledgling campaign faced immediate problems. As longtime DFL ally Eugenie Anderson warned, the public viewed Humphrey as an "ardent liberal in the New Deal tradition," a label that belonged to the past. The current era was one of "unprecedented prosperity and conservatism," and people sought fresh thinking. Similarly, *Time* in July 1959 questioned Humphrey's brand of "wildcat liberal" that would use his Phi Beta Kappa key to open the floodgates of the US Treasury when enthusiasm for big farm supports, big housing dreams, or big labor was gone. Newer liberals were committed to "pay as you go."[33]

Truman said that Humphrey lacked presidential bearing, a "strange" comment, McCarthy retorted, given the insults that the former president had suffered. But as a Minnesota journalist later wrote, Humphrey's "high forehead, darting eyes, snapping mouth, and slightly bulky figure" compared poorly with Kennedy: taller, strikingly handsome, always fashionably dressed, and six years younger at age forty-two. (Even Humphrey complained that "I am no longer a 38-year-old young man.") More important, the Humphrey campaign lacked money, and when a reporter asked where it would get it, McCarthy, in a swipe at Kennedy, said only that "it would not be financed by his father."[34]

Repeated trips by Anderson and others to New York to woo Eleanor Roosevelt and her liberal friends proved unavailing. This circle, which included Humphrey's wealthy benefactor, former senator William Benton, still favored Stevenson who, despite his refusal to declare, was "keeping his group of loyal supporters and heavy contributors firmly in his own bondage," and his large contributors were "sitting on their hands and their wallets." Humphrey complained bitterly that he had raised nearly all of his campaign money himself and that a recent fund-raising dinner in Minnesota seemed "more like a wake than it was a party." If that lack of enthusiasm continued, he said, it was better "to bury Humphrey than to try to run him."[35]

The senator was further distressed that Minnesota's labor movement was attacking him for having voted for the recent Landrum-Griffin labor management bill—coming after revelations about corruption among Teamsters, Longshoremen, and United Mine Workers unions—that imposed new obligations on unions for frequent secret elections and stricter control over finances. Humphrey, no longer on the Labor Committee, had tried to help moderate the bill but viewed its passage as inevitable given Congress's view that labor was "corrupt" and had to be "punished." Kennedy, who had favored more union regulation, escaped harsher labor criticism because he helped to mitigate some of the bill's excesses.[36]

Lack of support from New York liberals also disheartened Humphrey, who attributed this to the fact that they were always looking for a "Messiah" rather than someone possessed of "good glands" and a strong mind and body and able to run a campaign. He complained that liberals regarded him as "expendable," even though Stevenson could not win. Meanwhile, organization people, like Tammany Hall boss Carmine DeSapio, were leaning toward Kennedy, and Humphrey's friend, Wisconsin governor Gaylord Nelson, who believed the Minnesotan would make the best candidate and the best president, determined to stay neutral because he feared that a bitter party battle would hurt his own reelection chances in 1960. The Wisconsin state Democratic chair, Patrick Lucey, was working hard for Kennedy, and he was able to put political pressure on Ohio governor Mike DiSalle, who got the strong Democratic machine in Cleveland to back Kennedy.[37]

Humphrey suffered another sharp blow when he visited Johnson at his ranch in December 1959. The Texan's campaign committee had announced itself in October, although he said that his Senate duties precluded his entering any primaries. But after setting out an elaborate breakfast for his house guest, Johnson bellowed, "Hubert, you going to do me out of the nomination?" indicating that he intended to seek the presidency despite his disclaimers and general belief that the party would not nominate a southerner. Humphrey could only reply, "Lyndon, you have all this. Let me have the nomination." Johnson did accompany him to Houston, where Humphrey gained respect and funds from Texas oilmen, but also recognized his need for a "little miracle" to compensate for a "completely inadequate organization and inadequate money."[38]

Intent to gain an edge over his opponents, Humphrey formally announced from the Senate Appropriations Room on December 30—a poor time, given public focus on New Year's revelries—that he was the "candidate of the plain people" who would speak for those who, like himself, were of modest origins and means and "lack the power or influence to fully control our destiny." He pledged to "balance the moral budget as well as the fiscal budget" through stronger human rights guarantees, to work toward a responsible disarmament program, and to wage war on poverty and disease. At the National Press Club in Washington the next week, he attacked the Eisenhower administration's "age of complacency" policies and compared himself to his wealthy Democratic opponents, such as Kennedy, who could spend unlimited amounts of his own money in the primaries. Later, in Wisconsin, he would liken himself to "a corner grocer running against a chain store."[39]

Kennedy waited until he could dominate the news on January 2, 1960, and used the imposing Senate Caucus Room to declare his intention to reinvigorate the nation's material well-being and moral purpose. He also addressed his Catholicism: the issue was whether one believed, as he did, in the Constitution and separation of church and state. Moreover, despite his negligible legislative record, he had gained significant publicity from his 1956 run at the vice presidency and his 1957 largely ghostwritten *Profiles in Courage*, a best-selling, Pulitzer Prize-winning book about senators who made brave decisions. The public seemed far more enamored than resentful of Kennedy and his chic wife, Jacqueline Bouvier, and his family's wealth, Hollywood ties, and glamorous lifestyle. Further, the senator's good looks, charm, and wit made him "emblematic of a new breed of celebrity politician," whose writings increased sales of every magazine in which they appeared and whose personal appearances drew large crowds.[40]

Both Humphrey and Kennedy viewed the April 1960 primary in Wisconsin, with its 32 percent Catholic electorate, as crucial. Humphrey had the benefit of proximity and his third senator status, although this applied more to the rural, agricultural, and Protestant western regions than the largely Catholic and more heavily populated eastern urban areas. Humphrey also had a strong liberal following in Madison, home of the university and the state capital, although Mayor Ivan Nestingen was chairman of the Wisconsin Democrats for Kennedy. But Humphrey's funds were limited, his campaign headquarters in Milwaukee was subject to closings, and he had to replace Rolvaag, a poor organizer, with Gerald Heaney, a DFL leader from Duluth and DNC member.

The Humphrey campaign built cadres of weekend volunteers from Minnesota, but their unpaid status meant time-limited efforts and led to conflict with Freeman, who faced a tough reelection fight. Humphrey, the diligent senator, spent less time than needed in Wisconsin, traveling and sleeping on a rented bus during six weeks of cold winter campaigning. By contrast, Kennedy spent sixteen days in Wisconsin

1958–59, and now traveled on his private plane, the *Caroline*, accompanied by family members and political supporters. His organization had an advance man, a large staff, and its own pollster, Louis Harris. Humphrey's effort to analogize this highly organized campaign to efficiency in Nazi Germany played poorly, and he never could decide whether to follow Rowe's counsel to "go after" Kennedy on farm and labor issues or ADA leader James Rauh's advice to avoid party-splitting tactics.[41]

Humphrey tried to contrast his long-term commitment to liberalism and support for farmers and laborers to Kennedy's only recently having adopted similar positions, while Kennedy refused to debate him on grounds that they had no clear-cut differences over policy. Instead Kennedy pointed to his lead in the polls and alleged that he had a far better chance to defeat the likely Republican nominee, Vice President Nixon, in November. He also called Humphrey a stalking horse for Stevenson, Johnson, or Stuart Symington. Historian Arthur Schlesinger Jr., Humphrey's ADA ally but a Stevenson supporter who now was part of Kennedy's circle, publicly contended that the Minnesotan was a reflexive liberal who contrived reasons for his positions, whereas Kennedy arrived at his policy views after rational analysis and thought. The Kennedy campaign also alleged that reviled Teamster leader Jimmy Hoffa was funding Humphrey.

His campaign also suffered a bitter blow during the last week of the primary when Charles P. Greene, a former Wisconsin state Democratic chairman— without a word to Humphrey's aides—placed an ad, signed by a so-called Square Deal for Humphrey Committee, in newspapers across the state that urged Protestants to vote for the Minnesotan to offset Republican Catholics (chiefly Nixon supporters) who might cross over in this open primary to vote for Kennedy. Humphrey, who had sought to defuse the religious issue, sharply disavowed the ad but hinted that it might have been a Kennedy campaign trick to alienate him from Catholics. Kennedy absolved Humphrey of blame for the ad but questioned if Hoffa had been behind the scheme.[42]

Humphrey, Muriel, and their eighteen-year-old son Skip campaigned hard during the last two weeks, buoyed by Minnesota volunteers and funds raised by grass-roots organizers. But Kennedy won a clear-cut, though not definitive, victory on April 5 with 478,901 votes (56.5 percent) to Humphrey's 372,034 votes (43.5 percent). Humphrey did best in the highly Protestant western regions and Madison area.

Kennedy won six of the state's ten congressional districts; five districts were on the eastern border, with two of them in Milwaukee, which had large Irish and Polish Catholic working-class, or labor, constituencies that typically voted for Humphrey. Kennedy also noted publicly that he won Milwaukee's three

African American wards by a two-to-one margin, which augured well for him in a national election. Moreover, even Humphrey's team recognized that many Protestant Republicans in the western areas had crossed over to vote for him but that Catholic Republican crossovers had not provided Kennedy with his margin of victory; he would have won even in a closed primary.[43]

Nonetheless, Humphrey appeared more buoyant than Kennedy when they met the press on election night. Wisconsin was just a "warm-up," Humphrey said; he had been closing the gap in the last days of the campaign and looked forward to the West Virginia contest. Kennedy said he was delighted to have won, especially since his brother Robert had cautioned against running in Wisconsin, so close to Humphrey's base. But candidate Kennedy also knew that his failure to win in largely Protestant areas meant that he still had to prove to party leaders that he could triumph in a national election. As he told his sister Eunice, now he had to go into heavily Protestant West Virginia and "do it all over again"—and win in Michigan, Indiana, Oregon, and elsewhere.[44]

Humphrey's loss in Wisconsin and lack of funds—his campaign owed $17,000—provided reason to withdraw from West Virginia and perhaps to seek the vice presidency, as Schlesinger suggested. But Humphrey had no interest in that office. He ignored calls to step aside and was angry and hurt by the Kennedy campaign's charges that Hoffa was funding him and that he was a stalking horse for Stevenson or Johnson. He believed that Kennedy had played the religious issue to his advantage and felt that he had experienced Kennedy's "ruthlessness and toughness that I had trouble accepting or forgetting."[45]

Humphrey had already paid his $1,000 filing fee, so he borrowed another few thousand dollars from a New York lawyer friend, Marvin Rosenberg, and headed to West Virginia, which was 95 percent Protestant, highly blue collar, labor oriented, and terribly poor. As a Humphrey adviser wrote, its resources had been "plundered by robber barons from within and outside the state," and its taxing system was wholly inadequate. The setting seemed right to campaign as a self-made "man like the mountaineers" in contrast to the Bostonian Kennedy's "Bourbon background."[46]

Johnson, too, wanted to stop Kennedy. The Texan had New York businessmen raise money that was funneled to Robert Byrd, a three-term congressman from West Virginia elected to the Senate in 1958 who was becoming the most powerful politician in his state and an ally of the majority leader. Kennedy quickly recognized Byrd's work in behalf of Humphrey, but Johnson rejected the Massachusetts senator's call to get Byrd "out of West Virginia." When Byrd told voters that if they were for Stevenson, Symington, or Johnson, they should vote for Humphrey to "stop Kennedy," the Massachusetts senator challenged them to "come and run themselves." Humphrey in turn called on "poor little Jack" to "stop acting like a boy. What does he want, all the votes?"[47]

Humphrey sought to effect a winning strategy by telling West Virginians that although he knew the days of anyone but a millionaire seeking the presidency were likely over, he brought a "brand of liberalism learned in the Dust Bowl and depression" and a "lifetime of experience" confronting the state's problems. He proposed an eight-point "Marshall Plan" for West Virginia, including an Area Redevelopment Act, a Coal Research and Development Commission, a Youth Conservation Corps, and a Food Stamp Program. One month later—and five years before enactment of Medicare—he used the state to call for a national government health insurance program funded through Social Security to provide for hospital and nursing home care, and drugs for people over age sixty-five. But his campaign slogan, "Over the Hump with Humphrey," was amateurish, and he sidestepped the advice of his former graduate school mentor Evron Kirkpatrick to seize on the religious issue with a national address that went beyond merely calling for tolerance and instead pointed to his own strong record of fighting for religious and racial tolerance as a mayor, at the Democratic Convention in 1948, and in the Senate.[48]

Humphrey shied from this course, however, while the Kennedy people, fearful of getting less than 40 percent of the vote, determined to challenge the nation and West Virginians on the religion issue. In a major speech to the American Society of Newspaper Editors in Washington on April 21, Kennedy claimed that the press was overemphasizing the religious issue as opposed to taxes, inflation, price supports, and disarmament. Further, the only legitimate question regarding his religion was whether as president he would allow "ecclesiastical pressures or obligations" to influence his decisions bearing on the national interest. His repeated answer "was—and is—no." He opposed federal aid to parochial schools and sending an ambassador to the Vatican, and he did not intend to explain or defend every pope's or priest's statement. He drew an ovation from the four hundred journalists present and an outpouring of statements from religious organizations around the country. Humphrey was left to declare, "I would not want to be President if it meant my own party might be torn apart on this extraneous issue."[49]

Kennedy further insisted to West Virginia audiences that his religion had not been a barrier to his service as a naval officer in World War II, and "nobody asked my brother if he was a Catholic or a Protestant before he climbed into an American bomber to fly his last mission."[50]

Kennedy and his aides hammered at Humphrey as a man "who could not be nominated . . . and could not carry a state right next to his own" but was being used by other candidates to "stop Kennedy." Franklin D. Roosevelt Jr., whose father was revered in West Virginia, agreed to Joseph Kennedy's call to campaign for his son. Robert (Bobby) Kennedy prevailed on FDR Jr., who drew large audiences, to use material suggesting that Humphrey was a World War II draft dodger despite his efforts to enlist in 1944 and deferments because of color blindness and a hernia. By early May, as one West Virginian columnist wrote, Humphrey "is being pummeled so ferociously" by Kennedy campaign speeches, statements, and political cartoons "that an innocent bystander might think he was a Republican."[51]

Humphrey called FDR Jr.'s draft dodger charge "gutter politics." Kennedy said only that he regretted that the issue had been raised without his knowledge; he did not say it was false. Humphrey insisted that he was running not against FDR Jr. but Kennedy, "the son of Joe Kennedy, a mortal enemy" of the party's "great" and "beloved" FDR. He also insisted that he was pitting "my ideals and my faith against the wealth of my opponent." He hesitated to say much about religion but privately attributed talk about "Protestant bigotry" to journalists and believed that it was "Kennedy who keeps raising the religious issue"[52]

Humphrey's best opportunity to challenge Kennedy directly came when he finally consented to a one-hour debate to be broadcast statewide and to major US cities on radio and television on May 4. Lawrence O'Brien, a key Kennedy Senate staffer and campaign organizer, and Humphrey's senior aide, Herb Waters, agreed that their two "tigers" should not attack each other but focus on the Republicans. Both candidates blamed West Virginia's economic ills on the Eisenhower administration and agreed on the need to keep Nixon from the presidency. Both said that they favored "peaceful" civil rights protests, reducing the oil depletion allowance, maintaining church-state separation, denying the PRC a UN seat, and dealing cautiously with Moscow on disarmament.

"All was sweetness and light," the press complained, except for Kennedy's charge that Humphrey could not get the nomination and was being used by other candidates. Three days later at a Jefferson-Jackson Day dinner in Clarksburg, Johnson boosted Humphrey by emphasizing the ties between Democratic social programs and those the Minnesotan promoted, but otherwise stressed that any of the Democratic candidates being mentioned could defeat a Republican in November, a comment suggesting that Humphrey was a stalking horse for someone else.[53]

It was money, however, that separated Humphrey from his current rival. Kennedy's family fortune permitted him to dominate radio, television, and print media and, most notably, the support of local officials who sold their crucial services. Traditionally on Election Day in West Virginia, sheriffs, precinct captains, and other workers gave voters a list of their party's approved slate of candidates, including for governor and president. This form of slating required payment (extortion money) to local officials for alleged printing costs and wages lost due to time away from work and also provided them with walking around money.

Humphrey's campaign had nowhere near the funds needed to deal with the state's 2,900 precincts, which cost about $100 each for Election Day loyalty, while each of the several hundred sheriffs might cost hundreds, or a few thousand, dollars. Moreover, even when a Humphrey campaign worker offered to complete a $5,000 pledge to a county office, he was told that it was not close to the Kennedy camp's offer. Six years later, Boston's Richard Cardinal Cushing confided to Humphrey that in 1960 he and Joseph Kennedy (whose funding of his son's campaigns was legendary) had decided together which Protestant churches in West Virginia would now receive contributions from the Catholic prelate.[54]

Humphrey's campaign spent "peanuts"—$25,000—the candidate said, compared to Kennedy's expenditures, which included $40,000 for radio and television alone during the last three days, and a reported total of $92,000. But the actual sum was more likely ten times greater, as Humphrey wrote at the time, given lax reporting requirements and costs for vast advertising, twelve campaign offices, and hundreds of campaign workers. A *Charleston Gazette* investigative team, however, concluded that it could not find any spending illegalities.[55]

Humphrey's campaign staff operated on an ad hoc basis and failed to highlight enough of his senatorial achievements, and many of his usual supporters declined to help. AFL-CIO leaders told him they had to save their fire and funds to fight their real opponents, and liberal contributors held out for Stevenson. Johnson had raised some money, and Byrd provided introductions at rallies, but he made clear that he was for Johnson first, Symington second, and Humphrey for vice president. Humphrey's silent partnership with these men hurt him.[56]

Humphrey suffered a crushing and humiliating defeat on May 10: Kennedy won 60.8 percent of the tally with 236,000 votes to 152,000 votes. He took forty-nine of fifty-five counties, and most cities, towns, farm areas, and coal regions. Newspapers and magazines called the result "stunning" and one that "confounded the experts." The press quickly recognized, however, that Kennedy was an unusually adept campaigner with "kinetic charm" whom "women found irresistible." He also gained by taking on the religious issue directly and by responding with great empathy to the poverty he was viewing for the first time. Meanwhile his organization called every home with a telephone and offered voters a ride to and from the polls.[57]

Election results were clear shortly after the polls closed. Rowe pressed Humphrey to contend that the election had been bought, but after a few phone calls to friends, he graciously congratulated Kennedy for his "significant and clear-cut victory," and in a breaking voice concluded, "I am no longer a candidate for the Democratic presidential nomination." Bobby Kennedy came to Humphrey's headquarters, strode across the room to kiss Muriel — to her evident anger — on the cheek, and asked the Humphreys to come to his brother's headquarters. Muriel refused, but Humphrey dutifully walked with Bobby in the rain to meet with John Kennedy, who was flying in from Georgetown. After a short wait, Humphrey shook hands with the triumphant Kennedy, exchanged pleasantries, and left the stage, and the press, to him.[58]

Like *Sputnik*, Humphrey's presidential quest had crashed to earth. He was thoroughly disheartened and somewhat embittered: he never fully forgave FDR Jr. or Bobby Kennedy for assailing his lack of military service, but he accepted John Kennedy's claim that he did not know about the attack. He also sought to put the best public face he could on the primary loss, telling the Minneapolis press that Kennedy "got more votes than I did." He added that he had to get home for his daughter Nancy's wedding the next weekend to Bruce Solomonson, a young man from Waverly who had served as a driver during the Wisconsin campaign. "I lost a primary and gained a son-in-law. I think I'm ahead," he concluded. Humphrey intended to wield influence at the Democratic convention in Los Angeles and win reelection to the Senate to assure that the Democratic presidential nominee carried Minnesota in the November election.[59]

10

THE INSIDER AS OUTSIDER

In spring 1960, John Kennedy seemed poised to win the Democrats' presidential nomination on the first ballot. Humphrey's supporters, including ADA head Joseph Rauh, labor leaders George Meany of the AFL-CIO and Walter Reuther of the UAW, and Arthur Goldberg, counsel to the Steelworkers, promoted him for vice president, and Kennedy told Rauh that he would choose Humphrey or another midwestern liberal. Kennedy told Humphrey he was "strong" where, Kennedy confessed, he was "weak": with Jews, labor, and farmers. "What do you think?" Kennedy said.[1]

Humphrey was noncommittal, but family members, especially Muriel, were still angry at the Kennedys and strongly opposed joining forces. Humphrey knew he could not afford another defeat, but his announcement was ambivalent: "I do not want it. I wouldn't run for it—I did that once. I would not reject it. My candidate is Orville Freeman."[2]

The Democratic convention began on July 11 in Los Angeles. The party's platform, grandly entitled "The Rights of Man," strongly criticized the Eisenhower administration for allowing growth of alleged gaps in space, missile, and limited war capacity and proposed to contest the Soviets globally. The platform also featured programs that Humphrey had long advocated: medical insurance for older persons through Social Security; increases in parity payments and the minimum wage; repeal of right-to-work laws; federal funding of low-income housing; abolition of literacy tests and poll taxes; establishment of a Fair Employment Practices Commission; and requiring segregated school districts affected by the *Brown* decision to submit plans for first-phase compliance by 1963.[3]

Humphrey called this "the best statement on civil rights ever made by any political party in America." He was reminded of 1948, when his electrifying speech led the Democrats to adopt his minority plank and southerners to bolt the party. Now the southerners would try, but fail, to substitute their minority plank limiting federal authority and again warned that Democrats would suffer at the polls in November in the South.[4]

Humphrey's friends urged him to seek the vice presidency, but when he arrived in Los Angeles, he told his former legislative aide Max Kampelman, "I'm not running for vice president." Meany and Reuther urged Kennedy to choose Humphrey. The ADA leader Joseph Rauh visited Humphrey's hotel suite to press the Minnesotan to endorse Kennedy as a way to seek the second slot, but when he knocked on the door, no one answered, despite hearing the senator's laughter. He spotted Pat O'Connor, a Minneapolis fund raiser and political confidant of Humphrey, peering out from the next doorway, but when Rauh tried to enter, O'Connor slammed the door shut. Rauh left, certain he had glimpsed Humphrey, Johnson, former Kentucky senator and Johnson's chief campaign strategist Earle Clements, and Humphrey's recent campaign manager Jim Rowe; he presumed the group was trying to devise a "stop Kennedy" plan.[5]

Humphrey, who was inclined to support Stevenson, viewed Kennedy's nomination as inevitable. However, Johnson, who had declined to announce his candidacy until a week before the convention, insisted that he would get enough first-ballot support to win on a later vote. Kennedy was too young and politically inexperienced, he argued, and was in the race only because of his father's money.[6]

Humphrey encouraged Johnson to publicize his presidential effort by naming a vice presidential choice: Gene McCarthy. Humphrey knew his protégé was friendly with Johnson and regarded Kennedy as a "spoiled rich kid" who was intellectually inferior to him and was stealing his self-envisioned future role as the first Catholic president.[7]

Humphrey also encouraged Freeman to seek the vice presidential nomination, which the governor greatly desired. Freeman briefly favored Stevenson for president, but Stevenson's refusal to declare led to a shift to Kennedy, whose camp, seeking geographic balance and a first-ballot win, was courting the Minnesota governor. They sought to gain his state's delegation—committed to Humphrey as a favorite son but divided between Stevenson and Kennedy supporters—and perhaps the delegates Humphrey had won in the District of Columbia and Wisconsin primaries. On the first day of the convention, Kennedy named Freeman as high on his list of vice presidential candidates and offered to have him second his presidential nomination.[8]

Freeman asked Humphrey to help him turn their state delegation to Kennedy, insisting, "Now it's my turn." Humphrey agreed, but urged Freeman to get

Kennedy to commit firmly to his making the more attention-getting speech nominating him for president. Humphrey promptly released his delegates and, as Freeman noted, "made quite a talk about Kennedy" to the Minnesota delegation and urged it to support their governor for vice president. But McCarthy, meeting alone with Humphrey, pointedly reminded him of how badly the Kennedys had treated him in West Virginia and moved him to reconsider his support for his former rival.

At a closed Minnesota caucus, McCarthy charged that Kennedy had a poor legislative record and neither led nor followed his party on matters of principle. Humphrey said nothing then or afterward to the press, causing an anguished Freeman to conclude that his ally was backing away from supporting Kennedy and breaking his commitment to work for him to be Kennedy's running mate. Humphrey recognized he was jeopardizing his long personal and political relationship with Freeman, but their lengthy discussion, Freeman noted, achieved "nothing."[9]

Kennedy's camp got wind of these events and the next morning asked Freeman to nominate their candidate, provided that Humphrey, whose ability to rouse an audience they feared, did not nominate Stevenson. Humphrey said he was about to endorse—but would not nominate—Stevenson. He did not say, however, that in declining requests to nominate Stevenson, he had proposed that his backers call on McCarthy, whose liberal record and Catholicism would stand Stevenson in good stead.[10]

Humphrey's protégés, Freeman and McCarthy, nominated Kennedy and Stevenson, respectively, for president on July 13. Freeman described Kennedy as a "proven liberal" and a "man of courage and drive" who would bring the Democrats' platform to life. Speaker of the House from Texas Sam Rayburn nominated Johnson as a leader and a winner who belonged to no class or section, and Missouri's governor, James M. Blair Jr., spoke for his home-state compatriot, Senator Stuart Symington, as a symbol of strength who would keep the nation free.[11]

McCarthy spoke last in prime national television time about 8:00 p.m. With a passion that reminded many of Humphrey at the 1948 convention, McCarthy depicted Stevenson as a man who was the favorite son of "fifty states and of every country on earth," who "talked sense to the American people," and who did not prophesy or speak falsely. McCarthy implored the delegates not to turn away "this man who made us all proud to be Democrats" and who moved people's minds and stirred their hearts. "Do not leave this prophet without honor in his own party. Do not reject this man."

A historic twenty-five-minute demonstration followed, although the cheering came chiefly from the spectator galleries packed with Stevenson supporters, not delegates on the convention floor. Kennedy still managed a first-ballot victory with 809 votes, Johnson got about half as many votes, mainly from the South, and Symington and Stevenson trailed far behind; Humphrey got 31 of his 41 votes from faithful Minnesota delegates despite having released his favorite son commitment. Numerous liberals still wanted Humphrey for vice president, but the bitter primaries and his endorsement of Stevenson ruled him out. The forty-three-year-old Kennedy also balked at selecting the forty-two-year-old Freeman: "We would look like a pair of rover boys running for president," he said.[12]

Instead, Kennedy chose Johnson—likely his first choice—despite his aides' assurances to labor and liberals that he would not be selected. Candidate Kennedy viewed Johnson as necessary to win votes in the South, where religion was a major concern, and especially in the key state of Texas, which had voted for a Republican in the last three presidential elections. Kennedy worried that Johnson might reject the vice presidential offer, but Rayburn assured acceptance by Johnson, who worried about losing his majority leader's hold on the large, and more liberal, post-1958 Democratic ranks. A distraught Robert Kennedy tried to get the Texan to withdraw and instead chair the DNC, but Johnson rejected this, and the deal was sealed.[13]

"All hell broke loose" when word came to the convention, with liberals and labor protesting vociferously. Both Humphrey and McCarthy immediately reassured Johnson of their support; Humphrey worked furiously to calm liberal delegates, and McCarthy scotched District of Columbia delegates' effort to nominate him for vice president. Kennedy's aides arranged to have the rules suspended to allow a voice vote as the roll call reached Michigan, and after the question was called, the "ayes" and "nays" were about even, but the convention chairman declared that the motion carried, with Johnson nominated by acclamation.[14]

No Minnesotan was on the ticket, but Senator John Stennis of Mississippi said afterward, "You can never count that old Hubert out. Here he is, a defeated presidential candidate without a bit of power and the first thing you know, one of his boys is nominating the winning candidate, another of his boys gives the best speech of the convention, and his delegation still votes for Hubert"— including Freeman, despite his having nominated Kennedy.[15]

After the convention, Stevenson thanked Humphrey for his contribution to his "finest hour" and for "all you did to enliven my moribund political career." Humphrey replied that he had "no regrets, no second thoughts. I did what was

right and I felt like a free man—clean, alive, and happy." Still, he feared that
the Democrats' national ticket would be subject to "Nixon's demagoguery on
Communism and Socialism and the whispering rumors of religious intolerance." He also worried that the current brief session of Congress that Johnson
had scheduled to try to pass legislation to enhance the Democrats' electoral
prospects or permit them to campaign against "do-nothing" Republicans was
not helping any Democrat.[16]

Democrats faced a strong national Republican ticket. Vice President Nixon
swept the Republican presidential primaries. He chose as his running mate
Henry Cabot Lodge Jr., who had been elected senator from Massachusetts
three times before losing to Kennedy in 1952 and since 1953 had been ambassador to the United Nations. The Republicans hoped to capitalize on their
presumed foreign policy expertise, with their platform emphasizing nuclear
retaliatory power against any aggressor, and using Humphrey's PL 480 program
(Food for Peace) to assist "hungry peoples" around the globe.[17]

Humphrey returned to Minnesota to run for reelection against Minneapolis
mayor P. Kenneth Peterson. Humphrey's campaign well was almost dry because
his chief financial supporters had gone "all out" during the presidential primaries,
and he worried that Catholic voters, especially in neighboring St. Paul, might be
angry at him because of his battles with Kennedy. Republicans controlled the
state legislature, and Freeman, seeking his fourth term, was seen as a liability. He
had raised taxes, tried to institute withholding, and in 1959 had used the National
Guard to curb violence between striking workers and strikebreakers in Albert Lea,
only to have a court rule as illegal his seizure of the Wilson and Company meat-
packing plant.[18]

From the start of his campaign, Humphrey attacked the Eisenhower administration for a weak economy and avoided debating Peterson, who followed him
from city to city but said little more than that the senator voted to spend too
much federal money and abused his franking privileges. When Kennedy came
to Minnesota in late September, Humphrey, McCarthy, and Freeman worked
hard in succeeding to draw Twin City crowds that exceeded the 100,000 people
who had greeted Nixon two weeks earlier. The DFL leaders also took Kennedy
to barnstorm in Duluth and on the Iron Range, where high Election Day
turnout would prove vital to his winning this important swing state. At Kennedy's
behest, Humphrey went to New York City in early October to chair their party's
two-day National Conference on Constitutional Rights and American Freedoms,
where he criticized the Eisenhower administration for "inexcusable inertia"
on civil rights and pledged that with Kennedy as president federal action would
be far greater than ever. The conference report stressed the need for major

legislative enactments and enforcement of voting rights and antidiscrimination policies.[19]

Peterson released a surprising private poll that showed him narrowly winning over Humphrey, but at the candidates' only debate on October 30 in Rochester, he mainly charged that his opponent had missed more than half of his Senate roll calls in the last session and had shifted from criticizing Kennedy to praising him. Humphrey readily attributed his Senate absences to the presidential primaries and his seeming switch on Kennedy to "that's politics"; moreover, Kennedy would be a "far superior" president than Nixon. And when Peterson praised the Food for Peace program, Humphrey gleefully interjected, "I sponsored it." He also blamed the Eisenhower administration for Fidel Castro's rise to power in Cuba in 1959.[20]

Kennedy campaigned on the need to get the nation moving again after three recessions in eight years and to end the alleged missile gap between the United States and the Soviet Union. He also alleviated concerns about his religion by affirming before some three hundred largely Protestant ministers in Houston his belief in the absolute separation of church and state; he was not the Catholic candidate for president but the Democrats' candidate for president who was Catholic.[21]

In the first presidential debate on September 26, Kennedy appeared calm and confident. Nixon began by combatively contrasting himself and Kennedy and appeared tired and tense; in fact, he was sick. Millions of television viewers gained a lasting impression of Kennedy as a more appealing and winning candidate, whereas Lodge said of Nixon at the conclusion, "That son-of-a-bitch just lost us the election."[22]

Civil rights came to the fore on October 19, when Martin Luther King Jr. was jailed while attempting to integrate a department store in Atlanta. A judge sentenced him to four months of hard labor. Humphrey called it a "gross miscarriage of justice" and a "farce." He sought to have Johnson intervene but got no response. King's transfer to a rural maximum-security prison caused Coretta Scott King to fear for her husband's life. She called a civil rights aide to Kennedy, Harris Wofford, who called the candidate's brother-in-law Sargent Shriver, who was with him in Chicago and prevailed on him to call Coretta King to offer his sympathy and willingness to help.

Robert Kennedy grew angry when he learned of this because he feared it might cost his brother southern votes. But despite his outrage at a "bastard" judge's refusal to grant King bail, he soon called him to provide the political cover he demanded to release King on $2,000 bond. In turn, the Reverend—and Republican—Martin Luther King Sr. announced that he had a suitcase full of votes to put in John Kennedy's lap. Tens of thousands of pamphlets that described Kennedy as the "Candidate with a Heart"—as opposed to "No Comment Nixon"—went to African American churches and helped Kennedy win close races in South Carolina, Delaware, Michigan, Illinois, and New Jersey.[23]

Johnson campaigned hard from Virginia ("What's Nixon ever done for Culpeper?") to Louisiana and Texas, while during the fourth and final presidential debate on October 21, Kennedy spoke so forcefully about the US need to aid Cuban refugees to overthrow Castro that Nixon believed that his opponent had been informed about secret administration planning to support an invasion of Cuba. But the vice president, concerned not to reveal this project, said only that an attack would violate international law, despite his having privately advocated an invasion during the election.[24]

Kennedy won the tightest presidential race to date in the twentieth century on November 8 by 34,220,000 to 34,108,000 votes, a margin of 0.1 percent. His crucial Electoral College margin of 303 to 219 votes included extremely close victories in Illinois (27 electoral votes), where Chicago mayor Richard Daley's machine held sway, and in Texas (24 electoral votes), where Johnson's allies excelled at filling ballot boxes. If Nixon had won these states, he would have gained the presidency with 270 electoral votes.

Kennedy owed his victory to strong support from African Americans, Catholics, and other minorities in northern cities, midwestern Democrats (especially Humphrey's DFL in Minnesota), and Johnson's help in corralling southern votes. The Democrats lost a couple of seats in both houses but retained control of the Senate by 66–34 and the House by 283–154.[25]

Humphrey was "exuberant." He easily won reelection by 884,000 to 648,000 votes, his largest margin ever. He also carried Kennedy to a narrow victory in Minnesota by just 22,000 votes. Walter Mondale, a Humphrey protégé who as a college undergraduate worked to help him win control of the DFL in 1947–48, gained a resounding victory to become Minnesota's attorney general. Freeman was the only major DFL political casualty, losing reelection by just 23,000 votes. But he would soon join Kennedy's cabinet as secretary of agriculture, while Humphrey would become the shepherd of the administration's legislative program.[26]

The Humphrey family's political joy was tempered, however, when Hubert's and Muriel's first grandchild, Victoria, born to their daughter, Nancy, and son-in-law, Bruce Solomonson, on November 9, was diagnosed with Down syndrome, about which little was known. The Humphreys would quickly take "Vicky" close to their hearts and begin to work with medical specialists, teachers, and families to promote knowledge about retardation and other disabilities, particularly those affecting children.[27]

✦ ✦ ✦

Vice President–elect Johnson told Humphrey that Kennedy and key senators, including the newly designated majority leader, Mike Mansfield of Montana, wanted him to serve as majority whip. His friend and benefactor William Benton, and especially Stevenson, urged Humphrey not to surrender his independent voice by taking on "wheelhorse chores," but his acceptance was a "foregone conclusion," he later said. As he told a reporter, "I have made mud pies and dream houses long enough—now I want to do something."

He also aspired to join the political establishment and work with Mansfield, who had taught Asian history at the University of Montana before being elected to the House in 1943 and to the Senate in 1953. Humphrey viewed him as a "quiet, contemplative, leader" who did not "bully, punish, or even reward" senators for their vote but was "effective without being oppressive"—whereas Johnson had used every detail, "salacious or salutary," about a senator to "bargain, persuade, pressure, punish or reward." Humphrey felt free to operate as majority whip on his own terms, although there would be "no more oratorical flights." He had to urge colleagues to be brief; but as Jim Rowe told him, he was still a young man who "will be 57 in '68."[28]

By contrast, Johnson seemed to regret having been elected to a powerless position. He proposed to retain his role as chairman of the Democratic caucus and his majority leader's seven-room office, known as the Taj Mahal. He bluntly told his former aide Bobby Baker, now Senate secretary, that this would allow him to help "Mike Mansfield and Hubert Humphrey pass the Kennedy program" because "all those Bostons and Harvards don't know any more about Capitol Hill than an old maid does about fuckin'." Baker was horrified that Johnson believed the legislators would cede their power to an executive branch official, but Mansfield went along with him when he proposed his plan privately to a group of senators. Humphrey and the others indicated that the plan would not fly; but it was "not easy," he later said, to tell Johnson he could not do something. At the first Democratic caucus on January 3, 1961, the senators unanimously elected Mansfield as majority leader, and he moved that Johnson preside at future meetings.

Liberal and conservative senators contended that a vice president could not constitutionally preside at their meetings, but Mansfield gained passage of his resolution by threatening to resign. Johnson angrily left the meeting knowing that his victory was pyrrhic. Humphrey told him afterward that it was best for him not to seek to preside, but it took his mentor, Senator Russell, to dissuade him. He retained his old Senate office, however, and occupied new and large vice presidential quarters in the Executive Office Building next to the White House. Humphrey called the real estate vestiges of lost glory.[29]

The new majority whip reveled in his status and renewed political engagement. Even before Kennedy took office, Humphrey reiterated his call to finance health insurance for older persons through Social Security, and he sought once again, without success, to change the infamous Rule XXII to require a majority vote, not two-thirds, to end a filibuster.[30]

Humphrey found Kennedy's inaugural address "eloquent and challenging," especially his call to Americans to "ask not what your country can do for you—ask what you can do for your country." The senator believed that the new president's words inspired national unity or determination, although the address stressed foreign policy, informing friend and foe that "we shall pay any price, bear any burden, meet any hardship, support any friend, oppose any foe, to assure the survival and success of liberty." Kennedy also said, "Let us never negotiate out of fear. But let us never fear to negotiate."[31]

The president appointed moderate conservatives to senior cabinet posts, including Dean Rusk, a former State Department official and president of the Rockefeller Foundation, as secretary of state, and Robert McNamara, a nominal Republican and president of the Ford Motor Company, at Defense. More liberal officials included Freeman at Agriculture and Connecticut governor Abraham Ribicoff at Health, Education, and Welfare. Robert Kennedy, the president's closest confidant, became attorney general.[32]

Humphrey viewed his majority whip role more as an extension of the administration than an agency of the Senate. He delighted in his Tuesday morning breakfasts with the president and congressional leaders and soon wrote to his brother Ralph, "I am in the thick of things. . . . I find the President wants to consult with me," while legislative planning "made my juices flow." He also recognized that the president had "a few insiders who shared his personal and social life, as well as his political life. The rest of us were outsiders."

He carried out his whip's work in a small office in a corner of the Capitol, with a view of the East Front. He had to master the Senate's legislative rules and the political and personal needs of his colleagues, Democrats and Republicans, especially minority whip Thomas Kuchel of California. Humphrey was far more politically aggressive than Mansfield and unabashed about pursuing legislative votes, even from conservatives. While negotiating for an area development bill favored by his friend and colleague Douglas of Illinois, he said, "I'll bargain for you—I'm not so pure." Similarly, he told ADA friends who said he backed too many conservative presidential appointees, "I don't have to prove I'm a liberal."[33]

Humphrey was a far more advanced liberal than Kennedy, whose narrow election increased his caution about legislation, especially when it came to dealing with powerful southern conservatives. Though students and other activists were beginning their Freedom Rides into the South and undertaking sit-ins in restaurants, theaters, and department stores, the new president would not send a major civil rights bill to Congress. He would only call for recruiting more African Americans into the coast guard and sign an executive order in March establishing a Committee on Equal Employment Opportunity (CEEO) to eliminate discrimination in federal hiring and deny contracts to firms that refused equal opportunity to blacks. Despite having criticized Eisenhower for failure to desegregate federally financed housing with "a stroke of the pen," Kennedy refused to sign such an executive order.[34]

Humphrey, who insisted that discrimination was the "most glaring flaw in the moral fiber" of the nation, generously called Kennedy's establishment of the CEEO a "bold" move, but it did not compare to the bills the majority whip now proposed to outlaw discrimination in employment and interstate transportation; outlaw the poll tax and make lynching a federal offense; and provide servicemen with the same protection against bodily harm as members of the coast guard. But without White House support, the legislation remained in limbo.[35]

Humphrey provided the creativity and political drive for Kennedy's two most significant successes in 1961: establishment of the Peace Corps, which came to symbolize American idealism, and an arms control agency that would promote the historic Nuclear Test Ban Treaty in 1963. Humphrey had spoken for several years about having young people go abroad to help people in poorer nations, and in June 1960, he introduced legislation to establish a "Peace Corps of American young men" to assist peoples in underdeveloped nations to master the basic skills needed to "wage war" on poverty, disease, illiteracy, and hunger. He warned that the world was rapidly approaching an explosive situation as rich nations grew richer and poor nations became poorer, with Communism thriving on underdeveloped nations' growing frustration.

Humphrey did not want his proposal to be seen as an anti-Communist measure; rather, he hoped it would be a reflection of "our own elevating visions of the kind of world in which we would like to see mankind live." He proposed to start with a core of five hundred volunteers in the first year, building to five thousand in the fourth year, who would be sent only to countries that invited them. To assure skeptics and conservatives that the volunteers were not draft dodgers, they would serve for three years (not two, as in the military), be subject to call-up in time of war or national emergency, be paid the same as enlisted men, and have to serve in the reserves after leaving the corps, but not receive veteran's benefits.[36]

Kennedy established the Peace Corps on a pilot basis by Executive Order on March 1, 1961, and named his brother-in-law Sargent Shriver, who had managed Kennedy family enterprises in Chicago, as executive director. The goal was to promote American values over those of the Soviets. Humphrey introduced legislation to the Senate Foreign Relations Committee to make the Peace Corps permanent, with an initial appropriation of $40 million. The president signed the bill in September. Volunteers would undergo full FBI field investigation, be paid $50 to $75 per month, and serve for about two years.

Within three years, 7,500 Americans were working in forty-five countries, with demand far exceeding supply. The Peace Corps became a mainstay of American institutions, drawing bipartisan political support over the next half-century, with some 200,000 volunteers, chiefly younger people, but many older persons, serving in 139 countries. The Peace Corps' enduring success—although it raised American prestige more than the economies of recipient nations—has been cited as a major Kennedy administration legacy, but Humphrey was the one who envisioned, authored, and promoted this agency that reflected his strong belief in people-to-people diplomacy as a means to advance a more peaceful world.[37]

Humphrey's second major achievement in 1961 was the creation of the Arms Control and Disarmament Agency (ACDA). He was a strong national defense proponent but branded the Soviet-American nuclear arms race a "mutual suicide pact" and led all politicians in promoting arms control. As a member of the Foreign Relations Committee, he had managed to establish his Disarmament subcommittee in 1955, and he scored a major political coup in 1958 by sponsoring hearings that led to disarmament talks in Geneva and American-Soviet accord on voluntary suspension of atomic testing. But the 1960 U-2 episode halted further disarmament talks.[38]

President Kennedy stressed the urgency of arms control in his first State of the Union address in January 1961 and named John J. McCloy, former high commissioner to Germany, as his disarmament adviser. In May, Kennedy proposed to Congress to create a disarmament agency and privately assured Humphrey in July the administration supported establishing such an agency to foster arms control.[39]

Humphrey promptly introduced legislation, written with McCloy, to create an Arms Control and Disarmament Agency with its own director and staff.

Humphrey cultivated bipartisan support that included Rusk, McNamara, Chairman of the Joint Chiefs of Staff (JCS) General Lyman Lemnitzer, and Eisenhower and former high-ranking civilian and military leaders of his administration. Humphrey publicly contended that military preparedness and diplomatic preparedness were two sides of the same coin called "national security." Working for peace required long-term planning, paying, and sacrificing. But the alternative to arms control was nuclear war, when there would be "no place to hide" and "someone might crawl out from under a rock and say 'I think we won.'"[40]

The legislation made it through Congress despite growing international tension over the building of the Berlin Wall in August 1961, the Soviets ending their suspension of atomic testing in September—which Humphrey denounced as a "war against humanity"—and opposition of conservative senators Russell, chairman of the Armed Services Committee, and Republican Barry Goldwater of Arizona, who disdained a new "mother-love type of agency." Kennedy signed the bill into law in September; he termed its passage a "political miracle," which he attributed chiefly to Humphrey and McCloy. The ACDA was to be housed in the State Department, with its director reporting both to Kennedy and to Dean Rusk, and serving as Rusk's principal arms control adviser.

ACDA's purpose was to propose how to limit nuclear weapons, create a stable deterrence, and burnish the American image. The agency was to carry out federal research on arms control, manage US participation in international negotiations, keep the public informed, and help to establish and operate control systems to monitor treaties. Humphrey's former staffer Betty Goetz, well versed in arms control issues, was named as deputy to the first director, William C. Foster. The agency would have difficulties getting reports from the Pentagon, but it played the lead role in the next decade in promoting the 1963 Limited Test Ban Treaty, the 1968 Nuclear Non-Proliferation Treaty, and the 1972 Biological Weapons Convention—signal achievements resounding to Humphrey's lasting credit.[41]

Humphrey strongly supported the administration's successful effort to raise the federal minimum wage from $1.00 to $1.25 per hour and broadening the definition of interstate commerce to include companies doing more than $1 million per year of business, thus adding 4 million new workers covered by the bill. But conservatives "washed out," or excluded, 150,000 poorly paid workers in large laundries in the South.[42]

Humphrey, who had long supported federal aid to education, helped push through a modest White House bill providing $2.6 billion over three years for teachers' salaries and construction for primary and secondary schools despite conservatives' long-standing insistence this would bring federal control over local schools. Kennedy's bill, however, did not include aid to religious schools, which he viewed as unconstitutional and also worried that as a Catholic he would be charged with favoritism. Conservatives on the House Rules Committee initially blocked the bill with help from the Catholic Church, which wanted aid for parochial schools included. Humphrey favored this and helped fashion a compromise, with an NDEA bill amended to permit long-term, low-interest government loans to parochial schools for special projects, including building math, science, and language facilities.

Kennedy took a hands-off stance, but Catholic religious leaders insisted on one inclusive bill, fearful that if the education bill passed first, loans to Catholic schools would be rejected, but if the loans bill went first, the three liberal Catholics on the House Rules Committee who voted for it would face political challenges. The deadlock enabled conservatives on the committee to table both bills. Humphrey and Senator Wayne Morse, who chaired the Education subcommittee, were embittered at the House Rules Committee and the Catholic Church for blocking their Senate-passed aid to education bill, and many others blamed Kennedy for having lost Congress.[43]

Humphrey remained Kennedy's firm supporter, however, despite events in 1961 that seemed to undercut the president's standing and the nation's prestige. On April 12, the Soviet Union became the first country to put a man in space when cosmonaut Yuri Gagarin orbited the earth in ninety minutes. Humphrey said that the United States had to "wake up completely" to the Soviet challenge on every domestic and world front, and he soon lent support to the president's call in late May for the United States to become the first nation to land a man on the moon.[44]

Kennedy signed on to a CIA plan developed in the Eisenhower era to support an invasion of Cuba by some fifteen hundred exiles—trained by the United States chiefly in Guatemala—that was intended to spur uprisings that would topple Fidel Castro's government. Numerous advisers warned Kennedy that the attack would not succeed and would inspire anti-American antagonism and undermine his presidency. But his strong anti-Communist, anti-Castro views, combined with smooth CIA presentations, led the president to approve this plot. The consequence was the "perfect failure" at the Bay of Pigs on Cuba's southern coast on April 17, when Castro's forces quickly captured most of the invaders. Castro and Latin American leaders were enraged at US action, Europeans were dumbfounded, and Khrushchev pledged to protect Cuba against a future attack.[45]

Humphrey publicly conceded that the invasion was a "fiasco" and lamented privately, "Oh, how we botched it—and for no reason." His chief concern was harm to US prestige, but he believed that Kennedy would learn from his "biggest mistake." He also said that the United States had to learn to make "common cause" with the non-Communist Left that included labor, students, intellectuals, and other reform leaders or face "certain revolution" that would make Castro's regime seem tame. "We must learn . . . to understand the revolutionary spirit where it burns."[46]

Humphrey also stood by Kennedy after the president's stormy meeting with Khrushchev in Vienna in early June. The Soviet leader brushed off a test ban treaty and again insisted that the United States sign a peace treaty with the GDR (East Germany) that would allow Berlin to become a demilitarized, free city; otherwise, the Soviets would soon sign a separate treaty with the GDR, forcing the United States to renegotiate its access to West Berlin with Walter Ulbricht's Communist government. Kennedy said that the United States would not allow itself to be expelled from Berlin; Khrushchev replied that the United States would have to choose between war and peace, and the president retorted that it was "going to be a cold winter." He also confided to *New York Times* columnist and Washington bureau chief James Reston that Khrushchev "just beat the hell out of me."[47]

Humphrey was more sanguine; he said that the conference gave America's allies new confidence in its leadership and in Kennedy's ability to direct US foreign policy. The senator went to Geneva to assess the "hopelessly bogged down" disarmament talks and upon return repeatedly emphasized that the Soviet Union confronted a major food crisis, Khrushchev was struggling to stay in power, and the Soviets would not go to war over Berlin. He urged Kennedy to take the play over Berlin away from Khrushchev by coordinating an allied demand for free elections in Eastern Europe and to use a national address to warn Americans about the dangers posed by Khrushchev's threat to sign a separate treaty with the GDR. Humphrey also urged the president to increase the number of Strategic Air Command planes on alert and deploy more submarines with Polaris missiles.[48]

In a speech on July 25, Kennedy called Berlin the "great testing place of Western courage and will" and insisted that the Communists would never be allowed to drive the Americans from the city. He asked Congress for $3.5 billion in defense funding, and he called up the reserves. The speech led Khrushchev to tell Ulbricht to go ahead with his long-proposed plan to seal the East–West Berlin border. On August 13, the GDR put down a barbed wire barrier between East and West Berlin, and four days later soldiers began to erect a twelve-foot-high concrete block wall, with crossing points and guard towers.[49]

Humphrey contended this decision derived from weakness. East Germany lagged well behind West Germany economically and faced a critical, growing exodus—mainly through Berlin—of its people, especially its most skilled workers, that ran to one hundred thousand in the first half of 1961 and more than a thousand people daily by August. Khrushchev sought to "save" the GDR by allowing it to erect a wall that prevented its own people from leaving while allowing Western allies access to East Berlin through established checkpoints. "It is not a very nice solution but a wall is a hell of a lot better than a war," the president said to an aide.[50]

Humphrey agreed. He urged against retaliation, insistent that Khrushchev had suffered a major psychological and political defeat. The barrier did not harm West Germany, he said, only East Germany, whose people were restless under Communist rule. But the United States, he told his Senate colleagues, had to make clear to everyone that West Berlin and its two million inhabitants were a vital interest for the United States, which would not bargain away the rights of others even at the prospect of war.[51]

There was no confrontation, although in October, US and Soviet tanks faced off at the midcity "Checkpoint Charlie" crossing when GDR guards demanded that US officials show identification despite riding in a US military car that entitled them to unobstructed passage. Kennedy communicated through a back channel with Khrushchev to end the brief crisis—the only direct US-Soviet military confrontation of the Cold War—and thereafter both countries accepted their separate spheres of influence in the two Germanys.[52]

✦ ✦ ✦

After Congress adjourned in late September 1961, Humphrey traveled for six weeks in Europe and the Middle East and in Latin America for three weeks. He spoke with numerous heads of state and foreign ministers, as well as a broad array of politicians and citizens from all walks of life, and he gave numerous public talks, held several press conferences, and wrote three newspaper articles and memoranda for Kennedy and Rusk. He enjoyed press coverage that referred to him as one of the most influential members of the Senate and the president's "right hand man" there.[53]

His first major stop was Rome, where he met with twenty-five East-West parliamentarians, with more than half of them having come from Eastern Europe and the Soviet Union, including Khrushchev's son-in-law, Alexei Adjubei, editor of *Izvestia*, and prominent Soviet journalist Ilya Ehrenburg. Humphrey emphasized that disarmament was the most important issue of the day, touted his role in creation of the ACDA, and said that the Americans and Soviets had to be catalysts for disarmament. Asked directly by Ehrenburg about

Berlin, he urged moderation of the "tone of vituperation and rhetoric," but the United States would not allow a free city to "die on the vine." If the Soviets pushed the Americans too far, "there will be conflict," he said.

But Humphrey did not rule out resolving the Berlin issue as part of a larger settlement of the German problem; nor did he try to preclude—to Adjubei's surprise—the Soviets signing a separate treaty with East Germany. Humphrey reiterated that the wall was "a sign of weakness." He told the East European group that they worried too much about a rearmed Germany, which had only twelve divisions contained within NATO. His remarks earned enthusiastic applause.[54]

In London, Humphrey told Prime Minister Harold Macmillan that it was better for all of the allied leaders, not just Kennedy and Macmillan, to consult on Berlin, and that there was no "German problem, only one with the Kremlin." In Bonn, Humphrey urged Chancellor Konrad Adenauer to support Kennedy's negotiating with the Russians to preclude later charges of "appeasement," and at a press conference labeled the Berlin Wall the symbol of a "prison state."[55]

During a quick stop in Brussels, Humphrey said that the United States and the European community together constituted the most powerful political, economic, and military power in history, and there was no reason to yield to Soviet pressure. In Warsaw—where he was the first American to speak on Polish national television—he talked at length with Edward Ochab, deputy chairman of the Polish Council of State and second in command to Communist Party chieftain Wladyslaw Gomulka. Humphrey tried to make the case for Poland serving as a bridge or buffer between East and West, but Ochab was unrelenting in his support for the Russian position on Berlin and the threat of FRG militarism, despite Humphrey's insistence that West Germany's military strength was contained.[56]

Humphrey summarized his European findings in a long memorandum to Kennedy in which he urged the president to reach out to Adenauer, who he said was prepared to support the president's taking the lead in NATO in demanding assurance from the Russians regarding access to West Berlin and the right of the city's inhabitants to maintain close ties to West Germany. He also cautioned that Europeans were concerned that the United States was not thinking enough about nonmilitary responses to harassment over access to Berlin. West Berlin had become "a showcase for the success of Western Germany," and Europe's resurgence was "an eye-opener even for an American." No one who saw this, he concluded, would believe that Communism was the wave of the future.[57]

Humphrey reiterated his view in several newspaper articles that the United States would back its commitment to West Berlin with force if necessary, that the Berlin Wall was an "act of despair," and that Khrushchev's action was designed to prevent the GDR from "bleeding to death" as a result of its citizens fleeing the country. Most important, the economic tidal wave of the New Europe was now "lapping at the shores of Khrushchev's empire," and the United States needed to weigh forging a new Atlantic Community.[58]

Humphrey continued his travels with a trip to Cairo, where he met with Egyptian leader Gamal Abdel Nasser, whose 1958 merger of his country with Syria to form the United Arab Republic had just been ended by Syrian military officers who charged the Egyptian leader with monopolizing power. Nasser stressed his need for economic aid, which Humphrey pledged to seek through the Agency for International Development for public and private development and he let pass his host's charge that Israel intended to attack Egypt. From Cairo, Humphrey made brief trips to Lebanon, where again he was appalled at the state of Arab refugee camps, and to Syria, which he believed was in great need of capital and technical assistance. In Jordan, he found Amman to be a developing city, but the rest of the country appeared terribly poor, with no help coming from other oil-rich Arab states, and King Hussein seemed unable to act in advance of problems, although privately he spoke in friendly terms about Israel.[59]

In Israel, Humphrey found Prime Minister David Ben Gurion "not too flexible" in his belief that his country could not absorb more than one hundred to five hundred Arab refugees a month; the vast majority needed to be resettled in Arab lands, statements Humphrey did not dispute. His talks with Foreign Minister Golda Meir and other high officials, as well as his travel throughout the country, left him impressed with Israel's housing projects, educational, medical, and scientific facilities, and treatment of elderly and young people. The United States had a great stake in the country as an ally, he wrote, not because of its military strength or the American Jewish community, but because "the Israelis know how to find water." Humphrey was disappointed in Turkey because this NATO member seemed "too neutralist" in its Cold War stance, but he was delighted that in Greece, another NATO ally, the Communists had just taken a "good licking" in recent elections, and he called for the United States to help the country with its heavy defense expenditures.[60]

His final trip after a brief stay home was to South America. His reports called for raising the living standard of the underprivileged and poor people: "I have never seen so many of them as I have seen here," he said in speaking about Chile, but it was equally important to lift up the indigenous people in Ecuador, Colombia, and Peru—where "the Communists are working day and night."

He urged the United States to increase its foreign aid and help Latin America undertake genuine land reform, diversify its agriculture, establish price supports for its produce, stabilize the prices of its raw materials exports, step up assistance under the recently established Alliance for Progress, and look to establish an inter-American free trade program—"a Common Market for the Western Hemisphere that would rival Europe's Common Market." This, the cold warrior in him noted, "would put Castro and Communism on the run."

In a further moment of optimism, he urged President Kennedy and his wife, Jacqueline, to undertake a major tour of Latin America to signal that the Alliance for Progress was as much a historic program as the Marshall Plan. The southern hemisphere needed not only a New Deal but a program of "New Hope"; if the test for liberalism in the 1930s was the domestic economy, he said, the test of liberalism in the 1960s would be foreign policy.[61]

11

TRAGEDY AND TRIUMPH

Throughout 1962, Humphrey said that "an alliance between conservative Republicans and Dixiecrats, who are nothing but Republicans with a southern accent," was blocking key administration bills. He and Vice President Johnson told McGeorge Bundy, the president's national security adviser and White House confidant, that Kennedy had to become more visible on Capitol Hill. Bundy reported to the president that both men spoke with great commitment to him and his program, and former president Truman wrote to Kennedy that it was time to "cuss 'em & give 'em hell."[1]

Kennedy took to the campaign trail for Democrats in September just as Central Intelligence Agency (CIA) reconnaissance by U-2 planes spotted high-riding Soviet ships with huge crates on deck traveling to Cuba. Khrushchev denied rumors of Soviet missiles and sent word through Ambassador Anatoly Dobrynin that he would not put "offensive weapons" in Cuba or cause trouble before the elections. He denounced the stationing of US missiles across Europe, including thirty Jupiter missiles in Italy and fifteen in Turkey near Russia's border. Khrushchev also declared the Monroe Doctrine an invalid basis for US action in Latin America. Kennedy warned on September 4 that Soviet missiles in Cuba would raise the gravest issues and asked Congress for standby authority to call up 150,000 reserves, but he said on September 13 that Cuba posed no imminent threat.[2]

Humphrey chastised "swaggering irresponsibles" in Congress for seeking "to make political capital" and supported a near unanimous Senate resolution on September 29 authorizing the president to use force if necessary to deal with a Cuban or externally supported military threat. Humphrey also rebutted Khrushchev: the Monroe Doctrine still enabled the United States to resist any

European nation's effort to extend its system to Latin America, he said, and to act unilaterally against any security threat.[3]

When told at a State Department briefing on October 5 that the United States was talking to Caribbean nations about how to deal with Cuba, Humphrey demanded to know why the United States had not already decided on means "to help the freedom fighters inside Cuba." He proposed using tactics that "Red" guerrillas had adopted in South Vietnam and fixing a "program to over-throw Castro." If he did not get word quickly of a proper plan, he threatened to raise the issue on the Senate floor.

He went to the White House to complain that his State Department briefing was a "disgrace" and that Democrats' lack of an "affirmative policy" toward Cuba would harm them in the coming elections. He urged supplying "arms and money" to Cuban exiles and others to overthrow Castro, but when Kennedy did not respond, he took it as a sign to leave. On October 16, amid persistent claims about missiles in Cuba, Humphrey brushed aside charges that Kennedy was not being tough enough. The United States, he said, had "more power in Turkey today, on Russia's border, than Khrushchev will ever be able to put into Cuba."[4]

The White House received its first U-2 surveillance pictures of the ongoing installation of Soviet medium- and intermediate-range missile launchers and presence of IL-28 nuclear-capable bombers in Cuba on October 16. Kennedy formed an Executive Committee (ExComm) of the National Security Council (NSC), consisting of senior cabinet officers and diplomatic, military, and intel-ligence officials, to weigh a response to the Soviet action. Nearly all the ExComm members and the Joint Chiefs of Staff favored a military strike but drew back out of concern about a "Pearl Harbor" attack and likely Soviet retal-iation at the United States. Kennedy chose to begin with Defense Secretary McNamara's proposed "quarantine" of Cuba to stop and search ships and remove weapons. The president noted that the United States might need to express willingness to remove its missiles from Italy and Turkey if the Soviets raised this issue.[5]

The president informed congressional leaders, including Humphrey, of his quarantine decision on October 22. He said a military strike would kill Russian soldiers in Cuba, and it would be "*one hell* of a gamble" to assume missiles would not be fired, and the Soviets might also seize Berlin. The congressmen reluctantly deferred to Kennedy's course despite pressure from some senators for immediate strikes on Cuba.[6]

Humphrey was far more cautious; he inquired about the prospect of a UN-sponsored conference with Khrushchev. Kennedy said that the United

States had already asked the United Nations to request that the Soviets remove their missiles and added that US missiles in Turkey and Italy would complicate America's bargaining position. He joked with Humphrey that if he had known in 1960 how hard his job would be, he would have let the senator win. Humphrey said that was why he had let Kennedy win. Shortly, the president informed the nation about missiles in Cuba and said that the United States would regard an attack from there as coming from the Soviet Union.[7]

Humphrey said that the United States could not tolerate Soviet missiles in Cuba or a "squeeze play" in Berlin, and it was better to risk war than do nothing. Taking a cue from Kennedy about the Jupiter missiles, he warned that pressure for their removal could lead to war, although he added that thus far Soviet action had been limited.[8]

Khrushchev declared the quarantine "banditry," but Russian tankers stopped well short of its line, while the United States halted some ships and let others pass. On October 26, the Soviet leader wrote Kennedy that if the United States pledged not to invade Cuba, there would be no need for Russian military specialists or missiles there. The president, unable to get the ExComm to agree to exchange removal of Turkey's Jupiters (despite their being obsolete) for dismantling the Cuban missiles, sent his brother Robert to discuss this with Dobrynin. A second, curt Khrushchev to Kennedy note, however, demanded this swap, but the president feared adverse public and NATO reactions.[9]

The ExComm spent October 27 weighing every option, including a strike on Cuba, when Kennedy and his advisers decided to ignore Khrushchev's second letter demanding a missile swap and instead accept his first proposal for an American pledge not to invade Cuba—insisting the Russians dismantle their missiles in Cuba and that they reply by the next day.[10]

The president again sent Robert Kennedy to tell Dobrynin about this decision. When Dobrynin asked about the Turkish missiles, the attorney general said that if they were the only obstacle to agreement, the president, bound by NATO protocol, would withdraw them in four or five months—but this accord had to remain secret.[11]

The next morning, Khrushchev, ignoring Castro's overnight message urging the firing of nuclear missiles from Cuba, informed his Presidium members that it was necessary to "retreat" to save the world from a "nuclear catastrophe" and dictated a public letter to President Kennedy agreeing to return—with UN verification—the missiles in Cuba to Russia in exchange for the United States pledging the island's safety. He said nothing then or later of the deal on Turkish missiles.[12]

Humphrey publicly praised the president's "firm and resolute diplomacy" as having achieved one of America's "greatest victories without firing a shot." The senator also gloated that Khrushchev was surprised that America's allies stood by it, whereas the Soviet leader had no support. But although Kennedy deserved credit for gaining a peaceful solution, Humphrey overlooked that he and other hardline liberals had supported the president's constant attacks on Castro and Cuba from the Bay of Pigs invasion to secret Operation Mongoose efforts to assassinate the Cuban leader, which reinforced Khrushchev's belief that he had to act to preserve Castro and his revolution and fend off PRC charges about not aiding Marxist states.[13]

Happily for Humphrey and the Democrats, the missile crisis did not, as they had feared, adversely affect their party in the November 6 elections. They added 4 Senate seats to hold a 68–32 margin and lost only 4 House seats to retain a 258–176 margin. Humphrey was especially gratified that his DFL ally, liberal state senator Donald M. Fraser, defeated ten-term incumbent Republican congressman Walter Judd in Minneapolis, and DFL lieutenant governor Karl Rolvaag narrowly upset Governor Elmer Andersen. Most rewarding for Humphrey was his successful campaigning in his native South Dakota for his protégé, Food for Peace director George McGovern, who won a very close Senate race and became a strong ally on domestic issues, although later the two men would battle over the Vietnam War and presidential nominations.[14]

The missile crisis also brought talk of disarmament. Humphrey, the foremost congressional exponent of arms control, had been enthused in March 1962 at the start of the eighteen-nation Geneva disarmament conference when he said that it was America's "moral obligation" to pursue control of "weapons of mass destruction." The United States proposed a "General and Complete Disarmament" plan to be monitored by an international agency, but the Soviets refused onsite inspections for existing weapons systems and underground tests. Humphrey assailed Moscow for having built a "monster [state] of secrecy and fear" and warned that when "Communist China" got nuclear weapons capability, "all mankind will live in the shadow of death." By August, he concluded that the United States had to focus on an attainable ban, without onsite monitoring, on testing in the atmosphere, outer space, and underwater, thus curbing radioactive pollution.[15]

Kennedy sought accord with Khrushchev, whose letter ending the nuclear standoff noted that it was time to talk disarmament. The United States pressed its comprehensive test ban proposal. After Khrushchev mistakenly believed that American emissaries said that the United States would lower its demand for eight to ten onsite inspections to three, he hinted at an accord in early 1963. But Humphrey said that the Senate would not ratify a treaty with so few inspections, and Senator Russell's hawkish Armed Services Committee and the JCS opposed virtually any agreement.[16]

Humphrey took heart in spring 1963 after Norman Cousins, *Saturday Review* editor and exponent of limiting nuclear weapons, and Averell Harriman, former ambassador to the Soviet Union and now undersecretary of state for political affairs, reported that Khrushchev was amenable to an accord. Humphrey surprised his Senate colleagues by enlisting Connecticut Democrat Thomas Dodd, an Armed Services Committee member and known hardliner toward the Soviet Union and a test ban, to cosponsor a resolution urging a ban on underwater and atmospheric tests that "contaminated the atmosphere and the oceans." The two senators got thirty-three colleagues, including six Republicans, to join with them—far fewer than the sixty-seven votes needed to ratify a treaty, but a major advance given the support of Dodd, who called Humphrey a "champion of peace and disarmament" and Nobel Peace Prize candidate.[17]

Humphrey had introduced a resolution in early 1961 calling on the United Nations to inquire about Soviet steps to prevent accidental nuclear war, an issue that gained great appeal after the missile crisis and led to US and Soviet negotiators signing an accord in June 1963 establishing direct telegraphic communication (later upgraded to telephone lines) between the United States and Soviet Union to prevent nuclear war by accident or miscalculation. Humphrey could claim to be the "father" of the hot line.[18]

Kennedy made a last push for an arms accord in a speech at American University on June 10, 1963, insisting the United States and Soviet Union were caught in a dangerous and costly cycle of increasing mutual suspicion and weapons rivalry with money that could be better spent fighting "ignorance, poverty, and disease." Most important, he reminded, "we all breathe the same air. We all inhabit the same planet. And we are all mortal." Khrushchev told Harriman that it was "the best statement made by any president since Roosevelt," although in late June, Kennedy, addressing an enormous crowd at the Berlin Wall, challenged anyone who thought Communism the wave of the future to "come to Berlin," and said that freedom's proudest boast was to declare, "Ich bin ein Berliner."[19]

Khrushchev, unfazed, promptly called for a ban on nuclear tests in the atmosphere, outer space, and underwater, all detectable from afar without onsite inspection. Kennedy, supported by Prime Minister Harold Macmillan, sent the experienced Harriman to Moscow, where an agreement was quickly reached, and Humphrey and a bipartisan group of senators accompanied Secretary of State

Dean Rusk for the signing of the American-British-Russian Limited Test Ban Treaty on August 15 in Moscow. The gregarious Humphrey walked the streets and visited parks and train stations, and came away convinced, as he reported to the Senate, that the real American-Soviet contest was not in weapons rivalry but in the societies' lifestyles. The Soviets had a larger population and armies but an obsolete economy, and people in the street who admired his fifty-nine-dollar Botany suit were shocked to learn that it would take two months of their pay to buy it. And foreign students attending the "so-called Moscow Friendship University" longed to attend American schools.[20]

On his return to Washington, Humphrey was met by Kennedy's challenge: "Well, Hubert, now that we have your test ban treaty signed, let's see you get it ratified by a big majority of the Senate." The senator assured this would be done, but asked, "What happens then?" "Then it becomes my treaty," the president replied.

Humphrey's chief concern was not ownership but gaining ratification of the first post-1945 nuclear accord. He emphasized to his colleagues that the treaty was a first step in altering the arms race toward mutual destruction to one that would come to grips with economic, technological, scientific, and political change. He was certain that confronting Khrushchev over Cuba had caused him to back down and to seek a test ban treaty. National security depended not only on weapons but on a society's strength and ability to adapt to a changing world — one in which "we would eulogize the peacemaker as much as we eulogize the warrior." Senators had the right to criticize the treaty, he said, but he quickly rejected as "partisan mischief" Arizona senator Barry Goldwater's proposal to hinge ratification on withdrawal of all Soviet troops from Cuba.[21]

Armed Services Committee members, the military — especially the JCS — and scientists like Edward Teller (father of the hydrogen bomb) alleged that the treaty ceded advantages to the untrustworthy Soviets. The Kennedy administration, however, stressed that it would deepen the growing Sino-Soviet divide, although the president had also appeased the JCS by agreeing to step up underground testing and a weapons buildup. Even skeptics like conservative Senate minority leader Everett Dirksen would say that he did not want his tombstone inscription to read that "he knew what happened at Hiroshima but he did not take a first step." The Senate ratified the treaty by 80–19 in late September, and Kennedy signed it on October 7, remarking to Humphrey, "Hubert, this one is for you. It had better work."[22]

It did. Eighty-six nations soon signed it (but not France or the PRC), and it became the first crucial step toward the 1968 Nuclear Non-Proliferation Treaty, the 1972 Strategic Arms Limitation Treaty (SALT), and later arms accords. Nonetheless,

France, the PRC, and other nations—including Israel, India, Pakistan, and North Korea—would gain nuclear capability.

Nothing defined Humphrey and his liberalism so much as the personal commitment and political energy he brought to securing passage of a historic civil rights act. The battle would be seen as a test of his leadership and, most important, complete the "revolution" he had touched off with his 1948 speech to the Democratic convention.[23]

But the president was at best a "bystander" regarding civil rights. His primary focus was on foreign affairs, and he spoke more forcefully about anti-Communism and even his proposed tax cut than he did about civil rights. He had supported President Truman's "To Secure These Rights" program and accepted—but never endorsed—the 1954 *Brown* decision regarding school desegregation. He was also extremely hesitant to challenge the southern oligarchs who dominated the Senate.

He took civil rights advocate Harris Wofford as a special assistant in 1961, but inaction led to his leaving a year later. Kennedy cajoled Vice President Johnson in 1961 to chair the new President's Committee on Equal Employment Opportunity intended to encourage hiring and promotion of African Americans in government agencies, businesses working under government contract, and labor unions' apprentice programs, but its annual budget was a $425,000 "pittance." And despite having charged during his 1960 campaign that President Eisenhower could have ended discrimination in federally financed housing with "the stroke of a pen," Kennedy waited until after the 1962 election before he issued his executive order, which applied only to future housing construction.[24]

The administration also hesitated to act when the first Freedom Riders, who traveled by bus in spring 1961 to give life to the 1960 Supreme Court decision in *Boynton v. Virginia* banning segregation in interstate travel facilities, were often met by violence from mobs and local police and the National Guard. Only after frightful incidents in Alabama in Anniston, Birmingham, and Montgomery, where Attorney General Kennedy's assistant John Siegenthaler was beaten unconscious, did the administration send US marshals to restore order, but it also sought to have the civil rights groups end their protests. In late 1961, Kennedy had the Interstate Commerce Commission issue and post new rules banning discrimination in interstate travel.[25]

Humphrey praised the Kennedy administration for acting "courageously and efficiently" on behalf of the Freedom Riders. He backed the administration's amendment outlawing the poll tax and legislation making the completion of the sixth grade equal to a literacy requirement to vote in federal elections. Congress would ratify the poll tax bill as the Twenty-Fourth Amendment in January 1964, but southern Democratic and Republican senators filibustered the literacy test bill. Humphrey was disappointed but remained quiet as Kennedy came under fire for not campaigning personally for the bill.[26]

After intransigent city officials in Albany, Georgia, arrested thousands of marchers protesting segregation in summer 1962, Humphrey and nine other senators pleaded for Justice Department intervention, but Attorney General Robert Kennedy insisted that local leaders had to resolve the problems. This brought release of the jailed people but no improvement in African American conditions.

In September 1962, a mob assaulted a team of federal marshals sent to protect James Meredith, an African American air force veteran, whose court-ordered enrollment at the University of Mississippi in Oxford had been forcibly blocked by an unyielding Governor Ross Barnett and state troopers. Weeks of tedious negotiations with Barnett produced no result, and a riotous armed mob assaulted the marshals, wounding twenty-seven by gunshot, with two civilians killed. The president reluctantly agreed to send several thousand US Army troops to restore order and enroll Meredith. Kennedy was appalled at southern whites' treatment of blacks, but he could not identify with the African Americans' passion to gain equal rights.[27]

Humphrey, Democrat Paul Douglas of Illinois, and Republican Kenneth Keating of New York called for substantive congressional action, and the Minnesotan told ADA head Joseph Rauh he would press the president to commit to strong civil rights action. When Congress convened in January 1963, Humphrey again proposed to alter Rule XXII to require only a majority, not two-thirds, vote of all senators to end a filibuster. Southerners blocked this effort, and, much to Humphrey's ire, the White House refused to back his move. Johnson declined to make a parliamentary ruling as Senate president, insisting that the senators had to vote for any rules change.[28]

Humphrey and five other senators urged the president to submit a comprehensive civil rights bill, but he refused. In February 1963, however, concerned that liberal New York Republican governor Nelson Rockefeller might be his opponent in 1964, Kennedy sent his best legislation to date. It aimed to increase black voter registration, make a sixth-grade education proof of literacy in federal elections, provide financial aid to school districts desegregating, and extend the Civil Rights Commission for four years. Humphrey defended the administration against African Americans' complaints that the bill did not address critical issues such as public accommodations, employment, and housing. He warned the DNC that failure to act on civil rights would hurt Democrats in 1964, although he and liberal allies such as Douglas, Joseph Clark of Pennsylvania, and Philip Hart of Michigan agreed not to make legislative proposals without administration backing.[29]

Violent confrontations broke out in April in Birmingham, the nation's most segregated city. King led major protests, was arrested, and penned his "Letter from Birmingham Jail" justifying the civil rights struggle and civil disobedience and warning that the "cup of endurance" was near running over. After his release, King led more marches, and Police Commissioner Eugene "Bull" Connor brought national outrage by ordering lawmen to use clubs, German shepherd dogs, and high-powered water hoses to assail the protesters. Humphrey denounced Connor for "the most shameful attack in American history" that put a "blotch" on the nation's face and warned that Congress had to choose between "a quickened pace of reform or violence."[30]

President Kennedy was appalled by a *New York Times* photo on May 4 of a dog attacking a youngster but was uncertain how to act. He sought to alleviate matters by having his cabinet officers and others press Birmingham business leaders to integrate their stores and provide some white-collar jobs, and he looked to foster voting rights legislation but was doubtful that southerners would allow passage. After bombs exploded at the home of King's brother, the Reverend A. D. King, and at a black-owned motel where civil rights leaders stayed, and sparked riots, Kennedy dispatched troops and federalized the National Guard to restore order. The administration also sent Assistant Attorney General Nicholas Katzenbach and federalized National Guardsmen to compel Alabama governor George Wallace to desist from denying admission to two black students at the state university.[31]

Humphrey did not mince words when he went to the White House in early June to tell the president that he had to lead on the civil rights issue or it would be settled not by the courts but "in the street." He urged submission of a comprehensive bill to cover voting rights, with the attorney general empowered to file civil rights suits as per the Title III stricken from the 1957 bill; desegregation of public facilities; the cutoff of federal funds for state programs that discriminated; and establishment of an FEPC. He pressed Kennedy to solicit support from labor, business, religious, and educational leaders.[32]

The president, laying the groundwork for his bill, declared on June 11 that the nation confronted a "moral issue," namely, whether all Americans would have the equal rights that had been delayed since the Emancipation Proclamation. Kennedy sent his civil rights bill to Congress, despite concern it would have to go to the Senate Judiciary Committee chaired by Mississippi segregationist James Eastland. The bill included provisions to desegregate all public accommodations, withhold federal funds from state programs that discriminated, make a sixth-grade education proof of literacy, empower the attorney general to use a modified Title III to file school desegregation suits, and establish a community relations department to take up local disputes. The major omission was an FEPC.[33]

Humphrey was delighted at this increased civil rights commitment. Speaking to Brandeis University alumni and friends in Washington, he said that America had closed the missile gap and the space gap but not the citizenship gap, "the nation's most tragic failure." Discrimination was not a local problem but a national and international one that "weakens us at home and embarrasses us abroad." But "full citizenship" would soon be won either by law or by violence. He told his Senate colleagues that he and the minority whip, liberal Republican Thomas Kuchel of California, would cosponsor the administration's "bold, courageous, and comprehensive" bill, but it was only the "minimum necessary" to close the citizenship gap. He soon added forty-two more sponsors' names, said that the "ugly" television scenes from Birmingham had helped to arouse a national "awakening," and stated that the only question was when Congress would catch up.[34]

Humphrey was determined to make his case for a labor bill that went far beyond creating an FEPC. Discrimination, he told the Senate, was not the sole barrier to African Americans sharing in the general prosperity. He urged a "totally new approach," an "Equal Employment Opportunity Act" that would rest on an "affirmative philosophy" of equal education and job opportunity and development rather than merely enforcement of nondiscrimination. Black unemployment at 11 percent was more than double white unemployment, which was near 5 percent, but even worse, "production" jobs were decreasing while professional, white-collar, managerial, and technical jobs were increasing steadily. African Americans held only a small fraction of these positions.

Most significant, job disparity derived not just from "intentional" discrimination that an FEPC would police but "impersonal institutional processes" such as an ever-changing job market and lack of sufficient education and job training for African Americans. It was necessary to provide "parity of access" to job creation through federally supported job training programs, with employers managing them, a Labor Department official overseeing them, and an Equal Employment Opportunities Board able to seek redress in federal court in discrimination cases.

Humphrey opposed preferential treatment for any group; he aimed at "affirmative" action regarding equality of education and job training to provide equality of opportunity. He believed gainful employment to be essential to people being integrated into the American mainstream. "People do not feel free so long as they are denied jobs and their families are in want," he said. But he also knew when he submitted his bill on July 24 that the administration was focused chiefly on its civil rights bill—and on averting a riot in Washington.[35]

The president and almost every official and politician, including Humphrey—and some civil rights leaders—initially resisted the "March on Washington for Jobs and Freedom" that King and his supporters planned for August 28. Humphrey feared that violent incidents would derail the civil rights bill. But after the Kennedy administration realized that the march could not be halted, it sought to keep it orderly, while Humphrey told his colleagues that the best way to avert the march was to quit the "endless statements" and "get on the march" to pass a bill aimed at moral and political justice. He hailed the march leaders' "courageous and historic" call for self-discipline.[36]

Humphrey spoke with several hundred Minnesota church members and political representatives who came to march, and he went to the Lincoln Memorial to witness, along with 250,000 people, King's majestic "I Have a Dream" speech. Humphrey extolled this "blessed event." The "experience will live in my memory as long as I live," he told his Senate colleagues. He exhorted them to pass Kennedy's civil rights bill and said he hoped that they would become as excited about abuses of freedom in America as they did about injustice in Cuba. "Let us clean our own house" and come to the world with "clean hearts and consciences."[37]

But on September 15, four Ku Klux Klansmen exploded a bomb at a Birmingham church, killing four young girls attending Sunday school. Humphrey and Senators Kuchel, Philip Hart of Michigan, and New York Republican Jacob Javits asked the president to declare the next Sunday, the one hundredth anniversary of the Emancipation Proclamation, a day of national mourning, but Kennedy issued only a statement of remorse and sent army secretary Kenneth Royall and former West Point football coach Earl "Red" Blaik to mediate the Birmingham crisis.[38]

Humphrey delivered his most scathing civil rights speech, targeting not the "uneducated, the poor, and ill-informed white citizen," but the business and professional leadership of the South who—with their northern counterparts— owned the banks, factories, newspapers, and radio and television stations, and deliberately exploited black Americans through poor education, discrimination, and segregation for the sake of money. He added that this same North-South establishment also opposed improving education, working conditions, and social security for all other Americans. These were "strong words," but

Humphrey said he had considered them carefully. He also read into the *Congressional Record* a letter published in the *Washington Post* from Charles P. Morgan, a thirty-three-year-old white lawyer in Birmingham, who asked of the church bombing: "Who did it?" His answer: "We all did it." Humphrey agreed; this included a political-economic-religious establishment that preserved segregation and discrimination and failed to comply with Supreme Court rulings and "every Senator and Representative" who denied to the world the way things were back home.[39]

Humphrey's primary goal now was to secure a civil rights bill, but the president remained focused on his proposed tax cut and wished to avoid a fight with southern congressmen. He urged Birmingham officials to accept a slim Royall-Blaik proposal to hire some black policemen and firemen and integrate motels and hotels and quickly accepted a weakened version of his original civil rights bill that did little for voting rights, eliminated retail stores from public accommodations, and had no FEPC. But the House Judiciary Committee added provisions to desegregate all public accommodations, withhold federal funds from state programs that discriminated, and create an Equal Employment Opportunity Commission to prevent discrimination by employers. It sent the bill to the Rules Committee, a major barrier chaired by the reactionary Howard Smith of Virginia.[40]

Any further efforts to secure a stronger civil rights bill were postponed as the nation was thrown into a state of shock and despair on November 22 when Kennedy was assassinated in Dallas. He had gone to Texas to try to heal the deep political rift between conservative governor John Connally and liberal senator Ralph Yarborough. As the president's motorcade approached Dealey Plaza at the edge of the city's downtown, Kennedy was shot from a sixth-floor window of the Texas School Book Depository overlooking the plaza by Lee Harvey Oswald, a deeply disgruntled twenty-four-year-old who had served in the marines, defected to and from the Soviet Union, and taken up various causes, including that of a group dedicated to "Fair Play for Cuba."[41]

At the time of the shooting, Hubert and Muriel Humphrey were at a luncheon at the Chilean embassy in Washington with Edward P. Morgan of ABC News and Kennedy aide Ralph Dungan. Morgan got word of it from a telephone call from ABC News; he told Humphrey, who asked Dungan to call the White House, which confirmed the news. Dungan immediately went to the White House and soon called the senator to say that the president was dead. Grief-stricken and struggling to regain his composure, Humphrey informed the luncheon guests. He and Muriel drove to the White House, where they talked with aides before going to his office, and then to Andrews Air Force Base. There, they witnessed—along with McNamara, Bundy, key officials and congressmen, and millions of Americans watching on television—the arrival of Air Force One bearing the slain president's coffin, Jacqueline Kennedy in her blood-stained pink suit, and the newly sworn-in President Lyndon Johnson and his wife, Lady Bird, who kissed Hubert and Muriel, and said, "We need you both so much."[42]

The Humphreys viewed Kennedy lying in state at the Capitol Rotunda on Sunday, November 24, and later hosted dinner for friends—Adlai Stevenson, Orville and Jane Freeman, and Max and Maggie Kampelman. Interrupting the meal, Johnson called to ask Humphrey why the Democrats were allowing a vote on conservative South Dakota Republican senator Karl Mundt's bill blocking government guarantee of credits for the sale of American goods to Europe's Communist nations. Humphrey said that the agreement to vote had been set two weeks earlier, and he was unsure if he had enough votes to defeat the bill. Johnson replied with his usual disdain (most often for liberals): "You fellows don't count votes."

The next day, Humphrey called him to say that he had a 56–37 margin to defeat the bill, and later that night, "dripping satisfaction," he called again to report a final 57–35 vote. Johnson invited Humphrey to his Washington home for a late dinner that included Abe Fortas, his longtime friend, personal attorney, and partner in the influential firm of Arnold, Fortas, and Porter. They reviewed the speech the new president was to give to a joint session of Congress the next day, with Humphrey and Fortas making revisions until 2:00 a.m. Humphrey recalled adding language that reiterated the US commitment to its allies and, where Kennedy had said, "Let us begin," in his Inaugural Address regarding enactment of his New Frontier agenda, Humphrey had Johnson say, "Let us continue," the phrase that would mark the administration's legislative drive in the coming years.[43]

Johnson hailed Kennedy as "the greatest leader of our time" and said that "no memorial oration or eulogy could more eloquently honor" his memory than the earliest passage of a civil rights bill that would make equal rights the law of the land. Americans had talked about this for more than one hundred years, and now it was "time to write it in the books of law." Humphrey thought it a "fine" address, and readied to shepherd through the Senate, despite its hostile southern phalanx, legislation that would transform the civil rights revolution that he had helped to engender sixteen years earlier.[44]

The advanced civil rights bill that the House Judiciary Committee finally agreed upon in November 1963 might not have been reported out of the Rules

Committee had it not been for Ohio Republicans William McCulloch and Clarence Brown, who were committed to their party's Lincoln heritage and led a revolt against Chairman Smith. He gave way on January 30, 1964, but sought to derail the bill by adding the category of "sex" to the prohibition of discrimination based on "race, color, religion, or national origin" in Title VII (Equal Employment) in the belief that this would be a "poison pill" to cause moderate and conservative Republicans and Democrats to oppose the bill—or at least excise the crucial Title VII—because they objected to a perceived expansion of federal authority over workplace hiring. But the House accepted the amendment and on February 10 passed the most sweeping civil rights bill in the nation's history, by 290–132, with the support of 138 Republicans.[45]

No one was happier than the impatient Humphrey. He told Johns Hopkins University students in January that they should be as angry as he was at the "extremism and hatred" that had prompted the bombings, riots, and killings in Alabama and Mississippi and at the indifference of public officials that led to the breakdown of law. But anger had to be translated into action, and when the House passed its civil rights bill, he made clear publicly that he and the president planned a "fight to the finish," with "no wheels, no deals, no compromise."[46]

Humphrey relished becoming the "generalissimo"—as his Louisiana colleague Russell Long dubbed him—of the civil rights bill. He did not hesitate when Majority Leader Mike Mansfield and Johnson asked him to be the bill's floor manager, although the president launched into his usual taunt: "You have got this opportunity, Hubert, but you liberals will never deliver." Liberals did not know the Senate rules, he said, and were always off making speeches instead of counting Senate votes. Johnson insisted that he and Humphrey had to "get" Everett Dirksen, the veteran Senate minority leader from Illinois, who imagined himself an orator—and loved to hear himself talking. He had to be given "a piece of the action," Johnson said; Humphrey would have to "spend time with Ev Dirksen. You've got to play Ev Dirksen. . . . He's got to look good all the time."[47]

Humphrey knew better than Johnson how to play Dirksen: by bearing with his many meaningless amendments and insisting that the issue was "a moral, not a partisan one" to win the necessary twenty to twenty-five Republican votes from the Midwest and West to reach sixty-seven votes to end a filibuster. There were sixty-seven Democrats in the Senate, but twenty-one were southerners who would follow Georgia's Russell, a segregationist and leader of the "Dixie Association" and skilled parliamentarian adept at marshaling three cadres of six senators for floor presence to sustain a filibuster. Not once in eleven efforts since the Senate had adopted Rule XXII in 1917 had liberals been able to halt a filibuster of a civil rights bill.[48]

Humphrey organized civil rights supporters as never before. He and Kuchel named Democratic and Republican floor captains to master the intricacies of each of the bill's titles; held morning "skull sessions," with Justice Department officials and civil rights leaders present, to discuss issues likely to be debated; and published a daily bipartisan newspaper outlining developments. Six Democratic senators were given "military police" duty to keep tabs on every senator's whereabouts (including travel) and to post daily duty rosters to assure that thirty-six Democrats and fifteen Republicans were always on hand to meet a quorum call (fifty-one) to prevent adjournment. The Humphrey forces fell short only once in the next five months on April 4, when a group had to be rushed back from a Washington Senators baseball game. "We have returned," Humphrey playfully said. He resisted around-the-clock sessions out of respect for every senator's well-being and agreed to allow a vote on a bill providing price supports for wheat and cotton growers before dealing with the civil rights bill to try to win support from senators from western states.[49]

Humphrey mastered every title of the bill, met challenges—often barbed— with knowledge and wit, and never lost his temper. When Senator A. Willis Robertson of Virginia droned on while waving a Confederate flag, which he handed to Humphrey as he concluded, the majority whip praised Robertson for his knowledge and graciousness and called the flag a symbol of bravery. Humphrey also "got" Dirksen by allowing him more than ample time to talk and to offer amendments, and he agreed to meetings at the hideaway in the Republican minority leader's office rather than in the Democratic majority leader's suite or in his own office.

Humphrey cared only about the meeting and not whether it was in a "night-club," the "bottom of a mine," or a "manhole." Above all, he afforded the egocentric Dirksen the limelight. During a joint appearance on *Meet the Press*, Humphrey predicted victory for the civil rights forces but said that Dirksen "would not be found wanting" when the crucial vote came because "he is not only a great senator but a great American" who would become the bill's "champion." Johnson promptly called Humphrey: "You're doing right now. . . . Don't let those bomb throwers, now, talk you out of seeing Dirksen. . . . You drink with Dirksen. You talk with Dirksen. You listen to Dirksen."[50]

Humphrey listened. The House-passed bill was delivered to the Senate on February 17, and nine days later Mansfield maneuvered to have it placed directly on the calendar rather than, as customary, have it sent to the hostile Eastland's Judiciary Committee. Liberal Democrat Wayne Morse of Oregon, a former law school dean, expressed concern about precedent and the need to have a committee establish legislative intent, vital for future lawsuits. But

Humphrey stood with Mansfield: the Judiciary Committee was "the graveyard of civil rights bills" and had buried Kennedy's bill in 1963. Debate on whether to take up this new bill began on March 9, with Humphrey insistent that a century had passed since the Emancipation Proclamation, and it was time to deal with civil rights: "Let us begin. We are already very late."[51]

Southerners began to filibuster the motion to take up the bill, but for the first time, Humphrey and other senators challenged their statements rather than allow endless talk. When Democrat Allen Ellender of Louisiana said that few Negroes were registered in the South because there were no expensive voter registration drives, Humphrey retorted that there were five southern counties where no Negroes were registered but white registration ran from 65 percent to 118 percent. Ellender admitted that Negroes were kept from voting because they might be elected to office. And when Democrat John Stennis of Mississippi said that the bill would upset the South's social relationships, Humphrey said that the bill was not about social relationships but "better educational opportunity and better jobs." Civil rights was a "moral issue" and a "national issue," and he importuned church leaders, who would play a vital role, and big business— which stood to gain better trained workers—to lobby their congressmen. Finally, the southerners decided to save their energy to filibuster the legislation itself, and on March 26 they allowed the Senate to vote 67–17 to make the bill pending business and 50–34 not to send it to committee.[52]

Humphrey opened the formal debate on March 30, with southerners absent. For almost three and a half hours, he explicated the constitutional basis and purpose of each title of the bill. The most significant ones were: equal application of voting requirements in federal elections (I); nondiscrimination in public accommodations (II) and in municipal and state facilities (III); assistance for desegregation of public schools (IV) with the attorney general authorized to bring suits in all four titles; expansion of power and four-year tenure of the Civil Rights Commission (V); prohibition of discrimination by agencies that received federal money, with loss of funds for violations (VI); and no discrimination by employers and unions on the basis of race, color, religion, sex, or national origin, with an Equal Employment Opportunity Commission (EEOC) vested with enforcement power (VII). Other provisions dealt with collecting voting data, moving cases from state to federal court, establishing a Community Relations Service to deal with local claims of discrimination; and later, after protracted debate, an eleventh title would provide for jury trials in criminal contempt cases arising from Titles II–VII.[53]

Humphrey deftly explained constitutional issues, such as the federal government's use of the commerce clause to prohibit discrimination in public accommodations and shrewdly pointed to absurdities such as motels in Georgia and South Carolina that accepted dogs but not blacks. He was emphatic that the denial of human dignity (a "Fifth Freedom") demanded legal redress and that vast discrepancy between spending on white schools and black schools had grave implications for education and ultimately employment, where discrimination was rampant, as it was in public places. This had created a vast reservoir of anger, he warned, that would lead to radical action. America was amid an anticolonial struggle, and it had to give up the "yoke of superiority" that it imposed on Negroes "or it will be torn from us—and rightly so."[54]

Humphrey had to be accommodating, but when South Carolina's J. Strom Thurmond called the Fourteenth Amendment, providing equal protection of the laws, illegitimate because it was ratified during Reconstruction, Humphrey was openly disdainful that anyone would not regard the amendment in the same vein as the Bill of Rights. By contrast, he assured critics that under Title V, the cutoff of funds to municipal or state programs that discriminated would occur only "as a last resort." He also sought to assure his colleagues and working-class voters that Title VII's ban on employment discrimination would not compel employers to "hire on the basis of percentage or quota related to color, race, religion, or national origin." Merit was the sole determinant, he said.[55]

Humphrey was confident of public support. More than 60 percent of all Americans (70 percent in the North) favored the bill, and major Protestant, Catholic, and Jewish organizations held demonstrations, prayer meetings, and packed House and then Senate galleries. Humphrey courted and encouraged the clergy and told Rauh and Clarence Mitchell Jr., chief lobbyist of the NAACP, that "the secret of the passage of the bill is the prayer groups. . . . Just wait until [senators] start hearing from church people."[56]

Humphrey worried, however, when Alabama's segregationist governor George Wallace won 34 percent of the vote in April in the Democratic primary in Wisconsin, indicative of anti–civil rights views in a northern state. He feared that civil rights protests might cause violence, such as the Congress of Racial Equality's mid-April threat to block traffic on the Long Island Expressway leading to the opening of the World's Fair in Queens, New York. "Civil wrongs do not bring civil rights," Humphrey intoned, although similar tactics were employed in the South.[57]

Humphrey's chief legislative concern was dealing with Dirksen, who introduced forty amendments to Title VII (Equal Employment), giving state employment agencies primacy over the EEOC and denying it power to gain court injunctions to halt discriminatory hiring practices. No one was certain whether Dirksen aimed to gut the bill or sought, as he claimed, a "workable" and "equitable" one. The minority leader soon backed off his proposal to stifle the EEOC and reduced his amendments to a dozen minor ones. But Georgia Democrat Herman E. Talmadge opened a new front by proposing to amend the Federal Criminal Code to require a jury trial in all criminal contempt cases—not just civil rights ones—with southerners wrongly arguing, as they had during debate on the 1957 Civil Rights Act, that the Constitution guaranteed jury trials in these cases. Humphrey promptly outflanked Talmadge by having Justice Department lawyers work with Mansfield and Dirksen to craft a new amendment that they cosponsored allowing jury trials in all criminal contempt cases arising under the proposed law, but only at the discretion of the judge (not the defendant), with penalties in nonjury cases limited to thirty days in jail and three hundred dollars.[58]

Dirksen proposed to make desegregation in public accommodations virtually voluntary, and he sought to negotiate directly with Johnson in exchange for providing Republican votes to end the filibuster, which Humphrey called "the subject of national disgust and shame." He urged the president to "lay down the law" to Dirksen, who went to the White House on April 29 but got no concession. Humphrey grew weary at the lack of legislative progress, and he warned of a long, hot summer and "wild men" taking over. He carelessly remarked that the White House was amenable to bargaining over the bill, which led Johnson to give him "unshirted hell."[59]

The filibuster was tiring Humphrey's forces, and when on May 6, Russell maneuvered a vote on Talmadge's slightly amended original noxious jury trial amendment, they barely defeated it by a 46–45 vote. An angry Humphrey blamed Senate inaction on civil rights, not just on the southerners' "adult delinquency," but 81 other senators' failure to show more than "jelly for a spine" and to vote cloture, which now seemed to be doubtful.[60]

Dirksen and many Republicans, however, appeared ready to pass a modified civil rights bill, which they thought would increase their party's appeal to voters in November. On May 5, Humphrey, Dirksen, and their backers, along with Attorney General Kennedy and his chief lawyers, began serious talks that soon led to accord on two major issues. In public accommodations cases, state agencies would be used first to try to resolve a conflict before the federal government became involved, but only if there was a "pattern or practice of discrimination." Similarly, in employment cases, individuals would have to file their complaints with the EEOC, which would look to extant local or state law for resolution. Failing that, an individual had to file suit, again with the attorney general able to intervene only if there was a pattern or practice of discrimination. "Pattern or practice" pointed to the law's focus on the South, but the emphasis on need to seek local resolution before allowing federal action gave a nod to states' rights. Humphrey would give no more; and he arranged that when Dirksen proposed another amendment to Title VI, liberal senator Joseph Clark would yell, "It's a goddamn sellout," and storm out of the room. The minority leader halted his tactics.[61]

The negotiators agreed on May 13 on a "clean bill" that included the Mansfield-Dirksen jury trial amendment. Kennedy said that the bill was "perfectly satisfactory," and the group proposed to substitute it for the original House measure to avoid the inevitable delays of reconciling two separate bills in a conference committee. Humphrey immediately called Johnson to say that they now had "a much better bill than anyone ever dreamed possible" and that Dirksen had been "terrific." The president told the Illinois senator he was "worthy of the land of Lincoln," and "I will see that you get proper attention and credit for passing this bill."[62]

Humphrey, still worried about mustering sixty-seven votes to end the filibuster, asked Mitchell to get his NAACP friends and AFL-CIO people to "put their fingers on those eighty-one senators" who were not part of Russell's bloc. Humphrey also rejected Dirksen's proposal to hold a cloture vote for each title of the bill, fended off Johnson's call for "round-the-clock" sessions, and publicly denounced the "lies" that the "peddlers of fear" and "demagogues" were telling about the bill. On May 20, he issued his own "special newsletter" to rebut falsehoods and establish the legislative intent in critical titles regarding school desegregation and employment.[63]

Although afterward many civil rights advocates would make differing arguments regarding the latter two issues, Humphrey said that the bill did not permit "transportation or busing of students to end racial imbalance," nor was school segregation arising from housing patterns illegal. Nor did the bill permit the government to require an employer or union to hire or accept for membership a quota of employees for any particular minority, nor give preference to "Negroes or to any other group" to "maintain racial balance." And inadvertent or accidental discrimination was not a violation; there had to be intent.[64]

Russell sought delay, hoping that if Wallace, who had done well two weeks earlier in Indiana's primary, did well in Maryland's primary on May 19 that support for the bill would wane. The Alabaman won 43 percent of the vote and proclaimed that "we'd have won it all if it hadn't been for the nigger bloc vote." Dirksen told his constituents that nothing was eternal except change and, borrowing words from Victor Hugo that Humphrey had entered in the *Congressional Record* in August 1957, declared that "stronger than all the armies is an idea whose time has come"—and that was true for the 1964 Civil Rights

Act. Democrats and Republicans soon voted in separate caucuses to put the bill before the Senate.[65]

Humphrey graciously ceded to Dirksen the honor of introducing the bill on May 26. The Minnesotan and Mansfield lavished praise on the Republican and announced a vote on cloture for June 9. Russell said that the southerners would allow voting on amendments, but Mansfield rejected this ploy to delay the vote on cloture, for which Humphrey said he had the votes "by a shade." Then conservative Iowa Republican Bourke Hickenlooper, who Humphrey suspected was jealous of the publicity Dirksen was getting, threatened to spur a revolt unless three proposed changes were put to a vote. Humphrey agreed, in return for assurance that four conservative Republicans whose cloture votes were uncertain would vote to end debate. When Russell complained to Humphrey that he had recently refused to bargain with him over amendments, the Minnesotan replied candidly: "Well, Dick, you haven't any votes to give us in cloture and these fellows do." Two of Hickenlooper's amendments, regarding school desegregation and employment, were defeated on June 9, but the third, calling for a jury trial in all criminal contempt cases (except for voting rights), carried by 51–48 despite Humphrey's sharp critique that this undermined the power of courts to enforce their rulings.[66]

Humphrey remained in his office late into that night readying for the cloture vote the next day. He called Johnson around 7:30 p.m. to say he had "66 soldiers" lined up, one less than required to win, but two or three other senators had promised their votes if needed. Johnson was skeptical, while Humphrey remained to make more calls and got commitments from three Democrats and two Republicans. He was on the phone again in the early morning of June 10, and en route to the Senate floor he handed Hart of Michigan a slip of paper with "69" on it. When the session started at 10:00 a.m., CBS News television cameras were running, and the galleries were full, plus about 150 standees, including many House members. When the quorum call came an hour later, nearly all of the one hundred senators were present, with the others close by.

Mansfield spoke first: the Senate stood at the "crossroads of history," he said, and read a letter from a Montana mother who said she thanked God that her four children were white but that their birthrights of justice, freedom, and ambition had to be given to all people. Russell made his final arguments that the bill infringed constitutional and property rights.

Humphrey, given just two minutes, had a red rose in his lapel and was buoyant, despite limited rest and recently having lost twenty pounds. He recalled that Henry V at Agincourt in 1415 had rallied his greatly outnumbered English troops to victory over the French by telling them that they would always remember having "fought with us on St. Crispin's Day."

So, too, Humphrey told his Senate colleagues, "perhaps in your lives you will be able to tell your children's children that you were here for America to make the year 1964 our freedom year . . . of full freedom, full justice, and full citizenship for every American. . . . It will be remembered until the ending of the world." Dirksen countered Russell: civil rights were a "moral issue," and "an idea whose time had come," and the time was now "for equality of opportunity in sharing in government, in education, and in employment." As Dirksen sat down, Humphrey moved across the aisle to shake his hand.[67]

The voting took only ten minutes; Mansfield said he had never seen the chamber so quiet. The most unexpected moment came when Democrat Clair Engle of California, absent since April 13 due to surgery for brain cancer and soon to die, was brought to the floor in a wheelchair. After the clerk called his name, he tried but could not speak, so he moved his left arm toward his eyes and nodded, and the clerk called "Aye."

The roll call soon reached Republican John T. Williams of Delaware, whose commitment Humphrey had gotten the night before, and he cast the critical sixty-seventh vote for cloture. Humphrey bit down on his tally sheet and beamed. The final tally was 71–29, 4 votes more than the required two-thirds margin, consisting of 44 Democrats (only 3 from outside the South voted no) and 27 Republicans, including 15 conservatives. This ended the record-setting seventy-five-day filibuster and marked the first time cloture was invoked on a civil rights bill.[68]

An angry Russell tried to delay the bill's final passage by calling up many southern amendments eligible for roll call votes, but these were all beaten back; Humphrey agreed only to a stipulation allowing an employer to give an "abilities test" to all prospective employees despite some concern that "culturally deprived" groups might be disadvantaged. Finally, on June 17, Humphrey got the revised bill—technically the "Dirksen-Mansfield amendment in the form of a substitute" with Humphrey and Kuchel cosponsors—for the original House bill to be voted by 76–18 as pending business of the Senate, with a final vote to come in two days.[69]

The joy of the day was bittersweet, however. Humphrey was summoned from the Senate floor by a telephone call from a tearful Muriel telling him that doctors had discovered that the swelling in their twenty-year-old-son Robert's neck was a malignant tumor requiring immediate surgery. Humphrey "desperately" wanted to be with Robert, but he chose to remain in Washington, comforted in his office that night by friends Rauh of the ADA and Mitchell of the NAACP.[70]

Later that night, the two last southern holdouts, Thurmond and North Carolina Democrat Sam Ervin, informed Humphrey that they were giving up.

Goldwater, the presumptive Republican presidential nominee, announced that he would oppose the bill as unconstitutional and leading to a "police state." But the final vote, which came after a long day of skirmishing over amendments on June 19, was not in doubt. In the early evening, Mansfield praised Dirksen—"his finest hour"—and lauded Humphrey for his "herculean feats," and signaled that the time to vote had come. Russell again attacked the bill as violating states' rights and aimed at the South, while Dirksen thanked Mansfield for his patience and tolerance and pointedly criticized Goldwater for his "extreme opinion" about the bill and failure to recognize its "moral basis."

Humphrey hailed "the greatest piece of social legislation of our generation." He reminded everyone that it relied on voluntary conciliation and state and local officials before providing for federal intervention. But most important, he said, the current struggle was "too vast for bitterness" and the real battle was to overcome "irrational legacies" and the "bondage of ignorance and poverty" and create a community "where justice rolls down like waters and righteousness is a mighty stream." Passage of the bill was occasion to be "exalted but not exultant" and to preserve a sense of "oneness" and "mutual dependency."[71]

The final vote on the bill on June 19 was 73–27. Again, Engle voted from his wheelchair. West Virginia senator Robert Byrd voted against the bill, as did nearly all southern Democrats, but only five Republicans joined Goldwater in opposition. Congressman Emanuel Celler, chair of the House Judiciary Committee, and ranking minority member McCulloch immediately said that they would accept the Senate bill as being the same as the original House bill, avoiding any conference committee delay.

Humphrey joined Mansfield, Dirksen, and civil rights advocates in the majority leader's office to celebrate their victory. As Humphrey left the Capitol that night, he was met by a small but largely African American crowd that cheered and thanked him for giving them "freedom" and "justice." The senator, as he told *New York Times* columnist James Reston, felt that a "heavy load" had been lifted from his shoulders. He carried it graciously, with even the angry Russell conceding that it was not only Humphrey's legislative skill but his fairness that had been so critical to gaining passage of this historic legislation.[72]

Humphrey flew back to Minneapolis on June 20, where he was greeted at the airport by a relatively small but enthusiastic crowd carrying posters with pictures of his earlier return by train after his dramatic 1948 Democratic convention speech. He told his admirers that the bill was "an expression of the beauty of the country" but that the battle for racial justice was not over. It was not helpful to be able to sit at a lunch counter "if you don't have the dime to buy the cup of coffee."[73]

After spending three days with his family and son Robert—whose surgery proved successful over the long term—the senator returned to Washington, where he and his Republican counterpart, Thomas Kuchel, addressed the NAACP. Humphrey, a longtime member, was careful to lavish praise on Johnson—a man who does not "dither" or "agonize" but "decides" and "acts"—for passage of the Civil Rights Act, and drew an ovation for the president. Humphrey eschewed extremism, indicating that it was time to put away the banners of protest and effect an NAACP-style "white and Negro American partnership" to make the law work. His and Kuchel's speeches were frequently interrupted by applause, and both men received standing ovations at the end. But as the *New York Times* reported, Humphrey was "clearly the hero," and as an NAACP official said, "He has won our support for the vice presidency, if he wants it."[74]

The House Judiciary Committee accepted the Senate civil rights bill as a substitute for its original one, and sent it to the House Rules Committee, where Chairman Smith delayed action until committee members took control on June 30 and sent the approved bill to the full House, which passed it 289–126 on July 2. Johnson signed the Civil Rights Act of 1964 into law that evening on national television in the East Room of the White House. He linked the bill to the same quest for the "rule of justice" that had motivated the signers of the Declaration of Independence, and he called on all Americans to "close the springs of racial poison," end the racial discrimination the new law made illegal, and make the nation whole again. Johnson told his aide William (Bill) Moyers, "I think we just delivered the South to the Republican Party for a long time to come."[75]

That remained to be seen. But now Humphrey could mull the fruits of his two-decades-long labor in behalf of equal rights.

In August 1964, a Mr. Virgil P. Lacy, claiming to represent the "National Association for the Advancement of White People," wrote to Humphrey to ask why he "failed to be impressed" by his petition, with three thousand signatures, opposing the Civil Rights Act. Humphrey answered: "Bigotry has never impressed me favorably and never will."[76]

Humphrey was set to become his party's choice for vice president.

12

THE BEST MAN IN AMERICA

After President Kennedy's funeral in November 1963, Humphrey told his closest advisers that his goal was to be president, but as a poor man from a small state and without rich friends, his only route to that office was the vice presidency. One old friend, New York lawyer Marvin Rosenberg, recalled the advisers' belief that if he were vice president, Humphrey would lose his freedom and Johnson would "cut his balls off." But his friends gave in and began weekly meetings at Max Kampelman's house.[1]

Humphrey hired Ted Van Dyk, an American journalist who worked in the European Economic Community's Washington office and regarded Humphrey as his "childhood hero," after he brought to the senator's office his seven-page blueprint for a behind-the-scenes political and media campaign titled "How Hubert Humphrey Can Become President by First Becoming Vice President." This was meant to underscore Johnson's need to choose a vice president able to step into the president's role "in event of a tragedy" and to promote Humphrey's standing. Van Dyk urged changing the senator's neighborly image to one of an experienced congressional leader. Humphrey said that this was "the plan I was looking for."[2]

Humphrey's leadership with the Civil Rights Act thrust him to the forefront of the race. In January 1964, Johnson authorized Jim Rowe, who managed Humphrey's primary campaigns, to tell him he could seek support for the vice presidency, but wanted to be kept up to date. Rowe cautioned that the president would give other men the same license.

During spring 1964, Rowe talked with Humphrey several times to convey Johnson's view that "everything being equal, you're the candidate," although the emissary always tempered the message to preclude the senator's suffering the disappointment he had with Stevenson in 1956. However, things were never as they seemed when dealing with Johnson, who began to mention other people, including Secretary of Defense Robert McNamara, a lifelong Republican who had neither a political following nor interest in the vice presidency, and politely declined an offer he did not trust Johnson to fulfill.[3]

Johnson also showed up unexpectedly at a McCarthy reelection fund raiser in January in Washington attended by Humphrey, cabinet officials, and many leading Democratic congressmen. Then on his trip to Minnesota in late June following passage of the Civil Rights Act, the president praised Humphrey ("Where is life there is Hubert," Lady Bird Johnson wrote in her diary) but made a point to include McCarthy and Freeman, two other vice presidential hopefuls, in his comments.[4]

That summer, Humphrey published two books spelling out his liberalism. In *The Cause Is Mankind: A Liberal Program for Modern America* and *War on Poverty*, he declared the strength of liberalism to be its recognition of need to seize challenges and opportunities and creating a "welfare state which assured a decent standard of living and human dignity to every citizen." This required public aid to education, job training, responding to technology's impact on jobs and manpower, assuring good housing and health care, and providing foreign aid, such as his PL 480, which would pay for itself by fostering trade with recipient nations.

He viewed the era of trust-busting as over and said it was time for intellectuals and management to end their mutual hostility and focus instead on how to develop programs and ways of doing business that promoted investment in human potential. He insisted on the need for a vital labor movement that had long supported not just collective bargaining gains but civil rights, aid to education, foreign aid, and scientific research.[5]

Reviewers applauded Humphrey's command of societal needs and legislative acumen but suggested that this longtime critic of corporate malfeasance calling for intellectuals to shelve their traditional hostility toward management sounded like "extremism in pursuit of moderation"—or the vice presidency.[6]

Many of Johnson's Texas associates, including Governor John Connally and White House aide Walter Jenkins, urged Johnson to choose McCarthy to be his vice president. As a member of Harry Byrd's Finance Committee, he had voted for oil depletion allowances and, despite voting for civil rights, was more acceptable to the South than Humphrey. McCarthy was also a Catholic, which Johnson deemed important to attract voters who sought a replacement for President Kennedy. Moreover, McCarthy's wife, Abigail, and Lady Bird Johnson were "best friends," which the senator thought gave him an inside track to the vice presidency. The president told McCarthy to take on Goldwater over foreign policy and to seek out important Democratic Party leaders such as Jesse Unruh, Speaker of the California State Assembly, and Richard Daley, mayor of Chicago. McCarthy welcomed this as a clear message to seek the vice presidency.[7]

McCarthy mounted a fairly extensive campaign with financial support from Stephen Currier, heir to a banking fortune and a civil rights activist. McCarthy supporters established headquarters in Washington and hired a campaign manager and press secretary. He publicly said that he was neither seeking nor running away from the vice presidency, but traveled to California to seek Unruh's support; this failed, but the Speaker "hasn't come out against me either," he quipped.[8]

Robert Kennedy, too, sought the vice presidency. He wanted to continue his brother's agenda and believed that Johnson needed him politically. But the attorney general and the president had a long record of mutual contempt that dated to the early 1950s, when Kennedy worked for Senator Joseph McCarthy's witch-hunting committee, and continued through his 1960 efforts to block Johnson's nomination for vice president. Kennedy believed that Johnson had been too quick to be sworn into office in Dallas when John Kennedy was assassinated in November 1963 and begin working in the Oval Office before his predecessor's belongings had been removed. The attorney general viewed Johnson as "mean, bitter, and vicious—an animal in many ways."[9]

Johnson had grown angry over his increasing isolation from President Kennedy's cabinet officials and White House staff when he was vice president, feared being dropped from the 1964 ticket, and as president was insulted when Robert Kennedy came late to his first cabinet meeting. Johnson would not choose Kennedy as his running mate, he told White House aide Kenneth O'Donnell, unless that was the only way he could win in 1964.[10]

Johnson's paranoia caused him to fear having a vice president—any vice president—who might run against him in four years. Whomever he chose, he said, "I want his pecker to be in my pocket."[11]

A national poll of Democratic County chairmen gave Humphrey a modest lead over Kennedy for vice president, with McCarthy and a few others running far behind. Humphrey was quick to say that the convention would accept Johnson's choice, but also wrote his DFL supporter Eugenie Anderson that "the president calls on me a great deal. . . . The political pot is boiling, and I'm in the middle of it." He sought political support from East Coast leaders and Eugene Wyman, the liberal state chairman of the California Democrats. At Kampelman's request, Humphrey went to Jamaica to meet with Ambassador Thomas Loughery, former head of the Letter Carriers' Union and George

Meany's friend, who arranged for the senator to meet with the AFL-CIO president in Florida and speak to a closed gathering of union presidents. Later, when Johnson asked Meany for his three choices for vice president, he replied, "I have only one choice—Hubert Humphrey." Seven liberal governors, including Edmund "Pat" Brown of California, also urged Johnson to choose Humphrey.[12]

Kennedy's supporters organized a write-in vote in New Hampshire's March 10 primary in which Johnson, who had not entered the contest, barely outpolled him by 29,317 to 25,094 votes. Whether Kennedy sought the vice presidency, or to unseat Johnson, remains uncertain, but the president continued to vent about that "little shitass" and "grandstanding runt," while in April a survey in the *Minneapolis Morning Tribune* showed Democrats, even in Humphrey's Minnesota, seemed to favor Kennedy for vice president.[13]

When Republicans nominated for president archconservative Arizona senator Barry Goldwater, who ran strongly only in the South, and he chose as his running mate William E. Miller, an extremely conservative and acerbic, largely unknown six-term congressman from upstate New York, Johnson said of Kennedy, "I don't need that little runt to win." He summoned Kennedy to the Oval Office on July 29 and told him that Goldwater's nomination required choosing a running mate who would help the ticket in the South, the Border States, and the Middle West.[14]

Kennedy did not withdraw publicly or tell Johnson that he intended to run for the Senate from New York. Thus, the president put out his transparent announcement on July 31 that he would not be choosing a cabinet officer or anyone who met regularly with that body. Kennedy joked that he was "sorry that I had to take so many nice fellows down with me."[15]

Stevenson, who professed to being "disappointed" at being eliminated from the vice presidency, immediately telephoned Humphrey to say, "It's you, Hubert," and to offer to do all he could to ensure his getting the nomination. Kennedy and his supporters also lobbied for Humphrey.[16]

Johnson's arbitrariness and fear of anyone whose political standing and record of achievement was as high as Humphrey's meant that his nomination was not a certainty. Johnson had already instructed Rowe to get Humphrey's reassurance that he would be a loyal vice president—that "there ain't gonna be nobody running against me for eight years and gonna be following my platform and gonna be as loyal to me, like I was to [President] Kennedy."

Rowe assured Johnson of Humphrey's loyalty, but the president still fretted. Once he made up his mind, he said, "I don't want to have to kiss the ass of a vice president" and also sought assurance that "he won't be running against me in four years." Rowe told him there was no reason to worry Humphrey would be disloyal or run against him. Johnson said he should inform him of the forth-coming important announcement and say that Rowe himself told Johnson that Humphrey would be loyal, support his platform, and " 'He'll be *your man.*' " The president concluded the talk: "And if he don't [sic] want to be my wife, he oughtn't to marry me."[17]

Johnson insisted on floating other names, but said this did not mean he was a "double crosser." He would mention McCarthy, Majority Leader Mike Mansfield, Connecticut senator Thomas Dodd, New York City mayor Robert Wagner, and Governor Brown. Rowe promptly sent the president a memo-randum stating Humphrey's "precise" response about his commitment: namely, having called Johnson "a real liberal" years earlier, when northern liberals opposed him, there was no reason for him to be disloyal now.[18]

Johnson had Rowe subject Humphrey to a "horse shredding" — that is, answer questions about every aspect of his political, financial, and personal life, including marital fidelity (an ironic test given John Kennedy's and Johnson's serial philan-dering). Humphrey angrily exclaimed that he had been in public life for twenty years and subject to intense scrutiny, but Rowe insisted that now he was "in the big leagues," and Republicans would soon ask the same questions.[19]

In early August, Humphrey told reporters that "nobody has to woo me. I'm old reliable, available Hubert." Still, he traveled to New York, Chicago, and Detroit to impress major business and banking leaders that he was a "moderate" who saw government's role as "smoothing the way for new men and ideas" and providing needed credit to encourage competition. He favored a "business-government partnership" akin to that during World War II, with government planning to provide "proximate goals," not "stubborn goals." Humphrey won over many business leaders, including Roger Blough of US Steel, Henry Ford II of the Ford Motor Company, and Keith Funston, head of the New York Stock Exchange. They viewed him as a moderate who could get things done — and they feared Goldwater's radicalism.[20]

Johnson had Rowe subject Humphrey to another session in which he professed to be cognizant of the relationship between a president and subordi-nate vice president — with Rowe handing the senator the telephone to call Johnson to declare that he understood his concern about the issue, and "you can rely on me. I will be loyal." This virtual bullying took its toll on Humphrey, who told friends he thought Johnson would not offer him the vice presidency, but only a larger whip's office and two more clerks. In mid-August, Eric Goldman, a prominent Princeton University historian who had replaced Schlesinger as the president's special consultant, noted that Humphrey appeared emotionally drained and given to repeating the sad story of the girl whom the handsome football team captain always called—to ask her opinion of another girl, never for a date.[21]

Shortly before the Democratic convention in late August, Humphrey asked Gerald Heaney—a Duluth lawyer long active in DFL politics and former DNC member who had managed the senator's Minnesota campaign in 1960—to come to Washington to ask McCarthy to leave the vice presidential race. The junior senator refused, however, and his staff insisted that Connally and Lady Bird were on his side. But Heaney believed that unless Johnson thought he needed a Catholic on the ticket, McCarthy had no chance to be chosen.

Just before Heaney was to leave Washington, McCarthy called him to ask what he thought was going to be the most important issue. "Vietnam," he said, mindful that two weeks earlier Congress had passed the Gulf of Tonkin Resolution authorizing the president to take necessary action to support US forces in response to alleged attacks by North Vietnamese torpedo boats on two US destroyers. McCarthy agreed and said that the vice president had to be committed to seeing the president's policy through to the end, which he was prepared to do, but if the battle got rough, Humphrey likely would let it be known that he would be taking a different stance. Heaney agreed to call Johnson on McCarthy's behalf—only after informing Humphrey—but when he reached the White House, he was told that the president had gone to Texas, and the matter ended.[22]

A bitter political controversy swirled about Mississippi and its Democratic convention delegation that threatened to upset the meeting and Humphrey's vice presidential prospects. In the spring, civil rights groups, led by the Student Nonviolent Coordinating Committee, began their "Freedom Summer" campaign to educate and register black voters in Mississippi, whose population was almost half African American but only 5 percent were registered to vote. The civil rights workers were subject to great violence, notably three young activists who were murdered by Ku Klux Klan members but whose bodies were not discovered until August.[23]

Civil rights leaders formed the interracial Mississippi Freedom Democratic Party (MFDP) and, following Democratic Party rules, elected delegates to its national convention. MFDP leaders insisted that their delegates be seated instead of the all-white, segregationist regular Democrats, who had excluded them from voting and were led by antiblack governor Paul Johnson. The president panicked, and Texas governor Connally told him, if you "seat those black jigaboos, the whole South will walk out."[24]

As the convention neared, Joseph Rauh Jr., Washington's most prominent civil rights lawyer who was MFDP counsel as well as Humphrey's supporter and ADA compatriot, sought to force a roll call on the issue. But as he neared mustering the required number of states and credentials committee members, a friend of Humphrey's in the administration called him to warn that he would not be vice president if Rauh succeeded. Humphrey's staff informed Rauh, and Johnson called UAW president Reuther—whose union employed Rauh as its counsel and contributed to the MFDP cause—to insist that if "you and Humphrey have got any leadership you'd get Rauh off that damn television." Seating the MFDP will "really screw us good," the president complained, and cost the Democrats fifteen Deep South and Border States in the election. Reuther agreed Mississippi would be lost, but not all the other states; however, he did call Rauh to say that if he did not stop, he would have "Humphrey's blood on his conscience."[25]

Humphrey, too, called Rauh, as well as David Lawrence, former Pennsylvania governor and credentials committee chair, to propose seating both delegations, as was done for rival Texas groups in 1944. But Johnson told Humphrey, "You can't do that at all. There's no compromise. You can seat one delegation or the other," but there was "no justification for messing with the Freedom Party" that was "elected to nothing." To throw out the regular Democrats would mean "writing a blank check to [Goldwater] for fifteen states." The MFDP, he said, had to realize that they had the president, "they'll have the Vice President," and the law and the government for the next four years. "Why in the living hell do they want to hand—*shovel*—Goldwater fifteen states?" Humphrey replied that they were not dealing with "emotionally stable" people on this issue.[26]

Johnson repeated his argument the next morning to NAACP head Roy Wilkins, rhetorically asking, "Do you know how much trouble I'm gonna have when I name the Vice President? It's going to be almost like naming the Freedom Party to these folks." Further, the ADA had already "sent out this thing with Hubert's name on it . . . for Vice President to every Southern delegate." Johnson said he would not panic, but "if I were the Negro I'd let Mississippi sit up on the platform . . . and I'd salute the son of a bitch. Then I'd nominate Johnson for President and my Vice President . . . and the next four years I'd see the promised land."[27]

Despite virtually settling on Humphrey for his running mate, Johnson sought to stir matters by asking White House aide Kenneth O'Donnell how much stronger he was for the Minnesotan rather than widely respected Mansfield—a Catholic who might appeal to Kennedy's supporters and Catholic voters—but who refused to run for vice president "under any circumstances." O'Donnell showed no interest in pursuing the matter, and Johnson told Jenkins, his most trusted White House aide, to call Humphrey to tell him he had better get Reuther and Rauh to "quit causing these goddamn troubles" because they were going to make for a bad convention—and if "you [Humphrey] haven't got any influence with this ADA crowd, tell us who has."[28]

Tension increased the next day when the credentials committee in Atlantic City heard nationally televised testimony from both Mississippi delegations. Fannie Lou Hamer, a black sharecropper and MFDP organizer, dramatically described how her voter registration work had led to losing her job and being arrested and beaten in jail by black inmates acting under white guards' orders. "Is this America?" she asked. Johnson was so upset, he hastily called a press conference to interrupt Hamer's testimony, but the news stations rebroadcast it at night. He also called Humphrey to complain that he was doing a "lousy job" in gaining a solution.[29]

Humphrey was caught in the middle. He was by far the strongest vice presidential candidate, but Johnson's arbitrariness made his choice uncertain. The senator was confident that the Democrats would triumph in November but, after hearing Hamer's testimony, foresaw a hard battle with the "almost fanatical Goldwaterites," he wrote to his DFL friend Eugenie Anderson. Perhaps it was time to consolidate civil rights gains rather than press forward, but "we always have people who want to go a little bit further than it seems possible to go at the moment. . . . I too have done the same." Given the many problems in the cities owing to racial tensions, "it seems to me . . . we ought to let what we have sink in and be digested."[30]

Humphrey urged acceptance of the administration's proposed two MFDP guest seats, a loyalty pledge from seated regular Democrats, and a commitment to end segregated delegations. When the credentials committee rejected this, Walter Mondale, Humphrey's protégé and Minnesota's attorney general, proposed forming a five-member subcommittee to find a solution. That night, Rauh pleaded with Humphrey to press the White House to offer more than guest tickets, which the MFDP regarded as a "back of the bus" slap in the face.[31]

Humphrey and Rauh talked nearly all night, but the senator knew he could not offer the MFDP more than guest seats. The next day, he met with Rauh, Mondale, King, and members of the MFDP and credentials committee. Humphrey rejected seating both Mississippi delegations if they took a loyalty oath because he knew that Johnson would not allow MFDP legal recognition. Instead, the senator urged the MFDP to give way, allowing him to become vice president and continue working to advance civil rights. Hamer rebuked him for putting his position ahead of that of 400,000 black people; moreover, she had lost her job, but "God's taking care of me." If Humphrey continued to act as he was, she said, he might become vice president, but he would not be able to do any of the good things he was talking about. "I'm going to pray to Jesus for you," she concluded—so unnerving Humphrey that he had her excluded from further talks.[32]

Johnson sent Jenkins to the convention to resolve matters, only to have him report he had "walked into the lion's den" and was certain the MFDP people would force a floor fight. Johnson said that the Negroes were irrational and setting themselves back to Reconstruction, while he was trying "to get a Vice President for 'em. And I want him accepted by the country." When the convention opened on August 24, Humphrey arranged for MFDP members to be seated in the public gallery, even though the regular Democrats refused the same accommodation. That night Humphrey confessed to Rauh that the MFDP issue and his vice presidential prospects were taking a heavy emotional toll on him and that the administration would not budge.[33]

Talks continued the next morning, with Jenkins, Mondale, credentials chair Lawrence, Martin Luther King Jr., and Reuther, who, at Johnson's behest, had left contract talks in Detroit with Ford, Chrysler, and General Motors to fly overnight to Atlantic City. Humphrey made a seeming last-ditch suggestion: grant the MFDP two delegates-at-large seats even though they were not technically from Mississippi and allow the administration to name Aaron Henry, the African American head of the MFDP, and Edward King, a white clergyman, as delegates, with Hamer excluded. The regular Democrats would be seated only after taking a loyalty oath, and a commission would be created to eliminate future discrimination. Humphrey, with Reuther's support, got Johnson to agree to this plan and asked Mondale to get his subcommittee and then the credentials committee to sign off.[34]

Humphrey and Reuther called Johnson in midafternoon to say that a deal was at hand and that opposition would be "microscopic." The president was greatly relieved; the Democrats were always ready to help the "downtrodden," he said, and Humphrey and Rowe should tell the MFDP people that they were going to have a president and a vice president they could trust. He cryptically hinted to Humphrey that he was his choice: he was not "sadistic" or playing coy, but wanted the senator to know that there would be no more talks such as the one he had with Rowe on July 30 and no need to spell out the reason. The president also did not want anyone to know that he had been part of the MFDP talks: "It's your proposal."[35]

Humphrey, King, and several civil rights leaders took their plan to the MFDP leaders, who recoiled at having the White House choose their two delegates; they insisted on more than one black delegate. Humphrey vainly said that the aim had been to show an interracial party. Rauh had no better luck with another MFDP group, and when he said that their intransigence might cause Johnson to deny Humphrey the vice presidency, they said that they did not care about "traitors" like him.[36]

Talks later that afternoon led only to more enmity. Humphrey said Johnson would never allow that "illiterate" (a word he attributed to the president) Hamer to be a delegate; the MFDP leaders retorted that Humphrey was a "racist." Finally, MFDP officials asked for more time to weigh their decision. Humphrey sensed this might be a slight opening allowing them to accept the proposal. But just as he was about to grant an hour's delay, an aide rushed into the room and told him to turn on the television. A newscaster was announcing that the credentials committee had ruled in favor of the two MFDP delegates-at-large compromise. Humphrey and everyone else was stunned—it was his plan, and he had wanted it carried out, but not before the MFDP leaders had another chance to agree to it. He and others now realized the administration had used him to gain time to ensure that the credentials committee was on board, but the MFDP people believed that Humphrey always knew what was occurring and had "cheated," one member screamed.[37]

The convention delegates ratified the decision, which did not satisfy Humphrey or the Mississippi delegations, and it revealed profound differences in their life experiences and perspectives. Humphrey thought his two-delegates-at-large proposal would lead to major gains for the MFDP over the next four years, especially if a winning Johnson-Humphrey ticket could take on voting rights and housing issues. He was also keenly aware that his vice presidency was on the line, but as Rauh stated afterward, during all of their discussions, the senator "never appealed" to him for a solution so that he could gain his coveted nomination, and "that represented the highest standard of political ethics that I have witnessed in my lifetime."[38]

Mondale, who steered the compromise through his subcommittee and the credentials committee, always maintained that he was "proud" of the solution. He thought that the MFDP people were somewhat "naïve" not to recognize that this was a political convention, not a political science meeting. But MFDP leaders and many civil rights workers had suffered every abuse and degradation imaginable— job loss, beatings, imprisonment, and murders. They viewed the current fight as one for basic freedom and equality, not merely the right to participate in a political convention. As Hamer said, "We didn't come all this way for no two seats."

The MFDP delegates rejected the credentials committee decision, although many of them, aided by friendly delegates who supplied credentials, pushed their way into the seats vacated by the regular Democrats, who had bolted the convention. King and numerous civil rights leaders grudgingly accepted the decision, but the divide increased between the MFDP leaders and more militant civil rights activists on the one side and white liberals on the other.[39]

Johnson was the apparent winner; he would have the smooth convention he craved. But the MFDP fight undermined him, at least briefly. On August 25, he called A. W. Moursund, a Texas insurance man and close friend, to say he was considering withdrawing as a presidential candidate because he could not govern with a Democratic Party deeply divided between African Americans and white southerners. Similarly, he told his press secretary, George Reedy, he could not govern without the support of his own state and section, and "the Negroes are not going to follow a white Southerner." He told Jenkins he doubted whether a man born and raised where he was could "ever satisfy the Northern Jews and Catholics and union people."[40]

Moursund, Reedy, and Jenkins all urged Johnson to remain in the race; so did Lady Bird Johnson, who told her husband, "You are as brave a man as Harry Truman—or FDR—or Lincoln," and she and the country honored him for this. Retirement would be "a lonely wasteland," with "your enemies jeering."[41]

Johnson's "depression" ended after an hour or two when the credentials committee—at his bidding—voted to impose Humphrey's two-delegate compromise. It is doubtful he ever intended to quit the presidential race. What he feared was that the MFDP battle would disrupt the convention and call attention to his not being a beloved or well-liked leader. He could gain respect for mastery of politics, but his ruthless exercise of power and frequent inflicting of pain on others alienated many people. He was jealous not only of his idol, FDR, and of John Kennedy but also of Humphrey, who was highly respected and well liked even by those who opposed his ideas, and Johnson worried that as vice president he might become an independent power center, as *New York Times* Washington bureau chief James Reston said.[42]

Johnson used the seemingly unsettled vice presidential issue to act coyly with the main aspirants. McCarthy and Humphrey each appeared on *Meet the Press* on August 23. McCarthy said that anyone who was a member of a political party was obligated to accept the vice presidency, but he had never spoken about it to Johnson, who he assumed would make a decision in the Democrats' best interest. Humphrey spoke similarly, except that he denied ever having spoken about the position to Johnson, whom he praised effusively as a patriot committed to national unity. The president rated each man an A+ for his performance, while Lady Bird told McCarthy, "You're my candidate."[43]

Johnson heard reports that McCarthy supporters at the convention were saying he had the nomination wrapped up and told his aide Bill Moyers to tell them that four or five people were still being "very, very seriously" considered. He also wanted Humphrey to stay off the television "firing line" or his opponents would soon "make a real, full-grown Communist with a bastard baby out of him."[44]

On August 25, just after the MFDP issue had been settled and Johnson indicated to Humphrey he was his choice for running mate, the president again began to inflict perverse demands on him. Johnson called Jenkins at the convention to ask that Rowe get Humphrey to read and comment on a story in the *Washington Star* and *Washington Post* in which the president said he wanted a vice president who would do his bidding, possibly voice contrary views in conferences, but then follow Johnson's policies, be self-effacing, avoid press conferences, and be as loyal as the Texan had been to President Kennedy. Humphrey was told to expect to fly to Washington that night to meet with Johnson the next morning. Rowe brought the newspaper story to Humphrey, who said that the content was excellent and assured his loyalty. He said he would be ready to go to Washington on short notice.[45]

Humphrey insisted over Rowe's objections, however, that he be allowed to tell Muriel what was occurring and then went with her, Kampelman, and William (Bill) Connell to Rowe's hotel room to await word from the White House. Reedy called to say that fog precluded landing a plane in Washington; Kampelman proposed that they drive, but Johnson refused. A nerve-wracked Humphrey cursed out loud, and Rowe calmed him: today he was just a senator, he said, but tomorrow he would be a candidate for vice president, and then "we can both tell Johnson he's a shit."[46]

The president demanded that Humphrey stay off television and stop telling people he and Reuther had resolved the MFDP issue—which was antagonizing the South—although the president knew it was the newscasters who were touting the senator's work. Rowe called Humphrey's room at 1:00 a.m. to warn that the nomination was off if word of it leaked, while Johnson was content to delay Humphrey's trip to Washington to late afternoon.[47]

McCarthy was now certain he would not be the nominee and early on August 26 had his top aide, Jerome Eller, send Johnson a telegram—released to the press—stating while McCarthy recognized the president's need to choose his vice president, Humphrey met "most admirably" the qualifications Johnson had set out and recommended that he be given "primary consideration" for the position. McCarthy's own unstated "withdrawal" and lukewarm recommendation of Humphrey reflected his anger, which increased when he heard that Johnson had thought to have both Minnesota senators on the convention stage when he announced his choice of vice president. The president was "a sadistic son-of-a-bitch," he said. After first refusing Johnson's demand that he nominate Humphrey for vice president, McCarthy gave in, although the humiliation he felt would be reflected in his speech nominating Humphrey at the Democratic convention—and in his willingness three years later to challenge the president over Vietnam.[48]

After McCarthy "withdrew" his candidacy, Humphrey waited impatiently for a phone call from Johnson, who told White House reporters only that a vice presidential decision was imminent. He brooded to aides about his failure to get Kennedy, who had just announced his New York Senate candidacy, to agree to nominate him for president and said he would remember this when Kennedy needed him. Johnson had Jenkins call Humphrey to come to the White House. Rowe told him Senator Dodd would also be on the plane but reassured the presumptive vice-presidential nominee that this was to keep the press guessing and give Dodd a reelection boost.

After the plane landed in Washington, Johnson's aide Jack Valenti had the two senators driven aimlessly about Washington for fifteen minutes to allow television coverage of Lady Bird Johnson and daughters Lynda and Luci arriving at the convention. The president called Mayor Daley to say he was going to meet with Humphrey in order to choose him for vice president—what did he think? "He's a good man," Daley said. "I love him and think he'll do a good job. Just as you did in '60." But more important, Daley added, Johnson had to put life into the convention and deflect attention from the MFDP squabble.[49]

Shortly before 6:00 p.m., Humphrey and Dodd arrived at the White House. Dodd entered first, and Johnson told him his choice was Humphrey. The Minnesotan—who had dozed off in the limousine—was awakened to go to the Cabinet Room, where Johnson asked him if he wanted to be vice president. He said yes; Johnson then said that most presidents and vice presidents did not get along—at least after the first year or so—but that the vice president had to help the president achieve his goals and learn to stay out of the headlines. The relationship was like marriage, but "with no chance of divorce," and "I need complete and unswerving loyalty." Humphrey persisted that he would remain trustworthy and loyal, while Johnson recounted that despite his own loyalty to President Kennedy—who always treated him well, he said—JFK's staff had looked down on him and sought to stir trouble, and that was in the nature of things.

Humphrey held to his decision, and the deal was sealed, with Johnson again needlessly badgering the senator, saying if he did not realize a month before that the job was his, he was "too damn dumb" to have it. More important, Johnson's unrelenting questioning about Humphrey's "loyalty" said far less about the senator's outspokenness on issues than about the Texan's personal insecurity, reflected in his need to dominate everyone around him. The two men went to the Oval Office, where Johnson called and swore to secrecy a few Democratic leaders. The president and Humphrey returned to the Cabinet Room, where Rusk, McNamara, and Bundy offered their congratulations to the senator. Johnson called Muriel to tell her, "We're going to nominate your boy for vice president," and he handed the phone to his running mate to speak to his elated wife and make sure that she would be in the convention hall that night.[50]

Humphrey and Dodd flew back to Atlantic City under Johnson's orders to say nothing about their meetings, although the president told newsmen of his choice. Humphrey referred questioners to the president. He returned to his hotel suite for an interview with radio station WCCO in Minneapolis, only to be interrupted by a newsflash: the president—heeding Daley's advice—was unexpectedly heading to the convention that night, with no statement of his intention. As Humphrey recalled, "Johnson had drained every bit of juice out of the nomination, and he had drained a good bit out of me."[51]

The president micromanaged the convention proceedings: "the second coming of Lyndon," Mondale said, or as Humphrey later reflected, an effort to "erase the ghost of John Kennedy's presidency." Johnson arrived at the convention hall just after Governors Connally (a Protestant) and Brown (a Catholic) had "co-nominated" him, with the delegates affirming their choice by acclamation. Johnson headed to the rostrum, with two huge portraits of him hung on its walls, to be greeted by Broadway star Carol Channing singing "Hello, Lyndon" to the tune of "Hello, Dolly." He said he was proud to run on his party's "prosperity and peace" platform—and he wished to "recommend" for vice president a man who was neither a sectional choice nor intended to balance the ticket but "simply the best man in America for this job," namely his "close," "long time," and "trusted" colleague, Hubert Humphrey.[52]

Humphrey bounded to the platform; the first person from Minnesota to run on the national ticket was welcomed by cheering delegates. When the roll call began, Alaska yielded to Minnesota, and McCarthy nominated his DFL colleague for vice president with a perfunctory speech praising him and Johnson as men of energy, ability, and time-tested experience who had known hardship and poverty and were "qualified to provide leadership." He spoke of the

Democrats as the party of plenty, progress, and history and said that by contrast the Republican leader Goldwater was living in a "strange world" of his own in which the clocks had no hands, the calendars had no years, and "the pale horse of death and of destruction and the white horse of conquest and of victory are indistinguishable."[53]

Despite McCarthy's tepid praise for the Democratic ticket, the delegates cheered mightily, previously hidden Johnson-Humphrey buttons and banners appeared, and the next day newspapers noted that Johnson's coming to the convention had pumped life into a dying meeting. Most notably, as President Eisenhower's former speech writer Emmet John Hughes stated, Johnson deserved great praise for choosing Humphrey, someone so qualified to assume presidential responsibilities and who offered "a choice, not an echo" compared to the Republican vice presidential candidate.[54]

Humphrey's first leadership test came the next, and final, evening of the convention, after Robert Kennedy had taken the stage to speak about his brother John, before a showing of *The Thousand Days*, a film memorializing the deceased president. Johnson, who feared the film might be used to stampede the convention to the attorney general, had had its showing moved from the first to the last night, after nominations were completed. Kennedy's appearance drew thundering applause and cheering that he tried seven times to halt, but lasted over twenty minutes, until the convention chair, House Speaker John McCormack, banged his gavel for silence. Kennedy spoke mostly extemporaneously, asking the delegates to support the Johnson-Humphrey ticket as they had his brother. But his closing lines, taken from Shakespeare's *Romeo and Juliet*, imagined his deceased brother as having been cut into little stars shining from heaven that make people love the night, as opposed to their paying no worship to the "garish sun," and expressed his sentiment about Johnson.[55]

In the wake of this profoundly emotional moment, Humphrey delivered a rousing acceptance speech demonstrating that he was "the best man in America" to define Goldwater indelibly and set the political tone for the campaign. Humphrey paid tribute to "that great President" and "patriot" John Kennedy, who also had the wisdom to choose as his vice president Johnson, whose early presidential words—"Let us continue"—rallied the American people after Kennedy's death and whose policies had transformed the Democrats into a national party of "hope for all mankind." By contrast, the Republicans had been "kidnapped" by people who made it the party of "stridency" and "extreme radical language."

Humphrey depicted Goldwater as "facing backward against American history." He pointed out major legislative proposals, from the Nuclear Test Ban

Treaty to tax cuts, from civil rights, poverty programs, and aid to primary schools and higher education to UN peacekeeping efforts that "most Democrats and Republicans" voted for, *"but not Senator Goldwater,"* a refrain the delegates quickly seized upon to repeat in thunderous tones as Humphrey carefully cited the vote on each important bill. Finally, Humphrey reached out to "forward-looking" Republicans to join Democrats in building a "great society" and more peaceful world.[56]

Humphrey reveled in the tremendous applause and cheering his speech brought, especially in the presence of his family: Muriel and their four children with their respective spouses and his brother Ralph and his wife. The candidate's sole regret was that his father had not lived to see this day.[57]

Johnson looked on dourly while Humphrey enthralled the audience. The president then took the stage, having asked his staff to prepare a speech comparable to FDR's first inaugural. But his writers produced only a definition of the coming campaign as between those who wanted to see what can be done and those who wished to maintain the status quo. As White House aide Goldman later wrote, the speech had neither vitality nor a memorable phrase and left television viewers in their late-night lethargy.[58]

At the convention's end, the four thousand delegates and dignitaries adjourned to the grand ballroom of the convention hall—and to the boardwalk, beaches, and ocean waters—to celebrate Johnson's fifty-sixth birthday, which included a huge fireworks display that drew the president's portrait in red, white, and blue in the sky above New Jersey.[59]

Humphrey was told by the Johnson camp that he and Muriel were to fly the next morning to the president's ranch—"our own plans a matter of indifference," the vice presidential nominee recalled—in Stonewall, Texas, about fifty miles west of Austin and sixty miles north of San Antonio, to discuss campaign strategy. Humphrey would be forced to be an actor on Johnson's "permanent repertory theater," where he exercised total control over every person and event, despite the reluctance, and often revulsion, of those subjected to his outrageous behavior.

At the ranch, Johnson compelled Humphrey to go horseback riding wearing a ridiculously oversized outfit astride an extremely spirited horse that filled him with fear and left him "hanging on for dear life" before reporters and cameramen. Humphrey remembered an earlier episode when Johnson forced him to hunt deer; he was repulsed at killing two deer, but his host congratulated him for having "shot one more than [Gene] McCarthy, and the same number as Bobby [Kennedy]." The president also insisted that he would have the carcasses cut into steaks and sent—with antlers—to his guest's home, whether he wanted them or not.[60]

As for campaign strategy, Johnson told Humphrey to raise his own money, rent his own plane and crew, make his own plans—the Kennedys had told him that in 1960, he said—and never refer to Goldwater as a Republican. The president urged Humphrey to court businessmen. The Democrats had an antibusiness reputation, Johnson said, because of that "young fellow" (Robert Kennedy) in the Justice Department, whom he had recently told that this was the "last damn day of that behavior." Humphrey was advised to head to the South to show people there that he "did not have horns" and to talk farming to win them over. Johnson intended to remain in Washington, speak from the Rose Garden, act presidential, and avoid debating Goldwater.[61]

Johnson acknowledged that Humphrey would bear the main burden of the campaign. But nothing energized the man soon dubbed the "Happy Warrior" so much as marching into political battle under the banner of liberalism to advance what he viewed as humankind's causes.

13

LBJ VERSUS HHH: THE GREAT SOCIETY AND VIETNAM

On Humphrey's return from Texas to the Senate in September 1964, a spectator broke protocol by applauding when he entered the chamber, and his colleagues quickly joined in and escorted him to witness a Johnson bill-signing—the "job of a vice president," he quipped. The applause followed him to Minnesota, where he received a rousing reception at the Minneapolis airport and was welcomed by McCarthy and Val Bjornson, the Republican state treasurer, whom he had defeated in 1954. At the University of Minnesota, Humphrey's speech was interrupted by applause thirty times as he praised Johnson as a "can-do president" and "a giant of a man" and attacked Goldwater as someone who "scorns the path of moderation and accommodation" and sows distrust and disunity even in his own party. "A great beginning," Johnson wired. "Proud to be on the same team." As Humphrey approached his home in Waverly, virtually all of its 570 residents greeted him.[1]

Humphrey and the Democrats were confident about the upcoming campaign. The economy had been good for four months, unemployment was relatively low, and the administration's "war on poverty" seemed to be off to a good start with passage of the Economic Opportunity Act and a Food Stamp Act that significantly helped low-income households buy groceries.

By contrast, Goldwater had voted against every civil rights and social welfare bill, expressed willingness to "lob" an atomic bomb into the Kremlin or use one in Vietnam, and in accepting his Republican presidential nomination said, "Extremism in defense of liberty is no vice," and "moderation in pursuit of justice is no virtue." This confirmed for many that his views were outside the political mainstream, resulting in endorsements for the

Johnson-Humphrey ticket in many newspapers, including staunchly Republican ones.[2]

Humphrey was happiest on the campaign trail. Muriel wrote to their friend Eugenie Anderson that now they had a "wonderful airplane" with *"The Happy Warrior"* painted across its nose and a lot of operating money, which the senator raised easily, including from businessmen, a marked turnabout from the cash-strapped days of the 1960 primaries. The White House tried to impose a set text on Humphrey's speeches, but the felicitous improviser would not be contained, although he made some use of the White House's prepared text that was sharply critical of Goldwater's opposition to nuclear arms control and seeming willingness to use nuclear weapons.

In early September the Democrats ran their soon infamous "Daisy" ad showing a three-year-old girl plucking petals from a daisy and counting from one to ten, with a booming voice cutting in at nine to count down, a mushroom cloud flash coming at zero, and President Johnson's voice warning, "We must love each other or we must die." Public protest about using the threat of nuclear war to attack Goldwater forced the Democrats to pull the ad after one showing, and Humphrey said on *Meet the Press* that he had not been asked to approve the ad but had requested that it be removed from the air. News broadcasts replayed it many times, however, and it scared the public about Goldwater, as "we Goddamned set out to do," Johnson said.[3]

Humphrey began campaigning on Labor Day in Ohio—a "must-win" state for Republican presidential candidates. Democratic senator Stephen Young introduced him as "the man who tamed Khrushchev" in 1958. He accused Goldwater of waging a "war on progress," hailed the 1964 Civil Rights Act as morally, politically, and spiritually right, and, simulating his convention speech, said most Americans would vote for Johnson: *"but not Senator Goldwater,"* the audience chanted at once.[4]

In New Mexico, Humphrey accused Goldwater of injecting race into the campaign and appealing to backlash voters by saying the Democrats and the Civil Rights Act inspired urban riots when the real issue was high unemployment among African Americans, especially young people. Greeted by an admiring crowd of six thousand at the Watertown airport in South Dakota, Humphrey said he had "come home" to gain inspiration, drove to Doland to pay a sentimental visit to his former high school, where his eyes misted over as he recounted his pranks there—and assailed Goldwater's lack of knowledge about farming. In Huron, he visited his eighty-four-year-old mother, Christine, and his brother Ralph in the family drugstore—telling his sibling to send Goldwater some "happiness pills."[5]

In Kansas City, Missouri, Humphrey attacked Goldwater for suggesting that President Kennedy had played politics with the Cuban Missile Crisis to influence the 1962 congressional elections, voting against the 1963 Nuclear Test Ban Treaty, and criticizing installation of a hot line with Moscow. Humphrey's next stop was Independence, Missouri, where he visited Harry Truman, who said he had known vice presidents from Grover Cleveland's era but had "never known a better candidate than you." Humphrey responded in Trumanesque language that he and Johnson would "do their damnedest" to win.[6]

Traveling to Arkansas, Humphrey said he had not come to "squabble" with Governor Orval Faubus over civil rights, and he won applause by focusing on Democratic policies that helped farmers and cotton growers. From there, Humphrey moved on to Texas—Wichita Falls, Waco, and San Antonio—where he hit Goldwater on farm policy: he "did not know the difference between a ukulele and a corncob." A test of sorts came at the Houston Club, where Johnson had ordered Governor John Connally to gather leading Texas businessmen, especially oil executives. After Humphrey arrived, the president telephoned the group to say his running mate had no peer in energy, compassion, and devotion to his country—a "true patriot" Texans respected—and had the vision and vitality to become president. Humphrey again ripped Goldwater on farm and especially foreign policy, insisting he was impulsive and too often threatened military intervention. Humphrey was careful to say he thought the 1964 Civil Rights Act went far enough, and states needed time to adjust to the Supreme Court's 1962 *Baker v. Carr* "one man, one vote" ruling regarding need for reapportionment.

He begged the inevitable question as to whether he favored eliminating the oil depletion allowance or cutting it from 27.5 percent to 22.5 percent. He would ask Johnson, he said, and "if the oil man can't trust President Johnson, he's never had a friend." A new Texas admirer said Humphrey fielded tough questions the way the great Dodger shortstop Harold "Pee Wee" Reese fielded grounders.[7]

Humphrey reminded Michigan voters that it was their Republican senator Arthur Vandenberg Jr. who had set in motion the bipartisan foreign policy that Goldwater threatened and derided his proposal to cut individual and corporate taxes by 25 percent over five years as "economic and political quackery." In Cleveland, he assailed Republican vice presidential candidate William Miller's claim that the administration's proposed immigration reform bill eliminating the old national origins quotas would open the "floodgates"; it would open the "fair gates."[8]

In Kentucky and Tennessee, Humphrey said "equal rights" (rather than civil rights) were as great a national problem as poverty. He warned that Goldwater's aim to sell the Tennessee Valley Authority (TVA) would harm the South more than General William Tecumseh Sherman did in the Civil War. Humphrey met some boos and "Communist" charges when talking about civil rights in Moultrie and Tifton, Georgia, but he responded forthrightly and drew cheers assailing Goldwater's opposition to Food for Peace, the Rural Electrification Agency, and farm price supports.[9]

Humphrey fended off Republican vice presidential candidate William Miller's charge that the deed to his Maryland home had a racially restrictive covenant; he had learned of this only recently when auditors assessed his net worth, he said, and his lawyers had already declared his moral objections and intention not to honor the covenant, which the Supreme Court had ruled in *Shelley v. Kramer* (1948) was not legally binding. Humphrey was also unfazed that South Carolina senator J. Strom Thurmond, who defected to the Republican Party in mid-September, now led "truth squads" following him and charging that he was an "extremist."[10]

Humphrey's southern campaigning ended in late September, except for brief trips to the Border States of Kentucky and Tennessee. His civil rights record precluded his winning the minds and hearts of most voters below the Mason-Dixon Line, despite his equally strong support for farm and cotton price supports, public power, and Food for Peace export of southern produce. But no liberal Democrat would have fared well in the South in 1964, when views there were hardening against integration efforts and Democratic Party sponsorship of increased federal social welfare programs, economic regulations, and immigration reform. Many southerners were inclined to more conservative Republican views or Alabama governor George Wallace's racist populism.[11]

Humphrey was most critical of Goldwater outside the South. When the Republican said Johnson was "soft on Communism," Humphrey exclaimed, "Shades of Nixon," and called the charge "the last dying gasp of a desperate politician." He repeatedly hit at Goldwater's expressed willingness to give military theater commanders control of tactical nuclear weapons and his failure to repudiate the right-wing John Birch Society, which he likened to the Ku Klux Klan and the forces of "hate." Goldwater was the "Unhappy Candidate."[12]

Humphrey enjoyed campaigning with Robert Kennedy in his race for the Senate in New York against moderate incumbent Republican Kenneth B. Keating. Kennedy was uneasy on the stump and subject to "carpetbagger" charges despite living until age thirteen in suburban Bronxville, New York. Many Reform Democrats, Jewish leaders, and rank-and-file party members disliked him because of his work for Senator Joseph McCarthy in the 1950s and the reputed anti-Semitism of his father, Joseph P. Kennedy. Humphrey crisscrossed

New York with Kennedy, insisting that without him "there would never have been a civil rights bill" and helped ease his acceptance among liberals and Jewish voters.[13]

In late September, Johnson decided to hit the campaign trail to win a "front-lash" victory that demonstrated that people voted for Great Society programs, not just against Goldwater's extremist ideas. The president also wanted to ensure that people were voting for him: when campaign buttons appeared with equally sized likenesses of him and Humphrey, he had them replaced with ones that relegated his running mate to a smaller size in the background. Johnson went first to New England, then to the Midwest and Upper South and hit hard, if not always accurately, at the "opposition candidate" for having proposed to sell TVA, quit the United Nations, and use atomic bombs against enemies.

Johnson also said that "unlike Goldwater," he had no intention of "going North in Vietnam" or of dropping bombs that might involve American troops in a war with "700 million Chinese." In New Orleans, he told his audience the alleged story of a southern politician who said his constituents had not heard a real Democratic speech at election time for thirty years; it was always "nigra, nigra, nigra." The president's words stunned his listeners, until they grasped that he meant that the South had to put race behind it and join the rest of the nation.[14]

Johnson also campaigned for Kennedy, despite his reluctance to see him establish a political base in New York. While in Harlem and in Brooklyn—places Johnson did not want to go—he lauded Kennedy's knowledge about slum clearance, education, battling crime, and fighting for jobs in the Brooklyn Navy Yard. And when Kennedy's campaign seemed to be flagging in late October, Johnson and Lady Bird returned to Long Island and New York City, drawing huge crowds.[15]

Johnson routed Goldwater on November 3 by 41,129,484 to 27,178,188 votes, the biggest percentage (61 percent) and largest absolute margin ever received by a presidential candidate. The Democrats won forty-four states, losing only five Deep South states and Goldwater's Arizona by a tiny margin, which a last-minute Humphrey foray almost overcame. The Democrats added 37 House seats, increasing their lead to 295–140, and gained 2 Senate seats, raising their margin to 68–32, with McCarthy reelected in Minnesota by a 60 percent majority. Kennedy won narrowly in New York.[16]

The Democrats had won a major "frontlash" victory, although the South had moved toward the Republican Party. Medicare, Medicaid, the Civil Rights (Voting) Act, and comprehensive immigration reform were soon likely to pass.

Humphrey was virtually speechless—perhaps for the first time—when a reporter asked if this was worth all his efforts of the past twenty years. "Well, I guess so. I can't help but be moved," he said. "It was a victory, and I don't care if it disturbs somebody's sleep."[17]

Humphrey had contributed strongly to the Democrats' victory. They won in each of the forty states, except Georgia, in which he had campaigned, including in six midwestern states where John Kennedy had lost in 1960 and where Humphrey lambasted Goldwater over farm policy. The vice-president-to-be and his supporters got little sleep as they celebrated long into the night; there was constant cheering as he and Muriel and his friends and benefactors Dwayne and Inez Andreas watched the results at the Sheraton Ritz Hotel in Minneapolis. There was also some consternation because Goldwater would not concede until the next morning and Johnson delayed claiming victory for three and a half hours on election night. But when the president acknowledged victory, he credited his "Happy Warrior" and—with a laugh in his voice—made use of a Goldwater bumper sticker slogan to say of Humphrey, "In your heart you know he's right."[18]

Humphrey's longtime DFL partner Orville Freeman flew from Washington to join him. The agriculture secretary, who had aspired to be vice president in 1960 and 1964, admitted to himself that he wished he were in Humphrey's shoes. But he also acknowledged him as "a remarkable man," who fought his way up the ladder despite disappointments, and while at times he could be politically ruthless, he was never "mean." He had "made it" and was a true "happy warrior," who, Freeman noted, made a "special point of asking Jane and me to go with him and Muriel" when his entourage left the Sheraton to drive to the Radisson in St. Paul. This reminded the agriculture secretary of the days they first organized the DFL Party, and now they were together on national television. It was a heady feeling, even more "thrilling" for Humphrey when shortly after midnight Secret Service agents began to surround the area where he and his friends were rejoicing; now he was "Vice President-elect" and ready to do "great things" with Johnson for America.[19]

Humphrey knew he needed to manage his relationship with Johnson carefully. "LBJ v. HHH," Freeman wrote in his diary in late November. The president was extraordinarily self-centered, highly abusive of people, and given to paranoid reactions. Humphrey remembered that as majority leader, Johnson used every "salacious and salutary" bit of information to "bully, punish, or reward" senators. The vice president–elect told Freeman that to gain the president's attention, one had to come at him with something specific or simple; he would react or file it away and then make it his own idea and be welcoming—"but it was all about him."

He also warned his chief administrative assistant, Bill Connell, that asking for eleven rooms for the vice president in the Executive Office Building (EOB) would not work—but let him do it to learn a "lesson." Johnson rejected the plan, insisting that as vice president he had only four rooms in the EOB, without mentioning that in 1960 he also sought to remain as leader of the Democratic caucus and keep his majority leader's "Taj Mahal" office. Humphrey settled for EOB space similar to what Johnson had. But the critical point, Humphrey said, was, "From now on out there are no Humphrey rooms, there is no Humphrey staff, there is no Humphrey program, there are no Humphrey ideas. From now on there simply isn't any Humphrey." And that was how they had to "play it to get anything done."[20]

Freeman was not surprised, having recently visited Johnson's ranch and witnessed his "crudeness and thoughtlessness" toward people around him, constantly yelling at the help and telling Lady Bird ("an angel") to "shut her mouth." He was "rude and crude" with Sylvia F. Porter, the brilliant economist and widely read *New York Post* columnist who was seated next to him at dinner. She was "appalled" when he refused to talk seriously with her about the federal budget and persisted in telling off-color stories. But she told Freeman that despite Johnson's being a "crude, cruel, man," he would likely be a great president because he would not let anything stand in his way and "people didn't matter, it was really only reaching his objective." As Freeman wrote, Johnson might not destroy someone if he can help it, "but we're all expendable, we're all tools, he makes the decisions and he moves people around as he sees fit. . . . Everyone else is an instrument and often an unknowing one."[21]

Humphrey tended to get out front on newsworthy developments, such as his office's premature announcement that Minnesota governor Karl Rolvaag intended to appoint Attorney General Walter Mondale to the vice president–elect's Senate seat—a position Freeman dearly wanted—and his statement that the administration intended to provide significant aid to education in 1965. Humphrey's words about federal funding brought about Johnson's pointed comment at his November 28, 1964, news conference that nothing had been decided about education. But the president also announced that the vice president would have a large portfolio, including the chairmanship of a Humphrey-designed President's Council on Equal Opportunity (PCEO)—established by executive order in early 1965—consisting of sixteen major officials, including six cabinet officers, that would deal with civil rights issues as they affected education, employment, housing, and other critical areas. Humphrey would also chair an expanded Space Council and less important committees related to the Peace Corps, Jobs Corps, physical fitness, and tourism. More significantly, Johnson said Humphrey's long Senate experience meant that he would not just preside over that body but would help the legislative and executive branches formulate the administration's program for the coming year.[22]

However, Johnson soon reverted to his cruel manner when meeting with Humphrey and Freeman in early December 1964. The "sadistic" president showed them an obviously false letter stating that he would die of a fatal liver disease within six months. "You'd like that, wouldn't you, Humphrey?" he exclaimed. "What are you going to do about it? But if it happens sooner than January 20 [Inauguration Day] it won't do any good, will it?"[23]

The resilient Humphrey responded with a joke. Two days later, at a cabinet meeting, he not only demonstrated his "uninhibited free range of mind," Freeman noted, but with the president pressing to keep the budget below the $100 billion mark, he also "jacked up the Bureau of Budget boys in terms of a go, go instead of a no, no approach." And when everyone agreed on the need to act because 80 percent of price-support funds went to 20 percent of the farmers, Humphrey pushed for a commission, free from producers or their supporters, to weigh reductions and redistribution of funds to small businesses and rural development.[24]

No one was happier than Humphrey on January 20, 1965, when Chief Justice Earl Warren administered the oath of office to President Johnson and Massachusetts Democrat and Speaker of the House John W. McCormack swore in the new vice president. Fred Gates, longtime Minneapolis penny arcade owner and Humphrey benefactor, had the honor of holding the Bible for the new vice president. Humphrey's entire family was present, along with "dozens of cousins" and the Doland High School marching band, which had raised $8,000 for the trip and brought along the baritone horn young Humphrey used to play. That night, he went to numerous post-inaugural parties. Arthur Schlesinger Jr., former White House assistant to President Kennedy, noted that Humphrey appeared to be the "happiest man in the world"—in striking contrast to the "somber" Johnson—and when the vice president danced, "it was so filled with gaiety and charm and life that everyone else stopped, formed a circle around him, and clapped."[25]

Humphrey's mood shifted at about 3:00 a.m. on January 24, when White House press secretary George Reedy telephoned to say that Johnson—who had suffered a heart attack in 1955—had been admitted to Bethesda Naval Hospital. Humphrey was given no other medical information or instruction about whether to proceed to St. Paul as scheduled later that day. He could only mull the situation with Muriel, until Reedy called a couple of hours later to say that

Johnson—suffering from a heavy cold and chest pains—was fine and "Hubert" should carry on with his work. The episode sharply reminded Humphrey and his aides of his dependency on the president and Johnson's "irrational secretiveness" and suspicions about loyalty. They soon would discover that the president had put wiretaps on the telephones in Humphrey's EOB office.[26]

Winston Churchill died the same day Johnson fell sick, and the president left Humphrey off the delegation headed by Chief Justice Earl Warren that included Secretary of State Dean Rusk and Ambassador to Great Britain David K. E. Bruce. This prompted American and British press queries as to whether Johnson was "downgrading his vice president," to which he responded testily that he had never been reminded so vividly that it was the vice president's duty to attend all official funerals. When Muriel Humphrey incautiously asked him at a White House dinner why he had not sent Hubert to the funeral, the reply was silence.[27]

Johnson's need to control or humiliate was evident again in May when he saw the vice president cruising with a group of newsmen in a presidential yacht on the Potomac. The president ordered Humphrey to have his military aide, Colonel Herbert Beckington, forward all future requests for use of presidential ships and planes to White House aide Marvin Watson for Johnson to check "yes"—or "no," as he sometimes did.[28]

Johnson acted arbitrarily again in June 1965 when the Soviets, led by famed Soviet cosmonaut Yuri Gagarin, the first man to orbit Earth, were dominating the International Air Show in Paris. Humphrey suggested the United States should be represented. Johnson said no, but then suddenly dispatched the vice president and two American astronauts, Edward White 2nd and James McDivitt, to Paris, where Humphrey gained an interview with French president Charles de Gaulle; Johnson's order not to do this came too late. The vice president emerged from the Elysée Palace looking grave after de Gaulle expressed his firm opposition to the United States waging war in Vietnam but publicly insisted that American-French friendship remained intact.

After UN ambassador Adlai Stevenson died of a heart attack in London on July 14, Johnson did send Humphrey, as head of the US delegation, to bring his body back, and both men attended funeral services in Illinois.[29]

Humphrey was far less interested in attending air shows and funerals than in serving as a "Super Salesman" for the Great Society legislation. He had long been an advocate for nearly every piece of administration legislation put before the Eighty-Ninth Congress, and as Johnson told a congressional delegation early in 1965, "Hubert is my man on the Hill. I want you to deal with Hubert."[30]

Humphrey was present at every cabinet, NSC, and legislative leaders meeting and spent fourteen to sixteen hours a day lobbying for the president's

programs, attending fund raisers—especially with major contributors to the
"President's Club"—and bailing out legislators or administrators dealing with
constituents over difficult issues. Although humorous singer-songwriter Tom
Lehrer had more reason than he knew to record a song in July 1965 asking
"Whatever Became of Hubert?" that same month prominent Washington journalist Peter Lisagor wrote a *New York Times Magazine* feature story—"Ask Not
'What Became of Hubert Humphrey?' "—stating that he had achieved more
political influence as a vice president than Richard Nixon or Johnson had.
Johnson described Humphrey as "my strong right arm on everything from
beautification to Vietnam," although Vietnam policy marked a sharp, but
publicly hidden, divide between the president and vice president.[31]

Humphrey delighted in passage of Great Society legislation. After enactment in April 1965 of the Elementary and Secondary Education Act, providing
major federal funding for poor students in underfunded school districts, he
likened the Eighty-Ninth Congress to that of the "historic" Seventy-Third,
which had passed FDR's first New Deal programs. He urged action on the
administration's Immigration Reform Bill and Medicare-Medicaid legislation,
which both passed in summer 1965. The immigration bill ended the noxious
national origins quotas and Asian exclusion and permitted 170,000 immigrants
annually from Europe, Asia, and Africa, as well as 120,000 immigrants from
North and South America, with family members allowed to join those already
here. Medicare provided health insurance for people over sixty-five, including
hospitalization and outpatient care, and Medicaid established federal-state
partnerships to provide health care for poor and disabled citizens. Johnson
signed the bill at the Truman Library in Independence, Missouri, with the
former president signing up as the first Medicare member; Humphrey managed
to hitch a flight to the ceremony.

Humphrey also supported the Higher Education Act, which provided federal
funding for scholarships, guaranteed loans, and work-study opportunities for
college and university students, as well as funds for libraries. It wasn't a surprise
that all of this legislation passed, given the Democrats' two-to-one majority in
both houses of Congress.[32]

But ironically, Humphrey suffered acute embarrassment over civil rights.
The fault was partly his but more the result of changing times, bureaucratic
politics, and Johnson's cruelty.

The South had long used many devices, notably alleged literacy tests, to
prevent African Americans from registering to vote. In response, Martin Luther
King—who had just won the Nobel Peace Prize—and other civil rights leaders
sponsored a proposed fifty-mile march in March 1965 from Selma to

Montgomery, Alabama, to register voters. Governor George Wallace issued an order prohibiting the march, and as the marchers crossed a bridge leading out of the city, Selma sheriff Jim Clark and his deputies viciously attacked them. A second march fizzled, and in the aftermath, white racist hoodlums attacked three white Unitarian ministers who joined the marchers, killing one of the clergymen.

Johnson likened the marchers to heroes, and the administration submitted to Congress the Voting Rights Act, which prohibited states or political subdivisions from using any practice or procedure to deny people the right to vote based on race or color. In places where fewer than 50 percent of eligible voters were on the rolls as of 1964, federal registrars would be assigned to register voters. The Senate and the House passed the bill after considerable debate, and Johnson signed it into law in August. Humphrey called it "one of the great days in the life of the nation." By 1968, the percentage of registered African American voters in the South rose dramatically from 22 percent to 57 percent in Alabama and from 7 percent to 59 percent in Mississippi.[33]

A few days after the Voting Rights Act became law, an arrest for drunken driving in Watts, the black ghetto in Los Angeles, led to a scuffle with police and six days of rioting, which required fourteen thousand National Guardsmen to quell. Thirty-four people were killed, about a thousand injured, and four thousand arrested, with some $30 million in property destroyed—to cries of "Burn, Baby, Burn." Republicans cited this as the worst episode of racial violence in the nation's history and due to the failure of the War on Poverty.

Humphrey, however, in a speech for a White House conference on equal employment, insisted that the real issue was lack of jobs, with black unemployment near 40 percent in some communities. Moreover, the gap was widening between African Americans' education and labor market requirements. "What can we expect," he said, "when hope is resolutely crushed for the young, and even for the educated there are no jobs and no homes in good neighborhoods for the hardworking?" The African American community was near "a major economic crisis," and government, business, and labor were obligated to "go out and affirmatively seek" qualified people and begin to train those who were not to make "the other America" cherish and respect law and order.[34]

Humphrey's hopes for more constructive responses to the growing crisis were caught between the movement toward more militant Black Power confrontations and Johnson's beginning to draw back from his civil rights commitment. This growing divide was intensified by release that summer of Assistant Secretary of Labor Daniel Patrick Moynihan's *The Negro Family: The Case for National*

Action, which argued, as Humphrey did, that African Americans suffered from prejudicial racism and lack of education to compete with other Americans. Moynihan's emphasis, and that of the press, however, on the break-up of the Negro family—frequent lack of a male head of household (the result of an eligibility requirement for Aid to Families with Dependent Children, or welfare)—plus the high rate of children born out of wedlock and crime and dependency on drugs in African American communities called into question support for the welfare state and the civil rights movement.[35]

Johnson decided to pull back from civil rights advocacy and remove Humphrey from any prospective spotlight. He told Joseph Califano, an ambitious new White House assistant, "You know the difference between Hubert and me? When Hubert sits across from Reuther and Reuther's got that limp hand [owing to a prospective assassin's bullet] in his pocket, and starts talking about burning down the cities if billions of federal dollars aren't poured into them, Hubert will sit there smiling away and thinking all the time 'how can I get his hand out of his pocket so I can shake it?' Well, when Reuther is sitting in the Oval Office and telling me that, I'm sitting in my rocker, smiling and thinking all the time 'How can I get that hand out of his pocket—so I can cut his balls off.'"[36]

Johnson instructed Califano—anxious to accrue more power—and Attorney General Nicholas Katzenbach to eliminate the PCEO established earlier in the year and chaired by Humphrey. They quickly planned to transfer its functions to existing departments, including the Labor Department, to oversee federal contractors, and the Civil Service Commission, to monitor government employment. Humphrey would be limited to troubleshooting or program evaluation. But to avoid criticism from civil rights leaders, Johnson summoned an uninformed but not unsuspecting vice president to the White House in late September to "ask" if he agreed with shifting civil rights enforcement to the Justice Department and other agencies. Humphrey knew he had no choice, after which the president further humiliated him by forcing him to sign a memorandum claiming that the proposed transfer of PCEO functions was his idea. He dutifully gave a White House news conference announcing the changes and demise of the PCEO and told skeptical news reporters that it would improve civil rights enforcement.[37]

This was unlikely, although the PCEO had not matched Humphrey's high hopes, owing partly to his legislator's style of consensus leadership as opposed to executive-style command. More important, Humphrey had limited funds, no power to enforce affirmative action policies, and thus little influence over agencies.

Johnson gave no support and sacrificed his vice president to try to demonstrate that black extremism would make the country and his administration less rather than more prepared to address the problems of African Americans.[38]

◆ ◆ ◆

Vietnam brought an even greater Humphrey-Johnson divide as the president was bent on a war by stealth and the vice president sought a different course. But Humphrey lacked both the power and the political and personal capacities to resist more forcefully Johnson's domineering.

Humphrey accepted the Cold War domino theory that the "loss" of Indochina to Communism meant the loss of all of Asia, but he criticized the French in 1954 for failing to build proper civilian and military leadership in Vietnam, which he thought should be given independence. He also believed that the time for US involvement in "localized peripheral struggles was over" but complained the Eisenhower administration had let the "Red Chinese run off with half of Vietnam" at the 1954 Geneva Conference. He supported the US policy of blocking the scheduled 1956 unification elections and backed the effort to build a non-Communist state in South Vietnam to rival Ho Chi Minh's North Vietnam.

Humphrey had supported President Kennedy's "nation-building" efforts in South Vietnam, the strategic hamlet program intended to limit Communist control of the peasantry; putting pressure on President Ngo Dinh Diem's regime for political and economic reform; and sending sixteen thousand US military "advisers." But Diem's balking at reform led US officials to accede to a military coup in which he was killed on November 1, 1963, and Kennedy, who had ordered the withdrawal of a thousand marines, was assassinated three weeks later.[39]

When Johnson became president in 1963, Humphrey worried about the Texan's limited knowledge of the world beyond American borders and that his views were conditioned by his Senate service on military-related committees. Johnson, like most Democrats of his era, was determined not to be called an "appeaser" and was keenly aware that President Truman had suffered from charges of having "lost" China and failing to conclude the Korean War. Not surprisingly, Johnson chose to rely on Kennedy's foreign policy advisers; this seemed politically reassuring at the time, but the Texan's obsessive concern with loyalty led him to question the motives of anyone who called for rethinking a chosen course.[40]

Humphrey began to rethink US policy in Vietnam in spring 1964 after he was introduced to Major General Edward Lansdale, a former advertising executive who worked for the Office of Strategic Services during World War II and

Hubert Humphrey Sr. and Christine
Sannes Humphrey, ca. 1910.
Minnesota Historical Society

Hubert Humphrey Jr. as a child.
Minnesota Historical Society

Hubert Humphrey with his older brother Ralph (b. 1907) and younger sister
Frances (b. 1914) in front of their house in Doland, South Dakota.
Minnesota Historical Society

(Left) Minneapolis Mayor Hubert Humphrey in his office. Minnesota Historical Society

(Below) Humphrey speaks at the Democratic Convention on July 14, 1948. Minnesota Historical Society

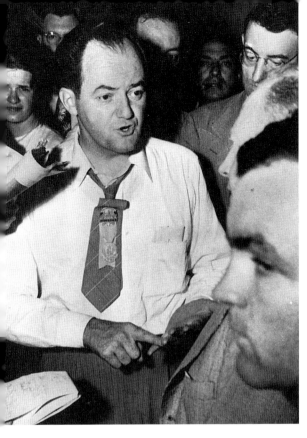

(Top) Humphrey at the Democratic Convention with reporters in July 1948. Minnesota Historical Society

(Left) Humphrey is carried by admirers at the train station on his return from the Democratic Convention in July 1948. Minnesota Historical Society

(Right) Humphrey and President Harry Truman campaign in Minnesota in October 1948. Minnesota Historical Society

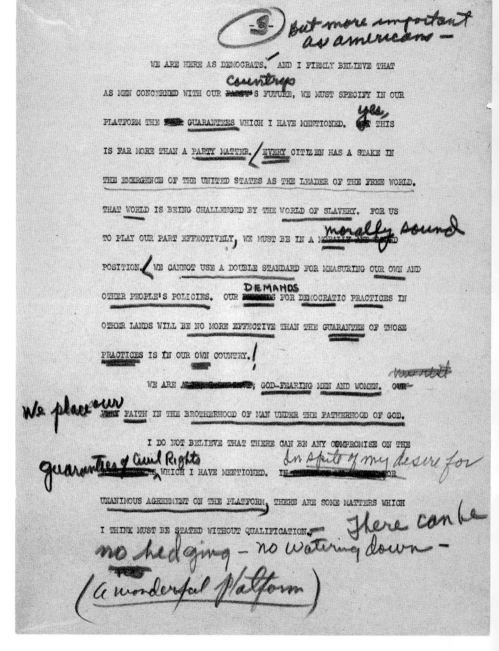

(3) *but more important as americans —*

WE ARE HERE AS DEMOCRATS. AND I FIRMLY BELIEVE THAT

Countries

AS MEN CONCERNED WITH OUR ~~PARTY'S~~ FUTURE, WE MUST SPECIFY IN OUR

yes,

PLATFORM THE ~~BASIC~~ GUARANTEES WHICH I HAVE MENTIONED. ~~AND~~ THIS

IS FAR MORE THAN A PARTY MATTER. / EVERY CITIZEN HAS A STAKE IN

THE EMERGENCE OF THE UNITED STATES AS THE LEADER OF THE FREE WORLD.

THAT WORLD IS BEING CHALLENGED BY THE WORLD OF SLAVERY. FOR US

morally sound

TO PLAY OUR PART EFFECTIVELY, WE MUST BE IN A ~~MORALLY AND GOOD~~

POSITION. / WE CANNOT USE A DOUBLE STANDARD FOR MEASURING OUR OWN AND

DEMANDS

OTHER PEOPLE'S POLICIES. OUR ~~DESIRES~~ FOR DEMOCRATIC PRACTICES IN

OTHER LANDS WILL BE NO MORE EFFECTIVE THAN THE GUARANTEE OF THOSE

PRACTICES IS IN OUR OWN COUNTRY. /

WE ARE ~~A RELIGIOUS PEOPLE;~~ GOD-FEARING MEN AND WOMEN. OUR

We place our

~~VERY~~ FAITH IN THE BROTHERHOOD OF MAN UNDER THE FATHERHOOD OF GOD.

I DO NOT BELIEVE THAT THERE CAN BE ANY COMPROMISE ON THE

guarantees of civil Rights   *In spite of my desire for*

~~GUARANTEES~~, WHICH I HAVE MENTIONED. IN ~~~~

UNANIMOUS AGREEMENT ON THE PLATFORM, THERE ARE SOME MATTERS WHICH

There can be

I THINK MUST BE STATED WITHOUT QUALIFICATION. *no hedging — no watering down —*

(a wonderful platform)

Page 3 of Humphrey's speech to the Democratic Convention on July 14, 1948. On the facing page is Humphrey's handwritten continuation of the same speech. Minnesota Historical Society

④

There are those who say to you —
~~that~~ we are rushing this issue
of Civil Rights — I say, we are
172 years late —

There are those who say — this
issue of Civil Rights is an infringement
on States Rights —
The Time has arrived for the
Democratic Party to get out of the
shadow of States Rights and walk
forthrightly into the bright sunshine
of Human Rights —

People — Human beings, this is
the issue of the 20th Century
People — all kinds & sorts of
people — look to america
for leadership — for help
for guidance

~~It is party _____ _____ principles —~~

Humphrey, surrounded by his wife, Muriel, and children, reads telegrams after winning a Senate seat in November 1948. Minnesota Historical Society

Humphrey, his wife, Muriel, and the Minnesota delegation return from the 1952 Democratic Convention. Minnesota Historical Society

From left, Humphrey, Lyndon Johnson, and John Kennedy at the
Legislative Leaders Breakfast on Feb. 7, 1961. Abbie Rowe, White House
Photographs, John F. Kennedy Presidential Library and Museum, Boston

Humphrey speaks at the dedication of the Freedom Forest in his honor in Tel Aviv,
Israel, in 1961. Minnesota Historical Society

(Right) Humphrey and
Soviet premier Nikita
Khrushchev celebrate the
signing of the 1963 Nuclear
Test Ban Treaty at the
Kremlin in August 1963.
Minnesota Historical
Society

(Above) Humphrey at work in
his Senate office. Minnesota
Historical Society

(Right) Humphrey and John
Kennedy look at a magazine
entitled *Minneapolis* in
September 1963. Cecil
Stoughton, White House
Photographs, John F.
Kennedy Presidential Library
and Museum, Boston

(Above) Humphrey and the Reverend Martin Luther King Jr. discuss the 1964 Civil Rights Act. Minnesota Historical Society

(Left) President Lyndon Johnson speaks to the nation before signing the 1964 Civil Rights Act on July 2, 1964. LBJ Library/O. J. Rapp

(Above) Humphrey on the
telephone at the
Democratic Convention in
August 1964. Minnesota
Historical Society

(Right) Humphrey and
Senator Eugene McCarthy
at the 1964 Democratic
Convention. Minnesota
Historical Society

(Above) Humphrey on his campaign plane in 1964 with (left to right) chief of staff William (Bill) Connell, adviser Max Kampelman, and aide William Sims. Minnesota Historical Society

(Left) Hubert and Muriel Humphrey walk from the White House on Inauguration Day, January 20, 1965. LBJ Library photo

The Reverend Martin Luther King Jr., left, meets with Vice President
Humphrey, center, and Attorney General–designate Nicholas Katzenbach
in Humphrey's office to discuss the 1965 Voting Rights Act. Bettman/Getty
Images

President Johnson, right, leans toward Humphrey to make a point.
Minnesota Historical Society

Humphrey, left, and President Johnson, September 1965. Minnesota Historical Society

From left, Humphrey, President Harry Truman, and President Johnson at the signing of the Medicare Bill on July 30, 1965, at the Harry S. Truman Library in Independence, Missouri. LBJ Library/Yoichi Okamoto

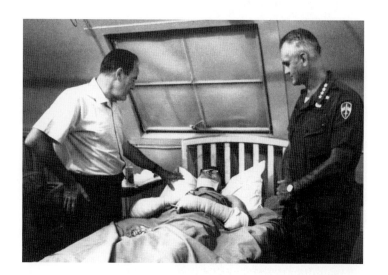

(Above) Humphrey and
General William Westmoreland
visit a wounded soldier in
Vietnam on November 1, 1967.
Minnesota Historical Society

(Right) Humphrey appears on
The Tonight Show with Johnny
Carson on July 31, 1967.
Minnesota Historical Society

(Below) Humphrey and
Richard Nixon in 1968.
Minnesota Historical Society

Humphrey campaigns in Ohio on October 28, 1968. Minnesota Historical Society

Senator Walter Mondale, left, and Humphrey wave to the crowd on their way to the 1976 Democratic Convention. Minnesota Historical Society

(Top) Muriel Humphrey kisses Humphrey as Senator Mondale watches during a taping of NBC's *Today* show on May 27, 1977. Minnesota Historical Society

(Center) Senator Humphrey, with his wife, Muriel, announces on April 29, 1976, that he will not enter the New Jersey presidential primary as Senator Mondale looks on. Minnesota Historical Society

(Below) Senator Humphrey and President Jimmy Carter, 1977. Minnesota Historical Society

the CIA afterward. Lansdale specialized in harsh counterinsurgency to combat Communism in Asia and was a strong proponent of democratic government and political-economic reform. During 1957–63, he worked in the Defense Department, but the Joint Chiefs of Staff abolished his position because he opposed the emphasis General Maxwell Taylor, JCS chairman and President Kennedy's military representative in Saigon, put on use of US troops to defeat the Viet Minh. He became a consultant to the Humphrey-generated Food for Peace program—and to the senator.[41]

Humphrey was pushed in two directions. His staff foreign policy adviser, John E. Rielly, counseled against speaking publicly about Vietnam or sending Johnson memoranda and said he should not become the administration's chief policy defender against Senate critics, including Majority Leader Mike Mansfield. Rather, he should hew to the position President Kennedy had taken: the United States was overcommitted in Southeast Asia and did not seek "victory" but wished to leave gracefully. This meant no more ground troops and no bombing in the North. The United States should seek a negotiated settlement that would protect South Vietnam from Communist assault and leave Southeast Asia stabilized and neutral.[42]

Lansdale and an associate, Rufus Phillips, who had headed the Agency for International Development in Vietnam and regarded Humphrey as one of the few Washington officials who understood the limits of American policy in Vietnam, drew up and passed along to the vice president a lengthy proposal titled "Concept for Victory." They delineated a long-term reform program that included a system for orderly change in the government, transfer of power from the military hierarchy to civilian leaders, empowering of provincial authorities, teaching the army to fight the Viet Cong (also known as the National Liberation Front, NLF) at night, increasing agricultural production and home and school building, and sending a small team of "winners" with experience in the Philippines and Vietnam to direct operations. But ultimately, they said, only the Vietnamese could win their war.[43]

Despite Rielly's advice, Humphrey sent Johnson both his own proposal for US policy in Southeast Asia and Lansdale's "Concept for Victory." The senator said it was not necessary to choose between pulling out of Vietnam and fighting a "Korea type conventional war." The United States should "stay, stabilize, and build" in Vietnam and Southeast Asia, but not just an "anti-Communist bastion." The Saigon government needed to work with a team experienced in counterinsurgency and political-economic reform to win "people's minds and hearts"; military action alone was fruitless. The government also had to make clear its caretaker status and push greater democratic governance and land reform. The US military had to halt its indiscriminate use of napalm and heavy weapons, and its troops had to stop shooting anything that moved on the theory that it was Viet Cong. Last, the government had to meet North Vietnam's challenge by announcing its goal was unification. All of this would take about a decade to complete.[44]

Johnson took Humphrey's advice in stride, although he would not commit to a decade of work in Vietnam. He sent the memoranda to his military aide Major General Chester "Ted" Clifton, who deemed the proposals "nothing contrary" to US current or planned efforts. Humphrey's democratization proposals were "admirable" but not necessarily what Vietnamese leaders wanted, although his points about better training for the military and less indiscriminate killing were well taken. Clifton judged Lansdale and Phillips skilled at their work but too given to a "lone wolf" approach to manage a large contingent, and he said that their ideas, and Humphrey's, should be made available to Taylor, who was about to return as ambassador to Vietnam.[45]

There matters rested until August 2, when the administration announced that the destroyer *Maddox* had been attacked without provocation in "international waters" in the Gulf of Tonkin by North Vietnamese torpedo boats and declared on August 4 that the *Maddox* and another destroyer, the *C. Turner Joy*, had been fired on. After the first attack on the *Maddox*, the administration warned North Vietnam that further assaults would have "grave consequences." After the alleged second attacks, Johnson quickly gained support of the NSC and congressional leaders for major air strikes that night on North Vietnam's torpedo boat harbors and oil storage facilities and denounced North Vietnam's "open aggression on the high seas"—yet insisted, "We still seek no wider war."[46]

Whether the *Maddox* was in international waters on August 2 is unclear. Johnson did not mention that the destroyer had long been involved in secret electronic surveillance for South Vietnamese commando raids on North Vietnam or that Hanoi had reason to assume this was the case. A CIA study concluded there had been no attack, and Johnson told an aide a few days later, "Hell, those sailors were just shooting at flying fish."[47]

Yet Johnson now had a pretext to put before Congress on August 6 a joint resolution authorizing him to take "all necessary steps" to repel attacks on US forces and to prevent aggression. The administration's version of events went unchallenged. The Senate passed the so-called Gulf of Tonkin Resolution on August 7 by 88–2, and the House followed with a vote of 417–0. Thus Johnson protected himself against any "soft on Communism" charges during the election campaign, raised his public approval, and gained authority to wage war without declaring it.[48]

Humphrey supported Johnson's swift action with the Tonkin Gulf Resolution; he also warned that there "were people in the Pentagon who think we ought to send 300,000 troops over there." He told a Los Angeles town hall forum on August 18 that the resolution was consistent with policy of the Eisenhower and Kennedy administrations. The near unanimous vote, he said, meant no partisan divide and no need to choose between "inglorious retreat or unlimited retaliation." The United States was in Vietnam to protect "the freedom and security of Asia." He also noted, as in his June memorandum, that land reform and rural development were essential for Vietnam, whose people were responsible for their country's peace and security. The next month, Humphrey insisted that US action in the Gulf of Tonkin was part of a continuing struggle "to preserve free civilization as we know it." Little more was said about Vietnam during the presidential campaign as Goldwater chose not to make it an issue.[49]

After Humphrey's election as vice president, Rielly cautioned him to "listen and learn" at NSC meetings and not to participate in discussions to avoid the "grave risk" of clashing with the president. Rielly also warned about avoiding a dispute with Secretary of State Rusk, who chaired the important "Committee of Principals," consisting of key State, Defense, NSC, CIA, and arms control officials. The vice president might chair the committee one day, but Rusk was not ready to step aside. The president's national security adviser, McGeorge Bundy, who headed the "extremely powerful" Intelligence Policy Committee, stated forcefully that the vice president "has no independent responsibilities" in national security affairs. Rusk and Bundy were "very wary of permitting the Vice President's office to become a source of independent, critical judgment." Rielly advised Humphrey to work with agencies he could influence, such as the Space Council and the Arms Control and Disarmament Agency, and to "avoid like the plague" association with "soft" Third World issues. Further, he said that efforts to influence the president should be limited to contacts "before and after" formal meetings. Above all, the vice president needed to be "as independent as possible and as compliant as the President thinks necessary."[50]

Since Vietnam was not an issue during the election campaign, Johnson let pass a Viet Cong attack on a US air base on November 1, and in his State of the Union address on January 4, 1965, he merely reaffirmed a US commitment to help South Vietnam fight "communist aggression."[51]

But later that month, Air Marshal Nguyen Cao Ky and General Nguyen Chanh Thi carried out another coup, setting off riotous protests and rumors that a new government might negotiate with the North. Johnson and his major advisers decided to strike at the North regardless of who governed in the South. When NLF forces attacked a US barracks in Pleiku and a nearby helicopter base in central Vietnam on February 6, the administration concluded it had the basis to begin bombing the North.[52]

Humphrey's immediate public response to the Viet Cong attack was to say it was in America's national interest to protect South Vietnam. But he was in Minnesota and not called back to Washington to attend the three crucial NSC meetings February 6–8 that resulted in expanded US military involvement in Vietnam. Johnson gained approval for major air attacks on North Vietnamese targets; only Majority Leader Mansfield (invited by Johnson and sitting in Humphrey's vacant chair) dissented on the grounds that the attack on US facilities indicated local support for the NLF and that US action might bring conflict with the PRC. He proposed that the United States go to the United Nations or seek an international conference. But Johnson, backed by the NSC, insisted on immediate air attacks.[53]

Bundy, having been in Vietnam, returned late on February 7 to urge a policy of "sustained reprisal," despite not knowing what this would achieve given the weakness of South Vietnam's government. Johnson seemed of similar view: "Ol' Ho isn't gonna give in to any airplanes," he said then and later.[54]

The next day, Johnson told the NSC that he approved Operation Rolling Thunder—major B-52 attacks on North Vietnam—and brushed off concerns from Mansfield and Llewellyn Thompson, former ambassador to the Soviet Union, about making North Vietnam dependent on Moscow or Beijing.[55]

Humphrey returned to Washington in time to attend another NSC meeting after a second Viet Cong attack on an American barracks at Qui Nhon, seventy-five miles east of Pleiku, on February 10. He spoke beforehand to several of the president's most "intimate" advisers, and they told him they opposed further bombing of North Vietnam, especially because Soviet premier Alexei Kosygin was in Hanoi. But at the meeting, the president's primary advisers all favored immediate reprisals.

When Johnson asked if everyone agreed, Humphrey immediately proposed to delay US action until Kosygin had left not only Hanoi but the Far East. Undersecretary of State George Ball, a longtime proponent of a negotiated settlement, and Thompson similarly urged being cautious and a limited number of attacks to minimize the Soviet reaction and warning North Vietnam that further attacks would bring a major military response.[56]

The next day, Humphrey and Ball agreed that each would try to show Johnson the perils in his policy. Ball and Thompson wrote the president on February 13 that bombing was acceptable to establish a stronger bargaining position but insisted that North Vietnam could not be coerced into ending the insurgency in the South and that American allies would not support military escalation. They urged seeking a negotiated settlement. Neither Johnson nor his advisers were upset by the memorandum.[57]

Humphrey's advice would draw a markedly different reaction. After the February 10 NSC meeting, he told Rielly he needed to "sit down soon" with the president and his advisers to discuss the implications of US policy in Southeast Asia and then left for a weekend trip to Georgia to visit Charles H. Ball, the board chairman of the Minneapolis-based General Mills Company, at his vacation lodge. Thomas Hughes, a former Humphrey staffer and now director of the State Department's Bureau of Research and Intelligence, called to warn him that "the die is cast," and only immediate action might halt a major military escalation.

Hughes flew to Georgia, and the two men spent the weekend discussing how to deter Johnson from expanding the war and instead seek a negotiated settlement. Hughes put their ideas on paper on his return flight, but Humphrey's handwritten notes show how he shaped the final document.

Humphrey's memorandum of February 17 was one of the era's most incisive and prescient documents; had Johnson heeded it, he might have averted national and personal political tragedy. Humphrey began by pointing out that Republicans, especially Goldwater, had always emphasized fast and total military victory in Vietnam by military escalation, whereas Democrats focused on the political, social, and military complexities of the conflict and recognized that the war would be won or lost chiefly in South Vietnam. Democrats always sought to leave opponents with face-saving options, as in Cuba in 1962, whereas an escalated conflict would have derailed US efforts to promote arms control, better US-Soviet and US-PRC relations, and perhaps required calling up reservists and increasing defense expenditures. The same would be true if the United States escalated the conflict in Vietnam.

Most significantly, the public always required politically understandable reasons for fighting wars, as with two world wars and Korea, where the United Nations supported repelling aggression. But now the public was being asked to accept the "simple argument of national interest." Further, the public could not understand why the United States would enlarge the conflict and "risk World War III" to support a country that was "totally unable to put its own house in order." In addition, the Korean conflict had shown air power's limitations, the prospect of PRC intervention, and the difficulties of "G.I.'s fighting a land war against Asians in Asia"—which had led President Eisenhower to compromise in 1953.

Humphrey said it was hard to justify "large-scale U.S. air bombardments" across borders in response to ten years of "small scale terror" that looked largely like a "civil war in the South." Further, Democrats, not Republicans, were the primary objectors to US involvement, and if it deepened, criticism would increase among "Democratic liberals, Independents, Labor, and Church groups." Cutting losses was always hard, he said, but the administration appeared to be the "prisoner of events," and this was eroding confidence in its domestic policies and jeopardizing the American image and progress toward "Democratic internationalist programs" such as arms control and improved UN relations.

Humphrey appealed to Johnson's greatly admired "political ingenuity" and public expectation he would use his "unrivalled talent" on the world scene. The best time to gain a settlement, he said, was in the first year after his decisive electoral triumph, and the best possible outcome would be a settlement that turned out to be better than what was perceived to be in the cards. This would be credited to the president and bring "enormous" domestic political benefits. Finally, Humphrey added the US goal should be limited to restoring the military balance between North and South Vietnam in order to achieve a negotiated settlement, which required immediately developing "*a political track in addition to the military one*" leading to the conference table, rather than appearing to be dragged to negotiations. Above all, the United States had to avert military action that might bring conflict with the PRC, which the Soviets would feel obligated to support.[58]

Whether Humphrey intended to give his memorandum directly to Johnson or, as he said in his memoir, he had prepared it "for use with the president" in future conversations is uncertain. But the vice president handed a copy to Bill Moyers, the president's favored special assistant, who made the "mistake," he recalled, of giving it to Johnson, which led to an extremely harsh attack on Humphrey.[59]

Johnson was "infuriated" at the memorandum, Humphrey told Hughes a few days later, and in paranoid fashion presumed that the vice president had put his views in writing in order to leak them to gain political cover later. Johnson was wrong; he knew well before he chose Humphrey for vice president that he doubted the utility of bombing North Vietnam and looked instead to a long political-economic process of reform in South Vietnam. Further, Ball, Mansfield, and Thompson had stood with Humphrey at the February 10 NSC meeting in which he proposed not bombing North Vietnam until Kosygin had left the Far East, and various Democratic senators, including McCarthy, McGovern, and Idaho's Frank Church, also questioned US bombing policy.[60]

Humphrey had not broken the pledge he made earlier to Johnson not to speak against a presidential decision. The vice president's suggestion of a bombing delay came in response to Johnson's direct query and was an honest answer. Moreover, he did not intend to leak his February 17 memorandum. But it may have angered Johnson because he was highly intent to begin major bombing and introduce US troops and now was being forced to recognize that he was going to escalate and fight a war by stealth on behalf of an unrepresentative and repressive regime. Finally, Johnson always needed to "beat up" on someone—ranch hands, White House staff, even senators—and Humphrey, who always had significant ideas and was universally well liked, made a convenient target.[61]

Regardless, Humphrey, who may not have grasped the depth of Johnson's ire, tried soon again to persuade him to alter Vietnam policy after hearing that he intended to deploy a large contingent of US troops. Humphrey's new memorandum to the president cautioned that "we do not see yet where we are going," and the "dangerous" bombing policy and injection of troops should be made secondary to seeking out "weaknesses on the other side that might tend to negotiation." Johnson threw a fit. "We do not need all these memos. I do not think you should have them around your office," he yelled at Humphrey. To others, he said that "in a choice between Humphrey and General Taylor as our major strategist, I am disposed toward Taylor."[62]

Most significantly, Johnson now excluded Humphrey—a statutory member—from NSC meetings or, rather, held such meetings infrequently and took up major foreign policy matters at "Tuesday luncheons" with Rusk, McNamara, Bundy, Director of the Central Intelligence Agency John McCone, and General Earle Wheeler, who had replaced Taylor as JCS chair. Humphrey was also no longer privy to Johnson's Vietnam decisions or other signal matters. He would spend the rest of 1965 as persona non grata at the White House—to his, Johnson's, and the nation's detriment. And worse, in seeking to regain his political standing, Humphrey would fruitlessly try to link the war against Communism to the war on poverty.[63]

14

HUMPHREY'S VIETNAM WARS

Humphrey had his first brush with administration control over his public view of Vietnam while preparing a speech for a UN conference in February 1965. Johnson forced Humphrey to permit hawkish national security adviser McGeorge Bundy to review the text, and he excised three "new and constructive" sections, including a proposal for Vietnam negotiations. Humphrey was limited to saying that the United States sought to return to "the essentials" of the 1954 Geneva Accords and prevent "subversives" from controlling the whole country. This ignored the US role in blocking the Geneva Accords commitment to unification elections and Johnson's decision to bomb North Vietnam. "Hubert, that is the worst speech I have ever heard you give," his old friend Bill Benton told him; it smacked of State Department pabulum. Most important, Humphrey's role in Vietnam policy talks was ended.[1]

Humphrey had no part in the administration's decision in March to send 3,500 marines—the first US combat troops—to protect the US airbase at Danang. Fearing a collapse in South Vietnam and/or the United States being perceived as a "paper tiger" (as Bundy said), the administration committed another 20,000 troops on April 1, with orders to begin offensive actions as opposed to defending enclaves. Americanization of the war was under way.[2]

Johnson sought to use his vice president to quiet critical senators and growing public restiveness. In late March, the president sent Bundy to meet with him and five liberal senators, all Humphrey's friends: Gene McCarthy, George McGovern, Frank Church of Idaho, Gaylord Nelson of Wisconsin, and Stephen Young of Ohio. The senators were unmoved as Bundy lectured them about their *Congressional Record* statements, arguing that they gave the world the impression that the country was not fully behind the president. Humphrey remained silent during the meeting and arranged to have twenty-two members of his beloved Americans for Democratic Action meet with the president at the White House on April 2, but Johnson's virtual monologue about US policy proved unconvincing.[3]

Five days later, in an address at Johns Hopkins University, the president proposed "unconditional discussions" but maintained that North Vietnam, inspired by the PRC, was waging war against South Vietnam. He said that the United States was defending that nation's independence and "freedom" as it had done for Europe during World War II. He offered a billion-dollar, vast TVA-style Mekong River project for all of Vietnam, insisting to his aide Bill Moyers that "Old Ho can't turn me down." But he did and countered with North Vietnam's "Four Points," which included ending the bombing, eventual US military withdrawal, allowing the South to solve its own problems, and unification elections. Johnson, however, had no interest in negotiations.[4]

Humphrey began to speak favorably about administration policy. At a flower festival in Norfolk, Virginia, in April, he said that unless Americans had the "patience to work and bleed and die five thousand miles from home," Communists would take over the world "bit by bit." Two days later at Duke University, he insisted that the United States "will not sacrifice small nations in the false hope of saving ourselves."[5]

When Johnson sent 23,000 troops to the Dominican Republic to help the military-backed regime crush a revolt led by Juan Bosch, the ousted left-leaning former president, Humphrey backed Johnson up, saying that the move would protect American nationals. He also felt that because the Organization of American States and United Nations refused to be the world's policemen, the United States had to act because "communist violence and revolution will not be permitted to gain the ascendancy."

The vice president was "chagrined" about not being consulted on the Dominican matter. His contacts with Bosch supporters had led him to warn the State Department months earlier about a possible revolt. He seemed even angrier about publicity focused on US military "shooting and killing" of insurgents rather than on their food distribution. Above all, he was "being careful not to get crosswise with anyone in the White House or in the operating agencies," agriculture secretary Freeman wrote, and constantly lavished praise on the president, did everything he wanted, and was being "a good boy at all times."[6]

This meant increasingly strong defense of Vietnam policy. In mid-May, he reassured a group of Democratic financial backers in Dallas that a nearly "disastrous" situation in Vietnam was improving. In a pep rally–style speech cleared with Bundy at the National War College on June 1, he said that bipolar

American-Soviet confrontations, such as over Cuba and Berlin, had been transformed into "less obvious confrontations stretching from Vietnam to Santo Domingo." He called on Americans to be of "sound mind, strong heart and will of steel" in battling these new Soviet, and especially PRC, sponsored wars, where "leaders could not be located, supplies could not be easily cut off, and enemy forces were indigenous troops who did not respect truces." The South Vietnamese and others would have to protect their own countries, he said, but he cited Johnson's April 7 address assuring the nation that the United States would be "the defender of non-Communist nations under attack." He told a conference of governors of western states that the stakes were too high in Southeast Asia either for withdrawal or general war.[7]

Humphrey's advocacy of administration policy continued as Johnson decided in July to send 40,000 more troops to Vietnam and permit a buildup to 180,000 troops by year's end. In mid-July, Humphrey told a county officials' meeting in San Diego that the United States would halt its military action only when "the aggressor stops his aggression." Two weeks later, he asserted to a national governors' conference in Minneapolis that the Vietnam War would "touch the lives of a thousand American families" and Americans' capacity to withstand more "sadistic warfare" than they had ever known. But the nation could still have "guns and schools" and "ammunition and medical care" in abundance. He denied that the White House had excised from his speech a statement that the war would mean expending "great resources—of money, materials, and yes, human life," even though this appeared in the advance text given to the press.[8]

Humphrey wrote Johnson that his July 27 announcement ordering the First Air Cavalry Division and supporting forces into Vietnam—with "additional forces to be sent later"—was "tremendous" and that he could not have been "happier if Christmas came every day." Further, when Oregon senator Wayne Morse warned the buildup of forces meant "sliding into the morass of war" and proposed negotiations at the United Nations, Humphrey told the president he could not understand how the senator could say that "when you are using every opportunity to achieve meaningful negotiations." In birthday greetings to Johnson in late August, Humphrey said he felt "privileged to be your Vice President and partner," and he included a letter from a Columbia University faculty friend stating that the "great majority of the academic community supported current national policy in Southeast Asia." In late October, Humphrey declared, "The tide has turned, the Vietcong has been stopped. They cannot win."[9]

Humphrey took an aggressive stance toward younger people who asked critical questions or protested. He appeared unnerved by the teach-ins that began at the University of Michigan in late March and quickly spread nationwide to

Columbia, Pennsylvania, Chicago, Wisconsin, and Berkeley. After a University of Pittsburgh student asked about "American atrocities" in Vietnam, Humphrey replied, "I am really going to tear into you," and asserted, "Only the Vietcong had committed atrocities," as well as "the most unbelievable acts of terrorism the world has ever known." He had yet to hear students ask "what is this barbarism?" he chided; "keep your mind on the enemy and the enemy is not in Washington."[10]

In July, after speaking in San Diego, where protesters' signs read "War on Poverty, Not People" and "Life—Not Death," Humphrey reported to Johnson's close White House aide Jack Valenti that only about twelve of the twelve hundred attendees dissented, and after he spoke to the former, three briefly applauded him: "In other words, they confessed their sins and were saved." At the University of Wisconsin, he called on picketers to replace "destructive demonstrations with constructive action" and insisted that the United States could not leave Vietnam "because the Communists would take over."[11]

Johnson took note of Humphrey's defense of administration policy. During an extended hospital stay for a gall bladder operation, he put the vice president in charge, adding that Humphrey would be accompanied everywhere by a Secret Service officer with the necessary nuclear codes. Muriel Humphrey sent Johnson a pair of blue pajamas that he wore during Humphrey's visit to the hospital.[12]

Humphrey continued to speak harshly of war opponents. He told the advisory committee to the Peace Corps in late October that he wished the young activists could be enlisted in the corps and alleged that their demonstrations were organized "with Communist help." At Washington University in St. Louis, he said those who raised their voices against the war should instead "do something for those who suffer rather than proclaim themselves experts on matters of national security and foreign policy." After a talk at West Virginia State College, he sent Johnson a declaration of support signed by more than half of the two thousand undergraduates and said that the president should be encouraged by the "rising tide of support for your policy in Vietnam among college students."

Humphrey entertained Swedish prime minister Tage Erlander at the palatial Greenbrier Hotel in White Sulphur Springs, West Virginia, where he pitched Johnson's Vietnam policy to his often critical, and unmoved, guest. Still, the president praised Humphrey for making US policy "crystal clear." On Veterans Day at Arlington Cemetery he called for rejecting the protesters' "counsel of despair and defeat" and told a Catholic Youth Organizations conference that the "behavior of some young Americans in recent weeks did not deserve serious attention."[13]

By late 1965, Humphrey's rapid and striking change from opponent to advocate of war in Vietnam had gained Johnson's approval. In December, the president told Bundy that no one was to review or censor Humphrey's speeches. But when a Gallup poll indicated that 58 percent of the public did not want Humphrey to become president, Johnson, seeing a chance to increase his control, told his "partner" he did not need a press secretary and should focus more on being a good vice president. Humphrey promptly pushed his press aide to take a position in an obscure government agency.[14]

Despite Humphrey's eroding public standing, Johnson believed that his felicitous vice president would be a highly effective envoy abroad. In mid-December, the president told Humphrey that he might be sent on a mission to Asia, perhaps to Vietnam. But after a press leak, Johnson blamed the vice president and canceled the trip, although it was Freeman who had inadvertently tipped the journalist. Yet when Bundy asked who should represent the United States at the upcoming inauguration of President-elect Ferdinand Marcos of the Philippines, Johnson wrote, "Send the VP." The White House announced this on December 19 and asked Humphrey to pay courtesy calls to the heads of state in Taiwan, Japan, and South Korea as well.

Johnson likely wanted the ensuing publicity to take headlines away from Senator Mansfield, who opposed the Vietnam War and was leading a group of senators to Asia. As *New York Times* columnist Arthur Krock wrote, the president also may have hoped that if Humphrey made a statesmanlike impression and raised his low public standing, he could be a foil to Senator Robert Kennedy. Either way, "the eyes of Texas"—and those of Jack Valenti, who was charged with reporting on the trip—would be on Humphrey. Johnson also announced a Christmas bombing halt: "We're going to try Hubert's way now," Valenti heard him say—which led to a month's truce.[15]

✦ ✦ ✦

Humphrey left for Manila on December 27, 1965, with his wife, Muriel, eighteen-year-old son Douglas, and Valenti—whose role Humphrey discovered when an admiring African American NSC staffer "mistakenly" delivered a copy of one of Valenti's reports to one of his advisers. The vice president also carried a document, prepared largely by Rusk, to use in talks with other leaders that concluded, "We have put everything into the basket of peace except the surrender of South Vietnam."[16]

Humphrey stopped briefly in Japan to assure officials that the US bombing halt was a genuine peace effort and ask that they use their good offices to help end the fighting. In the Philippines, the eighty thousand people attending Marcos's inauguration gave Humphrey a standing ovation far louder and longer than accorded any other delegation head. He was the only foreign representative to stand in the receiving line with Marcos, who agreed to send two thousand troops to Vietnam. Humphrey praised the Filipinos for having attained the "highest political achievement within the reach of man—the orderly and peaceful transfer of power." But a hospital visit to an American soldier—"just a little older than our Dougie," Muriel said—wounded in Vietnam by machine-gun fire left Humphrey barely able to muster "bless your heart" before departing.[17]

Humphrey stopped in Taiwan on New Year's Day to talk briefly with President Jiang Jieshi (Chiang Kai-shek). In Seoul, he brushed off inquiries as to whether the trip was intended to raise his political profile and insisted, in a nationally televised speech, that the United States was opposing "aggression" and guarding people's "right to choose" there and in Vietnam and sought peace but would not sell out "other people's freedom." Korean officials, who had already sent twenty thousand troops, agreed to a modest increase and warned the United States not to repeat the "mistake" it made in agreeing to peace talks in 1951 rather than pressing its advantage to seek better terms than it ultimately got in 1953.[18]

Back in Washington, Humphrey briefed the president and told reporters he had not seen any sign that North Vietnam wanted a peaceful settlement but that he had assured every leader he met that the United States would not "sell out" South Vietnam. Johnson declared Humphrey's mission a success and said he demonstrated his "capacity for leadership in foreign policy." Two days later, the vice president told the NSC that although the four nations he had visited doubted that the US "peace offensive" would succeed, their attitude toward US policy was summed up in Marcos's statement that "those who fight for liberty fight for us."[19]

A week later, Humphrey headed a delegation, including Rusk and two former ambassadors to India, economist John Kenneth Galbraith and former Republican senator John Sherman Cooper, to attend the funeral of India's prime minister, Lal Bahadur Shastri. While out for a walk in New Delhi, Humphrey met Soviet premier Alexei Kosygin, which led to several lengthy private talks, presumably about Vietnam, and generated several days of speculative headlines—but the Russians had no interest in helping the United States out of its deepening quagmire. The effusive Humphrey, however, presented the Soviet leader with a pair of vice presidential cuff links and asked him to hold up his wrists for a picture. The cuff links were never seen again.[20]

Humphrey offered his gloomiest estimate to date in January 1966, according to journalists, when he said Hanoi gave no indication that it sought peace. He attributed that to the "euphoria of its so-called 'inevitable victory.' " A couple of weeks later, he charged that "Asian communism" viewed coexistence with the West as a "fraud" and sought to subjugate South Vietnam. He claimed it was because of this that Johnson had to end the bombing halt in order to put military pressure on North Vietnam. Americans had to face the prospect of a war "that can go on for years."[21]

Johnson feared this, as he did Mansfield's bleak report on his return from Asia and Senator Fulbright's Senate Foreign Relations Committee nationally televised hearings on Vietnam. The White House announced on February 4 that the president would attend a Honolulu "summit" with South Vietnam's leaders, the so-called Young Turks, Generals Nguyen Cao Ky (now prime minister), and Nguyen Van Thieu (a figurehead president), who had taken power in spring 1965 after several coups. Johnson would focus on political-economic-social reform, not military matters, although this was "just a cover," as he told Rusk. The president quickly discovered that Ky, who recently expressed admiration for Hitler, was less interested in reform than flashy uniforms, drinking, gambling, womanizing, and using the US Air Force to his benefit. As William Bundy, assistant secretary for Far Eastern affairs, recalled, the Ky-Thieu directorate "seemed to all of us . . . absolutely the bottom of the barrel."[22]

Johnson promised General William Westmoreland all the military support he would need and sought assurance that he would not "pull a MacArthur" by appealing to congressional hawks to wage all-out war on North Vietnam. The president then met with Ky, who said that his goal was to defeat the Viet Cong and achieve greater social and economic justice and democracy in South Vietnam. Johnson insisted on "results, results" and the need "to see those coonskins nailed to the wall"—a frontier analogy that baffled his host. On February 8, they issued a Honolulu Declaration—far more hollow than real—committing their governments to seeking an honorable peace and a reformed South Vietnam, although Ky ruled out ever admitting the NLF to the government.[23]

Johnson summoned Humphrey to meet him on his way back from Hawaii at the Los Angeles airport, where they had a ninety-minute briefing, during which Johnson emphasized "the other war"—reform in Vietnam. Humphrey found himself embarking on a two-week, nine-nation, 41,000-mile journey to Asia that began in "chaos": Johnson's sudden decision had left no time for planning or briefing papers.[24]

In Honolulu, Humphrey's plane picked up Ky and Thieu and the US officials who had been with Johnson. The vice president's large entourage also included his chief of staff, Bill Connell; foreign policy adviser John Rielly;

McGeorge Bundy and his NSC expert on China, James (Jim) Thomson; elder statesman Democrat and ambassador-at-large Averell Harriman; Orville Freeman; various Agency for International Development officials; Colonel Edward Lansdale; and the ever-present Jack Valenti. Johnson also persuaded the White House press corps, which usually did not cover the vice president, to travel with him. Before taking off for Saigon, Humphrey reiterated to the reporters his "two wars" thesis: the struggle in Vietnam was against "the terror and tyranny of the aggressor" and "the age-old enemies of disease, hunger, and social and economic deprivation." Once airborne, he declared himself "a representative of the Great Society, not a representative of the Pentagon."[25]

From the start, Humphrey occupied "center stage every minute," en route to becoming the "chief exponent" and "star statesman" of the administration's Asian policy. As a diplomat in Vietnam said, "This is the President of the United States, in a sense, setting foot here to assure the world the United States would meet its commitments." But Humphrey's robust advocacy of US policy now differed strongly from his 1964–65 advice to Johnson to disengage from Vietnam and would increasingly alienate the vice president from his devoted liberal political allies and friends.[26]

Humphrey was greeted at Tan Son Nhut Air Base with a twenty-one-gun salute (usually reserved for heads of state), reviewed an honor guard, plunged into a tour of "self-help" projects in a recently pacified village, and inspected housing projects in slum districts in Saigon. An embassy aide said that he also gave "high priced instruction" in American-style politicking to the accompanying General Ky, who—to the amazement of the South Vietnamese—followed along with his sleeves rolled up and made impromptu speeches. At the day's end, Humphrey proclaimed, "The two wars, to defeat the Viet Cong and to achieve a social revolution, are being won."[27]

On his second and last day in Vietnam, Humphrey met with US and other troops, toured the demilitarized zone near the North-South border in a plane with Westmoreland, whose views about winning the war he tended to take at face value, and talked with various officials and reporters. He would recall that Philip Habib, an embassy official and later assistant secretary for Far Eastern affairs, told him to reach out to people other than those scheduled to brief him in order to hear more critical views of the war. Afterward, Humphrey claimed that the "glimmers of dissent" he heard were not enough to dispute the presentations of Westmoreland and Lodge, although he seems to have determined in advance to liken the Vietnam War to his 1940s battles in Minnesota with the extreme left in the DFL Party. As he told reporters, "I fought those bastards then and I'm going to fight them now. We licked them then and we can lick them now." The war in Vietnam was not a civil war, but one "backed by Hanoi and Peking just as Moscow backs East Germany. You can never let the aggressor have his way."[28]

In Thailand, he assured leaders that US emphasis on socioeconomic reform did not mean diminishing its military aid to fight Communists and that the United States would not press South Vietnam to negotiate with the NLF. "The closer one gets to the Communists," he told newsmen, "the less obscurity there is about their aim to take over all of the governments of Asia by force." In Laos, where Prince Souvanna Phouma's government sought to remain neutral, Humphrey said he would do his best to have the US ship tractors rather than weapons. He was also authorized to announce, when meeting with President Mohammed Ayub Khan in Pakistan and Prime Minister Indira Gandhi in India, that their governments would be receiving economic aid loans of $50 and $100 million, respectively.[29]

In Australia, Humphrey attended a late-night dinner during which Walter Jenkins, who had repeatedly said, "The President wants optimism," began to rail about the PRC threat and the US need to win in Vietnam or fend off the Chinese in Honolulu or San Francisco. When Jim Thomson strongly disputed these views, a tired vice president's sharp response ended the meeting, with everyone's feelings bruised. Humphrey threw away a speech Thomson prepared for him, calling it "soft," and the next day, while facing "War Criminal" taunts from protesters, blamed the PRC for directing the "Communist juggernaut" in Asia and called on "every non-Communist nation" to send troops to Vietnam. This "hardline harangue," one aide said, was one of the worst speeches Humphrey had ever made. And while en route to New Zealand, the vice president, always quick to forgive, rejected a gracious apology note from Thomson (long a Humphrey admirer) and—admittedly despaired by growing criticism from former liberal allies— insisted that his views were "intellectually honest" and "strategically correct."[30]

Humphrey garnered major headlines when reporters asked for his response to Robert Kennedy's comment that giving the NLF a "share of power" was the best hope for a negotiated Vietnam settlement. Humphrey likened a coalition government to putting a "dose of arsenic" in a prescription for South Vietnam's ills or putting "a fox in the chicken coop" or "an arsonist in the fire department." Further, "Communists working from within" had always taken over or paralyzed popular-front governments. His remarks, especially "fox in the chicken coop," were more widely reported than those of anyone else (including criticisms from Kennedy family friend Bundy and the dovish Ball). Humphrey's publicity reflected his rising status as the president's spokesman and a leading contender— perhaps versus Kennedy—for the White House in a post-Johnson era.[31]

The vice president thanked the Australians for their support of the US effort in Vietnam and made two final stops in the Philippines and South Korea, whose leaders agreed, respectively, to send an engineering battalion and twenty-five thousand troops to Vietnam. These decisions, Humphrey said, were best made by the people of those countries.[32]

Humphrey's return to Washington on February 23 was carefully orchestrated. His transfer from Andrews Air Force Base to the White House South Lawn coincided with national television's evening news hour. As he descended from his helicopter, Johnson, accompanied by Dean Rusk and McGeorge Bundy, welcomed his emissary with a bear hug and thanked him for his great service "in the mission of peace." Humphrey said he returned with "a deep sense of confidence in our cause—and its ultimate triumph," and the "tide of battle has turned in our favor."[33]

The next morning in the Cabinet Room, he told the president, his senior advisers, and leaders of both parties that he had gone to Vietnam as "a researcher, not an advocate," and that US objectives were clear: to "stop aggression" and provide a better life for all. There were no easy or speedy solutions, but "if we don't veer—don't weaken," the United States could achieve its goals. Westmoreland was "a great soldier," Ky and Thieu were "men of high leadership," and the B-52s were doing a "superlative job" blasting Viet Cong redoubts. He again opposed dealing with the NLF: it "is neither national nor liberating, but it is a front," and its Communist creed was "terror, murder, and assassination." Finally, Humphrey expressed anger at the "dastardly" news stories criticizing Asian leaders who supported US goals and at people in the United States who "resent victory." But "the tide has turned" in Vietnam, which was part of the larger struggle.[34]

The vice president restated his views about the tide turning and his opposition to negotiating with the NLF to members of the Senate and House Committees on Foreign Relations, Armed Services, and Appropriations. He spoke similarly to the rest of Congress the next day. Afterward, he was pleased that there had been "no antagonistic questions," although he evaded such queries by declining Fulbright's invitation to testify before his Foreign Relations Committee. When reminded that Vice President Johnson had done so in 1961 after his Vietnam trip, he smugly replied, "That was his privilege. My name is Hubert Humphrey." But a week later, he spoke with Fulbright's committee in a three-and-a-half-hour closed session, which a disdainful McCarthy left in the middle because he had "heard it all before."[35]

Humphrey's self-satisfied manner did not ward off criticism. Senator Morse said, "I think that he [Humphrey] has lost all of his persuasiveness with people who think," and "I never expected my vice president to make this plea for war."

Sharp criticism also came from former ADA compatriots—who began to promote a reluctant Kennedy—and the editors of the *New Republic* and the *Progressive*. The *New Republic* said Humphrey had gone overboard in an unsophisticated way for a "kind of export ADA—Asians for Democratic Action," and the *Progressive* charged that he had become "more royalist than the crown" and Johnson's "hatchet man."[36]

Humphrey's final report for Johnson hung like a "war cloud" over him and his cotravelers, who were polarized. Connell and Valenti wanted to speak positively about the South Vietnamese government's civilian and military policies, but Rielly, Thomson, and others were much more critical. The vice president sided with the hawks; he told the group he wanted the report to show Fulbright, Mansfield, and Morse had missed the "big picture": there was a PRC-led Communist master plan, which was "a plague, an epidemic" that had to be stopped.[37]

His first report on February 25 declared there were no "indigenous" Communist movements: Peking or Moscow controlled them, and the Viet Cong were "terrorists, assassins, and murderers." The Honolulu Conference was possibly a "historic turning point" that might foster victory "on both the battlefield and in the village." This would discredit "wars of national liberation as an instrument of fear and force" and allow Asia to anticipate an era of political and socioeconomic revolution. The United States had to make a major effort to win the military and "the other war" in Vietnam, which was the "immediate battleground" for the larger struggle for all of Asia.[38]

Johnson dismissed the report. Ten days later, the White House issued what Humphrey termed a "pro forma" seven-page summary referring chiefly to the "historic" Honolulu Declaration, the turn in the tide of battle, and the US-South Vietnamese effort to defeat Communist aggression and effect a socioeconomic revolution. Nothing was said of how this would be done, the cost to the United States, and its term of commitment. "We had labored hard," Humphrey reflected, but had brought forth only "a mouse."[39]

Further, despite his claim that the White House's scrubbed version of his report omitted the "more pessimistic passages" and recommendations for personnel and policy changes, no such proposals appear either in his initial report or in the forty-four-page one he filed later in March. This second report emphasized Asian leaders' willingness to battle Communist-backed (mainly PRC) subversion, "notable [military] progress" against North Vietnam, growing success of the "Revolutionary Development" (pacification) program, and the Ky government's commitment to "the other war." There is no mention of bitter dissatisfaction among Buddhists, students, labor groups, and many others with the Ky regime, the pacification program's lack of trained personnel, or that members of South Vietnam's army (Army of the Republic of Vietnam, or ARVN) and local officials extorted taxes and livestock from the villagers. As McNamara would soon report after traveling in Vietnam, pacification had "gone backwards": the B-52 bombings were not halting infiltration from the North but were killing many civilians; ARVN forces were apathetic about fighting; and the war could not be won soon.[40]

✦ ✦ ✦

Humphrey's Asian trip significantly affected him, his reports on Vietnam, and his public positions in coming years. As Rielly reflected, after Johnson sent Humphrey into virtual political exile in 1965 (a hurtful reminder of his earlier Senate isolation) because of his dovish Vietnam views, the vice president yearned to return to the president's good graces. He believed that a vice president has "a constituency of one" and was a realist about political power. As he told Emmet John Hughes, a *Newsweek* columnist and former speech writer for President Eisenhower, in 1966, "Look closely at the eagle of the Vice Presidential seal. . . . It holds just one arrow. The President's clutches a whole phalanx. And there you have the measure of this office: great responsibility, no authority." Later, Humphrey stated bluntly that a vice president has "few and feeble weapons," a president "has an arsenal," and could exclude his subordinate from the corridors of power and subject him to ridicule. The president could also choose a new running mate, even an archrival (Kennedy), as some politicians predicted, if the Vietnam War demanded political compromise.[41]

Humphrey was highly dependent emotionally on Johnson's goodwill. He was extremely happy when Johnson gave him a watch and some "wonderful pictures" for his birthday in May 1966 and invited him for breakfast or afternoon talks at the White House and both Humphreys to private dinners. Humphrey said his frequent travels and speeches in support of the Vietnam War made him "Johnson's Eleanor Roosevelt," a remark that respected *New York Post* columnist Mary McGrory said indicated that he lacked pride. Still, when Johnson gave him a friendly wink as he walked his daughter Luci down the aisle at her wedding in August 1966, Humphrey told Muriel, "I'm back in good standing." And after the president put his arm around him at the White House reception, he said "I was just like his son," which revealed more about his dependency than he realized.[42]

When Humphrey traveled as Johnson's alter ego in early 1966, he was treated as though he might become president one day, a thought always in mind. His reception on his return from Asia added to this: he occupied center stage in

briefing executive branch officials and Congress, and he was widely sought by
the media, political groups, and organizations. He was unmoved by the idea that
the war could not be won soon. He was a long-distance political runner, as his
two-decade battle for civil rights proved, and now he could make winning the
Vietnam wars—the military contest and the "other war"—America's objective.

He would view and report on Vietnam events through politically tinted glasses
and discard his former anticolonial concerns that the United States was replacing
the French and taking sides in a civil war. Instead, he believed the struggle to be
between North Vietnamese Communists and their southern agents (the NLF)—
both aided by the PRC and the Soviet Union—and the non-Communist South
Vietnamese, who sought to form a more democratic society to which the United
States had made a commitment. He also drew analogies between US support for
Great Britain in 1940 and the current need to back South Vietnam.[43]

The astute *New York Times* reporter Tom Wicker, who traveled in Asia with
Humphrey, wrote that he had earned an "A+" as a goodwill ambassador and
would not only share his findings with the American people but seek to set
himself apart from Kennedy, increasingly seen as a rival for vice president in
1968 or president in 1972. The administration used Humphrey as its "liberal
hawk" to counteract the growing liberal Democrats' revolt against the war. On
ABC's *Issues and Answers* in February 1966, Humphrey derided Kennedy's idea
of dealing with the NLF, or Viet Cong, as legitimizing their "banditry and
murder." A week later, he declared, "The NLF is not national and it liberates
no one. The only honest word is that it is a front . . . for the Communist Party
out of Hanoi, backed by the Peking Communist Party." He also tried to stake
out a more moderate position on the PRC by promoting "containment without
isolation," allowing American scholars and journalists to travel to China,
although the Beijing government rejected this "kiss of Judas."[44]

Humphrey told Minnesota Democrats that it was not possible to talk with
the PRC because it wanted the United States to hand over Taiwan—but "we
are not about to give away anybody's freedom." He added that US senators who
opposed current Vietnam policy but favored West Berlin's defense were making
it appear that Americans would keep their commitments "only to white people,
not to brown or yellow people." (The DFL leaders promptly voted unanimously
to support administration policy in Vietnam.) He told AFL-CIO leaders:
"Vietnam is as close to the U.S. as London was in 1940" and was entitled to the
same support. Communism in Asia is "not a subject for academic discussion. It
is a matter of survival."[45]

Humphrey's increasing outspokenness gave him "a place at the White House
table," Tom Wicker wrote in April 1966, even if it was "just above the salt." But

the vice president soon began to push his arguments beyond credible limits. Interviewed by Eric Sevareid on a CBS News special on April 19, Humphrey termed the Honolulu Declaration more than a commitment only to South Vietnam; it was a "Johnson Doctrine" opening the way to creating "a great society in the great arena of Asia." The declaration also signaled the same US relationship to Vietnam as the Atlantic Charter did for the United States to Europe—and when an incredulous Sevareid asked if American ties to Asia were "as fundamental, as long-lasting, intimate, and possibly as historic" as those with Europe, Humphrey replied, "I think so." The next day, he told Democratic Party leaders concerned about the impact of Vietnam on the coming midterm elections they should "not apologize": the war was "morally right" and "aggression unchecked is aggression unleashed." And if the war overshadowed the administration's domestic achievements, it was up to them to "put it in perspective."[46]

On April 23, Humphrey entered the so-called lion's den to address the ADA's annual meeting, which condemned the administration's stepping up of the war and called for a bombing halt and negotiations that included the NLF. He spoke of "we" in referring to his past ADA ties, insisted that the Johnson administration sought to effect "an Asian New Deal," and was following Roosevelt-Truman principles in seeking peace. Older ADAers, long-standing friends, applauded politely; younger members were displeased.[47]

Two days later, Humphrey, distraught over his growing breach with liberals, heatedly told newspaper executives at the Associated Press's annual meeting he would not discuss the basis for the US presence in Vietnam. "We are there," he said, and "I'm not going to argue about that because it's ancient history and can't be repealed." He also insisted, after referring to France's 1954 withdrawal, that "we are not colonialists. We have no empire to save" and were fighting only for the freedom of South Vietnam's people. Critics who called the contest a "civil war ought to know better," he said; the NLF, a "front for Hanoi," was waging the war, and the United States was battling Communists and "poverty, disease, and despair."[48]

The next day, a group of leading writers—including John Hersey, Lillian Hellman, Alfred Kazin, and Louis Untermeyer—presented Humphrey with a petition calling for a bombing halt and peace talks (including with the NLF) and criticizing Johnson for waging an undeclared and disastrous war. But their harshest criticism was for Humphrey, whom they accused of double talk and abandoning liberalism and to be suffering from Ernest Hemingway syndrome: "never thinking he was masculine enough."[49]

On April 29, *New York Times* Washington bureau chief James Reston, in his "Alas, Poor Hubert" column, depicted Humphrey as condemned by his liberal

friends, while praised by former conservative enemies for his "all out" support
of the war. He was trapped politically between Johnson and Kennedy, Reston
said, and given to making interminable speeches "laying it on about Vietnam as
if there were nothing to be said about the other side." But the real tragedy was
that "the mind that was more creative than almost any other in the Senate in
the fifties" was now focused on small chores, ceremonial greetings, and "repetitive political arguments." Humphrey was crushed, and when a senior aide said
that the column was not personal, but about policy, the vice president retorted,
"No, it's about me."[50]

Humphrey had better luck contending the United States should seek to
contain, but not isolate, the PRC. In June, he told the West Point graduating class
the United States needed to "build bridges to keep open the doors to communication to communist states," especially the PRC. The *New York Times* editorial
board praised his speech, which put him in lockstep with Fulbright and his
Foreign Relations Committee, whose recent hearings prompted public discussions and teach-ins at colleges and universities about China, and lessened the
past fifteen years of concern that the PRC was an aggressive international outlaw.[51]

Humphrey grew increasingly estranged from his liberal allies over the Vietnam
War, and by spring he appeared to stake his career on a victory, which Johnson and
his advisers thought possible only by stepping up US bombing of North Vietnam's
petroleum, oil, and lubricant (POL) facilities. They believed that this would slow
North Vietnam's increased infiltration of troops and supplies into the South, raise
ARVN troops' sagging morale and reduce defections, and perhaps pressure Hanoi
to start peace talks. At a June 17 NSC meeting, Johnson's national security advisers
nearly unanimously favored increasing POL bombing; only UN ambassador
Arthur Goldberg said that the Soviets and PRC would make up any losses and that
US public and world reaction to enlarging the war and increasing civilian casual-
ties would be highly negative.

Humphrey sided squarely with bombing POL sites. "We have been up and
down this hill many times," he said, and although increased bombing "will play
hell" in Europe and at the United Nations and "would be a catastrophe" if a
Russian ship were hit, he "reluctantly" accepted this action as necessary to
complicate North Vietnam's logistical problems and perhaps force Hanoi to
negotiate. He reaffirmed his position at a second meeting on June 22, and Johnson
gave final approval after military officials assured bombing POL sites near Hanoi
would cause only minor civilian casualties and strikes would not hit Soviet ships
in the Haiphong harbor. Goldberg remained the lone dissenter.[52]

The POL bombing lasted only until September, when intelligence reports
said it had no impact on North Vietnamese infiltration, morale, or supplies owing

to increased Soviet and PRC support. The next month, McNamara reported pacification in Vietnam had "gone backwards," confirmed intelligence findings about the POL bombing's lack of impact, and noted that the Viet Cong controlled the countryside while ARVN troops remained apathetic. His only proposal was to increase US troops from 325,000 to 470,000, with more to follow, and continue Operation Rolling Thunder bombing with the hope that Hanoi might negotiate.[53]

Humphrey continued to support the war. At President Joaquín Balaguer's inauguration in the Dominican Republic in July, he told the 1,400 US troops still stationed in Santo Domingo that "here it was primarily civil strife," but in Vietnam "it is naked aggression." In mid-August, he said fortitude and perseverance in Southeast Asia might ultimately convince leaders of the PRC and other Communist nations in Asia their aggressive expansion would not succeed. Two weeks later in Atlantic City, he told a Jewish War Veterans meeting that critics of the Vietnam War were advocates of "a new isolationism" and were too young to remember "Nazism, Fascism, and Hitler."[54]

Protesters constantly confronted Humphrey. He usually tried to ignore them, but at Rutgers University in September, he said that the dissenters were dishonoring their academic profession because their arguments rested on "untutored emotion" rather than "knowledge" and "hard analysis." In October at Boston College and Harvard University, he said he had been in more protest movements than those picketing and that the United States was practicing "restraint without appeasement" against North Vietnam's aggression.[55]

Defending the Vietnam War was taking a personal and political toll on Humphrey. When admiring columnist William Shannon sought to defend him against charges that he had flip-flopped on the war and hinted that his view differed from Johnson's but he could not express it, the vice president wrote, "If somehow I should become President tomorrow I would follow essentially the same pattern." Humphrey sent a copy of this letter to White House aide Valenti and was told that Johnson thought it "excellent." When ABC newsman Edmund Morgan asked Humphrey if he had been "in the doghouse" in 1965 for opposing the bombing, he said only that he—and the president—thought the bombing had "certain limitations."[56]

Similarly, when Humphrey advocate and *New York Post* columnist James Wechsler wrote that the vice president's "righteous rhetoric" was almost "reminiscent of Richard Nixon," he said that others had made this false charge, but "this too shall pass." However, when Wechsler later said Humphrey was "at war with himself," he asserted that "it is not Hubert Humphrey who became personal . . . or who cast the first stone. But constantly I receive reports that people who once claimed to be friends of mine in the liberal community now attack me viciously, accuse me of selling out, aping Johnson, violating liberal principles."[57]

Humphrey struggled to find his political bearings in spring 1966. When told that a former Senate colleague had said he had ninety-eight new ideas every week as a senator but now talked only about old ones—"it's not the same man"—Humphrey responded, "Now I am seeing things happen as well as dreaming up what might happen." By this he meant domestic affairs: his strong public support for the president's $2.4 billion Model Cities Program, enacted in the fall and intended to transform urban transportation, schools, and housing, as well as his own calls for states and communities to "wage war against slumism." At the same time Humphrey held to his mainstream NAACP views in opposing recent Black Power calls for "separation and exclusion," which led the press to note that this was "the old Humphrey who spoke," and not as Johnson's agent but as "an independent liberal speaking to other liberals"[58]

Nearly every important Democratic primary race in 1966 for a Senate seat or governorship—in Wisconsin, Florida, Tennessee, Alabama, and California— was perceived as a contest between Humphrey and Kennedy supporters, raising Kennedy's status to a challenger to the vice president or possibly to Johnson in 1968. As *New York Times* journalist Warren Weaver wrote in late May, Humphrey had gained prestige as Johnson's surrogate but had lost his ability to speak freely about issues, whereas Kennedy could openly critique policy. By mid-August Gallup polls showed that Democrats far preferred Kennedy over Humphrey as Johnson's running mate—even in Minnesota, by a two-to-one margin. The president said only that he could not explain this or assure that this "fine and excellent" public servant would be on the ticket in 1968.[59]

Humphrey said Kennedy's rise made him happy to see another Democrat so popular. But in September he declared that Johnson had assured him that as long as he was president, he wanted only him " 'by my side.' " He quickly added, however, that political reality required a president to have "many options" and that his "constituency of one" owed him nothing—"and I'm going to cause him as little trouble as possible." The White House offered "no comment," and James Reston wrote that Humphrey's lagging so far behind Kennedy in the polls was "almost humiliating."[60]

Humphrey not only ran behind Kennedy in Minnesota but could not broker a bitter political battle between incumbent governor Karl Rolvaag and his young and ambitious lieutenant governor, A. M. "Sandy" Keith, who secured the DFL's gubernatorial endorsement at its convention in June. Humphrey coun- seled Rolvaag to accept the verdict, but the governor won the nomination, with

Humphrey remaining neutral. Humphrey was the "biggest loser," Keith said, because unlike the Kennedys, he had not "laid it on the line" for his candidate.[61]

Humphrey was prepared to "lay it on the line" for Democrats in the November elections and planned to campaign in at least thirty-five states to help Johnson, who had "lost Congress." The vice president urged candidates to "run on Vietnam" and insist that the war there was "against hunger, poverty, illiteracy, and disease." He had to remain in Washington after the White House announced that Johnson would be going to Asia on October 17 to meet with America's allies—with a summit in Manila on October 23–25—and would not return until November 2, six days before the election. Humphrey was virtually alone—except for Robert McNamara—among Johnson's senior advisers to argue that the public would see his trip as politically diversionary and vent their anger on the Democrats at the polls. But the president, seeking to boost his own morale and sell the war to the public, would not be deterred, leaving Kennedy as the most prominent Democrat available to campaign for party members and earn their support.[62]

Johnson returned from his trip—after a surprise visit to Vietnam—with nothing achieved despite his repeated argument that if North Vietnam gave up the war, the United States would join with Hanoi to fight hunger and disease. A seven-nation communiqué from Manila said that allied forces would leave Vietnam within six months after the other side withdrew its troops to the North, ceased infiltration, and the "level of violence subsides." Johnson vainly hoped that this "Manila Formula" might induce Hanoi to negotiate and allow the United States to leave Vietnam.[63]

As 1966 drew to a close, Humphrey had reason to worry. During the election campaign, Richard Nixon had predicted that if the Democrats fared poorly, especially in Minnesota, and Johnson remained as weak as he now was, he would choose another running mate in 1968. Despite Humphrey's campaigning, only Senator Mondale, who was seeking his first full term, won in Minnesota; Republicans defeated all the other DFL candidates and swept their party from control in both houses of the state legislature. Democrats also did poorly nationally; Republicans gained three Senate seats, forty-seven House seats, and eight governorships, although the Democrats held firm control of Congress.[64]

Even though Humphrey publicly disdained Nixon's prophecies, polls showed that the vice president's support for the Vietnam War—which had an approval rating of only a 43–40 margin—had cost him at least a third of his liberal supporters and far more among academics, his most vocal constituency. As Reston wrote, Johnson had given Humphrey the "impossible task" of persuading liberals that

Vietnam policy was not only right but "moral and even successful." Further, Humphrey's former backers now favored Kennedy, who led him in national polls by 61–39 as their vice presidential choice and even led Johnson by 44–39 for presidential nominee.[65]

Humphrey remained optimistic. He was the "Best Prepared No. 2 Man" in US history, one columnist wrote. He "still speaks in exclamation points" and is "an uncapped volcano of ideas" who has become a major coordinator of enterprises for the administration and retains the ability to "grab an old friend's arm" to whisper winning words. Humphrey recognized the growing opposition to the war and the shift of many Americans, especially younger ones, to Kennedy. But he was now closer than ever to the center of power and had just moved his family from their Chevy Chase home to a six-room condominium in a new high-rise building overlooking the Potomac River in southwest Washington, where more than two thousand new neighbors greeted him in numerous gatherings. He had resisted the move initially, he said, but after returning from the campaign trail, he discovered that Muriel had gone "high hat, aristocratic" and chosen an apartment on the eighth floor of a nine-story building—"but you know, I never dare think, talk, or even dream about getting to the top."

Humphrey entered the new year with a president who did not use his cabinet for advice so much as to ratify decisions he had made and was unlikely to change course once he set on it, especially regarding Vietnam. Humphrey would soon confront increased urban racial violence, antiwar protests, and growing conflict with his most ardent liberal constituents.[66]

15

NORTHWEST'S PASSAGE

Humphrey's new year began unhappily. Johnson ordered his staff not to consult the vice president about his January 10, 1967, State of the Union address or show him an advance copy until the press had been briefed. Every reporter in Washington knew the contents of the speech before Humphrey did. Even worse, when Humphrey and his former aide Thomas Hughes jogged out of earshot of the ever-trailing Secret Service agents, he told Hughes that the president had put wiretaps not only in his offices but also in his new condominium in Washington. And Jack Valenti and his aides were reporting not only on him but on his staff, who Johnson complained were "wild men."[1]

When the Humphreys invited the Johnsons to their new home for dinner, the president pulled his host aside to tell him that by all reports he was "our greatest national resource" when it came to explaining US policy in Southeast Asia to the public and insisted that Humphrey recite one of his Vietnam speeches verbatim—to his audience of one. Humphrey balked at first, but then gave in to Johnson's persistence, even as the president moved from the sofa to the bathroom, calling over his shoulder, "Keep talkin', Hubert, I'm listenin' "— until the summons to dinner ended this absurd humiliation.[2]

The shortest answer to the question why Humphrey continued to endure Johnson's perverse behavior is most likely found in Humphrey's remark to reporters in early 1967: "I'm Vice President because he made me Vice President"—the office the Minnesotan viewed as providing his best route to the White House, given that he came from a small state and lacked wealth. Humphrey also felt indebted to Johnson for easing his initial pariahlike isolation imposed by the Senate's Old Guard southerners, putting him on the prestigious Foreign Relations Committee in 1953, and helping him become majority whip in 1961. As vice president, he could not contest the president's power, and he personally could not stand up to Johnson, who he had said in 1966 seemed to regard him "almost as a son." Or perhaps better said, Humphrey viewed Johnson as a father figure too powerful for him to fight.[3]

Humphrey was prepared to live with the consequences of his choices. As Max Kampelman, his former legislative aide and now a successful Washington lawyer, said in January 1967, Humphrey was "a fatalist who tries to maximize his opportunities," and he believed that "if you do everything you're capable of, virtue will triumph. He gives the President eighteen hours a day, he doesn't play golf, he's working all the time and when he's not working he's thinking. So while he would be disappointed if history decided he's not to be President, he wouldn't be a beaten, depressed man. He's service oriented and he would want to serve in some other way."[4]

Humphrey delighted in being the administration's chief public spokesman. In February, he toured the western states, with a stop in Minnesota, to remind his DFL compatriots that, contrary to rumors, Johnson intended to head the party's ticket in 1968. Democrats had better "give up the luxury of dropping poison in the water pitchers," he warned, and remember that the "magnificent program of the past two years was the work of your Party . . . and your President." In California, he met with reporters, publishers, and media managers and stressed the "realities of the situation in Vietnam," where the United States had almost half a million troops and, as Johnson conceded in his State of the Union address, the war would continue for at least another few years, although the president was "completely dedicated to peace."[5]

At Stanford University, Humphrey said he was sorry about the recent revelation that the CIA had been secretly funding the National Student Association in order to monitor its liberal activists, but his own efforts to secure private funding for the group had gotten "zilch" due to concern that Communists were subsidizing it. He was pleased that the students gave him a standing ovation for his speech about Vietnam, although when he left, the Secret Service had to get his car through several hundred protesters, and it "takes all of my self-discipline to keep me from letting some of these characters have it." He also said that students at Harvard University who jostled Defense Secretary Robert McNamara's car called up memories of "Hitler Youth" and Communists who broke up meetings in the 1930s.[6]

At a black-tie dinner for the Arizona "power structure" hosted by conservative newspaper publisher Eugene Pulliam, Humphrey gave his audience "both barrels on foreign policy" and drew a "stirring ovation," although he acknowledged that most of the people in Arizona "are hawks." Oklahoma businessman John Criswell, whom Johnson had installed as DNC treasurer, wrote the president that Humphrey had made seven speeches in twenty-six hours in his home state and "took the issues, especially Vietnam, to the folks." He was strong and persuasive, and although Oklahoma was "not Humphrey country," Criswell wrote, "it is a helluva lot more so than before," as well as more "pro-Johnson." Similarly, a White House aide reported that Humphrey was extremely well received in Birmingham, where radio, television, and newspaper editors were now reversing their views to favor the US war effort. Further, the vice president said that the administration was too focused on the eastern press and advised that Rusk and McNamara should spend one day a week taking the case to other parts of the country.[7]

Humphrey was inclined, even at friendly gatherings, to dispute or ignore criticism. After telling an AFL-CIO Council meeting in late February 1967 that South Vietnam's national elections, set for September, might be the "turning point" in the war, he responded to a query as to whether mining of North Vietnam's rivers by the United States was an escalation of the war by calling it a "military decision" that would slow infiltration of troops and arms into the South and hasten peace talks. Asked again if US action was an escalation, he said he had already answered the question. A week later, as he prepared to address a large audience at the National Book Awards ceremonies in New York, about fifty people, including several prominent writers and publishers, walked out; Humphrey grudgingly acknowledged their "free speech" right to protest but carefully spoke only about his literary preferences, largely Mark Twain.[8]

Humphrey's hewing to the Johnson line on Vietnam was evident when a clearly distraught and perhaps somewhat intoxicated president called him in mid-March to advise what he should say to Europe's leaders on his upcoming trip to repair frayed relations. In a long, rambling, frequently digressing monologue, the president urged Humphrey to tell the Europeans how many men the governments of Indonesia, Malaysia, and the Philippines had lost to Communists and how China's Cultural Revolution had become a "blood bath." The president proposed that Humphrey draw up charts in "red, white, and blue" to show Europe's leaders how many times the United States had undertaken bombing pauses, only to have the other side say, "No, no, no, hell, no," to any reciprocal gesture. Neither Prime Minister Harold Wilson nor Premier Alexei Kosygin had sought to start peace talks or gotten Hanoi to say yes to anything—but if they wanted peace, "by God, let them deliver their client." Humphrey's only responses throughout were an occasional "Yes, sir," "No, sir," "That's what I want to do," and "Very good."

Humphrey also said nothing while Johnson angrily reported that he had spoken to Harold Wilson about "the Goddamned bombing" and wanted to know why "nobody says anything about their bombing"—that they needed to "quit bombing the airport . . . and the Embassy in Saigon," and "our bases every day with these Russian rockets. Goddamn it, if they quit bombing, we quit bombing." The president advised Humphrey to get "a damn good staff" and good publicity that "will make you look very substantive . . . and going at the President's request." Above all, Johnson said, "I wouldn't apologize for one Goddamn thing. I'd just take the offensive on everything." Humphrey should let them know that the United States had stood up to others who had tried to "enslave folks"—in Greece and Turkey and Berlin—and that the Europeans should not forget it now. "Just because it's not in their backyard there's no reason to think that by God they ought to let it go off in their brother-in-law's yard." Again Humphrey responded, "Yes sir. Very good."[9]

While Humphrey prepared for his European trip, Johnson flew to Guam to introduce South Vietnam's leaders, Generals Thieu and Ky, to his new ambassador, career diplomat Ellsworth Bunker, and presidential aide Robert Komer, who would head the pacification program and give highly desired "sunny side up" reports, whether justified or not. The president urged Thieu and Ky to ensure that the coming September elections were free and fair, to step up South Vietnamese participation in the war, and to accept likely NLF representation in some fashion in peace talks—a point Humphrey had long proposed, although he publicly denounced the group. But despite General Westmoreland's warning that the war might continue indefinitely even as the bombing took a toll on North Vietnam, Johnson gave no thought to a contingency plan for withdrawal or disengagement from the conflict, which he viewed as a test of his wisdom or judgment for having entered. He lacked ability to admit that he might have made a mistake.[10]

Humphrey, Muriel, ever-present friends Dwayne and Inez Andreas, and some fifty staff members, reporters, and Secret Service men embarked on their seven-nation European journey on March 27. French president Charles de Gaulle and most other European leaders viewed US policy in Vietnam as badly misguided, a huge waste of resources, and worried that a proposed US-Soviet nuclear nonproliferation agreement would create a duopoly of nuclear power. They were also reluctant to negotiate on tariff reductions as Congress's 1962 Trade Expansion Act proposed. Humphrey undertook a near-impossible mission to win minds and hearts—and agreements.

The vice president loved traveling to Europe, where he was often more in tune—especially on social welfare issues—with Social Democrats and British Labourites than with many American politicians. At his first stop in Geneva, he heeded Johnson's advice to give a "pep talk" to US officials on Vietnam, insisting that "we have nothing to apologize for" and that "this is a peace Administration, but a peace-with-honor Administration." He spoke similarly wherever he went, adding that while the United States was subject to opprobrium, European lack of "moral judgment" about North Vietnam's "aggression" or the Viet Cong's "terrorist" actions provided no incentive for them to "turn off" the war.[11]

At The Hague, even Dutch officials, who usually supported American policy, politely called for "rethinking" of issues and a bombing halt in Vietnam, advice Humphrey labeled "very friendly." There was no mistaking, however, the public hostility and throngs of protesters in Italy who threw yellow paint and smoke bombs at the vice president's car in Rome and eggs and tomatoes at it in Florence, which Humphrey did his best to ignore. He presented briefing books detailing US efforts to start peace talks and fight "the other war" in Vietnam to Italian officials and Pope Paul VI, who favored Johnson's war on poverty but clearly disapproved of his Vietnam policy, especially the bombing.[12]

In England, Labourite prime minister Harold Wilson hosted the vice president at his country retreat at Chequers and then at Windsor Castle, where the two politicians delighted in talking of their humble origins and drinking "the Queen's whiskey." Humphrey amiably answered questions from college students on a BBC program and smoothly addressed two hundred members of Parliament, replying with quick and genial wit to questions from hostile Labourites. He drew applause, but also cries of "shame" and "rubbish," when he said that fighting Communism in Vietnam was "reason enough" to be there. Still, Conservative leader Ted Heath praised his "magnificent performance."[13]

West Germany's conservative chancellor Kurt Georg Kiesinger, concerned that the US-Soviet nonproliferation agreement augured a "nuclear confederacy," pointedly did not greet Humphrey at the Bonn airport. But the vice president, who had taken care earlier to visit with and bring greetings from Kiesinger's daughter and her family, who were living in Washington, elicited a warm response from his host, who soon seemed more willing to listen to assurances that the United States did not intend to "leapfrog" over Europe to reach a nuclear accord with the Soviet Union. The chancellor also did not fuss about US withdrawal of 12,000 American troops from Germany, and his government agreed to buy $500 million in US bonds to offset costs of maintaining the 225,000 forces that remained there.

In West Berlin, where US officials always drew large crowds, the police arrested eleven Far Left persons accused of plotting to assassinate Humphrey, who steered clear of the Berlin Wall to avoid any East-West provocation. At the House of Representatives, he drew robust applause for his speech comparing the US presence in Vietnam to defending West Berlin, while he also called for "reconciliation" with Eastern Europe and turning the Iron Curtain into an open door.[14]

Humphrey's biggest test came upon landing at Paris's Orly Airport, where large, hostile crowds confronted him, threw paint and objects at his motorcade, smashed the windows of the American Express and *New York Times's* International Edition buildings, and clashed violently with police, leading to hundreds of arrests, including Americans. Humphrey knew he could not resolve strong US-French differences over Vietnam or de Gaulle's challenge to US predominance over the West's diplomacy.

But the vice president won great respect—and changed the tenor of the talks—with a speech about American and French ties dating from the age of the Marquis de Lafayette through World War II and the Marshall Plan era that called up two centuries of mutual amity, subtly reminding his audience of all the United States had done to keep France a free nation. At an Elysée Palace luncheon, he discarded his prepared text to deliver an extemporaneous tribute to Charles de Gaulle as a "man of courage" whom history would remember as a great leader that brought tears to his host's eyes, and a response—"Thank you"—in English that even skeptical French attendees remarked upon. Humphrey focused on tariff and nuclear nonproliferation—not Vietnam—in talks with Prime Minister Georges Pompidou and Foreign Minister Maurice Couve de Murville, while his public speeches emphasizing "peaceful engagement" with Communist nations were consistent with the emergence of European détente and his own call for containment, but not isolation, of the PRC.[15]

Johnson hailed Humphrey's personal diplomacy. "I have read your reports to me, every word," he wrote to him. "I want you to know that we think you've done a perfectly wonderful job for the country. Your political skill, your good will and good humor have helped us turn an important corner in our relations with Europe. I want you to know how grateful I am."[16]

Despite European leaders' high regard for Humphrey, they remained convinced that the United States was obsessed about Vietnam, and they did not send one soldier.[17]

Humphrey's travels exceeded personal expectations. CBS news commentator Charles Collingwood said on Walter Cronkite's *Evening News Hour* that the vice president was as successful with Europe's elder statesmen as he was with university "kids" on the BBC. He can "smother you with rhetoric, numb you with statistics, surprise you with humor . . . and disarm you with candor." Johnson had him delay his return for a day in order to welcome his envoy himself, along with a large gathering ranging from cabinet officers to secretaries—plus full military honors—on the White House lawn.[18]

After briefing officials, Humphrey whisked off to New York to address a Boys Town Jerusalem dinner as well as a gathering of business executives by the foundation of publishing magnate Gardner Cowles's family and to appear on the *Today* show. He also met with Georgia's governor Lester Maddox, a segregationist who had gained notoriety in 1964 by confronting a group of African Americans attempting to enter his restaurant with a bare-handle ax in his hand. Clearly looking toward the 1968 election, Humphrey proclaimed Maddox a "good Democrat" and said that the "party is like a big house. It has lots of room for all of us."

The vice president told students at the University of Georgia that Martin Luther King had erred by aligning the civil rights movement with the growing peace movement and that the media's focus on bombing in Vietnam was presenting a distorted view of the war. These remarks, especially about Maddox, along with a front-page picture of the vice president holding the governor's arm as they went down a flight of stairs, angered the liberal community, despite Humphrey's effort to explain this "journalistic disaster"; he said he told Maddox that he had to comply with federal civil rights law and that his grip on the governor's arm was not a sign of friendship, only an effort to help him as he stumbled on a step.[19]

By spring 1967, Humphrey had become the administration's chief foreign and domestic policy spokesman, having logged over twenty thousand miles in the United States alone in the first three months to seek support for Great Society programs, justify the war, and prepare for the 1968 election. Ironically, he was now more readily received in the South than Johnson, who underscored the vice president's role at a cabinet meeting on April 19 by declaring that regarding all legislation, it was necessary to "clear it with Hubert." A few weeks later, a national Harris poll showed Humphrey leading Robert Kennedy as the Democrats' choice for vice president by 51 percent to 49 percent, a "remarkable" turnabout from having trailed by 31 percent to 69 percent six months earlier. Further, Humphrey's job rating had risen to a 60 percent to 40 percent favorable margin, while Johnson's was negative at 46 percent to 54 percent.[20]

✦ ✦ ✦

Despite his political celebrity, Humphrey knew that many of his long-standing and most liberal friends—"who I really care about," he told an aide—were deeply at odds with him over the Vietnam War. After his return from Europe, he asked prominent civil rights lawyer Joseph Rauh Jr., whose friendship dated to the founding of the ADA in 1947 and writing of the 1948 Democratic Party civil rights plank that launched Humphrey's national career, to arrange a meeting with disaffected liberals to air their differences. Rauh invited eight others to his home for dinner on April 17, including Arthur Schlesinger Jr., historian and former assistant to President Kennedy; John Kenneth Galbraith, noted economist and former ambassador to India; *New York Post* columnist James Wechsler; syndicated columnist Clayton Fritchey; and *New Republic* editor Gilbert Harrison. Ironically, Schlesinger, having reminded his colleagues that Humphrey had to support the president's policies and that their old friend deserved a polite reception, would engage in bitter exchanges with him.

Dinnertime conversation about farm issues, Minnesota politics, happier ADA days, and Humphrey's European trip was polite. But the "grim subject" of Vietnam was unavoidable, and after the vice president mentioned that the pope had expressed great personal sympathy for Johnson, Wechsler asked if he also said he opposed the bombing of North Vietnam. Humphrey paused, and then said, "Yes, he did." The conversation grew heated. Schlesinger sharply charged that the administration was clinging to an outmoded view of a monolithic Communist world. Humphrey retorted that his friends did not understand the reason for the conflicts, that there had been "less demagogic Russian-baiting" under Johnson than in modern presidential history, and that movement toward détente was under way, although, he conceded, the Vietnam War jeopardized this. As Schlesinger recalled, when pressed to explain what was the US vital interest in Vietnam, Humphrey "lapsed into Ruskese," repeatedly talking about "militant aggressive Chinese communism."

Humphrey also drew strong fire for his remark that the US presence in Vietnam had spurred resistance to Communism in Indonesia, a reference to the October 1965 military coup and ensuing bloodbath led by General Suharto that seized control of President Sukarno's intensely nationalistic and broadly based government. After Schlesinger said that the revolt related to internal politics, not Vietnam, Humphrey repeated his claim, leading the historian to retort, "Hubert, that's shit, and you know it," and they continued to argue, as an observer noted, "like a couple of barroom brawlers."

Humphrey's statement that it was necessary to accept the generals' view of the bombing in Vietnam caused another flare-up, with Schlesinger insisting that the JCS had been wrong about several things, notably the Bay of Pigs. Humphrey asked him if he thought he was better equipped than the military to assess matters, and Schlesinger retorted, "I damn well do." The vice president then asked, rhetorically, if he were president, would everyone in the room advise him to end the bombing to help get the United States out of its "morass." The unanimous answer was obvious, after which Humphrey agreed that the "risks" in this action were "less significant than other factors." But Johnson's advisers "obviously don't agree," he said, and his own participation in foreign policy discussions was only "fragmentary." When Galbraith and Fritchey added that ending the war would require not only halting the bombing—which might not lead to negotiations—but a change in US public opinion, meaning a complete overhaul of the State Department, Schlesinger chimed in that everybody associated with Secretary Rusk had to be "thrown out." Humphrey angrily shot back, "Arthur, these were your guys. You were in the White House when they were chosen. Don't blame them on us." Schlesinger made no reply.

Humphrey's chief concession was his preference for "slowing down" the war by moving toward an undeclared reciprocal military deescalation, although his proposal to build a barrier across northern South Vietnam to curb infiltration was unlikely to succeed. But his repeated use of the word "morass" when referring to the war led one observer to think that this reflected "his own deepening despair about the entrapment." The vice president was moved by the strong arguments made by Fritchey, Galbraith, and others about how bitterly divisive the war was. Everyone agreed that the Vietnam War had to be put in a totally new perspective for the public, but when asked if Johnson could ever imply, in the fashion of Kennedy after the Bay of Pigs, that military escalation had been a mistake, Humphrey remained silent, and then said, "I don't know."

The meeting ended long after midnight; Humphrey went out of his way to put his arm around Schlesinger, who openly apologized for his behavior and afterward wrote that he had been far more discourteous than the vice president. But he was depressed that Humphrey had said nothing about the "human wreckage wrought by American policy," and he lacked any sense "of the concrete human dimension of problems which characterized the old Hubert." As another participant wrote, Humphrey had been "far less optimistic and self-righteous" than on other occasions, although it was clear that "if he had to choose between his old liberal constituency and supporting the president, he would do the latter." As Rauh later said, almost everyone was "struck by the sense that he was increasingly conscious of the dead end into which his own political life might be headed as a result of the war." But despite the efforts of the vice president's long-standing friends and liberal allies, they could not persuade him to take their stance on the Vietnam War, and their political paths would continue to diverge.[21]

❖ ❖ ❖

The rest of 1967 proved unsettling for Humphrey. In June, he noticed blood in his urine. His friend and personal physician, Dr. Edgar Berman, sent him to Bethesda Naval Hospital, where exploratory surgery discovered nonmalignant polyps in his bladder. To be certain that cancer was not developing, Humphrey had to undergo—then and every six months thereafter—a cystoscopy. He remained cancer-free until symptoms recurred seven years later.

Humphrey recovered quickly enough to represent the United States at the inauguration of South Korea's president Park Chung Hee in July. But the vice president was soon deeply saddened when his older brother Ralph died in August of cancer at age sixty-one. A few days later, however, Hubert and Muriel happily witnessed their son Robert's graduation from Mankato State College in Minnesota.[22]

The summer proved long, hot, and deeply distressing for the vice president, who watched the nation experience the most destructive urban racial violence in its history, involving more than a hundred cities, while Humphrey's relations with Johnson further deteriorated.

One of the earliest, and worst, explosions came on July 12 in Newark, New Jersey, where the arrest of a black taxi driver and rumors of his being beaten to death brought several days of rioting. Governor Richard Hughes summoned the National Guard to restore order, but more than twenty-five African Americans were killed, a thousand others were wounded, and $10 million in property was destroyed.[23]

As the rioting began, Humphrey was flying to Missouri for a speaking engagement and from his plane called Hughes—a friend—to tell him not to hesitate to call on him if he thought he could be of help. When newspaper reports erroneously said that Humphrey had offered federal aid, Johnson barked at his White House aide Joseph Califano that the vice president had no authority— "N-O-N-E"—to do that. After further incorrect reports suggested that Humphrey had offered federal marshals, a nearly hysterical president screamed that Humphrey would "bring down the administration" and had Califano call him to provide a transcript of the vice president's conversation with Hughes. When Humphrey—who at first thought Califano was joking—asked, "By whose authority?" Johnson's aide hung up, but called back to say, "By authority of the President." Humphrey provided the transcript and a letter apologizing to the president for having caused concern. Seemingly assuaged, Johnson named Humphrey to head a cabinet committee to work on urban crises.[24]

But before anything could be done, the arrest of a group of African Americans for selling liquor after hours in a nightclub set off six days of arson and rioting in Detroit, a city with a strong economy and a progressive mayor, James Cavanaugh. He called Humphrey to inquire about federal troops. Appalled that if this could happen in Detroit, "it can happen anywhere," and still smarting from the Newark riots, the vice president told Cavanaugh to call Attorney General Ramsey Clark. Michigan senator Philip Hart also called Humphrey, who then took the matter to Johnson, but he flatly refused help. Deeply distraught, Humphrey dropped out of touch with everyone for the next several hours, while Michigan governor George Romney summoned the National Guard to restore order. Six days of rioting led to forty-three deaths, a thousand people wounded, and some thirteen hundred buildings destroyed.[25]

Humphrey addressed a conference of state and local officials in Detroit, where he boldly called for a new "American plan" equal to the postwar Marshall Plan to rebuild the nation's impoverished cities. He insisted on the need for law and order but proposed large investments of public and private capital in housing, jobs, education, and transportation. Injustices of the past century could not be wiped away quickly, he said, but the nation could show that it was as committed to building free and safe communities as it had been to rebuilding postwar Western Europe. And whatever the cost, "we must be willing to pay the price."[26]

Johnson immediately dressed down the vice president: "Hubert, what makes you think you can go around announcing programs like that? I've got all the problems I can handle." The president, worried about Vietnam War costs, insisted that Humphrey's cabinet committee recommend funding only programs under way and then be "tactfully disbanded." The vice president, at the American Bar Association meeting in Hawaii, said that he was not talking about spending billions and "checkbook solutions haven't always worked." He urged American business to provide more opportunity to those who lacked it and warned African Americans not to fall "into the trap of extremists, black or white."[27]

Distraught as Humphrey was by growing urban racial violence in 1967, he was equally torn by increasing public opposition to the Vietnam War. Shortly before his difficult dinner in April with his liberal, antiwar allies, some three hundred thousand people "mobilized" in New York in Central Park to hear Martin Luther King and the famous Dr. Benjamin Spock speak against the war and then lead a march to the United Nations, while fifty thousand people gathered in San Francisco at Kezar Stadium, where Coretta Scott King and Julian Bond—a founder of the Student Nonviolent Coordinating Committee and one of eight African Americans elected to the Georgia state legislature in 1966— assailed US policy in Vietnam. Soon, several of the vice president's liberal compatriots, including Rauh and Schlesinger, founded "Negotiations Now!" to demand an immediate bombing halt and cease-fire in Vietnam, while a group led by Gar Alperovitz—a fellow at the Kennedy School at Harvard University who had quit the State Department to protest the war—organized Vietnam Summer, modeled after the 1964 Mississippi Summer civil rights movement, to inform the public about the Vietnam conflict.

Increasing numbers of young people refused to register for the draft, burned their draft cards, or fled to Canada. On October 21, about 100,000 people gathered to protest peacefully at the Lincoln Memorial in Washington, while another 35,000 marched on the heavily guarded Pentagon, which brought many violent clashes and several hundred arrests—dramatized in Norman Mailer's Pulitzer Prize–winning *Armies of the Night*—while concurrent antiwar protests took place in London, Paris, Berlin, and other capital cities.[28]

Johnson never understood the antiwar movement, which spurred chants from younger protesters of "Hey, hey, LBJ, how many kids did you kill today?" He assumed that subversives, likely Communists, directed the movement, and since 1965 he had asked FBI director J. Edgar Hoover—always searching for alleged Communists—to monitor antiwar dissidents. In mid-1967, he authorized the CIA—in violation of its charter and federal law—to infiltrate (Operation Chaos) many organizations, such as the civil rights group CORE (Congress of Racial Equality), the antinuclear group SANE, and Mothers against the War, in order to undertake disruptive activities ("dirty tricks") to try to discredit them.[29]

Humphrey did not suffer from Johnson's animus or near paranoia, but he sharply criticized war opponents. Americans were not "whiners or quitters," he told a large gathering of Democratic legislators in August, and in early September he said that Johnson's appointments of African Americans such as Thurgood Marshall to the Supreme Court and Robert Weaver as secretary of Housing and Urban Development proved that the "tired people" who believed the war sapped US energy to help the impoverished were wrong. In mid-October, he spoke to 24,000 people at the National Shrine of Our Lady of Czestochowa in Doylestown, Pennsylvania, saying that American involvement in Asia dated at least to the Pearl Harbor attack in 1941, the issue in Vietnam was the "fate of free Asia itself," and those who urged withdrawal would give the impression that Chinese Communism was the wave of the future.[30]

The vice president told 2,500 business executives in Washington on October 23 that Americans had to recognize that the United States was involved in a protracted struggle that would not end until Hanoi recognized that Americans had the "will, the determination, the perseverance, patience, and strength" to see it through. "Dissent" had been intensifying, he said, and had even led to "useful understanding of past mistakes," but it had not offered a "realistic alternative" to Vietnam and subtracted from "intelligent, well-reasoned discussions." Vietnam critics were "poor students of history" who had to be reminded of the need to check "international aggression." The next day, Humphrey told a meeting of AFL-CIO leaders that in 1951 a poll indicated that two-thirds of Americans favored withdrawal from Korea, and he attacked newspaper critics of the Vietnam War as "weekend wonders."[31]

New York Times columnist Tom Wicker wrote that Humphrey's recent remarks did "not suggest a serenely convinced mind," despite his claim that if he did not believe his own comments, "I could not come before mothers and fathers. . . . It would be beneath a man's decency." The vice president was undergoing "an emotional struggle," Wicker said, and the issue was more than war tactics or the number of troops required. The question was whether the war was worth the "indisputable costs," which were running to $24 billion a year and had already claimed twelve thousand American lives, all of which blunted the hopeful beginnings of the Great Society, brought profound discontent to the postwar generation, and added to the climate of violence in the world. This challenged "Hubert Humphrey's sense of decency" and raised the issue that even if the war was right in principle, "can these costs be decently borne?"[32]

Humphrey's response was to double down on his position. He looked to South Vietnam's September elections for the presidency and legislature as the means to establish a viable and relatively democratic state that would justify the war costs, as well as bolster his and Johnson's political standing. Defense Secretary McNamara, increasingly disillusioned, urged an unconditional bombing halt or restriction of bombing to the southern areas of North Vietnam; refusal of further troop increases; and end of search-and-destroy missions in favor of protecting South Vietnam's population. Johnson rejected this, although in a speech in San Antonio in late September, he agreed to a bombing halt if North Vietnam assured that this would bring prompt and productive negotiations and it would not use the halt to infiltrate more men or supplies into South Vietnam. The proposal produced no result, however.[33]

The vice president (codename "Northwest") made his second trip to South Vietnam on October 27, 1967, to represent the United States at the political inaugurations and urge reform and a stronger war commitment on the new government. At the same time, Senator Eugene McCarthy announced that he might contest Johnson in the 1968 primaries, and Secretary of Defense McNamara resigned—or was pushed out by Johnson. Thus, Humphrey's trip and reports seem to have been directed less to the Vietnamese people than to the American public. As his staff indicated to the press, unless the administration could persuade voters of significant progress in Vietnam in the next six months, the vice president and the entire administration would suffer "sure political death."[34]

En route to Vietnam, Humphrey received two briefings. The first, by the US Pacific Command, emphasized the alleged effectiveness of pinpoint bombing of North Vietnam. The second, by marine colonel Herbert Beckington, the vice president's former military aide now stationed in Vietnam, detailed the pervasive corruption of the Saigon government, the popular support for the Viet Cong, and the lack of success of General Westmoreland's "search and destroy" strategy, whereby US military units won daytime battles but effectively ceded the territory to the Viet Cong at night. Humphrey had heard much of this before, but now he seemed agitated to the point of saying, "I'll be damned if I will be part of sending American kids to die for these corrupt bastards."[35]

The vice president arrived in Saigon on October 29 "as a witness," he said, for millions of Americans who trust in the "remarkable progress being made in Vietnam," symbolized by the inaugurations. His official greeter, Vice President Ky, reciprocated by chiding American critics of the war as being unable to distinguish between self-defense and "external aggression." Humphrey attended the inauguration of President Thieu—who expressed willingness to engage in peace talks but insisted that South Vietnam remain independent, all but ruling out negotiations—and returned for a reception to Independence Palace, where three Viet Cong mortar shells hit in the garden where he, Thieu, Ky, Ambassador Bunker, and Westmoreland would have been standing had rain not forced them inside.[36]

Humphrey spoke first with Ky, who said he was powerless to effect policy as vice president, a point Humphrey said he well understood. Next he sought to impress on Thieu the need for greater government reform and for the Vietnamese to take on more of the fighting because neither Congress nor the American public would continue to support the war at current high levels. Thieu listened, while smoking a Gauloise cigarette, and then flicked the ash in a manner suggestive of also flicking away Humphrey's advice. "We have appreciated your help," Thieu said, "but we also know that you must maintain your current levels of support for several years, and perhaps even increase them for a time." A startled Humphrey responded that perhaps his host had not understood him—it would be impossible to sustain present US support levels without significant improvement in his regime's policies. Thieu waved the hand holding the cigarette, said, "Oh yes . . . yes," and rose from his seat to escort his guest from his office.[37]

Despite the abrupt treatment, Humphrey asked Bunker if he had been too rough on Thieu; the ambassador assured him that the Vietnamese needed to hear what had been said. That night, Humphrey wrote Johnson—in language that did not reflect what had transpired or that Thieu and Ky were bitter rivals who were unlikely to cooperate—that both leaders were "determined to move strongly not only militarily, but in building a responsive, representative government. Both feel that the Viet Cong can hold out no longer than our November 1968 elections, but will fight in smaller units, until the death. Both were concerned as much as anything else, with U.S. opinion. I assured them of our continued support in the face of unfavorable opinion."[38]

The vice president told the US embassy staff and military personnel that they were fighting not just for South Vietnam's freedom but for the "ultimate freedom of the United States." He said that in wartime, America was always marked by both "disagreement and valor," but now he charged that "ugly dissent" in the United States refused to see the "remarkable" political, military, and economic progress being made in Vietnam. "Our business is to make history," he said, and great American leaders from Washington to Lincoln to Truman had faced tough challenges. "I saw nation building this morning," he said, and now in Vietnam the "family of man" had gained the time needed to break through to a new era of human development and justice. "This is the chance we have. This is our great adventure—and a wonderful one it is." These final words, spoken with thoughtless enthusiasm amid the gruesome Vietnam War, would soon be hurled back at him.[39]

Afterward, Humphrey flew with a military escort to various bases, including those under heavy fire near the demilitarized zone (DMZ), to bring news from home, award medals, and lavish praise on the troops. "We are winning the struggle," he said, "I don't say it has been won. I say we are winning it." Departing from Danang, he told a press conference that he had not heard one word of complaint from the troops in Vietnam and that "building a nation is the work of generations, not of days." As had become his habit, he cautioned friends back home "not to put poison in the soup you are going to have to eat."[40]

Humphrey went next to Kuala Lumpur, where he pledged to seek greater US aid for the strongly anti-Communist Malaysian government in return for increased help with rural development (but no troops) in South Vietnam. He then spent almost three days in Indonesia, the first high-ranking US official to visit there since General Suharto's forces overthrew President Sukarno's government in October 1965. Humphrey wrongly denied any US role in that coup, but again insisted that the presence of US troops in Southeast Asia provided a shield for anti-Communist forces. He also praised the strongman Suharto as a "tough and shrewd leader" who was bringing recovery to the economically distraught country—a judgment one reporter said reflected Humphrey's ability to "spot a silver lining in even the stormiest clouds."[41]

Humphrey returned to Washington from his eleven-day trip on November 7 to a modest White House reception. Just before he briefed NSC, cabinet, and congressional officials, Johnson passed him a note: "Hubert, keep it upbeat, short, then sit down." The vice president complied; he said that he had seen significant changes and an improved US military situation in Vietnam since his first trip in February 1966 and that US commanders were certain they could handle anything thrown at them. He also added his frequent, and inaccurate, claim that US forces in Southeast Asia gave confidence to the Indonesians to destroy their Communist Party.[42]

In his memoirs, Humphrey wrote that he told Johnson the United States had to help the Thieu-Ky government build popular support and establish a constructive relationship with the legislature. But at the time, he said publicly that it was not important that Thieu had not appointed any major political opponents to his cabinet or that he had named as Prime Minister Ky's close ally. The major goal, he said, was to gain control over the military corps commanders, who ran their regions like "war lords"; meanwhile, he added, the Saigon government had opened numerous new seaports and airports. Most important, he claimed that the new spirit in Vietnam was "nationalism," which was not there earlier—a statement that ignored the Vietnamese people's battle against French colonialism from the 1930s to 1950s.[43]

Humphrey was even more emphatic in a lengthy report he sent to Johnson. The vice president hailed the "extraordinary performance of American and Free World forces" that had transformed a stalemate into "the rollback" of the Viet Cong and North Vietnamese troops, an "outstanding victory," although the Viet Cong remained "largely intact in the countryside" and were "moving aggressively" in Saigon. The government there needed to focus on pacification, but now he insisted that this could be done only by the armed forces, including the dreaded corps commanders, because they were the nation's principal political structure and because, despite his and Johnson's earlier proclamations, there was no "other war," only an integrated effort led by the military to establish order.

Most significantly, Humphrey proposed an end to calling for negotiations; he said this only strengthened the North Vietnamese belief that the US government was weakening under public opinion. He advised, instead, continuing the "relentless air effort" against North Vietnam's supply lines and forces in the South, which would lead to "demonstrable and self-evident victory in the coming year." He also insisted on avoiding Americanization of Vietnam's undertaking so that responsibility would fall to the people there, thus allowing the administration to say that Vietnam was made "by and for the Vietnamese."[44]

Humphrey spoke with equal optimism to the public. He told a business executives' meeting in Washington that he had "not forgotten the lessons of the '30s, when men cried peace and failed a generation," and when talking to AFL-CIO leaders, he lambasted administration opponents as a "coalition of retreat." In New York in mid-November, he told another gathering of businessmen that the enemy was being "systematically defeated" and that North Vietnam's only hope for victory was "division, despair, and defeatism" in the United States. In Minneapolis, addressing a journalists' society, he deplored the emergence of an alleged "new isolationism" in the United States and worried that if it abandoned its role in Asia, the people there would be subject to "aggressive Asian communism, which they have resisted for twenty years." Humphrey disputed Robert Kennedy's charge that the South Vietnamese—who had recently left it to the Americans to "charge up the hill" to defend the military base at Dak To near the DMZ—were not fully supporting the war effort. But the vice president did not respond to the senator's second complaint that the Johnson administration had changed the rationale for the war from defending South Vietnam against aggression to protecting larger US interests in Asia.[45]

In December, Humphrey, who in early 1966 had deplored Robert Kennedy's proposal to allow the NLF a role in South Vietnam's government as putting "the fox in the chicken coop," now said that negotiations between Saigon and the NLF were a possibility, although only with non-Communist NLF members, a virtually self-defeating requirement. A few days later, addressing a DFL convention in Minneapolis, Humphrey sought to dispel rising opposition to current policy with a vigorous two-hour speech that ran through arguments ranging from the consequences of appeasement to the need for nation-building in Vietnam and defense against aggressive Asian Communism. But when he again analogized the Vietnam conflict with the failure to resist Hitler, one aggrieved DFL official shouted that her objection was not to World War II but to the Vietnam conflict.[46]

Humphrey had come full circle in his position on Vietnam. In 1964–65, he had urged Johnson to disengage and then opposed expanded bombing. He proposed stepping up the pacification program, seeking major reform of the government, and looking to negotiations that somehow would include the NLF. But by 1967 he had become a hawk on Vietnam, and in his memoirs he sought to explain this evolution by relying on the old saw that "where you stand depends on where you sit." His views would have been different had he remained a senator and not become vice president, he said. But listening every day to the president's advisers—Rusk, McNamara, McGeorge Bundy, Walt Rostow, and Generals Westmoreland and Earle Wheeler, the last chairman of

the JCS—meant becoming part of an increasingly closed society. Once a decision was made, there was an irresistible impulse to become more "locked in,"
or hardened like cement. To this, he added that all but two senators had voted
for the Gulf of Tonkin Resolution—with no mention that Johnson had lied
about what had happened in August 1964—and that critics of US policy rarely
saw anything wrong with Viet Cong or North Vietnamese actions, an argument
that begged the question of the merit of US policy.[47]

Humphrey was privy to more information, public and private, than any
congressman or ordinary citizen, and with good reason he referred to the
Vietnam situation as a "morass," as his liberal friends noted in April 1967.
Moreover, on his latest trip to Vietnam, his former military aide, Colonel
Beckington, briefed him on the pervasive corruption of the South Vietnamese
government, public support for the Viet Cong, and the failure of Westmoreland's
search-and-destroy missions. The vice president knew that little progress had
been made with pacification, and President Thieu had virtually blown away
like cigarette smoke his advice about needed governmental reform. Humphrey
was well aware of all the public testimony before Congress and statements in
the media about the lack of political reform and military success in Vietnam,
and his aides and friends in the State Department, such as his former staffer
Tom Hughes, kept him well informed.

Humphrey's passage from dove to hawk on Vietnam was not the result of one-
sided White House briefings or of his ability, as one journalist had noted, to see
silver linings in the stormiest clouds. His change in position derived from a case
of willful mind over matter, from his strong anti-Communism combined with
political expediency driven by ambition, namely desire to remain in Johnson's
good graces and perhaps succeed him whenever his presidency ended. At the
same time, Humphrey wanted the outcome in Vietnam to reflect genuine nation
building and democratic advancement so badly that he forced himself to see such
results wherever he went, despite the reality before him. This was self-delusion.

He could not bring himself to resist Johnson's importuning him to "keep it
upbeat"; thus, he tailored his words—and perhaps his thoughts—to conform to
what he knew his political superior wanted to hear. He also lacked the personal
and political strength, or assets, to contest the president and his power. Having
suffered near-pariah status during his early Senate years and exile from the
White House's inner circle in 1965, he was determined never to suffer such
isolation again.

Rather than cross or disappoint Johnson, he tied his political fortune to
staying the course with him and his Vietnam policy in the hope that the
outcome in Southeast Asia would justify his decision and ultimately allow him

to run for the White House on his own terms. He would gain this latter goal far sooner than anticipated, but under unimagined frightful terms or circumstances that would splinter his liberal constituency and the Democrats while he remained political captive to a discredited but domineering, and somewhat paranoid, president.

16

LAST MAN IN

From late December 1967 to early January 1968, Humphrey led a large delegation, including his wife, Muriel, Associate Supreme Court Justice Thurgood Marshall, numerous aides, government employees, business and organization leaders, and twenty reporters, on a nine-nation, 22,000-mile journey across Africa. The vice president largely dispensed Export-Import Bank loans and PL 480 food grants and urged African leaders facing sharp cutbacks in US foreign aid to open their nations to private US investment.

On his return to Washington, Humphrey happily reported to Johnson that it would have "gladdened your heart" to hear "praise and friendship for you" in Africa, where the United States did not suffer the "colonial image" of European nations. Humphrey told reporters that he was delighted not to have spent even "30 minutes" discussing Vietnam with his hosts, although members of his party said that the issue "came up everywhere" with young people.[1]

Vietnam was becoming the predominant issue, especially for Democrats after Senator McCarthy made it known that he intended to challenge Johnson in the 1968 primaries. His decision to contest a powerful and vindictive president was audacious and of complex motivation. Admittedly bitter toward Johnson for not choosing him as his vice president in 1964, he later said, "I vowed I would get that son of a bitch, and I did." McCarthy was also tired of Senate life: he had not initiated major legislation and saw Humphrey and Johnson as blocking a route to the presidency.[2]

Humphrey credited McCarthy's challenge to his "change of mind" about the war. The senator was a traditional Cold War liberal who supported US policy in Vietnam until late 1965, when he grew concerned about the militarization of US foreign policy and concluded that Johnson had lied about Tonkin

Gulf events in 1964 and grossly misused Congress's resolution to expand the war in Vietnam. McCarthy began to rethink the conflict as a civil war rather than a Sino-Soviet inspired aggression and viewed Undersecretary of State Nicholas Katzenbach's August 1967 statement to the Senate Foreign Relations Committee equating the Tonkin Gulf Resolution with a war declaration allowing the president to use the armed forces as he saw fit as akin to establishing a "dictatorship in foreign policy." This called for a "showdown challenge."[3]

In early October, McCarthy agreed to be the candidate of the National Conference of Concerned Democrats, or "Dump Johnson" movement, a group of young activists led by Allard K. Lowenstein, a University of North Carolina and Yale Law School graduate and former foreign policy assistant on Humphrey's staff in 1959. McCarthy likened his effort to Humphrey's having forced the Democrats and a sitting president to confront civil rights at their 1948 convention and after two months of speech-making gained enough support from prominent ADA leaders and wealthy Democratic contributors to agree to challenge Johnson. "There are some things that are just so wrong, that you have to take a stand, no matter what," he said.[4]

Humphrey told the president that he was "very much upset" at McCarthy's decision but initially regarded it as a "lark," given the senator's casual manner toward major undertakings. The vice president, acting first on his own and then at Johnson's behest, tried but failed to dissuade his fellow Minnesotan from his campaign. "I guess I have no influence on these friends of mine," Humphrey told the president, meaning the many Senate liberals who now opposed the war. But McCarthy "is my friend," he told the press, "and no matter what happens we will continue to have lunch together."[5]

In November, McCarthy formally declared that he would enter four primaries. He sought an "honorable, rational, and political solution to the war," which he termed too costly in terms of lives lost on both sides, the destruction of Vietnam, and could not be justified morally or before "the decent opinion of mankind."[6]

Longtime DFL colleague Agriculture Secretary Orville Freeman said that McCarthy would soon be "a very small footnote, if a footnote at all, in history." The White House attributed his chief support to East and West Coast liberals, Johnson led him by 62 percent to 17 percent in an early Harris poll, and New Hampshire Democratic senator Thomas McIntyre, cochair of Johnson's reelection campaign, branded him "an appeaser" who would get less than 10 percent of the vote in his state's primary.[7]

Humphrey was equally confident, as he wrote after returning from Africa, that Johnson would be renominated and reelected; he was a "strong man who knew how to get things done in a rough competitive world" and was "the kind of President the times called for." The vice president supported him "without equivocation," felt closer than ever to him, and would campaign for him regardless of whether he was still his choice for running mate.[8]

Humphrey flew to California at Johnson's behest in mid-January to contest McCarthy's effort to gain support of the liberal California Democratic Council. Humphrey denied that he was the White House's designated "stop McCarthy" spokesman and vigorously insisted to a thousand delegates at a regular Central Democratic Committee conference that the United States was in Southeast Asia "not to make war but to maintain peace" and to build a nation. He warned that "disunity" might bring a Republican victory in November and used his too familiar refrain: "Don't put poison in the well whence you're going to have to drink, fellow Democrats."[9]

Humphrey could not contain the downward spiral of events, however. On January 23, 1968, North Korean ships captured the USS *Pueblo*, an intelligence ship, in international waters and interned its crew. Johnson, intent to avert another crisis abroad, would have to endure eleven months of tortuous negotiations, and an ambiguous US apology, to get the crew returned.[10]

North Vietnamese and Viet Cong forces launched their Tet (lunar New Year) Offensive on January 31: major assaults on five of six of South Vietnam's biggest cities, including Saigon, and eighty provincial and district capitals. The offensive did not spark major rebellions against the Saigon regime as the North Vietnamese and Viet Cong had hoped, but American and South Vietnamese troops battled for weeks to beat back enemy forces, who were soon rebuilt and able to carry out "mini-Tets" in the next couple of years.[11]

The Tet Offensive stunned the US military and gave lie to the administration's claim of progress in the war. Republican senator Thruston Morton of Kentucky quoted Humphrey's 1951 remark that it was "outright political stupidity and national suicide" to fight a land war in Asia and branded US Commander General William Westmoreland's assertion of "light at the end of the tunnel" as "grossly misleading." Similarly, at the start of the offensive CBS News's Walter Cronkite snapped, "What the hell is going on? I thought we were winning the war," and weeks later he declared on his "Special Report" on Vietnam that the United States was "mired in stalemate." Johnson said, "If I've lost Cronkite, I've lost the country."[12]

The president now told his military advisers to lay out what was needed to meet a crisis request from Vietnam. The Joint Chiefs of Staff asked first for 45,000 more troops—Johnson sent 10,500—and on February 27, they and Westmoreland requested another 206,000 troops to join the 500,000 forces deployed.[13]

The ever-optimistic Humphrey drafted a paper for Johnson, "Regaining the Initiative," proposing to fund the troop increase with a special 1 percent war tax, step up the South Vietnamese army's arms modernization, and demand better battle performance. But Johnson, already concerned about his political credibility and an imbalance of payments that had devalued the dollar and caused a sharp run on gold, rejected imposing new taxes or mobilizing the reserves in an election year. He turned the issue over to his new secretary of defense, Clark Clifford, a former counsel to President Truman and a highly influential Washington lawyer and Democratic operative.[14]

Clifford, a foreign policy hawk, formed a task force composed of experienced civilian analysts in the Pentagon, while his own questioning revealed that the military had no plan for "victory" even with 206,000 more troops — which North Vietnam could match — and increased bombing. By March 4, his group was convinced of the need to start peace talks.[15]

Even in Humphrey's Minnesota, the political landscape shifted sharply against the administration. DFL chair Warren Spannaus had predicted that in the March precinct caucuses McCarthy's supporters would win no more than six of the fifty-two delegates. But the senator's supporters won convincingly in the three congressional districts in the Minneapolis–St. Paul area and made inroads in Minnesota's five other, largely rural districts, assuring McCarthy at least sixteen Democratic convention delegates.

Minnesota's secretary of state, Joseph Donovan, said, "never in 50 years in politics" had he seen such a large and diverse turnabout in the Twin Cities, which cost even Humphrey's son Hubert III ("Skip") and son-in-law, Bruce Solomonson, their DFL precinct positions. McCarthy was also assured that Massachusetts's seventy-two delegates would cast their first ballots for him because Johnson failed to file for the April 30 primary.[16]

McCarthy's "tremendous showing," as Humphrey called it, in the March 12 New Hampshire primary stunned the political world as his largely young people's movement gained him 42.4 percent (and within 230 votes of defeating Johnson after Republican write-in votes were counted) against Johnson's 49.5 percent. Kennedy jumped into the race, while McCarthy was poised to win a major triumph in Wisconsin's primary.[17]

Humphrey was torn: he worried his career was being destroyed by the defection of key Democratic constituents, such as African Americans, who, led by Martin Luther King, were turning against the war. But despite the New Hampshire results, he still believed that "when the chips are down," the American people would stick with the "hard task" of the Vietnam War. He told a Democratic regional conference in Rhode Island that McCarthy's challenge was just the party's way of debating issues: Johnson would be renominated and reelected and bring peace in Vietnam "without appeasement."[18]

Humphrey urged Johnson to use the impact of the Tet Offensive—and public opposition to the war—to press South Vietnam's president, Nguyen Van Thieu, to propose UN supervision of a cease-fire, withdrawal of all foreign troops from South Vietnam, and general elections that included all parties. In turn, the United States would halt bombing above the 20th parallel, sparing densely populated Hanoi and the port of Haiphong. Humphrey hoped to induce North Vietnam into peace talks, despite doubts that Ho Chi Minh would accept, but at least Johnson would gain politically for his effort. The president, however, rejected his proposal.[19]

Johnson also rejected the military's expensive request for 206,000 more troops on March 22 and summoned the so-called Wise Men, whom he had been consulting since 1967, to weigh war options. The group, which included former secretary of state Dean Acheson and former national security adviser McGeorge Bundy, met with State, Defense, and CIA briefers and then with the president, Humphrey, Clifford, Rusk, and Generals Wheeler and Maxwell Taylor. Acheson admitted that he had changed his mind on the war and spoke for nearly all in insisting on a bombing halt to induce peace talks.

Johnson was surprised and afterward—using Humphrey's phrase—asked Clifford and Rusk, "Who poisoned the well with these guys?" and remarked to an aide, "The establishment bastards have bailed out." He called an extra briefing with Humphrey and several civilian and military advisers, only to hear George Carver, special assistant for Vietnamese affairs to CIA director Richard Helms, reiterate the grim assessment. Humphrey was "effusive" about the briefing, however; he walked Carver—who had feared to bring bad news—and Helms out of the White House to assure them that Johnson had appreciated the presentation. Two eventful weeks later, Humphrey would again thank Carver for his "brutally frank and forthright analysis," which had a "profound effect" on US policy in Vietnam.[20]

The March 25–27 briefings compelled Johnson to change course, as even his close aides and Texas governor John Connally now advised him against seeking reelection. He ordered his speechwriters to craft a "peace with honor" address he planned for March 31 and had his aide Horace Busby secretly craft a possible alternative ending stating that he would not seek reelection in order to focus on securing peace.[21]

Humphrey still believed in Johnson's presidential viability and in talks alone at night advised him to assuage the public by offering a full bombing halt in North Vietnam and calling for a cease-fire and reconvening of the 1954 Geneva

Conference. But Johnson again rejected his proposal. Humphrey reported after meeting in North Carolina with seven southern governors that all but Alabama governor Lurleen Wallace had assured him that their convention delegates would be either pledged or favorably disposed to the president. "Strange as it seems," Humphrey added, he now got on well with the southern leaders, even Georgia's fiery segregationist Lester Maddox. Clifford pressed Johnson's advisers to urge him to announce a full bombing halt, but the JCS, Johnson's close friend and Supreme Court Justice Abe Fortas, and Ambassador to Vietnam Ellsworth Bunker successfully pressed him to settle on a partial halt.[22]

Early on March 31, the Humphreys were packing for a flight to Mexico City, where he was to lead a delegation to witness his signing of a protocol to the 1967 Treaty of Tlatelolco pledging US respect for the Latin American nations having agreed to keep their region free of nuclear weapons. Shortly before noon, Johnson, his wife, Lady Bird, and their daughter Luci and her husband, Patrick Nugent, an air force enlisted man, having attended church in Washington, stopped at the Humphreys' apartment. The president pulled Humphrey into his den to have him read the speech he would deliver that night announcing a partial bombing halt. The vice president said it was "just great, the best thing I have ever heard you say." Johnson then handed him his alternative ending announcing his withdrawal from the presidential race. "You're kidding, Mr. President. You can't do this," a startled Humphrey said. "You can't just resign from office. You're going to be reelected."

Johnson indicated his uncertainty about withdrawing but said that his peace-seeking efforts would be seen as political moves if he ran for president. He added that men in his family had died early from heart trouble, and he wished to live a while longer. He swore Humphrey to secrecy—not a word even to Muriel—and told him he had "better prepare to run for president." The vice president, "inwardly thunderstruck," said only, "There's no way I can beat the Kennedys." On leaving, Johnson again urged, "You've got to get moving."[23]

As the Humphreys sped to Andrews Air Force Base, Muriel asked if something was wrong with Johnson; the vice president said no, he was only tense about his impending speech. But as Humphrey boarded his plane, his fellow travelers noted that he was unusually silent. After the dinner he hosted that night for Mexico's president, Gustavo Díaz Ordaz, at Ambassador Fulton Freeman's residence, he asked Díaz Ordaz and a few others to join him in the library to listen to Johnson's speech, a surprising protocol breach that took attention away from the honored guest.

In the speech, Johnson proposed a start to peace talks by announcing a bombing halt above the 20th parallel, ending attacks on Hanoi and Haiphong but continuing them in the DMZ area. As the president neared closing, Humphrey was summoned from the room to take a call from White House aide Marvin Watson, who said Johnson would state that he would not seek reelection. "Oh, my God, he shouldn't do that," the vice president blurted, but Watson said that the president had made his decision. Humphrey returned to the library, and muttered, "You shouldn't do this," as Johnson spoke his final words. Muriel Humphrey burst into tears, angry at her husband for not forewarning her and at Johnson for not having given him time to prepare for his coming political life. Clifford, too, was angry, he later said, because he would have pressed harder for a full bombing halt had he known Johnson was leaving the presidential race, or so it seemed.[24]

US reporters began to pound at the embassy door to ask Humphrey if he would enter the presidential race. His press secretary, Norman Sherman, told them and countless callers that the issue had not been discussed. Humphrey spoke on the telephone that night only with Margaret Truman Daniel, the former president's daughter, and Patrick O'Connor, a Minneapolis friend and lawyer, both of whom urged him to run. He thanked them but said he had not made a decision. He also telephoned Johnson to say he was sorry.[25]

Members of Humphrey's delegation urged him to run. This included Organization of American States ambassador Sol Linowitz, who said it was inevitable; foreign policy adviser John Rielly; political aide Ted Van Dyk; Senator Morse; and Dr. Berman. Humphrey insisted, however, that he needed to talk with Muriel and to think things through. He feared being "destroyed again in a fight with the Kennedys," he told an aide, and worried that they had already moved into the power vacuum.[26]

Humphrey told Berman he was still uncertain about the domineering Johnson's motives, whose stepping down was so uncharacteristic, although he recalled that the president had told him earlier that day that despite what he had done for "the Negro and the poor, even they're against me." Humphrey ran through a list of Democratic governors, mayors, and union leaders for whom he had done so much, and said, "I'm not begging. They know where to get in touch with me. So we'll wait and see." Still, he said presciently, "If I run, Johnson's not going to make it easy."[27]

In Washington, Humphrey's chief of staff, Bill Connell, had already telephoned fifty Democratic leaders around the country—often finding that a Kennedy backer had already called—to ask they hold for the vice president. He had not been able to talk to him, Connell said, but indicated that he was likely to run.[28]

The next day, Humphrey attended the protocol signing and, quietly brooding, flew to Washington. As his plane taxied to a stop, several hundred people greeted him, including Rusk, Freeman, Labor Secretary Willard Wirtz, and numerous White House aides, with "Humphrey for President" signs. "Oh, no, oh, no," he sighed. A more buoyant Muriel said, "Well, Daddy, there they are once again." As he stepped onto the tarmac, his first words to Connell were, "Has Bobby got it locked up yet?" His chief of staff reassured him that all the officials he had called had agreed to delay any decision. He added that Kennedy's bandwagon had stalled and that only Humphrey could capture the center of the Democratic Party.[29]

Connell met earlier that evening with a group of the vice president's long-time friends and advisers, including Max Kampelman, Evron Kirkpatrick, Gus Tyler, head of the International Ladies' Garment Workers' Union, and staffer William Welsh. They agreed to urge Humphrey to declare at once. The next morning, Louisiana congressman Hale Boggs and Humphrey's old friend Senator Russell Long pressed him to commit "or Kennedy will wrap it up." Oklahoma senator Allmer Stillwell "Mike" Monroney called with the same message. AFL-CIO president George Meany arrived at Humphrey's office to demand an immediate announcement and went to the White House to urge Johnson—in vain—to call on Humphrey to run.[30]

The vice president attended a dinner that night in New York at the Waldorf-Astoria sponsored by Minneapolis publishing magnate Gardner Cowles and agribusinessman Dwayne Andreas. Afterward, at Andreas's apartment at the Waldorf Towers, a group of major business figures, including Henry Ford II, Jacob Blaustein, head of Amoco, and Sydney Weinberg, leader of Goldman Sachs, pledged support for Humphrey. These men, and others present, all feared Kennedy and were uncertain about McCarthy, who that day beat a noncampaigning Johnson in the Wisconsin primary by a 56 percent to 35 percent margin.[31]

The next day, the president reluctantly received Kennedy (that "grandstanding little runt," Johnson remarked) and declared himself "no king maker." He said he would remain neutral because that was the only way to achieve his goals, including peace in Vietnam. Kennedy likely was disbelieving, although when Humphrey told the president he had not announced his candidacy so as not to "demean" Johnson's withdrawal statement, he retorted that was Humphrey's choice. He also sought to blame him for McCarthy's Wisconsin win by saying that if the vice president intended to run, he would have to do a better organizing job than had been done for him. Further, Johnson—unaware of Humphrey's Waldorf meeting—said money would be an issue, a sure sign he would not help, and added that the vice president would have to fight hard to win in big northern states such as New York, New Jersey, Pennsylvania, and

Illinois. And when Humphrey said New Jersey's governor Richard Hughes and Chicago's powerful mayor Richard Daley had made no decision, Johnson said they would go for Kennedy.[32]

Humphrey was pleased the next day to hear Johnson tell his cabinet he rated him a "triple A-plus" as vice president and himself only a "B-minus." Humphrey agreed that the president had to appear neutral regarding Democratic presidential candidates, although he told a friend he was certain that Johnson "did not renounce the presidency in order to be succeeded by Robert Kennedy." Still, Humphrey was disappointed by Johnson's lack of private encouragement and wanted more time to get his "ducks in a line" before declaring. He continued to worry about contesting a Kennedy again but knew that delaying meant he would miss the filing deadline for the only two primaries he could still enter, in New Jersey and South Dakota, thus averting the need to debate his rivals about the highly unpopular war. He also worried about a bad vote in a primary and hoped that Kennedy and McCarthy, without Johnson as their main target, would weaken each other. He would rely on Democratic officials—many of them old friends or indebted to him for past favors—in the thirty-six nonprimary states that would choose about three-fourths of the convention delegates, with most of them likely to favor his candidacy.[33]

Humphrey "loved" the attention he was getting and was elated when Pittsburgh's mayor, Joseph Barr, introduced him on April 4 to the Pennsylvania AFL-CIO convention as the next president of the United States. Several thousand union members staged a six-minute demonstration and repeatedly interrupted his speech with cries of, "Tell us what we want to hear," to which he replied that he was not one to shirk a decision. He was tempted to announce his candidacy, but that evening Martin Luther King was assassinated in Memphis, where he had gone to aid striking sanitation workers.[34]

King's murder set off rioting, arson, and looting in more than a hundred cities—including Washington, as Humphrey saw on flying home that night—and it took a week and more than twenty thousand federal troops and thirty-four thousand National Guardsmen to restore order. The vice president, whom Johnson agreed only at the last minute to allow to fly to Atlanta to King's funeral, was deeply moved by his murder, which he said "brings shame to our nation."[35]

Humphrey immediately pleaded with black Americans not to strike out in rage and retaliation because this would "make a mockery" of everything for which King lived, and he sent messages to numerous business and political groups urging them to fight to eliminate discrimination and segregation and to help with "healing the torment of our poor and hungry, our deprived and our illiterate." This would cause the tragedy of King's death to be remembered "not as the moment when America lost her faith, but as the moment when America found her conscience."[36]

Politics, however, were not put on hold, as acclaimed *New York Times* columnist James Reston wrote on April 5 that despite Humphrey's failed presidential run in 1960 and his having become a "loudspeaker" for the war, he was the "most creative legislative mind to come out of the Senate in a generation," and "if Presidents were elected by the thousand best-informed men in Washington on the basis of who would make the best President, he would be No. 1 at last." Governor Harold Hughes of Iowa urged him to resign as vice president to dissociate from Johnson's war policy, and staff members and others pressed him to run.[37]

Humphrey's continued calls to Democrats around the country drew mostly encouraging responses from governors such as Hughes, Ned Breathitt of Kentucky, and Connally of Texas. Support also came from Los Angeles mayor Sam Yorty; California congressman Chet Hollifield; and even conservative Republican newspaper magnate Eugene Pulliam, who said he would praise him to Johnson. So, too, did organized labor, farmers, northern African Americans, and Wall Street and the business community indicate their support.[38]

However, Humphrey remained "strangely flat and detached" from debate about a campaign, Van Dyk noted, and by mid-April even Kampelman was thinking that, having run before and been hurt, the vice president was letting his indecision become his decision. Van Dyk reminded him that he had long aspired to the presidency and had a vision for the nation; the best place to achieve it was from the White House. Humphrey agreed, despite his "intuitive feeling" that if he ran, "bad things" would continue to happen, and "I'll be engulfed by them."[39]

Yet Humphrey spent Easter weekend in Key Largo, Florida, on Andreas's yacht, planning his campaign. His first choice for campaign manager, Postmaster General Lawrence O'Brien, had gone with Kennedy. Looking to appeal to younger people, Humphrey chose as comanagers the forty-year-old senator Walter Mondale—who had said when Johnson withdrew that "Bobby's nominated. Hubert shouldn't even get into the race"—and thirty-seven-year-old liberal and civil rights–oriented senator Fred Harris of Oklahoma. The vice president told Harris to lead the hunt for delegates, and Mondale would do convention planning. Humphrey pledged not to interfere with their work, except "as necessary."[40]

Humphrey prevailed on Harry Truman to be honorary chairman of the emerging United Democrats for Humphrey (UDH), and others who took on roles included prominent Washington lawyers Max Kampelman and Jim Rowe, while Bill Connell—who leaned on the Democratic officials he had lined up for a later Humphrey campaign—brought in another DC attorney, former DNC treasurer Richard Maguire.[41]

Further support came from Robert (Bob) Short, a friend and wealthy Minnesota businessman and contributor, and Freeman, a masterful organizer who headed an "advisory council" to keep tabs on the inexperienced young managers and hunt for delegates. Freeman and Labor Secretary Willard Wirtz promptly announced for Humphrey, only to have Johnson insist that no cabinet officer attend his formal declaration—and, later, that they play no role in the campaign. An agitated agriculture secretary called Califano to threaten resignation, and Johnson allowed exceptions for Humphrey's longtime friends. He and Freeman also attributed Johnson's initial action to his desire always to be in control and his regret he was not the candidate—but he would be even more domineering and undermining than they imagined.[42]

Humphrey finally declared his candidacy on April 27 in Washington's Shoreham Hotel ballroom before seventeen hundred cheering supporters and hundreds more outside. Harris introduced him as a man whose record was "unmatched in public life" and who was "so far ahead of his time" that bills he had introduced two decades ago had only recently become law.

Clearly excited as he stood on the cusp of history, Humphrey began by stating, "Here we are, the way politics ought to be in America, the politics of happiness, politics of purpose, politics of joy; and that's the way it's going be," words—especially "politics of joy"—he would regret. He spoke about his record as mayor, senator, and vice president, having worked with presidents for twenty years, his intent to reach across racial, regional, and socioeconomic divides, and to focus on a "new American patriotism" to advance the "unfinished, peaceful American revolution." He limited foreign policy references to narrowing the gap between rich and poor nations, slowing the "dangerous, spiraling arms race," and strengthening the United Nations. His only mention of the Vietnam War was his hope for successful peace talks. In a jibe at his opponents, he pledged to avoid "inflammatory rhetoric" because the next president had to unify his party and the nation.[43]

His relatively brief speech provided little to criticize, but newspapers headlined his words about the politics of "happiness" and "joy," and critics derided them as callous so long as there were "children starving to death in the Delta of Mississippi," as Kennedy commented, and Americans were "dying in record numbers in Vietnam."[44]

The vice president attributed his politics of "joy" and "happiness" to John Adams's words, but the Library of Congress could not verify this. An aide said he had taken the words from a 1964 McCarthy speech, but the senator had spoken of the "joylessness of American politics" to the National Conference of Concerned Democrats in December 1967 and in Cleveland on April 22 had quoted Adams's words about a "spirit of happiness" among the American people before the 1776 revolution. McCarthy refrained from criticizing Humphrey, whose words ignored the sense of powerlessness among so many Americans and indicated that he had grown distant from his liberal base.[45]

African Americans, Catholics, and other minorities and poorer people moved toward Kennedy, while McCarthy drew backing from legions of young people, the middle class, and professionals. The Minnesotan even seemed to take a page from Humphrey in an April speech at Boston University by calling for a "new civil rights" program that included not only voting but the right to decent housing, a job, and medical care, as well as massive government investment in the inner cities. McCarthy also defined the "New Politics" of 1968 as concern not with political leadership or organized politics but with a "politics of participation," of "personal response," and of confidence in democracy.[46]

Nonetheless, Humphrey was in a far stronger position to win the Democratic nomination than most people, even he, realized. As vice president, he had gathered countless political IOUs traveling more than 250,000 miles to fifty states and some six hundred cities and towns. Where once he was anathema in the South, now he had backing from Connally and leading governors from his region and from 600 southern delegates, almost half of the 1,321 votes needed for the nomination. House majority whip Boggs of Louisiana told him, "I think we've changed a lot, and you've changed a little." As *Time* correspondents wrote when he declared, "His stature and potential delegate strength have multiplied almost magically."[47]

Humphrey also stood to benefit from the McCarthy-Kennedy contest. McCarthy had always felt upstaged by President John Kennedy and never forgave Robert Kennedy for jumping into the current contest after the New Hampshire primary. Soon after Humphrey joined the race, McCarthy vaguely told him that if he lost to Kennedy, he would support the vice president " 'when the time was ripe.' " Later, McCarthy said he would have given his delegate votes to Humphrey had Robert Kennedy lived to take part in the convention. Similarly, Kenneth O'Donnell, a key Kennedy aide, told Humphrey early on that if the New York senator lost to McCarthy, he would support the vice president at the convention. Humphrey's backers funneled money to McCarthy's campaign to enable him to compete with Kennedy's spending, although Humphrey opposed doing anything to "hurt Bobby because he's a good liberal senator and we'll need him later" and to leave it to the press to reveal his "tough tactics."[48]

At the start of his campaign, Humphrey's managers used arm-twisting and the unit rule to secure all of Maryland's 49 votes and won over nearly all of Delaware's 22 delegates by bringing them to meet the vice president in Washington. In Pennsylvania, where McCarthy had won 71 percent of the nonbinding primary vote in April, Mondale teamed up with Pittsburgh mayor Joseph Barr and former governor David Lawrence, and Harris worked the political scene at the Democrats' meeting in Philadelphia to secure 83 of the 125 delegates, the largest group after New York and California. The press called this the "political coup of the year"; McCarthy labeled the vote a "Pennsylvania railroad." In Florida, a slate of delegates pledged to favorite son Senator George Smathers but "favorable" to Humphrey won 55 of the 63 delegate slots. One month after Humphrey had become a candidate, a *Newsweek* survey had him within 32½ delegate votes of the nomination.[49]

He refused to debate McCarthy or Kennedy and said little about Vietnam, except that peace talks would begin soon. They did, on May 13, but quickly deadlocked. Humphrey went to West Virginia—where his campaign had run aground in 1960—to tell an audience, "I am my own man," and thereafter persisted that as vice president he was a "member of the team" but as president would be the "captain." He denied that the United States was guilty of "an arrogance of power"—as Fulbright charged in a recent book—and said it had "nothing to apologize for." He drew large crowds in Tennessee and Mississippi, where he called for integrated delegations to the convention, but added that there were a lot of people "who would rather point at you than look in the mirror."[50]

Humphrey pushed his liberal domestic agenda: getting rid of "slumism" and "the grey cemeteries of public housing" by ending the "artificial division" between cities and suburbs and redesigning antipoverty programs to include preschool training, health and nutritional services, improved schools, high national standards for teachers' salaries, and "some form of guaranteed national income." In a triumphal return to his hometown of Doland, South Dakota, in late May, Humphrey insisted that it cost less to put people to work than to fight poverty's costs: disease, crime, and welfare payments. In Detroit, he bluntly reminded Democrats, especially union workers, he had been with them in "dark days" and—poking at Kennedy—stated, "Liberalism is not a short and frenzied outburst of emotion, but the steady dedication of a lifetime." And peace "requires a lifetime of dedication."[51]

After a month of campaigning, Humphrey was doing extremely well, and "better than he deserves," Reston wrote, because his refusal to debate McCarthy and Kennedy about the war or answer questions about it was misleading supporters and opponents of the conflict into thinking he was with them. Reston said there were rumors the vice president had opposed escalation several times but had put loyalty to Johnson over revealing his doubts about the war. This strategy might win the nomination and even the election, Reston wrote, but it had lost Humphrey his old friends and ruined Johnson's presidency, and it was time the vice president told voters where he stood.[52]

Humphrey did not criticize either Kennedy or McCarthy during their Indiana and Nebraska campaigns. Kennedy won in Indiana by 42 percent to 27 percent and again in Nebraska by a 52 percent to 31 percent margin. McCarthy won 44.7 percent to 38.8 percent in Oregon, home to a large suburban population with few African Americans, and two senators, Democrat Wayne Morse and Republican Mark Hatfield, who were doves on Vietnam.[53]

During the crucial California primary, the two candidates' closely watched lone debate on June 1 proved to be a draw. Three days later, Kennedy, with a huge vote from minorities, won by a close 46 percent to 42 percent margin and declared his determination "to get Humphrey. I'm going to *make* him debate me. I'm going to chase his ass all around the country."[54]

Humphrey was in Colorado Springs that day to give the commencement address at the US Air Force Academy. He had surprised an aide by saying that he hoped to see Kennedy win "decisively" in California and knock McCarthy out of the race, whom he saw as "a spoiler" who would "plague Bobby and me all the way to the convention," and "I want him gone tonight." He added that he and Kennedy had agreed to campaign for whichever of them won the nomination. The vice president went to bed before the full returns were in.[55]

An aide awakened Humphrey with the news that Kennedy had been shot. Horror-struck and disbelieving, Humphrey turned on the television and watched the pandemonium at the Ambassador Hotel, wondering aloud how much tragedy the Kennedys could suffer and what had happened to American politics. He put in calls to Kennedy's aides to offer help, and Pierre Salinger, the senator's press secretary, soon called back to ask for a military plane to fly a Boston neurosurgeon to Los Angeles. Humphrey telephoned air force chief of staff General John McConnell to request a plane. When asked "by what authority," he made up a title: "as Vice Commander-in Chief." The plane was ordered—and a second to fly Kennedy's children from Washington. But a call from the White House informed Humphrey that the planes had been canceled. He was infuriated and humiliated but more distraught over Kennedy's shooting, which he viewed as a national tragedy whose "poison" permeated society. He informed his air force hosts he was canceling his speech and, despite their "macho" protests, returned to Washington the next morning.[56]

At the White House on June 6, presidential assistant Watson "raised hell" asking Humphrey why he had not sought clearance before ordering the planes. He said he had acted because "I knew that's what the President would have wanted." When Johnson asked the same question, the vice president let silence be his answer."[57]

Kennedy died early that day; funeral services were held in New York on June 8, and he was buried that evening at Arlington National Cemetery, close to his brother John.[58]

The president assured Humphrey that there was "no question" about his nomination and that he was "1 million percent" for him. He would do "exactly" what he wanted. Humphrey was not deceived, but he worried that Johnson might try to impose his choice of vice president, such as Connally. Instead, Johnson advised using the choice—as he had in 1964—to enliven a likely dull convention and minimize focus on Edward (Ted) Kennedy, who would be memorializing his brother Robert, with others paying tribute to John Kennedy and Martin Luther King.[59]

McCarthy came to Humphrey's office the next day. The senator's face was "white and ravaged," and he looked "weary beyond belief," reporters noted. He said he viewed Humphrey's nomination as inevitable and wanted a graceful exit. But his supporters would denounce him if he left without at least "symbolic" concessions on Vietnam. Humphrey, still tied to Johnson's hard line and fearing his wrath, declined the proposal, despite Van Dyk's view that it was not to be lightly refused and that McCarthy's endorsement would be valuable. The vice president now declared a campaign moratorium and returned home to Minnesota.[60]

Four days later, McCarthy, after meeting with Johnson at the White House, said he could not support Humphrey unless he changed his position on the war. On June 17, the senator added, "The time had come to take our steel out of the land of thatched huts." But in the coming months he did not reach out to the bereft Kennedy supporters and campaigned as though he had given up.[61]

Muriel Humphrey told her husband, "Daddy, the shot that killed Bobby has wounded you, maybe very seriously." People were going to be tired of politics and of the Democrats, she said, and "it's just going to be impossible to do anything." She was right. Kennedy's murder took a great psychic toll, not only on his family and friends but on his supporters, many of whom, along with McCarthy backers, would vent their anger at Humphrey. He also experienced a sense of "profound and personal loss," was noticeably pallid when he attended Kennedy's funeral services in New York, and continued to fret about the "poison" and "irrational hate among us." Joy in politics was gone.[62]

Humphrey's nomination was virtually certain, although in the New York primary on June 18 McCarthy's delegate candidates won sixty-two slots, Kennedy supporters took thirty seats, and the vice president's backers got only twelve. But Democratic State Committee leaders gave fifty of sixty-five delegate-at-large seats to Humphrey's people. Similarly, despite McCarthy's strong showing in Minnesota's March caucuses, DFL Party leaders gave all of the state's twenty at-large delegates to Humphrey, who also won over Kennedy delegates from Indiana, Nebraska, and California and now named Kennedy's former shrewd campaign manager, O'Brien, to head his campaign. As a key Mayor Daley lieutenant said, "You'd have to be crazy not to get on the Humphrey bandwagon."[63]

But as columnist Reston noted, Humphrey's campaign crowds were small, and he often met great hostility, notably from young people furious at his support for the Vietnam War and from African American communities, where Kennedy had taken hold. Reston did not think that the vice president could win in November unless he dealt with his differences with Johnson over the cities and, above all, the war. As Bill Moyers, Johnson's former press secretary and now *Newsday* publisher, said in seeking to flush Humphrey out, he had to speak for himself and "say publicly what he has been feeling privately."[64]

The journalists were right but overlooked that Johnson, who no longer feared that Robert Kennedy might succeed him, felt freer than ever to harass Humphrey to conform strictly to official Vietnam policy—and also secretly weighed reentering the presidential race. He worked with his young friend John Criswell, the DNC treasurer and convention manager, and Chicago mayor Richard Daley to arrange an unannounced invitation to address the August convention that he hoped would spur a "draft." He also planned to announce a fall Moscow summit meeting with Soviet prime minister Alexei Kosygin to discuss nuclear nonproliferation and begin strategic arms limitation talks. Humphrey, suspicious of the president's intentions, initially responded to Moyers by saying that he was "not a hypocrite" and was not "living a lie." At the National Press Club on June 20, he reaffirmed his "Marshall Plan for the Cities" but downplayed differences with Johnson over the war.

Humphrey said he always favored a negotiated rather than a military solution and reverted to his view that as vice president he was "a member of the team" but that as president he would be "captain of the team. There's a lot of difference." Further, "one does not repudiate one's own family to establish his identity," but his administration would have its own program. He congratulated McCarthy for his New York success but continued to evade a debate, saying that he was saving his "best remarks" for the Republican candidate. Two days later, Humphrey conceded to the *New York Times*'s editors that occasionally he differed with other cabinet members about Vietnam but supported policy because "you can't always have it your way." He regretted the loss of many old political friends but was sure they would support him if he were nominated, as he would back McCarthy. Most important, as president he would bring a "new Administration and new policies."[65]

Humphrey knew it would be difficult to convince people his policies would differ from Johnson's. In June, he told his staff that Johnson had not run "because he knew he could not make it. And he had clothed me with nothing" and subjected him to "the worst type of calumny and humiliation" and being "spit on" and "having filth thrown at me" on college campuses. But it was time to "pull ourselves up from the ashes" and "break out of this cocoon, without repudiating my father."[66]

By July, Humphrey recognized he had to propose a Vietnam policy that would satisfy McCarthy-Kennedy followers but not bring Johnson's wrath just at the time the administration had stepped up bombing of North Vietnam and its supply routes to the South. Hanoi refused serious talks without a bombing halt.[67]

Arthur Schlesinger Jr. wrote to David Ginsburg, a New York lawyer, ADA ally, and Humphrey supporter, on July 9 that the vice president was making a "disastrous error" by seeking "backroom manipulation" of the Democratic delegates to win the nomination without "public confrontation in the primaries" and "public confrontation in debates." If he got the nomination that way, Schlesinger wrote, he would face a bitter party, with bitterness "greatest among the issue-oriented activists." The Republicans' nomination of Nixon would not unify the Democrats; they would rather oppose a "reactionary foreign policy" from a Republican administration than one from a Democratic presidency. Schlesinger also said that the vice president's speech in Doylestown, Pennsylvania, in October, in which he blamed the war on "militant, aggressive communism" headquartered in China, led one to conclude that "Hubert really believes in this ghastly war" and would never overrule the Joint Chiefs of Staff.[68]

Humphrey responded passionately and at length that he was seeking the nomination "exactly" as John Kennedy had in 1960 by working with political leaders in key states, although he evidently ignored or forgot that his opponent had defeated him in the early and crucial Wisconsin and West Virginia primaries. More to the point, Humphrey confessed that he could not have entered any primaries until after Johnson withdrew on March 31, which left no time to organize. He referenced the countless speeches he had given across the nation as vice president about urban affairs, liberalism, and East-West relations, although none directly addressed the crucial Vietnam War issue and led

Schlesinger to respond that Humphrey's failure to recognize that his old friends opposed his candidacy on principle because of his position on the Vietnam War meant that "you had lost your own sense of reality and are in deep trouble."[69]

Ironically, Humphrey had been planning to give a speech titled "The Next Era in Foreign Policy" in July at San Francisco's prominent Commonwealth Club to declare that the Vietnam War had "consumed our energies, divided our people, tarnished our reputation, and limited our vision." The policies of tomorrow could not be limited to "the policies of today," and "no more Vietnams" had to become a US objective, with recognition that the nation could not be a "global policeman" or prevent people from choosing their own rulers, "even if that is a communist government." A bad case of the flu, however, prevented him from delivering his speech, which was released as a statement and largely escaped public notice, even by the White House. But eminent journalist Walter Lippmann soon wrote that the undelivered address represented a "total repudiation of the fundamental concept" of Johnson administration foreign policy—and "the kind of American conception of the world that would have been natural in Hubert Humphrey had he not become Lyndon Johnson's Vice President." But little more was said.[70]

Humphrey suffered a further blow when the president met with South Vietnam's leaders in Honolulu on July 19–20 and Johnson formally declared support of their government, with no mention of a bombing halt or negotiations to include the NLF, which Saigon's leaders refused to consider.

Humphrey was "crushed" by Johnson's speech: "He pulled the rug right out from under me. It gave me an awful wallop," he told syndicated columnist Drew Pearson, while the *New York Times*'s Tom Wicker wrote that it added to the vice president's "politically painful" identification with the war. And the National Governors' Conference viewed the president's action as preventing Humphrey's campaign from exciting the public, with Vermont Democrat Philip Hoff calling on the vice president to resign to separate from Johnson's policy.[71]

Humphrey's "Vietnam Task Force," a group of staff members and academic specialists, had been working for two months to craft a statement to establish his independent position on resolving the Vietnam War without contravening Johnson's policy. The draft—"Toward a Political Settlement and Peace in Southeast Asia"—called for cutting back US forces in Vietnam, taking mutual steps to reduce the fighting, and indicating that if North Vietnam continued to decrease its infiltration and shelling of Saigon, this might be the requisite "reciprocal action" to bring an immediate bombing halt. Humphrey agreed to issue the statement promptly—but only after showing it to the president.

The vice president told Johnson on July 25 that as a presidential candidate he had to explain publicly his position on Vietnam. But for most of the next hour, the president insisted that the statement would endanger peace prospects and the lives of his two sons-in-law serving in Vietnam—and Humphrey would have "blood on his hands." Johnson threatened to "destroy" his presidential chances publicly if he made his statement. On return to his office, the vice president told Van Dyk that the president had been too busy to discuss his paper. But Humphrey's repetitive handwashing—a sign of tension, friends knew—led his aide to press him to reveal the truth, and to confess, "You know, I've eaten so much of Johnson's shit in this job that I've grown to like the taste of it." He vowed to try to persuade Johnson later, while Van Dyk told the press that Humphrey had not yet discussed his proposal with the president.[72]

The president continued to undermine Humphrey. Whereas Johnson had spoken earlier of his eloquence and "broad range of knowledge" and said he had chosen "the best man in America" to be his vice president, now he often derided him to others as being "disloyal" and lacking "balls" and "the ability to be President."[73]

Humphrey also was under fire from usually supportive constituents. At an African American voter registration rally in Los Angeles in early August, catcalls—including "Honky Go Home"—quickly drove him from the stage. In Detroit, rising African American leaders Michigan representative John Conyers and Mayor Richard Hatcher of Gary, Indiana, complained bitterly that the war was consuming funds vital for domestic programs and having a disparate impact on young African Americans who were being drafted while better-off white students in college were being deferred. Humphrey defensively pointed to Great Society programs and said he had never favored military escalation and now sought a political compromise. He left shaken and feeling that the charges against him were undeserved "after all I've done."[74]

Political allies and friends continued to urge him to separate from Johnson on the war. From Paris, Harriman urged Humphrey to "get out from under" current policy, or just to "get out" by resigning his office. Similarly, his friend David Ginsburg, who would be his liaison in shaping the Democratic platform on Vietnam, pressed him to "make the break now," before the convention in late August. So, too, did O'Brien exhort him to call for a bombing pause; it was "the right thing to do," and he should act "come hell or high water" and despite southern defections or objections from the White House—which "seems to be doing everything not to help him," Berman noted.[75]

Humphrey remained torn; he told Democrats at a Washington dinner he did not intend to run for president "by turning my back on those people who have stood with me" or by repudiating "the work of my Party, my President, and my predecessors." He told *Newsweek*'s editors, "I make no apologies" for being a "loyal supporter" of administration policy, and "I do not fundamentally disagree with resistance of aggression from the North." The problem, he claimed, was that the United States had provided South Vietnam's army with poor military equipment and insufficient training and had not stressed enough to Saigon's leaders the importance of economic and political developments, statements that belied his own urgings in Vietnam in September 1967. His views kept him distant from McCarthy and Senator George McGovern, who had entered the race to harness Robert Kennedy's supporters, and the increasing number of war opponents who sought a bombing halt and negotiations that would include the NLF and who now viewed the conflict as a civil war the United States should not have entered.[76]

Humphrey was upset with McCarthy followers' New Politics, which he defined as "not very new" and consisting of "breaking up meetings . . . being dogmatic, unwilling to listen, and demanding an open convention when you have a closed mind. . . . Storm troopers are storm troopers." Still, he believed that most of McCarthy's supporters would accept a Vietnam plank "designed by the convention" that "would not repudiate the President."[77]

But the vice president, given to procrastinating, as Berman said, now told him he preferred to wait "another week or ten days" before issuing his own statement. He suspected, as Harriman had warned, that the president and his aides had not been briefing him fully on the Paris talks. He also properly guessed—while having returned to his Minnesota home to wait out the Republican convention in Miami Beach during August 5–8 that would nominate Nixon for president—that Johnson would seek to connect with the candidate even though his party's platform termed US policy in Vietnam a military, political, and diplomatic failure.[78]

The vice president, soon to campaign in Texas, had Van Dyk call Johnson at his ranch, where he was suffering from diverticulitis, to ask if he would like company. Told he would be most welcome, Humphrey, Muriel, and his hawkish senior aide Bill Connell flew to Texas, where Vietnam briefings confirmed that information had been held back earlier. Humphrey showed Johnson his "revised" Vietnam statement calling for a bombing halt when "reciprocity" was obtained from North Vietnam. The president, surprisingly cordial throughout, said that perhaps reciprocity was too strong a term, with "restraint and reasonable response" agreed upon.

But Johnson said that although the speech might "get a headline," Humphrey should let the president work for peace. Events were imminent, he said, and "I

think I can pull it off" and this would do more for the vice president and his
election prospects than anything else. Johnson added that Nixon would be
coming the next day. Humphrey left the ranch feeling better about the president, but knew he had been put "very definitely on the spot" about a statement
and grew angry over having been told not to bring reporters only to see Nixon
arrive with a press entourage.[79]

Despite Humphrey's surmise that Johnson would reach out to the Republican
presidential nominee, his immediate invitation to him to come to his Texas
ranch was perceived as a "political bombshell" and "almost throwing Hubert to
the wolves," columnist Drew Pearson and many Democrats concluded. The
president told aides that Nixon "may prove to be more responsible than the
Democrats" on Vietnam.

At their meeting, the Republican nominee told the president that although
his own advisers favored a bombing halt, he viewed bombing as America's only
leverage. As a candidate, he needed to be assured the United States would not
abandon Saigon, in which case he would not attack Johnson or his policy
during the campaign, and "I do not intend to advocate a bombing pause."
Reinforced in his view, Johnson soon rejected as "mush" a bombing halt
proposal from Harriman, his chief negotiator in Paris, and said he would "like
to see us knock the hell out" out of the North Vietnamese, and publicly threatened increased military action.[80]

Johnson was greatly mistaken in dealing with Nixon. As Clifford told his
staff, "Nixon has outmaneuvered the President again, digging him in more
deeply" on a war the Republican intended to hang "so deeply around the
Democrats' neck that it can't be loosened." Worse, Nixon's "game plan" to
secure inflexibility in Johnson's policy—as opposed to Humphrey's change—
was intended to "freeze poor Hubert out in the cold." As Clifford recognized,
"at some inner level of his psyche," Johnson was "ambivalent" about a preferred
successor and had already told aides that if Humphrey did not firmly back his
policy, "Nixon would be better for the country."[81]

Humphrey's advisers continued to insist he would help himself the most by
issuing his Vietnam statement before the Democratic convention began on
August 26. But he continued to hold back, avoiding direct answers to questions
about a bombing halt on CBS's Face the Nation on August 11 and telling his
staff—based on his visit with Johnson—"events may be on our side," and "I
don't want to say something that will screw things up and have the President
come down on me hard."[82]

Humphrey hoped that progress at the Paris talks would resolve his Vietnam
problem, but fear of Johnson's wrath was the major barrier that kept him from

establishing his own position on the war. He viewed the president as a father figure and persisted that one did not repudiate one's parent or family to establish one's independence. Although he said he felt better about the president after his visit at his ranch, Muriel had a darker view. "Things were not as before," she told Berman. Her husband and Johnson had a good relationship during their Senate years through their 1965 inauguration, but the president soon grew distant. She said Humphrey had "worshipped" his father but had a difficult period after his father drove him to Minneapolis and left him on his own, and she had never seen anyone as "forlorn" as her husband after his father died in 1949. Now the same process was at work with Johnson, she said, questioning whether Humphrey would be able "to get out of a tough situation where he has indoctrinated himself for almost four years to be this man's son." She also doubted whether "Johnson really wanted him to break away" because every time a story appeared about an issue, he called the vice president in a "bitchy mood and raises him up and down and back."[83]

Humphrey continued to behave more like a son who feared a punitive father than a man certain to become "captain" of the Democrats' team. He balked at a Vietnam statement, while McCarthy, despite his lackluster campaigning, drew ever larger enthusiastic crowds in cities across the country and even in the South. Nixon surged in the Gallup poll from running just behind Humphrey in late July to a sixteen-point lead in mid-August.[84]

A North Vietnamese offensive on August 17 led Johnson to call Humphrey immediately to say that developments intended to advance peace talks were not going to materialize. The vice president "looked as if he had been kicked," Berman noted. "He just seemed to sag all over." Even worse, two days later, the president declared to the Veterans of Foreign Wars annual meeting that he alone was responsible for the presidency and executive policy toward Vietnam until January 20, 1969. He said that because Hanoi had not responded to his March 31 bombing cutback with military deescalation or halting infiltration of the South, the United States would take no further deescalation steps until North Vietnam showed its willingness to seek peace. Humphrey and his advisers saw this as one of Johnson's "hardest line speeches" that would hurt the vice president and preclude any Democratic presidential candidate from helping to shape US policy.[85]

The next day, as Freeman recorded, Johnson "launched into almost a tirade about Humphrey and Vietnam," insisting that the vice president was "all over the place" on the war and should not be seeking to get McCarthy's delegates. Johnson claimed that North Vietnam had not offered even one concession in return for a bombing halt, and he had two sons-in-law in Vietnam, and one of them had "more than half of his men shot out from under him." He added that Mayor Daley, who would be hosting the convention, had relatives serving in Vietnam, and he and Connally were "equally ready to walk out on the whole business," meaning they would not support Humphrey's nomination.[86]

Later that day, Soviet tanks and thousands of Warsaw Pact troops moved into Czechoslovakia to suppress the Prague Spring political liberalization, which Moscow feared might spread to other Eastern Bloc countries or even its own republics. This "bombshell," Johnson told an emergency NSC meeting that evening, surprised the Americans, but nothing could be done. Humphrey said that the Czechs had "touched at the heart of the Communist revolution," but "all we can do is snort and talk." He told his staff, "We have our Cuba here, and they [the Soviets] have their Yugoslavia there, and they don't want any more of either." The administration ruled out action, the Czechs quickly accepted Soviet demands, and Johnson had to cancel his planned fall summit with Moscow.[87]

Humphrey viewed the Czech crisis as briefly pushing news of Nixon's lead in the presidential race off the front pages but ultimately helping him due to his strong anti-Communism and opposition to dealing with the Russians. Johnson ostentatiously called Nixon to inform him of US deliberations but did not include the vice president in the post-NSC meeting picture session that included UN ambassador George Ball and members of the Joint Chiefs of Staff.[88]

At an August 22 cabinet meeting, Johnson expressed "again and again" his determination to remain firm on his position, assailed the Russians for not getting Hanoi to moderate its position, and "in effect lectured and challenged Humphrey, saying that the only way they [the North Vietnamese] would talk was if they are faced with a tough, hard position and perhaps we'll have it after the National Convention." The vice president now knew that Johnson would fully control the Democrats' convention, including its crucial platform committee decisions, while Mayor Daley readied an army of forces to crack down on any individual or group protesting proceedings or policies. Humphrey's key advisers believed that the stage was set for him to win the Democratic nomination—but to lose the election.[89]

17

THE SIEGE OF CHICAGO

In fall 1967, Johnson chose to hold the 1968 Democratic convention in Chicago, where Mayor Richard Daley prevailed with an iron hand. The city's major lakefront convention center had burned down, however, compelling the Democrats to meet at Chicago's International Amphitheater, five miles west of downtown, while nearly all attendees would be housed at the Conrad Hilton Hotel on Michigan Avenue and nearby hotels. Telephone and transportation workers were on strike that summer, and numerous antiwar groups, such as the National Mobilization to End the War in Vietnam and Students for a Democratic Society, along with social protest movements such as the Youth International Party ("Yippies") and "Hippies," were threatening to send thousands of protesters to the convention.[1]

Humphrey, concerned about possible violence, proposed to Johnson that he move the meeting to the more insular Miami Beach, where the Republicans were to meet first in early August, a request strongly seconded by the media, which faced strike-related logistical problems and expensive new start-up costs in Chicago. Johnson insisted that Daley would be insulted, and Humphrey's call in early August to the mayor to provide facilities for the protesters went unanswered. Daley built up a virtual army of 12,000 Chicago police on twelve-hour shifts, 6,000 National Guardsmen, 1,000 FBI and Secret Service agents, and 6,000 heavily armed US Army troops, although no more than 10,000 protesters—despite estimates running to 50,000—showed up, with the majority peacefully inclined. The Daley administration allowed a permit for only one demonstration and forbade sleeping in the city's parks, although protesters could have been accommodated in large Lincoln Park, four miles from the convention center, which was surrounded by barbed wire fencing and looked like a prison or nuclear installation.[2]

Violence was so likely that Senator McCarthy urged his young followers to stay away, and many did. But confrontations began on Sunday, August 25—the day before the convention opened—when fifty baton-swinging police routed from Lincoln Park some one thousand demonstrators shouting, "Peace Now," "Dump the Hump," and "Hey, hey, LBJ, how many kids did you kill today?" News reporters were driven off, and far worse scenes followed during the next two days.

Daley and John Criswell, Johnson's chosen DNC treasurer and convention manager, installed extremely tight security inside the amphitheater, including electronic identification cards for entry and exit, and strict guards almost everywhere. Administration-friendly delegations were seated nearest the podium, and McCarthy or McGovern supporters were located in the building's outer reaches. The mayor was determined to keep television cameras focused on the podium and away from protests on the floor.[3]

Before flying to Chicago on August 25, Humphrey appeared on *Face the Nation*. He insisted that he was his own man and that Johnson's Vietnam policies were "basically sound," supportive words that left a little "wiggle room" to raise the hopes of stronger peace advocates. But the convention proved disastrous for everyone: Humphrey was undermined by Daley, who kept rigid control of the meeting, and by Johnson, who dominated the platform committee regarding the Vietnam plank. Further, Humphrey's excessive insecurity about his pending nomination led him to fail to take charge of events or grasp reasons for the protesters' anger.[4]

The vice president was upset on arrival at the Chicago airport that neither the mayor nor a crowd greeted him; there was only a bagpipe band, whereas, he noted angrily, some ten thousand supporters had turned out for McCarthy. Humphrey hurried to meet with the Illinois delegation, but Daley withheld his expected endorsement. The vice president and many others speculated that this politically powerful Democrat intended to seek another candidate who he thought stood a better chance to win—Senator Ted Kennedy, despite his dovishness on the war. Kennedy had reentered politics on August 21 with a speech deploring the deep divisions in American society and calling for an unconditional bombing halt and mutual withdrawal of US and North Vietnamese troops.[5]

The morning after the speech, Humphrey quietly went to Kennedy's home in McLean, Virginia, to ask him to be his running mate, insistent that Democratic polling showed that together they would readily win but that otherwise the race against Richard Nixon would be very close. By choosing Kennedy, who would bring his family name and charisma and the nation's peace advocates, Humphrey would signal a break from Johnson, who would be angry but unable to halt a move that would appeal both to old-line Democrats like Daley and peace progressives.

Kennedy declined; despite having gotten on well with Humphrey in the Senate, he was responsible for his deceased brothers' families and reluctant to join with a man his brother Robert had sought to defeat because of his Vietnam War position. Still, Humphrey found Ted Kennedy "very warm" and committed to working for his election, and was also convinced that he not only did not want the second slot on the ticket but "absolutely will not run for President."[6]

Nonetheless, Daley called Kennedy on August 24, two days before the convention, to ask him to become a candidate for presidential nomination or agree to accept a draft. He declined both options but said that his brother-in-law Stephen Smith would be coming to Chicago as a New York delegate and would report on events. The next day Daley and Jesse Unruh, Speaker of the California State Assembly and fervent Robert Kennedy backer, met and tried to lure Kennedy into the presidential race. But he again cited family responsibilities, which he repeated when historian Arthur Schlesinger Jr. called to query him about running, and he remained at his family compound in Hyannis Port on Cape Cod.

Humphrey still feared a draft Kennedy movement despite having enough delegate support to gain the 1,312 votes needed for the nomination even without Illinois's 118 votes, and he had assurance from Larry O'Brien, who had spoken to the senator, that Kennedy would not run. Humphrey grew worried when on the first day of the convention former Ohio governor Mike DiSalle said he was setting up a Kennedy for President office, and then the cochairmen of the Michigan delegation, Senator Philip Hart and state Democratic chairman Sander Levin, announced for him.[7]

Humphrey was also distressed on checking into his suite at the Conrad Hilton Hotel that Secret Service agents had to whisk him past a less than friendly crowd carrying McCarthy signs. Further, Johnson's control over convention minutiae compelled the vice president to send his son-in-law, Bruce Solomonson, to one of the president's functionaries' rooms daily to secure extra tickets for his family and friends to enter the amphitheater. On hearing of McCarthy's displeasure at the lack of space for his staff, Humphrey exclaimed, "What the hell's he complaining for? I'm the Vice President of the United States and I'm being treated like a Yugoslavian peasant."[8]

Humphrey began "waffling all over the place," Berman noted, when Texas governor John Connally, who spoke for southern governors, said his peers in the region opposed the rules committee's intention—spurred by the more liberal Democrats—to jettison the unit rule allowing governor-controlled majorities to cast all of their delegations' votes for one candidate. The vice president, through his chief of staff, Bill Connell, had let Connally know he favored waiting until 1972 to abolish the unit rule. But as his preconvention delegate vote increased, Humphrey wrote the rules committee that he backed changing the rule for the current meeting, causing Connally to threaten to start a "draft Johnson" movement, soon disavowed by the president.

Fearing loss of support among the South's 527 delegates, Humphrey again changed course with a letter to the rules committee proposing not to drop the unit rule until 1972. But on the second night of the convention the assemblage voted to end the unit rule at once, opening the delegate selection procedure to much greater—and more diverse—public participation.[9]

Humphrey sought to make amends with southerners in credentials fights. His supporters helped seat "as is" Connally's delegation, defeating a challenge from a delegation led by his arch-opponent, liberal senator Ralph Yarborough, and consisting of many African Americans and Mexican Americans. The vice president also helped to gain a limited "compromise" over the Georgia delegation, with half the seats awarded to segregationist governor Lester Maddox's choices and half to a group led by the young civil rights leader and state representative Julian Bond. North Carolina and Alabama delegations withstood their challenges, with only the old-line, lily-white Mississippi delegation pushed aside. Still, the changes in the unit rule and make-up of delegations proved monumental. McCarthy and his minions got most of the credit; Humphrey's mixed responses diminished liberals' respect for him.[10]

The vice president continued to worry about a Kennedy draft, even though no one had nominated him and the large southern bloc was opposed. McCarthy came to the convention convinced he could not get the nomination but on the first day rejected the idea of his campaign manager, Richard Goodwin, a former adviser to Robert Kennedy, to woo southerners by offering the vice presidential slot to Connally. The next morning McCarthy asked Goodwin about "this Teddy thing," but Goodwin's four calls to Smith got no clear response, although later that afternoon Smith met briefly with McCarthy, who offered to withdraw in favor of Kennedy (gratuitously adding that he could not have done that for Robert Kennedy). Smith said he thought McCarthy's action would make the nomination fight "a real ballgame," but he needed to check with Ted Kennedy.[11]

The matter ended there. That afternoon Daley, upset that Kennedy would not declare, pulled back, and offered his support to Humphrey. With a nudge from the White House, every southern leader but one endorsed the vice president that evening. Kennedy, who had a "gut feeling that this is not the year"—informed his closest advisers that he would not run, and a draft was impossible without his prior commitment. He delayed a public announcement and a call to Humphrey, perhaps hoping to influence the Democrats to vote for the minority "peace" plank on Vietnam.[12]

This was the most difficult, and detrimental, issue for Humphrey. Although now certain of the nomination, he hoped to avert a divisive platform battle. McCarthy, McGovern, and others were calling for an unconditional bombing halt intended to have Hanoi agree to negotiations. The vice president's advisers and supporters were urging him to separate from Johnson by proposing a bombing halt and perhaps resigning his office to run as a candidate separate from the administration. This latter strategy risked charges of Humphrey abandoning a sinking ship; further, he was too emotionally and politically tied to the president to do this and fearful he would "come down hard" on him if he broke ranks. After North Vietnam's August 17 offensive and the Soviet invasion of Czechoslovakia three days later, Johnson had halted further Vietnam peace efforts, excluded Humphrey from pictures with him and NSC officials, and challenged him in cabinet meetings to take a hard line on Vietnam. As Berman noted, Johnson was doing "nothing but harming the VP all the way."[13]

The president also controlled key convention proceedings. He named a political ally, House majority leader Carl Albert of Oklahoma, as permanent chairman, and rejected Humphrey's choice of Maine senator Edmund Muskie to chair the platform committee. Instead the president chose his staunch advocate Louisiana congressman Hale Boggs. The platform committee began hearings on August 19. Humphrey sent New York lawyer David Ginsburg and staffer William Welsh to work with the committee and its drafting group, hoping to strike a balance between Johnson hard-liners and dovish spokesmen. The doves comprised about one-third of the committee, thus ensuring a minority report, and included Goodwin; Kenneth O'Donnell, an aide to Presidents Kennedy and Johnson who managed Robert Kennedy's 1968 campaign and then Humphrey's before O'Brien took over; Ted Sorensen, counsel and speechwriter for President Kennedy; and Ohio congressman John Gilligan, a Humphrey admirer who sought a plank that would satisfy the administration and the Kennedy-McCarthy-McGovern forces and bolster the vice president's presidential campaign in the way his 1948 victorious minority civil rights plank had helped President Truman.[14]

This "peace" faction's plank included four points: an unconditional end to bombing of North Vietnam while continuing to aid US forces in the South; a phased mutual withdrawal of US and North Vietnamese forces from South Vietnam; encouragement of the Saigon government to negotiate a "broadly representative" government with the NLF; and reduced US military action leading to early, significant withdrawals of US troops. McCarthy approved the plank, and Ginsburg, preparing a Humphrey draft, said that there was "not ten cents worth of difference between this and the vice president's policy." He cleared the plank with the southern governors, who said they "could live with it." The Vietnam conflict was not cited as a civil war, nor was "coalition government" mentioned; the only sticking point might have been setting terms for an "unconditional" bombing halt.[15]

Ginsburg called Humphrey in Washington, who, as per Johnson's instruction, read the statement to Secretary of State Dean Rusk and National Security Adviser Walt Rostow. They proposed minor edits and said that they could "live with this." Humphrey also got backing from AFL-CIO president George Meany, a Johnson supporter. The vice president flew to his Waverly home for a brief stay before going to Chicago, thinking he had a consensus position on a Vietnam platform plank in hand.[16]

Johnson soon destroyed the accord. Two days earlier he had summoned to Washington the convention and platform committee chairs, Albert and Boggs, and platform committee member West Virginia senator Jennings Randolph. The meeting was ostensibly called to brief them on the Czech crisis, but Johnson instead read them a riot act, buttressed by cables from the US commander in Vietnam, General Creighton Abrams Jr., asserting that a bombing halt would vastly increase North Vietnam's military capabilities in the DMZ and facilitate the NLF's third major offensive of the year. Boggs and his compatriots returned to Chicago determined to resist the peace plank.[17]

Humphrey heard "audible rumblings from the ranch in Texas" on his arrival in Chicago. Johnson's representative, White House aide Charles Murphy, had secured a copy of the peace plank from the vice president's aides, and that night he told Boggs, Ginsburg, and Welsh that the president held the peace plank's proposed bombing halt unacceptable despite its proviso that its timing would "take into account the security of our troops and the likelihood of a response from Hanoi."

Early on the morning of August 26, Murphy called Johnson to express Boggs's concern that he would have to go to his colleagues with a disagreement between the vice president and president. Johnson was unmoved. He would not agree to a bombing halt: "I had rather vote for Nixon than to kill my boys" and would not allow "a bunch of draft dodgers and pacifists who had never seen a uniform" determine when the United States would stop bombing. Instead, he would allow a bombing halt only "when the action would not endanger the lives of our troops in the field," and only the president and National Security Council would determine the crucial "when." The president did not intend, as did the framers of the peace plank, a bombing halt to be a first step to induce Hanoi to negotiate seriously, and while the peace plank proposed to start a mutual troop withdrawal, Johnson insisted that there would be no withdrawal until hostilities were ended, or nearly so.[18]

Boggs immediately told the platform committee drafting group that Johnson's Vietnam plank was not negotiable, while Ginsburg and Welsh talked with O'Brien about their drafting problems. Coming on their discussion, an agitated Humphrey said, "I don't want to hear any more about it—they're just haggling over words." But he soon learned that far more was at stake when Marvin Watson, a close Johnson aide and now postmaster general, came from Washington to tell him the president refused to accept the peace plank. Taken aback, Humphrey called Johnson in Texas, who said he did not want it known that this was being cleared with him and insisted that the peace plank undercut government policy and him. When Humphrey replied that he had cleared the plank with Rusk and Rostow, Johnson said it had not been cleared with him.[19]

Humphrey and his advisers still inclined to stick with the peace plank until Boggs made it clear that he was as "immovable" on the issue as the president. The vice president backed down completely, although he later wrote, "I should have stood my ground." He defended himself by saying, "The Vice President has very few guns in a battle with presidential artillery. He can be shot down before he takes off," and that to fight Johnson would have been "suicidal." But more revealing, as Humphrey confided to Berman at the time, he feared that fighting Johnson over the Vietnam plank would be "suicidal," and he "would cut me up and out of the nomination." Consequently, as columnist Tom Wicker wrote, this meant that if the vice president went into the campaign with the president's Vietnam plank rather than his own, he would be viewed as presenting "his master's voice."[20]

Humphrey undoubtedly would have faced trouble from the president had he rejected his plank, although the vice president believed that Johnson had not run himself because "he could not make it." But the president, working through White House aide Watson, Criswell, and Connally, had been secretly planning to have Daley invite him to deliver an address to the convention that he hoped would spur a presidential draft. Yet the next day, August 27—with a plane at the ready in Texas—his aides and Daley "roundly" told him not to come, even for the gala birthday party the mayor had planned for him at Soldier Field stadium. Humphrey was greatly relieved; he now knew the presidential nomination was likely his since neither Johnson nor the big southern bloc would throw support to Kennedy, McCarthy, or McGovern, all of whom favored the peace plank.[21]

In dealing with Johnson, the vice president underestimated his own strength and high regard among longtime Democrats despite having become the president's captive spokesman for the war. Thus Humphrey, who had defied a sitting president, party officials, and the South in daring to put his minority plank before a national convention in 1948, meekly yielded to Johnson. As he confessed at the time, "I had become the oldest son and could not make the break."[22]

On Monday evening, August 26, the platform committee supported the president's Vietnam plank by 65–35, opening the way to the bitter convention floor fight Humphrey dreaded. As McCarthy said, "Now the lines are clearly drawn between those who want more of the same and those who think it is necessary to change our course in Vietnam." Most important, the vice president looked "weak and vacillating," Orville Freeman noted, and the nomination he had seemingly secured "might not be worth taking." Berman agreed; now Humphrey's "Democratic support melted away," he later wrote, with few of his faithful to return before Election Day.[23]

Humphrey further alienated liberal and antiwar supporters the next morning while debating McCarthy and McGovern before the big California delegation. "I did not come to repudiate the president," he said. No one on the American side of the war had sought to escalate it, he stated, and "the roadblock to peace is not in Washington, D.C. It is in Hanoi." He drew shouts and boos, whereas McGovern got a standing ovation when he repudiated Humphrey's defense of Johnson's policies and said that the Democrats had pledged "no wider war" four years earlier. McCarthy, strangely diffident, said little, insisting the delegation already knew his views as expressed in their primary. He said he could not support a Democratic candidate "whose views did not come close" to his own but told reporters he would probably give Humphrey support in "a couple of weeks."[24]

Boggs delayed introducing the Democrats' platform until 12:37 a.m. on August 28. Proponents of the minority Vietnam plank—calling for an unconditional bombing halt—suspected that the administration had waited until the television viewing audience was small, and they fought to gain adjournment. But when the delegates reassembled around noontime, they found "fact sheets" on their seats warning that the minority plank was an attack on the president and on "rational" US policy in Southeast Asia.

An unprecedented three-hour debate followed, with spokesmen for the majority, or so-called Humphrey-Johnson plank, such as Muskie, insisting that the two planks differed only over means, not ends, while Boggs repeated Johnson's dire warnings about a bombing halt. Minority spokesmen such as Oregon senator Wayne Morse viewed the war as ill-conceived and destructive of the fabric of American society. The late afternoon 1,567¾–1,041¼ vote in favor of the Humphrey-Johnson plank was never in doubt, however. The New York and California delegations were joined by others that promptly donned black armbands and sang "We Shall Overcome."[25]

During Humphrey's breakfast with Daley on that Wednesday morning, Kennedy called to inform the vice president he would absolutely not be a presidential candidate. Humphrey asked Kennedy again to be his running mate—"together we can win this, easily," he said. But the senator again cited "family reasons" as making this impossible, and when Humphrey asked, "Is the door locked and the key thrown away," Kennedy said, "Yes." But he would come out strongly for Humphrey and work for him "with everything I have." Not even word that Daley wanted Kennedy to join the ticket moved him. Humphrey's best chance, short of his own strong action, to unify the party and to win the election had passed.[26]

The vice president spent the rest of the day reviewing San Francisco mayor Joseph Alioto's speech nominating him for president, weighing vice-presidential choices, and having lunch with African American athletes Jackie Robinson and Elgin Baylor, to whom he insisted that he would not be silent, no matter the price, about his belief that Nixon's emphasis on "law and order" was "subdued racism." He complained to *Time-Life* interviewers that the press had unfairly charged him with hardening his line on Vietnam by insisting that Hanoi show "restraint" before a bombing halt; he was saying only that "you shouldn't sell anybody out."[27]

The debate about the Vietnam plank spurred protest that turned violent. The National Mobilization, using its only demonstration permit, gathered a large crowd in Grant Park, across Michigan Avenue from the Hilton. When a demonstrator was arrested for lowering an American flag from its stand, forty or more police pushed rapidly in wedge formation through the crowd, swinging clubs and hurling tear gas canisters, with the fumes wafting through air conditioning ducts of nearby hotels, including into Humphrey's Suite 2225A in the Hilton. Angry and with his eyes irritated, he complained about television coverage of "the kooks and rioters" and then went to take a shower, order dinner, and prepare for the night's proceedings.[28]

Protesters gathered again in the early evening in Grant Park, intent to march to the convention site with chants ranging from "Peace Now" to "Fuck LBJ" to "The Whole World Is Watching" coming through squawk boxes. But squads of police charged them—and National Guard troops cut off escape routes—swinging their clubs, using an overturned barricade as a battering ram, and hurling tear gas grenades. The brutal "battle of Michigan Avenue" lasted only about fifteen minutes, with dozens of protesters and bystanders badly beaten—and considerable blood spilled (including that of police)—while hotel plate-glass windows were smashed and hundreds arrested.

The police, or "Pigs," as protesters yelled as they threw bricks, bottles, and other objects at them, were provoked. But their behavior constituted a "police riot"—as an investigative committee later judged—that the "whole world" would watch when filmed versions of the events were run on national television that evening. Humphrey, distressed that the day of his nomination was being disrupted, called in reporters to say that the protesters did not represent Chicago but had "been brought in from all over the country," although half came from the city and the convention was a national one.[29]

Amid the street chaos and convention floor battles between zealous security forces, delegates, and news reporters, the nominations began. Governor Harold Hughes of Iowa spoke for McCarthy as the people's candidate, and Connecticut senator Abraham Ribicoff, nominating McGovern, said that if McGovern was president there would be none of the Chicago police's "Gestapo tactics," causing Daley—with ninety million shocked Americans watching—to mouth a four-letter expletive and reference to Ribicoff's Judaism, to which the senator retorted, "How hard it is to accept the truth. How hard it is."[30]

Humphrey found it equally hard to accept the way his nomination appeared on national television. Alioto formally nominated him as an "extraordinary man" who had become practitioner of the "art of the impossible" in achieving passage of the 1963 Nuclear Test Ban Treaty and 1964 Civil Rights Act. But as Cleveland mayor Carl Stokes, the first African American to lead a major city and proof of Humphrey's continuing civil rights commitment, rose to second his nomination, NBC News cut away from the speech to broadcast footage of the police action in Grant Park. Humphrey and his staff were furious. "I'm going to be President someday," he blurted out, "and I'm going to appoint the FCC and we're going to look into all of this."[31]

There was little joy as Humphrey watched the roll call, although he grinned when Minnesota gave him 38½ votes to McCarthy's 13½. As his tally mounted, however, he went into another room, where Berman found him, alone and crying, although why remains uncertain. He returned in time to see Pennsylvania (where McCarthy had won 70 percent of the primary votes) give him enough votes to put him over the 1,312 required for victory. His final tally reached 1,760¼, with McCarthy finishing at 601, and McGovern at 146.

As television cameras scanned the amphitheater to focus on Muriel Humphrey, her husband, who was watching on TV in his room, said, "See how pretty she looks," and kissed her image on the screen, a moment photographers captured. But the picture played poorly in the press the next day as another unfortunate "joy of politics" moment.

Humphrey took congratulatory calls from Johnson ("Bless your heart, thank you," the vice president said) and Nixon. The traditional motion to make the nomination unanimous was not voted, however, although the convention chair, Albert, declared it passed.[32]

Humphrey's nomination was not a stolen one, as McCarthy later claimed, although the senator had won nearly 40 percent of the primary votes, Robert Kennedy had 31 percent, and Humphrey got just 2 percent. Primaries selected only 900 of the 2,600 convention delegates, however, and 76 percent of the nonprimary delegates favored Humphrey, along with most party officials. But Humphrey, who had not broken from Johnson's grip, may not have been his party's strongest candidate. As Schlesinger had warned, the most liberal and activist core of the Democratic Party needed for election would be unforgiving about the overriding issue of the Vietnam War.[33]

Humphrey now had to choose a running mate. His clear first choice, Ted Kennedy, had declined. Strained Humphrey-McCarthy relations precluded their running together; the senator had told the vice president shortly before the convention that he would not accept the second slot. Humphrey had allowed feelers to go out earlier to New York governor Nelson Rockefeller, who chose to remain a Republican, and McGovern, a spokesman for the minority Vietnam plank, who had no interest in the position.

The southern governors pressed the vice president to choose one of their own, but he did not want anyone from that region, including progressive governor Terry Sanford of North Carolina. Humphrey also passed over New Jersey governor Richard Hughes, a liberal and a friend, as not adding to the ticket, and objections from the extended Kennedy family ruled out Sargent Shriver, currently ambassador to France and a former head of the Peace Corps and Office of Economic Opportunity.[34]

The choice narrowed to Humphrey's campaign cochair, Senator Harris—young, liberal, civil rights–oriented, and dovish—who greatly wanted the role, and Muskie, a former two-term governor and twice-elected senator from usually Republican Maine. His state had only four electoral votes, but the son of Polish Catholic immigrants was seen as playing well with the Democrats' constituency in the larger northern states. He had a liberal record and had been a Senate friend of McCarthy's, though he stood with Humphrey on the Vietnam plank. The vice president judged Muskie to be the most reliable person to direct domestic policy and to move, in an emergency, from the vice presidency to the White House. Further, his calm demeanor and height led to his being perceived as "Lincolnesque," and his reticence contrasted with Humphrey's garrulousness. The vice president felt more comfortable with Muskie than with any other prospective candidate.[35]

Humphrey nearly backed away from his choice when Muskie, after being told of his selection, revealed that his unwed daughter was pregnant. Distraught at this eleventh-hour bad news, the vice president delayed his announcement for over four hours while he consulted advisers, who were divided, but at last opted to stick with him and to ask the aspiring Harris to nominate him, which — ever the good soldier — he did.[36]

Humphrey had made a principled choice that brought no enthusiasm. Harris would have had greater appeal to younger people, minorities, and antiwar proponents; the liberal Hughes might have helped to avert a narrow loss of New Jersey to Nixon; and Sanford might have helped in the South's Border States. Notably, Humphrey had failed to seek someone who would appeal to crucial disaffected constituencies: antiwar liberals, young people, and African Americans. Perhaps it was symbolic that just as Humphrey was introducing Muskie to the press on August 29, McCarthy was walking across Michigan Avenue, past lines of armed National Guardsmen, into Grant Park to address the protesters as the "government of the people in exile."[37]

Humphrey's acceptance address also posed a major dilemma. Nearly everyone in his camp thought that he needed a "shocker" speech to rouse the country; otherwise, O'Brien said, "he may win the nomination with the president, but lose the election because of it." The vice president's closest advisers, except for chief of staff Bill Connell, had been urging him to separate from Johnson by declaring his own plank on Vietnam. Even the president's former aide Jack Valenti told Berman that Johnson's "hard line" on Vietnam with Humphrey was "ridiculous," and no one could hold a candidate after his nomination: "any nominee would go the other way."[38]

A group of Humphrey's closest longtime friends and advisers had devised a plan, approved by O'Brien, to have him "go the other way" from Johnson after being nominated by flying to Hyannis Port to persuade Teddy Kennedy to run with him and then to give his sealed acceptance speech to reporters with the proviso that it not be opened until he delivered it. He would fly to Washington to give a copy of the speech to Johnson, but too late for him to do anything about its distributed content. Humphrey would deliver his address, pay tribute to Johnson for standing aside on March 31 in order to seek peace, and announce that he was resigning as vice president so that his words on Vietnam and other issues would be taken as his own and not those of the administration. Thus he would separate himself from Johnson and be free to lay out his own position on Vietnam.

This unprecedented action was highly risky — especially without Kennedy as a unifier on the ticket — and subject to criticism as a cynical move to abandon a sinking ship. When O'Brien presented the proposal to Humphrey, he viewed it as a "gimmick" and, perhaps most important, feared that "it would enrage the President."[39]

Humphrey held to a standard script but viewed as disappointing the acceptance speech his writers and friends had produced, and worked alone to the last minute to craft a revised address. He feared that "violence, disorder, and repudiation" might mark the day he had dreamed about, and he sought to offer inspiration and reconciliation through recalling the prayer of Francis of Assisi that proposed to sow love in place of hatred, hope over despair, and light rather than darkness. His staff excised this reference with each redraft, but the vice president discovered the omission en route to the amphitheater and wrote it back in.[40]

Standing before the delegates, the nominee feared rejection until he received the first of several ovations during his speech, which was good, but far from his usual stem-winder. He began by disapproving of violence, "whatever the source," and quickly summoned Francis's prayer while calling on Americans to reaffirm their love of country and to continue their "revolution" marked by the traditions of Franklin Roosevelt, Harry Truman, Adlai Stevenson, John Kennedy—each name drew cheers—and Lyndon Johnson, whose mention produced as many loud boos as cheers. Still, Humphrey praised him for having accomplished more of the nation's unfinished business than any modern predecessor, and "I say thank you, thank you, Mr. President," drawing more boos.

Humphrey said that the party's hard and "sometimes bitter" debate over issues had been decided by "majority rule," with minority rights preserved. Three issues most needing to be addressed remained: the need for peace in Vietnam and in American cities and Democratic unity. Vietnam was foremost, but he offered only the pledge that "the policies of tomorrow need not be limited by the policies of yesterday." He decried "mob violence and police brutality" and attacks on the courts as unacceptable and said that all Americans were entitled to a job, a decent home and neighborhood, and a good education. He called on his "two good friends" McCarthy and McGovern, who had given "new hope to a new generation," to join with him in effecting Martin Luther King's "dream" and Robert Kennedy's "vision." McGovern came to the platform to stand with Humphrey, but McCarthy did not.[41]

The presidential nominee and his entourage attended a celebratory party, and he returned to his suite at 2:00 a.m. for a good night's sleep. But the "nightmare" or "catastrophe" of Chicago was recurring. Around 5:00 a.m. Friday, a swarm of Chicago police and some National Guardsmen, without warrant or writ but having been pelted by some hard objects thrown from the McCarthy campaign's operational base on the fifteenth floor of the Hilton, burst in, brutally assaulted the young staff workers, and began to arrest them. The attack slowed to a halt only after Goodwin happened to stop by, intending to bid fare-well to the senator's campaigners. He had them sit quietly on the floor, ordered calls made to summon McCarthy and Humphrey, and warned the attackers that print and television reporters were coming.

McCarthy came quickly, called a halt to the police action, and, on advice of his Secret Service detail, delayed leaving the city in order to protect his departing staffers. But the "siege of Chicago," as novelist Norman Mailer termed it, would haunt Humphrey throughout the campaign. More than 700 civilians were injured, along with 83 police, and 653 people were jailed, many for little or no reason. When McCarthy finally left the city aboard a chartered aircraft, the pilot announced over the intercom, "We are leaving Prague."[42]

Norman Sherman, Humphrey's press secretary, had refused to wake him when told of the police attack, although how he would have reacted is uncer-tain, given his view of protesters as "storm troopers" whose "new politics" consisted of "breaking up meetings." When CBS television reporter Roger Mudd interviewed Humphrey the next day, he said he was "sick at heart" over the conflict between the police and young people, "but I think we ought to quit pretending that Mayor Daley did anything wrong. He didn't." The demonstra-tions "were planned, premeditated by certain people that feel all they have to do is riot and they'll get their way," he said. "They don't want to work through the peaceful process." The profanity they uttered "was an insult to every woman, every mother, every daughter, indeed, every human being," he added. "You'd put anybody in jail for that kind of language. . . . Is it any wonder that the police had to take action?" His focus on traditional politics and lifestyle put him "on the far side of the generation gap," as a sympathetic biographer has written.[43]

Humphrey left Chicago for his Waverly home feeling as if "we've been pushed off the rim of Grand Canyon," he told Muriel, "and now we have to claw our way up the sides." Later in the campaign he would remark to news reporters that "we went out of there [Chicago] destroyed." Only about three hundred people, including numerous protesters carrying signs, greeted him at the Minneapolis airport. Shortly, after returning to his Waverly home, he told a gathering of a couple of thousand friends and supporters that if Americans needed to protest against anything, it was the tendency of some people "to take to the streets to settle their problems." A couple of days later, he backtracked slightly on his view of the Chicago protests and proposed a blue-ribbon commis-sion investigation. He conceded that the police had "overreacted" and insisted that neither he nor Daley condoned "beating of those people with clubs."

Nonetheless, three years later—well after an investigatory committee issued its report on the Chicago "police riot"—Humphrey again assailed as "just not decent people" those who had spit on his wife, "called her every filthy name in the book," and "threw bags of urine and human excreta" on him. These were people who claimed to believe in peace and brotherly love, he said, "but I don't consider that peace-making. ... I think it was a terrible thing." Notably, Humphrey did not mention the impact of Vietnam War violence on American society.[44]

✦ ✦ ✦

Humphrey left the Democratic convention trailing Nixon in polls by sixteen or more points and subject to Johnson's continued harassment. The vice president admitted to Soviet ambassador Anatoly Dobrynin, "I don't even know who Johnson would prefer as the next president, Nixon or me." Similarly, Defense Secretary Clifford wondered on more than one occasion if in his *"heart of hearts Lyndon Johnson really wants Humphrey to win,"* and another prominent Democrat felt compelled to say to the press, "Johnson is not running against Humphrey."[45]

Nixon was a strong candidate who, despite earlier losses to John Kennedy in 1960 and Edmund "Pat" Brown for governor of California in 1962, won the Republican presidential nomination over George Romney, the moderate governor of Michigan; the more liberal New York governor Nelson Rockefeller; and Ronald Reagan, elected governor of California in 1966 and the new darling of extreme conservatives. At the Republican convention during August 5–8 in Miami, Nixon's ranks held, especially in the South, with a key assist from South Carolina senator Strom Thurmond, former Democratic segregationist turned Republican. Nixon gained a close first-ballot victory, and the party closed ranks behind him.[46]

Nixon chose as his running mate the largely unknown governor of Maryland, Spiro Agnew. He had begun his term in 1966 as a relative moderate and a Rockefeller supporter, but after protest movements and riots in black neighborhoods, he became outspoken on "law and order," blamed "misguided public compassion" for urban conflict, and said that police should shoot fleeing rioters. Nixon chose Agnew to please Thurmond and increasingly conservative southern voters who disliked federal government programs and Supreme Court rulings that promoted school desegregation, voting rights, open housing, and affirmative action. Agnew would also assail war protesters, newsmen, and political opponents, and presumably would also counter George Wallace, candidate of the American Independent Party, who was on the ballot in every state and would seek southern votes and eat into the Democrats' traditional blue-collar, labor union base in the North.[47]

The Republican platform blamed the "Johnson-Humphrey" administration for "lawlessness" in America and called for "liberating the poor" from welfare programs that allegedly stifled the work ethic. The GOP further charged that the administration's Vietnam policy "has failed—militarily, politically, diplomatically, and with relation to our own people," and proposed to settle the war based on self-determination and US interests while moving to civil and military "de-Americanization" of the conflict. In his acceptance speech, Nixon claimed to speak for "the great majority of Americans, the forgotten Americans, the non-shouters, the non-demonstrators," said it was time to get tough on crime, and decried the United States being "tied down in a war for four years with no end in sight."[48]

During the New Hampshire primary in March, Nixon said he would "end the war and win the peace in the Pacific," a statement taken to mean that he had a "secret plan" to achieve this. He sought to appear to take the political high road by insisting that he would not say anything that might upset the Paris negotiations and shrewdly played to Johnson's vanity by assuring him that he would never embarrass him over the conflict during his remaining time as president or afterward.[49]

Secretly, Nixon sought to forestall a settlement, or announcement of an "October surprise" portending one, which he feared would turn the election to Humphrey. During the Republican's vice presidential years and on a business trip to Taipei in 1967 he had come to know Anna Chennault, the wealthy Chinese-born widow of Lieutenant General Claire Chennault, World War II commander of the "Flying Tigers" that had defended China against Japan. In 1958, she moved to Washington, DC, where she became a prominent hostess and Republican Party contributor, and in 1968 she would cochair with Mamie Eisenhower the "Women for Nixon-Agnew" committee. Chennault was also connected to Asian political leaders, including South Vietnam's president, Nguyen Van Thieu, and Saigon's ambassador to the United States, Bui Diem, who transmitted her messages to and from his government.

Nixon arranged for Chennault and Diem to meet in Manhattan on July 12, 1968, with him and his campaign manager, John Mitchell. Then and later, Nixon made clear that he was "committed to winning the war," that if he was elected president South Vietnam would "get a better deal" from him than from Humphrey, and that Chennault was to be the "sole representative" between him and South Vietnam's government. William Bundy, assistant secretary of state for East Asian and Pacific affairs at this time, later wrote that Nixon's action "may have been unique. The opposition party's candidate for president was setting up a private channel to the head of state of a government with whom the incumbent President was conducting critically important and secret negotiations!"[50]

Humphrey decided to forego the Democrats' usual kickoff of marching on Labor Day with UAW members and other labor people in Detroit's Cadillac Square because so many union workers were sporting Wallace buttons or hats. Instead, he flew to New York City to take part in a union parade that drew far more marchers than observers and many antiwar protesters carrying "Dump the Hump" or other hostile signs. His Secret Service detail had to slip him into his hotel through a side door.

His bland statement to an educational television station interviewer that he favored a blue-ribbon commission investigation of the violent behavior of the Chicago police was unlikely to win endorsement from Senator McCarthy (who would spend most of September on the French Riviera) or his liberal supporters. By contrast, when Nixon opened his campaign in Chicago, Mayor Daley gave city workers the afternoon off, and his police orchestrated an orderly reception for some 400,000 people.[51]

Humphrey could not begin campaign planning until he returned home from New York. He persuaded O'Brien to stay on as manager by also naming him DNC chairman, although he regarded his new task as "hopeless" and said he stayed out of "sympathy" for the candidate. Humphrey's DFL compatriot Freeman was made to feel part of the inner circle by being put in charge of issues, scheduling, and travel, which allowed him to keep his cabinet post and the status he craved.[52]

O'Brien and his aides hastily drafted a "very basic . . . flying by the seat of your pants" plan, but lack of money was a constant problem despite the efforts of Humphrey's campaign treasurer, wealthy Minneapolis businessman Bob Short, and agribusinessman Dwayne Andreas. Humphrey's and O'Brien's first phone calls to Johnson and Arthur Krim, movie producer mogul and head of the President's Club, whose coffers the vice president had helped to fill, went unanswered. When Humphrey finally reached Krim, he was told that the lack of aid was due to Johnson's ire over the naming of O'Brien to head the DNC; the president believed that O'Brien would turn the party over to the Kennedy family. Johnson also objected to Humphrey's choice of Short as his treasurer rather than the president's man, Criswell. Angry and frustrated, Humphrey— assuming the call was being recorded—yelled that if he had to raise the money himself he would, "and it will make the goddamnedest story you ever heard. I have the Communists, the Republicans, and now the White House against me. I'll go it alone."[53]

The struggle with the White House had just begun. Humphrey flew back to Washington for a September 4 NSC meeting—the last one Johnson would let him attend—where the vice president, looking for a possible break in the war, asked JCS chairman General Earle Wheeler why he viewed a cease-fire as dangerous. Wheeler replied that it would allow the enemy to organize politically in the area he controlled in South Vietnam and keep it from the Saigon government's rule. The vice president's campaign was not going to get help on the military front, and the meeting ended without the talk he sought with Johnson.

Humphrey told White House aides that he would raise his own campaign funds even if he had to drive a car across the country himself. "I am not going to let the chance [to be president] go because the Administration [the president] doesn't want it." Humphrey did decline a subtle offer from Soviet ambassador Anatoly Dobrynin to have Moscow supply funds, asking only for Russia's good wishes.[54]

Johnson did tell Humphrey he would help in any way asked and would also release the cabinet to do so. The vice president doubted this. In fact, Krim's offer to help with funds was as a consultant only, and he soon began to dismantle the President's Club, with none of the $600,000 in its accounts going to the vice president's campaign. Nor would Johnson ask his wealthy Texas friends to contribute. Thus Short looked to have twenty friends pledge $100,000 each to start things, while he put up $2 million of his own money, and O'Brien borrowed another $3 million for national advertising. Still, the Republicans would outspend the Democrats by about $20 million to $10 million.[55]

Humphrey and Johnson divided over more than money. The vice president hoped to make his candidacy a "referendum on human rights," as he told a B'nai B'rith gathering in Washington on September 8, and he intended to assail Nixon and Wallace for exploiting the "fears and hates" that social justice issues brought to the fore. Humphrey's remarks were well received, and the next morning he began a cross-country dash. At the first stop, at John F. Kennedy Plaza in Philadelphia, the crowd was thin, with "Dump the Hump" hecklers all around and repeated questions about Vietnam. During a meeting with students, Humphrey responded to a query that "negotiations or no negotiations," he thought "we could start to remove some American forces early in 1969 or late 1968." In Denver that day he said that the minority plank—with its proposed bombing halt—was so "mildly different" from the majority one on Vietnam that he could have run on the former one. Secretary of State Rusk immediately stated that a bombing halt was unlikely to improve things quickly and even denied having approved the dovish plank Humphrey had run by him before the convention.[56]

Unnerved, Humphrey sought to recoup in Houston the next day by holding up the Houston *Post*, which headlined the return of a marine regiment to the United States. He repeated his claim that troops might soon be coming home, although, as aides soon pointed out, two paragraphs later the story revealed that the troops had been on temporary assignment and were already being replaced by others. Before he could issue a retraction, Johnson publicly rebuked him.[57]

The president, greatly on edge over lack of progress at the Paris talks, took out his anxiety on Humphrey. Johnson had told Clifford that he wanted a "new initiative" to move negotiations along and would "pay a premium" for this. He also knew his chief Paris negotiator, Averell Harriman, favored a bombing halt, as did many State and Defense officials, but the president thought that if the United States held firm, a "break" would come from North Vietnam. Johnson worried, however, that "some of Hanoi's work" was being done by Americans, including the thousand delegates who backed the Democrats' minority plank in Chicago—but "I am the only President until January 1969," he insisted, and he did not want anyone telling him what to do.[58]

Thus, immediately after Humphrey's remarks about troop withdrawals and the minority plank, Johnson raced to make a surprise, unyielding speech at an American Legion Convention in New Orleans on September 10. He insisted that his policy derived from those of Presidents Truman, Eisenhower, and Kennedy, who had intervened in small conflicts to ward off larger wars. He likened Vietnam critics to 1930s isolationists and said that everyone yearned to bring home US troops, but "no man can predict when that day will come."[59]

The speech was "not an act of friendship," an angry vice president told friends, while Johnson aide Harry McPherson said that everyone took it as "a real blast at Humphrey." But his remark about troop withdrawals "wasn't really very far off," Freeman noted, since Rusk, Clifford, and even Johnson had spoken hopefully about bringing US troops home. They gave Humphrey "almost no leeway," however, and could have gone "much easier" on him. Further, many analysts viewed the majority and minority planks as not far apart "semantically."

Johnson was intransigent, as Freeman learned after talking with trusted aide Charles Murphy, who "was convinced that the President would rather see Nixon elected than to see any equivocation on this very key issue" of being "tough as can be" with Hanoi. Johnson "really went after Humphrey," Freeman wrote. "He called him a coward," accused him of "trying to back off his family [the administration]," and charged him with "ogling McCarthy. . . . On and on he went. A lot of the language was four letter words," after which the president asked Freeman not to tell Humphrey about this—they needed to "help him." The agriculture secretary left "with my ears still ringing." They would have rung more had he heard Johnson tell Clifford twelve days later that he doubted Humphrey had the ability to be president and would have respected his vice president more if he "showed he had some balls."[60]

Nixon sought to maneuver Johnson by sending the popularly renowned Reverend Billy Graham to see him on September 15 with a message—read to him "point by point"—in which the Republican pledged never to embarrass him after the election, to seek his counsel, to send him on special assignments, to give him "a major share of the credit" when the Vietnam War was settled, and to seek to ensure his deserved place "in History." Johnson said he would support Humphrey, but if Nixon won, he would cooperate fully with him. The president was "touched and appreciative" of Nixon's "generous gesture," Graham reported to him. In fact, when Clifford soon pressed at an NSC meeting for a bombing halt and Rusk, opposed, argued that if it brought no result many Democrats would vote for Nixon, Johnson sharply cut in to say Nixon should not be part of the discussion.[61]

Hecklers greeted Humphrey everywhere he went as though he were Johnson, who admitted that the press took out their hostility toward him and the Vietnam War on the vice president. On Humphrey's arrival in Texas in mid-September, Democratic leaders—including the president and Governor Connally—were notably absent, as were California's more liberal Democratic officials when the vice president spoke in San Francisco and Los Angeles. As the *New York Times* reported, most of Humphrey's campaign stops consisted of airport to hotel to television studio, and he spoke only of the "Kennedy-Johnson," not "Johnson," administration. The vice president also inclined to shift voters' attention to the choice between Muskie and Agnew, whom the Republicans had openly designated to take the "low road," as Freeman noted, and who remarked after Humphrey's troop withdrawal remarks that the vice president was "squishy soft" on Communism. Nixon made Agnew apologize, but he was branded "the Joe McCarthy of 1968."[62]

By mid-September, Humphrey appeared to be "coming apart at the seams," Freeman wrote, and internal campaign analyses revealed severe defections "from the left, anti-war liberals, and leftists comprised of University Students, intellectuals, and better educated middle class once liberal Democrats." So, too, were "Negro militants" gone, "but even more serious is the defection from the right. This is white workers both in the North and the South." They "see a threat from inflation, from taxes, from Civil Rights, to wit, open housing and school desegregation and their physical safety," Freeman noted. They also believed that their taxes were being spent on "lazy people," meaning Negroes, who could get a job "if they really wanted to." These voters would support Wallace and, if not, would go to Nixon because, as one analyst reported, "These people don't think Humphrey is white—they really think he's black."

Humphrey knew of his difficulties but "ripped into everyone connected to the campaign," especially about keeping him from the crowds that had always inspired him, although he seemed to ignore the anger directed toward him over the war. But in mid-September he gave "absolute authority" to Freeman to revamp his campaign staff and scheduling. Still, as his old DFL compatriot realized, "Poor Humphrey is swimming against the stream, but he's sure battling," and "He's best when the tide runs against him."[63]

That same day, O'Brien told Humphrey, "Let's face it, as of now we've lost. It's on every newsman's lips. You're not your own man. Unless you change direction on this Vietnam thing, and become your own man, you're finished." The vice president agreed, and estimated the odds were three-to-one against him. He blamed himself for his mistaken troop withdrawal comments and Johnson for "undercutting me" in New Orleans. He needed "some[thing] positive," a compelling stroke to hammer home that "Nixon represents resistance and apathy" and Wallace "apartheid"; Humphrey offers an economy that will lead people to vote their pocketbooks, and he will tell the people that "we have to start pulling our ground forces out as soon as the Vietnamese are ready— de-Americanization." O'Brien quickly pointed out this last proposal meant a break with Johnson: "a clean break this week or never. Do it now—even a white paper," he urged. Humphrey balked: "I don't know."[64]

"The press wants to divide us—me and the president. That makes their stories," Humphrey said. Johnson told Humphrey that it was not "proper for the VP or an ex-VP [Nixon] or an ex-President [Eisenhower] to play commander-in-chief." Humphrey agreed that neither he nor Nixon would do anything like that before January 20, 1969. Johnson added that "tactics, strategy, peace conferences, [and] troop withdrawals" were delicate matters to be left to the president. Humphrey noted only that when he became president, "I'll spend every day finding peace. Re-examine everything."[65]

The vice president sought to reenergize his campaign on September 19 by flying to Boston, where Ted Kennedy surprised him by greeting him at Logan Airport. But even when this Democratic heartland's favorite son addressed a large crowd on the Boston Common, boos rang out from more than five hundred protesters at mention of Humphrey. When he spoke, the loudspeakers had to be turned up to project his voice over cries of "Dump the Hump" and "Shame." The vice president insisted that his hecklers' behavior would "disgust" the American people, and he cut his speech short. Massachusetts's Democratic leaders feared he might even lose in their state, despite its overwhelming orientation to their party.[66]

Humphrey headed west, stopping in South Dakota to endorse McGovern's reelection. But even in the state where the vice president was born and raised, he was running so far behind Nixon that there was concern he would drag his former protégé to defeat. In Independence, Missouri, he heard Truman urge him to "give 'em hell" and likened his own campaign to that of the former president's 1948 stunning upset of a front-running Dewey. In Toledo Humphrey sought to start regaining voters from George Wallace by labeling his "law and order" slogan a "hoax," and in Minneapolis, before an AFL-CIO convention, he pointed out that Wallace's Alabama ranked at the nation's bottom in wages, unemployment benefits, and workmen's compensation but was near the top in sales tax and crime rate.[67]

Humphrey pressed Nixon to clarify his stance on key issues such as school integration (which the Republican said he favored though he questioned use of federal power to enforce this); law and order (with Nixon insisting that "black capitalism" was the answer to crime); and the pending Nuclear Nonproliferation Treaty (which Nixon said he favored though he wanted to delay ratification). Humphrey said that Nixon straddled issues so much, "he must be saddle sore."

Humphrey also argued that a Republican victory portended a return to the Herbert Hoover era and economic depression. This view appealed to traditional Democrats, but as *Time* noted, it was unlikely to win back vital Robert Kennedy and McCarthy voters who wanted Humphrey to break with the president on the war and believed that he had become Johnson's "bond servant."[68]

As Humphrey headed into the crucial electoral state of California in late September, Johnson and the war remained the critical issue. Numerous leading Democrats shied from contact with Humphrey, including Los Angeles mayor Sam Yorty; Speaker of the California Assembly Jesse Unruh, who was urging a write-in vote for McCarthy, which the highly liberal California Democratic Council (CDC) was promoting; and Alan Cranston, a CDC founder running for the US Senate.

Further, while in Los Angeles, Humphrey spent four hours at the small, conservative, Christian-affiliated Pepperdine College rather than at the large and diverse UCLA campus, where, an aide conceded, he would have been subject to "uncontrollable rudeness or total indifference." Only in San Francisco, where the United Nations was founded, did he offer even a nod to peace-oriented advocates by proposing that organization might send peacekeeping forces to administer free elections in Vietnam and monitor withdrawal of all foreign troops.[69]

Humphrey's challenges to "Richard the Silent" and "Richard the Chicken-Hearted" to debate him went unanswered, and when McCarthy returned from France on September 27, he declined to endorse the vice president, insistent that he had not changed his basic views on Vietnam. Humphrey's campaign, which had lost many big Democratic contributors who had once feared Robert Kennedy's nomination, was almost broke and unable to run television ads, while Nixon's smooth commercials flooded screens.

Johnson remained totally aloof from Humphrey, even hostile, and adamant that senior officials keep Nixon's name out of policy discussions. *Time* reported that "the President might even prefer a Nixon victory," which he could explain as a repudiation of the Democratic Party, given that he viewed the Republican candidate as more steadfast on the war than Humphrey, whose triumph would suggest "a repudiation of Johnson personally." There was also a "Bourbon sense of 'après moi, le déluge' " in the White House.[70]

In late September, the Gallup poll showed Nixon leading Humphrey by 43 percent to 28 percent, with the vice president leading Wallace by only 7 percent and in danger of coming in behind him in the Electoral College vote. Historian Arthur Schlesinger Jr. was amazed at how many "New York intellectuals"—journalists and writers—had gone "soft" on Nixon out of anger toward Humphrey over Chicago and his failure to separate from Johnson on Vietnam. Even the eminent Walter Lippmann endorsed Nixon, finding him to be "maturer and mellower" than before, and left-oriented columnist Murray Kempton said that the Democratic Party needed to lose in order to be reorganized with new leadership.[71]

Humphrey's downward spiral continued as he moved from California to Oregon, where at Portland's Civic Arena several hundred college students rose as one to shout at the vice president "End the war" and "Murderer," and walked out en masse. In Seattle fewer than six hundred supporters greeted him at Boeing Field, and on September 28, before an overflow crowd at Seattle Center Arena, several hundred militant protesters booed or shouted down his introducers, including the popular and powerful senator Warren Magnuson.

Several times Humphrey bellowed "shut up" at his opponents, only to have them respond, with a bullhorn, that "Vietnam is a scream [of death] that does not end" and that they had come to arrest and try him for "crimes against humanity." He insisted that he would not be driven from the platform by people who "believe in nothing" but was unable to speak uninterrupted until federal agents and local police removed about thirty protesters. His speech emphasized his usual "underdog" status in his fights for progressive legislation from the Peace Corps and Food for Peace to Medicare, and he won sympathy and an ovation, but there were pickets at his hotel.[72]

The vice president seemed "bewildered by his youthful enemies," and "a desperate and angry figure," *New York Times* columnist Robert Semple reported, and "an air of sadness hangs over his campaign." Later, Humphrey would write that although Seattle was his campaign's low point, public "outrage" over his mistreatment began to turn things his way. But it was not public outrage that turned his campaign; it was his willingness at last to distance himself, if only in a small way, from Johnson on the war and to demonstrate, as O'Brien had pleaded, that he was his own man.[73]

18

BATTLING THE TORRENTS—AND JOHNSON

Aware that Johnson had been keeping the vice president uninformed regarding Paris negotiations, Undersecretary of State Nicholas Katzenbach and Executive Secretary of the State Department Benjamin Read began drafting a statement for Humphrey, explaining what he might do about Vietnam after becoming president. This included giving the Saigon government a schedule for US troop reduction ("de-Americanization of the war") based on Communist respect for the DMZ between North and South Vietnam. Read, a friend of Humphrey's aide William Welsh, gave him the draft statement to pass along. "My God, this is what I need," the vice president exclaimed.[1]

UN ambassador George Ball—who with Humphrey had opposed Johnson's bombing escalation in February 1965—told the vice president that the Paris talks were "sterile" and that he needed to help himself by speaking about Vietnam. Determined to break Johnson's "psychological grip" on Humphrey, Ball resigned on September 26, 1968. Deeply discouraged but intent to secure peace, Humphrey conceded that he had "loused up the situation" by failing to stand firm on troop withdrawals and a bombing pause. Ball told him he should have "stuck to your guns," but thought they could still make a fight of the election. Arthur Goldberg, who resigned as UN ambassador in April 1968 in disagreement about Vietnam, announced the formation of a "National Citizens Committee for Humphrey-Muskie" and called for a complete bombing halt.

Humphrey committed $100,000 of the campaign's dwindling funds to buy a half-hour on NBC television on the evening of September 30, which prompted rumors that the candidate was about to make a major statement.[2]

Ball and Welsh prepared a draft speech; the former diplomat assured Humphrey that it would refer only to action he would take after he was president. It became a group effort, with Humphrey's speech writer Ted Van Dyk, Averell Harriman in Paris, Senator Fred Harris, Johnson's former press secretary Bill Moyers, and Labor Secretary Willard Wirtz contributing. When Harris asked Humphrey if he would seek Johnson's accord, he replied, "Hell, no. I'm not going to ask. I did that once." The group worked on the address long after an exhausted Humphrey took a tranquilizer and went to bed.

O'Brien cabled a blistering memorandum to the vice president calling Ball's speech—heavily focused on Europe—an "abomination," and joined Humphrey in Seattle, where the group continued working for a day before traveling to Salt Lake City.[3]

O'Brien, Harris, and Van Dyk favored a dovish approach, including an unconditional bombing halt, as the best way to win over McCarthy-Kennedy voters and get North Vietnam to agree to serious talks. Goldberg and Governor Richard Hughes of New Jersey telephoned their support for this view. But Humphrey's chief of staff, Bill Connell, hawkish on the war and wanting not to offend Johnson, resisted compromise. He was supported by two of the president's confidants who had joined the group: Jim Rowe, the Washington attorney who vetted Humphrey for Johnson in 1964, and John M. Bailey, head of Connecticut's Democratic Party and DNC chair the past four years. Welsh and Ball sought a compromise: a bombing halt that would continue based on North Vietnam's respect for the DMZ. Ball also sent word from Harriman and his conegotiator, former deputy secretary of defense Cyrus Vance, that a bombing halt had to be contingent on North Vietnam's reaction.

Humphrey said he had to know *before* he offered a bombing halt that North Vietnam would respect the DMZ. He was concerned about Johnson's reaction, but he chiefly did not want to say anything that might upset the Paris talks. This was his speech; he was the one running for president, he said, and he finished the draft himself at around 5:45 a.m. Van Dyk would smooth it over before the vice president taped it in the afternoon. After the press and major politicians were briefed, Humphrey would inform Johnson of the main points just before the speech aired, and, as Ball recalled, he would call the president to "get him down off the ceiling."[4]

Humphrey spent the morning of September 30 with Utah Democrats, conceding he would "not have a prayer" if the election were held that day. He spoke briefly at the Mormon Tabernacle, returned to his hotel to review the final text of his speech, and went to the television station for the taping. At 6:45 p.m., Nixon called Johnson seeking assurance the speech would not reveal a dramatic change in current policy. The president said he could not speak to the issue because he had not read the speech but informed Nixon—while insisting he not be quoted—that the US commander in Vietnam, General Creighton Abrams, had written a memorandum contending that a bombing halt would greatly increase North Vietnam's military threat.

Johnson told Nixon he had not shared Abrams's memorandum with Humphrey, allegedly because he did not want to be accused of "coaching" him, and the best thing Nixon could say publicly was that only the president and the State and Defense Departments were responsible for making US foreign policy. Johnson also had his national security adviser, Walt Rostow, assure Nixon that the United States was not changing its policy and would insist on its three points: in return for a bombing halt, North Vietnam had to respect the DMZ, not shell South Vietnam's cities, and accept the Saigon government at the negotiating table. Nixon pledged continued support of current policy.[5]

Moments before his speech was to air, Humphrey called Johnson to tell him what he would do as a "new President" facing "new circumstances"—but assured him that he did not intend "unilateral withdrawal." He wanted to de-escalate the war and take a "risk for peace," as the Democratic platform proposed, by ordering a bombing halt if he had prior evidence that North Vietnam would respect the DMZ and enter good-faith negotiations. When the president said that his position included North Vietnam admitting Saigon to the talks and not shelling southern cities, Humphrey said that the DMZ was his only specific point and that "good faith negotiations" included the other two points. Johnson said, "Okay," and promised to watch the speech. He did not mention his conversation with Nixon.[6]

Humphrey's speech aired at 7:30 p.m. He chose not to have the vice president's seal or flag on display—he spoke as a "citizen" who was a "candidate" for president. He charged that "protesters" had "drowned out" his prior messages and undermined the "democratic process," and he had "paid for" this television time to tell "my story" uninterrupted. He acknowledged that Johnson as president would make all Vietnam decisions until January 20, 1969, and he hoped to see peace achieved by that date. But if not, a "new President" would need a "complete reassessment," and "the policies of tomorrow need not be limited by the policies of yesterday."

The people had a right to know, Humphrey said, that if he became president he would not opt for unilateral withdrawal or military escalation but would be willing to halt the bombing as an "acceptable risk for peace." He would need advance evidence by "deed or word"; however, the Communists would respect the DMZ, and he reserved the right to resume bombing if they showed bad faith. The South Vietnamese would have to be ready to meet their self-defense obligations, and he would begin "de-Americanization" of the war—namely, setting a specific timetable to begin troop withdrawals within the next year, followed by a cease-fire, mutual troop withdrawals, and free elections in South Vietnam to include the NLF and all dissidents. Humphrey called out Nixon for favoring the military intervention in Vietnam in 1954 that Eisenhower had repudiated and challenged him to reveal his "plan" to end the war as well as a debate.[7]

"I feel good inside for the first time," the vice president said immediately after the speech, which did not seem to ruffle feathers but chastised war protesters. Ball called Johnson to say he had told reporters that Humphrey assumed both North and South Vietnam would want to bring "the other side" (the NLF) to the negotiations, but that was their decision. The president seemed satisfied and told Ball he was doing a "superb" job with the press, especially his line that "Johnson is not running against Humphrey."[8]

However, the president told Republican Senate minority leader Everett Dirksen, a conduit to Nixon, that Humphrey aimed to gain McCarthy voters and that the Republican candidate would do best to say that the current administration was responsible for running the war. Two days later, Johnson complained to Rusk that Harriman ("a damned fool") and Vance had collaborated with Ball in drafting the speech, and Nixon fell into their trap by publicly criticizing Humphrey for taking away the negotiators' "trump" card, a bombing halt. Now the North Vietnamese were unlikely to act until after the election, and if Humphrey won, "they're in clover." Three days later, Johnson vented about recalling Harriman from his post and said that if he were Hanoi, he would ask himself, "Can I get a better deal out of Humphrey than I can Johnson?"[9]

Clifford, Rusk, and Rostow, however, believed that "the speech need not give us trouble" and that the White House should not "look for marginal differences." Reporters were told that the address was not a departure from policy, and the president—unlike his earlier blast at Humphrey's call for troop withdrawals—remained publicly quiet. Most important, as even a still disaffected Arthur Schlesinger wrote, Humphrey had "come out for himself, or rather as himself."[10]

Humphrey's appearances were met no longer with protest signs but ones saying, "If You Mean It, We Are with You," and "Hecklers for Humphrey—We Came Back." Major polls began to shift in the vice president's favor. Connell floated joint Humphrey campaign–DNC-commissioned private polls skewed to show that Gallup and others had overstated Nixon's lead and that Humphrey was closer than they realized to carrying the states needed to win 270 electoral votes and the presidency.[11]

A revitalized vice president headed to Nashville and Knoxville, Tennessee— Wallace country—where he assailed the Alabaman as the "apostle of hatred and racism" whose own state had frightful working conditions and the nation's highest murder rate. Humphrey also charged that Nixon "appeals to the same fear, the same passions, the same frustrations which can unleash . . . unreasoning hate and repression." In North Carolina and West Virginia—where Wallace was estimated to get 40 percent of the vote in the coal counties— Humphrey, seeking to win back working-class blue-collar voters who had defected to the Alabaman or to Nixon, hammered at Republican failure to do anything for Appalachia.[12]

Humphrey sought to motivate AFL-CIO leaders (who now formally endorsed him) and UAW officials to step up their voter registration and campaign efforts. He also got a break on October 3 when Wallace introduced his vice presidential choice, former air force chief of staff General Curtis LeMay, who said he did not think "it would be the end of the world if we explode a nuclear weapon." The vice president promptly labeled Wallace and LeMay "the bombsy twins."[13]

Goldberg took over Humphrey's campaign in "must win" New York, where his longtime liberal ADA allies, including Senate candidate Paul O'Dwyer, began to return—if unenthusiastically—to his fold, bringing along McCarthy and Robert Kennedy voters. The *New York Times* endorsed Humphrey, citing his social welfare and civil rights legislation and internationalist foreign policy perspective and saying he was the only candidate with strong support in both white and black communities. The editors urged McCarthy to endorse his DFL compatriot, but the senator said that Humphrey first had to call for a new government in South Vietnam that included the NLF and a revamped US draft law.[14]

Johnson, prodded by the ILGWU, taped a short speech for the campaign committee to broadcast over NBC television on October 10 that endorsed Humphrey based on his long-term leadership of progressive forces and "unique" understanding of foreign policy. Johnson—or the ILGWU—also pointedly noted that four presidents had died in office in the twentieth century, highlighting Humphrey's choice of Muskie, as opposed to Agnew or LeMay, being a "heartbeat away from the Presidency." Later, Humphrey would ask voters to "contemplate a President Agnew."[15]

The vice president's September 30 speech brought his campaign increased energy and support and more than $300,000 in desperately needed funds, with more to come—although not from Texas's big-money Johnson-Connally benefactors. The president refused requests from Rowe and North Carolina governor Terry Sanford to campaign for Humphrey in New Jersey, Texas, Kentucky, and

Tennessee. "You know that Nixon is following my policies more closely than Humphrey," he said.[16]

Johnson refused to help Humphrey by revealing, as he learned from O'Brien in early October, that the Nixon-Agnew campaign received more than half a million dollars from the Greek military junta that had overthrown the government in Athens in 1967. The president was still feeling the effects of Billy Graham's neutralizing interview and harbored his own fear that if Nixon were elected, "he will indict all of us," he told an aide, although he never said why he would be indicted.[17]

Despite Johnson, by mid-October Humphrey and his campaign had taken on new life, aided by a hard-hitting advertising campaign orchestrated by Joseph Napolitan, a shrewd political consultant O'Brien brought in who advised the vice president to omit black people from his advertisements because they were costing him votes. Humphrey took on the law-and-order issue by contending that there could be "no compromise" on everyone's right to a "decent and safe neighborhood"—but that for every jail Nixon would build, "Humphrey would also build a school," and for every policeman Wallace would hire, "Humphrey would also hire a good teacher." The word "also" suggested building a jail and a house and hiring a policeman and a good teacher, a "guns and butter" approach to the crime problem. This led, however, to Humphrey's cutting Nixon's large lead to just 5 points, 40 percent to 35 percent, as a Harris poll showed, mainly by reclaiming Democrats who had defected to Wallace.[18]

Humphrey adapted Johnson's 1960 campaign query, "What Has Nixon Ever Done for Culpeper [Virginia]?" to stops in St. Louis and elsewhere. In big cities, such as New York, which had been the center of McCarthy or Kennedy support, many former dissidents—including Allard Lowenstein, who had brought McCarthy into the presidential race—now returned to Humphrey's camp, if only because they despised Nixon and regarded Agnew as a "disaster," as did many Republican officials, at least privately.[19]

Even the cautious Freeman, who had worried that Humphrey's September 30 speech would be met with a "yawn," noted an "upbeat" public response to him. Polls were showing that he was tied or had a small lead in most of the key industrial states, whereas Nixon's stilted campaign formats, vagueness on issues, and ducking of a debate were catching up to him. For the first time Freeman believed, "We are going to win." But he still thought that Humphrey's road back would be a long one and removed North and South Carolina and Florida from his schedule because he trailed so badly there; so many people were "irritated" with African Americans and thought the candidate was "more black than white." After a trip to Missouri, Freeman wrote that farmers in the West were given to vote the same way as "city people" on "Vietnam, and law enforcement, and race relations." Optimism aside, he concluded, "I can't help but feel very sorry for Humphrey. If ever there was a man battling the torrents, it's more than a tide, it's him."[20]

The "torrents" included Johnson, who continued to go out of his way to diminish his vice president. As Humphrey returned from campaigning on October 19 and headed to meet with the president, a press inquiry led Johnson to cancel abruptly their get-together. Even Freeman, who usually gave Johnson the benefit of doubt, was "appalled" by his "petulance and pettiness," which had cost him his "personal popularity" and "affection of the people." It was hard to believe that the president was "so mean and petty"—his behavior was "incredible."[21]

Johnson's behavior grew even more problematic just as the Paris negotiations began to seem fruitful, perhaps partly due to Humphrey's bombing halt speech. Ten days later, the Soviets and North Vietnamese proffered a major concession to the Harriman-Vance team: admission of the Saigon government to the talks in exchange for a bombing halt. Johnson, after a series of intense meetings with his senior diplomatic and military advisers, agreed, provided that North Vietnam pledged not only to admit the Saigon government to the talks but not to attack across the DMZ or shell South Vietnam's cities; otherwise, the United States could resume "unlimited" bombing. Harriman devised a clever "your side–our side" term for negotiations to allow the presence of both the Saigon government and the NLF without being named. Johnson doubted that Hanoi would take the deal or honor it. But Clifford persisted that "the time has come," and the president, aware that his time to gain an accord was running out, finally said, "Let's try it"; but negotiations had to begin the day after the bombing halted.[22]

Johnson feared, however, that his effort would be viewed as a ploy to aid Humphrey's election, and "Nixon will be disappointed." The conservative Democratic senator George Smathers of Florida told Johnson, "The word is out that we are trying to throw the election to Humphrey" and that Nixon said "he did not want the President to be pulled into this, that wrong results could flow," and he "is afraid we could be misled." Rusk claimed, mistakenly, "Nixon has been honorable on Vietnam. We must give him a chance to roll with this. . . . He has been more responsible on this than our own candidate." He added that Ball was coming to the State Department but would be given "nothing."

Clifford, however, insisted that most people had already made up their minds about the election, and even though he agreed to give Nixon notice of the negotiations, the important point was, "Nixon doesn't want anything that could possibly rock the boat. He likes the shape that it is in now. . . . But what's the matter with rocking the boat?"[23]

Johnson called Senate majority leader Mike Mansfield on October 16 to complain bitterly about Humphrey's proposed bombing halt—"period, no comma, no semi-colon, just plain outright stop it," a phrase the president used repeatedly—and about the October 12 "fool speech" of former national security adviser McGeorge Bundy calling for a bombing halt and start of US troop withdrawals. Later that morning in a conference call, Johnson ("amazingly" without prior word to Humphrey, Clifford recalled) told the three candidates in "absolute confidence" of the US proposal being sent to the Paris negotiators. He stressed that it was consistent with past policy, it would not be changed until he left office, and he wanted silence on the matter. Anything the candidates might say would be "injurious to your country." In an obvious slap at Humphrey's September 30 address (and Bundy's speech), he said, "We're not going to get peace through speeches, and we're not going to get peace through the newspapers." He added that he had weighed, but jettisoned, a plan to have all three candidates sign a statement to be read to the North Vietnamese, pledging support for this position as long as Johnson was president. Humphrey said nothing, but Wallace spoke for a "strong" position on Vietnam, and Nixon—lying, as the White House would soon learn—assured him that he would not say anything to "undercut" negotiations.[24]

Humphrey was dispirited. *New York Times* reporter Max Frankel attributed the vice president's evident discomfort to his being "only one of three equals at the end of a telephone line." Or perhaps less than an equal, as Johnson's abrupt cancellation of their scheduled October 19 White House meeting suggested.[25]

Humphrey persevered. He now insisted that he had never favored "massive escalation" in Vietnam, only "de-escalation and bombing pauses." He repeatedly chided Nixon for refusing to debate and got a break on October 26 when New York's courts denied McCarthy supporters' last-minute effort to put his name on the ballot. Three days later, the senator finally endorsed him. McCarthy still believed that Humphrey's position on Vietnam was lacking but credited him with better understanding of America's domestic needs than Nixon and more likely to scale down the arms race.[26]

By late October, Humphrey had so sharply reduced Nixon's lead in the Gallup poll that some Democrats began to talk of an upset. This led an unsettled Republican nominee to charge that the vice president had at first favored an unconditional, and then a conditional, bombing halt in Vietnam, thus prompting an enemy confused about US intentions to escalate the war. Nixon also stepped up unfounded law-and-order charges: Humphrey was "sitting on his hands" while the United States became a nation "where 50 percent of American women are frightened to walk within a mile of their homes at night," and crime "is rising ten times as fast as the population." The "old Nixon" was back, analysts said, and running scared.[27]

Most important, Johnson and Humphrey learned that Nixon's pledge not to say anything to undermine Vietnam negotiations was a lie. First, Nixon knew more about the Paris talks than they realized because a chief campaign aide was passing him material obtained from an unnamed White House informant. So, too, was Henry Kissinger, then a Harvard University professor who had consulted to the Kennedy and Johnson administrations and taken part in 1967 in high-level Vietnam negotiations, secretly sending Nixon information gleaned from his contacts in Paris. Kissinger, who served as Rockefeller's foreign policy adviser and helped write the Republican platform, hoped for a position in either a Humphrey or a Nixon administration and twice warned the GOP candidate that "something big" would happen around October 23, thus fueling his suspicion about an October surprise intended to throw the election to Humphrey.[28]

In late October, Nixon falsely said that Humphrey had called for a dangerous unconditional bombing halt and claimed to have been told of a "cynical, last minute attempt" by the Johnson administration to salvage Humphrey's candidacy "through a bombing halt and perhaps a ceasefire"—adding sanctimoniously, "This I do not believe." Johnson assailed Nixon's "ugly and unfair charges," while the Republican inveighed against the idea of a coalition government in Vietnam, although neither Johnson nor Humphrey had advocated this.[29]

On October 31, Nixon—aware that Johnson was about to announce a bombing halt—had Mitchell call Anna Chennault, the Republicans' liaison with the Saigon government, to say that he was speaking on the candidate's behalf, and "it's very important that our Vietnamese friends understand our Republican position and I hope you have made that clear to them." Chennault claimed, however, that her role was to relay messages, not, as Mitchell's words implied, to try to influence Saigon's policy. But she said South Vietnam most likely would not take part in the Paris talks. At the same time, Ambassador Diem cabled his superiors: "Many Republican friends have contacted me and encouraged us to stand firm. They were alarmed by press reports that you had softened your position." The ambassador also said he was "regularly in touch with the Nixon entourage" and had made clear "our firm attitude." He added, "The longer the impasse continues, the more we are favored."[30]

Johnson knew that South Vietnam's government had little support and depended on 550,000 US troops and a constant supply of US dollars and was likely to try to wait out his term to seek a better deal from a hardline Nixon administration. Thus, Thieu first objected to NLF representatives being treated as a separate government and, when told that was not to be the case, insisted that the NLF come as part of North Vietnam's delegation. Hanoi first said it could not ensure NLF presence but finally indicated that if a bombing halt came on October 30, it would be ready to begin talks on November 2.[31]

Johnson responded again in almost paranoid terms: "November 2 is a bad date, a dangerous date. Nearly everyone will think it was connected to the election." The Russians were behind the proposal—"shoving us"—he argued, in order to elect Humphrey, who had said only "thank you" after the last conference call to the three candidates, whereas Nixon had said, "We all speak with one voice." The president was also angry at Harriman for having said that South Vietnam should not have "veto power" over US policy and charged that his chief negotiator and Vance were for "peace at any price," barking at his advisers that "all of you are playing with this like you are in another world—with a bunch of doves."[32]

Nonetheless, even the hawkish Rusk said, "I smell vodka and caviar in this [Hanoi's] proposal"—namely, Russian pressure on Hanoi to negotiate. It would serve US interests to negotiate, and it would be "serious to reverse our field." The hardline Rostow said that if Johnson waited until after the election to act, "I cannot even be sure the deal will be there to pick up." Clifford also pressed the president to negotiate: whether the deal came two weeks or one week before the election, the country would "applaud him," media support would be overwhelming, and only an "obtuse man" would see it as political stratagem. And North Vietnam "had taken eight steps for every one the U.S. had to get to this point."[33]

Further support came from former ambassador to Saigon General Maxwell Taylor and JCS chairman General Earle Wheeler; both viewed Hanoi's willingness to talk as a sign of military weakness. Johnson's highly conservative political mentor, Georgia senator Richard Russell, also thought "the election will turn around pretty good now." Still, the president demanded a delay to recall General Abrams from Vietnam to give his approval, despite Clifford's pointing out that even if a bombing halt helped Humphrey, continued bombing benefited Nixon. But Johnson would not relent, causing Clifford to wonder again: *"In his heart of hearts, does Lyndon Johnson really want Humphrey to win?"*[34]

The answer is "no." Johnson was highly ambivalent toward Humphrey: he admired, and was jealous of, his intelligence, facility with words, and amiability. But he humiliated and denigrated him to others from the day he became his vice president and deliberately undermined his campaign. As Clifford recalled, Johnson told one confidant that if Humphrey did not stand firm on Vietnam, Nixon's victory "would be better for the country." Later Johnson would write, even after having labeled Nixon's behavior "treason" in 1968, that he was "a much maligned and misunderstood man . . . a tough unyielding partisan and a shrewd politician, but always a man trying to do his best for the country."[35]

The president knew better. On October 28, 1968, FBI, CIA, and National Security Agency (NSA) reports revealed Nixon campaign efforts to influence the Saigon government not to take part in the Paris talks. Rostow confirmed this, forwarding a letter sent to his brother, Eugene Rostow, undersecretary of state for political affairs, that related comments attributed to a prominent New York banker, Alexander Sachs, a Democrat who was also "very close" to Nixon. Sachs held that the Republican candidate hoped to thwart negotiations, with the expectation that the costs in lives and money of continued fighting would make it easier for him as president to settle the war on terms Johnson could not accept. "It all adds up," Johnson said after reading the letter.

Walt Rostow added in a separate memorandum that another source at the banker's meeting said that Nixon was letting Hanoi know that when he took office, "he could accept anything and blame it on his predecessor." Overall, the national security adviser judged the information "so explosive" that it could gravely damage the country whether Nixon was elected or not, and he urged the president to "talk with Mr. Nixon" to let him know that while he did not hold him personally responsible, some of his advisers may have been "inflaming the inexperienced South Vietnamese" about the US Constitution or political life.

At the same time, Johnson was assured by General Abrams, who had returned from Vietnam, that he backed a bombing halt, only to have Ambassador Ellsworth Bunker in Saigon send word that Thieu would not agree to a joint announcement of a bombing halt on October 31. "That's the old Nixon," Johnson said.[36]

The president proposed to have the FBI wiretap Chennault's telephone and put a listening device on the Republican nominee's campaign plane. But Cartha "Deke" DeLoach, deputy director of the FBI, warned that it was too risky to wiretap Chennault's apartment in the busy Watergate building or Nixon's plane and that it would discredit his agency and the administration if it were found out. Johnson settled for CIA, NSA, and FBI intercepts of messages to and from South Vietnam's embassy in Washington and surveillance of Chennault.[37]

Johnson told Senator Russell that Nixon "has been playing on the outskirts with our allies," telling them they "will get sold out by the current administration," which will recognize the NLF. The president continued to vacillate about a bombing halt: on October 29, he blamed Humphrey's and Bundy's speeches for Saigon's resistance to negotiations and said that they "may think this [a bombing halt and talks] would help Humphrey. They know the Vice President would be softer. I do not want to help them [North Vietnamese] put over a man who has this attitude toward us. . . . Thieu and the others are voting for a man they see as one who will stick with it—Nixon."[38]

The president knew that he could no longer wait for Bunker to persuade the Saigon regime to go along. The ambassador could only report on October 30 Thieu's message that despite South Vietnam's dependence on US support, "you cannot force us to do anything against our interests. This negotiation is not a life or death matter for the US but it is for Vietnam."

"Horseshit," Clifford said, and even Rusk added that the United States had fought to get Saigon the right to sit at the negotiating table, "but if it pisses it away, it is all on their back."[39]

Johnson finally agreed to announce his bombing halt on October 31—at a time he conceded "bombing ain't worth a damn" now that the monsoon season had started. But first he called Dirksen, who he knew would inform Nixon, to say it was "dirty pool" for his party's nominee to tell both Hanoi and Saigon that they would get a better deal from him than a Democrat. "I've played it clean," Johnson said, "I told Nixon every bit as much, if not more, as Humphrey knows. I've given Humphrey nothing." Then he half-warned that Nixon had better "keep Mrs. Chennault and this China crowd tied up for a few days."[40]

Two hours later, Johnson, again by conference call, told the three presidential candidates that his decision rested on Hanoi's willingness to deal with South Vietnam, respect the DMZ, and not shell southern cities. He gratuitously slapped Humphrey by referring to problems made by speeches about troop withdrawals and a bombing halt "without getting anything in return," but only hinted at Nixon's perfidy by referring to "old China lobbyists" promising a better deal to both North and South Vietnam. Humphrey remained silent, while Nixon got Johnson to assure that the bombing halt applied only to North Vietnam, not to the South or Laos, and that Hanoi understood its pledges about the DMZ and cities.[41]

Less than an hour later, Johnson called Humphrey, ostensibly to discuss Nixon's chicanery but chiefly to browbeat the vice president into giving the president sole credit for the coming negotiation breakthrough. Initially, Johnson said that the old China Lobby and Nixon were encouraging South Vietnam to reject talks to ensure Humphrey's defeat, while telling North Vietnam that the Republican would be more amenable to settling with them because he had no commitment to the war. But the president again said he had no hard proof of Nixon's involvement, and Rusk even worried that the bombing halt would be seen as a ploy to elect Humphrey. Johnson pressed his vice president to "let all the laurels come to me," to say everyone supports the president, and the bombing halt follows his 1967 San Antonio speech promising a halt if "productive" talks promptly followed.

Further, Humphrey should not attack the other candidates over Vietnam and—in the coming hour before the president's 8:00 p.m. bombing halt announcement—should tell reporters that Johnson had briefed the presidential candidates but "enjoined us to secrecy." After the speech, Humphrey was to stress that the issue was an "American matter," not a party one, and that all three nominees supported the president. In this way, Johnson added—disingenuously—no one could attack Humphrey because they thought "you and I were trying to fix something."

Humphrey, as always, assented to Johnson's order, aware that his spurious claim of lacking proof of Nixon's actions meant that he would not provide the tapes, or copies of them, to the vice president. Thus, any charge he might make about Nixon's treasonous activities would be dismissed as a desperate campaign ploy. Johnson thereby disarmed Humphrey, limiting him to talking about Democratic programs. The president's conference call once again failed to distinguish Humphrey from the other two presidential candidates. The vice president could not take implied credit for his proposed bombing halt on September 30 or for being in concert with current initiatives. Nor was he to criticize Nixon over Vietnam.[42]

Johnson's taped address, "the most important decision he had ever made," he told aides, aired at 8:00 p.m. on October 31. He announced a bombing halt to begin in twelve hours and serious negotiations to begin on November 6—the day after the election—with the NLF included but not formally recognized, while the Saigon government was free to attend.[43]

The next day, the president called his Democratic confidant Rowe, who was campaigning with Humphrey in Illinois, to inform him about "the most explosive thing you have ever touched in your life." He was almost hysterical in pressing Rowe to keep Humphrey "from mentioning Vietnam until Tuesday [election] night" and in charging that his September 30 statement, "that he would stop the bombing of Vietnam, period, North Vietnam, period, no comma, no semi-colon," had cost the administration two weeks of time to bring around President Thieu to weigh peace talks, after which "Nixon picked up that ball right quick and started going into them through your China Lobby friend [Anna Chennault]. So he is in deep telling Thieu . . . and [South] Korea and all of them not to go along with me on anything" because Humphrey has said "he wouldn't pay a damn bit of attention to them so they better wait for him [Nixon] and he'll never sell them out."

When Rowe asked if he should have Thomas Corcoran, his law partner and constant companion of Chennault, "pull her out," the president said, "I don't care now. I've already done it" (the bombing halt). Johnson was more concerned that Humphrey appeared to be "jubilant," leading reporters and Republicans to question whether politics was involved in the halt. Rowe tried to reassure the president that the "comment on the street" was he had been "tough" and gotten the United States a "good deal."

But nothing seemed to lessen Johnson's fear that either a growing belief that his action was politically motivated or a military attack by Hanoi would create "pandemonium" and cause Asian allies to "dump us." He demanded that Humphrey say only that he "prays for peace" and that all the candidates back the president. The vice president remained silent, although Rowe recalled that Humphrey asked him to use the Corcoran channel to let the South Vietnamese know that he expected to win the election and that they would shun the Paris talks at their peril. Johnson again pressed Humphrey to keep silent.[44]

Humphrey, of course, lacked access to the proof needed to make a public case against Nixon and knew that the president would not help him counter inevitable charges of a desperate election ploy. Nor did Johnson act even after Walt Rostow showed him materials "so explosive they would gravely damage the country" even if the Republican were elected. Johnson also kept silent following a report that Thieu had told a US official he could not agree to a bombing halt "in the interest of the number of votes for Mr. Humphrey" or allow the "ruination" of his nation "for the sake of one person."[45]

Whether Johnson would have acted differently about Nixon's actions had the president been seeking reelection remains unknown. But Clifford believed that almost certainly Johnson would either have called in Nixon or told him to send a "countervailing" signal to Thieu to get a team to the Paris talks, or else the Republican would be charged with interfering with negotiations. Johnson could also have had the information leaked to the public and bet that national security claims would prevail over charges of illegal government wiretapping. But the president did not support Humphrey's election, held Nixon's views on Vietnam to be closer to his own, and, as in the case of the Greek junta's contributions to the Republican's campaign, likely feared that exposing his deceitful behavior might bring post-presidential retribution in event that he was elected.[46]

Despite Johnson's harassment, Humphrey had been campaigning "like the Happy Warrior of other years." He questioned whether voters could trust Nixon to sustain the nation's progress from the New Deal's Social Security Act to the Great Society's Civil Rights and Medicare Acts. Organized labor, which regarded Humphrey as its favorite son, responded to his call for help and had greater impact than at any time since it had become the mainstay in 1936 of the Democratic Party. The AFL-CIO alone registered 4.6 million voters, printed and distributed 105 million pamphlets, got 26,000 union workers and their families to staff 638 telephone banks, and enlisted 72,000 house-to-house canvassers and 94,000 people to poll watch and assist voters on Election Day.

Labor took aim at George Wallace, pointing out that Alabama was a union-busting, right-to-work state with no minimum wage, paid workers less than almost everywhere else, and ranked forty-ninth in welfare payments. Thus, it was necessary to accept Humphrey's view of civil rights, including for black people. The result was to ravage Wallace's base, at least in the North.[47]

Endorsements, however late, finally came from McCarthy and prominent liberals such as Schlesinger, who said that failure to vote for Humphrey meant being an "accomplice" to Nixon's election, and Senate aspirant O'Dwyer, who campaigned with the vice president and helped draw an enthusiastic packed house at Madison Square Garden. By late October, polls showed Humphrey so close to Nixon that the anxious Republican began again to make spurious charges about crime rising ten times as fast as the population under Democrats, as well as alleging that the Supreme Court had freed thousands of "known murderers" and that the administration's emphasis on nuclear parity meant superiority for America's enemies.[48]

Nixon was confident—overly so—that he would win the popular vote handily, but he feared that Wallace's victories in the Deep South would keep him from gaining the requisite 270 Electoral College votes, sending the election to the Democratic-controlled House of Representatives, where each state had one vote. Nixon disingenuously challenged Humphrey to allow "the voice of the people" to determine the election, but he held to following the Constitution. The bombing halt announcement added to Humphrey's momentum, and by November 2 he had cut Nixon's once robust Gallup poll lead to 42 percent to 40 percent and even led in the Harris poll by 43 percent to 40 percent, with Wallace down to 13 percent.[49]

Johnson remained a problem. After Humphrey finished campaigning in Maryland on a rainy November 2 and headed to a midday meeting with the president, he paused to change his clothing and was a few minutes late. On the vice president's arrival outside the Oval Office, Johnson's aide, Jim Jones, told him the president had already departed for Texas. Certain Johnson was still present, Humphrey said loudly that he had had enough of this stuff, and the president could "cram it."[50]

The next morning, November 3, Assistant Secretary of State Bundy arrived at Humphrey's Washington apartment to summarize what he knew of the intelligence information. He advised against going public, partly because he mistakenly believed Nixon was not personally involved. The vice president's staff divided over outing Nixon; press secretary Norman Sherman begged "to tell all" and offered to be fired as an "unauthorized leaker" if matters went badly.

But once again, Humphrey, lacking proof or Johnson's support, passed over what he later called his "last chance" to win the election. He appeared on ABC's *Issues and Answers* and, seemingly anticipating defeat, said that he and his campaign staff had acted from their hearts as well as their minds, perhaps had made a few mistakes, but overall had "done a pretty good job."[51]

Afterward, Humphrey flew to Texas to make his first joint campaign appearance with Johnson at a Houston Astrodome rally, where it now seemed "all different" from his last encounter with the president. Fifty thousand lightbulbs on the world's largest scoreboard blinked "HHH" and transformed into fireworks as he and Johnson strolled about the field and the crowd of 58,000 roared and the president pointed to the vice president as if to direct the cheers to him.

Johnson acknowledged Humphrey as "my friend and co-worker for twenty years" and as a "healer and builder" who never sought to generate "suspicion or fear" among people but always inspired them about their ability to work together. "President Humphrey" would never disappoint them, he promised, nor would Vice President Muskie, even if an accident should thrust him into the White House, which he warned could not be said for a Vice President Agnew.

That night, in a prerecorded national television broadcast, Johnson urged for "the sake of our American Union, Humphrey should and must become the 37th President of the United States."

Humphrey told the Texas crowd that 1968 had been filled with too much "shock" and "violence," but he was confident that the "basic decency" in the nation would soon "lift the veil" from people's eyes so they would see one another not as black or white, rich or poor, but as one people standing equally together, without hate or suspicion. And although no one person could lead the nation out of the current crisis, "if you trust me . . . I shall call forth from America the best that lies within it."[52]

Humphrey later wrote that there was "no ambiguity about Lyndon Johnson that day. He strongly supported me, and his message got across to Texans. That afternoon, at least, we seemed to have resolved whatever difficulties we had." Still, as soon as Johnson finished his Astrodome speech, the crowd began to drift out and continued to do so during the vice president's address. Humphrey left for a final day and night of campaigning in California with a new sense that victory might be possible.[53]

His difficulties with Johnson were not resolved, however, and winning depended on the economy, fear of a Nixon administration (especially Agnew as vice president), and peace—meaning Vietnam. Johnson said he had done all he could with Thieu, who had declared on November 2 that despite its earlier agreement, South Vietnam would not attend the Paris talks. The same day, the FBI intercepted Chennault's message to Ambassador Diem that "her boss" had just called to advise her to tell Thieu to "hold on. We are gonna win."[54]

An angry Johnson again called Dirksen to say, "This is treason." The senator responded: "I know." Johnson continued that it would "shock America," he said, to learn that "a principal candidate" and his people were "contacting a foreign power in the middle of a war," and "if they don't want it on the front pages, they better quit it."[55]

Nixon, fearful that Johnson was "ready to blast him" for collaborating with Chennault, got Senator Smathers to tell the president this was not so. Nixon was also quick to say on *Meet the Press* the next day that peace prospects were less bright than earlier, adding deceitfully that although many people, including in his own campaign, saw Johnson's bombing halt as an election ploy, he did not share this view. But if elected, he would be willing to help him gain peace even by going to Paris or Saigon.[56]

Nixon called Johnson to tell him that he had given assurance on *Meet the Press* of his cooperation. "My God," he said, "I would never do anything to encourage Hanoi—I mean Saigon—not to come to the table. . . . We've got to get them to Paris, or you can't have a peace." Johnson insisted that "the old China Lobby" was telling some people they would get "a better deal" from Nixon—he did not hold him responsible, he said—but this had created problems, such as Thieu's refusal to negotiate.

Nixon insisted that if he won the election, a Democrat and a Republican united in pressing for peace might achieve a "breakthrough" before the inauguration, something that might not be possible later. He, too, wanted "this damn war over with," but Humphrey's people had been "gleeful" in claiming that the bombing halt had helped them politically. Johnson said Nixon's people should not tell Saigon that it would get a better deal from him, to which the Republican added, so Hanoi should know it would not do better with him. The president told Rusk he did not believe that Nixon's people had spoken without his knowledge and asked what he thought they should do. "I would think we ought to hunker down and say nothing," Rusk answered, which also meant leaving Humphrey uninformed.[57]

Walt Rostow sent word the next day to Johnson at his ranch that the *Christian Science Monitor* was considering publishing a story that the Nixon campaign had influenced Thieu's decision to boycott the Paris talks. The president got Rusk, Rostow, and Clifford on the telephone. Clifford balked at releasing information so "shocking" that if Nixon were elected it could undermine his administration to the detriment of US interests and might also hurt Johnson's post-presidential relations with him. Rusk added—without explanation—that there was no public "right to know" about material so harmful to American politicians. The last chance to expose Nixon's "treason" had passed.[58]

Humphrey was en route to California when he heard from Rowe that the efforts to get the South Vietnamese to join the Paris talks had failed: they were "waiting for Nixon." Infuriated, Humphrey declared that the "China Lobby is not going to decide this election" and said he would issue a statement saying that, if elected, he would withdraw support from the Saigon government. But aides saw this as an emotional outburst; Humphrey said publicly only that the United States would enter the talks without South Vietnam.[59]

A tumultuous reception in Los Angeles on November 4—the day before the election—buoyed Humphrey. Blacks and Latinos, in particular, surged about his motorcade, and even the once cool press corps left their buses to run alongside his car. The previously aloof California politicians, such as the powerful Unruh, joined in. After an exhilarating but exhausting ride, Humphrey returned to his Century Plaza Hotel suite in midafternoon to prepare for his telethon that night, joined by his running mate, Muskie. The program included a taped tribute from Ted Kennedy and scenes of Humphrey playing with his granddaughter, Vicki Solomonson, who was afflicted with Down syndrome and taught him about "love." The Democratic candidates responded to screened questions from viewers, including one from McCarthy, who said he hoped to inspire his followers to vote for Humphrey.[60]

The vice president appeared at ease as he roamed about, microphone in hand, talking for hours about strengthening social welfare programs, revitalizing cities, and regaining people's trust. At the same time, Nixon, seated alone, held a structured telethon, with a taped appearance from young David Eisenhower saying that his grandfather, Dwight Eisenhower, favored the Republican's election. Nixon agreed on the need for Social Security and Medicare but hammered away at the administration's failure to bring an end to the Vietnam War.[61]

Following the broadcast, Humphrey went to a Beverly Hills dinner-dance that seemed like a victory party, but he recalled thinking, "I doubt we can win." At 2:00 a.m. the vice president and his party flew to Minneapolis, arriving at 7:41 a.m., where the cheering crowd of fifteen hundred stood in marked contrast to the few hundred who met his return from the convention. Then it was an hour's drive west to Marysville Township, where the Humphreys voted ("Please, God, let our efforts be successful," he thought), talked with well-wishers, and drove a short distance to their Triple H Ranch in Waverly. After a long nap, Humphrey sought to cheer himself by thinking of what he would do as president, including appoint Clifford as secretary of state and Vance as secretary of defense and, unaware of Kissinger's duplicity, make him a White House adviser. Muskie would handle domestic affairs, and President Humphrey would focus on getting the United States out of Vietnam. "Fast. It's ripping the country apart." He wondered "why Johnson shot me down when I said troops would be withdrawn in 1969? I was right. . . . Ruined my credibility and made me look like a damn fool. Never really recovered from that." Humphrey also questioned whether he should have "blown the whistle" on Nixon and Chennault.[62]

In the afternoon, the Humphreys did errands, then had dinner with his benefactor-friend Dwayne Andreas, heard some early East Coast election returns, and drove to campaign headquarters at the Leamington Hotel in Minneapolis, arriving around 11:00 p.m. Humphrey sensed that the crowd was looking at him as though he were president—but "I'm not going be." Early results in Connecticut and New York were encouraging, but the Border States vote was "awful." It was not just that Nixon would win Kentucky, Tennessee, North and South Carolina, and Virginia but that the Wallace vote was so high, North and South—"an ugly part of American politics." Soon he recognized reality: "We're losing. We're losing. . . . It's gone."[63]

He knew he had lost by 2:30 a.m., exactly when the ever-cautious Nixon was summoning his aides to say he was positive he would win in the Electoral College. Humphrey was desperate for sleep—"alone, away from it all"—but first he went downstairs to encourage his supporters: "They've given me so much. I've failed them." When he awoke around 8:00 a.m., crucial states from Illinois and Missouri to California were in Nixon's column, and newscasters were conceding his victory. Not even a call not to quit from Mayor Daley—known to hold back Cook County results to see how many votes he needed to rustle up to swing Illinois to the Democrats—was consoling. It was time to accept defeat. First, there was the "difficult assignment" of a congratulatory call to Nixon, who was "gracious," but "to lose to Nixon. Ye Gods, no warmth, no strength, no emotion, no spirit. No Heart. Politics of the computer. Probably if I had more of it, I'd be President."

Next, it was necessary, with Muriel at his side, to address his supporters, "the worst moment of my life. . . . We could have won it. We should have won it." There were some "who did not help" but "got to hide the bitterness." He thanked family, friends, supporters, and Muskie, and promised to continue his work in their behalf regarding civil rights and peace. "I have done my best. I have lost. Mr. Nixon has won. The democratic process has worked its will. So let us get on with the urgent task of uniting our country. Thank you."[64]

Admittedly "numb," "heartbroken," ready "to cry," and desperate to get away from it all, the defeated candidate set out on the drive home, alone but for Muriel, Freddy Gates, his long-devoted guardian-benefactor, and the Secret Service detail. They stopped for a late afternoon lunch at a favorite delicatessen: "Not the way I planned it," he thought. But it was pointless to rethink it all: starting out so far behind, the "stupid campaign mistakes," and the lack of another week when "we were coming on so fast." Humphrey arrived home at 4:30 p.m., bringing an end to the "longest day" of the "longest year" of his life. Some people had failed him, but he had failed others, he thought. Above all, he had lost the chance he dreamed of: to implement his ideas and ideals as president.[65]

Humphrey began the 1968 presidential campaign in desperate political straits. The Democrats were bitterly divided over the war, social welfare issues, and party governance, and recovery from their disastrous convention was near impossible. Humphrey admitted that he had lost "some of my personal identity and personal forcefulness" during his vice presidency and had failed to establish himself soon enough as his own person—especially regarding Vietnam—and as "captain of the team." Johnson cared only about his own agenda and reputation and virtually betrayed the vice president's campaign, preferred Nixon's election, and failed to confront the Republican's "treason."[66]

As syndicated columnist Drew Pearson wrote in his diary, when Johnson received President-elect Nixon at the White House on November 12, the photos made it look as if the Texan "was more for Dick than for Hubert."[67]

The vice president lost the popular vote by less than 0.75 percent, the slim margin most likely due to his sheer determination to gain the presidency, seemingly inexhaustible campaign energy, and a relatively small but critical shift on Vietnam policy. Nixon received 31,785,000 votes, or 43.4 percent; Humphrey received 31,275,166 votes, or 42.7 percent; and Wallace got 9,903,473 votes, or 13.5 percent.

Significantly, Nixon and Wallace gained a combined 57 percent of the popular vote, a major turnabout from the Johnson-Humphrey ticket having won 60 percent in 1964. Issues of race, law and order, and growing objection to Great Society programs and civil rights enforcement led the "silent majority," or the "unyoung," "unblack," and "unpoor," to vote for Nixon or Wallace. Still, the Democrats lost only 5 Senate seats and 5 House seats and kept control of each body by 57–43 and 243–192 margins, respectively.[68]

Nixon clearly won in the Electoral College with 301 votes from thirty-two states running from the upper South across the Midwest to the West Coast; Humphrey got 191 votes from the District of Columbia and thirteen states, mainly in the East (including New York and Pennsylvania), and Wallace got 46 votes from five Deep South states and Arkansas. Humphrey later wrote that he believed he might have won the election, or thrown it into the Democratically controlled House of Representatives, if McCarthy had endorsed him earlier and more enthusiastically, which might have brought victory in closely contested states such as New Jersey, Ohio, and Illinois (a combined 69 electoral votes), or perhaps even in California, where Nixon's loss of its 40 electoral votes alone would have put him 9 below the required 270 votes.[69]

Humphrey's contention about McCarthy, however, ignores the vice president's failure to gain the backing of the senator and his followers at the Democratic convention, or sooner than his September 30 speech. Humphrey, who in June 1964 and February 1965 had warned Johnson against a Vietnam War, too readily became a "loudspeaker" for administration policy. Further, despite knowing Johnson had withdrawn from the presidential race in 1968 because he "could not make it," the vice president resisted most of his advisers' urgings to state his own position on the war early, to fight harder for his own platform plank at the Democratic convention, or to declare his position as soon as he became the nominee. His failure to break with Johnson, despite his threat to "destroy" him if he departed from administration policy on Vietnam, reflected not just political misjudgment but Humphrey's having become too much the "elder son" who feared to resist a punitive father figure.

What Humphrey lacked most was the spirit and courage he had shown as a young mayor and aspiring Senate candidate who twenty years earlier had successfully challenged a Democratic convention and an incumbent president to adopt his civil rights plank for their party platform. Had he done this over Vietnam in 1968, he might have won the presidential election.

A defeated vice president returned to Minnesota, deeply regretful about loss of the election and the presidency. But after a short period of reflection and recovery, he would eagerly run again for public office and return to the nation's capital.

19

Resurrection and Defeat

After his 1968 defeat, Humphrey thought he had failed not only himself but everyone who had believed in him and worked hard for him. "Now I know what Adlai Stevenson felt," he said, but the governor had lost to Dwight Eisenhower, not Nixon, "the one man who should never be allowed to head the nation." Humphrey blamed his loss on "the liberal deserters" and the likes of California's State Assembly leader Jesse Unruh and Senator Gene McCarthy. He asked himself repeatedly whether he should have distanced himself sooner from President Johnson on the war. The answer was all too obvious.[1]

When Johnson alleged in an interview with renowned CBS news anchor Walter Cronkite in December 1968 that Humphrey's September 30 speech was the "fatal mistake" that cost him the election because he seemed to be offering an "unconditional" bombing halt that led South Vietnam to shun peace talks, Humphrey responded only, "I did what I thought was right and responsible." He listened in quiet disgust at a final White House meeting in January 1969 as the outgoing president repeatedly charged him with sole responsibility for losing the election.[2]

"The most ebullient and resilient man in public life," as the *New York Times* called Humphrey, would have to console himself with praise for having resisted the "philistine calls for law and order" and having stressed instead the links between crime and poverty and need for a Marshall Plan for the Cities. As columnist James Reston said, Humphrey was one of the few American politicians able to take on the century's most significant issues and emerge respected and liked by both supporters and critics—but as in the case of his hero, Adlai Stevenson, he was the right man at the wrong time.[3]

Time opined that Humphrey would remain a major Democratic Party figure. "Count me in for the future," he said as he sought to lift his and his family's postelection spirits, as well as those of running mate Ed Muskie and his wife Jane and numerous staff, by taking them to a favorite resort at Caneel Bay in the Virgin Islands. On the way, he stopped in Florida to visit briefly with President-elect Nixon, who seemed ill at ease but offered him the post of UN ambassador, with power to veto Democratic appointments to the new administration and the right to rebuild his party. Humphrey politely declined; he had no interest in joining Nixon's administration and viewed the meeting as a ploy to show unity.[4]

At midnight on December 31, 1968, Humphrey flushed a bathroom toilet in his home, a "silly gesture," he recalled, but it reflected his feelings about the year. A week later, he represented the United States at the funeral of Trygve Lie, the first UN secretary general, in Oslo and visited relatives in Kristiansand, his mother's birthplace. In New York, he pitched *Beyond Civil Rights*, his account of events leading to passage of the 1964 and 1965 Civil Rights Acts, with a plea for continuing that "American revolution" that aimed at true equality for all.[5]

Humphrey returned to Washington to clean out his offices, pack belongings and mementoes of the past two decades, and say many good-byes. On January 20, 1969, he stood grim and unsmiling at President Nixon's and Vice President Agnew's inauguration. He returned on a Nixon-provided 707 jet—an Air Force One–type plane far larger than any Johnson had ever ordered for him—to his own Triple H Ranch in Waverly, Minnesota. Disconsolate, he wrote to his son Douglas, a student at Hamline University, that he was sorry to have been so "irritable" during their family's Christmas gathering. It was not just the flu, but an emotional letdown after coming so close to the presidency. "I could almost feel it. . . . I thought I almost touched it. It was like reaching for the top rung of the ladder, and your fingernails scratch the surface, but you fail to put your fingers around it and hang on to it. You just slip away." After twenty-five years in public office, he had to design "a whole new life," leaving him with a "sad feeling."[6]

His life was extremely comfortable and more secure financially than ever before. He had a $19,500 annual federal pension; $75,000 plus travel and enter-tainment expenses annually for a board membership and a roving ambassador-ship for the *Encyclopaedia Britannica*'s Educational Corporation; a $70,000 publisher's advance for memoirs and a book on foreign policy; and many proposed speaking engagements at $2,500 each. Humphrey declined more than fifty job offers, including numerous in high finance, a professorship at Brandeis University, where he became a trustee, and a chance to become pres-ident of Columbia University. He also rejected running for governor of Minnesota because it would take his focus away from national politics.

Malcolm Moos, a political scientist and friend from college who was now president of the University of Minnesota, secured funds to pay Humphrey $10,000 annually for a professorship at their alma mater, while De Witt Wallace, publisher of *Reader's Digest*, donated $500,000 to his alma mater, Macalaster College in St. Paul, to endow a political science chair for the former vice president. This paid $30,000, bringing his annual income to about $200,000, and included a spacious four-room office suite where a secretary and several aides worked on his writings and a two-story stucco house on campus where he lived while teaching at the two Minnesota campuses. He taught one seminar at the university during the 1969 spring quarter and one course at Macalaster. This allowed time for speaking engagements and travel and kept Humphrey close to his DFL political base.[7]

He was ambivalent about returning to the classroom, despite being a charismatic teacher as a graduate student in the 1940s, and remained a dynamic public speaker. He said he looked forward to having his "mind and senses" stretched by students who questioned society's basic premises. But "I am not here by design," and this was not his ultimate goal, he declared at his first lecture at the University of Minnesota. He admitted to having developed a "Pavlovian reaction" to "Dump the Hump" students who bedeviled his 1968 campaign. This was reinforced when Macalaster students and faculty met the arrival of "New Man on Campus" with skepticism and "barbed" questions, challenged his moral standing, and staged a short-lived takeover of his office.

At the start of his teaching venture, Humphrey admitted he was overly defensive, given to acting like a vice president defending his administration. He emphasized his ties to powerful leaders, blamed the 1968 riotous Democratic convention — "I was a victim" — on Mayor Richard Daley, and sought to justify having defended US policy in Vietnam. When a large audience at the University of Massachusetts in April 1970 shouted him down, he left the stage — saying he had already gotten his "dinner and fee" — and returned to his hotel, where he spoke to a small group of students who had followed him. He told them, and many others, that it was especially incumbent on liberals to protect speech and eschew violence, its deadly enemy. He had a point, but his behavior revealed the great divide between someone who had been part of the national political power structure and a younger generation angry that the nation's leaders had lied to them about the causes and purposes of a war they were helpless to stop.[8]

Eventually, he took a student's advice to stop being defensive about the past and "just teach." He emphasized significant differences between the theory and practice of politics and listened closely to students' views. Within a year, he stated that the new generation of students were the people most concerned about the "role of the university" and its ties to big business and the government and about the "values of society." He conceded that it was "those kids" who were part of McCarthy's 1968 campaign "who blew the whistle on our use of power as the main instrument in our international relations" and "raised the question" about the proper role of the United States in world affairs. History would remember "those kids," not the 1968 candidates.[9]

After his first semester of teaching, Humphrey took a long European vacation with Muriel, their friends Dwayne and Inez Andreas, Ben Read, his former aide and State Department official, now head of the recently created Woodrow Wilson International Center for Scholars in Washington, whose board Humphrey chaired, and Dr. Edgar Berman. Humphrey attended the investiture of Prince Charles as Prince of Wales and in London underwrote high-end lodging, dining, and entertaining with his *Encyclopaedia Britannica* business expense account. The Humphrey group traveled to Copenhagen, Geneva, and the Soviet Union, where they toured Leningrad, Odessa, and Kiev before settling in Moscow for thirteen days. There, Humphrey collected on a long-ago promised boar-hunting and vodka-consuming venture at the lodge of the defense minister General Andrei Grechko. At his Moscow hotel on July 20, Humphrey listened over a short-wave radio and provided his commentary to a small crowd as three American astronauts on the Apollo 11 mission became the first people to land on the moon.

The next morning, the former vice president, with prior instruction from the Nixon administration, went to the Kremlin to inform Premier Alexei Kosygin that the United States was interested in slowing the nuclear arms race. The Soviet leader's positive response soon led to the start of SALT talks. After the meeting, he took reporters' questions. The first wanted to know his opinion about Senator Ted Kennedy driving off a bridge on July 19 on Chappaquiddick Island, resulting in the drowning death of his young passenger, Mary Jo Kopechne. Startled, Humphrey said he had to give the matter "a great deal of thought."[10]

While flying back to Washington on July 26, he learned that Eugene McCarthy had announced that he would not seek reelection to the Senate in 1970. "It's a resurrection. I'm high as a kite. I'm on the run. I'll win in a walk," Humphrey shouted to Berman. On landing, he declined to comment to waiting news reporters. He knew that McCarthy was bored with his Senate role and feared a primary challenge. DFL and labor leaders had been urging Humphrey to run, and polls showed him with a strong lead over the senator. Humphrey didn't have to say anything: he had just had a "fantastic week," a Minnesota newspaper said, and now saw a clear way to return to the Senate, perhaps running against Nixon in 1972, since Ted Kennedy, the most apparent Democratic nominee, had knocked himself out of the race.[11]

Humphrey delayed announcing for the Senate for almost a year. But in September 1969, he wrote to an old college friend, Anton (Tony) Thompson, "There's a rumor around I might run for the Senate. Could be," and in November, he told longtime DFL associate Eugenie Anderson that although the presidential race had taken something out of him, "I heat rapidly." He arranged to teach all of his classes on Wednesdays and Thursdays, piled up endorsements from DFL and labor officials, and in mid-September agreed to chair the seventy-six-member Democratic Policy Committee, which monitored Nixon administration policies.[12]

Humphrey modulated criticisms of Nixon's policies, convinced that economic issues would determine the 1972 presidential race and that the incumbent would be difficult to beat if he had tamped down inflation and achieved a foreign policy breakthrough. He labeled as "traditionally progressive" Nixon's proposed Family Assistance Plan, which augured a minimum income for poor families while requiring job training and work—presumably ending traditional welfare, with its social workers. The president would have to work hard to get it through Congress, he said, but he was "coasting" on domestic economic issues and lacked broad vision. Humphrey endorsed the administration's willingness to begin SALT talks but firmly opposed its proposed deployment of antiballistic missiles (ABM) and multiple independently targetable reentry vehicles (MIRV).[13]

Vietnam remained Humphrey's most difficult subject. Wherever he went, he would emphasize domestic issues—hunger, health care, and housing—but he was inevitably asked why he had supported US policy in Vietnam and whether it had been worth the cost. Repeatedly, he said his decisions were based on the information he had, no one had foreseen how high the costs would be, his mistakes were "of the heart," and only "history" could judge whether the United States had acted properly. But he had learned that "the world is not our pie, our plum, our lake."[14]

He approved Nixon's reducing US troop levels in Vietnam by 25,000 in May 1969 and by another 60,000 by year's end as consistent with his own 1968 proposals. He sought to put the Vietnam issue behind him and appear to be part of a bipartisan foreign policy tradition. He arranged, through National Security Adviser Henry Kissinger, to meet with the president. Humphrey told Nixon on October 10 that the war was having a far more "divisive" impact on the nation than he and Kissinger—and Humphrey himself, while in office—realized. He warned that broadening the conflict would spur even more massive protests than those already planned for October and November: not only college kids, but "everyone," was opposed to the war, which had to be resolved quickly. Humphrey offered to support the president publicly if he began a real "peace offensive." But Nixon, contemplating a major bombing increase in North Vietnam—Operation Duck Hook—and an expanded blockade of its ports, insisted that a swift US pullout would bring a Communist takeover, assassinations, and recriminations against his administration. He did say he intended to keep US casualties at their current three-year low.

Humphrey surmised that the president was weighing a cease-fire and told waiting news reporters that Nixon was "proceeding on the right path" to end the war and would have his support if he began a systematic withdrawal. The United States had only one president at a time, he insisted, and the "worst thing we could do is undermine his position." The public should accept his "good faith." Both liberal Democrats and Republicans sneered that Humphrey was naive—or merely repeating the lines he had used to defend President Johnson.[15]

Major moratoriums—the largest such gatherings in US history—took place on October 15 and November 15, with millions of people protesting the war. Vice President Spiro Agnew attacked the antiwar movement as "an effete corps of impudent snobs," and Nixon said that no moratorium would influence his policy, although he canceled Duck Hook. On November 3, Nixon publicly outlined his plan—"Vietnamization"—to increase training and supply of South Vietnam's army and its share of the fighting, with US forces to be steadily withdrawn. He called on the "great silent majority" to support his policy and declared that North Vietnam could not defeat or humiliate the United States: "only Americans can do that."[16]

Humphrey said that the proposed policy was consistent with what he would have done as president but called Agnew's attacks on the moratoriums a "calculated, premeditated" assault on free speech and dissent aimed at creating "an atmosphere of suppression and call it patriotism." In mid-November, he said, "Nixon wants to get out [of Vietnam] just as fast as he can and a lot sooner than most people think. I keep telling my liberal friends who attack him for not getting out faster 'You're gonna' lose—he's gonna' get out.' But they won't listen."[17]

Nor would the Democratic Policy Committee, which he chaired, and it demanded that the Nixon administration make "a firm and unequivocal commitment to withdraw all American troops from Vietnam within eighteen months." Humphrey and several Johnson supporters fought for a vaguer commitment and beat back stronger proposals. But now the Minnesotan claimed that the resolution had healed the wounds inflicted on the Democratic Party and "defused Vietnam as a political issue" and that "the economy" would determine the 1970 elections. Two weeks later, however, Humphrey would be jeered off the platform at the University of Massachusetts over his support for the Vietnam War.[18]

The US military incursion into Cambodia on April 30—intended to halt North Vietnamese attacks on South Vietnam—shattered any hope that the war would not be a major issue. Humphrey said, "No amount of explanation can erase the fact that the level of combat and casualties has been increased" and "the war has been expanded and the hope for peace seriously damaged." He would soon call for a "speedy, systematic, responsible disengagement and withdrawal, a cease fire, and use of the UN or an expanded Geneva Conference to effect a negotiated settlement."[19]

That would not occur; the invasion sparked nationwide protests, especially on college campuses. National Guardsmen killed four students at Kent State University in Ohio on May 4, and Nixon called student protesters "bums." Bipartisan congressional efforts to cut off military funds for Cambodia and an amendment sponsored by Senators George McGovern and Oregon Republican Mark Hatfield to compel withdrawal of US troops from Vietnam by the end of 1971 failed, although the Senate made a symbolic gesture by repealing the Tonkin Gulf Resolution. US military action enlarged the theater of war and forced diversion of vital resources to a client state in Cambodia, which would be destabilized by attacks from the recently formed extreme Khmer Rouge Communists.[20]

Humphrey suffered his own Democratic difficulties. As the party's titular head, he appointed Senator Fred Harris as chair of the DNC, partly to compensate for not having chosen him as his 1968 running mate. Harris was in tune with the younger and more liberal members of the party and sought to broaden its constituency and reform the process for choosing convention delegates. He picked McGovern to chair the commission assigned to achieve this goal, and McGovern got liberal Iowa senator Harold Hughes to serve as his vice chairman. They soon assembled a staff of young liberals—ironically, to Humphrey's disadvantage—to set the rules for choosing convention delegates.[21]

Harris resigned suddenly in February 1970, under pressure from Humphrey for failing to reduce the party's large $9.3 million debt and being too focused on his own 1972 presidential aspirations. Humphrey offered the post to former North Carolina governor Terry Sanford, who declined but recommended Larry O'Brien, the Minnesotan's 1968 campaign manager, who now ran a consulting firm. O'Brien agreed tentatively but backed away after learning both the size of the Democratic debt and that not every segment of the party was as happy to have him as Humphrey had said. DNC executive committee members rebuffed

Humphrey's next choice, former Indiana governor Matthew Welsh, bringing charges of "bungling" and "ineptitude" and forcing him to go back to O'Brien, who now set his own terms and became a power center. The former vice president's political stock was seen as diminished.[22]

Humphrey told a group of Washington-based reporters in March 1970 that he was tired of academic life, thirsted for political office the way an alcoholic did for drink, and saw Minnesota as an inadequate base to attract national attention. He said he intended to run for the Senate and perhaps the presidency in 1972, hopefully with Senator Ted Kennedy as a running mate. This would bring charges of using the Senate as a stepping stone, he said, but most Minnesotans would be happy to have a native son seeking the White House again.[23]

Humphrey established a campaign headquarters in Minneapolis and announced his candidacy on June 13. He said he had "every intention of serving out a full six-year term," but "I would be less than candid if I tried to pretend that I would turn away from the [presidential] nomination if it came my way." He scorned Nixon's failure to end the war and misdirection of the economy. His future Republican opponent, Clark MacGregor, a five-term conservative congressman from the Minneapolis suburbs, immediately assailed Humphrey as a big spender whose "Johnson-Humphrey administration" policies had pushed the nation deeply into debt, and he pointedly reminded that as vice president Humphrey had called the Vietnam War America's "great adventure."[24]

DFL Party leaders were united behind Humphrey, but a cadre of McCarthy supporters determined to battle his nomination in the primary. The only willing candidate, however, was Earl Craig, an eloquent, soft-spoken thirty-one-year-old black instructor in the University of Minnesota's Afro-American Studies Department. He helped establish a New Democratic Coalition and was now endorsed by Minnesota's ADA chapter. Humphrey viewed having an African American opponent as a "testing" and "ironic," telling Anderson: "I've been attacked all my life for being too liberal and today I've got a black running against me and I'm told I'm not liberal enough." Craig said he was not "hung up" over Humphrey and assumed his Vietnam position was just "doing Johnson's bit."

But Craig, who like Humphrey rejected separatism and violence, said that while his opponent subscribed to a melting pot theory and wished to ignore racial differences, he himself wanted to be dealt with in terms of his self-identity—that is, as black—within the context of American history, a perspective he thought the former vice president, or in fact most Americans, did not understand. Humphrey campaigned as an underdog: "Been away from here for four years. I've had to reacquaint myself," he said. In mid-September, he rolled to a huge victory: 338,000 to 88,709 votes. "I feel as if I had a whole new set of glands," he said. "I'm the most emancipated man in politics. Relaxed not driven by anything, not mad at anybody."[25]

Humphrey now faced MacGregor, who posed little threat despite strong ties to Nixon. The congressman regarded Humphrey as an "institution" and later said he would not have declared for the Senate seat had he known that the former vice president, rather than McCarthy, would be his opponent. Humphrey had 99 percent name recognition in Minnesota; a well-organized campaign headed by Jack Chestnut, a thirty-seven-year-old Minneapolis attorney who had done excellent organizational and advance work for him in his 1968 race; sophisticated mailing and get-out-the-vote technology brought in by Norman Sherman, his former press secretary who now led a consulting firm; a helicopter loaned by Dwayne Andreas to traverse the state quickly; and, for the first time, ample campaign funds. Humphrey also had a new look: twelve pounds slimmer, hair dyed blacker, and a New York–style designer wardrobe. He was still able to campaign with his old abandon and reminded every crowd that but for a few more votes they would now be seeing him in the White House.[26]

"You Know He Cares" was his campaign theme, and his issues included the cost of living, education, health, labor, rural America, pollution, and, to the surprise of many, "law and order." Humphrey spoke of this concern to the American Bar Association on August 11 in a speech written by campaign adviser (and later neoconservative) Ben Wattenberg. In his address, Humphrey said that liberals had to let "the hardhats, Mr. and Mrs. Middle America, know that they understand what is bugging them, that they too condemn crime and riots and violence, and scorn extremists of the right and left." Some liberal critics, including many still angry at his Vietnam War support, viewed his statements as bending to Nixon administration rhetoric despite his claim that his speech was common sense.[27]

Humphrey's views reflected his long-stated belief that liberalism was the first casualty of violence, and it might be time to "conserve our gains, and plan for new advances." There always had to be "people on the left pushing you all the time," he said, but perhaps his role now was to "reconcile our differences, to be a healer but also to show a better way." Regardless, "I've spent a lifetime trying to point out you can't have civil order without civil justice."[28]

MacGregor, who sought to establish himself as moderate on the Vietnam War by calling for the withdrawal of all US combat troops by the end of 1971, hoped that a last-minute visit on October 29 to Minnesota by President Nixon would make a difference. But Humphrey won by 778,000 to 550,000 votes (60 percent) and carried to victory on his DFL coattails thirty-seven-year-old Wendell Anderson, who became the nation's youngest governor. The DFL took the critical state attorney general's office and made sufficient gains in the state legislature to challenge the long-dominant Republican conservatives. Colleagues hailed Humphrey as the greatest vote-getter in DFL history.[29]

He suggested that Democrats ought to spend the next year seeking a presidential candidate whom they could rally behind and avoid the divisive 1968-style primaries. Numerous liberals rejected this as self-serving advice from someone seeking to have his support for the Vietnam War forgotten. Piqued, he said that he saw no reason to disavow his 1972 prospects when others, "whom I consider less able," affirmatively stated their intentions.[30]

"A Freshman Named Humphrey Is 'Home,'" the *New York Times* headlined when he returned to Washington to be sworn in, again, as a US senator on January 21, 1971. Colleagues gave him an ovation, and friends feted him at a welcoming party at Washington's Shoreham Hotel. But the cheering soon stopped. He now ranked ninety-third out of one hundred senators in seniority—he had been seventeenth in 1964—and his hopes were promptly dashed that the Democrats would treat him with the same deference Republicans had shown Barry Goldwater, who after his 1964 presidential loss returned to the Senate in 1969 and was given his former committee assignments.

By contrast, Humphrey, whose Vietnam War support had damaged his relations with Senate majority leader Mike Mansfield, was denied his former seats on the powerful Appropriations and Foreign Relations Committees. He gained the Agriculture Committee, crucial to his midwestern farm constituents, but otherwise was put on the minor Government Operations Committee and the Joint Economic Committee. Moreover, the major issues he cared about most, such as health care, education, and foreign relations, were now the purview of other senators, and civil rights was on the back burner. There were twenty-eight new senators he did not know.

Humphrey was given McCarthy's old, relatively small office and was limited to twenty-two staff members—he had more than eighty-five as vice president. Further, Senate rules had changed, to his dislike. Previously, senators could speak spontaneously on an issue; now they had to register in advance. The new senator missed the Senate camaraderie in pre–Vietnam War years and the frequent White House calls to promote crucial legislation. He bridled at seeing Agnew, whom he loathed, preside as vice president over the Senate. Humphrey was further distressed by the death of sixty-two-year-old Freddie Gates, his "guardian angel and protector" since his Minneapolis mayoral days.[31]

The new senator, who at first said he needed to be a leader but act "with humility," offended Democratic colleagues by calling on them to "put their minds not only on how to attack Nixon, but on how to attack problems." He introduced a spate of legislation designed to put him at the forefront of domestic liberalism, including a multibillion-dollar Revenue Sharing Bill that, unlike current Nixon administration policy, increased the total funds going to each state that raised its own tax rates to boost state revenue, and he pressed the administration to sponsor a Full Employment Budget with enough spending to lower the 6.2 percent unemployment rate.[32]

Humphrey returned to the critical issue of national health insurance he first addressed in May 1949. He decried that the United States was the only Western industrial nation not to have such a program and that its low ranking with regard to infant mortality and life expectancy was unacceptable. On January 26, 1971, he introduced a sweeping National Health Security Act calling for the federal government to pay 50 percent of the yearly premiums, employers to pay 36 percent, and individuals to pay 14 percent, with no coinsurance or coverage limits and 40 million currently uninsured people—20 percent of the population— included. He also added legislation to provide prescription drug coverage under Medicare.[33]

In May, Humphrey proposed creating a National Development Bank, modeled after the World Bank and capitalized at $35 billion, to underwrite building of state and local public facilities. But his legislation drew little news coverage or political support.[34]

He opposed continued funding of the SST (Supersonic Transport), despite its strong support from a key constituency, George Meany and the AFL-CIO. The senator gave Meany two days' notice of his March 24 vote, which was determined by the plane's polluting effect on the upper atmosphere and its continued cost overruns and need for perpetual subsidies. Some analysts accused Humphrey of seeking to regain favor with liberals and environmentalists who opposed the bill, but his stance risked losing labor's backing in California and Washington if he were to enter the Democratic primaries there in 1972.[35]

Humphrey called for a constitutional amendment to provide for direct election of the president and for the Senate to change its cloture rule from a required two-thirds majority to sixty votes. He also proposed to mandate automatic voter registration upon the filing of a federal income tax return in order to bypass obstructive state voting requirements, especially in the South, and to facilitate the registration of millions of those age eighteen or older newly eligible to vote under the Twenty-Sixth Amendment, ratified in July 1971. Humphrey voted not to confirm Nixon's nomination of Assistant Attorney General William Rehnquist to the Supreme Court because as a lawyer in segregated Phoenix, Arizona, he opposed a public accommodation law in 1964 that would have assured all people service in restaurants. Humphrey believed that Rehnquist supported the so-called right of business owners to deny service to others over the constitutional rights of individuals.[36]

Speaking at the dedication of the Lyndon Baines Johnson Library and Museum in May 1971, Humphrey paid tribute to a "great leader," hailing the Texan's administration for passing the landmark 1964 civil rights and 1965 voting rights legislation and establishing Medicare and major Model Cities, urban renewal, educational, and poverty programs. He noted the administration had set in motion negotiation of the SALT and Nuclear Nonproliferation treaties and an opening to China.[37]

Humphrey drew sharp criticism from his labor supporters in August 1971, however, for backing Nixon's ninety-day freeze on prices and wages intended to tamp down inflation. This was one part of the president's New Economic Program that included suspending the convertibility of the dollar, devaluing it, and taking the United States off the gold standard; a 10 percent investment credit; and a 10 percent surcharge on imports, the so-called Japan shocks, intended to increase exports and reduce unemployment. The program was largely consistent with what Humphrey and the Joint Economic Committee had counseled, but long-serving UAW secretary-treasurer Emil Mazey ripped into his old friend for having "blindly endorsed the freeze" with his "usual overenthusiasm." Humphrey responded only that he had not issued the order and that Nixon was "tough" and had "many resources," including "the valuable one of surprise."[38]

Humphrey strongly advocated a détente-oriented foreign policy, with caveats, especially about Soviet policy. He urged the administration to continue meetings on SALT and to propose a mutual freeze on further deployment of nuclear weapons. He opposed further MIRV and initial ABM deployments but voted "with a heavy heart" with the Senate majority to approve building two ABM sites because that was the best he could get. He opposed Mansfield's proposed reduction of NATO forces without comparable Soviet cuts and argued against the administration's refusal to supply Israel with Phantom jets, citing Moscow's buildup of Egyptian and Syrian air forces. He criticized as anachronistic the Nixon government's resistance to the United Nations' decision to expel the Taiwan regime—the old Kuomintang—and seat the PRC in its place.[39]

Returning to the Senate had renewed Humphrey; even at age sixty-two, he was "more serious, more amusing, and more effective than all the old boys and new boys put together," wrote influential journalist James Reston. Humphrey's "disbelief in President Nixon is almost total," and it was a near "obsession" with him that five more years of Nixon in the White House would prove a "disaster" for the young, the poor, and African Americans. He longed to run against him again for the White House.[40]

The senator knew that he first had to distance himself from his former ties to the Vietnam War, although he hesitated to criticize Nixon's policy "because I'm not without sin in that area." During his recent Senate campaign, he had called for bringing all US troops home by the end of 1971, and he was certain that Nixon, if only for political reasons, would do that. On entering the Senate that January, he said, "The President is missing a golden opportunity for the American people. We just have to make a decision to get out and then get out. We don't have to apologize for that at all."[41]

In March, Humphrey formally endorsed the Democratic Policy Committee's call for withdrawal of all US troops from Vietnam, with military funding cut off by the year's end, assuming safe return of American POWs. He cheered this as breaking Johnson's hold on the party. "My God," he said, "it finally happened." In June, he co-sponsored the second bipartisan McGovern-Hatfield amendment calling for the Senate to legislate the same withdrawal of all troops and cutoff of military funds by December 31, which was defeated again. Humphrey generously praised McGovern as the one senator "who has never veered for one moment from his conviction that we ought to disengage from the struggle in Vietnam."[42]

Humphrey and liberal Democrat Alan Cranston of California cosponsored an amendment to prohibit the president from sending conscripted troops—but not volunteers, as were most air force and navy personnel—into a combat zone after June 30, 1972, unless Nixon deemed it necessary to protect forces already there, in which case he would have to seek Congress's approval within thirty days. He said that the measure was intended not just to set an end date for the Vietnam War but to constrain the president's historically growing power to send forces to places where conflict would likely escalate. The bill, however, was defeated 66–23.[43]

Humphrey had reverted to his pre-March 1965 views on Vietnam, but after a Gallup poll in March 1971 showed him running not far behind Senators Ed Muskie and Ted Kennedy as a choice for 1972 presidential nominee, the *New York Post's* Pete Hamill charged that this "wormy artifact from a wormy year" had returned to politics despite deserving to be tried for war crimes. Similarly, *Village Voice* writer Stephanie Harrington said that Humphrey had "retreated from the vanguard to the rearguard of American liberalism." Rather "cruel and tough" criticism, he told a friend, "but I can take it."[44]

His past ties to Johnson and the war were further highlighted on June 13 when the *New York Times* began to publish portions of the Pentagon Papers. The study that former defense secretary Robert McNamara commissioned about US involvement in Vietnam from 1945 onward was now being leaked to the press by former Defense Department employee Daniel Ellsberg. The published documents showed that the Johnson administration had been planning before the 1964 election to bomb North Vietnam and had undertaken covert military action against the North to provoke it to strike at South Vietnam and American forces, providing a rationale for major US military retaliation.

Humphrey initially denied knowing about the plan to bomb; otherwise, he said, he would not have campaigned against Goldwater as trigger-happy and in favor of bombing. "I am not a liar," he said, and insisted that many of the revealed documents may have been memoranda or advice, not policy or decisions. He regretted that the Pentagon Papers did not emphasize Johnson's anguish over his decisions and efforts to achieve "a negotiated settlement." Humphrey refused to say what course he had recommended, accepted responsibility for supporting Johnson's policies, and said, "I do not now intend to try to make myself look good at his expense." If that proved costly to his current political prospects, he had lived through "the harassment of 1965–1968" and the presidential campaign.[45]

Humphrey soon realized that his stance was not helping him, and he confessed to *Baltimore Sun* reporter Philip Potter "to tell the truth, I didn't have a helluva lot to say about things." He permitted Potter to reveal the content of his February 1965 memorandum to Johnson urging against bombing and a wider war. He told *St. Paul Pioneer Press* reporter Albert Eisele, "I was informed about key Vietnam decisions" and had always believed as "Vice President it was my job to support those decisions." He later added, he knew "some people won't forgive me for the war and for being with Johnson. I am not sure that I forgive myself for that, but I have a right to grow and learn"[46]

Humphrey now wanted the war ended swiftly, which he thought Nixon would do. But he told a Jewish War Veterans' convention in Minneapolis in August, "Only history will proclaim the verdict as to whether US military engagement in Vietnam was a costly, tragic and incredible mistake, or whether it had increased regional security in Southeastern Asia." In September, he told a large California gathering that the war in Vietnam, Laos, and Cambodia "saps our energy and our will," has "consumed our spirit and voided our moral strength," and has "depleted our resources." It was time "to end the war."[47]

Humphrey wrote more sweepingly in March 1972—by then seeking a presidential nomination—in "The Hard Lessons of Peace and War" in *World Affairs*, that during the past twenty-five years the United States had pursued "a foreign policy for the whole world with a half-world understanding," that Americans were "almost totally ignorant about the developing world," and that, had they known more, they would not have become involved in Vietnam. Too often "schools are so intent on teaching the myths of American destiny" and for too long Americans assumed "they were the center of the world." It was time to abandon "the self-righteousness that has stigmatized much of our foreign policy" and to be rid of a great nation's usual "myopia of power" and "cultural imperialism," and to "learn to be involved in the world without trying to dominate it."[48]

In April 1972, North Vietnamese forces, led by Soviet tanks, launched a major assault across the demilitarized zone and knocked South Vietnam's army on its heels. Nixon, convinced that South Vietnam's defeat would ruin his credibility, responded with vastly increased bombing, the mining of Haiphong harbor, and a naval blockade of North Vietnam. Humphrey firmly aligned with Senate doves: the war had gone on too long and was too brutal, he insisted, and "we owe [President] Thieu nothing—he owes us everything." Nixon should "disengage quickly" and resolve the conflict at the conference table, pending assured safe return of US POWs. He supported a measure sponsored by his Minnesota protégé and colleague Senator Fritz Mondale to have Congress cut off all funds if the president did not end the bombing of North Vietnam and the mining of Haiphong. US action was a "dangerous escalation," Humphrey said, and would neither compel the North to negotiate nor halt its troop reinforcement.[49]

The public largely sided with Nixon's strong action against North Vietnam, however, and the Soviet Union and China pressed Hanoi to enter negotiations, which began in the early fall during the election campaign.

✦ ✦ ✦

Despite being "scarred and battered," Humphrey told Berman in March 1971, he would seek the 1972 Democratic presidential nomination. A run for the White House was in his blood; he regarded himself as far better qualified than all the other candidates and could not forget how close he had come to winning in 1968. Muriel Humphrey agreed; she told him in early 1971 that "your whole life has been a preparation for the presidency" and "you came so close last time."[50]

In March, he ran third behind Muskie and Kennedy in the Gallup poll, and the Harris poll put him second to Muskie if Ted Kennedy did not run. Journalist William V. Shannon said that many Democrats preferred Humphrey, wanting a reassuring candidate even while he led them toward change. This formerly perceived "flaming liberal" was now viewed as a "progressive" who could get things done. On May 26, two hundred of Humphrey's most ardent and wealthy supporters gathered in Washington to celebrate him on the eve of his birthday, with actress-singer Edie Adams toasting his "sixtieth birthday going on seventy-two"—a clear message to everyone, including the Washington reporters present. At the National Press Club the next day, Humphrey said, "I've got the sails up . . . I'm not salivating. But I am occasionally licking my chops."[51]

He spent the July 4 weekend at his Waverly home, weighing whether "I ought to run" with Jack Chestnut, who had managed his recent Senate campaign and now promised a vigorous organization and young blood if he sought the presidency. "There won't be any talk about a tired Humphrey," he said. "We did it for you in Minnesota in 1970 and we can do it nationally in 1972." Back in Washington, the senator met with his major financial backers— wealthy businessmen John Morrison of Minneapolis and S. Harrison Dogole of Philadelphia—along with his former chief of staff, Bill Connell, friend and lawyer Max Kampelman, and former press secretary Norman Sherman. Humphrey said he would travel about the country to speak to political gatherings and party leaders and have a poll taken in September to see where he stood. He would skip the early primaries in hopes that the other candidates would do each other in, save his money and energy for the big California and New York contests in June 1972, and win the nomination at the convention in July. Chestnut ("my new Freddie Gates") would head the campaign.[52]

Humphrey spent early August in Minnesota making plans and feeling encouraged. The front runner, Muskie—a moderate liberal who had become a war critic—had not "wrapped up" the nomination, Kennedy kept saying he would not run, and no one else seemed to be gathering significant support. This included McGovern, the most outspoken critic of the war; Senator Henry "Scoop" Jackson of Washington, a Cold War anti-Communist hawk who had strong labor backing; former Alabama governor George Wallace, returned to the Democrats and still rousing audiences with racially tinged attacks on welfare recipients and school busing; Representative Shirley Chisholm of Brooklyn, the first black woman elected to Congress; the liberal and telegenic John Lindsay, mayor of New York City, a Republican turned Democrat in 1971; and former senator McCarthy, who had added an extended social welfare platform to his antiwar position, although many of his supporters and financial under-writers had switched to less enigmatic candidates, and he was often criticized for not supporting Humphrey in 1968.[53]

Humphrey campaigned hard across twenty-six states, where he still had legions of ardent supporters, although many officials did not believe he could win the nomination. But his admirers who had celebrated at his Washington birthday party met in Minneapolis and pledged another $800,000, and Muriel told him that as long as she had to campaign for a Democrat for president, "I want you as my candidate."[54]

Humphrey opened his campaign headquarters in Washington in mid-November; he also wrote Eugenie Anderson that he realized many Democratic leaders "are hungry for a new face even if there isn't much behind it." Despite viewing primaries as an "ordeal," he knew he had to enter at least a few, because the post-1968 election Democratic commission had sharply changed the party's rules for choosing convention delegates. They would be apportioned to the states based on total population and the Democratic vote in the past presidential election, but with "affirmative steps" to ensure reasonable proportional representation of minority groups, young people, and women. Delegates also had to be selected in the year of the convention, with state party officials naming just 10 percent of them; these rules brought a rapid surge in state primaries, in place of party caucuses, to choose delegates. Humphrey knew that the best thing for his image was "to win a few."[55]

Rather than wait as planned until late January 1972 to announce his candidacy in Florida, which put all candidates on the ballot, he gave in to his advisers to declare earlier to foreclose anyone building an insurmountable lead and to see if he had cast off his identity with Johnson and the war. "I'm as confident and eager as a young colt," he stated, and "I don't believe there's any substitute for winning." He seemed to be the best financed candidate; Dogole had lined up other wealthy backers, and Beverly Hills attorney Eugene Wyman, longtime head of the California Democrats and the state's leading fund raiser, was on board. A couple of national polls showed that Democrats regarded Humphrey as their party's most experienced candidate, and he led everyone.[56]

Standing in front of a "We the People" banner at the Poor Richard Club in Philadelphia on January 10, 1972, Humphrey declared his candidacy for the presidency for the third time in twelve years. "America is not sick," but it lacked leadership and vision. His task was "reconciliation, rebuilding, and rebirth," which he said he knew how to achieve given his tenacity and persistence. The reception was not enthusiastic, but his "old zeal for combat, awesome energy, a quick creative mind, and joyous spirit" were still on display, the *New York Times* editors said. And he would be "false to himself if he campaigned as other than the happy warrior of contemporary politics."[57]

Humphrey bypassed the New Hampshire primary but gained a break when the front-running Muskie from neighboring Maine ran a cautious campaign and was out-organized by McGovern's insurgency, which was fueled by young, liberal, antiwar advocates who campaigned zealously door to door. Three days before the March 7 vote, Muskie appeared to shed tears at a press conference after the archconservative editor of the *Manchester Union-Leader* accused him of insulting French Canadians in Maine by referring to them as "Canucks," and alleged that his wife, Jane, tended to drink and tell off-color jokes. Muskie's 46 percent to 37 percent margin over McGovern was far smaller than predicted, and his image and reputation as the candidate the Nixon White House most feared was seriously damaged.[58]

Humphrey campaigned hard in Florida, seeking to come in a strong second to the heavily favored Wallace. He surprised observers with cool responses to young hecklers; when an angry student said he was "full of shit" as he spoke at the University of Florida in Gainesville about ending the war and rebuilding America, Humphrey broke the sudden audience silence by saying that he did not think the words "added much grace to the English language." He drew student praise for being "a lot looser than in 1968," and as incisive columnist Anthony Lewis wrote, "the emasculated vice president is gone," free of the tie to Johnson and the war.[59]

Humphrey, however, seemed to move to the right on critical issues such as school busing when the Supreme Court ruled that busing was an appropriate means to end racial imbalance in schools. The Nixon administration was constitutionally mandated to enforce this effort to desegregate schools, but the president ordered the Justice and Health, Education, and Welfare Departments to delay as long as possible, and Wallace told Floridians he would "take the batteries out of the buses."[60]

Humphrey sought to finesse the issue by saying that busing was not the answer to high-quality education and should not be seen as the "sole way" to get "racial balance" in schools. Similarly, he took a tough law enforcement view regarding drug use, despite the recognized failure of US policy. He also insisted that the nation was helping the rest of the world more generously than Americans, and "for the next ten years it was time to help ourselves," a striking change for a pioneer proponent of foreign aid. Wallace ran away with the Florida primary on March 14 with 42 percent of the vote; Humphrey ran a distant second with 19 percent but shed his "has been" image. Jackson gained 13 percent, and a fading Muskie got 9 percent. McGovern, who barely campaigned, won just 6 percent, as did Lindsay, whose campaign never gained traction.[61]

"Hubert Humphrey is a viable candidate," he now self-proclaimed. Asked to define "viable," he said, "Alive," "Active," "With it"—and he promptly put in

grueling nineteen-hour campaign days in Wisconsin, where he had enthusiastic support from organized labor. He approved Nixon's March 16 speech
calling for a "moratorium" on busing and instead proposed spending a few
billion dollars on improving inner-city schools. Humphrey would "rather be
president than be right," the *New York Times* opined, and he soon withdrew
support for Nixon's plan after he saw that the "fine print" revealed that the
moratorium would be permanent and that school renewal money would not be
new dollars but mostly previously allocated funds.[62]

McGovern's supporters tapped into a rich vein of economic discontent with
a populist message that resonated even with Polish American workers presumed
to be for Muskie. Wallace, who did not plan to campaign in Wisconsin, drew
such a strong response to his right-wing populist message in Milwaukee's civic
center, he spoke at eleven more rallies. On April 4, McGovern won a clear
victory with 30 percent of the vote, but Wallace startled everyone by coming in
second with 22 percent, helped—as Humphrey feared—by a heavy Republican
crossover vote. The former vice president fell to a close but disappointing third
place with 21 percent. His only consolation was the prospect of gaining "centrist"
votes in upcoming primaries from a fading Muskie.[63]

Humphrey skipped the next primary in Massachusetts on April 25, where
Muskie earlier won the support of the state's political leaders. But McGovern's
campaign mobilized the state's liberal base, especially young and student voters,
to defeat Muskie decisively by 53 percent to 21 percent, driving him from the race,
although his name was on the ballot for the Pennsylvania vote the same day.[64]

"Winning is everything," Humphrey declared as he won his first primary
ever in Pennsylvania on April 25 with 35 percent of the vote, owing to major
support from the AFL-CIO and other labor groups. McGovern surprisingly
edged Muskie for second place, with both at a fraction over 20 percent. Muskie
suspended his campaign, and Humphrey claimed to have captured the "vital
center" of the party. He looked to defeat McGovern in a head-to-head match in
Ohio. He made several forays into Indiana to confront Wallace directly in the
May 2 primary and defeated him, if only by a disappointing 47 percent to 41
percent margin. Humphrey also narrowly topped McGovern in Ohio by 41
percent to 40 percent, owing to overwhelming margins in African American
areas around Cleveland. A McGovern aide questioned this, but the gracious
senator apologized for this allegation. The Humphrey campaign and other old-
line Democrats increasingly attacked McGovern as a "radical" who would
bring devastating defeat on the party in a race against Nixon.[65]

McGovern was highly favored in the May 9 primary in Nebraska, where he
had a strong grassroots operation. But Humphrey's strategists rushed in vital

resources and sought to win the conservative Catholic vote in Omaha, the state's most populous city, by hypocritically attacking their opponent as favoring legalizing abortion and marijuana, granting amnesty to draft evaders, and opposing federal aid to Catholic schools. McGovern, like Humphrey, believed abortion to be a state issue and postwar amnesty an American tradition, and the former vice president had proposed two years of public service as recompense for draft evasion. McGovern denied the other allegations, but Humphrey's strategy prevailed. He won heavily in Omaha and lost overall by a respectable 35 percent to 41 percent margin, with McGovern winning in the more liberal university city of Lincoln and in rural areas. Humphrey's camp stepped up attacks on McGovern as a radical, even as the Minnesotan claimed they were good friends, and he was "not going to let the people around us louse up our relationship."[66]

The poor state of Humphrey's campaign compelled him to concede the next two primaries on May 16 in Maryland and Michigan to Wallace, who was running well ahead by denouncing busing, welfare "handouts," and foreign aid. But tragedy struck at the end of a political rally on May 15 in suburban Laurel, Maryland, when a young sociopath, Arthur Bremer, shot Wallace, paralyzing him. A horror-struck Humphrey, finding the shooting reminiscent of the tragic assassinations of the Kennedy brothers and King, rushed to see the Alabaman, who, despite no longer being a viable candidate, won both primaries the next day by larger than expected margins: 38 percent of the Maryland vote to Humphrey's 27 percent and McGovern's 22 percent, and—most surprising—51 percent in Michigan, a labor bastion, to McGovern's 27 percent and Humphrey's 16 percent.[67]

The results were a "slap in the face" to Humphrey, the press said. He learned that his campaign was virtually broke, and he had to fly to New York to plead for $50,000 from a wealthy supporter in order to meet payroll and campaign expenses. He canceled his plans for the June 20 primary in New York and conceded most of the state's 248-delegate bloc to McGovern, who now also won in Oregon with 50 percent to the stricken Wallace's 20 percent. Humphrey, who did not campaign, received a mere 12 percent.[68]

The Minnesotan's last prospect was the "winner take all" 271 delegates in California's June 6 primary. This was the "Superbowl," Humphrey told Steelworkers president I. W. Abel. "If we win, we go on to win [at the convention] in Miami. If we lose, that will be like falling in a ditch with a bulldozer filling it in." Humphrey also said on national TV that only a "spoilsport" would dispute California's winner-take-all rule, despite the long odds he faced: McGovern's $1.5–2 million campaign chest was over three times larger than his

$500,000, which was soon depleted when he sent $200,000 intended for local television ads to cover his Washington headquarters' overdrafts. Dwayne Andreas made nineteen phone calls for funds and came up empty-handed, leaving Humphrey to say that he would rely on the free television time that the three upcoming debates would provide.

This was no match for McGovern's extremely well-run campaign led by Gary Hart, then a thirty-six-year-old Denver lawyer, and supported by a broad-based, vibrant, young new voter campaign force, which used computer technology to send get-out-the-vote letters and had 153 area offices. Humphrey's campaign had only 30 area offices and relied on older African Americans, labor, Jewish leaders, and senior citizens, who used notecards for voter information.

Coretta Scott King, widow of Martin Luther King Jr., and Cesar Chavez, head of the United Farm Workers, backed McGovern, as did numerous Hollywood stars, who were able fund raisers. By late May, McGovern led by eight points in the California polls. Humphrey had to rely on his indefatigable campaign energy, and despite having told his staff not to attack McGovern personally—"He's my friend and I'm proud of his success"—he now agreed to his advisers' demand to step up their Nebraska-style branding of his opponent as a dangerous "radical" on domestic and foreign policy.[69]

Humphrey fired his first salvo on May 24 before six thousand Lockheed workers by denouncing McGovern's alternative defense budget that proposed a 10 percent, $34 billion reduction in planned military spending of $343 billion as a threat to their jobs and the nation's security. He would not seek the presidency "at the expense of America becoming a second rate power," he said.[70]

At their first nationally televised debate on *Face the Nation* on May 28, McGovern, whose campaign slogan "Right from the Start" referred to his long opposition to the Vietnam War, began by insisting the people were tired of "a war that never ends" and a "tax system that favors the powerful and penalizes the rest of us." Citing Lincoln, he proposed to offer leadership that "appeals to our better angels."

A hyperaggressive Humphrey responded with a broadside attack that stunned his opponent, who had expected a collegial colloquy. The former vice president charged, several times, that "we were both wrong on Vietnam," that McGovern's proposal to provide every American with a $1,000 grant to assure a family of four an annual income of $4,000 was a "massive, unrealistic outside welfare program" that would cost a budget-shattering $72 billion annually, and that he was "wrong on defense cuts," which would "cut into the muscle, in the very fiber of our national security." He added that McGovern's defense cuts jeopardized Israeli security, an obvious pitch to Jewish voters.

McGovern found it almost "impossible to believe" that Humphrey would attack his record on Vietnam, having publicly recognized the decorated World War II B-24 pilot in 1971 as the one senator who had never veered from his early belief that the United States had to disengage in Vietnam. McGovern pointedly reminded everyone watching that Humphrey had said in fall 1967 that Vietnam "is our greatest adventure, and a wonderful one it is."

McGovern also made it clear that he never hesitated to vote for the arms and aircraft Israel needed for its security, as well as US military appropriations, but like President Eisenhower, he felt the resources could be better used more constructively on job-producing housing, day care, infrastructure, and education projects.

Humphrey struggled to respond to McGovern. He continued to say, "We were both wrong" about Vietnam, because the South Dakotan had voted for the Gulf of Tonkin Resolution and military appropriations until 1967, although McGovern noted that one had to vote for the appropriations bills as a whole, which included funds for medical and other vital supplies for the troops as well as armament. Humphrey falsely charged his colleague of having voted against the repeal of the Gulf of Tonkin Resolution in July 1970 and failed to note McGovern's cosponsorship with Senator Hatfield of an amendment to remove all US troops out of Vietnam by that year's end.

Humphrey's attack on McGovern's complex welfare proposal—soon derided as a "demogrant"—ignored the fact that it derived from current minimum income schemes, Nixon's unpassed Family Assistance Plan, economist Milton Friedman's negative income tax concept, and progressively reduced grants as family income approached twelve thousand dollars. McGovern was unprepared to provide a total cost figure, but he said this was due largely to the need to reform the tax code, including higher income and inheritance taxes for the wealthy, and to be rid of the current welfare system. He pointed out that Humphrey had long advocated sweeping tax reform, social welfare bills, and cutting the oil depletion allowance.[71]

Journalist Tom Wicker wrote that the "most devastating" comment of the evening was McGovern's rejoinder to Humphrey that he had called the Vietnam War "our greatest adventure," although he thought Humphrey had won on debating points due mainly to McGovern's failing to cost out his welfare plan. Still, McGovern was "spouting new ideas and pointing to new directions," while "Humphrey peddles the old politics and old banalities." Significantly, James Reston, who viewed Humphrey as the best qualified person to be president, said that Humphrey's implication that McGovern was "soft on the poor and soft on Communism" was "desperation"; the titular head of the Democrats, Reston wrote, had divided the party and given Republicans criticisms to use in the coming election, making Nixon the winner of the debate.[72]

The confrontation also took a great personal toll. Terry McGovern, the senator's twenty-three-year-old daughter, returned to her motel in tears, asking political aide Ted Van Dyk, "Did Dad get a chance to talk to Uncle Hubert after the debate?" McGovern would forgive, but not forget, how his political mentor and longtime family friend and next-door neighbor in Chevy Chase, Maryland, had savaged him. Their friendship was never the same.[73]

Humphrey toned down his manner and criticisms during the second debate two days later, claiming "careless language" for having said the day before that McGovern's taxation system was "confiscatory" and that his welfare proposal was the work of a "fool." He also admitted that like McGovern, he would be willing to cut off support for South Vietnam's troops because the United States had no reason to be involved in that continuing war.

McGovern stood by his positions and insisted that his ideas were not "radical"; they only seemed so "to people so wedded to the past, so caught up in old assumptions," that they could not envision new solutions. The third debate, on June 4, lacked confrontation as court challenges led to including other candidates: Representative Chisholm; conservative Los Angeles mayor Sam Yorty; and a stand-in for Wallace.[74]

The damage had been done. McGovern's camp felt betrayed, if not doomed, come November. Ironically, on June 3, a Field poll showed Humphrey trailing by a shocking 26 percent to 46 percent, with half a million new eighteen- to twenty-one-year-old voters, out of an estimated 3.5 million California voters, expected to side largely with McGovern. "Unbelievable," exclaimed a dispirited Humphrey.[75]

McGovern won the primary by 44 to 39 percent, a solid five-point margin. Humphrey lamented to Eugenie Anderson that if his campaign had another $150,000 to use on media ads, "the results would have been different." That was unlikely. McGovern won most constituencies: 74 percent of those aged eighteen to twenty-four, and a majority of union workers, African Americans, Mexican Americans, and poor voters. More than 80 percent of these people said that his antiwar stance was a big factor in their vote. Humphrey won among people over age fifty-five and aerospace workers.

McGovern also won primaries in both candidates' native South Dakota— Humphrey did not run there—New Mexico, and New Jersey. Democratic voters had settled on McGovern as their nominee, Wicker wrote, and despite many party leaders believing that he would lose in a landslide to Nixon, that would not happen if Humphrey and other leading Democrats now supported him. He had shown himself to be an astute politician and would accommodate moderate ideas.[76]

AFL-CIO supporters, however, pressed Humphrey to align with a Jackson-Chisholm-Wallace bitter-end struggle, "Anybody But McGovern," or "ABM," to deny McGovern the nomination, although he had 1,364 of the 1,509 required delegates and needed only a big win in New York's June 20 primary to go over the top. Humphrey, despite his "spoilsport" epithet for anyone who disputed California's winner-take-all rule, joined his Democratic colleagues' court challenge to the rule as denying equal protection of the law to candidates who got a minority of the vote. He claimed he did not want his supporters to feel that he had "copped out" on them and said that by criticizing McGovern now he would be a stronger advocate for him later. And, he told him, "If you think it was rough in California, wait until Nixon comes at you."[77]

Humphrey reversed an earlier view and said he might be willing to accept Wallace, who had won 358 delegates, as a vice presidential candidate, which led the former governor to send an agent to talk with the senator's staff. The idea quickly came to naught, however, and Humphrey later said he had never intended to join forces. He decided to campaign in New York—despite not even having filed a delegate slate—where his supporters again said that McGovern's defense positions threatened America's and Israel's security. But on June 20, McGovern won 226 of New York's 248 delegates, ensuring his nomination, and two days later, a federal district court judge threw out the California lawsuit on grounds that in American elections some candidates win and others lose.[78]

Humphrey was ready to concede, but his staff urged him to take his case to the Democrats' credentials committee, which awarded him 151 of California's 271 delegates. "A rotten political steal," McGovern said, and threatened a third-party run if denied the nomination. Humphrey said his chances were "remarkably improved," but a federal appeals court restored the winner-take-all rule, and on July 7 the Supreme Court ruled that the Democratic convention was the authority on delegates. On the eve of the convention's start on July 10, DNC chair O'Brien put the issue to the credentials committee, which, bolstered by McGovern's uncontested 120 California delegates, restored the winner-take-all result, assuring his first-ballot victory.[79]

Tearful but relieved, Humphrey ended his candidacy. He said he took this loss harder than his 1968 election defeat, although columnist Reston wrote that the 1972 nomination was really lost at the 1968 convention when Humphrey showed greater loyalty to Johnson than to his deeper Vietnam War beliefs. A good friend wrote he was deeply disappointed that despite Humphrey's "fantastic drive, energy, and stamina," he was seen as a "tired old representative of the establishment," but "unfortunately a lot of Johnson rubbed off on you, and that was the critical poison." Humphrey replied, "It is not easy for me to accept the analysis . . . but I am afraid that it is true." Yet "I'll be damned if defeat is going to shut me up. I have something to say, and I am going to say it even if no one will listen." The *New York Times* opined that this "modern happy warrior" was now better enabled to devote his "remarkable energy and intellectual power" to work in the Senate.[80]

Humphrey should have been happier than he was. The Democratic convention's credentials committee expelled Mayor Richard Daley's handpicked Illinois delegation on the grounds that it was not representative of African Americans, women, and minorities, and installed a more diverse and reformist group. Humphrey might as well have written his party's platform, which spoke strongly to issues he had long addressed: a guaranteed job for every American, with the government as employer of last resort; an assured family income above the poverty level; national health insurance; welfare recipients' right to form organizations to represent them; use of transportation as one means to effect school integration, as well as redistricting and building larger facilities; tax reform, including ending the oil depletion allowance, to redistribute income and wealth; and, above all, the United States to leave Vietnam by October 1972, or after a Democratic administration took power in January 1973.[81]

The McGovern camp, however, committed a near-fatal error in choosing a vice presidential candidate. McGovern, like Humphrey, had sought as his running mate only Kennedy, whose final refusal late on July 12 left little time to find a nominee on the convention's last day, July 13. Humphrey's protégé Mondale declined an offer; the next choice, Boston mayor Kevin White, an urban Catholic with Old Guard ties, was vetoed by Massachusetts political rivals; and Wisconsin senator Gaylord Nelson refused but strongly recommended Missouri senator Thomas Eagleton, who was on a short list.[82]

McGovern hardly knew Eagleton, a Catholic with a liberal voting record and strong labor support. There were rumors, but no damning evidence, of alcoholism problems, and in a brief vetting session he said nothing in his background would embarrass the party. Eagleton was nominated, but McGovern's acceptance speech was delayed until 3:00 a.m., long after most television viewers had gone to bed.

McGovern's address said little that Humphrey had not articulated earlier, and the nominee sought to minimize any "radical" perception of him by emphasizing that the nation was safest in the hands of people who governed openly and spoke truthfully. But his dramatic, repeated call, "Come home,

America," from wasteful military spending that weakened the nation, special privilege and tax favoritism, and conflict in Southeast Asia that "maims our ideals as well as our soldiers," gave him more of a radical taint than was the case.[83]

More damaging, rumors soon circulated that Eagleton had been hospitalized for depression and treated with electroshock therapy in the 1960s. Yet a week passed before McGovern's aides were able to get him to admit to this. McGovern, perhaps influenced by the fact that his daughter Terry suffered from depression, announced that he backed Eagleton "1,000 percent." But continuing political pressure and increasing concern that Eagleton would be a liability finally led McGovern to force him to resign on July 31.[84]

Eagleton's cover-up of his bouts with depression irreparably damaged McGovern's campaign. Almost three weeks after the convention, he needed a running mate. Kennedy again said no, as did Muskie, which led McGovern to turn to Humphrey. But he declined with a painful response: "I just can't take the ridicule any more. You know that if I take that nomination they'll just say: 'There goes old Hubert over the track again. He just can't resist running.' "[85]

Finally, Sargent Shriver, now ambassador to France, agreed to run, by which time McGovern's poll numbers had plummeted to 34 percent.[86]

McGovern was as hopelessly behind Nixon as Humphrey was after the 1968 Democratic Convention. Nixon had gained highly favorable publicity from his February 1972 historic trip to China, a Moscow summit in May that led to accord on the first SALT agreement, putting a cap on intercontinental ballistic missiles, and resumption of Vietnam peace talks. Nixon also signed legislation boosting Social Security payments by 20 percent and providing funds for higher education and student loans. He openly opposed busing, while his surrogates attacked McGovern as the candidate of "acid, amnesty, and abortion." The president campaigned as little as possible, seeking to appear "above the battle," advice a bitter Lyndon Johnson tendered, adding, "And don't worry, the McGovern people are going to destroy themselves."[87]

Nixon's chief worry occurred after five men were arrested for breaking into Democratic National Committee headquarters in the Watergate building in Washington on June 17, 1972. One man, James W. McCord, was a security coordinator for the Republican National Committee and the Committee to Reelect the President, which suggested White House complicity. The Nixon administration denied knowledge about this "third-rate burglary," as press secretary Ronald Ziegler termed it, although the president and his senior White House aides almost immediately became involved in a cover-up intended to keep McCord and others from admitting to administration ties. But there was insufficient public evidence or knowledge of "Watergate" in 1972 to affect the election.[88]

McGovern's advisers told him his only hope was to turn himself into another Humphrey and to talk about "what the bowling alley audience wants to hear." Humphrey gave similar advice at a private dinner in St. Paul, urging his former protégé to "emphasize economic issues almost exclusively." He pledged to campaign hard for him and moved tirelessly from "small airport to small airport" trying to stir voters in behalf of McGovern, who, he told West Coast news reporter Thomas Braden, "would not go off into the wilderness" as McCarthy had. Humphrey detested Nixon, but also said, "I'm through" ever again seeking the presidency. Instead, "I want to be Mr. Democrat" and after the election "step in and pick up the pieces" for the party.[89]

McGovern lacked Humphrey's emotional ability to appeal to the "bowling alley," or blue-collar, crowd, and George Meany and the AFL-CIO leadership steadfastly opposed him, especially his antiwar position. By late fall, nearly all US combat forces were gone from Vietnam, and the public supported bombing of the North. On October 26, Kissinger, having reached a tentative accord with North Vietnam's negotiators, proclaimed, "Peace is at hand," although a few days before the election, Nixon said that South Vietnam rejected the peace accord. Still, nearly every newspaper endorsed Nixon.[90]

The Republicans ran national television ads sponsored by "Democrats for Nixon" and chaired by Texas's John Connally, who had recently resigned as treasury secretary; these ads featured, among others, Humphrey's voice denouncing McGovern's welfare proposals and assailing his proposed defense budget.[91]

Nixon won with a vast margin over McGovern: 47,168,710 votes (60.7 percent) to 29,173,222 (37.5 percent). The president took every state except Massachusetts and the District of Columbia and was the first Republican to win a majority of Catholic and blue-collar votes. He ran strongly among the "unyoung, unpoor, and unblack," but also won 46 percent of first-time voters. The Democrats gained 2 Senate seats, however, to increase their lead to 56–42 and lost only 12 House seats and held a 242–192 margin, marking the first time anyone had been twice elected president without his party carrying a branch of Congress.[92]

Humphrey called Nixon on election night to congratulate him for "racking up" such a victory. The president thanked him for being a "statesmanlike man" and not criticizing his Vietnam maneuvers and added, "Speaking as friends, people ask privately to compare this with '68, and I said the difference is that when Senator Humphrey and I were campaigning and we had this terrible issue of Vietnam, we both put the country first. And this time I said we had a problem where one fella said any goddamned thing that came into his head." Nixon absolved Humphrey for having campaigned for McGovern: "You had to fight for your man." The senator said, "I did what I had to do. If not, Mr. President, the whole defeat would have been blamed on me and some of my associates." Nixon replied that Winston Churchill returned to be prime minister at the age of sixty-eight, and "What the hell, you're still in your sixties." As the president's chief of staff, H. R. Haldeman, noted, the two men had "quite a friendly conversation."[93]

Whether Nixon's comments caused Humphrey to think about another presidential run in 1976 is not known. But he agreed to an unusual request by Nixon's inauguration committee to make a sixty-second television spot calling for national unity to be run at the start of the New Year. Right after Humphrey agreed, however, the Nixon administration ordered heavy bombing of Hanoi and Haiphong. The so-called Christmas bombing brought intense public criticism, even by members of Nixon's own party, with some wondering if he had gone mad. Negotiations resumed in early January 1973, and Humphrey allowed release of his taped unity message before the inauguration. Many Democrats sharply criticized him for permitting this, especially in the wake of the bombing; he responded defensively that his statement was "not a policy endorsement."[94]

It was unusual, however, and reflected Humphrey's need to be liked, if not loved, by the nation's political leadership and to be perceived as a major figure in Washington who might still harbor hopes of inhabiting the White House.

20

A Time for Everything

Humphrey found the period from November 1972 to fall 1974 extremely difficult. Harry Truman died on December 26, 1972, and Lyndon Johnson died on January 22, 1973. The senator did not need to be reminded that both men were chosen for vice president for politically expedient reasons, and both men gained the White House on the incumbent's death in office, won election in their own right, and left their respective Fair Deal and Great Society legacies. He hailed Truman as a modest "giant" of a man who had made "monumental" domestic and foreign policy decisions but whose "greatness" was recognized only after he had passed from the scene.[1]

Humphrey said that Johnson was a "unique" individual who had mastered the art of persuasion and politics and had befriended him—a new and lonely senator—and used him as a link to his "bomb thrower" friends. He credited Johnson for being a southerner who did not sign the Southern Manifesto and who fought for civil rights, waged war on poverty, and provided education for the young and Medicare for the elderly. He said that Johnson did not seek military victory but sought to preserve political self-determination in Vietnam, and that "history" would be the ultimate judge.[2]

Humphrey viewed himself as the guardian of the New Deal–Fair Deal–Great Society tradition. At a symposium at the Lyndon Baines Johnson Library in Austin in December 1972, he said that the concept of civil rights had to include the rights of the mentally and physically handicapped and the elderly—and the right of every American to live in good health. Despite Nixon's "impressive" victory that November, Humphrey was prepared to fight him "day in and day out" on the Senate floor if the president tried to "cut the heart out" of the human resources programs that aided the "sick, the indigent, and the elderly."

He deplored Nixon's having secreted himself and his budget-making with a group of White House counselors who claimed executive privilege to avert oversight and produced budgets that slashed social welfare programs. The president was "waging war on the poor" by proposing to dismantle the Office of Economic Opportunity and its myriad poverty programs.[3]

The senator successfully pressed a bill to allow individuals to keep their full Social Security cost-of-living increases without, as the administration proposed, losing equivalent food stamp, housing, or veteran's benefits. He assailed the president's "one man rule" in cutting back Rural Electrification Agency subsidies, failing to increase the Medicare budget to match inflation, and not providing Congress with notice and a rationale, as a recent Humphrey amendment to a debt ceiling bill required. He dismissed as "blackmail" the administration's threats to veto Labor and Health, Education, and Welfare Departments' appropriations if Congress did not block state and local community lawsuits against the government for impounding federal appropriations. And he vigorously opposed the president's call for a line-item veto, which would allow him to cancel programs Congress had voted for.[4]

He also fought the administration's proposed budgeting of $2.1 billion in 1973 for military aid to the South Vietnamese, who already had one of the "most lavishly equipped" armed forces in the world. But he was amenable to reconstruction aid pledged to North Vietnam if taken from the Defense Department budget. He strongly supported Congress's cutting off all military spending in the Indochina region in June 1973 and generously credited McGovern with this result.[5]

Humphrey resisted Nixon's request for a $5.6 billion military budget increase to $87.3 billion while the administration was ignoring "pressing domestic needs." He praised the president and Secretary of State Henry Kissinger for furthering détente with the Soviet Union and its allies and fostering increased commercial and economic relations. He backed the administration's SALT negotiations with Moscow but urged against deployment of ABM and MIRV systems. More arms do not bring more security, he said. "As fast as we build, they build." At the start of the Arab-Israeli Yom Kippur War in early October 1973, however, he urged resupplying Israel with vital military equipment, especially Phantom jets that enabled it to beat back attacks of the Russian-supplied Egyptian and Syrian forces, with military disengagement coming at the end of the month.[6]

Humphrey was an early and strong supporter of the joint congressional War Powers Resolution requiring the president to notify Congress within forty-eight hours of his use of troops abroad, with this action limited to sixty days before requiring Congress's authorization. Humphrey viewed the "steady accretion of Presidential war-making authority" since World War II as having led to actions detrimental to US interests and said that the executive branch's claim to need to act speedily was not a substitute "for rational policy judgment and Congress' approval." Congress had been "woefully guilty of permissiveness" in allowing "Presidential war" for more than a decade in Asia, and he voted with the Senate majority to approve the War Powers Act. The House followed suit, but Nixon vetoed the bill—and Congress overrode his action in November 1973.[7]

Humphrey was deeply concerned that "a small group of men" around Nixon were displaying contempt for the norms of governance and the political process, a view derived from the growing Watergate crisis. This included discovery in August 1972 of a $25,000 check made out to Nixon's Committee to Reelect the President deposited in the bank account of a Watergate burglar, Bernard Barker; and a revelation that former campaign manager and attorney general John Mitchell controlled a fund to pay for spying on Democrats. In January 1973, the Watergate burglars pleaded guilty, and former White House aides E. Howard Hunt and G. Gordon Liddy, who had planned the break-in, were convicted of conspiracy, burglary, and wiretapping.

Testimony to the Senate committee investigating Watergate by the president's White House counsel, John Dean, implicated Nixon's top White House aides, Chief of Staff H. R. Haldeman and domestic counselor John Ehrlichman, in the effort to cover up the crime through bribes and misleading FBI investigators. They and Attorney General Richard Kleindienst were forced to resign in April, and Nixon named to the post of attorney general Defense Secretary Elliot Richardson, with authority to appoint a special prosecutor. He chose Harvard Law School professor Archibald Cox.[8]

Humphrey was "appalled" by the revelations, as he wrote in an article commissioned by the *Washington Post* in May 1973. Many presidents were responsible for the growth of executive war-making power, he said, but recent abuses of power "originate in the philosophical heart" of an administration that demanded "personal loyalty for its life blood." For the first time in the nation's history, a small group of powerful men were "so aloof, so remote from the people, and so contemptuous of the institutions of government and the recognized norms of the political process." Watergate was "not politics as usual" but "a flagrant violation of the law" that may have been rooted in the president's "determined political and institutional confrontation with the Congress" over impounding funds and "recklessly eliminating entire programs established by law." Humphrey's solutions were standard fare: appointment of a special prosecutor and revision of campaign finance law to require greater disclosure.[9]

Dean testified in June 1973 that he had spoken to Nixon numerous times about the "hush money" paid to the jailed burglars and conspirators, and former White House aide Alexander Butterfield revealed that Nixon had installed a voice-activated taping system in the Oval Office. Cox sought access to the recordings, but the president claimed executive privilege and separation of powers. At the same time, Vice President Agnew, under investigation by the US attorney for Maryland for continuing to take bribes from businessmen who sought state contracts while he was Baltimore County executive and governor, was allowed to plead no contest to income tax evasion in return for resigning.

Humphrey disdained Agnew and was dismayed at the corruption. He and other leading Democrats blocked Nixon from naming his former treasury secretary John Connally as vice president because he might be a strong presidential candidate in 1976. Humphrey voted to confirm thirteen-term Michigan congressman Gerald Ford, a well-liked, cautious conservative without significant national political standing.[10]

Humphrey was incensed that the president, despite a federal appeals court ruling, still refused to give Cox the requested White House tapes. The senator opposed Nixon's proposal to have conservative Republican senator John Stennis of Mississippi provide summaries of them. Nixon asked Richardson to fire Cox, but the attorney general refused and resigned, and his successor, Deputy Attorney General William Ruckelshaus, followed the same course. Finally, the highly conservative solicitor general, Robert Bork, became acting attorney general and fired Cox, and the president put the special prosecutor's office and functions under control of the Justice Department's Criminal Division.[11]

Humphrey was appalled at what journalists quickly labeled the "Saturday Night Massacre" and lambasted Nixon for "having brought us to the brink of Constitutional and governmental crisis" by exercising power "without restraint" in the fashion of "authoritarian executives." Addressing the AFL-CIO national convention that demanded Nixon resign, Humphrey cautioned against a "political lynching party." But he called Nixon "a man 'obsessed' with power" who was acting in "dictatorial" fashion. He urged Congress to impose a new special prosecutor and hold "full and complete" hearings on the many impeachment motions already filed, and he urged Stennis to recant his willingness to summarize White House tapes. Above all, Humphrey the politician said that Americans had to elect a "veto-proof Congress" that would end "government by one— government by edict" and allow Congress to return to an agenda of energy, health care, transportation, education, and security.[12]

Mounting public and political pressure led Nixon to name a new special prosecutor, Leon Jaworski, a prominent Houston trial lawyer with close ties to

Johnson as well as many former Kennedy administration officials. Congress set terms assuring that the president could not remove Jaworski without first consulting that body.[13]

At the same time, Humphrey had to confront his own difficult questions, especially about fund raising, which he called "the most demeaning, disgusting, depressing, and disenchanting" chore in public life. He was greatly embarrassed in early 1973 at the disclosure that the $25,000 Nixon campaign contribution check found in Watergate burglar Bernard Barker's bank account had come from Humphrey's longtime close friend, benefactor, and agribusiness millionaire Dwayne Andreas. Republicans on the Senate Watergate Committee subpoenaed Humphrey's campaign contributions records, and Nixon wondered if Andreas might "go in and scare Hubert," presumably not to criticize the president or seek his impeachment.[14]

Another Humphrey supporter, the prominent banker John L. Loeb, was convicted under the Federal Election Campaign Law of 1971 of having failed to disclose his $25,000 California primary campaign contribution that the senator had flown from the West Coast to New York to solicit. Loeb reimbursed each of eight employees he instructed to write $6,000 campaign contribution checks, action that violated the law's disclosure terms. He was fined $3,000.[15]

Even more unsettling were Watergate Committee revelations about former Humphrey aides' connections to the Associated Milk Producers, Incorporated (AMPI), a large dairy farmers' cooperative that lobbied politicians to vote for high dairy price supports. After Humphrey left the vice presidency in 1969, AMPI hired as consultants his chief of staff, Bill Connell, and his speech writer, Ted Van Dyk, and former campaign manager Jack Chestnut's law office handled its legal affairs in Minnesota. Chestnut in turn hired the political advertising firm formed by Norman Sherman, Humphrey's former press secretary, to prepare voter registration lists for the 1970 and 1972 campaigns. Although legal, this appeared to be political payback. The Watergate Committee learned that Chestnut had destroyed all of Humphrey's political contribution records before April 7, 1972, the effective date of the new campaign disclosure law. This, too, was legal but appeared to be intended to obfuscate.[16]

More damaging was the 1974 charge that Chestnut broke the law in 1970 by agreeing to have AMPI pay $12,000 to cover Humphrey's Senate campaign advertising expenses owed to the New York–based Lennen and Newell (L&N) advertising firm. As a corporation, AMPI was barred from making political contributions, although it could solicit money through its Trust Agricultural Political Education (TAPE) fund for political campaigns. Since AMPI did not want the Nixon administration to know that it supported Democrats, especially

Humphrey, corporate officials chose to avert contributing through TAPE and sent four AMPI checks for $3,000 each made out to L&N directly to Chestnut's office. The checks were then forwarded to L&N's New York bank. After an L&N official testified to the Watergate Committee about this, Chestnut invoked the Fifth Amendment, and Humphrey denied knowledge of the matter. Chestnut was convicted in May 1975, fined $5,000, and sentenced to four months in prison; AMPI was fined $35,000 for its illegal corporate contribution.[17]

Humphrey was "embarrassed to tears" about the AMPI matter, he wrote in August 1974 to *Denver Post* publisher Palmer Hoyt. "I didn't need that. I've been for 90 percent parity since 1949." Moreover, "I was one of the first to advocate that we have a checkoff on our income tax to establish public financing." He suffered additional indignity when asked where he got the funds to support his last-minute entry into the 1972 presidential primary campaign. He admitted to selling $116,000 worth of stock—his own money, he claimed—from his blind trust run conjointly with Andreas, who, along with a daughter and her friend, contributed $348,000 of ADM stock proceeds to the campaign, far beyond the legal limit. Humphrey had not reported this in his filing in March 1972, one month before the new law required disclosure of such gifts.[18]

Campaign finances were the least of Humphrey's problems. A routine medical examination in October 1973 discovered a serious urinary bladder problem that dated to the 1967 finding of irregular, but nonmalignant, cells. This time, however, there were worrisome cell changes; his physician, Edgar Berman, sent the findings to eleven bladder cancer specialists. Nine recommended precautionary X-ray therapy, one suggested no action, and one proposed radical surgery, which might have been the best course. But Humphrey, advised by his personal urologist, Dr. Dabney Jarman, and Berman, opted for the X-ray treatment, which had an 80 percent to 85 percent chance of success. He underwent six weeks of intensive treatment at the Washington Municipal Hospital during November and December, with bad reactions requiring five blood transfusions during a sixteen-day stay at Bethesda Naval Hospital. He went home to Minnesota to recover from this exhausting ordeal, which included excruciating pain in his swollen legs and "the most God-awful spasms." It was "the most terrible experience of my life," he said, and admitted that he had even wished for death.[19]

By March 1974, however, Humphrey was back working his usual twelve- to fourteen-hour days in the Senate. He promptly pressed for a minimum-wage increase to offset inflation and extend coverage to seven million domestic and farm workers. He also proposed a Child Nutrition Act to establish a free, universal food service program—a "right" of all children to nutritious food—intended to match free textbooks and school transportation, and formation of a National Goals, Growth and Development Priorities Office to review all federal, state, and local legislation and report on trends, allowing House and Senate Budget Committees to plan and budget for long-range national growth and development.[20]

Addressing the Democratic governors in Illinois in April, Humphrey insisted that while Watergate had revealed the Nixon administration's "unprecedented corruption and governmental mismanagement," this was only a momentary reprieve from the president's threat to use his electoral mandate "to demolish our efforts to achieve greater social justice." He implored congressional Democrats to work with party leaders at every level of government to effect tax reform, a public employment program, national health insurance, and a national energy policy. In May, while accepting the AFL-CIO's Philip Murray–William Green Humanitarian Award, he called on the group to fight for campaign finance reform to be rid of "big money in politics" and to press to "close the income gap between the rich and poor" by urging legislation to achieve full employment, inflation controls, and high-quality education and health care for the "most deprived in our society." A month later, he assailed the Nixon administration's "bad arithmetic, false promises, and self-serving prophecies" about its handling of the economy.[21]

The Watergate investigation intensified. In February 1974, the House authorized its Judiciary Committee to weigh grounds for Nixon's impeachment, and in March, a significant group of the president's advisers, including Mitchell, Haldeman, and Ehrlichman, were indicted. Jaworski and the House Judiciary Committee subpoenaed a large number of tapes; Nixon sent transcripts after excising what he deemed irrelevant or nasty comments about individuals, making the phrase "expletives deleted" suggestive of a foul-mouthed president who tolerated burglary and obstruction of justice.[22]

In late July, the Supreme Court ruled unanimously that Nixon had to hand over all the subpoenaed tapes, and the House Judiciary Committee voted three articles of impeachment: obstructing justice, misuse of power, and violation of oath of office. One tape, dubbed the "smoking gun," revealed that Nixon agreed six days after the Watergate break-in to Haldeman's proposal to have CIA director Richard Helms press the FBI to back off its investigation based on national security concerns.[23]

Nixon was ready to resign, and on August 8, Republican senator Barry Goldwater, leading a Republican delegation, told him that the House would impeach him and the Senate would vote to convict him. That night, Nixon announced that the constitutional process had run its course and, in order not to take the nation's focus off the great issues, that he would resign the next morning, with Vice President Gerald Ford becoming president.[24]

Humphrey charitably termed Nixon's statement "his best hour and his best speech" and his resignation a "personal tragedy for the President and his family." But it was also "one of hope" for the nation and showed that "democracy works." He had not expected Nixon to admit to guilt, he said, but "the public record was clear." Humphrey doubted Americans would want to see Nixon punished. Resigning the presidency meant he had already "suffered a unique, very unusual form of punishment that brings with it great pain and personal agony."[25]

When Ford granted Nixon a "full . . . and absolute pardon" for any crimes he may have committed during his presidency, Humphrey, leading a congressional delegation abroad, called this the "right decision," although several members of the senator's group proposed their immediate return to the United States to protest Ford's action. But the ever-dutiful Minnesotan insisted that they had "a mission" and "a program": "We'll go home when we're scheduled to go home."[26]

Humphrey sought to cooperate with President Ford, whose approval plummeted from 71 percent to 49 percent after he pardoned Nixon. Humphrey and Ford, who both entered Congress in 1949, had always had a cordial relationship. Although the new president was a "Regular Republican," Humphrey said, "I don't hold that against him." Ford was also a "good, down-to-earth politician" who knew he could not govern without Congress, and he was "not a loner like Nixon" and would surely "reach out" to others. Humphrey did ask Ford to choose as vice president a man of "character and experience," words he said he wished to underscore—a clear swipe at Agnew. Nelson Rockefeller, three times elected governor of New York, met Humphrey's requirement. Washington had been "a sad city, no joy in politics down here for a long time. Mr. Nixon's politics did not allow that," the senator said, but now there was a chance to "get back to governing, to binding up the nation's wounds."[27]

The wound Humphrey most cared to bind in 1974 was the damage done by the decade's bitter "stagflation" arising from growing unemployment, slow economic growth, and inflation. People at the bottom of the economic ladder suffered most, he said, especially African Americans, who were clustered in the nation's increasingly neglected cities, where their unemployment rate was about double that of white Americans' 5 percent; black teenagers' unemployment ran to 32 percent. "Social justice" and economic necessity mandated that every American had a "right to work," Humphrey argued. "Unemployment knows no race," and it "threatened the life and well-being of millions of families" and augured more crime, alcoholism, drugs, educational loss, and racial tension.

Increased work opportunity, he said, would mitigate these problems and create a "climate of identity" and perhaps foster an interracial political coalition that would create a new bill of rights covering work, health care, housing, education, and environment, and freedom from discrimination or segregation. The private sector would be the employer of first resort, and public service jobs would fulfill remaining needs.[28]

In August 1974, Humphrey teamed with Democratic representative Hawkins of California, head of the Congressional Black Caucus, to introduce the Equal Opportunity and Full Employment Act of 1976, which was the year they intended enactment. Humphrey's legislative undertaking was rivaled only by his stewardship of the 1964 Civil Rights Act. The Humphrey-Hawkins bill rested on Roosevelt's 1944 Economic Bill of Rights that included the "right to a useful and remunerative job," Truman's 1946 Employment Act gutted by Congress that encouraged federal government policy to promote maximum employment, and the United Nations' 1948 Declaration of Human Rights that articulated everyone's right to employment and equal pay for equal work.

Humphrey-Hawkins proposed to guarantee every able-bodied American a job at a "fair rate of compensation" by creating local reservoirs of public service jobs; forming a Job Guarantee Office to fund private and public positions; requiring the president to submit to Congress annual budgets assuring full employment and production; permitting the Joint Economic Committee (JEC), which Humphrey would soon chair, to review the president's full employment program; and allowing qualified individuals unable to secure employment the right to sue for a job in federal court. Later versions of the bill would include mandating the Federal Reserve to establish monetary policy to maintain long-run growth and to minimize inflation (ultimately 0 percent) and unemployment (limited to 3 percent).[29]

Shortly after putting forth this major bill, Humphrey chaired a congressional delegation that traveled for two weeks across China, meeting with countless officials, although not with Chairman Mao Zedong (Mao Tse-Tung), whose picture was "in every conceivable public place." Humphrey, an early advocate of containing the PRC without isolating it, was concerned that American schools taught almost nothing about the PRC. He was impressed that the Chinese had brought crime, alcoholism, and drug addiction under relative control, offered all of its citizens free medical care, and had made exceptional industrial-economic gains, at least as measured against the standard of 1949—and would provide the United States with substantial commercial opportunities. But everything had been purchased at "the price of individual freedom and extra-ordinary political discipline."[30]

Humphrey returned to Washington in time to criticize Ford's proposal to whip inflation ahead of unemployment by imposing a 5 percent surtax on incomes over $15,000. The senator countered that there was "no justice" in imposing the same tax rate on low-income workers as high earners, and it made no sense not to address unemployment until it reached 6.5 percent. Ford's proposal never made it through Congress. Humphrey and the Democrats called for a major tax cut, which helped them in November to gain a stunning 49 seats in the House, raising their majority to 291, and add 4 Senate seats to reach a total of 60. These new and younger Democrats, however, were more inclined to liberal stances on social issues than on governmental social-welfare spending and business regulation. As Gary Hart, McGovern's former campaign manager and newly elected senator from Colorado, said, "We're not a bunch of little Hubert Humphreys."[31]

Humphrey became the Democrats' primary spokesman in challenging Republican governance. He told CBS News that Ford had failed to provide desperately needed leadership, that the "disease" infecting the nation was not inflation but "recession," and that the only antidote was a jobs program and a major tax reduction, with the "lion's share" going to the lowest income earners, not to the wealthy.[32]

As JEC chair, Humphrey deftly promoted his economic agenda. "Economic justice" was the new goal of the civil rights movement, and "a recession for white America is a depression for Black America." He introduced a revised version of his Humphrey-Hawkins bill that included establishing a Jobs Corps and authorizing the committee to initiate its own full-employment bill. He also proposed an Energy and Tax Relief Act, a $21 billion reduction providing tax cuts up to 60 percent for the lowest income earners tapering off to 7 percent at the high end.[33]

Ford's State of the Union address proposed only a $12 billion tax reduction that would mean an average cut of 12 percent, with a maximum of $1,000 for each return; the president also threatened to veto any new program or spending, except for energy. By contrast, Humphrey called for stronger "economic penicillin": a $20 billion cut skewed heavily to the lowest income brackets and authorization for half a million public service jobs. Americans want work, he said, "not WIN buttons," and unemployment "violates the promise of America."

Humphrey and thirteen other senators, including four Republicans, cosponsored legislation to create the Federal Full Employment Board to implement such a policy and strongly criticized the president's proposal to limit Social Security increases to 5 percent despite double-digit inflation. Humphrey pushed a bill to provide a free "nutritious lunch" to public school children, just as they had free school transportation and books. Finally, unyielding pressure from a Democratic Congress able to override Ford's veto forced him to accede in

March to a modified Humphrey-proposed $30 billion tax cut—reduced only to $28 billion—progressively skewed toward lower-income earners; there was no new spending, but none of Ford's threatened cuts.[34]

Humphrey's concern about the bitter 1970s recession, and his use of the JEC, soon extended to New York City. The city's expenses far outran revenues, owing largely to loss of its manufacturing base and middle-class flight to the suburbs. By fall 1975, New York appeared ready to default on its debt obligations, with the Ford administration unlikely to be of help. Humphrey had the JEC hold two weeks of public hearings to gather testimony from municipal and financial experts about the likely domino effect of the city's default on other municipalities and the national economy.

When Treasury Secretary William Simon balked at federal assistance, Humphrey shouted, "You can't stand there day after day and say that all [New York] can do is go bankrupt. I'm an internationalist, but I'm damn sick and tired of thinking you can save everybody else in the world but not the 8 million people in New York City." He proposed an Intergovernmental Emergency Assistance Act to allow states to borrow federal funds to bail out cities provided that they presented plans to balance their budgets and pay back their borrowings.[35]

Ford finally agreed to a $1.3 billion loan to the city that would be extended in 1978. *Business Week* credited Humphrey and his dynamic leadership of the JEC for this. He had made the JEC a major force in the legislative process and led the Senate, for the first time, to include the chair of this relatively minor committee in its leadership meetings. Ford's most conservative advisers publicly conceded that Humphrey was one of the most perceptive senators on economic issues. But as *Business Week* said, skeptically, he insisted that he would not be a candidate for president in 1976.[36]

April 1975 proved to be a cruel month. The US-supported Cambodian government faced defeat by advancing Communist Khmer Rouge forces. Ford asked Congress for another $228 million in military aid, but Humphrey argued strongly that $1.8 billion had already been provided in military and economic aid since 1970 and that General Lon Nol's government's "incompetent and irresponsible military strategies" had put it "beyond help."[37]

As the Khmer Rouge seized control in Cambodia, North Vietnamese troops were advancing in South Vietnam. Ford asked for an additional $300 million in military aid, and Kissinger insisted that Congress's failure to act would force President Nguyen Van Thieu's South Vietnamese regime to surrender. Humphrey led a legion of senators to refuse more military aid: he reminded the administration that the January 1973 peace accords were to end the military conflict and any further US obligation to the Saigon government.

Humphrey believed that the United States had long overstated its ability to control events in Vietnam and made the mistake of substituting power for wisdom and judgment. America's failure there, however, was due, not to presidential or congressional policy, but to "a failure of national policy." The only faint hope was a negotiated settlement, which was "up to the Vietnamese." The United States watched North Vietnamese forces overrun Saigon on April 30, which led to chaotic evacuation of remaining US forces and personnel and tens of thousands of fleeing Vietnamese. North and South Vietnam were soon united, with Hanoi as the capital.[38]

Humphrey was determined that Americans not repeat "the McCarthy era and the 'who lost China?' charge that poisoned our political dialogue for many years," as he told students at Yale University and Senate colleagues. Congress was not responsible for South Vietnam's failed military strategies or its army's lack of loyalty. He worried that "the scar of Vietnam has been etched too deeply into the American body politic to begin a new era of blame and recrimination. It is counterproductive and has poisoned our political process far too long." He said in another speech that "no outside force can save a country that lacks the will or political leadership" and "there aren't American answers for every problem in the world." After 1945, he said, "we were a world power with a half-world knowledge. It's clear that there's blame enough for all of us. I include myself."[39]

The Communist Pathet Lao completed their conquest of the Royal Lao government and its forces and proclaimed the Lao People's Democratic Republic in December 1975. Humphrey now turned his focus on US arms sales abroad, which totaled $110 billion since 1945 and was increasing every year. In Humphrey's view, arms sales had proved ineffective to halt the rise of Communism. Much of the weaponry had gone to governments that used it to deny their citizens basic rights, while drawing the United States into their conflicts. Humphrey called for the United States to change its policy from arms sales to arms control, become more transparent about its policies, and join with others, including the Soviet Union, to establish multilateral control of arms sales, lest the United States be drawn into regional wars of "ferocious intensity and devastating destruction fought with American weapons" and no benefit to national security.[40]

Humphrey's economic and foreign policy leadership again raised speculation that he intended another presidential run. Journalists noted in early 1975 that his "legendary zest and energy" had returned, and the "very warm feeling" he experienced wherever he spoke had given him the sense that he was no longer a divisive figure. But he had been campaigning almost nonstop since 1968 and did not want to be viewed as a "perennial." He thought that the more he bided his time, the less likely it was that his "natural coalition of Jews, trade unions, farmers, and blacks" would fragment. Above all, "I have no stomach" for the primary circuit, but he would accept his party's nomination from a brokered convention, a "possibility," if unlikely.[41]

His first presidential choice in 1976 was Walter Mondale, now Minnesota's senior senator, whom Humphrey had endorsed at Minnesota's AFL-CIO convention in September 1974. Mondale spent much of 1975 testing the waters and admitted to being "90 percent of the way toward running," but surprised everyone in November by declaring that he lacked the "overwhelming desire to be President" and could not imagine "spending all those nights in Holiday Inns."[42]

Humphrey's name came to the fore, especially after signs from Ted Kennedy that he would not run. Throughout spring 1975, Humphrey persisted that he was content in the Senate, where colleagues viewed him as "sensitive, energetic, encyclopedic in knowledge" and "passionate about jobs, medical care, world hunger, and arms control." He regarded himself as a "free spirit," and said he would not seek the nomination but would accept it from an unlikely deadlocked convention. When George McGovern stopped by in Waverly in June to suggest a Humphrey-McGovern unity ticket for 1976, a tearful Minnesotan noted that his former campaign manager, Jack Chestnut, had just been sentenced to prison for violating fund raising laws, and he had no intention of entering into that squalid world again.[43]

Still, as columnist James Reston wrote in October 1975, Humphrey was more qualified than anyone else by virtue of "experience, character, ability, and personality." Even President Ford and his cabinet agreed, Reston said; Humphrey "is our modern Happy Warrior" and the best candidate the Democrats could field if they wished to return to the White House. Humphrey reiterated on *Meet the Press* that he would not seek the nomination but would accept it in the unlikely event that the convention offered it.

Minnesota governor Rudy Perpich's office coordinated "draft Humphrey" petitions from the state's eight congressional districts, and in December, liberal representative Paul Simon of Illinois formed a "Draft Humphrey" committee in the House. Wisconsin senator Gaylord Nelson began to canvass senators. And Indiana senator Birch Bayh, who was seeking the Democratic nomination, said, "We're running against Humphrey."[44]

As 1976 dawned, the Gallup poll showed that a majority of Democrats favored the sixty-four-year-old Humphrey. Support increased when archconservative former California governor Ronald Reagan emerged as a challenger to Ford. Both

Republicans were about Humphrey's age, eliminating that as a factor. Further, Humphrey's status as his party's best speaker suggested that he was the one most able to take on the "smooth operator," Reagan, whom he called "just George Wallace sprinkled with eau de cologne." However, the senator balked at entering primaries and fund raising. Muriel Humphrey was focused on remodeling their Waverly home and, owing to her husband's earlier battle with cancer, said, "There are only a certain number of years left at this stage of life," and "We don't need the presidency."[45]

Democrats who sought the nomination, besides Bayh and Wallace, included former governor James Earl (Jimmy) Carter of Georgia, Senators Henry "Scoop" Jackson of Washington, Lloyd Bentsen of Texas, Fred Harris of Oklahoma, and liberal congressman Morris (Mo) Udall of Arizona. Carter, virtually unknown nationally, was a born-again Christian and an Annapolis graduate who left his promising naval officer career in 1953 after his father's death to take over his family's peanut farm business in Plains, Georgia. He won a state senate seat in 1962 and was elected governor in 1970. He had been outspoken about civil rights but backtracked when running for governor. He was a political moderate, although hawkish on foreign policy, and an outsider who railed against inefficiency and corruption in Washington and said he would never lie to anyone. His early and hard-driving campaign for the nomination surprisingly led to his leading all candidates in the Iowa caucuses and winning in New Hampshire, showing that a southerner could win in the North.[46]

Bentsen's withdrawal from the race led many of his supporters to call on Humphrey to run; this increased after Jackson won in dovish Massachusetts in early March. Liberals might be ready to forgive Humphrey for his Vietnam arguments, columnist Anthony Lewis wrote, while the senator said publicly that it "would only be prudent and sensible for a man of my position" to consider entering the race if no clear winner emerged after the California primary in June. Carter knocked Wallace out of the race by defeating him in Florida, North Carolina, and Illinois, leading Humphrey to say that anyone who campaigned against Washington and federal programs might be guilty of "a disguised new form of racism" by attacking blacks, the poor, and cities. Carter retorted that the senator was dishonest—citing campaign manager Chestnut's conviction—was too old, and had a "loser's image."[47]

Humphrey-Carter sniping continued. The Minnesotan's effort to help Udall beat the Georgian in Wisconsin on April 6 was perceived as part of a nascent "Anybody but Carter" movement led by liberals, Senator Frank Church of Idaho and Governor Edmund "Jerry" Brown of California. Presumably, Humphrey—still first choice in the Democratic polls—hoped to garner enough support in big states such as New York and California to get a deadlocked convention to turn to him. But he echoed Muriel in telling *New York Times* reporter Jeff Greenfield in early April that he had found a personal "sense of happiness with my family, my friends, my wife," and recognized after his bout with cancer that there was "not much time left," and he was a respected senator and able to travel the world recognized as such.

The Democratic Party mainstream seemed to have adopted his views about jobs, the economy, agriculture, and, Greenfield added, civil rights and arms control, which, in contrast to Jackson and Carter, made him acceptable to liberals. He could unite the party unlike anyone else; even Earl Craig, his 1970 opponent for the DFL nomination for senator, headed to the convention as a Humphrey delegate. As thirty-three-year-old senator Joseph Biden of Delaware put it, if Carter faltered, "I'd go with Humphrey because, for all his shortcomings, all of the others have them in spades, without the benefits of Humphrey." But Carter did not falter; despite Humphrey's efforts for Udall in the Wisconsin primary, the Georgian managed a narrow victory, 36.6 percent to 35.6 percent, on April 6.[48]

It was time for a decision. Five days before New York's June 6 primary, Humphrey promoted his Full Employment bill and Marshall Plan for the Cities in Manhattan in a rousing speech to the National Conference of Democratic Mayors. "My fellow mayors," he said—referencing his Minneapolis days—if Americans could help to rebuild London and Berlin after the war, they could rebuild their own cities now, and "if you wished to govern America you have to know how to govern a city," implicit criticism of Carter, Jackson, and Udall, all present. Humphrey drew the most applause from the audience and attention from the reporters.[49]

Jackson won the New York primary but failed to gain the majority vote he had predicted; Udall ran second, and Carter a distant third. Joseph Crangle of Buffalo, the powerful Erie County Democratic chairman and DNC member, had put together three slates of uncommitted delegates who now declared for Humphrey even though he was not on the ballot, with many other "uncommitted" delegates believed to favor him. Crangle openly urged Humphrey to join the race, and he seemed ready to agree, having told one of his Democratic hosts while in New York, "I should have entered this primary. New York is where I could have shown my stuff." But he quickly backtracked: "I made my decision not to enter the primaries. I'm not going to change now. I've got a peace of mind I never had before."[50]

The last chance to stop Carter was in New Jersey's June 8 primary, and the required April 29 filing date was imminent. Humphrey had asked Bob Short, his Minneapolis friend, businessman, and former DNC chair, to organize a committee to search for uncommitted delegates, despite strong opposition from current DNC chair Robert Strauss. Humphrey admitted that unlike "the old days," when he had savvy Washington lawyer Jim Rowe as an adviser, now he had no one in particular to counsel him. "I end up talking with my wife, Muriel," he said. Rowe called him in late April, however, to say that the only way to stop Carter was to beat him in New Jersey, and "you will once again try."[51]

The phones on Humphrey's desk continued to ring as he gathered with advisers on the evening of April 28. Everyone urged him to run, including Mondale, McGovern, Berman, Short, and Kampelman. Muriel said she would support whatever decision her husband made. He seemed mainly concerned about how to enter the race after repeatedly saying that he would not, but the group said he had met his pledge by staying out for so long, and no one else had a chance. Humphrey left the office with a prepared statement saying he would run; the assembled group was certain he would, and he had a press conference scheduled for 1:00 p.m. the next day.

At home that night and early the next morning, he and Muriel assessed where they stood with regard to age, finances, health, and family obligations. He reminded her that past campaigns had been brutal; he would now be criticized for dividing the party and being a spoilsport, and he could bring at most 600 delegates to the convention, whereas Carter was close to the requisite majority of 1,129 delegates. But to Humphrey's surprise, the once highly reluctant Muriel was now ready for him to run, a "dramatic change," he noted. He remained uncertain as he arose early on April 29 to take more calls, including from southern Democrats—Senators Dale Bumpers of Arkansas and Wendell Ford of Kentucky and former governor Carl Sanders of Georgia—urging him to run. He talked with Muriel, who later recalled that he seemed "negative," and went to his office about 10:00 a.m.[52]

Staff and supporters were in political action mode, and an activist lawyer from New Jersey arranged a chartered flight to take Humphrey to Trenton to file his campaign papers. Journalists were gathering to attend his press conference, but after about an hour Humphrey called Muriel to say he would not run, for all the reasons he had given her. Instead, he would be the Democratic healer who would unify the party. She returned to her household chores "singing," which she never did before. Word of Humphrey's decision shocked and disappointed his staff and friends, but he calmly entered the Senate caucus room packed with reporters, legislative aides, and supporters.

Even as his eyes filled with tears, he got to the point quickly: he would be honored to be the party's candidate if the convention called, he said, but he would not be an active candidate. "I have no organization, no committee, and, frankly, no campaign funds for the presidency." He would not enter the New Jersey primary, nor would he authorize any committee to work for him in other primaries where others had entered his name.[53]

Berman later wrote he could never understand Humphrey's decision. The reasons he later gave him—failure of early supporter and AFL-CIO president George Meany to call back and warnings about "humiliation" from Strauss— did not suffice. But just after Humphrey's press conference, he told columnist Reston that he feared charges about his former aide's illegal fund raising, about dividing the party and losing the South by depriving Carter of the nomination, and about causing loss of the election to Ford. "It's ridiculous—and the one thing I don't need at this stage of my life is to be ridiculous."[54]

He also spoke truthfully to Muriel and Reston about a campaign's brutality, the squalid world of fund raising, and inevitable charges that he was divisive and a spoiler. By contrast, now he was a highly respected elder statesman among Democrats and Republicans, nearly all of whom believed he was the Democrat most qualified to be president, as Reston wrote. He also had a prominent polit- ical agenda all congressmen knew they had to reckon with, and a secure family life, including financially—and he was a cancer survivor. There was no need to chance appearing "ridiculous" with a fourth run at the presidency since 1960.[55]

Suspicion lingered that Humphrey was still working to achieve a deadlocked convention that would offer him the nomination. The shrewd New York Times political analyst Tom Wicker wrote in late April that Humphrey was not only playing a major, if subtle, role in the stop Carter movement by appearing on behalf of the other candidates but drawing larger audiences than any of them, creating the impression that they were his surrogates. Similarly, Reston wrote that on reading the Minnesotan's recently published Education of a Public Man, the despair Humphrey revealed over his narrow loss of the presidency in 1968 suggested that he still dreamed of redeeming that defeat and was not ready to let the "next generation take over."

Shortly before the New Jersey primary, journalist R. W. Apple wrote that Humphrey had spent far more time in that state, ostensibly campaigning for congressional candidates, than any presidential aspirant; allowed a group of "uncommitted" delegates to endorse him; and declared at a major fund raiser that the presidential race was "not over until the last vote at the convention is counted." It seemed as if Humphrey harbored hope that somehow Carter might be stopped and that deadlocked Democrats would turn to their elder statesman to battle Ford or Reagan, even if gaining the nomination without entering a primary would have raised bitter memories of 1968.[56]

In May, Carter won in Texas, Georgia, and Indiana. Church won in Nebraska and his home state of Idaho, and Brown won in Maryland, but this did not produce the "earthquake" Humphrey had predicted. Carter rebounded to win in Michigan, Kentucky, Tennessee, Rhode Island, and South Dakota. Brown would win, as expected, in California, but Carter swept New Jersey and Ohio, virtually assuring his first-ballot nomination at the Democratic convention in New York City.[57]

Edgar Berman later said that Humphrey believed this convention was harder on him than the chaotic one of 1968, but the senator and his political agenda got star billing at the Democrats' gathering. The adopted party platform made its major national program "Full Employment, Price Stability, and Balanced Growth," a paraphrase of Humphrey's major legislative initiative espousing the "right of all Americans" to a job; executive branch and congressional planning to effect this; legislation to reduce unemployment to 3 percent within four years; and a comprehensive anti-inflation policy, revamped tax system, and tax cut. The platform did not specify how to achieve the goals, or reference the Humphrey-Hawkins bill, and Carter would say little about it during the campaign. But the key point was establishing the bill's aims as the nation's agenda.[58]

Humphrey proffered his view of America's goal in a prime-time address on the two-hundredth anniversary of the American Revolution. "There are new Tories abroad in the land," he said, but it was time to bid farewell to their policies of "corruption," "inflation," and "callous indifference" to the nation's ills, along with the Vietnam War, which "ultimately poisoned the whole body politic of America." A Democratic administration would "destroy the cancer of unemployment," champion education for the young, enact national health care, and provide decent care for the elderly. "The ultimate moral test of any government," he insisted, "is the way we treat three groups of citizens. First, those in the dawn of life — our children. Second, those in the shadows of life — our needy, our sick, our handicapped. Third, those in the twilight of life — our elderly." The Democrats would win in November, he concluded, because the people knew that they would "dare to try" to meet this moral imperative.[59]

Carter gained the nomination the next night, and his acceptance speech reflected Humphrey's agenda. The nominee made the "test of government" how fairly it dealt with those dependent on it, and he called for universal voter registration, comprehensive national health care, an end to discrimination by race or sex, an overhaul of the tax system, and work for anyone able to do so. The following day, Humphrey nominated his protégé Mondale for vice president as a man focused on education, health care, and human rights and concerned about both farm and urban life. Humphrey was delighted when Carter chose

Mondale over his own 1968 running mate, Maine's Ed Muskie, and Senator John Glenn of Ohio and claimed that the ticket signaled the "final unification of North and South," although Mondale was selected largely to encourage liberals to vote for the cautious Carter.[60]

Humphrey set the tone for his own Senate campaign, and the Carter-Mondale ticket, in early September, insisting to a friendly B'nai B'rith audience in Washington that Americans had to have a government that respected the law, a clear swipe at the "Nixon-Ford administration." The United States could not support democracy by "cozying up to juntas in the name of security," nor could there be true freedom without freedom from poverty, hunger, and unemployment. Humphrey won overwhelmingly in the DFL primary on September 14, and the next day introduced Carter, campaigning in the Middle West, to a southern Minnesota audience as the "next President," who would provide farmers with the price supports and purchases of food for sale abroad that they needed to sustain themselves. The senator devoted the rest of the speech to his own record.[61]

Humphrey's reelection was certain; his Republican opponent, Gerald Brekke, was an unknown education professor at small Gustavus Adolphus College in St. Peter in southern Minnesota. He volunteered to run because no well-known Republican would do so. He labeled Humphrey the state's "patron saint" and said that he no more expected to defeat him than he "expected to be hit by lightning."[62]

Health was the senator's main opponent now, however. In late September, he called Edgar Berman to say that he was passing blood in his urine, the first time in three years. Berman had him admitted to Bethesda Naval Hospital, where bladder tissue biopsies revealed cancer. Surgery was required: a radical cystectomy that entailed removal of the bladder and nearby fatty tissue, the prostate gland, lymph nodes, and part of the urethra, and installation of tubing to carry urine from his kidneys to an external plastic bag that could be emptied. Humphrey was stunned when Berman broke the news and concerned for Muriel, but prepared to fight the disease.[63]

Humphrey entered Memorial Sloan Kettering Cancer Center in New York City. On October 7, Dr. Willet Whitmore, a leading urologist and pioneer in the cystectomy procedure, led a team that performed the seven-hour operation. "The patient is cured," he said afterward, but discovery of cancer in lymph nodes meant that the disease had metastasized, which required chemotherapy. Humphrey suffered considerable pain and discomfort, but his spirits were raised by visits from family, most Democratic leaders, Ford, Rockefeller, and Kissinger, and even a telephone call from Nixon, still in relative isolation in California. The senator also fraternized freely with other patients and, upon leaving, told reporters he would soon be "swimming, and walking, and God only knows, I'll be talking."[64]

Humphrey went home to Minnesota to watch the November 2 election returns. Carter had left the Democratic convention running about 30 percentage points ahead of President Ford, who chose conservative Kansas senator Robert Dole as his running mate. The Republican platform emphasized a minimal federal government role in the economy, blamed Democratic spending for inflation, and proposed little or no funding for social welfare or jobs programs, singling out the pending Humphrey-Hawkins bill for criticism.[65]

Carter repeatedly lambasted Republican corruption during the Nixon-Agnew years, said he would never lie to the public, and blamed the administration for the current economic malaise. Still, the race narrowed, especially after the moralist Carter was quoted in a *Playboy* interview in mid-September that he lusted after many women and had committed adultery "in his heart." But Ford matched this blunder during the second presidential debate by saying that there was "no Soviet domination of Eastern Europe" and his administration would never allow it. Carter gained a very narrow 50 percent to 48 percent popular vote edge and a 297–240 Electoral College margin. His victory rested on sweeping the South, except for Virginia, and narrow margins in New York, Ohio, Pennsylvania, and Wisconsin. It was a triumph without a mandate.[66]

Humphrey gained his own expected landslide with 67 percent of the vote, graciously thanked Brekke for not making health a campaign issue, and said he regretted only not being able to attend the DFL victory party in Minneapolis. There, Vice President–elect Mondale would announce that "President Carter" would become one of America's "great presidents," although their ticket's narrow victory was not a certainty until after 2:00 a.m.[67]

Humphrey thought he had a mandate, however, to become Senate majority leader, replacing the retiring Mike Mansfield. Despite his weakened condition and biweekly chemotherapy treatments in New York City, he chose to seek the post. Why did he run? "Why do fish swim?" Reston wrote. "Because Hubert can't help it." The columnist conceded that no one was better suited to speak to the nation, and, more important, to the president in weekly leadership meetings, about the issues of the day.

The leading claimant, however, was West Virginia's Robert Byrd, first elected to the Senate in 1958 and majority whip since 1971, when he won a surprising vote to oust Kennedy from the post. Byrd, an archconservative who had founded a Ku Klux Klan chapter in 1941 and vigorously opposed civil rights legislation, had mastered Senate history and legislative procedures and won colleagues' favor by expeditiously managing their bills without seeking to impose his views.

He also lined up the votes he needed for the position months before Congress would convene. Further, many Democrats believed that President Carter would be the party spokesman and agenda-setter, not the majority leader.[68]

With the result not in doubt, Humphrey called Byrd to withdraw before the Senate reconvened on January 4, 1977. As Alaska's liberal senator Mike Gravel said, Humphrey "did not need to be a Majority Leader to be a great voice in the Senate."

As the Minnesotan entered the Senate chamber to sign the register for reelected senators, his colleagues gave him a rousing ovation, and archconservative and longtime political foe Barry Goldwater embraced him warmly. Senate Democrats elected Humphrey to the newly invented post of deputy president pro tem of the Senate and afforded him a $7,450 pay raise (raising his salary to $52,000, equal to the majority leader's), a chauffeured limousine, an office in the Capitol, four additional staff, and—significantly—the right to attend leadership meetings with the president.[69]

Humphrey sought to work at full throttle. This included fourteen-hour days, sending Carter memoranda after leadership meetings about foreign aid and foreign policy, economic and energy policy, and schools for Native Americans, while also making television appearances. But as Humphrey admitted to his old friend Eugenie Anderson in late January, his continuing chemotherapy in New York was making him feel "lousy" for days at a time, with loss of appetite, weight, and hair, although his hair had begun to grow back, curly, for the first time. In February his right leg began to swell, causing considerable pain and discomfort. Berman advised him to elevate his leg when sitting at committee meetings to avoid pressure on it, but the cause of his pain was an as-yet-undetected tumor. Despite his remarkable work habits, his decline was evident to everyone.[70]

Regardless, Humphrey soon became the administration's "best friend in Congress," or as key presidential assistant Hamilton Jordan would say, "At first we hated this fellow, but now we love him. He is the greatest man alive." In April, Humphrey persuaded Carter that his campaign commitment to a fifty-dollar tax rebate was too expensive—it was "very, very wrong," the president publicly admitted the senator had told him. He also argued strongly against Federal Reserve chairman Arthur Burns's insistence on keeping interest rates high, a reason the president did not retain Burns as chair after 1977. Humphrey became the administration's "point man" in the Senate to win votes for the hotly contested Panama Canal Treaty returning control over the canal to Panama in twenty years' time. Even as he lay dying in Minnesota in early 1978, at Carter's behest Humphrey called Goldwater, a treaty opponent, to ask that he at least hold back in urging other Republicans to follow suit—which he agreed to do, "for you, Hubert."[71]

Carter sought to foster negotiations between Israel and Egypt. After Egyptian president Anwar Sadat made a historic trip to Israel in November 1977, Carter asked Humphrey in January 1978 to write Israeli prime minister Menachem Begin to see if he could be more flexible in dealing with issues of Jewish settlements in the Sinai Peninsula and perhaps in the West Bank. Humphrey, rapidly failing, dictated his views to his Washington office, which pulled together a letter on his behalf to Begin in which he praised the Israelis for having "opened up their arms" to Sadat in a "magnificent gesture of peace and honor," but "we cannot let this cup pass from our lips without doing what needs to be done." He urged "my friend" to weigh a transition program to "Egyptian sovereignty" over the Sinai as well as a "workable solution" for the West Bank, but with the understanding that neither Israel nor its neighbors could accept an "independent and potentially antagonistic state" there. If all parties recognized the need for "give," a solution was possible.[72]

The major goal remained: passage of the Humphrey-Hawkins bill, despite Carter's cool attitude. In March 1976, the senator and his cosponsor revised their bill, omitting price controls and the right to sue for a job. Both liberal and conservative economists contended that government provision of jobs meant increased spending and higher taxes; full employment at 3 percent would spur inflation; and paying private-sector wages for public jobs would cause lesser-skilled workers to move to the public sector. Humphrey countered that joblessness caused more suffering, especially for the poor, than inflation caused "inconvenience" to the well-to-do. Carter downplayed the bill during the election campaign, and despite AFL-CIO, NAACP, and ADA endorsements, his new administration remained opposed, with liberal economist Charles Schultze, now head of the Council of Economic Advisers, and conservative Budget Director Bert Lance strongly warning against inflation.[73]

Negotiations continued during spring and summer 1977. The administration, which did not want to appear dismissive of urban issues and African American communities, proposed to make 4.75 percent unemployment, rather than 3 percent, a "goal" to be achieved over four, rather than three, years and eliminate the government as "employer of last resort" concept. Humphrey's failing health kept him away from the political wrangling, while the president persisted that his chief concerns were inflation and a balanced budget. By November, compromise was at hand, with a "goal" of 4 percent unemployment for those over age sixteen to be set as "full employment" to be achieved within five years or longer, if the president deemed it necessary, and inflation to be reduced to 3 percent within five years and 0 percent in a decade. The president's budget was mandated to contain revenues and expenditures to promote full employment, with the

Federal Reserve Board required to report annually to Congress how its monetary policy related to full employment. There was no "right" to a job or to sue for one, and federal jobs as a "last resort" were limited to lower-end skills and pay scale.

The Humphrey-Hawkins bill was a far cry from its original proposal. But there was merit to criticism that federal government management of the macro-economy was more difficult than imagined, that joblessness often arose from constant changes in technology and the global economy, and that there was some link between full employment and inflation, and between personal behavior and unemployment.

Carter approved the bill in November 1977, Humphrey conceded that it was acceptable, and the Congressional Black Caucus and the Urban League and labor groups endorsed it. Congressional dealing over language delayed Congress's approval for nearly a year, with the president finally signing the bill on October 27, 1978. The Humphrey vote in favor, however, was cast by Senator Muriel Humphrey, who had been appointed by Minnesota governor Rudy Perpich to her husband's seat on his death the preceding January.[74]

✦ ✦ ✦

While at home in Minnesota during the summer of 1977, an ailing Humphrey experienced increasing abdominal pain. He was admitted to the University of Minnesota Hospital, and on August 17, Dr. John Najarian performed a four-hour operation to remove an obstruction from his large intestine that proved to be an inoperable tumor attached to a bone in his pelvis. It was necessary to cut off the large intestine above the tumor and connect the unobstructed section with a tube through the abdominal wall to an external pouch to permit defecation. Tests showed that the tumor, likely missed by Humphrey's doctors during his 1976 surgery, was malignant. The cancer could be called "terminal," Najarian said, but chemotherapy might contain it; life expectancy "could be months, it could be years."[75]

"Deep down, I believe in miracles," Humphrey said, and he intended to remain on the national stage "as long as I have the breath of life." He maintained his usual upbeat attitude while in the hospital, where he underwent radiation treatment before returning home in late August, but he still needed to take anticancer drugs. At a public appearance in September at the Minnesota AFL-CIO convention in St. Paul, he confessed, "I may start out a little wobbly, but I'm going to end up damned good and strong." The speech was a thank-you to Minnesota political allies who had backed the pending Humphrey-Hawkins bill and a paean to organized labor as a bulwark of a free society.[76]

The senator's absence from Washington, and increasing public awareness that he was dying, sparked a powerful bipartisan response among countless thousands of people who recognized that they were about to lose a beloved national treasure—their "Happy Warrior"—who had never won his way to the Oval Office but had more influence than most presidents. Three thousand to six thousand letters a week—ranging from penciled scribblings on lined paper to typed formal notes—poured into Humphrey's Senate office, and numerous awards, major public gatherings to honor him, and unique political and governmental recognition of his dedication to significant causes became the order of the day.[77]

The Pioneer Women, the Labor Zionists women's organization in the United States, honored his longtime commitment to Israel by giving him the first Golda Meir Award. His sister, Frances Humphrey Howard, spoke for him at the October 19 ceremony, expressing his admiration for the former prime minister's goal that Israel be not the only democratic state in the Middle East but one among a cooperative community. The next day, more than two thousand people gathered at the first of two celebratory dinners in Washington hosted by Mondale to honor Humphrey and begin to raise $20 million to endow the newly established Hubert H. Humphrey Institute of Public Affairs at the University of Minnesota. The senator, "heartsick" at being too weak to attend, instructed that the evening should not be a "maudlin" one but devoted to "dining, dancing, and laughing." Among the many luminaries who spoke, Senator Bob Dole best summed up the prevailing view: "When I think of Hubert Humphrey, I think of politics as it ought to be"—and they would remain friends for life.[78]

Returning from fund raising in California, the president stopped in Minnesota on October 23 to bring Humphrey back to Washington: a "free ride," the senator said, and his first on Air Force One. Carter welcomed "the greatest American I know" and announced that once airborne he would sign legislation, sponsored by Dole, naming the newly completed Health, Education and Welfare (now Health and Human Services) Building for Humphrey—the first time a federal building was named for a living American.

Two days later, he made his first appearance in the Senate since early in the summer. His colleagues, pages, and spectators in the packed galleries gave him a standing ovation and countless embraces, including Majority Leader Byrd, and South Carolina's Strom Thurmond, who had led the segregationists' fight against Humphrey's 1948 civil rights plank. Humphrey responded, briefly, that his greatest therapy and "the gift of life" was the "friendship and love" he had gotten in the Senate and "from across the land."[79]

On November 1, the Humphreys attended the dedication of the new HEW Building at 200 Independence Avenue, not far from Capitol Hill. They viewed the large plaque at the entryway explaining the building's dedication to the senator as due to his "contribution to the health, education, and welfare of the Nation." Inscribed high on a wall in the entryway reception area are Humphrey's words spoken at the 1976 Democratic convention that the "moral test of government" is how it treats its children, the elderly, and the "sick, the needy, and the handicapped." At the ceremony, with Carter, Mondale, and countless other political leaders present, Dole stated that in seeking to make America, the world, and life a little better, Humphrey had "overshot the Nation's highest office, and become instead one of the great world leaders—one of the major moral forces of our time or of any time." Humphrey thanked Dole for having "sparked" this event and reflected that few men ever enjoyed the honor of being so "lavishly praised" while still able to enjoy it. The occasion proved, he said in a self-reference, that people identified not only with winners but also "with folks who lose a round or two but who fight on against the odds."[80]

The House of Representatives gave Humphrey another unique honor by convening, for the first time, a special session to receive a senator. Speaker Thomas P. "Tip" O'Neill, Democrat of Massachusetts, welcomed Humphrey: "You are the most genuine liberal the country has ever produced," he said, and have "played a dramatic role in shaping . . . every major legislation initiative that has become law in the past twenty-five years"—and often "you have stood alone." Countless tributes followed from both sides of the aisle; Minnesota Republican Albert Quie noted that Humphrey was always at the forefront of discussion of the nation's most critical issues and spoke for the disadvantaged, the mentally challenged, the unemployed, and the oppressed, while Virginia Democrat Herbert Harris called him "a second Roosevelt" who showed "more imagination and originality in the uses of government on behalf of the people" than anyone since FDR. Humphrey wryly responded, "I am standing where the President of the United States gives the State of the Union address"—and pleaded with his colleagues to remain strongly committed to "the needy, and the sick, and the handicapped" and to a political-economic system that "will make it possible for us to care for the less fortunate."[81]

Humphrey had a touching reunion on November 8 at his Harbor Square apartment in Washington with former Israeli prime minister Meir, in town to see a preview of William Gibson's Broadway play *Golda*. Afterward, Humphrey entered a suburban Bethesda hospital for a week of chemotherapy and anti-cancer drug treatment and enjoyed the Thanksgiving holiday in Washington. Governor Rudy Perpich designated December 2 as "Hubert Humphrey Day" in Minnesota, a gesture thirty-nine other states matched.[82]

Hubert Humphrey Day brought a "National Tribute" $1,000-a-plate dinner and fund raiser sponsored by the Humphrey Institute at Washington's Hilton

Hotel attended by about 2,500 people, including cabinet members, Supreme Court justices, major civil rights, labor, and corporate leaders, and dozens of Hollywood stars. The evening, as Humphrey requested, was devoted chiefly to dining, laughing, and singing, the last led by 1970s star Helen Reddy, who sang his favorite song, "You and Me against the World." Carter, the main speaker, told tales of Humphrey's unusually kind gestures to the president and his family, and concluded, "I'm proud to be the President of a nation that loves a man like Hubert Humphrey and is loved so deeply by him." Humphrey briefly responded that the institute bearing his name was an effort to educate the younger generation of "public servants" to deal with problems such as housing, health care, energy, and the environment not only as domestic-national issues but as global in scope.[83]

Muriel Humphrey, exhausted from caring for her husband and attending all the public events, checked into the Washington Hospital Center for a week. His sister, Frances, traveled to California to accept on his behalf the first Eleanor Roosevelt Human Rights Award, which spoke to gainful employment and good-quality health care as a right.

At Mondale's suggestion, Carter invited Humphrey to spend the December 10–11 weekend with him at the presidential retreat, Camp David, in the Catoctin Mountains in Maryland, about sixty miles northwest of Washington. The senator had never been there. He spoke at length about his relationship with Lyndon Johnson, blaming their "disharmonies"—and the vice president's "exclusion"—on Vietnam War pressure. He said that the former president had treated him as well as President Kennedy had treated Johnson, but this ignored Johnson's repeated humiliation of Humphrey and his seriously undermining his 1968 campaign. Humphrey believed he should have been elected president in 1968 and 1972; he expressed disappointment that African Americans had not supported him over George McGovern, who he said had little role in the civil rights movement. Humphrey spoke with no bitterness, although he was angry that Eugene McCarthy had offered only last-minute support in 1968 and labeled him "cynical" and "disloyal."[84]

In mid-December, Muriel left the hospital and returned to the family home in Waverly. On December 22, Mondale escorted Humphrey there aboard Air Force Two, where the senator told waiting reporters, "I'm not resigning from anything," and "I still know how to talk." This he did daily on the WATS (wide-area telephone service) line his family gave him for a Christmas gift so that he could stay in touch with political colleagues and friends, and even Nixon, whom he invited to attend, when the time came, his funeral in Washington. Humphrey took calls from Carter to make his near-deathbed efforts to help secure passage of the Panama Canal Treaty and to try to help bring peace between Israel and Egypt.[85]

Visitors also came to Waverly, including former president Gerald Ford, civil rights organizer Jesse Jackson, and *Chicago Sun-Times* columnist Irv Kupcinet, whom Humphrey told "with all the parties we've had, they might as well cut back on the funeral because all the eulogies have been said." Edgar Berman also paid what he knew would be a last visit to his patient-friend, and he was with him on January 6 when Humphrey learned that a recent poll of one thousand former legislative aides and political reporters had voted him the most effective senator of the past seventy-five years. "Lyndon Johnson's going to be sore as hell about this," Humphrey said.

Two days later, the NAACP, citing his "crusade to eliminate poverty, bigotry, and discrimination," awarded Humphrey its first Walter White Award, named for its executive secretary. His sister, Frances, spoke for him again in conveying his belief that the full enjoyment of one's rights awaited the day when differences in income, education, housing, and health care would no longer be related to race. On January 13, Humphrey received the Public Health Services Workers Award commemorating the life of Dr. Martin Luther King Jr. This was the last award he would receive during his lifetime; on June 9, 1980, Jimmy Carter would posthumously award Humphrey the Presidential Medal of Freedom.[86]

On Friday, January 13, 1978, Betty Smith, his press aide in Minnesota, said that the senator was "quite tired" and had spent most of the previous day in bed. Muriel, his four children and their spouses, and numerous grandchildren were at his bedside, and he soon slipped into a coma. David Gartner, his friend and chief aide, announced that at 9:25 p.m. the last "breath of life" had passed from Hubert Horatio Humphrey.[87]

EPILOGUE: THE CONSCIENCE
OF THE COUNTRY

Humphrey's chief assistant, David G. Gartner, telephoned Mondale on January 13, 1978, to say that the senator had died at 9:25 p.m. CST. The vice president informed Carter. Then, his voice breaking, he told journalists that his political mentor—"more like a father to me"—was a man of "decency and commitment to human service" who had "set a remarkable example of how to die with dignity, courage, spirit, and meaning." The president ordered Air Force One to fly Humphrey's body from Minnesota to Washington to lie in state under the dome in the Capitol Rotunda. Carter said that from time to time the United States "is blessed by men and women who bear the mark of greatness and who help us see a better vision of what we are at our best and what we might become." Hubert Humphrey, he said, "was such a man."[1]

Humphrey's lying in state provided an occasion for national mourning. Tens of thousands braved the cold weather long into the night of January 14 to view his coffin in the Capitol Rotunda on the same bier on which the bodies of Abraham Lincoln and John Kennedy had rested. Those who came to pay last respects included a surprising number of young people who had not yet been born or were toddlers when Humphrey burst on the national political scene three decades earlier. "He was never elected President, but now he's being honored like one," said his former running mate, Senator Edward Muskie. "He'd like that."

He would have liked the unusual private, bipartisan gathering that Republican Senate minority leader Howard H. Baker Jr. of Tennessee hosted in his office on January 15 that brought together an array of prominent guests and their spouses, including Carter, Mondale, Senate majority leader Robert Byrd, Lady Bird

Johnson, former president Gerald Ford, former vice president and governor Nelson Rockefeller, former secretary of state Henry Kissinger, and Richard Nixon, who had made his first trip back to Washington since having resigned the presidency.[2]

In his eulogy, the president said again that Humphrey gave Americans a vision of what they might become at their best. At a time of impending social crisis thirty years ago, his was the "first voice . . . a passionate voice" that Carter heard confronting the nation's "most difficult and moral issue" and demanding equal rights for black people and "basic human rights for all Americans." He always spoke for "the weak and the hungry, and the victims of discrimination and poverty." He should have served in the Oval Office, but from Truman to Carter himself, he was "a conscience to us all" and he "may well have blessed our country more than any of us." He was the "most beloved of all Americans" and reason for Americans to celebrate, rather than mourn, because "the joy of his memory will last far longer than the pain and sorrow of his leaving."[3]

For Mondale, speaking at services for Humphrey was intensely personal. Humphrey's passing was "as great a loss as I've ever known," Mondale said, and he chose not to catalogue his myriad accomplishments but rather to seek to discover what had made this "unique person" such an "uplifting symbol of love and joy for all people." With tears in his eyes, he said that the answer appeared to be in the letter young Humphrey had written almost forty-three years earlier on his first visit to Washington to his then fiancée, Muriel, in which he said that perhaps if "you and I apply ourselves, and make up our minds to work for bigger things we can live here," and perhaps serve in Congress.

Humphrey had succeeded beyond his "most optimistic dreams," Mondale said, to become one of the greatest legislators in the nation's history and one of the nation's "most loved men of his time." His was a spirit "so filled with love there was no room at all for hate." When he said that life was "not meant to be endured but, rather, to be enjoyed," that signaled Humphrey's belief that it was "time for all Americans to walk forthrightly into the bright sunshine of human rights." He may not have realized his greatest goal, but he achieved something much rarer and more valuable than the nation's highest office. "He became the country's conscience."

Above all, Mondale said, Humphrey was "a man with a good heart," meaning in Shakespeare's words in *Henry V* that "a good heart . . . is the sun . . . for it shines bright and never changes, but keeps his course truly." So did "Hubert's heart keep its course truly," and in so doing "he taught us all how to hope and how to love, how to win and how to lose; he taught us how to live, and, finally, he taught us how to die." Famed violinist Isaac Stern, a friend of the classical-music-loving Humphrey, and Metropolitan Opera star baritone Robert Merrill led the audience in singing "America the Beautiful."[4]

Mondale accompanied Humphrey's family and his coffin on Air Force II back to Minnesota, where Governor Rudy Perpich had declared a thirty-day mourning period. Humphrey lay in state in the Capitol Rotunda in St. Paul, where into the night and the early morning, forty thousand people braved near-zero temperatures to pay their respects. Services the next day were held at the House of Hope Presbyterian Church. Humphrey—a not-often-practicing Congregationalist—had worked with the church's pastor, the Reverend Calvin Didier, on several projects and relied on him to help plan his funeral, which he wanted to be a "celebration" of his life, not a brooding.

More than three thousand people crammed into the church's pews, along with House Speaker Tip O'Neill, who led a two-hundred-member congressional delegation, while several thousand gathered outside to hear the eulogies. Carter spoke mainly about his Camp David weekend with Humphrey, the wisdom the senator imparted about foreign policy, nuclear arms control, foreign aid, the Peace Corps and Food for Peace, and the suffering that accompanied physical pain and "the pain of losing." Yet there was no bitterness in any of Humphrey's words, the president said, and the weekend together "was the greatest favor I ever did myself."

Mondale declared that this was "the day that Hubert comes home to Minnesota"—the place whose land and lakes and people fed the "springs of love and streams of ideas" that marked Humphrey's "great genius" and "immense humanity." He "never found a person who was not worth his time," Mondale said, and like Abraham Lincoln, "he could not be separated from his people." Above all, Mondale said as he did the day before, Humphrey taught everyone how to love, lose, win, "and finally, how to die."

Stern played, along with acclaimed pianist Eugene Istomin, while Merrill sang "Ave Maria" and "The Lord's Prayer," and the congregation sang "A Mighty Fortress Is Our God," as Humphrey had requested. An African American choir from Sabathani Baptist Church in Minneapolis sang a series of spirituals; as the press noted, Humphrey had been in more African American churches than any other white politician in America. The services, intended to last two hours, ran well past the allotted time, but as the Reverend Didier said, God was familiar with Humphrey's "loquaciousness" and his events running too long, but the Lord also knew that the senator "almost always had a good point."

At last, at sundown, the family, close friends, Carter, and Mondale, and perhaps a thousand friendly onlookers, went to lay the Happy Warrior to rest. An honor guard provided a nineteen-gun salute, and a bugler played taps as

Humphrey was buried in the frozen ground near the main gate of the Lakewood Cemetery in Minneapolis.[5]

Humphrey was the most successful legislator in the nation's history and a powerful voice for equal justice for all, although he did not attain the presidency he coveted. But when Dr. Berman informed him in 1976 of the severity of his cancer and grim prospects, he responded that he had not a single regret about his life, except "I'd have liked to see if I could run this country." But then he smiled and said, "I didn't quite make history, but they knew I was here."[6]

NOTES

ABBREVIATIONS

ACR	*Appendix to the Congressional Record*
BDD	*Brainerd (MN) Daily Dispatch*
CRH	*Congressional Record*, House of Representatives
CRS	*Congressional Record*, Senate
FP	Orville H. Freeman Papers, Minnesota Historical Society, St. Paul
FRUS, 1958–1960	US Department of State, *Foreign Relations of the United States, 1958–1960*, 28 vols. (Washington, DC, 1986–96)
FRUS, 1964–1968	US Department of State, *Foreign Relations of the United States, 1964–1968*, 34 vols. (Washington, DC, 1992–2006)
HP	Hubert H. Humphrey Papers, Minnesota Historical Society, St. Paul (documents cited by file number)
HT	Harry S. Truman Presidential Library, Independence, MO
JL	Lyndon Baines Johnson Presidential Library, Austin, TX
JP	Lyndon Baines Johnson Papers, Presidential Papers, LBJ Presidential Library, Austin, TX
NYT	*New York Times*
SP	Carl Solberg Papers, Minnesota Historical Society, St. Paul
WDN	*Winona (MN) Daily News*

PROLOGUE

1. Humphrey to Gael Sullivan, Jan. 17, 1948, HP, 150.A.8.3B.
2. Humphrey to William O'Dwyer, Apr. 15, 1948, HP, 150.A.8.4F.
3. Humphrey, *Education*, 41–42. All citations to Humphrey's memoirs are to the 1991 edition rather than the out-of-print 1976 edition.
4. Transcript of Platform Committee Meeting, July 13, 1948, HP, 158.A.8.2F.
5. Griffith, *Humphrey*, 154–55.
6. Humphrey, *Education*, 77; Solberg, *Hubert Humphrey*, 15–16.

7. Solberg, *Hubert Humphrey*, 16.
8. Humphrey, *Education*, 78; Solberg, *Hubert Humphrey*, 17; Thurber, *Politics of Equality*, 60–61.
9. Thurber, *Politics of Equality*, 61; Cohodas, *Strom Thurmond*, 166–67.
10. Douglas, *Fullness of Time*, 133.
11. The original text of the speech with Humphrey's handwritten emendations is at the MHS, Reserve 20; the text of the July 14, 1948, speech is taken from transcription of the audio version (which matches the original draft with Humphrey's changes) and can be accessed at http://www.americanrhetoric.com/speeches/huberthumphey1948dnc.html; a typescript, dated July 14, 1948, is in HP, 150.A.8.1B.
12. Douglas, *Fullness of Time*, 133; Bryan, of course, had given his speech many times beforehand; Solberg, *Hubert Humphrey*, 18–19.
13. *NYT*, July 15, 1948 (which notes that southerners in control of the convention kept the forty-piece band under the podium silent); Solberg, *Hubert Humphrey*, 19; Ross, *Loneliest Campaign*, 121–22.
14. *NYT*, July 15, 1948; *BDD*, July 15, 1948; Solberg, *Hubert Humphrey*, 19.
15. *NYT*, July 15, 1948; *BDD*, July 15, 1948; Cohodas, *Strom Thurmond*, 166–67; Ross, *Loneliest Campaign*, 121; Anderson quoted in Solberg, *Hubert Humphrey*, 19.
16. *NYT*, Jan. 16, 1978.

1. A NEW STAR IS BORN

1. Eisele, *Almost to the Presidency*, 11–12; Griffith, *Humphrey*, 34–35; Solberg, *Hubert Humphrey*, 23–26.
2. Solberg, *Hubert Humphrey*, 27–28; Eisele, *Almost to Presidency*, 13n.2.
3. Solberg, *Hubert Humphrey*, 30–31, 35; Eisele, *Almost to Presidency*, 13.
4. Eisele, *Almost to Presidency*, 14, 16; Solberg, *Hubert Humphrey*, 35, 41, notes that Humphrey's complexion was clear, not the color of his clothes; Humphrey, *Education*, 4, 6–7; Griffith, *Humphrey*, 40.
5. Eisele, *Almost to Presidency*, 12; Humphrey, "My Father," 83.
6. Eisele, *Almost to Presidency*, 15; Humphrey, *Education*, 17.
7. Humphrey, "My Father," 89; Eisele, *Almost to Presidency*, 37; Solberg, *Hubert Humphrey*, 42.
8. Eisele, *Almost to Presidency*, 14–15; Humphrey, *Education*, 9–10.
9. Humphrey, *Education*, 8.
10. Humphrey, "My Father," 83; Solberg, *Hubert Humphrey*, 45, 53.
11. Humphrey, *Education*, 8; Humphrey, "My Father," 89.
12. Humphrey, *Education*, 17; Eisele, *Almost to Presidency*, 19.
13. Griffith, *Humphrey*, 38.
14. Humphrey, "My Father," 81–82.
15. Humphrey, *Education*, 16.
16. Eisele, *Almost to Presidency*, 19; Humphrey, *Education*, 19–20.
17. Humphrey, *Education*, 21–23.
18. Ibid., 23–25.

19. Ibid., 27–28; Eisele, *Almost to Presidency*, 22–23.

20. Eisele, *Almost to Presidency*, 23–24; Solberg, *Hubert Humphrey*, 47–48.

21. Humphrey, *Education*, 30–31; Eisele, *Almost to Presidency*, 24.

22. Humphrey, *Education*, 31–32; Eisele, *Almost to Presidency*, 25.

23. Thurber, *Politics of Equality*, 161; American Presidency Project, Franklin D. Roosevelt, "Rear Platform Remarks at Huron, S.D., during a Drought Inspection Tour," August 28, 1936, http://www.presidency.ucsb.edu/ws/index.php?pid=15108; Humphrey later said that meeting Roosevelt was "the greatest thrill of my life," quoted in Solberg, *Hubert Humphrey*, 74.

24. Solberg, *Hubert Humphrey*, 52; Eisele, *Almost to Presidency*, 25–26.

25. Griffith, *Humphrey*, 61–62; Solberg, *Hubert Humphrey*, 51–53.

26. Humphrey, *Education*, 35–36; Solberg, *Hubert Humphrey*, 67–68.

27. Solberg, *Hubert Humphrey*, 68; Eisele, *Almost to Presidency*, 49–50.

28. Humphrey, *Education*, 36–38; Solberg, *Hubert Humphrey*, 70–71.

29. Humphrey, *Education*, 38–39.

30. Leuchtenburg, "FDR and Kingfish," 81, 88–91.

31. Humphrey, *Education*, 40–41.

32. Delton, *Making Minnesota Liberal*, 61; Humphrey, *Education*, 41–42.

33. Griffith, *Humphrey*, 66–67; Solberg, *Hubert Humphrey*, 73–74.

34. Solberg, *Hubert Humphrey*, 74; Griffith, *Humphrey*, 67.

35. Humphrey, *Political Philosophy of the New Deal*; Humphrey, *Education*, 42.

36. Humphrey, *New Deal*, xx–xxii, 17.

37. Ibid., 64–67.

38. Humphrey, *Education*, 45–47.

39. Humphrey, *New Deal*, 68–76, 99.

40. Ibid., xxii–xxiii.

41. Humphrey, *Education*, 42–44; Solberg, *Hubert Humphrey*, 72.

42. Solberg, *Hubert Humphrey*, 83–84.

43. Humphrey, *Education*, 45.

44. Eisele, *Almost to Presidency*, 52; Humphrey, *Education*, 46; Solberg, *Hubert Humphrey*, 84.

45. Humphrey, *Education*, 46–47.

46. Solberg, *Hubert Humphrey*, 84–85.

47. Griffith, *Humphrey*, 110; Humphrey, *Education*, 47; Solberg, *Hubert Humphrey*, 85–86.

48. Solberg, *Hubert Humphrey*, 86–87.

49. Reichard, "Mayor Humphrey," 52.

50. Solberg, *Hubert Humphrey*, 89–90.

51. Eisele, *Almost to Presidency*, 52–53.

52. Humphrey, *Education*, 50–51.

53. Eisele, *Almost to Presidency*, 53; Solberg, *Hubert Humphrey*, 90.

54. Eisele, *Almost to Presidency*, 53; Humphrey, *Education*, 49.

55. Griffith, *Humphrey*, 107–8; Solberg, *Hubert Humphrey*, 90.

56. Humphrey, *Education*, 50; Reichard, "Mayor Humphrey," 52; Eisele, *Almost to Presidency*, 53; Solberg, *Hubert Humphrey*, 91.

57. Solberg, *Hubert Humphrey*, 92; Eisele, *Almost to Presidency*, 53.

58. Solberg, *Hubert Humphrey*, 93; Reichard, "Mayor Humphrey," 52n.3.

59. Solberg, *Hubert Humphrey*, 93–94; Humphrey, *Education*, 52; Eisele, *Almost to Presidency*, 53.

2. THE PEOPLE'S MAYOR

1. Griffith, *Humphrey*, 110; Humphrey, *Education*, 54–55.

2. List of Speaking Engagements, 1943–1945, HP, 150.E.3.6F; Address to Minnesota Library Association, "The Strength of Democracy," Oct. 1, 1942, and Address to Minneapolis-Moline Employees, [1942], HP, 150.D.4.3B; Thurber, *Politics of Equality*, 9–21.

3. Griffith, *Humphrey*, 111; Gieske, *Minnesota Farmer-Laborism*, 268–75; Risjord, *Popular History of Minnesota*, 189–201.

4. Gieske, *Minnesota Farmer-Laborism*, 291–96.

5. Solberg, *Hubert Humphrey*, 94; Gieske, *Minnesota Farmer-Laborism*, 316–22, 325–27; Haynes, *Dubious Alliance*, 107–13; Hennepin County, the most populous one in Minnesota, comprises Minneapolis and numerous suburbs to the south and west.

6. Solberg, *Hubert Humphrey*, 94–95; Humphrey, *Education*, 53–54.

7. Gieske, *Minnesota Farmer-Laborism*, 326–28; Haynes, *Dubious Alliance*, 113–15; Wallace's speech was entitled "The Price of Free World Victory" but was soon known by its "century of common man" theme; Walton, *Wallace, Truman, and Cold War*, 10–13.

8. Gieske, *Minnesota Farmer-Laborism*, 329; Solberg, *Hubert Humphrey*, 96.

9. Solberg, *Hubert Humphrey*, 96; Haynes, *Dubious Alliance*, 116.

10. Haynes, *Dubious Alliance*, 116; Humphrey, *Education*, 56–57.

11. Humphrey, *Education*, 56–57; Solberg, *Hubert Humphrey*, 96–97, 99; Humphrey's hernia caused him to have to wear a truss to support weakened groin muscles, and this kept his whole body from flowing into his walk; see Manfred, "Hubert Horatio Humphrey," 98.

12. Humphrey Speech nominating Henry Wallace for vice president, July 23, 1944, HP, 150.D.4.3B.

13. Solberg, *Hubert Humphrey*, 97–98; Humphrey, *Education*, 58; Haynes, *Dubious Alliance*, 119.

14. Solberg, *Hubert Humphrey*, 98.

15. John Newman, "Hubert Humphrey on the Death of F.D.R.," citing Humphrey to Wallace, Apr. 12, 1945, and Wallace to Humphrey, Apr. 21, 1945, accessed at http://www.lib.uiowa.edu/spec-coll/Bai/newman.htm.

16. Haynes, *Dubious Alliance*, 119–20; Solberg, *Hubert Humphrey*, 53, 55.

17. Reichard, "Mayor Humphrey," 53, 55.

18. Thurber, *Politics of Equality*, 23–24.

19. Solberg, *Hubert Humphrey*, 101–2; Humphrey, *Education*, 60–62.

20. Griffith, *Humphrey*, 115; Reichard, "Mayor Humphrey," 52–53; BDD, June 12, 1945.

21. Reichard, "Mayor Humphrey," 54.

22. Solberg, *Hubert Humphrey*, 102–3; Griffith, *Humphrey*, 117–19; Humphrey, *Education*, 63–65.
23. Solberg, *Hubert Humphrey*, 104; Reichard, "Mayor Humphrey," 56.
24. Solberg, *Hubert Humphrey*, 104; Reichard, "Mayor Humphrey," 54–55; *Time*, Jan. 17, 1949; *Winona (MN) Republican-Herald*, Mar. 18, 1947, dates the shooting to Feb. 6, 1947, but at the time Humphrey declined to acknowledge the episode until rumors forced him to address it in March.
25. Reichard, "Mayor Humphrey," 55–56.
26. Ibid., 56–58.
27. Ibid., 59.
28. Morison, "His Honor," 4.
29. Ibid.; Reichard, "Mayor Humphrey," 60.
30. Morison, "His Honor," 4; Solberg, *Hubert Humphrey*, 105.
31. Thurber, *Politics of Equality*, 25–28; McWilliams, "Minneapolis," 61–65; Berman, "Political Antisemitism."
32. Reichard, "Mayor Humphrey," 62; Thurber, *Politics of Equality*, 29.
33. Reichard, "Mayor Humphrey," 62–66; Thurber, *Politics of Equality*, 28–33; Solberg, *Hubert Humphrey*, 105–6.
34. Reichard, "Mayor Humphrey," 62, 62n.32; Thurber, *Politics of Equality*, 38–41; see also Blood, *Northern Breakthrough*, 7; the law did not cover domestic workers, the lowest paid and most vulnerable employees.
35. Reichard, "Mayor Humphrey," 63.
36. Thurber, *Politics of Equality*, 45–48.
37. Solberg, *Hubert Humphrey*, 106–7.
38. Solberg, *Hubert Humphrey*, 108; Morison, "His Honor," 2, 4; "Education of a Senator."
39. Griffith, *Humphrey*, 121–23; Morison, "His Honor," 3; on polio and Sister Kenny in Minneapolis, see Oshinsky, *Polio*, 73–78.
40. Morison, "His Honor," 2; Solberg, *Hubert Humphrey*, 108–9; see also HP, 150.D.4.3B, 150.D.4.4F.
41. Solberg, *Hubert Humphrey*, 109; Reichard, "Mayor Humphrey," 63; BDD, June 10, 1947.
42. Reichard, "Mayor Humphrey," 64; *Time*, Jan. 17, 1949.
43. Reichard, "Mayor Humphrey," 64–65; Solberg, *Hubert Humphrey*, 109.
44. Reichard, "Mayor Humphrey," 60–61.
45. Ibid., 65.
46. Ibid., 66.

3. THE NEXT SENATOR FROM MINNESOTA

1. Haynes, *Dubious Alliance*, 131–32; Humphrey, *Education*, 71; Solberg, *Hubert Humphrey*, 113.
2. Haynes, *Dubious Alliance*, 135–36; Solberg, *Hubert Humphrey*, 113.
3. Humphrey quoted in James I. Loeb Oral History, June 26, 1970, 59, James I. Loeb Papers, TL; Delton, *Making Minnesota Liberal*, 98; Haynes, *Dubious Alliance*, 139.

4. Haynes, *Dubious Alliance,* 140; Offner, *Another Such Victory,* 165–73.

5. Haynes, *Dubious Alliance,* 175–77; Offner, *Another Such Victory,* 175–77.

6. Humphrey quoted in Solberg, *Hubert Humphrey,* 114.

7. Haynes, *Dubious Alliance,* 127, 141; Solberg, *Hubert Humphrey,* 115.

8. *BDD,* Nov. 6, 7, 1946; Reichard, *Politics as Usual,* 17–19.

9. Walton, *Wallace, Truman, and Cold War,* 75–76; Gillon, *Politics and Vision,* 16.

10. Gillon, *Politics and Vision,* 16–20.

11. Ibid., 20–21; Solberg, *Hubert Humphrey,* 115.

12. Solberg, *Hubert Humphrey,* 115; Offner, *Another Such Victory,* 200–202.

13. Gillon, *Politics and Vision,* 25–27; Solberg, *Hubert Humphrey,* 116; Humphrey, *Education,* 72.

14. Offner, *Another Such Victory,* 226–28, 235.

15. ADA Statement, Oct. 2, 1947, HP, 150.A.4F; Humphrey to Patterson, Dec. 4, 1947, and Humphrey to Judd, Mar. 15, 1948, HP, 150.A.8.3B.

16. Humphrey to Clarence O. Madsen, Mar. 26, 1947, HP, 150.A.8.1B; Humphrey to Dudley Partson, Mar. 26, 1947, quoted in Solberg, *Hubert Humphrey,* 116.

17. Haynes, *Dubious Alliance,* 152–53; Delton, *Making Minnesota Liberal,* 136.

18. Delton, *Making Minnesota Liberal,* 136–37.

19. Sandbrook, *Eugene McCarthy,* 37, 39; Humphrey to Matt Pelkonen, Dec. 16, 1947, HP, 150.A.8.2F.

20. Sandbrook, *Eugene McCarthy,* 36–37; Haynes, *Dubious Alliance,* 153–55.

21. Haynes, *Dubious Alliance,* 155–56; Solberg, *Hubert Humphrey,* 116–17; Humphrey, *Education,* 72, 351.

22. Eisele, *Almost to Presidency,* 65–66; Solberg, *Hubert Humphrey,* 118; Haynes, *Dubious Alliance,* 167–68.

23. Humphrey to David Dubinsky, Oct. 30, 1947, Humphrey to Gael Sullivan, Sept. 4, 1947, and Humphrey to Robert E. Hannegan, Sept. 4, 1947, HP, 150.A.8.3B.

24. Walton, *Henry Wallace,* 181–82; Mitau, "Democratic-Farmer-Labor Party Schism," 275; Clark M. Clifford, Memorandum for the President, Nov. 19, 1947, box 22, Clark M. Clifford Papers, TL; the memo was written chiefly by James H. Rowe Jr., a Washington lawyer, New Deal supporter, and ADA founder; Walton, *Henry Wallace,* 206–11; Karabell, *Last Campaign,* 66–67; Hamby, *Man of the People,* 436.

25. Offner, *Another Such Victory,* 237–40.

26. Haynes, *Dubious Alliance,* 179; Solberg, *Hubert Humphrey,* 118–19; Freeman quoted in Eisele, *Almost to Presidency,* 62; for Freeman, this included pushing aside his father-in-law, James M. Shields.

27. Haynes, *Dubious Alliance,* 174, 180; Solberg, *Hubert Humphrey,* 119–20.

28. Mitau, "Democratic-Farmer-Labor Party Schism," 276; George Demetriou to Jimmy Wechsler, Mar. 24, 1948, HP, 150.A.8.3B.

29. Haynes, *Dubious Alliance,* 182–83.

30. Ibid., 183–84.

31. "Message to DFL Liberals," [Apr. 17, 1948], HP, 150.A.8.1B.

32. *St. Paul Pioneer Press,* Apr. 19, 1948, quoted in Mitau, "Democratic-Farmer-Labor Party Schism," 277; radio address quoted in Bell, *Liberal State,* 79.

33. Humphrey, "Report to the National ADA on DFL Precinct Caucuses," May 7, 1948, HP, 150.A.8.1B; see also Haynes, *Dubious Alliance*, 184–89; Mitau, "Democratic-Farmer-Labor Party Schism," 277; and Sandbrook, *Eugene McCarthy*, 46.

34. *NYT*, June 12, 1948; Haynes, *Dubious Alliance*, 190–93.

35. Solberg, *Hubert Humphrey*, 121; Haynes, *Dubious Alliance*, 199–200; Delton, *Making Minnesota Liberal*, 153.

36. Address Delivered by Mayor Hubert H. Humphrey Accepting Endorsement of the D-F-L Party at State Convention at Brainerd, MN, June 13, 1948, HP, 150.D.4.4F.

37. Solberg, *Hubert Humphrey*, 151; Haynes, *Dubious Alliance*, 153, 199; *NYT*, June 13, 1948.

38. Mitau, "Democratic-Farmer-Labor Party Schism," 278–80.

39. Hamby, *Man of the People*, 435; Humphrey quoted in Gillon, *Politics and Vision*, 38–39; see also Haynes, *Dubious Alliance*, 197.

40. *Minneapolis Star*, Mar. 24, 1948; *Minneapolis Times*, Mar. 24, 1948; George Demetriou to Wechsler, Mar. 24, 1948, HP, 150.A.8.3B; Humphrey to Bowles, Apr. 9, 1948, HP, 150.A.8.8F.

41. Humphrey to S. M. Kelly, Mar. 31, 1948, and Demetriou to Public Relations Department, *Milwaukee Journal*, May 11, 1948, HP, 150.A.8.8F; on vice presidential hopes, see Solberg, *Hubert Humphrey*, 123; Gerald Heaney to Humphrey, July 3, 1948, HP, 150.A.8.2F; and Minutes of the ADA Executive Committee, June 28, 1948, HP, 150.A.8.5B.

42. Humphrey to O'Dwyer, Apr. 29, 1948, HP, 150.A.8.4F.

43. Hubert H. Humphrey Sr. to Hubert H. Humphrey Jr., July 2, 1948, HP, 150.A.8.2F.

44. *BDD*, Nov. 6, 1946; Delton, *Making Minnesota Liberal*, 113–14; Divine, *Second Chance*, 237–38; Stuhler, *Ten Men of Minnesota*, 139–42; within a month, Humphrey gained a permanent lead, although the *NYT*, Nov. 1, 1948, rated his chances of winning at "even."

45. Stuhler, *Ten Men of Minnesota*, 150–55; Delton, *Making Minnesota Liberal*, 167; Porter and Johnson, *National Party Platforms*, 450–52.

46. Humphrey to James B. Forrestal, Apr. 26, 1948, accessed at http://www.trumanlibrary.org; Humphrey quoted in Thurber, *Politics of Equality*, 55.

47. Thurber, *Politics of Equality*, 54–56.

48. *BDD*, July 13, 1948; Karabell, *Last Campaign*, 150; Hamby, *Man of the People*, 448.

49. Diary entries for July 12, 13, 1948, in Ferrell, *Off the Record*, 141–42; Hamby, *Man of the People*, 449.

50. Porter and Johnson, *National Party Platforms*, 435.

51. Ross, *Loneliest Campaign*, 124; *NYT*, July 15, 1948.

52. *NYT*, July 15, 1948; only two presidents, William Howard Taft and Woodrow Wilson, ever called an opposition-led Congress into special session; Taft lost reelection in 1912, and Wilson was not renominated in 1920; *BDD*, July 15, 1948.

53. Eisele, *Almost to Presidency*, 69; Humphrey, *Education*, 79; United Press Report by George Marder, [July 1948], HP, 150.A.8.8F; his campaign ordered five hundred copies for newspaper distribution.

54. Cohodas, *Strom Thurmond*, 174–77; Porter and Johnson, *National Party Platforms*, 466–68.

55. Walton, *Henry Wallace*, 235–36; Porter and Johnson, *National Party Platforms*, 436–47.

56. Karabell, *Last Campaign*, 187–88.

57. Humphrey quoted in Thurber, *Politics of Equality*, 64.

58. BDD, Sept. 15, 1948. Haynes, *Dubious Alliance*, 208–10, notes that regular DFL candidates won the primaries for governor, five lesser statewide offices, and six congressional seats, whereas left-wing DFL candidates won nominations for two lesser statewide offices and two congressional seats; U.S. Senate Primary Tally Sheet, HP, 150.A.8.8F.

59. Humphrey Press Release, Aug. 5, 1948, HP, 150.A.8.8F; Humphrey quoted in Thurber, *Politics of Equality*, 64; Haynes, *Dubious Alliance*, 205.

60. Stuhler, *Ten Men of Minnesota*, 142; Solberg, *Hubert Humphrey*, 126–27; Griffith, *Humphrey*, 160–61. Ball also lost some campaign support in August when the highly popular Stassen left Minnesota politics to become president of the University of Pennsylvania.

61. Solberg, *Hubert Humphrey*, 127–28; *Time*, Jan. 17, 1949.

62. Delton, *Making Minnesota Liberal*, 161; Griffith, *Humphrey*, 161–62.

63. Humphrey quoted in *Minneapolis Labor Review*, July 27, 2006, accessed at www.minneapolisunions.org; BDD, Oct. 27, 1948.

64. Haynes, *Dubious Alliance*, 206–7; Solberg, *Hubert Humphrey*, 126–29; Haynes, "Farm Coops," 201.

65. Humphrey Address, Oct. 5, 1948, HP, 150.A.8.8F.

66. Truman address, St. Paul, Oct. 13, 1948, www.trumanlibrary.org; BDD, Oct. 14, 1948.

67. Quoted in *Minneapolis Labor Review*, July 26, 2007; Solberg, *Hubert Humphrey*, 127; BDD, Oct. 15, 1948.

68. Ball and Freeman quoted, respectively, in Solberg, *Hubert Humphrey*, 127, 129; *Time*, Oct. 11, 1948.

69. BDD, Nov. 4, 6, 1948; Haynes, *Dubious Alliance*, 210; Sandbrook, *Eugene McCarthy*, 50 (who notes that McCarthy later claimed to have met Humphrey for the first time on election night, but this was not the case); Bell, *Liberal State*, 157.

70. Humphrey to Truman, Nov. 4, 1948, quoted in Thurber, *Politics of Equality*, 65; Hamby, *Man of the People*, 464–66; Karabell, *Last Campaign*, 260–62.

71. Goldish, "Minnesota Poll," 722–24; Karabell, *Last Campaign*, 254.

72. Delton, *Making Minnesota Liberal*, 157–59; Benton quoted in Bell, *Liberal State*, 151.

4. LONELY, BITTER, AND BROKE IN THE SENATE

1. Humphrey, *Education*, 86; *Time*, Jan. 17, 1949.

2. Humphrey, *Education*, 88–89; Griffith, *Candid Biography*, 182–84.

3. Eisele, *Almost to Presidency*, 88; *Time*, Jan. 17, 1949.

4. Humphrey, *Education*, 87.

5. Caro, *Master of Senate*, 447–48; Humphrey, *Education*, 87.

6. Thurber, *Politics of Equality*, 68; *Time*, Jan. 17, 1949.

7. *Time*, Jan. 17, 1949; Solberg, *Hubert Humphrey*, 148.

8. Solberg, *Hubert Humphrey*, 135; Caro, *Master of Senate*, 446; Thurber, *Politics of Equality*, 68.

9. Humphrey quoted in Michael Amrine, *This Is Humphrey*, 133–34.

10. Reichard, *Politics as Usual*, 48–49; on Feb. 7, 1949, Humphrey introduced a bill to permit states to include their employees in Social Security, *NYT*, Feb. 8, 1949.

11. ACR, Mar. 2, 1949, A1259; Myrdal, *American Dilemma*.

12. Thurber, *Politics of Equality*, 68; Solberg, *Hubert Humphrey*, 137–38.

13. Thurber, *Politics of Equality*, 69–70; CRS, Mar. 10, 1949, 2166–69.

14. Digest of Humphrey Speeches on Civil Rights, Mar. 14–Mar. 16, 1949, HP, 150.D.4.4F; for full details of the congressional maneuvering, see "Limitation of Debate, Congressional Almanac 1949," accessed at http://library.cqpress.com/cqalmanac/.

15. CRS, Mar. 11, 14, 1949, 2260, 2418–20.

16. Ibid., Mar. 15, 16, 1949, 2462–65, 2605–12.

17. Thurber, *Politics of Equality*, 70, also quotes Humphrey to Frank Paskowitz, Aug. 12, 1949; http://library.cqpress.com/cqalmanac/. Humphrey added a digest of his remarks of Mar. 14 and 16 to ACR, May 25, 1946, 3235–36.

18. CRS, Mar. 25, Apr. 29, 1949, 3150–51, 5291–92; Thurber, *Politics of Equality*, 71. Wagner was a prime mover of the 1935 National Labor Relations and Social Security Acts in 1935 and the first federal housing act in 1937.

19. Hamby, *Man of the People*, 493–94; Thurber, *Politics of Equality*, 72.

20. CRS, Feb. 17, June 10, 1949, 1334–35, 7542–61; Solberg, *Hubert Humphrey*, 138–41; see also Reichard, *Politics as Usual*, 51.

21. CRS, Apr. 19, 20, 21, 1949, 4737–61, 4803–6, 4853–60.

22. Hamby, *Man of the People*, 498; Donovan, *Tumultuous Years*, 127.

23. Poen, *Truman versus Medical Lobby*, 17, 31, 157, 160–61. Other parts of the omnibus bill were introduced as separate measures, including financing of medical education, research institutes, and hospital construction and grants to states to improve their public health systems; only the hospital construction measure was passed in 1949 as an amendment to the 1946 Hospital Construction Act. On Humphrey, see CRS, May 6, 1949, 5808–9, 6493.

24. Poen, *Truman versus Medical Lobby*, 125–30, 142–54, 163.

25. Ibid., 164, 176–77.

26. Patterson, *Mr. Republican*, 432–33; CRS, Apr. 29, May 3, 1949, 4908, 5474–80. For sharp public debate between New York's Francis Joseph Cardinal Spellman and Eleanor Roosevelt, see Lash, *Eleanor*, 156–61.

27. Solberg, *Hubert Humphrey*, 142.

28. CRS, Aug. 29, 30, 1949, 12404–62; Humphrey to Philip S. Duff, Aug. 31, 1949, quoted in Solberg, *Hubert Humphrey*, 143.

29. Humphrey, Oral History Interview (1971), JL; Solberg, *Hubert Humphrey*, 148–49; Humphrey, *Education*, 89; Hubert Humphrey, "My Father," *Atlantic Monthly* (November 1966), 82.

30. Eisele, *Almost to Presidency*, 92–93.

31. CRS, Feb. 24, 1950, 2328–29.

32. Ibid., Mar. 2, 1950, 2610–15.

33. Ibid., 2615–22.
34. *Time*, Mar. 13, 1950.
35. *CRS*, Mar. 2, 1950, 2622–30.
36. Humphrey, *Education*, 92; Eisele, *Almost to Presidency*, 92–93.
37. Humphrey, *Education*, 92; Solberg, *Hubert Humphrey*, 143; Humphrey said he never forgot Tydings's gesture but apparently did not remember that Douglas and Wisconsin Republican Alexander Wylie also backed him on the Senate floor.
38. Humphrey, Oral History Interview (1971), JL; Caro, *Master of Senate*, 450.

5. CONFRONTATION AND COOPERATION

1. Humphrey, *Education*, 86–87; Humphrey, "Civil Rights Program for America," Jan. 15, 1950, in *ACR*, A439–40; "Roosevelt Day Address," Jan. 24, 1950, HP, 150.D.4.4F.
2. Humphrey, "Congress and the Nation's Health," address to the DFL Party's Legislative Conference, Feb. 18, 1949; Humphrey, "The Welfare State," Speech at Harvard Law School Forum, Mar. 29, 1950, *ACR*, A1604–7, A2317–19.
3. Humphrey, "The Fair Deal in Virginia," Apr. 18, 1950, in *ACR*, Apr. 21, 1950, A2864–67; Humphrey and Holland, "Should We Adopt the Federal FEPC?" radio debate on American Forum of the Air, *ACR*, Apr. 26, 1950, A3025–28; *Baker v. Carr*, 369 U.S. 186 (1962), opened the way under the equal protection clause of the Fourteenth Amendment to judicial review of malapportioned electoral districts and reapportionment of legislative districts based on population, which would reflect the transformation of the United States from a rural to an urban society.
4. *CRS*, Feb. 7, 1950, 1560–76.
5. Ibid., May 17, 1950, 7143–47.
6. Ibid., May 17, June 22, 1950, 7147–53, 9074–77; Thurber, *Politics of Equality*, 75.
7. Thurber, *Politics of Equality*, 76; Nichols, *Matter of Justice*, 42–43.
8. *CRS*, May 26, 1950, 7781–82.
9. Douglas, *Fullness of Time*, 351–53; Fetter, "Exit Basing Point Pricing," 815–16, 826–27; *F.T.C. v. The Cement Institute et al.*, 333 U.S. 698 (1948).
10. Latham, "Politics of Basing Point Legislation," 294, 309–19; Douglas, *Fullness of Time*, 353.
11. *CRS*, May 26, 31, 1950, 7781–12, 7853–65; Humphrey used many arguments from Fetter, "Exit Basing Point Pricing"; Douglas, *Fullness of Time*, 354; *NYT*, June 17, 1951.
12. On the basing point system, see Soper et al., "Basing Point Pricing," 539.
13. Donovan, *Tumultuous Years*, 243–47; Helsinki, "Comments on Revenue Act," 455–57.
14. Humphrey statement, July 20, 1950, *CRS*, July 20, 1950, 10683–84.
15. Douglas, *Fullness of Time*, 424–25n.; see also Paul, *Taxation*, 554–71; economist quoted in Mann, *Walls of Jericho*, 115; Humphrey and Douglas quotations in *CRS*, Aug. 23, 1950, 13677, 136784, 13696.
16. *CRS*, Aug. 29, 1950, 13671–84, 13696–700.
17. Biles, *Crusading Liberal*, 76–77; on Heller comment, see Mann, *Walls of Jericho*, 116; Solberg, *Hubert Humphrey*, 147; Humphrey, *Education*, 106–7; on excess profits and tax laws, see Paul, "Excess Profits Tax," 44–45; Webster, "Taxpayer Relief," *Virginia Law Review*, 1039–42, notes Congress's failure to close loopholes.

18. Klehr and Haynes, *American Communist Movement*, 26–39, 50–58; Morgan, *Reds*, 312–19; *Dennis v. United States*, 314 U.S. 494 (1951). The Smith Act was also used in 1941 to prosecute in Minneapolis ideological supporters of Leon Trotsky (Stalin's rival in exile in Mexico who was assassinated in 1940), who urged workers to foment world revolution rather than fight in the world war.

19. Hamby, *Man of the People*, 429.

20. Oshinsky, *Conspiracy*, 109–10, 168–72; Caute, *Great Fear*, 313–14; Senator Smith's statement in *NYT*, June 2, 1950; Humphrey did not speak against McCarthy but publicized an article by *Washington Evening Star* columnist Thomas L. Stokes praising the Republican senators for standing up to McCarthy; see *CRS*, Sept. 15, 1950, 14883.

21. Oshinsky, *Conspiracy*, 207.

22. *CRS*, Sept. 11, 1950, 14457.

23. *ACR*, Aug. 12, 1949, A5242–43; *CRS*, Feb. 28, May 22, 1950, 2493–95, 7404–6; the file of the young writer, David Lloyd, was mistakenly sent to the House Appropriations Committee.

24. *ACR*, Sept. 7, 8, 1950, 14286, 14412–14; Humphrey's reference to Hoover derived from the FBI director having recently said that he could quickly name an additional twelve thousand Communists if his agency was given a $6 million appropriation boost; ibid., Sept. 11, 1950, 14491.

25. Ibid., Sept. 8, 1950, 14412–16.

26. Ibid., Sept. 11, 22, 1950, 14486–88, 14606; Biles, *Crusading Liberal*, 78.

27. Cotton and Smith, "Emergency Detention Act," 29–30.

28. Humphrey to Kefauver quoted in Biles, *Crusading Liberal*, 79; Humphrey in *CRS*, Sept. 23, 1950, 15520; Douglas, *Fullness of Time*, 307, says that he "failed morally" in voting for the McCarran Act.

29. *NYT*, Sept. 23, 1950.

30. *CRS*, Sept. 22, 23, 1950, 15520–25, 15709–26; Biles, *Crusading Liberal*, 79; on Lincoln's action and the Court, see *ex parte Merryman* (1861).

31. Truman on Hoover and FBI in Clifford, *Counsel to President*, 180. Clifford, Truman's counsel during his first term, later wrote that Hoover was "very close to being an American fascist"; ibid., 182. On Hoover's hatred of Eleanor Roosevelt and suspicions of Einstein, see Isaacson, *Einstein*, 501–2.

32. *ACR*, Oct. 15, 1949, A6350–53.

33. *CRS*, July 20, 1949, 9777–78.

34. Ibid., Apr. 8, 1949, 4150–51. Humphrey soon reiterated opposing aid to any European country [his reference here was to France in Indochina] seeking to preserve "an old, antiquated colonial system by continuing to subjugate the people of southeastern Asia"; *ACR*, May 31, 1949, A3340–50.

35. Logan, "Racism and Indian-U.S. Relations," 71–79.

36. *CRS*, Apr. 8, 1949, 4150–51.

37. Paterson, "Foreign Aid under Wraps," 124–25.

38. *CRS*, Jan. 5, 1950, 104–7.

39. Offner, *Another Such Victory*, 367–77. The Russians were boycotting the Security Council because that body was refusing to seat the PRC in place of the Nationalists,

but Stalin could have rushed back his delegate to veto the resolutions if he so desired; perhaps he thought North Korea would win a quick victory or envisioned a US-PRC conflict to Soviet advantage.

40. *CRS*, June 27, 1950, 9233–34.
41. Ibid., July 11, 1950, 9914–23.
42. Ibid., July 12, 1950, 9990–91.
43. Ibid., Feb. 12, 1951, 1207–9.
44. Ibid., Mar. 21, 1951, 2755–57.
45. Offner, *Another Such Victory*, 402–5.
46. *CRS*, Apr. 12, May 10, 1951, 4406–7, 5183–87.
47. Eisele, *Almost to the Presidency*, 93–94.
48. Humphrey, *Education*, 115.
49. Solberg, *Hubert Humphrey*, 151–52.
50. Ibid., 152.
51. Humphrey, *Education*, 125–37; *Time*, July 16, 1952; Youngdahl quoted in *Minneapolis Star Tribune*, June 22, 1978.

6. PROMINENCE AND COURTSHIP

1. Eisele, *Almost to Presidency*, 94–95.
2. "Legends in the Law"; Solberg, *Hubert Humphrey*, 157.
3. Eisele, *Almost to Presidency*, 98; Solberg, *Hubert Humphrey*, 157; "Statement by Senator Morse in Defense of Senator Humphrey," *CRS*, July 5, 1952, 9472–83.
4. Donovan, *Tumultuous Years*, 384–87; Hamby, *Man of the People*, 593–95.
5. Humphrey remarks and "Staff Report to the Subcommittee on Labor and Labor-Management Relations," *CRS*, Apr. 9, 1952, 3818, 3845–949.
6. *CRS*, Apr. 18, 1952, 4081–103.
7. *Youngstown Sheet and Tube Co. v. Charles Sawyer*, 343 U.S. 579 (1952); Donovan, *Tumultuous Years*, 386–87; McCullough, *Truman*, 900–901.
8. Eckerson, "Immigration and National Origins," 6–9.
9. Bennett, "Immigration and Nationality Act," 127–31; the law allowed officials to exclude many people whose ideas they deemed "subversive."
10. *CRS*, Mar. 12, 1952, 2140–44.
11. Bennett, "Immigration and Nationality Act," 130; Humphrey speech, Jan. 28, 1953, in Engelmayer and Wagman, *Hubert Humphrey*, 110–11.
12. Smith, *Eisenhower in War and Peace*, 508–10.
13. *Time*, Mar. 12, 24, 1952.
14. *BDD*, Mar. 19, 1952.
15. Davis, *Prophet*, 396; Hamby, *Man of the People*, 602–5.
16. *BDD*, Mar. 19, 1952; Grant, "1952 Minnesota Republican Primary," 311–15.
17. Porter and Johnson, *National Party Platforms*, 497–98; Ambrose, *Eisenhower: President-Elect*, 542n17.
18. Ambrose, *Eisenhower: President-Elect*, 543n18.
19. *CRS*, July 22, 1952, 9727; *BDD*, July 23, 26, 1952.

20. *BDD*, July 22, 1952; Thurber, *Politics of Equality*, 81–82.

21. *BDD*, July 24, 1952; Thurber, *Politics of Equality*, 82–83; Kampelman quoted in Mann, *Walls of Jericho*, 127; Porter and Johnson, *National Party Platforms*, 473–81.

22. Davis, *Prophet in His Country*, 400–401.

23. Thurber, *Politics of Equality*, 83; *BDD*, July 24, 1952.

24. *BDD*, July 26, 1952; Thurber, *Politics of Equality*, 84.

25. *NYT*, July 26, 1952; Davis, *Prophet*, 406–7.

26. Reichard, *Politics as Usual*, 84; see *BDD*, Sept. 30, 1952, for the advertisement.

27. Reichard, *Politics as Usual*, 85–86; Gellman, *President and Apprentice*, 31–54.

28. Oshinsky, *Conspiracy*, 236–38; *BDD*, Oct. 28, 1952; *NYT*, Oct. 28, 1952.

29. *BDD*, Oct. 8, 24, 1952; Davis, *Prophet*, 420–24; Hamby, *Man of the People*, 613–14.

30. Eisele, *Almost to Presidency*, 97; Humphrey to Benton, Sept. 30, 1952, quoted in Solberg, *Hubert Humphrey*, 155.

31. Reichard, *Politics as Usual*, 85; *BDD*, Nov. 5, 7, 1952.

32. Morgan, *Reds*, 424; Shermer, "Origins of Conservative Ascendancy," 685–89, 694; Taft would die in August 1953.

33. Woods, *LBJ*, 253–54; Humphrey quoted in Caro, *Master of Senate*, 480–81.

34. Caro, *Master of Senate*, 232–46.

35. Ibid., 247–48.

36. Ibid., 249–85; Hamby, *Man of the People*, 491; on the impact of anti-Communism, Dallek, *Lone Star Rising*, 375–76.

37. *CRS*, Oct. 12, 1949, 14370–75.

38. Caro, *Master of Senate*, 293–95; Truman appointed a former Senate crony, Monrad (Mon) Wallgren of Washington, to the post, and he proved a weak commissioner.

39. Ibid., 482; Humphrey, *Education*, 117; Humphrey, Oral History Interview, Aug. 17, 1971, JL.

40. Humphrey, *Education*, 117.

41. Caro, "Orator of the Dawn," 62–63.

42. Humphrey, *Education*, 117–18; Caro, *Master of Senate*, 502; Douglas would join the prestigious Finance Committee in 1956.

43. Caro, *Master of Senate*, 494.

44. Ibid., 503–4.

45. Caro, "Orator of Dawn," 63; Humphrey, Oral History Interview, June 21, 1977, JL.

46. Humphrey, *Education*, 118; Caro, "Orator of Dawn," 59.

47. Mann, *Walls of Jericho*, 51–53.

48. Ibid., 53–68. Johnson also lost an extremely bitter and controversial special Senate election in 1941 to Governor W. Lee "Pappy" Daniel; General MacArthur awarded Johnson a Silver Star for flying on a bomber that went on a mission over New Guinea in 1942 and came under fighter plane attack, but he only observed and was the only one on the plane to get a medal; Johnson had to know that MacArthur was engaging in political backscratching but nonetheless displayed the medal prominently during political campaigns; see Dallek, *Lone Star Rising*, 238–41.

49. On Johnson's business interests and likely conflicts of interest, see Dallek, *Lone Star Rising*, 247–52, 281–84.

50. Humphrey quoted in Solberg, *Hubert Humphrey*, 161; Reedy quoted in Caro, *Master of Senate*, 451; Humphrey, *Education*, 115; Russell quoted in Mann, *Walls of Jericho*, 144.
51. Humphrey moved so fast on the agriculture seat when North Carolina senator Clyde Hoey died in May 1954 that Johnson said, "Out of respect for the man, Hubert, you could have waited for somebody in his family to be notified before you were in here"; Humphrey, Oral History Interview, June 20, 1977, JL; Johnson to Humphrey, November 1957, Oct. 24, Nov. 5, 22, Dec. 9, 1958, Marvin Watson Files, box 24, JL.
52. Humphrey, Oral History Interview, Aug. 17, 1971, JL.
53. Woods, *LBJ*, 188–89, 326–27.
54. Caro, *Master of Senate*, 460; Humphrey, Oral History Interview, Aug. 17, 1971, JL.

7. THE PRICE OF LEADERSHIP

1. Thurber, *Politics of Equality*, 88–89, 271n.3.
2. Ibid., 90–91.
3. Stern, "Presidential Strategies," 784–88; Kutler, "Eisenhower, Judiciary, and Desegregation," 88–90.
4. Thurber, *Politics of Equality*, 90; on Eastland and Russell, see *BDD*, May 18, 1954; Stern, "Presidential Strategies," 788.
5. Thurber, *Politics of Equality*, 92–93.
6. Ibid., 94–95; *CRS*, Aug. 2, 1955, 12883–84.
7. Humphrey, *Education*, 219–20.
8. Solberg, *Hubert Humphrey*, 231–32; Andreas contributed to many prominent Democrats and Republicans, including the presidential campaigns of Humphrey (1968 and 1972), Richard Nixon (1972), and Bill Clinton (1992 and 1996); for a summary of his extraordinary political ties, see *NYT*, Nov. 16, 2016.
9. Humphrey, *Education*, 133–34.
10. *CRS*, Mar. 11, June 22, July 7, 8, 1953, 1857–59, 7055, 8109–11, 8178–79.
11. *BDD*, May 24, 1954.
12. Amrine, *This Is Humphrey*, 223; Cochrane, "Public Law 480," 14–15.
13. Humphrey, *Education*, 120; Solberg, *Hubert Humphrey*, 165–66.
14. Cochrane, "Public Law 480," 16–18.
15. Amrine, *This Is Humphrey*, 224–31; Kennedy speech to Young Democrats in Racine, WI, Mar. 19, 1960, accessed at www.jfklibrary.org; Schlesinger, *Thousand Days*, 168–70.
16. McCauliffe, "Liberals and Communist Control Act," 354–55; the ISA referred only to "Communist-action" and "Communist-front" organizations; the new term, "Communist-infiltrated," lacked clear definition.
17. *CRS*, Aug. 12, 1954, 14208–9.
18. Ibid., 14210.
19. Ibid., 14233–34.
20. Ibid., Aug. 12, 14, 1954, 14522–23; McCauliffe, "Liberals and Communist Control Act," 358–60.
21. Kampelman, "Hubert Humphrey," 235; *CRS*, Aug. 17, 1954, 15105–6.
22. McCauliffe, "Liberals and Communist Control Act," 364–65; young George McGovern, then teaching history at Dakota Wesleyan University, recalled hearing a

senior professor say that Humphrey's support for the CCA revealed a basic character flaw that would keep him from the presidency; Solberg, *Hubert Humphrey*, 159.

23. "Communist Control Act," 712; *CRS*, Aug. 17, 1954, 14718.

24. Oshinsky, *Conspiracy*, 385–87, 502–6; McCauliffe, "Liberals and Communist Control Act," 361n.35, 366; Amrine, *This Is Humphrey*, 179; Griffith, *Humphrey*, 222. The CCA was used only twice: to keep the CP off the New Jersey ballot and to deny the CP the right to participate as an employer in New York State's unemployment compensation program; *Time*, Aug. 30, 1954.

25. *Time*, Feb. 21, 1955; Griffith, *Humphrey*, 222.

26. Hoopes, *Devil and Dulles*, 135–51, 161–62.

27. Zubok and Pleshakov, *Inside the Kremlin's Cold War*, 154–57. West Germany's population was more than twice that of the East; the Russians wanted direct negotiations between two sovereign German states; *NYT*, Apr. 17, 1953.

28. *CRS*, Apr. 17, 1953, 3239–40.

29. Ibid., June 22, July 28, 1953, 6767–68, 6990–91, 10107.

30. Ibid., June 23, 1953, 7055.

31. Ibid., July 7, 22, 1953, 8109–11, 9461–62.

32. Ibid., Jan. 23, 1954, 788–90; Bowie and Immerman, *Waging Peace*, 198–201.

33. Herring, *America's Longest War*, 33–42. On Kennedy, see Dallek, *Unfinished Life*, 186–87.

34. *CRS*, Mar. 31, 1954, 4210–11.

35. Ibid., Mar. 14, 1954, 5116–18.

36. Ambrose, *Nixon: Education*, 344–45; *CRS*, Apr. 19, 1954, 5290.

37. Costigliola, *France and the United States*, 108; Herring, *America's Longest War*, 45–51, 54–58.

38. *CRS*, Apr. 28, May 2, 1955, 5239, 5289–91; the October 1954 report is included in the Apr. 28, 1955, statement.

39. Ibid., Feb. 4, 1953, Apr. 19, 1954, 872–73, 5290.

40. Tucker, *Taiwan and United States*, 40. The United States violated the Geneva accords by extending the pact to Vietnam, Laos, and Cambodia.

41. Ibid., 41; *CRS*, Jan. 27, 28, 1955, 827–29, 929–38. The Cairo Declaration called for return of Formosa to the ROC, which administers the territory but is not sovereign over it; this could be achieved only by a treaty.

42. *CRS*, Jan. 28, 1955, 939–40.

43. Zhang, *Deterrence and Strategic Culture*, 213–14; Humphrey speech in *ACR*, Apr. 19, 1955, 4763–64.

44. On this episode, see Herring, *From Colony to Superpower*, 662–64. It is unclear whether Jiang thought that the United States would not follow through or perhaps knew that his forces could not stand against the PRC.

45. *CRS*, June 17, 1955, 8595–96, 8609–10.

46. On the Republican desire to defeat Humphrey, see *BDD*, Oct. 8, 1954. On Republican candidates, see Fleeson, "Fight Shaping up in Minnesota"; and *CRS*, Mar. 30, 1954, 4047. On Bjornson and Humphrey campaigning, see Crippen, "Thoughts of Bjornson."

47. *BDD*, Sept. 9, 28, Oct. 8, 1954; Eisele, *Almost to Presidency*, 100.

48. Eisele, *Almost to Presidency*, 102; *BDD*, Oct. 25, 1954.

49. *BDD*, Sept. 17, 29, 1954.

50. Ibid., Nov. 3, 5, 1954; "Welder."

51. Reichard, *Politics as Usual*, 113.

8. LIBERAL WITHOUT APOLOGY

1. CRS, Mar. 12, 1956, 4490–91. Schapsmeier and Schapsmeier, "Eisenhower and Agricultural Reform," 153, notes that between 1948 and 1973 the number of farms in the United States declined from 5.8 million to 2.8 million.

2. *CRS*, Mar. 6, 1956, 4025–51.

3. Schapsmeier and Schapsmeier, "Eisenhower and Agricultural Reform," 147–53; *NYT*, Jan. 19, 1956.

4. *NYT*, Mar. 21, 1956; *ACR*, Mar. 26, 1956, A2640.

5. *CRS*, May 23, 1956, 8786–93; *Time*, June 11, 1956.

6. Johnson to Humphrey, Aug. 3, 1956, Marvin Watson Files, box 24, JL.

7. Humphrey, *Education*, 136; Solberg, *Hubert Humphrey*, 172.

8. Keillor, *Hjalmar Peterson*, 248–49; Solberg, *Hubert Humphrey*, 173; Eisele, *Almost to Presidency*, 103.

9. *Time*, June 11, 18, 1956.

10. Humphrey, *Education*, 136; Solberg, *Hubert Humphrey*, 174; Kampelman, "Hubert Humphrey," 232.

11. Kampelman, "Hubert Humphrey," 232; Eisele, *Almost to Presidency*, 103–4; Solberg, *Hubert Humphrey*, 174–75.

12. Humphrey, *Education*, 137; Thurber, *Politics of Equality*, 99–100.

13. Woods, *LBJ*, 310; Caro, *Master of Senate*, 824.

14. Goodwin, *Fitzgeralds and Kennedys*, 782–83.

15. Johnson quoted in ibid., 783; Caro, *Master of Senate*, 826; Davis, *Prophet*, 478–80; Dallek, *Unfinished Life*, 206 (who notes that Kennedy thought that Stevenson's action was a way to avoid choosing him for vice president); Kampelman, "Hubert Humphrey," 238.

16. Humphrey, *Education*, 137; Solberg, *Hubert Humphrey*, 176.

17. Solberg, *Hubert Humphrey*, 176; Caro, *Master of Senate*, 826–27; Dallek, *Unfinished Life*, 207–8; Goodwin, *Fitzgeralds and Kennedys*, 784.

18. Amrine, *This Is Humphrey*, 185; Humphrey, *Education*, 137; Eisele, *Almost to Presidency*, 104; Martin, *Adlai Stevenson*, 356.

19. Johnson to Humphrey, Sept. 18, 1956, Watson Files, box 24, JL.

20. Gellman, *President and Apprentice*, 122–24; Greenstein, "Eisenhower as Activist," 594.

21. Davis, *Prophet*, 482–85; Martin, *Stevenson and World*, 357.

22. Solberg, *Hubert Humphrey*, 177; *Mansfield (OH) News-Journal*, Oct. 7, 1956.

23. Martin, *Stevenson and World*, 366–67. The Republicans falsely charged that Stevenson had called for an immediate end to the draft and a unilateral halt to US atomic testing.

24. Ibid., 375–76.

25. Pach and Richardson, *Eisenhower*, 126–27.

26. Ibid., 127–30, 132–35; Martin, *Stevenson and World*, 387–88.

27. Pach and Richardson, *Eisenhower*, 131–32, 136.

28. Ibid., 136; Martin, *Stevenson and World*, 392; Mann, *Walls of Jericho*, 236–37; Aquiar, "Congressional Experiences," 51; *Austin (MN) Daily Herald*, Nov. 5, 1958; *NYT*, Nov. 5, 6, 1958.

29. Eisele, *Almost to Presidency*, 104; Thurber, *Politics of Equality*, 101; *NYT*, Nov. 10, 1956.

30. Caro, *Master of Senate*, 840; Solberg, *Hubert Humphrey*, 17. In the House, McCarthy was the primary author of a liberal manifesto calling for expanded social welfare programs and civil rights legislation. Eight representatives from twenty-one northern states signed the document. Speaker Rayburn said he approved it but could not say so publicly. McCarthy gained prestige with liberals and lost no standing with Democratic leaders. Sandbrook, *Eugene McCarthy*, 577–78.

31. *CRS*, Jan. 9, 1957, 358–60.

32. Biles, *Crusading Liberal*, 117; Caro, *Master of Senate*, 859–60.

33. Thurber, *Politics of Equality*, 95, 101 (quoting Humphrey); Caro, *Master of the Senate*, 845–46. On the Southern Manifesto, see *CRS*, Mar. 12, 1956, 4459–60.

34. *CRS*, Jan. 9, 1957, 358; Pach and Richardson, *Eisenhower*, 145–47. Brownell was conservative on most matters but believed in civil rights. The bill he crafted was originally introduced in July 1956 but had no chance of passage in an election year and was buried in the Judiciary Committee, chaired by James Eastland of Mississippi. See *Time*, May 13, 1957.

35. Stern, "Lyndon Johnson and Richard Russell," 693; Thurber, *Politics of Equality*, 102; Nichols, *Matter of Justice*, 151–53. On Johnson's claim, see Caro, *Master of Senate*, 898–900. For its refutation, see Gellman, *President and Apprentice*, 379–82, 401; and Humphrey, Oral History Interview, June 20, 1977, JL.

36. Caro, *Master of Senate*, 916–18; Biles, *Crusading Liberal*, 121. Nichols, *Matter of Justice*, 156–58, also writes that Eisenhower's secretary, Ann Whitman, noted that he was "not at all unsympathetic to the position that people like Senator Russell take," and that, when challenged, he would say, "I have lived in the South, remember."

37. Humphrey to J. L. Markham, July 23, 1957, quoted in Thurber, *Politics of Equality*, 103; *CRS*, July 22, 30, 1957, 12304–13, 12989.

38. *CRS*, July 23, 1957, 12429–30.

39. Nichols, *Matter of Justice*, 159.

40. *CRS*, July 24, 1957, 12557–58; Biles, *Crusading Liberal*, 122; *NYT*, July 15, 1957.

41. Humphrey, Oral History Interview, Aug. 17, 1971, JL; *CRS*, July 30, 1957, 12989. The inability to get an all-white jury to convict a white southerner for a crime against an African American was most dramatically demonstrated in September 1955 when an all-white jury quickly acquitted two southerners who had brutally murdered fourteen-year-old Emmett Till, an African American from Chicago who was visiting in Mississippi and who was alleged to have whistled at or flirted with a white woman. Thurber, *Politics of Equality*, 95.

42. *CRS*, July 30, 1957, 12988.

43. Caro, *Master of Senate*, 950–51.

44. Mann, *Walls of Jericho*, 973–74.

45. Biles, *Crusading Liberal*, 124, notes Douglas's objection that a jury trial set the stage for voting registrars to ignore court orders and then be acquitted of criminal contempt. Nichols, *Matter of Justice*, 164; Caro, *Master of Senate*, 985–86.

46. *CRS*, Aug. 2, 7, 1957, 13472, 13850–54.

47. Caro, *Master of Senate*, 994–96.

48. *CRS*, Aug. 14, 1957, 14726.

49. Caro, *Master of Senate*, 998; Nichols, *Matter of Justice*, 163–67.

50. Winquist, "Civil Rights Act of 1957," 619–30; Caro, *Master of Senate*, 1001–4; Mann, "Mild Reforms."

51. *CRS*, Aug. 29, 1957, 16479; Mann, *Walls of Jericho*, 221–22.

52. Humphrey to Anton Thompson, Aug. 17, Humphrey to Eugenie Anderson, Aug. 14, and Stennis to Humphrey, Aug. 2, 1957, quoted in Solberg, *Hubert Humphrey*, 180. Humphrey on civil rights beginning is quoted in Thurber, *Politics of Equality*, 105.

53. Nichols, *Matter of Justice*, 169–75.

54. Gellman, *President and Apprentice*, 404; Nichols, *Matter of Justice*, 180–83; Pach and Richardson, *Eisenhower*, 149–50.

55. Thurber, *Politics of Equality*, 106; *NYT*, Sept. 16, 1957.

56. Nichols, *Matter of Justice*, 196; Mann, *Walls of Jericho*, 226–28.

57. Thurber, *Politics of Equality*, 106–7.

58. *CRS*, Jan. 31, 1958, 1418; Thurber, *Politics of Equality*, 107.

59. Mann, *Walls of Jericho*, 231–32; Biles, *Crusading Liberal*, 136–37.

60. Mann, *Walls of Jericho*, 231.

61. Ibid., 232–33.

62. Ibid., 234–35; Dallek, *Lone Star Rising*, 537–38.

63. Pach and Richardson, *Eisenhower*, 170–77.

64. Ibid., 180–82; *Austin (MN) Daily Herald*, Nov. 3, 1958.

65. Dallek, *Lone Star Rising*, 538.

66. Sandbrook, *Eugene McCarthy*, 82–87; Eisele, *Almost to Presidency*, 127–29; *Austin (MN) Daily Herald*, Nov. 5, 1958.

67. Mann, *Walls of Jericho*, 237–38.

68. Solberg, *Hubert Humphrey*, 197–98, 438; Tom Roeser, "Flashback: Thanks to Dwayne Andreas' Management of Hubert's Blind Trust, Hubert Becomes a Rich Man; Then Scandal, Mostly Posthumous," Mar. 31, 2008, Tom Roeser's Blog, http://tomroeser.blogspot.com/2008/03/flashback-thanks-to-dwayne-andreas.html; and website of New Beginnings Minnesota at Waverly (an alcohol and chemical dependency treatment center) at www.nbminnesota.com.

69. Roeser, "Flashback"; Solberg, *Hubert Humphrey*, 198.

9. CANDIDATE IN ORBIT, 1958–1960

1. Humphrey, "Government Organization for Arms Control," 967; statement of Jan. 4, 1958, *ACR*, Jan. 27, 1958, A655–56; "What Hope for Disarmament?" *NYT Magazine*, Jan. 5, 1958, *CRH*, Jan. 27, 1958, 139–41.

2. Pach and Richardson, *Eisenhower Presidency*, 170–73, 177–78; CRS, Apr. 12, 1957, 5622; Woodring, *Literature*, 53; the NDEA was signed into law on Sept. 2, 1958; CRS, Jan. 9, 16, 1958, 189, 594.

3. CRS, July 13, 1956, Jan. 13, 1957, 12649–50, 189.

4. Humphrey, "Government Organization for Arms Control," 967; statement of Jan. 4, 1958, in CRA, Jan. 27, 1958, A655–56; "What Hope for Disarmament?," *NYT Magazine*, Jan. 5, 1958, CRH, Jan. 27, 1958, 139–41.

5. CRS, Feb. 4, 1958, 1607–31.

6. Ibid., Apr. 1, 2, 14, 1958, 5897–901, 6074–77, 6304–7; see also Solberg, *Hubert Humphrey*, 187–88.

7. CRS, Aug. 22, 23, 1958, 19092–96, 19792–93; Solberg, *Hubert Humphrey*, 188; Pach and Richardson, *Eisenhower Presidency*, 206; William V. Shannon, "Going Strong," *New York Post*, Apr. 23, 1958, in CRA, May 6, 1958, A4184.

8. CRS, Feb. 16, 17, 21, 1957, 2673–78, 2808, 3036.

9. NYT, Jan. 6, 1957; Humphrey quoted in Little, *American Orientalism*, 132–33; CRS, Feb. 11, 1957, 1871–83.

10. NYT, Feb. 20, 21, 1957; CRS, Feb. 27, 1957, 2695–97. See also Pach and Richardson, *Eisenhower Presidency*, 161; Little, *American Orientalism*, 133; and Woods, *Fulbright*, 221–22.

11. CRS, Feb. 26, Apr. 15, 1957, 2604, 5713–14. Over the past decade the refugee population had grown to nine hundred thousand.

12. *U.S. News and World Report*, May 17, 1957; *Time*, June 10, 24, 1957. See also Humphrey, "Middle East and Southern Europe."

13. CRS, Feb. 20, June 8, 1957, 2423–36, 9598–99; see also ibid., Apr. 15, 1957, 5713–14.

14. Ibid., May 27, 1957, 7715. See also manuscript of newspaper article, not printed, intended for *New York Post*, HP, 150.A.13.2F.

15. *Time*, June 10, 24, 1957.

16. NYT, Dec. 14, 1958; *Time*, Dec. 22, 1958.

17. Harrison, *Driving the Soviets*, 99–105.

18. Pach and Richardson, *Eisenhower Presidency*, 202; Harrison, *Driving the Soviets*, 114; Solberg, *Hubert Humphrey*, 189; *Life*, Dec. 1, 1958.

19. *Time*, Nov. 24, Dec. 16, 1958; Solberg, *Hubert Humphrey*, 189–90; Humphrey, *Education*, 143; "Notes on Senator Humphrey's Trip—Nov. 1958—Trip to Moscow," and on Humphrey's *Izvestia* article, see Howland H. Sargeant to Humphrey, Feb. 4, 1959, HP, 150.A.13.3B; see also *Time*, Dec. 15, 1958.

20. Humphrey, "Marathon Talk," 81–82.

21. Martin, *Stevenson and World*, 430–36; Humphrey, *Education*, 145.

22. Amrine, *This Is Humphrey*, 189–91; Humphrey, *Education*, 144; Solberg, *Hubert Humphrey*, 191–92.

23. US Embassy to the State Department, Dec. 3, 1958 [dictated by Senator Humphrey], *FRUS*, 1958–1960, 8:148–52; Humphrey, *Education*, 145.

24. Humphrey, *Education*, 147–48; Solberg, *Hubert Humphrey*, 193–94; Humphrey used the bathroom break to tell an off-color joke (likely an apocryphal story) about former prime minister Clement Attlee complaining that Winston Churchill had opted to use a

urinal far from where he had stopped and Churchill retorting that the problem with socialists like Attlee was that whenever they saw something big that functioned well, they sought to nationalize it; Khrushchev laughed hard, made Humphrey repeat the story for Mikoyan, and said that he would send it to Russian ambassadors around the globe.

25. See note 23, above; Humphrey's more informal account is in "Notes on Senator Humphrey's Trip, 1958," HP, 150.A.13.3B; *Austin (MN) Daily Herald*, Dec. 2, 1958; *Time*, Dec. 15, 1958; *U.S. News and World Report*, Dec. 19, 1958.

26. Taubman, *Khrushchev*, 408; *Time*, Dec. 15, 22, 1958.

27. *Austin (MN) Daily Herald*, Dec. 9, 1958; *Time*, Dec. 15, 22, 1958; Amrine, *This Is Humphrey*, 196–97; Roscoe Drummond, "Humphrey Moving In," *Syracuse Herald-Journal*, Dec. 22, 1958, wrote that the senator gave five major speeches drawing fifteen thousand people; CRS, Feb. 6, 1959, 2025–26.

28. Amrine, *This Is Humphrey*, 196.

29. CRS, Mar. 19, Apr. 13, 1959, 4611, 5739–41.

30. *Minneapolis Tribune*, Dec. 14, 1958; NYT, Dec. 14, 1958; Humphrey, *Education*, 148; *Time*, Dec. 22, 1958; Drummond, "Humphrey Moving In"; Baker article, NYT, Jan. 11, 1959; Muriel Humphrey quoted in Solberg, *Hubert Humphrey*, 195.

31. Humphrey, *Education*, 149, 360nn.1,2; Solberg, *Hubert Humphrey*, 201; Humphrey's staff in Washington included former legislative aide Max Kampelman, ADA founder Joseph Rauh Jr., and Robert Barrie, a Minnesotan and former aide to Senator Harrison Williams of New Jersey; Humphrey to Eugenie Anderson, Jan. 26, 1959, HP, 150.D.5.8H; *Time*, Mar. 2, 1959. The senator also hired an assistant for LaFever, Allard Lowenstein, a young former aide to University of North Carolina president Frank Graham; Lowenstein quit after a few months to pursue other interests in Africa; Chafe, *Never Stop Running*, 132–33.

32. Eisele, *Almost to Presidency*, 140.

33. Anderson to Humphrey, May 28, 1959, HP, 150.D.5.8H; *Time*, July 27, 1959.

34. Eisele, *Almost to Presidency*, 137–38, 140; Humphrey to Eugenie Anderson, Nov. 11, 1959, HP, 150.D.5.8F.

35. Eugenie Anderson Memorandum on Report on Trip to New York to See Mrs. Roosevelt, Oct. 15, 17, 1959; Anderson Memorandum, Nov. 17, 1959; Walter Butler Memo for Humphrey, Oct. 29, 1959; and Humphrey to Eugenie Anderson, Nov. 11, 1959, HP, 150.D.5.8F.

36. Humphrey to J. L. Markham, Sept. 9, 1959, HP, 150.D.5.8H; Solberg, *Hubert Humphrey*, 204.

37. Humphrey to Anderson, Nov. 11, 1959; Jim Loeb Memorandum, Apr. [?], 1959, HP, 150.D.6.9B (quotes Nelson); and Joseph Glazer (United Rubber Workers) to Congressman Joseph Karth, Joseph L. Rauh Jr., et al., Oct. 13, 1959, HP, 150.D.5.8H; Dallek, *Unfinished Life*, 247.

38. Eisele, *Almost to Presidency*, 141–42.

39. Solberg, *Hubert Humphrey*, 203; NYT, Dec. 31, 1959; Eisele, *Almost to Presidency*, 142.

40. Dallek, *An Unfinished Life*, 225.

41. Ibid., 249; Solberg, *Hubert Humphrey*, 201; *Charleston (WV) Daily Mail*, Mar. 4, 1960, on Rowe-Rauh divide.

42. *Appleton (WI) Post-Crescent*, Apr. 1, 1960; *Morgantown (WV) Post*, Apr. 4, 1960; Solberg, *Hubert Humphrey*, 204, 207.

43. *Time*, Apr. 18, 1960; Solberg, *Hubert Humphrey*, 206; Max Kampelman to James Rowe (enclosing election vote analysis from Richard Scammon), Apr. 16, 1960, HP, 150.D.6.H10.

44. *Sheboygan (WI) Press*, Apr. 6, 1960; Dallek, *Unfinished Life*, 251.

45. Schlesinger Jr., *Thousand Days*, 22; Eisele, *Almost to Presidency*, 144; Solberg, *Hubert Humphrey*, 208; Humphrey, *Education*, 152.

46. Solberg, *Hubert Humphrey*, 208; Harry W. Ernst to William Connell et al. [n.d.], 1960, HP, 150.D.5.8H.

47. Evans and Novak, *Lyndon Johnson*, 259; Caro, *Master of the Senate*, 85; *Time*, Apr. 25, 1960.

48. Humphrey Remarks in Huntington, West Virginia, Mar. 23, 1960, HP, 150.D.5.8H; Humphrey Press Release, Apr. 26, 1960, and Kirkpatrick to Kampelman, Apr. 14, 1960, HP, 150.D.6.9B.

49. NYT, Apr. 22, 1960; *Time*, May 2, 1960.

50. Dallek, *Unfinished Life*, 253.

51. *Appleton (WI) Post-Crescent*, Apr. 1, 19, 1960; on charge of FDR Jr., *Charleston (WV) Daily Mail*, May 5, 1960; *Sunday Gazette-Mail* (Charleston, WV), May 8, 1960; Doris Fleeson, "Kennedy Collects Dividends," *Charleston (WV) Gazette*, May 14, 1960; on veteran issue, *Charleston (WV) Daily Mail*, May 2, 1960; see also Caro, *Master of the Senate*, 85; on "pummeling" Humphrey, Arthur Edson, "Wisconsin Was Never Like W.Va.," *Charleston (WV) Daily Mail*, May 3, 1960.

52. *Charleston (WV) Gazette*, May 7, 1960; NYT, May 7, 1960; *Sunday Gazette-Mail* (Charleston, WV), May 8, 1960; *Charleston (WV) Gazette*, May 9, 1960. On the religious issue, see Humphrey to Chalmers Roberts, Apr. 18, 1960, HP, 150.D.6.9B.

53. *Charleston (WV) Daily Mail*, May 5, 1960, includes a full text of the debate; Dallek, *Lone Star Rising*, 567.

54. On the slating system, see David Ginsburg to Humphrey et al., Mar. 15, 1960, HP, 150.D.6.9B; Solberg, *Hubert Humphrey*, 158; Humphrey, *Education*, 157–58.

55. *Time*, May 23, 1960; Humphrey, *Education*, 158; Humphrey to Elmo Roper, May 31, 1960, HP, 150.D.6.9B; *Charleston (WV) Gazette*, May 27, June 4, 13, 14, 1960; reporting requirements did not include a candidate's personal expenditures (or use of the *Caroline*) or reimbursements for expenses (payments) to hundreds, perhaps thousands, of "volunteers"; see also Solberg, *Hubert Humphrey*, 211; and Dallek, *Unfinished Life*, 257–58.

56. *Weirton (WV) Daily Times*, May 4, 1960. On the labor issue, see Victor Riesel, "Humphrey and Friends," *Oakland Tribune*, May 6, 1960. On Byrd, see *Beckley (WV) Post-Herald*, Apr. 12, 1960, and *Morgantown (WV) Post*, June 3, 1960. *Time*, May 23, 1960.

57. *Charleston (WV) Gazette*, May 11, 14, 1960.

58. Ibid., May 11, 1960; Eisele, *Almost to Presidency*, 146; Solberg, *Hubert Humphrey*, 212.

59. Humphrey quoted in Eisele, *Almost to Presidency*, 147. FDR Jr. later said he had made the "biggest political mistake" of his life; see Caro, *Master of the Senate*, 86.

10. THE INSIDER AS OUTSIDER

1. *Time*, July 4, 1960; Solberg, *Hubert Humphrey*, 213.
2. Eisele, *Almost to Presidency*, 151; Solberg, *Hubert Humphrey*, 212–13; NYT, June 28, 29, 1960; Orville H. Freeman diary, July 11–15, 1960, box 14, FP (hereinafter cited as Freeman diary); see also Woods, *LBJ*, 357.
3. Johnson, *National Party Platforms*, 574–600.
4. Humphrey quoted in Thurber, *Politics of Equality*, 110; *Time*, July 25, 1960.
5. Pearson, "Humphrey Delegates Vital"; Pearson, "Freeman Is Too Young"; Eisele, *Almost to Presidency*, 151–52; Sandbrook, *Eugene McCarthy*, 103–4.
6. Woods, *LBJ*, 355–58; Dallek, *Unfinished Life*, 261–62.
7. Eisele, *Almost to Presidency*, 152; Sandbrook, *Eugene McCarthy*, 101–2; see also Pearson, "Humphrey Delegates Vital."
8. Freeman diary, July 11–15, 1960, FP; Eisele, *Almost to Presidency*, 152.
9. Freeman diary, July 11–15, 1960, FP; Humphrey, *Education*, 170–71; Johnson and Kennedy also debated each other before combined Texas and Massachusetts delegations, with Johnson accusing Kennedy of poor Senate attendance and Kennedy replying that Johnson's mastery of the majority leader's role meant that he should stay in that job; see Woods, *LBJ*, 359.
10. Freeman diary, July 11–15, 1960, FP; Sandbrook, *Eugene McCarthy*, 101–3; McCarthy had already spoken twice publicly for Stevenson, although Oklahoma Senator Robert Kerr had declared that the Minnesotan supported Johnson, a statement McCarthy said had not been cleared with him, Eisele, *Almost to Presidency*, 153; Eleanor Roosevelt and former Senator Herbert Lehman had asked Humphrey to nominate Stevenson, Humphrey, *Education*, 170.
11. NYT, July 14, 1960.
12. Ibid.; NYT, July 14, 1960; Sandbrook, *Eugene McCarthy*, 104–6; Martin, *Stevenson and World*, 527–28; *Berkshire Eagle*, July 14, 1960; Pearson, "Freeman Is Too Young."
13. Woods, *LBJ*, 360–62; Dallek, *Unfinished Life*, 269–72.
14. Eisele, *Almost to Presidency*, 156; *Troy (NY) Record*, July 16, 1960; Woods, *LBJ*, 364; Dallek, *Unfinished Life*, 273–74.
15. Humphrey, Oral History Interview, Aug. 17, 1971, JL; Eisele, *Almost to Presidency*, 156.
16. Stevenson to Humphrey, Aug. 10, 1960, and Humphrey to Stevenson, Aug. 19, 1960, HP, 150.D.15.2F.
17. Ambrose, *Nixon: Education*, 553–54; Johnson, *National Party Platforms*, 604–20.
18. BDD, Oct. 26, 1960; *Fergus Falls (MN) Daily Journal*, June 18, 1959.
19. BDD, Oct. 1, 2, 1960; Thurber, *Politics of Equality*, 111.
20. BDD, Oct. 26, 31, 1960.
21. Dallek, *Unfinished Life*, 283–84.
22. Ibid., 285; Thomas, *Being Nixon*, 114–15.
23. Branch, *Parting the Waters*, 350–71, esp. 361–67; Dallek, *Unfinished Life*, 293; Meriwether, " 'Worth a Lot of Negro Votes,' " 737–63, says that it was not the King episode but Kennedy's Algeria speech, frequent mention of Africa, and funding of

Kenyan students to study in the United States in 1960 that helped him gain 68 percent of the African American vote.

24. Ambrose, *Nixon: Education*, 590–96.

25. Woods, *LBJ*, 375; Dallek, *Unfinished Life*, 295–96.

26. *BDD*, Nov. 9, 22, 1960; Gillon, *Democrats' Dilemma*, 24–25, 54–55; Governor Freeman had appointed Mondale to that post months earlier when the incumbent, Miles Lord, retired.

27. Humphrey, *Education*, 173; *Fraser in Focus: A Newsletter for Friends of Fraser* (Winter 2006), 1; the Fraser School in Minneapolis focuses on children and adults with special needs, and is where Vicky Solomonson was enrolled; Muriel Buck Humphrey (she remarried in 1981 to Max Brown, an old schoolmate from Huron, SD) received the school's Whitbeck Fraser Award for enhancing the lives of people with special needs in 2006; on Muriel Humphrey's remarriage, see *People*, Feb. 16, 1981.

28. Humphrey, *Education*, 181; Solberg, *Hubert Humphrey*, 215.

29. Caro, *Master of Senate*, 1036–40; Woods, *LBJ*, 376–77; Humphrey, Oral History Interview, August 1971, JL; Humphrey, *Education*, 179; see also *Time*, Feb. 23, 1962.

30. *CRS*, Jan. 9, 1961, 377–78; *Time*, Jan. 13, 1961; Humphrey proposed to finance health insurance by slightly raising the taxable Social Security wage base from $3,800 to $4,000; this was not "socialized medicine," as some critics charged, he said, but "pre-payment" for health insurance and a way to minimize need for unpaid charity, see *CRS*, Sept. 19, 1961, 20223–24.

31. *NYT*, Jan. 21, 1961.

32. Schlesinger, *Thousand Days*, 127–45.

33. Humphrey, *Education*, 175, 181–82, 184; Solberg, *Hubert Humphrey*, 215–16.

34. Dallek, *Unfinished Life*, 380–83.

35. *CRS*, Mar. 18, 1961, 3476–77.

36. Ibid., June 15, 1960, 12635–38.

37. Ibid., Mar. 2, Apr. 12, June 1, Aug. 23, 1961, Sept. 28, 1962, Mar. 2, 1964, 3056–58, 5605–7, 9287–89, 9292–300, 16818–29, 21258–61, 3982–83; *NYT*, Apr. 2, 2009, and May 21, 2011; Hoffman, *All You Need Is Love*, 257, holds that the Peace Corps' primary contribution to nation building was to the United States, "by confirming its values and sense of mission as the world's first democratic country."

38. Humphrey, "What Hope for Disarmament?"

39. Clarke, *Politics of Arms Control*, 18, 20; Humphrey, *Education*, 186–87; Solberg, *Hubert Humphrey*, 217.

40. *CRS*, Aug. 29, 31, Sept. 5, 8, 1961, 17346, 17649, 18121–27, 18806–7.

41. Humphrey's denouncing of Soviet suspension of atomic testing, ibid., Sept. 16, 1961, 19889–90; Clarke, *Politics of Arms Control*, 19; *NYT*, Sept. 27, 1961; McDougall, *Heavens and Earth*, 324; on Goetz, see Solberg, *Hubert Humphrey*, 217.

42. Tom Wicker, *JFK and LBJ*, 54–82, 100–117.

43. Bernstein, *Promises Kept*, 229–34; Wicker, *JFK and LBJ*, 117–48; Humphrey views in *BDD*, Mar. 31, 1961.

44. *BDD*, Apr. 13, 1961; Dallek, *Unfinished Life*, 393.

45. Higgins, *Perfect Failure*.
46. *BDD*, Apr. 24, July 24, 1961; Humphrey to Anton Watson, May 1, 1961, quoted in Solberg, *Hubert Humphrey*, 218; *New York Herald Tribune*, May 14, 1961.
47. Reynolds, *Summits*, 207–10.
48. *CRS*, June 8, 1961, 9837; *BDD*, July 5, 15, 18, 26, 1961; Humphrey also said that Kennedy should seek a tax increase to pay for military expenditures; *Austin (MN) Daily Herald*, July 25, 1961.
49. Reynolds, *Summits*, 214–15; Harrison, *Driving the Soviets*, 206–7.
50. Harrison, *Driving the Soviets*, 207.
51. *Fergus Falls (MN) Daily Journal*, Aug. 17, 1961; *CRS*, Sept. 23, 1961, 19801–2.
52. Harrison, *Driving the Soviets*, 210–17.
53. *Rhein-Zeitung*, Oct. 5, 1961.
54. William Connell Memorandum, Sept. 28, 1961, HP, 150.A.13.6F.
55. Transcript of Press Conference, Oct. 9, 1961, HP, 150.A.13.6F.
56. *Le Soir* (Brussels), Oct. 14, 1961; Memorandum from Senator Hubert Humphrey, Oct. 16, 1961, HP, 150.A.13.6F.
57. Humphrey Memorandum for Kennedy, Oct. 23, 1961, HP, 150.A.13.6F.
58. "Germany and the West," "The Emergence of the New Europe," and "The Berlin Crisis," articles for North American Newspaper Alliance, HP, 150.A.13.6F.
59. Memorandum to Bill (William Connell), Dec. 26, 1961, HP, 150.A.13.7B.
60. Ibid.
61. Press Release for Hubert Humphrey, Dec. 5, 1961, Press Release, "Humphrey Suggests Common Market for Western Hemisphere," Dec. 6, 1961, and Press Release, "Humphrey Urges Liberal New Deal for Latin America," Dec. 7, 1961, HP, 150.A.13.7B; *Minneapolis Tribune*, Dec. 6, 1961; the Alliance for Progress, a Kennedy administration initiative, was signed at Punta del Este, Uruguay, in August 1961 and intended to advance Latin America economically through major US and Latin American investment and land reform; success was limited, however, because such countries as Argentina, Brazil, and Mexico did not want to submit their development plans to foreign scrutiny, political and military elites resisted reforms, US firms took more in profits and dividends than they invested there, and 70 percent of the US commitment of $18 billion was in loans rather than grants; see Herring, *Colony to Superpower*, 716–19.

11. TRAGEDY AND TRIUMPH

1. *Daily Plainsman* (Huron, SD), Oct. 17, 1962; Dallek, *Unfinished Life*, 577–78.
2. Dallek, *Unfinished Life*, 538–40; Beschloss, *Crisis Years*, 413–14; on the Jupiter missiles, made operational in 1961–62, see Nash, *Other Missiles of October*, 79, 103.
3. Humphrey quoted on Republicans in Paterson and Brophy, "October Missiles," 96; *CRS*, Sept. 11, 14, 1962, 19073, 19552–55; *NYT*, Sept. 30, 1962.
4. Reports of Humphrey's briefing appeared in numerous nationally syndicated columns, including Pearson, "Humphrey Stomps Out of Briefing," and Allen and Scott, "It's Off to Work We Go, Again!"; Humphrey comments on US power in Turkey,

Daily Plainsman (Huron, SD), Oct. 17, 1962; Senator Keating was the leading critic about alleged Soviet missiles in Cuba, but his source was never revealed; see Paterson and Brophy, "October Missiles," 98n.25.

5. Stern, *Averting "Final Failure,"* 30–34, 80–81, 86, 135, 169; Paterson and Brophy, "October Missiles," 98n.25.

6. Stern, *Averting "Final Failure,"* 159–73; Kennedy's "gamble" statement, p. 167, was made in response to Senator Richard Russell's call for an invasion.

7. Stern, *Averting "Final Failure,"* 74; Humphrey, *Education*, 184; *NYT*, Jan. 23, 1962.

8. *Press Telegram* (Long Beach, CA), Oct. 24, 1962.

9. Beschloss, *Crisis Years*, 516–27; Stern, *Averting "Final Failure,"* 289; Freedman, *Kennedy's Wars*, 207–9.

10. Stern, *Averting "Final Failure,"* 310–72; on Kennedy's letter, Freedman, *Kennedy's Wars*, 214–15.

11. The report of the Kennedy-Dobrynin meeting, based on the ambassador's cable to Moscow, is in LeBow and Stein, *We All Lost the Cold War*, 523–26; Dobrynin also reported Robert Kennedy was exhausted and not his usual argumentative self; ironically, he did not favor the Turkish missile swap.

12. Taubman, *Khrushchev*, 572–76; Khrushchev did send a letter through Dobrynin to Robert Kennedy seeking the president's acknowledgment of the missile swap, but this was refused; see Beschloss, *Crisis Years*, 546–47.

13. *Fergus Falls (MN) Daily*, Nov. 1, 1962. On Khrushchev and Cuba, see Taubman, *Khrushchev*, 541–46. The United States also completely underestimated Soviet troops and weaponry in Cuba; see Dobbs, *One Minute to Midnight*.

14. Paterson and Brophy, "October Missiles," 112–15; see also *Daily Plainsman* (Huron, SD), Oct. 17, 1962; Watson, *George McGovern*, 52–54.

15. CRS, Mar. 12, Apr. 19, 27, 1962, 4853–60, 7040–48, 17804–5.

16. Humphrey quoted in *Evening Tribune* (Albert Lea, MN), Feb. 26, 1963; Freedman, *Kennedy's Wars*, 263–64.

17. *Evening Tribune* (Albert Lea, MN), May 27, 1963; Marquis Childs' column, *WDN*, July 7, 1963; Freedman, *Kennedy's Wars*, 266–67.

18. CRS, June 28, 1963, 1201–15; see also *WDN*, June 6, 1963.

19. Freedman, *Kennedy's Wars*, 269. Dallek, *Unfinished Life*, 625, who notes Kennedy's error in having said, "Ich bin ein Berliner" ("ein Berliner" being colloquial for a jelly donut), rather than "Ich bin Berliner."

20. Freedman, *Kennedy's Wars*, 273–74; CRS, Aug. 8, 1963, 14538–39.

21. *Sunday Tribune* (Albert Lea, MN), Aug. 18, 1963; *BDD*, Sept. 6, 1963.

22. Freedman, *Kennedy's Wars*, 275; Humphrey, *Education*, 187.

23. *WDN*, Nov. 27, 1963; *Fergus Falls (MN) Daily Journal*, Nov. 27, 1963; *NYT*, Jan. 31, 1964.

24. Bryant, *Bystander*, 29, 172, 192–93, 227–28, 230, 314, 473.

25. Branch, *Parting the Waters*, 412–90; Thurber, *Politics of Equality*, 114.

26. Thurber, *Politics of Equality*, 114–15.

27. Ibid.; Bryant, *Bystander*, 332–53; Barnett's cynical goal was to be compelled to give way to federal force so as to appear politically correct to his constituents.

28. Thurber, *Politics of Equality*, 116; Bryant, *Bystander*, 366. Johnson, as Senate president, might have ruled on the issue based on the Constitution's allowing each house of Congress to set its own rules at the start of a new term.
29. Dallek, *Unfinished Life*, 589–90; Biles, *Crusading Liberal*, 157; Bryant, *Bystander*, 370–71.
30. Sitkoff, *King*, 94–102; Humphrey quoted in Thurber, *Politics of Equality*, 117.
31. Dallek, *Unfinished Life*, 396–97. Bryant, *Bystander*, 386–89, says that Kennedy, speaking to an ADA group, did not say, as historian Arthur Schlesinger claimed, that the picture of a dog attacking a youngster made him "sick," but called the picture "terrible" and Birmingham "the worst city in the South."
32. Thurber, *Politics of Equality*, 117–18.
33. Dallek, *Unfinished Life*, 604.
34. CRS, June 19, 1963, 11096, 11166–72.
35. Ibid., June 26, July 24, 1963, 11743, 13242–49; Thurber, *Politics of Equality*, 119–21.
36. CRS, July 9, Aug. 2, 27, 1963, 12275–76, 14040–44, 15917–18; Branch, *Parting the Waters*, 839–41.
37. CRS, Aug. 28, 1963, 16114–16. Humphrey's statement that he had been for the march ignored his early opposition; Kennedy invited King to the White House after the speech but declined a "crusade" for civil rights; Branch, *Parting the Waters*, 883–87.
38. Bryant, *Bystander*, 439–42; Dallek, *Unfinished Life*, 647–49.
39. CRS, Sept. 17, 1963, 17204–8.
40. Dallek, *Unfinished Life*, 649–51.
41. Humphrey, *Education*, 192; Woods, *LBJ*, 415; Secretary of State Dean Rusk, Agriculture Secretary Orville Freeman, and Commerce Secretary Luther Hodges were in a plane en route to Japan when word of Kennedy's death came; they immediately headed back to Washington; Freeman diary, Nov. 21, 23, 1963, box 14, FP.
42. Humphrey, *Education*, 191–92.
43. Ibid., 196–97.
44. *NYT*, Nov. 28, 1963.
45. Woods, *LBJ*, 472; Zelizer, *Fierce Urgency of Now*, 98–101; Zelizer notes that Smith may have underestimated the strength of the movement for gender equality, although even some liberals opposed including "sex" because they feared that this would cause others less committed to civil rights to oppose the bill.
46. *NYT*, Jan. 31, Mar. 9, 1964.
47. CRS, Mar. 12, 1964, 5059 ("generalissimo"); Humphrey, Oral History Interview, June 21, 1977, JL.
48. Woods, *LBJ*, 474; Dallek, *Flawed Giant*, 119; Humphrey, *Education*, 205.
49. *NYT*, Feb. 19, Mar. 22, Apr. 5, 1964; Humphrey, *Education*, 206–9; Zelizer, *Fierce Urgency of Now*, 110–11; on newsletters, CRS, Mar. 12, 1964, 5042–45; on the wheat-cotton bill, Thurber, *Politics of Equality*, 286n.6.
50. On the Robertson episode, Bernstein, *Guns or Butter*, 65; Humphrey, Oral History Interview III; *NYT*, Mar. 9, 1964; see also Thurber, *Politics of Equality*, 130.
51. CRS, Feb. 26, Mar. 9, 12, 1964, 3759–64, 4756–57, 5062–63. Humphrey's statement echoed his 1948 Democratic convention speech the United States was "172 years late" in dealing with civil rights.

52. *NYT*, Mar. 15, 21, 31, 1964.

53. Humphrey's speech in *CRS*, Mar. 30, 1964, 6528–53; see also *NYT*, Mar. 31, 1964.

54. Specific references in *CRS*, Mar. 30, 1964, 6532, 6542.

55. *CRS*, Apr. 9, 1964, 7420. When Thurmond said he knew many lawyers who had the same opinion he did, Humphrey asked if they were lawyers "of repute"; Thurber, *Politics of Equality*, 131.

56. Mann, *Walls of Jericho*, 412.

57. *NYT*, Apr. 15, 16, 1964.

58. Miles, "Art of the Possible," 102; *NYT*, Apr. 24, 25, 27, 1964. The 1957 Civil Rights Act provided for jury trials for criminal contempt cases only with regard to voting rights.

59. *NYT*, May 1, 12, 1964; Thurber, *Politics of Equality*, 139. As the newspapers reported, a contrite but smiling Humphrey stood before the senators and press and tugged on his ears, much the way Johnson was known to handle his beagles.

60. *NYT*, May 7, 12, 1964; Dan Carter, *Politics of Rage*, 210–12.

61. Thurber, *Politics of Equality*, 141. The law prohibited the EEOC from filing a suit; some twenty states had already adopted public accommodations and fair employment laws; Miles, "Art of the Possible," 1–3.

62. *NYT*, May 14, 1964; Dirksen Congressional Center, Civil Rights Act of 1964, accessed at http://www.congresslink.org.

63. *NYT*, May 15, 1964.

64. *CRS*, May 20, 25, June 4, 1965, 11486, 11846, 12702–18 (explication of the bill).

65. Mann, *Walls of Jericho*, 422, explains Dirksen's overly liberal "paraphrase" of Hugo's words taken from his *Histoire d'un crime*. Congressman Robert Michel, who represented Dirksen's former north-central district in Illinois, put the senator's report to his constituents into the *CRH*, May 27, 1964, accessed at http://www.congresslink.org. For Humphrey's use of Hugo, see *CRS*, Aug. 2, 7, 1957, 13472, 13850–54. On Wallace, see Carter, *Politics of Rage*, 210–12.

66. Mann, *Walls of Jericho*, 423–24; Thurber, *Politics of Equality*, 143. The Republican senators were Roman Hruska and Carl Curtis of Nebraska, Karl Mundt of South Dakota, and Norris Cotton of New Hampshire. Senator Morton said voting rights, once denied in an election, could not be replaced; hence he left the case to be expedited by a judge's decision. His amendment increased the maximum fine from $300 to $1,000 and the time in jail from thirty days to six months. The Morton amendment replaced the Mansfield-Dirksen amendment, which gave the judge the discretion to determine whether there would be a jury trial.

67. *NYT*, June 11, 1964; Mann, *Walls of Jericho*, 423–25; Bernstein, *Guns or Butter*, 75–76. Twenty of the twenty-three Democrats came from the South; the six Republicans included the leading conservative and soon-to-be presidential nominee Barry Goldwater.

68. *NYT*, June 11, 1964; Bernstein, *Guns or Butter*, 76.

69. *NYT*, June 11, 18, 1964; Thurber, *Politics of Equality*, 144–45.

70. Humphrey, *Education*, 211–12, 366n.13.

71. *NYT*, June 20, 1964; *CRS*, June 19, 1964, 14443–44.

72. *NYT*, June 20, 1964; Humphrey, *Education*, 211; Thurber, *Politics of Equality*, 146.

73. Thurber, *Politics of Equality*, 146.
74. NYT, June 24, 1964. The text of Humphrey's speech read, "Today we are fortunate in having a man in the White House who does not float on a cloud somewhere above the battle but plunges right into the struggle," but in speaking he said "men in Congress" rather than "man in the White House."
75. NYT, July 3, 1964; Dallek, *Flawed Giant*, 120.
76. Humphrey to Virgil P. Lacy, Aug. 18, 1964, letter in author's possession.

12. THE BEST MAN IN AMERICA

1. Eisele, *Almost to Presidency*, 198; Solberg, *Hubert Humphrey*, 240.
2. Van Dyk, *Heroes, Hacks, and Fools*, 26–27; Eisele, *Almost to Presidency*, 198.
3. Mann, *Walls of Jericho*, 435; Dallek, *Flawed Giant*, 136–37; see also Donaldson, *Liberalism's Last Hurrah*, 187–88.
4. Eisele, *Almost to Presidency*, 202; WDN, June 29, 1964; Lady Bird comments in Beschloss, *Taking Charge*, 443.
5. Humphrey, *Cause Is Mankind*, esp. pp. 47–60; Humphrey, *War on Poverty*. The former was an adaptation of prior speeches and articles, the latter largely the product of his staff. See also Solberg, *Hubert Humphrey*, 260–61.
6. Stone, "Everybody's Guide to Liberalism"; Eisele, *Almost to Presidency*, 198; Solberg, *Hubert Humphrey*, 240.
7. Solberg, *Hubert Humphrey*, 242; Van Dyk, *Heroes, Hacks, Fools*, 29, says he sent daily reports to Rowe, who forwarded them to Johnson. On McCarthy, see Sandbrook, *Eugene McCarthy*, 113–15.
8. Eisele, *Almost to Presidency*, 204–7.
9. On Kennedy's views, see diary entry for Dec. 13, 1963, Schlesinger, *Journals*, 214–15; Beschloss, *Taking Charge*, 388n.3.
10. Caro, *Passage of Power*, 374–75; entry for Nov. 23, 1963, Orville H. Freeman Diary, Nov. 23, 1963, box 14, FP (hereinafter cited as Freeman diary); Seshol, *Mutual Contempt*, 178–79; Woods, *LBJ*, 529. On Johnson taking Kennedy, see Beschloss, *Taking Charge*, 388.
11. Johnson's comment in Schlesinger, *Journals*, Aug. 29, 1964, 213.
12. Solberg, *Hubert Humphrey*, 242–43; Mann, *Walls of Jericho*, 434.
13. Thomas, *Robert Kennedy*, 290–92; NYT, Mar. 11, 12, Apr. 5, 30, 1964.
14. Thomas, *Robert Kennedy*, 295; Beschloss, *Taking Charge*, 405–6, 463–64, 466–69, 476–78; Dallek, *Flawed Giant*, 139–40; Eisele, *Almost to Presidency*, 205–6.
15. Seshol, *Mutual Contempt*, 207–9; Dallek, *Flawed Giant*, 141.
16. Martin, *Stevenson and the World*, 807, 816; Goldman, *Tragedy of Lyndon Johnson*, 200; Eisele, *Almost to Presidency*, 205.
17. Beschloss, *Taking Charge*, 484–86.
18. Eisele, *Almost to Presidency*, 203.
19. NYT, July 31, 1964 (Humphrey led Kennedy in the poll by 341 to 230 votes); Solberg, *Hubert Humphrey*, 243–44; Eisele, *Almost to Presidency*, 203.
20. Eisele, *Almost to Presidency*, 197; NYT, Aug. 4, 7, 1964.

21. Solberg, *Hubert Humphrey*, 246; Goldman, *Tragedy of Johnson*, 202.

22. Eisele, "Gerald Heaney"; the original version of this story, without naming Heaney, is in Eisele, *Almost to Presidency*, 208–9.

23. Sitkoff, *Struggle for Black Equality*, 161–63. The murder, abetted by Mississippi lawmen, of James Chaney, a black resident of the state, and Andrew Goodman and Michael Schwerner of New York, incited national outrage and spurred passage of the 1965 Voting Rights Act.

24. Sitkoff, *King*, 138; Thurber, *Politics of Equality*; Woods, *LBJ*, 524.

25. Beschloss, *Taking Charge*, 510–11; Thurber, *Politics of Equality*, 152.

26. Beschloss, *Taking Charge*, 515–16.

27. Ibid., 517.

28. Ibid., 520–21.

29. Thurber, *Politics of Equality*, 153.

30. Humphrey to Anderson, Aug. 22, 1964, quoted in Thurber, *Politics of Equality*, 154.

31. Ibid., 154.

32. Ibid., 154–55.

33. Beschloss, *Taking Charge*, 526–27; Thurber, *Politics of Equality*, 155.

34. Thurber, *Politics of Equality*, 156; Gillon, *Democrats' Dilemma*, 72–73; Freeman diary, Aug. 30, 1954.

35. Beschloss, *Taking Charge*, 524–25.

36. Thurber, *Politics of Equality*, 156–57.

37. Ibid., 157.

38. Solberg, *Hubert Humphrey*, 245–46.

39. Thurber, *Politics of Equality*, 158.

40. Beschloss, *Taking Charge*, 527–32.

41. Ibid., 534n.1; Johnson was also upset about unflattering news articles portraying his political style and accumulation of wealth; see Woods, *LBJ*, 536–37.

42. James Reston, *NYT*, Sept. 7, 1964.

43. *NYT*, Aug. 24, 1964; Eisele, *Almost to President*, 210–11.

44. Beschloss, *Taking Charge*, 522.

45. Ibid., 536; Solberg, *Hubert Humphrey*, 253–54.

46. Solberg, *Hubert Humphrey*, 254.

47. Beschloss, *Taking Charge*, 537; Humphrey, *Education*, 223.

48. McCarthy to Johnson, Aug. 26, 1964, box 25, JP; Sandbrook, *Eugene McCarthy*, 116; Eisele, *Almost to Presidency*, 216–17.

49. Beschloss, *Taking Charge*, 539; Humphrey, *Education*, 223; Solberg, *Hubert Humphrey*, 254; *NYT*, Aug. 27, 1964.

50. Beschloss, *Taking Charge*, 540–41; Humphrey, *Education*, 225–26; Johnson quoted in Dallek, *Flawed Giant*, 159.

51. Dodd comment in *Daily Messenger* (Canandaigua, NY), Aug. 27, 1964; *Fergus Falls (MN) Daily*, and *Galveston Daily News*, Aug. 27, 1964. Humphrey, *Education*, 226, notes incorrectly that the news flash said that Johnson was going to nominate Humphrey, but the president did not announce this until he spoke to the convention, although everyone knew what was about to occur.

52. Mondale quoted in Freeman diary, Aug. 30, 1964, FP. Freeman worried about Johnson's "all-pervading control" that he found "almost revolting"; Humphrey, *Education*, 227.

53. McCarthy speeches in "Humphrey Files," Eugene J. McCarthy Papers, Elmer L. Andersen Library, University of Minnesota, Minneapolis; see *Syracuse Post Standard*, Aug. 27, 1964. See also *Fergus Falls (MN) Daily Journal*, Aug. 26, 1964, which stated its long-term opposition to Humphrey's domestic policies but acknowledged Democrats accepted him with "open arms"; *Newsweek*, Sept. 7, 1964. McCarthy came to a Minnesota delegation party for Humphrey but was "very sarcastic"; Abigail McCarthy refused to attend; see Eisele, *Almost to Presidency*, 221.

54. *Newsweek*, Sept. 7, 1964.

55. Seshol, *Mutual Contempt*, 219–20.

56. *NYT*, Aug. 28, 1964.

57. Solberg, *Hubert Humphrey*, 258; Humphrey, *Education*, 226.

58. Beschloss, *Taking Charge*, 543–44; Eric Goldman, *Tragedy of Lyndon Johnson*, 217.

59. Woods, *LBJ*, 538.

60. Humphrey, *Education*, 227–29.

61. Solberg, *Hubert Humphrey*, 259–60; Donaldson, *Liberalism's Last Hurrah*, 243–44.

13. LBJ VERSUS HHH

1. *Fergus Falls (MN) Daily Journal*, Sept. 2, 1964; WDN, Sept. 6, 1964.

2. Donaldson, *Liberalism's Last Hurrah*, 146–47; Perlstein, *Before the Storm*, 391–92; *Newsweek*, Sept. 7, 1964.

3. *Newsweek*, Sept. 21, 1964; *NYT*, Sept. 21, 1964; Solberg, *Hubert Humphrey*, 260; Donaldson, *Liberalism's Last Hurrah*, 247–48.

4. *NYT*, Sept. 8, 1964.

5. *Newsweek*, Sept. 21, 1964.

6. Ibid., Sept. 28, 1964.

7. Thurber, *Politics of Equality*, 162; Moyers Draft of Johnson Telephone Call, Sept. 18, 1964, White House Aides File, Moyers, box 32, JP; *Newsweek*, Sept. 28, 1964; full text of all of Humphrey's Texas comments, HP, 150.E.1.5B.

8. *NYT*, Sept. 26, 28, 1964.

9. Thurber, *Politics of Equality*, 162; Solberg, *Hubert Humphrey*, 261; *NYT*, Sept. 27, 28, 29, 30, 1964.

10. On Humphrey, the restrictive covenant, and his net worth, see *NYT*, Sept. 26, 1964, and *Newsweek*, Oct. 5, 1964, which notes that this "Poorest Rich Man" in the race was worth $171,396. His Maryland house was assessed at $36,000, and his Waverly home at $28,000; he also owned three cars (a 1960 Pontiac, a 1964 Chevrolet, and a 1931 Ford) and had $100 in pocket money. By contrast, Lyndon Johnson's assets were worth $3.5 million, those of Barry Goldwater $1.7 million, and those of William Miller $270,000. Cohodas, *Strom Thurmond*, 361.

11. See Thurber, *Politics of Equality*, 163–64, on concerns of whites not only in the South but in the North.

12. *NYT*, Oct. 1, 6, 8, 15, 21, 1964.

13. Thomas, *Robert Kennedy*, 299–300; Seshol, *Mutual Contempt*, 222–25; *NYT*, Sept. 30, 1964. Kennedy apparently attracted great numbers of young people; many others in the crowds may have been paying homage to the memory of John Kennedy.

14. Dallek, *Flawed Giant*, 172, 182–83; Donaldson, *Liberalism's Last Hurrah*, 276–77; Woods, *LBJ*, 542–43.

15. Woods, *LBJ*, 552–53; Seshol, *Mutual Contempt*, 225–28; Thomas, *Robert Kennedy*, 301.

16. Dallek, *Flawed Giant*, 183–84; Seshol, *Mutual Contempt*, 229; Sandbrook, *Eugene McCarthy*, 115.

17. *Newsweek*, Nov. 9, 1964.

18. Ibid.; *NYT*, Nov. 9, 1964.

19. Orville H. Freeman diary, Nov. 9, 1964, box 14, FP (hereinafter cited as Freeman diary); Humphrey, *Education*, 230.

20. Freeman diary, Nov. 30, 1964; on Humphrey's recognition of dependence on Johnson, see also Eisele, *Almost to Presidency*, 227; Hannaford, *Pearson Diaries*, Jan. 13, 1965, 282–83; *NYT*, July 25, 1965; Humphrey's Senate president office was modest; Russell Long of Louisiana now occupied his previous, more spacious Majority Whip's office; there was talk in 1965 of buying or building an official vice president's residence but budget cuts precluded this.

21. Freeman diary, Nov. 22, 1964.

22. Ibid. The announcement of Mondale's appointment was put out prematurely not by Humphrey but by a staff person (Humphrey had resigned his Senate seat in early December 1964 to allow Mondale seniority over senators about to begin their first terms in January 1965); see Humphrey, *Education*, 261. On the education issue, see *NYT*, Nov. 29, 1964. Eisele, *Almost to Presidency*, 226. The PCEO was established in February 1965; *NYT*, Feb. 6, 1965.

23. Freeman diary, Dec. 12, 1964.

24. Ibid., Dec. 12, 23, 1964.

25. *NYT*, Jan. 21, 1965; Schlesinger, *Journals*, Jan. 20, 1965, 235–37. Schlesinger, a John Kennedy devotee, said that Humphrey was "the only thing that lifted my spirits," while Robert Kennedy told him that he "thanked heaven every day that the vice presidency had fallen through; it would have been a miserable and hopeless relationship, and nothing but trouble could have come from it."

26. *WDN*, Jan. 24, 1965; Berman, *Hubert*, 92; see also Humphrey, *Education*, 233–34. On the telephone taps, see Van Dyk, *Heroes, Hacks, and Fools*, 44.

27. *WDN*, Jan. 29, 1965; *Newsweek*, Feb. 1, 1965; Solberg, *Hubert Humphrey*, 266.

28. Eisele, *Almost to Presidency*, 237.

29. Humphrey, *Education*, 311–12; *NYT*, June 21, July 15, 1965; see also *Anderson (IN) Daily Bulletin*, June 21, 1965.

30. Eisele, *Almost to Presidency*, 225; *NYT*, Mar. 15, 1965.

31. Solberg, *Hubert Humphrey*, 277; *NYT*, July 25, 1965.

32. Dallek, *Flawed Giant*, 200–207; Woods, *LBJ*, 660–61; Zelizer, *Fierce Urgency of Now*, 174–201; *Newsweek*, Apr. 26, 1965.

33. Sikoff, *Struggle for Black Equality*, 175–82; Thurber, *Politics of Equality*, 178.

34. Humphrey speech, Aug. 19, 1965, HP, 150.E.2.1B; *Austin (MN) Daily Herald*, Aug. 19, 1965; Thurber, *Politics of Equality*, 179–80.

35. Thurber, *Politics of Equality*, 180.

36. Califano, *Triumph and Tragedy of Johnson*, 55–56; Califano admitted that he laughed at the remark, taking it to mean that Johnson thought Humphrey was not "tough enough" to deal with civil rights tensions.

37. Thurber, *Politics of Equality*, 182–83.

38. Dallek, *Flawed Giant*, 224–25.

39. For background on Vietnam policy, see Chapter 7.

40. Humphrey, *Education*, 194.

41. Currey, *Edward Lansdale*. See also Garrettson, *Hubert H. Humphrey*, 178–80, on Lansdale and Humphrey.

42. Rielly to Humphrey, June 8, 1964, HP, 150.D.10.1B.

43. Lansdale to Humphrey, May 20, June 8, 1964, HP, 150.D.10.1B; on Phillips's views about Humphrey and friendship with his chief of staff Bill Connell, see Garrettson, *Hubert H. Humphrey*, 173–75.

44. Humphrey to Johnson, June 8, 1964, HP, 150.D.10.1B. See also Memorandum from Senator Hubert H. Humphrey to the President, June 8, 1964, *FRUS, 1964–1968*, 1:477–84.

45. Clifton Memorandum for the President, June 25, 1964, National Security File, Vietnam, box 77, JP; Humphrey, *Education*, 368n.3, says Johnson solicited his views, although that does not seem to be the case; in addition, his insistence he ruled out direct military action does not appear in the documents, but it is clear neither he nor Lansdale intended to have US forces engage in major fighting.

46. Hess, *Presidential Decisions*, 85–86.

47. Lovegall, *Choosing War*, 196–98.

48. Hess, *Presidential Decisions*, 86–88; Goldstein, *Lessons in Disaster*, 126; only Senators Ernest Gruening of Alaska and Wayne Morse of Oregon voted against the Gulf of Tonkin Resolution.

49. *Van Nuys (CA) News* and *NYT*, Aug. 18, 1964; Perlstein, *Nixonland*, 400; Eisele, *Almost to Presidency*, 230–31.

50. Rielly to Humphrey, Nov. 16, 1964, HP, 150.D.10.4F.

51. Herring, *Longest War*, 148; *NYT*, Jan. 5, 1965.

52. Lovegall, *Choosing War*, 317–19, 362; Herring, *Longest War*, 152–53.

53. Humphrey quoted in *WDN*, Feb. 9, 1965; he did not return to Washington until Feb. 9; Memorandum for the Record, Feb. 6, and Summary Notes of NSC Meeting, Feb. 7, 1965, *FRUS, 1964–1968*, 2:158–60, 166–68; see also Lovegall, *Choosing War*, 326–27; Johnson, *Vantage Point*, 124–25.

54. Goldstein, *Lessons in Disaster*, 158–59; Lovegall, *Choosing War*, 328–29; Bundy Memorandum for the President, 7, 1965, *FRUS, 1964–1968*, 2:184–85.

55. Memoranda of NSC Meetings, Mansfield Memorandum to Johnson, Feb. 8, and Bundy to Mansfield, Feb. 9, 1965, *FRUS, 1964–1968*, 2:187, 188–92, 203–6, 208–11.

56. Humphrey, *Education*, 257; Memorandum of Meetings of the Principals, and Record of NSC Meeting, Feb. 10, 1965, *FRUS, 1964–1968*, 2:214–15, 216–18.

57. Lovegall, *Choosing War*, 344–45.
58. The file documents relating to Humphrey's memorandum, which bears the notation "Not Sent J.E.R. [John E. Rielly]," are in HP, 150.D.10.1B; the memorandum cited is in *FRUS, 1964–1968,* 2:309–10, and was apparently given to Moyers; Humphrey reproduces an earlier version, dated Feb. 15, 1965, in *Education,* 238–41.
59. Lovegall, *Choosing War,* 346; Solberg, *Hubert Humphrey,* 272; Humphrey, *Education,* 238; on Moyers, Garrettson, *Hubert H. Humphrey,* 181.
60. Solberg, *Hubert Humphrey,* 273; Humphrey, *Education,* 242; Eisele, *Almost to Presidency,* 234.
61. Solberg, *Hubert Humphrey,* 271, says that Humphrey erred on February 10 by speaking against the bombing; Van Dyk, *Heroes, Hacks, and Fools,* 41, seems to agree but says that Humphrey had given an honest answer to a direct question about a situation in which American lives were at stake. On Johnson's "stealth" war, see Lovegall, *Choosing War,* 333. Mann, *Grand Delusion,* 404–7, suggests that Humphrey's memorandum may have unintentionally encouraged Johnson to pursue a stealth policy by indicating people were talking about the bombing, but more likely this policy was already set; Solberg also points out that Johnson's advisers, such as Jim Rowe, Abe Fortas, and Mike Mansfield, preferred to remain independent and carefully avoided working under his direct control.
62. Solberg, *Hubert Humphrey,* 274; Dallek, *Flawed Giant,* 253.
63. Humphrey, *Education,* 242.

14. HUMPHREY'S VIETNAM WARS

1. NYT, Feb. 18, 1965; Humphrey, *Education,* 242.
2. Goldstein, *Lessons in Disaster,* 168–70; Herring, *America's Longest War,* 145–46.
3. Eisele, *Almost to Presidency,* 234–35.
4. NYT, Apr. 8, 1965; Mann, *Grand Delusion,* 426.
5. NYT, Apr. 23, 25, 1965.
6. Herring, *Colony to Superpower,* 735–36. Johnson's intervention was brought on by his administration's near hysteria that Fidel Castro or other Communists were behind the revolt and led in 1966 to twenty-five years of authoritarian rule by Joaquin Balaguer, an ally of former brutal dictator Rafael Trujillo; NYT, Apr. 25, May 18, 1965; Orville H. Freeman diary, May 9, 1965, box 14, FP (hereinafter cited as Freeman diary).
7. NYT, May 18, June 14, 1965; Humphrey Speech at National War College, June 1, 1965, Humphrey Vice Presidential Files, Foreign Affairs, HP, 150.D.10.1B.
8. Lovegall, *Choosing War,* 373; NYT, July 13, 29, 1965.
9. Morse and Humphrey quoted in Mann, *Grand Delusion,* 463; Solberg, *Hubert Humphrey,* 282; Humphrey to Johnson, Aug. 27, 1965, White House Central Files, FG 440, box 347, JP; NYT, Oct. 28, 1965.
10. NYT, May 14, 1965.
11. Ibid., July 13, Aug. 24, 1965. For Humphrey on those "saved," see Solberg, *Hubert Humphrey,* 281. Valenti had just said publicly that he slept better each night knowing that Johnson was president; *Wall Street Journal,* July 5, 1965.

12. Woods, *LBJ*, 667; Solberg, *Hubert Humphrey*, 283.

13. *NYT*, Oct. 22, 29, Nov. 12, 14, 1965. On West Virginia talk, and Humphrey and Erlander, see Solberg, *Hubert Humphrey*, 283.

14. *Time*, Jan. 7, 1966; Solberg, *Hubert Humphrey*, 283; *Newsweek*, Jan. 3, 1966.

15. Humphrey, *Education*, 245; Solberg, *Hubert Humphrey*, 284; *NYT*, Dec. 20, 22, 1965.

16. *NYT*, Dec. 27, 1965, Jan. 4, 1966; Van Dyk, *Heroes, Hacks, and Fools*, 47–48; Humphrey, *Education*, 246, omits this trip from his memoir and inaccurately notes his discovery of Valenti's reporting role on his third Asian journey (which included Vietnam in February); Valenti's reports on Humphrey were "glowing," said columnist Marianne Means, *Washington Post*, Feb. 16, 1966, in White House Central Files, FG 440, box 346, JP.

17. *NYT*, Dec. 29, 30, 1965, Jan. 16, 1966; on the reluctance of Asian nations, except Australia and South Korea, to commit troops, see Herring, *America's Longest War*, 167.

18. *NYT*, Jan. 2, 1966.

19. Ibid., Jan. 4, 1966; Summary Notes of NSC Meeting, Jan. 5, 1966, *FRUS, 1964–1968*, 4:19–22.

20. *NYT*, Jan. 11, 14, 15, 1966; Humphrey, *Education*, 316–17.

21. *NYT*, Jan. 17, Feb. 4, 1966.

22. Mann, *Grand Delusion*, 491–92; Woods, *LBJ*, 717–18; Herring, *Longest War*, 15.

23. Woods, *LBJ*, 317–19; Mann, *Grand Delusion*, 492–93; *NYT*, Feb. 9, 1966.

24. Humphrey, *Education*, 245–46; Eisele, *Almost to Presidency*, 242. Humphrey says that Johnson had forewarned him that he might be sent to Asia but that he was sworn to secrecy.

25. Van Dyk, *Heroes, Hacks, and Fools*, 47; *NYT*, Feb. 10, 1966.

26. *NYT*, Feb. 10, 1966; *Time*, Feb. 25, 1966; *Newsweek*, Mar. 21, 1966.

27. *NYT*, Feb. 12, 1966. Freeman now proclaimed that the way to the heart of South Vietnam's farmers was to help them get their troops to market.

28. Humphrey, *Education*, 237; Eisele, *Almost to Presidency*, 243; Solberg, *Hubert Humphrey*, 288, says that Humphrey's marine aide, Colonel Herbert Beckington, felt that the vice president's lack of military service inclined him to accept what military officials told him.

29. *NYT*, Feb. 16, 17, 1966.

30. Humphrey, *Education*, 250; *NYT*, Feb. 18, 19, 1966; Eisele, *Almost to Presidency*, 244.

31. *NYT*, Feb. 20, 21, 1966. Kennedy had cleared his statement with McNamara, and intended it as a "middle way." Initially Kennedy defended his statement by saying that refusal to allow the NLF into negotiations was imposing a precondition on "unconditional negotiations," but then said that he meant only that the NLF should not be "automatically excluded." See Seshol, *Mutual Contempt*, 289–91; and *NYT*, Feb. 22, 1966.

32. *NYT*, Feb. 22, 23, 1966.

33. Ibid., Feb. 24, 1966.

34. Ibid., Feb. 25, 26, 1966; Notes of Meeting, Feb. 24, 1966, *FRUS, 1964–1968*, 4:255–59; *Time*, Mar. 4, 1966.

35. *Time*, Feb. 26, 1966; Eiscle, *Almost to Presidency*, 248.

36. Eisele, *Almost to Presidency*, 248; *New Republic*, Mar. 6, 1966; *Time*, Apr. 1, 1966 (for "hatchet man").

37. Humphrey, *Education*, 250; Notes of a Meeting of the Vice President with His Staff, Feb. 18, 1966, Confidential Files, box 166, JP.

38. Vice President's Report to the President, Feb. 25, 1966, HP, 150.E.14.5B.

39. Humphrey, *Education*, 251.

40. Report of Vice President Humphrey on Asian Trip, Mar. 17, 1966, HP, 150.E.14.5B; McNamara Memorandum to the President, Oct. 14, 1966, attached to Minutes of the NSC Meeting, Oct. 15, 1966, NSC Files, NSC Meetings, box 2, JP; see also Herring, *Longest War*, 174–76.

41. Eisele, *Almost to Presidency*, 246; *Newsweek*, Apr. 4, 1966. On Humphrey's "constituency of one," see *Time*, Apr. 1, 1966; Glass, "Hubert Humphrey's One-Man Constituency," 27–30; and Humphrey, *Education*, 320.

42. Humphrey quoted in Solberg, *Hubert Humphrey*, 296–97; *NYT*, July 26, July 29, 1966; McGrory quoted in *New York Post*, July, 29, 1966.

43. On Humphrey's travels, see *Newsweek*, Feb. 28, Mar. 7, 1966.

44. *NYT*, Feb. 28, 1966; *Time*, Apr. 1, 1966 on NLF; on "containment without isolation" (an idea proffered by Columbia University China specialist A. Doak Barnett), *NYT*, Mar. 14, 1966.

45. *NYT*, Apr. 20, 25, 1966; *Time*, Apr. 1, 1966.

46. *NYT*, Apr. 17, 20, 21, 1966; see also Eisele, *Almost to Presidency*, 247–48.

47. *NYT*, Apr. 24, 1966; Eisele, *Almost to Presidency*, 248.

48. *NYT*, Apr. 26, 1966.

49. Ibid., Apr. 27, 1966.

50. Ibid., Apr. 29, 1966; Van Dyk, *Heroes, Hacks, and Fools*, 48.

51. *NYT*, June 9, 10, 1966; Woods, *Fulbright*, 412–13.

52. Notes of NSC Meetings, June 17, 22, 1966, NSC Files, NSC Meetings, box 2, JP.

53. McNamara Memorandum for the President, Oct. 14, 1966, NSC Files, NSC Meetings, box 2, JP.

54. *NYT*, July 5, 12, 26, 1966.

55. *NYT*, Sept. 23, Oct. 14, 1966; "unwashed" in Solberg, *Hubert Humphrey*, 299.

56. Solberg, *Hubert Humphrey*, 292.

57. Ibid., 293.

58. *NYT*, June 26, July 7, 19, Aug. 13, 1966. See also Thurber, *Politics of Equality*, 186–87; and on disappointing results of the Model Cities program, see Woods, *LBJ*, 688–92.

59. *NYT*, Apr. 11, 1966; *Newsweek*, Apr. 25, 1966; *NYT Magazine*, May 22, 1966; *NYT*, Aug. 25, 1966.

60. *NYT*, Sept. 2, 30, 1966; Eisele, *Almost to Presidency*, 250.

61. *Newsweek*, Sept. 26, 1966; Eisele, *Almost to Presidency*, 249.

62. *NYT*, Oct. 7, 17, 1966. On Humphrey's view, see Unsigned Memorandum, Oct. 16, 1966, White House Central Files, FG 44, JP. On Johnson, see Dallek, *Flawed Giant*, 393.

63. Gardner, *Pay Any Price*, 317–18. The seven nations were the United States, Australia, New Zealand, Malaysia, the Philippines, Thailand, and South Korea.

64. *NYT*, Sept. 18, Nov. 9, 10, 1966; *WDN*, Oct. 20, 31, 1966. Though Humphrey failed to get Rolvaag an ambassadorship to Sweden or Norway, he secured him a less prestigious appointment to Iceland; Eisele, *Almost to Presidency*, 249.

65. *NYT*, Oct. 30, Nov. 2, 1966; *Austin (MN) Daily Herald*, Nov. 26, 1966; *WDN*, Nov. 28, 1966. When Nixon predicted the Republicans would win forty House seats, Humphrey scoffed that the public did not buy him as a president in 1960 and now would not "buy him as a prophet"; *NYT*, Oct. 24, 1966.

66. *Austin (MN) Daily Herald*, Nov. 26, 1966; Eisele, *Almost to Presidency*, 227; Humphrey quoted in Solberg, *Hubert Humphrey*, 300; on Johnson and cabinet, see *Wall Street Journal*, July 6, 1965.

15. NORTHWEST'S PASSAGE

1. Eisele, *Almost to Presidency*, 251.
2. Solberg, *Hubert Humphrey*, 301–2.
3. Humphrey remarks in *NYT*, Aug. 7, 1966; Solberg, *Hubert Humphrey*, 296.
4. Eisele, *Almost to Presidency*, 251.
5. Humphrey to Johnson, Feb. 23, 1967, Marvin Watson Files, box 31, JP.
6. Humphrey to Douglass Cater, Mar. 2, 1967, White House Central Files, FG 440, box 38, JP.
7. Humphrey to Johnson, Feb. 23, 1967, and Criswell to Johnson, Mar. 14, 1967, Watson Files, box 31, JP; Robert Fleming to George Christian, Mar. 23, 1967, White House Central Files, FG 440, box 348, JP.
8. *NYT*, Feb. 28, Mar. 9, 1967.
9. Telephone Conversation between President Johnson and Vice President Humphrey, Mar. 18, 1967, *FRUS, 1964–1968*, 5:262–66.
10. Berman, *Lyndon Johnson's War*, 33; on Komer, see Woods, *LBJ*, 759–60; Dallek, *Flawed Giant*, 459–61.
11. *Newsweek*, Apr. 4, 1967; *NYT*, Apr. 4, 1967.
12. *Time*, Apr. 7, 1967; Humphrey, *Education*, 312.
13. Humphrey, *Education*, 313; *Time*, Apr. 17, 1967.
14. *NYT*, Apr. 6, 7, 1967.
15. Ibid., Apr. 8, 1967.
16. Johnson to Humphrey, Apr. 7, 1967, quoted in Solberg, *Hubert Humphrey*, 305; Solberg also quotes Humphrey's friend, William Benton, as saying in May 1968 that Johnson had told him he would gladly die the next day if he knew his vice president would succeed him for the next eight years; this is hard to believe given Johnson's narcissism and frightful personal and political treatment of Humphrey as vice president.
17. Humphrey's diplomacy may have contributed to the Europeans' soon agreeing to modest agricultural and industrial tariff reductions in 1967 based on the 1962 Trade Expansion Act, and in 1968 the United States, United Kingdom, and Soviet Union signed the Nuclear Nonproliferation Agreement (rooted in Humphrey's 1963 Nuclear Test Ban Treaty), which eventually included 190 nations; *NYT*, Apr. 10, May 16, July 1, 1967; Herring, *Colony to Superpower*, 755–56.

18. *NYT*, Apr. 11, 1967; Collingwood comments, Apr. 21, 1967, White House Central Files, FG 440, box 348, JP.

19. *NYT*, Apr. 11, 15, 1967; Eisele, *Almost to Presidency*, 252; Sitkoff, *King*, 215. The administration was concerned that Maddox might ally with Alabama governor George Wallace in a third-party run.

20. *NYT*, Apr. 24, 1967.

21. Eisele, *Almost to Presidency*, 253–55 (quoting from James Wechsler's memorandum of the meeting); Schlesinger, *Journals*, Apr. 18, 1967, 258–59.

22. Berman, *Hubert*, 274; *NYT*, Aug. 23, 1967; *WDN*, Aug. 25, 1967.

23. Sitkoff, *Struggle for Black Equality*, 187–88.

24. Thurber, *Politics of Equality*, 191–92; Solberg, *Hubert Humphrey*, 308–9; *Newsweek*, July 29, 1968.

25. Thurber, *Politics of Equality*, 192–93.

26. *NYT*, Aug. 3, 1967.

27. Thurber, *Politics of Equality*, 194; *NYT*, Aug. 9, Sept. 9, 17, 1967.

28. Woods, *LBJ*, 764–65; Small, *Johnson, Nixon, and the Doves*, 113–17; Mailer, *Armies of the Night*.

29. Woods, *LBJ*, 808–9.

30. *NYT*, Aug. 23, Sept. 9, Oct. 16, 1967.

31. Ibid., Oct. 23, 24, 1967; *Newsweek*, Nov. 6, 1967.

32. *NYT*, Aug. 24, 1967.

33. Herring, *Longest War*, 214–15. Conservative syndicated columnist William S. White wrote in "Task Force Humphrey," *Washington Post*, Oct. 23, 1967, that the vice president had been assigned to "counter-attack dissident Democrats" who assailed Vietnam policy, and that despite his loss of liberal support, he had new acceptance among moderate and conservative Democrats, and was prepared to "live or die" on the Vietnam issue; article in National Security Files, box 2, JP.

34. *Newsweek*, Nov. 11, 1967.

35. Van Dyk, *Heroes, Hacks, and Fools*, 55.

36. *Time*, Nov. 6, 1967. The legislature was inaugurated at the same time, while there was no formal inauguration for Ky, who was moving from the presidency to the vice presidency; security was so tight that there were almost no civilians present, only thousands of military forces.

37. Humphrey, *Education*, 260; Van Dyk, *Heroes, Hacks, and Fools*, 56–57.

38. Humphrey, *Education*, 260–61; Solberg, *Hubert Humphrey*, 311.

39. Text of address, Oct. 31, 1967, in HP, 150.E.14.10F; see also *NYT*, Oct. 30, 31, 1967; *Time*, Nov. 11, 1967; Solberg, *Hubert Humphrey*, 311–12.

40. *NYT*, Nov. 2, 1967; *Time*, Nov. 11, 1967; *Newsweek*, Nov. 13, 1967.

41. *NYT*, Nov. 11, 1967; *Newsweek*, Nov. 20, 1967. Humphrey may not have known of US aid, especially from the CIA, to Suharto, whose rule of Indonesia from 1967 to 1998 showed him to be one of Asia's most brutal and corrupt dictators. On US involvement, see Scott, "United States and Sukarno," 239–64.

42. Van Dyk, *Heroes, Hacks, and Fools*, 57; *NYT*, Nov. 9, 1967; NSC Meeting, Nov. 8, 1967, NSC Meetings Files, box 2, JP; Humphrey also denied having said that the PRC

was the enemy, but that the wounded South Vietnamese troops knew that Ho Chi Minh and the Viet Cong were the real enemy.

43. Humphrey, *Education*, 261; *NYT*, Oct. 31, Nov. 11, 1967.

44. Humphrey Report to the President: Visit to South Vietnam, Oct. 29–Nov. 2, 1967, HP, 150.F.18.10F; the vice president also sent this report to his chief aide, Bill Connell, on Mar. 6, 1968, with instructions to send it to their "Vietnam cadres" to gain support for South Vietnam's army.

45. *Newsweek*, Nov. 6, 1967; *NYT*, Nov. 11, 14, 27, 1967. Some people saw this as an effort on Robert Kennedy's part to suggest that Johnson had deviated from President John Kennedy's more limited goal.

46. *NYT*, Dec. 10, 1967.

47. Humphrey, *Education*, 261–63.

16. LAST MAN IN

1. Humphrey to Johnson, Jan. 12, 1968, National Security Files, Country Files, Africa, box 77, JP; Vice President's Report on His Trip to Africa, Jan. 12, 1968, HP, 150.E.13.4F; *NYT*, Jan. 13, 1968; *Newsweek*, Jan. 15, 22, 1968.

2. Sandbrook, *Eugene McCarthy*, 172.

3. Humphrey, *Education*, 281; Sandbrook, *Eugene McCarthy*, 125–29, 162; Woods, *LBJ*, 826. McCarthy made his remark to his chief of staff, Carl Marcy, and *NYT* reporter Ned Kenworthy.

4. Sandbrook, *Eugene McCarthy*, 167–70; Eisele, *Almost to Presidency*, 284–85; quotation in Chafe, *Never Stop Running*, 272.

5. Humphrey, *Education*, 281; Humphrey to Johnson, Nov. 28, 1967, quoted in Solberg, *Hubert Humphrey*, 313; Eisele, *Almost to Presidency*, 285n.3.

6. Eisele, *Almost to Presidency*, 283–84; Sandbrook, *Eugene McCarthy*, 173; McCarthy speech to NCCD, Dec. 3, 1968, HP, 150.E.13.4F.

7. Eisele, *Almost to Presidency*, 291, 304.

8. Humphrey notes, Jan. 19, 1968, HP, 150.E.13.4F.

9. *Ogden (UT) Standard Examiner*, Jan. 13, 1968; WDN, Jan. 14, 1968; Eisele, *Almost to Presidency*, 292.

10. Herring, *Colony to Superpower*, 752; Berman, *Lyndon Johnson's War*, 144–45; one member of the eighty-three-person crew was killed during the capture.

11. Herring, *America's Longest War*, 204–9; Berman, *Hubert*, 145–47; US and South Vietnamese troops killed 30,000–40,000 North Vietnamese and VC forces, while 1,250 US soldiers and 2,300 South Vietnamese troops were killed, and nearly 1 million people became refugees.

12. Senate Republican memo, Feb. 8, 1968, Marvin Watson Files, box 31, JP; Humphrey's remark appeared on April 15, 1951, in the *St. Paul Pioneer Press*, amid the controversy over President Truman's firing of General Douglas MacArthur; Brinkley, *Cronkite*, 367–79.

13. Woods, *LBJ*, 828–29.

14. Humphrey draft, "Regaining the Initiative," n.d., William Connell Files, HP, 150.F.18.6F.

15. Woods, *LBJ*, 829–31.

16. *Minneapolis Star*, Mar. 6, 1968; "The Minneapolis DFL Precinct Caucuses," Mar. 7, 1968, memorandum sent to Humphrey and White House Staff, HP, 150.F.18.6F; see also Nathanson, "Two Favorite Sons"; Eisele, *Almost to Presidency*, 297; the state party in Massachusetts declined to enter a stand-in candidate for Johnson.

17. Solberg, *Hubert Humphrey*, 319; on the New Hampshire campaign, Eisele, *Almost to Presidency*, 290–99; Sandbrook, *Eugene McCarthy*, 183–86.

18. Humphrey to Gerald Heaney, Mar. 14, 1968, and Humphrey speech to Democratic Regional Conference, Mar. 15, 1968, William Connell Files, HP, 150.F.18.6F.

19. Humphrey to Johnson, Mar. 20, 21, 1968, Watson Files, box 31, JP.

20. For Johnson quotations, Dallek, *Flawed Giant*, 512, and Woods, *LBJ*, 834; on the briefings, see Humphrey to George Carver, Apr. 19, and Carver to Humphrey, Apr. 26, 1968, and Carver Memorandum for the Director [of the CIA], Mar. 31, 1970, which recounts the briefings and Johnson's surprise at what he heard, HP, 150.E.17.B; Dallek, *Flawed Giant*, 513, contends that the president knew what the briefers were going to say and his questions were play acting; Clifford was a major force from March 4 on in seeking a way out of the war.

21. Woods, *LBJ*, 832, 837, on aides and Connally urging against seeking reelection.

22. Humphrey, *Education*, 266; Humphrey to Johnson, March 29, 1968, Watson Files, box 31, JP; Clifford, *Counsel to President*, 504–5; perhaps to assuage Johnson's pride, Humphrey also suggested that if North Vietnam refused to cooperate, the United States should raise its troop level sufficient to impose a military solution, an unrealistic idea.

23. Eisele, *Almost to Presidency*, 322–23; Solberg, *Hubert Humphrey*, 321–22; Humphrey, *Education*, 267.

24. Van Dyk, *Heroes, Hacks, and Fools*, 62–63, Berman, *Hubert*, 154–55; Humphrey, *Education*, 267–28; Clifford, *Counsel to President*, 525–26.

25. Humphrey, *Education*, 270.

26. Berman, *Hubert*, 156–57.

27. Ibid., 157.

28. Eisele, *Almost to Presidency*, 324–25; many of the officials were ones Humphrey's staff had put in place in anticipation of a presidential run in 1972.

29. Eisele, *Almost to Presidency*, 326; Berman, *Hubert*, 158.

30. Eisele, *Almost to Presidency*, 326; Solberg, *Hubert Humphrey*, 324.

31. Eisele, *Almost to Presidency*, 327; *NYT*, Apr. 3, 1968.

32. Solberg, *Hubert Humphrey*, 325–26; Thomas, *Robert Kennedy*, 341.

33. *Time*, May 3, 1968; Eisele, *Almost to Presidency*, 326–27, 327n.3, on cabinet meeting; Berman, *Hubert*, 162, confirms nonprimary strategy.

34. *NYT*, Apr. 28, 1968.

35. Sitkoff, *Struggle for Black Equality*, 207–8; Humphrey quoted in *NYT*, Apr. 5, 1968; on Humphrey and King's funeral, James Cross to Johnson, Apr. 6, 1968 (with Johnson note "Hold for now"), and Watson to Johnson, Apr. 8, 1968, White House Central Files, box 349, JP.

36. Humphrey to National Alliance of Businessmen, Long Island, NY, Apr. 5, Remarks to Jefferson-Jackson Dinner, Louisville, and Message to DFL Conventions, St. Louis,

Washington, and Clay Counties, MN, Apr. 6, 1968, HP, 150.E.3.4F; Humphrey, *Education*, 269–70, admits he did not know King well but "shared his dream."

37. Reston's column, "Pray Silence for Hubert Horatio Humphrey," *NYT*, April 5, 1968; Van Dyk, *Heroes, Hacks, and Fools*, 65–66.

38. Humphrey to Ken Birkhead, Apr. 8, 1968 (two memoranda), Connell Files, HP, 150.F.18.6F; *Newsweek*, Apr. 15, 1968.

39. Van Dyk, *Heroes, Hacks, and Fools*, 66.

40. Solberg, *Hubert Humphrey*, 331–32; Mondale and Harris were good friends personally, and Harris's wife, LaDonna, was half-Comanche and politically active.

41. Birkhead to Humphrey, Apr. 8, 1968, HP, 150.F.18.6F; Solberg, *Hubert Humphrey*, 329.

42. Orville H. Freeman diary, Apr. 17, 22, 23, 1968, FP (hereinafter cited as Freeman diary). Freeman hoped that Johnson would not take him up on his "threat" to resign if he could not work for Humphrey.

43. *NYT*, Apr. 28, 1968; Solberg, *Hubert Humphrey*, 332, wrongly says Humphrey added his "joy of politics" phrase spontaneously at the end; this language appears at the start of the speech distributed in advance by the Humphrey campaign, HP, 150.E.3.4F.

44. *NYT*, Apr. 28, 29, May 25, 1968; Kennedy also quoted in *Time*, May 24, 1968; *WDN*, Apr. 28, 1968.

45. *NYT*, May 25, 1968; *Time*, May 31, 1968; Eisele, *Almost to Presidency*, 311–12.

46. Eisele, *Almost to Presidency*, 311–12; Sandbrook, *Eugene McCarthy*, 197–98.

47. *Newsweek*, Apr. 29, 1968; Boggs quoted in *Time*, May 3, 1968.

48. Sandbrook, *Eugene McCarthy*, 192–93; Berman, *Hubert*, 166.

49. *Time*, June 7, 1968, and *NYT*, May 27, 1968, which cites *Newsweek* reporters on the "coup."

50. Fulbright, *Arrogance of Power*; *Time*, May 3, 1968.

51. *Time*, May 3, 1968; *NYT*, June 2, 1968.

52. *NYT*, May 30, 1968.

53. Sandbrook, *Eugene McCarthy*, 200–201. This was the first defeat for a Kennedy in twenty-eight elections.

54. On the debate and for the Kennedy quotation, see Thomas, *Robert Kennedy*, 386, 389.

55. Van Dyk, *Heroes, Hacks, and Fools*, 70; Eisele, *Almost to Presidency*, 331.

56. Eisele, *Almost to Presidency*, 331; Berman, *Hubert*, 173–75; Humphrey, *Education*, 278–79; Kennedy's assassin was Sirhan B. Sirhan, an unstable Palestinian who had fixated on him because of his support for aid to Israel.

57. Eisele, *Almost to Presidency*, 332n.6; Berman, *Hubert*, 176.

58. Thomas, *Robert Kennedy*, 390–94, notes that Johnson sought to prevent Robert Kennedy from being buried at Arlington but that he gave way when he was told this action would be "politically reckless."

59. Solberg, *Hubert Humphrey*, 341; *Time*, June 21, 1968.

60. Sandbrook, *Eugene McCarthy*, 206. Van Dyk, *Heroes, Hacks, and Fools*, 71, adds that he later discovered notes that Humphrey wrote suggesting that McCarthy had come with an ultimatum, but the vice president's aide doubted that was the case; rather, the meeting was as Humphrey had described it to him at the time.

61. *Time*, June 24, 1968; Sandbrook, *Eugene McCarthy*, 206–8. McCarthy told an aide after the meeting that Johnson had said the Viet Cong were "desperate" and the United States was negotiating from strength—"the same old stuff." Eisele, *Almost to Presidency*, 339–40, notes that an aide said that McCarthy was passive and self-absorbed all summer.

62. Eisele, *Almost to Presidency*, 341; *WDN*, June 6, 1968; *Time*, June 21, 1968.

63. *Newsweek*, July 1, 1968; McCarthy, *Year of the People*, 182–84; *Time*, June 21, 28, 1968; Nathanson, "Two Favorite Sons"; Humphrey to Connell, July 12, 1968, HP, 150.F.18.6F.

64. *NYT*, June 17, July 7, 1968; *Time*, June 21, 28, 1968.

65. On Johnson's plans, see Woods, *LBJ*, 862–63; *NYT*, June 21, 23, 1968; and *Time*, June 28, 1968.

66. Berman diary, June 19, 1968, quoted in Solberg, *Hubert Humphrey*, 342.

67. Herring, *Longest War*, 232.

68. Schlesinger to David Ginsburg, July 9, 1968, Schlesinger, *Letters*, 358–69.

69. Humphrey to Schlesinger, July 13, and Schlesinger to Humphrey, July 24, 1968, ibid., 365–69, 371–74.

70. Humphrey speech, "The Next Era in Foreign Policy," HP, 150.G.4.5B; *Newsweek*, July 29, 1968.

71. On the Honolulu Declaration, Clifford, *Counsel to President*, 551–53; Hannaford, *Pearson Diaries*, July 24, 1968, 598–99; *NYT*, July 22, 23, 1968.

72. Van Dyk, *Heroes, Hacks, and Fools*, 73–74; Solberg, *Hubert Humphrey*, 348; *NYT*, July 26, 1969.

73. Kearns, *Lyndon Johnson*, 133, notes Johnson's lasting respect for Humphrey's "brilliance, talent, and ability" and view that " 'he is truly a happy warrior.' " On Johnson's criticism, Clifford, *Counsel to President*, 563, 571.

74. *Newsweek*, Aug. 12, 1968; on California meetings, see Berman diary, Aug. 3, 1968, HP, 147.E.11.10F.

75. Berman diary, Aug. 2, 5, 1968.

76. *Newsweek*, Aug. 5, 1968.

77. Ibid.; Berman diary, Aug. 8, 1968.

78. Berman diary, Aug. 9, 1968.

79. Ibid., Aug. 12, 1968; Eisele, *Almost to Presidency*, 337; Solberg, *Hubert Humphrey*, 371.

80. Hannaford, *Pearson Diaries*, Aug. 9, 1968, 602–3; Gardner, *Pay Any Price*, 478–80.

81. Clifford, *Counsel to President*, 563–64.

82. *NYT*, Aug. 12, 1968; Berman diary, Aug. 12, 1968.

83. Berman diary, Aug. 10, 1968.

84. Eisele, *Almost to Presidency*, 341–42; *NYT*, Aug. 21, 1968.

85. Berman diary, Aug. 18, 1968.

86. Freeman diary, Aug. 20, 1968, FP.

87. Notes of the Emergency Meeting of the National Security Council, Aug. 20, 1968, NSC Files, NSC Meetings, box 2, JP; Berman diary, Aug. 20, 1968.

88. Berman diary, Aug. 22, 26, 1968.

89. Freeman diary, Aug. 22, 1968, FP.

17. THE SIEGE OF CHICAGO

1. Chester, Hodgson, and Page, *American Melodrama*, 515–17. During riots after Martin Luther King's assassination in April 1968, Daley told his police to "shoot to kill" arsonists and assailed antiwar protesters as "hoodlums and communists"; see Gould, *1968*, 125.

2. *Time*, Sept. 6, 1968.

3. Eisele, *Almost to Presidency*, 347–48; Chester, Hodgson, and Page, *American Melodrama*, 520–23; Solberg, *Hubert Humphrey*, 363; *Time*, Aug. 26, 1968.

4. *NYT*, Aug. 26, 1968.

5. Solberg, *Hubert Humphrey*, 358; Eisele, *Almost to Presidency*, 349; *NYT*, Aug. 22, 1968.

6. Kennedy, *True Compass*, 273; Dr. Edgar Berman diary, Aug. 23, 1968, SP; *Time*, Sept. 6, 1968, confirms Humphrey's trip to Kennedy's house.

7. Solberg, *Hubert Humphrey*, 357–58; Neustadt, "Democrats, Delegates, and Democracy," 128–29; Berman diary, Aug. 26, 1968, SP; Schlesinger, *Journals*, Aug. 24, 1968, 298–99.

8. Eisele, *Almost to Presidency*, 348.

9. Ibid., 355; Neustadt, "Democrats, Delegates, Democracy," 119; Wainstock, *Election Year 1968*, 141.

10. Eisele, *Almost to Presidency*, 355, Chester, Hodgson, and Page, *American Melodrama*, 551–58; Solberg, *Hubert Humphrey*, 359–60; Neustadt, "Democrats, Delegates, Democracy," 119.

11. Chester, Hodgson, and Page, *American Melodrama*, 572–73.

12. Schlesinger, *Journals*, Aug. 24, 1968, 297–98 (the entry was clearly written a few days afterward, as the reference to "calling off DiSalle" indicates); Neustadt, "Democrats, Delegates, Democracy," 125, 133–35; *NYT*, Aug. 28, 1968; *Newsweek*, Sept. 9, 1968; see also Chester, Hodgson, and Page, *American Melodrama*, 525.

13. Berman diary, Aug. 22, 1968, SP; see also Tom Wicker, "Fight Fiercely, Hubert," *NYT*, July 23, 1968.

14. Solberg, *Hubert Humphrey*, 352.

15. Chester, Hodgson, and Page, *American Melodrama*, 533–34; *NYT*, Aug. 29, 1968; Neustadt, "Democrats, Delegates, Democracy," 122.

16. Humphrey, *Education*, 291.

17. Chester, Hodgson, and Page, *American Melodrama*, 535–36.

18. *NYT*, Aug. 29, 1969; Eisele, *Almost to Presidency*, 346–47; Telephone Conversation Between President Johnson and the President's Counselor (Murphy), Aug. 26, 1968, *FRUS, 1964–1968*, 6:974–78.

19. Humphrey, *Education*, 292.

20. Berman, *Hubert*, 181–82; Humphrey, *Education*, 293; *NYT*, Aug. 29, 30, 1968.

21. On Johnson's Chicago plans, see Telephone Conversation between President Johnson and the President's Counselor (Murphy), Aug. 26, 1968, *FRUS, 1964–1968*, 6:978n.2; Dallek, *Flawed Giant*, 570–73; Woods, *LBJ*, 862–63; see also Berman diary, Aug. 27, 1968, SP. Humphrey told Berman that if Johnson came, he would go to Miami. See also Eisele, *Almost to Presidency*, 349; Neustadt, "Democrats, Delegates, Democracy,"

138; and Solberg, *Hubert Humphrey*, 361. *Time*, Sept. 9, 1968, notes that Johnson had to settle for coffee and cake at daughter Luci's house.

22. Sandbrook, *Eugene McCarthy*, 210. Reston, "Chicago," argued that most Democrats had great respect, even affection, for Humphrey despite his defense of Vietnam policy, whereas Nixon inspired little affection among Republicans. On Humphrey "oldest son," see Solberg, *Hubert Humphrey*, 354.

23. Chester, Hodgson, and Page, *American Melodrama*, 536–37; McCarthy is quoted in Eisele, *Almost to Presidency*, 347; Orville H. Freeman Diary, Aug. 28, 1968, box 14, FP (hereinafter cited as Freeman diary); Berman diary, Aug. 21, 1968, SP; and Berman, *Hubert*, 182.

24. *NYT*, Aug. 28, 1968; Sandbrook, *Eugene McCarthy*, 211; Mailer, *Siege of Chicago*, 123–25; Eisele, *Almost to Presidency*, 353–54; on McGovern, see *NYT*, Sept. 1, 1968.

25. *NYT*, Aug. 29, 1968; Chester, Hodgson, and Page, *American Melodrama*, 579–81.

26. Berman diary, Aug. 29, 1968, SP; *Time*, Sept. 6, 1968, confirms the conversation.

27. White, *Making of the President*, 291–94.

28. Chester, Hodgson, and Page, *American Melodrama*, 583–84; Solberg, *Hubert Humphrey*, 364.

29. Chester, Hodgson, and Page, *American Melodrama*, 582–83, 603 (for the commission headed by Daniel Walker, a Chicago lawyer, and later governor of Illinois, 1973–77), and White, *Making of the President*, 298–99; eight leaders of the various protest groups were also indicted, with five convicted for crossing state lines with intent to incite a riot.

30. Chester, Hodgson, and Page, *American Melodrama*, 585; *NYT*, Aug. 29, 1968; Perlstein, *Nixonland*, 327, quotes Daley as saying, "Fuck you, you Jew son-of-a-bitch."

31. Eisele, *Almost to Presidency*, 358.

32. Chester, Hodgson, and Page, *American Melodrama*, 585–86. A relative handful of votes went to favorite sons, the Rev. Channing Phillips from the District of Columbia, Governor Daniel Moore of North Carolina, and Kennedy; see Eisele, *Almost to Presidency*, 358n.10.

33. Sandbrook, *Eugene McCarthy*, 212–13.

34. McCarthy told Humphrey he would not accept the nomination, which his supporters would see as a betrayal, and Humphrey believed that party members were too angry at McCarthy to accept him; *Time*, Sept. 6, 1968, and Berman diary, Aug. 21, 1968, SP; see also Eisele, *Almost to Presidency*, 373. On Rockefeller, see *NYT*, Sept. 1, 1968, and Solberg, *Hubert Humphrey*, 351. Kennedy family members were angry that Shriver had sought the vice presidency in 1964 that Robert Kennedy had wanted and that he did not campaign enough for the senator in the 1968 primaries.

35. Humphrey, *Education*, 292–93; Eisele, *Almost to Presidency*, 361; White, *Making of the President*, 304–5. *Newsweek*, Sept. 9, 1968, quotes Muskie as saying to his wife, Jane, "Mommie, we're stuck with it."

36. Solberg, *Hubert Humphrey*, 367. Connell and Washington lawyer James Rowe, who had vetted Humphrey in 1964, opposed naming Muskie. Hughes, Daley, and O'Brien approved the choice.

37. Eisele, *Almost to Presidency*, 362.

38. Berman diary, Aug. 26, 29, 1968, SP; on Valenti, Solberg, *Hubert Humphrey*, 361.

39. Eisele, *Almost to Presidency*, 359n.12; Solberg, *Hubert Humphrey*, 361–62. The people urging Humphrey's resignation included former graduate school mentor Evron Kirkpatrick and his wife, Jeanne; staff person William Welsh; and lawyer and long-time adviser Max Kampelman. John C. Calhoun was the only vice president who had resigned to that time, and he had already won an open Senate seat from South Carolina. Vice President Spiro Agnew would be forced to resign in 1973.

40. Eisele, *Almost to Presidency*, 362–63.

41. *NYT*, Aug. 29, 1968; Solberg, *Hubert Humphrey*, 370.

42. White, *Making of the President*, 309–19; Eisele, *Almost to Presidency*, 363–64; *Newsweek*, Sept. 9, 1968; Mailer, *Siege of Chicago*.

43. *Newsweek*, Aug. 5, 1968; Solberg, *Hubert Humphrey*, 370.

44. Eisele, *Almost to Presidency*, 364, 367. Humphrey's statement conflated events of the first month of his campaign with the Chicago convention.

45. Dobrynin, *In Confidence*, 180–81; Clifford, *Counsel to President*, 581; George Ball comment in Telephone Conversation between President Johnson and George Ball, Sept. 30, 1968, *FRUS*, *1964–1968*, 7:107–9.

46. *NYT*, Sept. 1, 1968; Gould, *1968*, 99–105.

47. Gould, *1968*, 106–9; Ambrose, *Nixon: Triumph*, 173–75. Ambrose says that Nixon's first choice for vice president was his close friend and California lieutenant governor Robert Finch, who declined; this led to the choice of Agnew, who was not subjected to background checks that might have uncovered his having taken kickbacks as a Baltimore and state of Maryland official that led to his forced resignation as vice president in 1973.

48. Gould, *1968*, 109–10; *NYT*, Aug. 9, 1968.

49. Melvin Small, "Election of 1968," 524.

50. Chennault, *Education of Anna*, 168–76; Forslund, *Anna Chennault*, 52–62; Diem, *In the Jaws of History*, 235–37, says he informed Bundy that he would not discuss current peace talks, only general matters with Nixon; Bundy, *Tangled Web*, 35–48, esp. 38. See also Summers, *Arrogance of Power*, 298–99; and Farrell, *Richard Nixon*, 342–43.

51. Solberg, *Hubert Humphrey*, 372; Eisele, *Almost to Presidency*, 367; Sandbrook, *Eugene McCarthy*, 214.

52. Eisele, *Almost to Presidency*, 366; Freeman diary, Aug. 31, 1968, FP (Freeman hoped to be campaign manager); Sandbrook, *Eugene McCarthy*, 214–15; Ambrose, *Nixon: Triumph*, 182–83.

53. Eisele, *Almost to Presidency*, 368; Solberg, *Hubert Humphrey*, 374.

54. Summary Notes of the 590th Meeting of the National Security Council, Sept. 4, 1968, *FRUS*, *1964–1968*, 7:9–10; Solberg, *Hubert Humphrey*, 375; Dobrynin, *In Confidence*, 181; the ambassador opposed this proposal, which came from "top Soviet leaders," as far too risky politically.

55. Solberg, *Hubert Humphrey*, 375; *Time*, Oct. 25, 1968.

56. *NYT*, Sept. 9, 10, 11, 12, 13, 14, 15, 1968; *Time*, Oct. 25, 1968.

57. *NYT*, Sept. 11, 1968; see also Eisele, *Almost to Presidency*, 369.

58. Johnson-Clifford Telephone Conversation, Sept. 2, 1968; Notes of Meeting, Sept. 6, 1968, *FRUS, 1964–1968*, 7:1–6, 13–16.

59. *NYT*, Sept. 10, 1968. The conflicts Johnson mentioned were Korea in 1950, Lebanon in 1958, and Berlin and Vietnam in 1961.

60. Humphrey quoted in Solberg, *Hubert Humphrey*, 376; Freeman diary, Sept. 1, 12, 13, 1968; Clifford, *Counsel to President*, 571.

61. Ambrose, *Nixon: Triumph*, 183–84, on Nixon's maneuver. See also Dallek, *Flawed Giant*, 578; and Clifford, *Counsel to President*, 571–72.

62. Eisele, *Almost to Presidency*, 574; Freeman diary, Sept. 11, 16, 1968; *Newsweek*, Sept. 23, 1968; Ambrose, *Nixon: Triumph*, 191; Agnew's apology in *NYT*, Sept. 12, 1968.

63. Freeman diary, Sept. 16, 20, Oct. 9, 1968, FP.

64. Berman diary, Sept. 16, 1968, quoted in Solberg, *Hubert Humphrey*, 377–78.

65. Humphrey handwritten notes, cited in ibid., 378.

66. *NYT*, Sept. 20, 1968. Berman, *Hubert*, 201–3, expresses great hostility toward those he called "SDS dissenters," "dropouts," and "righteous professors" for their "undisciplined, irresponsible" opposition to Humphrey.

67. *NYT*, Sept. 20, 21, 22, 23, 1968; Eisele, *Almost to Presidency*, 371.

68. *Time*, Sept. 27, 1968; on Nixon's evasive positions, *Time*, Sept. 20, Oct. 4, 1968; *Newsweek*, Sept. 23, 1968; Ambrose, *Nixon: Triumph*, 187–88.

69. *Time*, Sept. 27, Oct. 4, 1968; Humphrey, *Education*, 299–300; on UN speech, Eisele, *Almost to Presidency*, 372.

70. Ambrose, *Nixon: Triumph*, 192–93; Dallek, *Flawed Giant*, 578–79; *Time*, Sept. 27, 1968; *Newsweek*, Sept. 23, 1968; White, *Making of the President*, 353. Reporter Neil Sheehan wrote in the *NYT*, Sept. 29, 1968, that Johnson's emotional pitch and shouting about his policy may have reflected his "inner doubt" about it.

71. White, *Making of the President*, 353; *Newsweek*, Sept. 23, 1968; Schlesinger, *Journals*, Sept. 25, 1968, 299–300; *Time*, Oct. 11, 1968. University of California, Berkeley, political scientist Aaron Wildavsky wrote that a Nixon victory was the best way to preserve the two-party system because it would put a "real Republican" in charge of his party and the Democrats would have to be rid of their discredited leadership; *Time*, Oct. 11, 1968.

72. *NYT*, Sept. 30, 1968; Chester, Hodgson, and Page, *American Melodrama*, 646; White, *Making of the President*, 353; Eisele, *Almost to Presidency*, 374–76.

73. *NYT*, Sept. 30, 1968; Eisele, *Almost to Presidency*, 375–76.

18. BATTLING THE TORRENTS — AND JOHNSON

1. Solberg, *Hubert Humphrey*, 377.

2. Clifford, *Counsel to President*, 572; *NYT*, Sept. 27, 1968; Solberg, *Hubert Humphrey*, 378–79.

3. Solberg, *Hubert Humphrey*, 380–81; Van Dyk, *Heroes, Hacks, and Fools*, 86; Chester, Hodgson, and Page, *American Melodrama*, 646–47.

4. Solberg, *Hubert Humphrey*, 382–84; Eisele, *Almost to Presidency*, 376–77; Van Dyk, *Heroes, Hacks, and Fools*, 86–87; Chester, Hodgson, and Page, *American Melodrama*, 646–48.

5. Telephone Conversation between President Johnson and Presidential Nominee Richard Nixon, Sept. 30, 1968, *FRUS, 1964–1968*, 7:94–103.

6. Telephone Conversation between President Johnson and Vice President Hubert Humphrey, Sept. 30, 1968, *FRUS, 1964–1968*, 7:103–6. Three years later Humphrey recalled that Johnson said, "Hubert, you give that speech and you'll be screwed," although in his memoirs, *Education*, 301, the vice president wrote that Johnson merely said "tartly" that he assumed he was being informed, not being asked for his advice, and was told, "That's about right"; Eisele, *Almost to Presidency*, 377–78. At the time a Humphrey aide told the press that Johnson's response was "very cool"; *Time*, Oct. 11, 1968. Ball, *Past Has Another Pattern*, 477, recalled that he called Johnson after the speech to inform him about it, and the president said he hoped that reporters would be told that it did not mark a departure from administration policy, but Ball replied, "I'm sorry Mr. President, that's not the name of the game."

7. *NYT*, Oct. 1, 1968.

8. Humphrey quoted in Eisele, *Almost to Presidency*, 378; Telephone Conversation Between President Johnson and George Ball, Sept. 30, 1968, *FRUS, 1964–1968*, 7:107–9; Gardner, *Pay Any Price*, 490–92; *NYT*, Oct. 6, 1968.

9. Telephone Conversations between President Johnson and Senator Dirksen, Oct. 1, and between President Johnson and Secretary of State Rusk, Oct. 1, 3, 6, 1968, *FRUS, 1964–1968*, 7:109–12, 130–37, 137–44; Nixon quoted in *NYT*, Oct. 6, 1968.

10. Clifford, *Counsel to President*, 572; Rostow to Johnson, Sept. 30, and Charles Murphy to Johnson, Oct. 1, 1968, box 25, JP. See also *Time*, Oct. 11, 1968; and Schlesinger, *Journals*, Nov. 19, 1968, 301–2. Schlesinger also termed the speech "half assed," but by this he meant that Humphrey would have done better to have supported the minority plank at Chicago or proposed a bombing halt earlier.

11. *NYT*, Oct. 5, 1968; Ambrose, *Nixon: Triumph*, 198; Eisele, *Almost to Presidency*, 380–81; Chester, Hodgson, and Page, *American Melodrama*, 711–13.

12. White, *Making of the President*, 365–68; *NYT*, Oct. 1, 1968.

13. Gould, *1968*, 147–48; *Time*, Oct. 25, 1968.

14. *NYT*, Oct. 2, 6, 11, 13, 1968 (on McCarthy demands). On ADA, see Gillon, *Democrats' Dilemma*, 22.

15. Johnson speech in *NYT*, Oct. 13, 1968; *Newsweek*, Nov. 4, 1968.

16. Rowe to Johnson, Oct. 10, 1968, box 25, JP. See also *NYT*, Dec. 27, 1969, in which Johnson also claimed that he could have won the election had he chosen to run.

17. Dallek, *Flawed Giant*, 579–81.

18. *NYT*, Oct. 13, 17, 1968; Thurber, *Politics of Equality*, 212-13.

19. *NYT*, Oct. 20, 1968.

20. Orville H. Freeman diary, Oct. 9, 12, 1968, box 14, FP (hereinafter cited as Freeman diary). Federal law requiring equal time for all presidential candidates meant having to include Wallace—which Nixon did not want—and Republicans in Congress blocked Democratic efforts to suspend temporarily this provision, just as Democrats had done the same in 1964 to prevent Johnson's need to debate Goldwater with Wallace included; *Time*, Oct. 18, 1964.

21. Freeman diary, Oct. 19, 1968, FP.

22. Herring, *Longest War*, 237–38.

23. LBJ et al. remarks in Notes of Meetings (3), Oct. 14, 1968, *FRUS, 1964–1968*, 7:173–74, 177–84, 196–98; Clifford, *Counsel to President*, 576.

24. Telephone Conversation between President Johnson and Senator Mike Mansfield, and Telephone Conversation among President Johnson, Hubert Humphrey, Richard Nixon, and George Wallace, Oct. 16, 1968, *FRUS, 1964–1968*, 7:213–16, 219, 226; *NYT*, Oct. 20, 1968. For Bundy's speech at DePauw University in Indiana on Oct. 12, see *NYT*, Oct. 13, 1968. "Amazingly" in Clifford, *Counsel to President*, 577.

25. *NYT*, Oct. 20, 1968.

26. Ibid., Oct. 21, 1968; *Newsweek*, Oct. 21, 28, 1968; McCarthy, *Year of the People*, 235–36, 241–43; see also Sandbrook, *Eugene McCarthy*, 214.

27. *NYT*, Oct. 24, 26, 1968.

28. Isaacson, *Kissinger*, 129–34. Kissinger said to one confidant, "Six days a week I'm for Hubert, but on the seventh day, I think they're both awful." In the fall of 1967 Kissinger had used French contacts in Paris in a vain effort (codenamed "Pennsylvania") to help start negotiations; see Gardner, *Pay Any Price*, 385–94.

29. *NYT*, Oct. 27, 28, 1968; Ambrose, *Nixon: Triumph*, 209–10.

30. Forslund, *Anna Chennault*, 64, 67–68; Summers, *Arrogance of Power*, 300. Diem, *Jaws of History*, 244, later wrote that he could see how his messages constituted circumstantial evidence for "anybody to assume the worst."

31. Clifford, *Counsel to President*, 578–79.

32. Johnson's remarks on bad date, and aides playing with doves, in Notes of Meeting, Oct. 27, 1968, *FRUS, 1964–1968*, 7:364–71. On Russians "shoving," see President Johnson Telephone Conversation with Secretary of State Rusk, Oct. 24, 1968, and Humphrey, President Johnson Telephone Call with Senator Richard Russell, Oct. 23, 1968, *FRUS, 1964–1968*, 7:321–25, 302–9.

33. Rusk's remarks in Notes of Meeting, Oct. 27, 1968, Memorandum from the President's Special Assistant (Rostow) to the President, Oct. 28, 1968, and Clifford Remarks in Telephone Conversation between President Johnson and Secretary of Defense Clifford, Oct. 22, 1968, *FRUS, 1964–1968*, 7:364–71, 373–74, 289–94.

34. Notes of Meeting, Oct. 27, 1968, *FRUS, 1964–1968*, 7:364–71; Clifford, *Counsel to President*, 580–81, italics in original.

35. Clifford, *Counsel to President*, 564; Johnson, *Vantage Point*, 548.

36. Gardner, *Pay Any Price*, 504–6; Information Memorandum from the President's Special Assistant (Rostow) to President Johnson, Oct. 29, 1968, *FRUS, 1964–1968*, 7:423–24.

37. Woods, *LBJ*, 872.

38. Telephone Conversation #13612, Lyndon Johnson and Richard Russell, Oct. 29, 1968, JL; Notes of Meeting, Oct. 29, 1968, *FRUS, 1964–1968*, 7:437–41.

39. Notes of Meeting, Oct. 30, 1968, *FRUS, 1964–1968*, 7:446–51.

40. Telephone Conversation #13617, Lyndon Johnson and Everett Dirksen, Oct. 31, 1968, JL.

41. Transcript of Telephone Conversation among President Johnson, Hubert Humphrey, Richard Nixon, and George Wallace, Oct. 31, 1968, *FRUS, 1964–1968*, 7:476–82.

42. Johnson-Humphrey Telephone Conversation, Oct. 31, 1968, *FRUS, 1964–1968,* 7:485–93. Solberg, *Hubert Humphrey,* 396, cites the Dr. Edgar Berman diary of October 31, 1968, which states that Johnson refused Humphrey's request to return from campaigning to attend an NSC meeting that evening because it would be seen as a partisan matter, and afterward Humphrey said, "I hope I can keep my Vice President in line as well as he does." Given that the NSC meeting preceded the Johnson-Humphrey call, perhaps Berman's reference was to a different meeting, although Johnson had excluded Humphrey from NSC meetings all fall.

43. *NYT,* Nov. 1, 1968.

44. Johnson-Rowe Telephone Conversation, Nov. 1, 1968, *FRUS, 1964–1968,* 7:505–11; Solberg, *Hubert Humphrey,* 397.

45. Woods, *LBJ,* 873–74; Gardner, *Pay Any Price,* 509; Clifford, *Counsel to President,* 591. Later Theodore White, *Making of the President,* 381, would write he knew of "no more essentially decent story in American politics" than Humphrey's not airing this information that might have led to his winning the presidency. White did not know, however, that Humphrey lacked access to proof to charge Nixon. Cohen, *American Maelstrom,* 326, mistakenly states that Johnson thought Humphrey should go public with the information.

46. Clifford, *Counsel to President,* 584; Gardner, *Pay Any Price,* 509. Solberg, *Hubert Humphrey,* 394, says that Humphrey's aide, Welsh, told the author in 1983 that the vice president was informed on about Sept. 27, 1968, of the Nixon matter but concluded that Johnson would not say anything about it. Welsh's recollection of when Humphrey was informed was off by one month; it was not until later October, but the vice president rightly thought that Johnson would not raise the issue publicly.

47. Chester, Hodgson, and Page, *American Melodrama,* 706–17; White, *Making of the President,* 364–69.

48. *NYT,* Oct. 24, 26, 1968; *Time,* Nov. 1, 1968.

49. *NYT,* Oct. 30, 31, 1968; Ambrose, *Nixon: Triumph,* 212; Gardner, *Pay Any Price,* 516.

50. Humphrey, *Education,* 303–4; Van Dyk, *Heroes, Hacks, and Fools,* 89–90.

51. Bundy, *Tangled Web,* 42; Sherman, *From Somewhere to Nowhere,* 195–96; Solberg, *Hubert Humphrey,* 398. See also Dallek, *Nixon and Kissinger,* 74–78, who concludes with Bundy that Nixon's actions "must be judged harshly."

52. *NYT,* Nov. 4, 1968.

53. Ibid.; Humphrey, *Education,* 304.

54. Forslund, *Anna Chennault,* 70–71.

55. Telephone Conversation #13706, Lyndon Johnson and Everett Dirksen, Nov. 2, 1968, JL. Nixon's action might have been prosecutable under the rarely invoked 1799 Logan Act prohibiting unauthorized persons to negotiate with foreign governments with intent to undermine US negotiations.

56. Telephone Conversations #13708 and #13709, George Smathers and Lyndon Johnson, Nov. 3, 1968, JL; *NYT,* Nov. 4, 1968; Ambrose, *Nixon: Triumph,* 212–13. Nixon's statement was meant to recall Eisenhower's "I Shall Go to Korea" statement in 1952.

57. Johnson-Nixon Telephone Conversation, Nov. 3, 1968, *FRUS, 1964–1968,* 7:538–44; Rusk comment in Parry, "LBJ's X File," 9.

58. Telephone Conversation #13714, Lyndon Johnson, Walt Rostow, Clark Clifford, Dean Rusk, Nov. 4, 1968, JL.

59. Van Dyk, *Heroes, Hacks, and Fools*, 91.

60. Ibid., 92–93.

61. Ibid., 93; White, *Making of the President*, 384–86.

62. Humphrey, *Education*, xviii–xix; Solberg, *Hubert Humphrey*, 403.

63. Humphrey, *Education*, xxi.

64. Ibid., xxii; Solberg, *Hubert Humphrey*, 406; NYT, Nov. 6, 7, 1968.

65. Humphrey, *Education*, xxiii–xxiv.

66. Humphrey quoted about a month after the election, in Solberg, *Hubert Humphrey*, 407.

67. Hannaford, *Pearson Diaries*, Nov. 12, 1968, 633.

68. LaFeber, *Deadly Bet*, 164–65. Cohen, *American Maelstrom*, 331–35, highlights racial divisions and crime as major factors in the Democrats' losses.

69. Humphrey, *Education*, 282. Humphrey would have had to win only two of the three states of New Jersey, Illinois, and Ohio to put the election into the Democratically controlled House.

19. RESURRECTION AND DEFEAT

1. For Humphrey on "liberal deserters," who he said he hoped "slept well" with Nixon as president, see NYT, May 28, 1972. Berman, *Hubert*, 230–31; Eisele, *Almost to Presidency*, 421.

2. Humphrey, *Education*, 320–23; *Time*, Nov. 14, 1969; NYT, Dec. 27, 1968; Eisele, *Almost to Presidency*, 421. In reflecting on the 1968 election in 1971, Humphrey told his chief speechwriter, Ted Van Dyk, he should have taken a stronger position on the war, but then — to his listener's amazement — said, "I should have stuck with Johnson"; Van Dyk, *Heroes, Hacks, and Fools*, 119.

3. NYT, Nov. 7, 8, 1968.

4. *Time*, Nov. 15, 22, 1968; Humphrey, *Education*, 326; *Time*, Mar. 7, 1969; Sandbrook, *Eugene McCarthy*, 230. Former New York governor and presidential nominee Thomas E. Dewey had arranged the meeting. It is not known if Humphrey knew Nixon had offered the UN position a month earlier to McCarthy, who was interested but refused to resign his Senate seat when Minnesota's Republican governor Harold LeVander would not agree to appoint a Democrat to the position.

5. Solberg, *Hubert Humphrey*, 414; Berman, *Hubert*, 241–42; Humphrey, *Beyond Civil Rights*.

6. Eisele, *Almost to Presidency*, 422–23; Solberg, *Hubert Humphrey*, 411–12.

7. Solberg, *Hubert Humphrey*, 412–13; Eisele, *Almost to Presidency*, 428–29; NYT, Feb. 22, 1969; *Time*, Mar. 7, 1969.

8. *Time*, Feb. 2, Mar. 3, 1969; NYT, Oct. 11, 1969, Apr. 30, 1971.

9. Solberg, *Hubert Humphrey*, 415–16; NYT, Mar. 3, 1969, Oct. 11, 1970, Apr. 11, 1971.

10. Solberg, *Hubert Humphrey*, 413–15; on Humphrey and the Wilson Center, CRS, Feb. 23, 1971, 3582–87.

11. *Chicago Tribune*, July 27, 1968; Sandbrook, *Eugene McCarthy*, 239–40; Berman, *Hubert*, 247; *St. Paul Pioneer Press*, July 27, 1968.

12. Solberg, *Hubert Humphrey*, 416; Berman, *Hubert*, 247.

13. *Time*, Aug. 15, 1969.

14. Humphrey address at UCLA, Feb. 25, 1969, UCLA Communications Studies Archives, accessed at https://www.youtube.com/watch?v=yzbxE1_SPvI.

15. BDD, Oct. 10, 1969; *NYT*, Oct. 12, 1969; Eisele, *Almost to Presidency*, 425, 425n.5 (which cites a confidential memorandum Humphrey sent to Kissinger offering to support Nixon's policy); Solberg, *Hubert Humphrey*, 417; see also Ambrose, *Nixon: Triumph*, 300–302; similar comments came from former Secretary of State Dean Acheson and Washington columnist David Broder.

16. *NYT*, Oct. 16, Nov. 4, 16, 1969.

17. *NYT*, Nov. 16, 1969; Solberg, *Hubert Humphrey*, 417–18.

18. *NYT*, Feb. 10, 1970; Eisele, *Almost to Presidency*, 427.

19. Humphrey quoted in Eisele, *Almost to Presidency*, 429; BDD, May 12, 1970. By contrast, Johnson said at a Democratic dinner in Chicago hosted by Mayor Richard Daley that he hoped President Nixon's voice would not be "drowned out by other voices that do not know the facts"; BDD, May 2, 1960.

20. Herring, *America's Longest War*, 293–95; *NYT*, June 25, Sept. 2, 1970.

21. *NYT*, May 2, 1971; Eisele, *Almost to Presidency*, 427; Solberg, *Hubert Humphrey*, 421–22.

22. Eisele, *Almost to Presidency*, 427; Solberg, *Hubert Humphrey*, 422; *NYT*, Mar. 4, 1970.

23. Eisele, *Almost to Presidency*, 428–29.

24. *NYT*, June 14, 1970. MacGregor had also said he now favored withdrawal of all US "combat forces" from Vietnam by June 1971; BDD, May 12, 1970.

25. Eisele, *Almost to Presidency*, 429–30; Solberg, *Hubert Humphrey*, 418; *NYT*, Oct. 11, 1970; quotation on election victory in *NYT*, Sept. 18, 1970.

26. Eisele, *Almost to Presidency*, 431; Solberg, *Hubert Humphrey*, 418; *NYT*, Sept. 18, 1970.

27. Scammon and Wattenberg, *Real Majority*; BDD, Oct. 15, 22, 30, 31, 1970.

28. Eisele, *Almost to Presidency*, 431–32; Solberg, *Hubert Humphrey*, 418.

29. MacGregor troop withdrawal statement in BDD, Mar. 12, 1970; election results in BDD, Nov. 3, 4, 5, 1970; Eisele, *Almost to Presidency*, 432.

30. November 1970 campaign statement quoted in Solberg, *Hubert Humphrey*, 423.

31. Solberg, *Hubert Humphrey*, 423–24; Eisele, *Almost to Presidency*, 432–34; Humphrey, *Education*, 60, 324–25, 329.

32. Eisele, *Almost to Presidency*, 433; CRS, Mar. 2, 1971, 4548–50.

33. CRS, Jan. 26, May 12, 1971, 573–74, 14660–61.

34. Ibid., May 26, 1971, 17062–65; Eisele, *Almost to Presidency*, 434n.12.

35. CRS, Mar. 24, 1971, 7617–18; Eisele, *Almost to Presidency*, 435.

36. CRS, Feb. 11, Aug. 5, Dec. 1, 1971, 2601–2, 2630–33, 29915, 43755–58.

37. Ibid., June 10, 1971, 19285–86. Humphrey omitted mention of Vietnam.

38. Solberg, *Hubert Humphrey*, 428; Ambrose, *Nixon: Triumph*, 458–59.

39. For Humphrey on SALT talks, nuclear weapons, and ABM, see CRS, Feb. 1, Sept. 2, 24, 1971, 1193–95, 33296–315, 34022–33; on PRC and UN, ibid., Oct. 29, 1971, 38224–25

(Humphrey held that the UN was based on states, e.g., the PRC, and not on governments, e.g., the regime in Taipei); on Mansfield resolution, ibid., May 19, 1971, 15296; and on Israel and jets, ibid., Oct. 12, 1971, 35723.

40. *NYT*, Apr. 21, 1971.

41. Ibid., Aug. 3, 1970, Jan. 21, 1971.

42. Eisele, *Almost to Presidency*, 435. As cosponsor of McGovern-Hatfield amendment, see *CRS*, June 4, 1971, 18221. On defeat of the amendment, see *NYT*, June 16, 1971.

43. *CRS*, June 24, 1971, 21960–68.

44. Hamill and Harrington quoted in Solberg, *Hubert Humphrey*, 426; Gallup poll and Humphrey in *NYT*, Mar. 30, June 13, 1971.

45. *BDD*, June 17, 1968.

46. Humphrey quoted in Solberg, *Hubert Humphrey*, 427; *NYT*, June 20, 1971.

47. Humphrey entered his August speech into the *CRS*, Oct. 12, 1971, 35723–26. His September speech is recorded in ibid., Sept. 28, 1971, 36333–34.

48. Reprinted in ibid., Mar. 1, 1972, 6201–6.

49. Herring, *Longest War*, 304–9; *CRS*, Apr. 7, 1972, 11784–86.

50. Solberg, *Hubert Humphrey*, 426, quotes Humphrey to Berman, Mar. 29, 1971; others are quoted in *NYT*, May 28, 1972.

51. Eisele, *Almost to Presidency*, 437–38; see also *Miami Herald*, May 28, 1971.

52. Eisele, *Almost to Presidency*, 438–39.

53. Ibid., 439; Sandbrook, *Eugene McCarthy*, 246–49.

54. Solberg, *Hubert Humphrey*, 428.

55. Ibid.; Eisele, *Almost to Presidency*, 440; Miroff, *Liberals' Moment*, 20–22; *NYT*, Dec. 12, 1971.

56. *NYT*, Dec. 12, 1971; Eisele, *Almost to Presidency*, 440.

57. *NYT*, Jan. 1, 11, 1972; Eisele, *Almost to Presidency*, 441.

58. Miroff, *Liberals' Moment*, 52–55; Ambrose, *Nixon: Triumph*, 522.

59. *NYT*, Mar. 11, 1972.

60. The Supreme Court empowered federal courts to do this in 1971 in *Swann v. Charlotte-Mecklenburg Board of Education*. *Time*, Mar. 12, 1972.

61. *Time*, Mar. 12, 1968; *NYT*, Mar. 13, 14, 1972.

62. *NYT*, Mar. 12, 23, 1972.

63. Ibid., Mar. 29, 1972; Miroff, *Liberals' Moment*, 59; *Time*, Apr. 15, 1972.

64. Miroff, *Liberals' Moment*, 69.

65. Ibid.; *NYT*, May 14, 1972; Carter, *Politics of Rage*, 432, cites Humphrey as winning by 40,000 votes out of 700,000 votes cast, a 5.7 percent margin.

66. Miroff, *Liberals' Moment*, 63–64; *NYT*, May 28, 1972. On May 15, 1972, syndicated conservative columnist Robert Novak wrote that an unnamed US senator had said that McGovern was the candidate of "acid, abortion, and amnesty" and would be dead politically once Catholics learned this. The senator, ironically, was Missouri's Thomas Eagleton, then a Muskie supporter. See Ganey, "Slice of History."

67. Carter, *Politics of Rage*, 444–46; *NYT*, May 17, 1968.

68. Solberg, *Hubert Humphrey*, 432; *NYT*, May 2, June 5, 1972. See *NYT*, June 8, 1973, and *Time*, June 18, 1973, for discussion of the illegal $48,000 contribution of Republican

banker John L. Loeb Sr. of Loeb, Rhoades, and Co., conjured from his employees in violation of the recently passed Federal Election Campaign Act of April 7, 1972. See also *NYT*, May 28, 1972, which discusses how Wallace cut into Humphrey's vote.

69. Humphrey to I. W. Abel, May 16, 1972, in Solberg, *Hubert Humphrey*, 432–33; *NYT*, May 4, 23 ("spoilsport"), June 5, 1972; *Time*, June 5, 1972; Humphrey, *Education*, 328; Miroff, *Liberals' Moment*, 220–21.

70. Miroff, *Liberals' Moment*, 178.

71. For text of the debate, Transcript of *Face the Nation*, May 28, 1972, HP, 150.D.3.10F, esp. 2–10, 20–21. For McGovern vote in the majority to repeal Tonkin Gulf Resolution, see *NYT*, July 25, 1970. On defeat of the McGovern-Hatfield Resolution, see ibid., Sept. 2, 1970.

72. *NYT*, May 29, 30, June 1, 1972.

73. Van Dyk, *Heroes, Hacks, and Fools*, 133.

74. Text of *Meet the Press*, May 30, 1972, HP, 150.D.3.10F, esp. 1–4, 19; Miroff, *Liberals' Moment*, 179.

75. *NYT*, June 1, 1972; Miroff, *Liberals' Moment*, 180; Solberg, *Hubert Humphrey*, 434; *Time*, June 19, 1972.

76. Solberg, *Hubert Humphrey*, 434–35; *NYT*, June 8, 1972.

77. *NYT*, June 23, July 1, 1972; Perlstein, *Nixonland*, 672.

78. *NYT*, June 23, 1972; Humphrey statement on Wallace in *Time*, June 19, 1972; see also Carter, *Politics of Rage*, 446. Wallace, debilitated and paralyzed from the waist down, was an unlikely vice presidential candidate.

79. Miroff, *Liberals' Moment*, 76–79; Schaff, "Clear Choice," 122. Ironically, McGovern had originally opposed the winner-take-all rule when he was on the Democrats' reform commission but agreed to allow it to stand until 1976; *Time*, June 19, 1972.

80. *NYT*, July 12, 13, 1972; Solberg, *Hubert Humphrey*, 435–36, which quotes Roger Kent to Humphrey, July 14, and Humphrey to Kent, July 21, 1972; *St. Paul Pioneer Press*, July 23, 1972.

81. Miroff, *Liberals' Moment*, 81–83. Humphrey and Muskie delegates also helped to excise planks they thought most voters would reject, such as legalizing abortion and same sex marriage, and ending all tax deductions, including the cherished home mortgage.

82. Van Dyk, *Heroes, Hacks, and Fools*, 138; Miroff, *Liberals' Moment*, 85–86.

83. Miroff, *Liberals' Moment*, 87–89.

84. Ibid., 89–96.

85. Solberg, *Hubert Humphrey*, 435; *Washington Post*, Aug. 4, 1972.

86. Schaff, "Clear Choice," 124–27, regarding the Eagleton affair.

87. Ambrose, *Nixon: Triumph*, 555, 586. The "acid, amnesty, and abortion" phrase was attributed to Republican Senator Hugh Scott of Pennsylvania, but Eagleton put forward the original line of argument during the primaries; Johnson sent his message to Nixon through the Reverend Billy Graham; doubtless Johnson was angry that the Democrats did not display his picture at their convention, and McGovern was an early and sharp critic of Johnson's Vietnam policy; on the "missing" Johnson picture—those of Roosevelt, Truman, and Kennedy were hung—see Schulman, *Johnson and Liberalism*, 155.

88. Ambrose, *Nixon: Triumph*, 560–67; Kutler, *Wars of Watergate*, 187–90. The exact purpose of the break-in remains uncertain; it may have been to rearrange wiretaps on telephones placed there earlier, or to glean Democratic political strategy and perhaps learn what O'Brien may have known about Nixon's financial dealings with reclusive business tycoon Howard Hughes. Possibly the purpose was to learn the whereabouts, and prevent release, of the tapes of Republican dealings in 1968 with Anna Chennault and the Saigon embassy in Washington intended to keep South Vietnam from the Paris talks.

89. Miroff, *Liberals' Moment*, 101; Braden column in *Redlands (CA) Daily Facts*, Nov. 11, 1972 (written the day before the election, when the results were fairly certain).

90. Ambrose, *Nixon: Triumph*, 605–7; Miroff, *Liberals' Moment*, 108–14; Herring, *Longest War*, 313–18, which notes the peace agreed upon in January 1973 was virtually the same as that of October 1972; Kissinger's 1972 "peace" statement is in *NYT*, Oct. 27, 1972.

91. Humphrey statement on McGovern's defense budget as used in ad by "Democrats for Nixon" accessed at http://www.youtube.com/watch?v=h7nfn9rIFJI.

92. Ambrose, *Nixon: Triumph*, 651–52.

93. Humphrey-Nixon talk at 1:30 a.m. on Nov. 8 accessed at http://www.youtube.com/watch?v=56dBfyeH2DM; Haldeman, *Diaries*, 531, which notes that it was "quite a friendly conversation" and that Nixon was pleased with Humphrey's view of national security as opposed to that of McGovern.

94. *Time*, Jan. 8, 1973.

20. A TIME FOR EVERYTHING

1. *CRS*, Feb. 6, 1973, 3487–88.

2. Ibid., Jan. 24, 1973, 2075–78. On February 10, 1973, however, Humphrey wrote to a retired banker friend, W. R. Biggs, that if the United States had not gone into Vietnam, "we would see today Indonesia in the hands of the Communist party, and surely all of Southeast Asia would have been taken over by North Vietnamese communist forces"; Solberg, *Hubert Humphrey*, 448.

3. Humphrey address on Dec. 11, 1972, at JL; "The Unfinished Agenda," HP, 150.H.1.1B; fighting Nixon, and "waging war on the poor," *CRS*, Jan. 9, Feb. 21, 1973, 434–35, 4773–74. On Congress's oversight, Humphrey Remarks to the American Political Science Association Fellows at Fletcher School of Law and Diplomacy, Jan. 26, 1973, HP, 150.H.1.B.

4. On Social Security, *CRS*, Feb. 8, 1973, 3997–98; on REA, ibid., Feb. 15, 20, 1973, 4217–18, 4690–92; on "one man rule" and impoundment, ibid., Feb. 8, 1973, 4100–4102; on "blackmail" and veto threats, ibid., Nov. 27, 1973, 38133–34; on line-item veto, ibid., Oct. 13, 1973, 35911–12.

5. On opposition to military aid budget for South Vietnam, *CRS*, Feb. 21, 1973, 4782–85; on cutting off military spending in Indochina area and praise for McGovern, ibid., June 29, 1973, 22316.

6. On opposition to Nixon's military budget, *CRS*, Sept. 20, 1973, 30671–73; on praise for Kissinger and détente, ibid., Sept. 6, 1973, 28715–17; on urging against deployment

of ABM, *CRS*, Sept. 20, 1973, 38133–44; on jets for Israel, and oil, ibid., Oct. 18, 1973, 34614.

7. *CRS*, Jan. 18, July 20, Oct. 10, 1973, 1415–16, 25094, 33552–53; *Washington Post*, Nov. 8, 1973.

8. Humphrey's concerns in *CRS*, May 7, 1973, 14487–88; Kutler, *Wars of Watergate*, 265–319; Kleindienst tearfully responded that it was unfair to link him to the others, but Nixon was seeking to appear to make a clean sweep of officials touched by the Watergate matter. See also Farrell, *Richard Nixon*, 510.

9. *Washington Post*, May, 7, 1973.

10. Thomas, *Being Nixon*, 468–69; WDN, Oct. 11, 1973.

11. Thomas, *Being Nixon*, 470–72; *Washington Post*, Oct. 21, 1973; Kutler, *Wars of Watergate*, 426–29.

12. *CRS*, Oct. 30, 1973, 19656–59.

13. Kutler, *Wars of Watergate*, 426–29.

14. Humphrey quoted in *Time*, Apr. 22, 1974; Haldeman, *Diaries*, Aug. 4, 1972, 490; *Time*, July 8, 1974; Haldeman, *Diaries*, Jan. 12, 1973, 567; see also Solberg, *Hubert Humphrey*, 442–43.

15. *NYT*, June 3, 1973.

16. Solberg, *Hubert Humphrey*, 443–44.

17. *Washington Post*, Aug. 3, 1974; *United States v. Chestnut*, 399 F. Supp. 1292 (S.D. N.Y. 1975); see also U.S. Court of Appeals, 533 F.2d 40 (1976); Torres-Spelliscy, "Got Corruption?"

18. Humphrey quoted in Solberg, *Hubert Humphrey*, 444–45. Nixon threatened to veto public financing legislation; meanwhile the milk cooperatives had pledged $2 million to his campaign as payback for increased price supports in 1971, and in 1972 archconservative Mellon family banking heir Richard Scaife contributed $990,000 tax-free dollars to Nixon's campaign in the form of 330 checks for $3,000 each; *Time*, Apr. 8, 22, 1974.

19. Berman, *Hubert*, 273–74; *NYT*, Apr. 15, 1974; Solberg, *Hubert Humphrey*, 448–50.

20. *CRS*, Mar. 7, 20, 1974, 5716–17, 5810–11, 7491–95.

21. Humphrey Remarks at Democratic Governors Conference, Apr. 22, Humphrey Address to AFL-CIO, May 9, 1974, HP, 150.H.1.2F; *CRS*, May 30, 1974, 16992–94.

22. Thomas, *Man Divided*, 482; Kutler, *Wars of Watergate*, 450–52.

23. Thomas, *Man Divided*, 490–91; Kutler, *Wars of Watergate*, 513–30.

24. Thomas, *Man Divided*, 492–96.

25. Humphrey statement for Winona radio stations and newspapers, Aug. 9, 1974, HP, 150.H.1.3B.

26. Humphrey on pardon in Cannon, *Time and Chance*, 385; Gerald Ford Oral History Project interview with Max Friedersdorf (Ford White House assistant for congressional relations), Jan. 30, 2009, accessed at https://geraldrfordfoundation.org/centennial/oralhistory/max-friedersdorf/.

27. Humphrey statement for Winona radio and newspapers, Aug. 9, 1974, HP, 150.H.1.3B. Rockefeller's nomination angered Republican conservatives, as well as others who wondered how such a wealthy man could respond to the average person; Wilentz, *Age of Reagan*, 13–14.

28. Humphrey speech, "The Unfinished Agenda," Dec. 11, 1972, at JL, HP, 150.H.1.3B; Thurber, *Politics of Equality*, 233–36.

29. CRS, Aug. 21, 1974, 29785–89; see also Ginsburg, "Historical Amnesia," 7–11.

30. CRS, Jan. 29, 1975, 1579–84.

31. Humphrey's Comments [Oct. 8, 1974] on President Ford's Speech of October 8, 1974, to Joint Session of Congress, HP, 150.H.1.3B; Hart quoted in Gillon, *Democrats' Dilemma*, 153–54.

32. Interview with CBS News, Dec. 12, 1974, HP, 150.H.1.3B.

33. Humphrey Remarks to Congressional Breakfast for Full Employment, Jan. 15, 1975, HP, 150.H.1.3B; CRS, Jan. 16, 1975, 577–78.

34. CRS, Jan. 23, 1975, 1107–9 (on "promise of America"); on Full Employment and $20 billion tax cut, ibid., Jan. 29, 1975, 1708–11; on nutritious lunch program, Feb. 28, 1975, ibid., 4833–36; on $30 billion tax cut, Mar. 3, 1975, ibid., 4913–17; on Ford tax bill, Wilentz, *Age of Reagan*, 38.

35. *Time*, Oct. 6, 1975; CRS, Oct. 9, 1975, 32819–22.

36. *Business Week*, Dec. 15, 1975.

37. CRS, Apr. 8, 1975, 9296–97.

38. Ibid., Apr. 7, 1975, 9088–99; Herring, *Longest War*, 332–40.

39. CRS, Apr. 8, 1975, 9296–97; *Time*, May 15, 1975.

40. Humphrey Remarks at Johns Hopkins School for Advanced International Relations, Feb. 5, 1976, HP, 150.H.1.6F.

41. NYT, Feb. 2, 1975.

42. Solberg, *Hubert Humphrey*, 451; WDN, Sept. 25, 1975; Gillon, *Democrats' Dilemma*, 152.

43. NYT, Apr. 27, June 22, 1975; Solberg, *Hubert Humphrey*, 449–52.

44. Solberg, *Hubert Humphrey*, 451; NYT, Oct. 17, Dec. 11, 1975.

45. NYT, Dec. 28, 1975, Jan. 25, 1976. Humphrey and Reagan were both born in 1911; Ford was born in 1913.

46. Wilentz, *Age of Reagan*, 69–70.

47. NYT, Mar. 4, 9, 23, 27, 1976; *Time*, Apr. 5, 1976. Humphrey later said that his remark was aimed at Ford and Reagan, not Carter.

48. Jeff Greenfield, "What Makes Hubert Not Run?," NYT, Apr. 4, 1976; *Time*, Apr. 5, 1976.

49. NYT, Apr. 2, 1976.

50. *Time*, Apr. 12, 1976.

51. Solberg, *Hubert Humphrey*, 412; *Time*, May 10, 1976.

52. *Time*, May 10, 1976; Berman, *Hubert*, 67.

53. Statement by Senator Humphrey, Apr. 29, 1975, HP, 150.H.1.5B; NYT, Apr. 30, 1976.

54. Berman, *Hubert*, 69; NYT, Apr. 30, 1976.

55. Reston column in NYT, Apr. 24, 1976.

56. NYT, Apr. 23 (Wicker), May 26 (Reston), and June 4 (Apple), 1976.

57. Humphrey had predicted an "earthquake" if Brown won the Maryland primary; WDN, May 11, 1976; NYT, June 9, 1976.

58. NYT, July 13, 1976.

59. Humphrey Address to Democratic National Convention, July 13, 1976, HP, 150.D.4.1B.

60. Carter address of July 15, and Humphrey Remarks Nominating Senator Mondale for Vice President, July 15, 1976, *NYT*, July 16, 1976; Humphrey nominating speech also in HP, 150.D.4.1B; see also Kaufman, *Presidential Profiles*, 213; Mondale, *Good Fight*, 165, who also recognized that what had occurred "meant we were turning a page in our own history."

61. Remarks of Senator Hubert H. Humphrey at B'Nai B'rith [Washington, DC], Sept. 7, and Remarks of Senator Hubert H. Humphrey, Farmfest, Lake Crystal, MN, Sept. 15, 1976, HP, 150.D.4.1B.

62. *WDN*, Oct. 12, Nov. 3, 1976.

63. Berman, *Hubert*, 275–79.

64. Ibid., 280–81; *NYT*, Nov. 15, 1976.

65. *NYT*, Aug. 19, 1976; conservative Republicans pressed Vice President Rockefeller to deny interest in the post.

66. Patterson, *Restless Giant*, 105–7.

67. *WDN*, Nov. 3, 1976; *BDD*, Nov. 3, 1976.

68. *NYT*, Nov. 25, Dec. 15, 1976; *Time*, Jan. 10, 1977.

69. *NYT*, Jan. 2, 3, 6, 1977; *Time*, Jan. 17, 1977. The newly invented post was designated for any former vice president or president who later served in the Senate; to date, only Humphrey qualified, and the likelihood that another person would qualify seemed doubtful.

70. Solberg, *Hubert Humphrey*, 454; *Time*, Jan. 17, Nov. 7, 1977.

71. Jordan comment in *NYT*, Jan. 16, 1978; Kaufman, *Carter Years*, 214; Jeff Taylor, *Where Did the Party Go?* 186; Carter Remarks on the Tax Rebate in *NYT*, Apr. 15, 1977. On the Humphrey-Goldwater exchange, see commentary by Fred Gates (not to be confused with Humphrey's longtime supporter and general aide-de-camp Fred Gates, who ran a penny arcade in Minneapolis), who managed Humphrey's Minneapolis office and was with him in Waverly during his last months there, in Herrera, "Humphrey Era Lacked Acrimony"; see also *NYT*, Jan. 15, 1978. Carter signed the Panama Canal Treaty in September 1977, but the Senate did not ratify it until March 1978, two months after Humphrey's death.

72. *JTA* (*Jewish Telegraphic Agency*), Jan. 30, 1978.

73. Thurber, *Politics of Equality*, 237–43; Ginsburg, "Historical Amnesia," 13–14.

74. *NYT*, Nov. 11, 1978; *Time*, Nov. 21, 1977; Humphrey-Hawkins Full Employment Bill, *Congressional Quarterly Almanac*, 34th ed. (1978), 272–79; *Washington Post*, Oct. 28, 1978.

75. Berman, *Hubert*, 282–83; *BDD*, Aug. 18, 19, 22, 1977.

76. *BDD*, Sept. 13, 22, 1977; Humphrey Remarks to Minnesota AFL-CIO, Sept. 19, 1977, HP, 150.D.4.2F.

77. On letters to Humphrey's office, *NYT*, Dec. 2, 1977; *WDN*, Dec, 19, 1977.

78. *BDD*, Oct. 20, 1977; *NYT*, Oct. 21, 1977; *WDN*, Oct. 21, 1977. Dole and Humphrey became good friends while serving together on the Agriculture Committee. Humphrey spoke briefly by telephone to the group to endorse the Humphrey Institute's mission to educate a "new generation of public servants" to seek to solve the nation's problems.

Remarks by Hubert H. Humphrey, III: An Evening in Honor of Hubert H. Humphrey, Oct. 20, 1977, HP, 150.D.4.2F.

79. Carter statement about Humphrey, and Carter remarks in Minnesota, Oct. 23, 1977, HP, 150.D.F.2F; WDN, Oct. 26, 1977; *Time*, Nov. 7, 1977.

80. Dole statement in *CRS*, Nov. 4, 1977, 37285–286; remarks of Senator Hubert H. Humphrey at Dedication of HEW Building, Nov. 1, 1977, HP, 150.D.4.2F; WDN, Nov. 2, 1977.

81. *CRH*, Nov. 3, 1977, 12130–38.

82. WDN, Nov. 8, 15, 23, 1977; see also Lawn, *You Wake Me*, 117.

83. NYT, Dec. 2, 3, 1977; *Washington Post*, Dec. 3, 1977; Remarks by Senator Humphrey at the National Tribute to the Honorable Hubert Humphrey, Dec. 2, 1977, HP, 150.D.4.2F.

84. WDN, Dec. 6, 1977; Carter, *White House Diary*, 146–47.

85. WDN, Dec. 23, 1977; NYT, Jan. 16, 1978.

86. *Washington Post*, Jan. 6, 1977; *Ocala (FL) Star Banner*, Jan. 6, 1977; Berman, *Hubert*, 284; Solberg, *Hubert Humphrey*, 456; Remarks of Frances Howard at NAACP Annual Awards Dinner, New York City, Jan. 8, 1978, HP, 150.D.4.2F; *NYT* June 10, 1980; see also Berman, *Hubert*, 284.

87. *Albert Lea (MN) Tribune*, Jan. 13, 1978; *NYT*, Jan. 14, 1978.

EPILOGUE

1. NYT, Jan. 14, 1978; *Time*, Jan. 30, 1978.

2. NYT, Jan. 15, 1978; *Time*, Jan. 30, 1978.

3. NYT, Jan. 16, 1978; *Washington Post*, Jan. 16, 1978.

4. NYT, Jan. 16, 1978.

5. Ibid., Jan. 16, 17, 1978; *Washington Post*, Jan. 17, 1978; *Time*, Jan. 23, 30, 1978.

6. Berman, *Hubert*, 279.

BIBLIOGRAPHY

ARCHIVES

Harry S. Truman Presidential Library, Independence, MO
   James I. Loeb Oral History, James I. Loeb Papers
Minnesota Historical Society, St. Paul
   Dr. Edgar Berman Diary
   Orville H. Freeman Papers
   Hubert H. Humphrey Papers
   Carl Solberg Papers
Lyndon Baines Johnson Presidential Library, Austin, TX
   Hubert H. Humphrey, Oral History Interviews
   Lyndon Baines Johnson Papers, Presidential Papers
Elmer L. Andersen Library, University of Minnesota, Minneapolis
   Eugene J. McCarthy Papers

GOVERNMENT DOCUMENTS

Appendix to the Congressional Record, 1949–78
Congressional Quarterly Almanac, 1978
Congressional Record, House of Representatives, 1958
Congressional Record, Senate, 1949–78
US Department of State, *Foreign Relations of the United States*, 1958–1960, 28 vols. (Washington, DC, 1986–96)
US Department of State, *Foreign Relations of the United States*, 1964–1968, 34 vols. (Washington, DC, 1992–2006)

NEWSPAPERS AND MAGAZINES

Albert Lea (MN) Tribune
Anderson (IN) Daily Bulletin

Appleton (WI) Post-Crescent
Austin (MN) Daily Herald
Baltimore Sun
Beckley (WV) Post-Herald
Berkshire (MA) Eagle
Boston Globe
Brainerd (MN) Daily Dispatch
Business Week
Charleston (WV) Daily Mail
Charleston (WV) Gazette
Chicago Tribune
Columbia (MO) Daily Tribune
Daily Herald (Provo, UT)
Daily Messenger (Canandaigua, NY)
Daily Plainsman (Huron, SD)
Evening Tribune (Albert Lea, MN)
Fergus Falls (MN) Daily Journal
Galveston Daily News
JTA (Jewish Telegraphic Agency)
Life
Lowell (MA) Sun
Manchester (NH) Union-Leader
Mansfield (OH) News-Journal
Miami Herald
Minneapolis Labor Review
Minneapolis Morning Tribune
Minneapolis Star
Minneapolis Star Tribune
Minneapolis Times
Minneapolis Tribune
Morgantown (WV) Post
New Republic
New York Herald Tribune
New York Times
New York Times Magazine
Newsweek
Oakland Tribune
Ocala (FL) Star Banner
Ogden (UT) Standard Examiner
People
Press Telegram (Long Beach, CA)
Redlands (CA) Daily Facts
Rhein-Zeitung (Koblenz, Germany)
St. Paul Pioneer Press
Sheboygan (WI) Press

Le Soir (Brussels)
Sunday Gazette-Mail (Charleston, WV)
Sunday Tribune (Albert Lea, MN)
Syracuse Herald-Journal
Syracuse Post Standard
Time
Troy (NY) Record
U.S. News and World Report
Van Nuys (CA) News
Village Voice
Washington Post
Washington Star
Weirton (WV) Daily Times
Winona (MN) Daily News
Winona (MN) Republican-Herald
Worthington (MN) Daily Globe

PUBLISHED SOURCES

Allen, Robert S., and Paul Scott. "Well, It's Off to Work We Go, Again!" *Daily Herald* (Provo, UT), Oct. 23, 1962.

Ambrose, Stephen E. *Eisenhower,* vol. 1, *Soldier, General of the Army, President-Elect, 1890–1952* (New York: Simon and Schuster, 1983).

———. *Nixon: The Education of a Politician, 1913–1962.* New York: Simon and Schuster, 1987.

———. *Nixon: Ruin and Recovery, 1973–1990.* New York: Simon and Schuster, 1991.

———. *Nixon: The Triumph of a Politician, 1962–1972.* New York: Simon and Schuster, 1989.

Amrine, Michael. *This Is Humphrey.* New York: Popular Library, 1960.

Aquiar, Gary. "Congressional Experiences, Congressional Legacies." In *George McGovern: A Political Life a Political Legacy,* edited by Robert P. Watson. Pierre: South Dakota State Historical Society Press, 2004.

Asselin, Pierre. " 'We Don't Want a Munich': Hanoi's Diplomatic Strategy, 1965–1968." *Diplomatic History* 36, no. 3 (June 2012).

Atkins, Annette. *Creating Minnesota: A History from the Inside Out.* St. Paul: Minnesota Historical Society Press, 2007.

Ball, George. *The Past Has Another Pattern: Memoirs.* New York: W. W. Norton, 1982.

Bell, Jonathan. *The Liberal State on Trial: The Cold War and American Politics in the Truman Years.* New York: Columbia University Press, 2004.

Bennet, Marion T. "The Immigration and Nationality (McCarran/Walter) Act of 1952, as Amended to 1965." *Annals of American Academy of Political and Social Science* 367 (September 1966).

Berman, Edgar, MD. *Hubert: The Triumph and Tragedy of the Humphrey I Knew.* New York: G. P. Putnam's Sons, 1979.

Berman, Hyman. "Political Antisemitism in Minnesota during the Great Depression." *Jewish Social Studies* no. 3–4 (Summer–Fall 1976).

Berman, Larry. *Lyndon Johnson's War: The Road to Stalemate in Vietnam.* New York: W. W. Norton, 1989.

Bernstein, Irving. *Guns or Butter: The Presidency of Lyndon Johnson.* New York: Oxford University Press, 1996.

———. *Promises Kept: John F. Kennedy's New Frontier.* New York: Oxford University Press, 1991.

Beschloss, Michael R. *The Crisis Years: Kennedy and Khrushchev, 1960–1963.* New York: HarperCollins, 1991.

———. *Taking Charge: The Johnson White House Tapes, 1963–1964.* New York: HarperCollins, 1997.

Biles, Roger. *Crusading Liberal: Paul H. Douglas of Illinois.* DeKalb: University of Illinois Press, 2002.

Bill, James A. *George Ball: Behind the Scenes in U.S. Foreign Policy.* New Haven: Yale University Press, 1997.

Bischof, Gunter, and Stephen E. Ambrose, eds. *Eisenhower: A Centenary Assessment.* Baton Rouge: Louisiana State University Press, 1995.

Bowie, Robert R., and Richard H. Immerman. *Waging Peace: How Eisenhower Shaped an Enduring Cold War Strategy.* New York: Oxford University Press, 1998.

Branch, Taylor. *Parting the Waters: America in the King Years, 1954–1963.* New York: Simon and Schuster, 1988.

Brinkley, Douglas. *Cronkite.* New York: HarperCollins, 2012.

Brinkley, Douglas, and Luke A. Nichter. *The Nixon Tapes, 1971–1972.* Boston: Houghton Mifflin Harcourt, 2014.

———. *The Nixon Tapes, 1973.* Boston: Houghton Mifflin Harcourt, 2015.

Bryant, Nick. *The Bystander: John F. Kennedy and the Struggle for Black Equality.* New York: Basic Books, 2006.

Bundy, William. *A Tangled Web: The Making of Foreign Policy in the Nixon Presidency.* New York: Hill and Wang, 1998.

Califano, Joseph A., Jr. *The Triumph and Tragedy of Lyndon Johnson: The White House Years.* New York: Simon and Schuster, 1991.

Cannon, James. *Time and Chance: Gerald Ford's Appointment with History.* Ann Arbor: University of Michigan Press, 1988.

Caro, Robert. "Orator of the Dawn." *New Yorker,* March 4, 2002.

———. *The Years of Lyndon Johnson: Means of Ascent.* New York: Alfred A. Knopf, 1990.

———. *The Years of Lyndon Johnson: Master of the Senate.* New York: Alfred A. Knopf, 2002.

———. *The Years of Lyndon Johnson: The Passage of Power.* New York: Alfred A. Knopf, 2012.

Carter, Dan. *The Politics of Rage: George Wallace, the Origins of the New Conservatism, and the Transformation of American Politics.* New York: Simon and Schuster, 1995.

Carter, Jimmy. *White House Diary.* New York: Farrar, Straus and Giroux, 2010.

Caute, David. *The Great Fear: The Anti-Communist Purges under Truman and Eisenhower.* New York: Simon and Schuster, 1978.

Chafe, William H. *Never Stop Running: Allard Loewenstein and the Struggle to Save American Liberalism.* New York: Basic Books, 1979.

Chennault, Anna. *The Education of Anna.* New York: Times Books, 1980.

Chester, Lewis, Geoffrey Hodgson, and Bruce Page. *An American Melodrama: The Presidential Campaign of 1968.* New York: Viking, 1969.

Clarke, Duncan. *The Politics of Arms Control: The Role and Effectiveness of the U S. Arms Control and Disarmament Agency.* New York: Basic Books, 1993.

Clifford, Clark, with Richard Holbrooke. *Counsel to the President: A Memoir.* New York: Doubleday, 1979.

Cochrane, Willard W. "Public Law 480 and Related Programs." *Annals of the American Academy of Political and Social Science* 331 (September 1960).

Cohen, Michael A. *American Maelstrom: The 1968 Election and the Politics of Division.* New York: Oxford University Press, 2016.

Cohodas, Nadine. *Strom Thurmond and the Politics of Southern Change.* New York: Simon and Schuster, 1979.

"The Communist Control Act." *Yale Law Journal* 64 (April 1955).

Costigliola, Frank. *France and the United States: The Cold Alliance since World War II.* New York: Twayne, 1992.

Cotton, Cornelius P., and Malcolm Smith. "The Emergency Detention Act of 1950." *Journal of Politics* 19 (February 1957).

Crippen, Ray. "Thoughts of Val Bjornson." *Worthington (MN) Daily Globe*, December 8, 2007.

Currey, Cecil B. *Edward Lansdale: The Unquiet American.* Boston: Houghton Mifflin, 1988.

Dallek, Robert. *Flawed Giant: Lyndon Johnson and His Times, 1961–1973.* New York: Oxford University Press, 1998.

———. *Lone Star Rising: Lyndon Johnson and His Times, 1908–1960.* New York: Oxford University Press, 1991.

———. *Nixon and Kissinger: Partners in Power.* New York: HarperCollins, 2007.

———. *An Unfinished Life: John F. Kennedy, 1917–1963.* Boston: Little Brown, 2003.

Davis, Kenneth S. *A Prophet in His Own Country: The Triumph and Defeats of Adlai E. Stevenson.* New York: Doubleday, 1957.

Delton, Jennifer. *Making Minnesota Liberal: Civil Rights and the Transformation of the Democratic Party.* Minneapolis: University of Minnesota Press, 2002.

Diem, Bui, with David Chanoff. *In the Jaws of History.* Bloomington: Indiana University Press, 1999.

Divine, Robert A. *The Triumph of Internationalism in America during World War II.* New York: Atheneum, 1967.

Dobbs, Michael. *One Minute to Midnight: Kennedy, Khrushchev, and Castro on the Brink of Nuclear War.* New York: Alfred A. Knopf, 2008.

Dobrynin, Anatoly. *In Confidence: Moscow's Ambassador to America's Six Cold War Presidents (1962–1986).* New York: Random House, 1995.

Donaldson, Gary. *Liberalism's Last Hurrah: The Presidential Campaign of 1964.* Armonk, NY: M. E. Sharpe, 2003.

Donovan, Robert J. *Conflict and Crisis: The Presidency of Harry S. Truman, 1945–1948.* New York: W. W. Norton, 1977.

——. *Tumultuous Years: The Presidency of Harry S. Truman, 1949–1953*. New York: W. W. Norton, 1982.

Douglas, Paul H. *In the Fullness of Time: The Memoirs of Paul H. Douglas*. New York: Harcourt Brace, 1971.

Eckerson, Helen F. "Immigration and National Origins." *Annals of the American Academy of Political and Social Science* 367 (September 1966).

"Education of a Senator." *Time*, Jan. 17, 1949.

Eisele, Albert. *Almost to the Presidency: A Biography of Two American Politicians*. Blue Earth, MN: Piper, 1972.

——. "How Gerald Heaney Might Have Changed the Course of History." *MinnPost*, Oct. 12, 2010. https://www.minnpost.com/politics-policy/2010/06/how-gerald-heaney-might-have-changed-course-history.

Engelmayer, Sheldon D., and Robert J. Wagman, eds. *Hubert Humphrey: The Man and His Dreams, 1911–1978*. New York: Methuen, 1978.

Evans, Rowland, and Robert Novak. *Lyndon Johnson: The Exercise of Power*. New York: New American Library, 1966.

Farrell, John A. *Richard Nixon: The Life*. New York: Doubleday, 2017.

——. *Tip O'Neill and the Democratic Century*. Boston: Little, Brown, 2001.

Fetter, Frank Albert. "Exit Basing Point Pricing." *American Economic Review* 38 (December 1948).

Fleeson, Doris. "Fight Shaping up in Minnesota." *Washington Star*, Mar. 19, 1954.

Forslund, Catherine. *Anna Chennault: Informal Diplomacy and Asian Relations*. Wilmington, DE: Scholarly Resources, 2002.

Freedman, Lawrence. *Kennedy's Wars: Berlin, Cuba, Laos, and Vietnam*. New York: Oxford University Press, 2000.

Fulbright, J. William. *The Arrogance of Power*. New York: Vintage Books, 1966.

Ganey, Terry. "A Slice of History." *Columbia (MO) Daily Tribune*, Aug. 19, 2007.

Gardner, Lloyd C. *Pay Any Price: Lyndon Johnson and the Wars of Vietnam*. Chicago: Ivan Dee, 1995.

Garrettson, Charles Lloyd, III. *Hubert H. Humphrey: The Politics of Joy*. New Brunswick, NJ: Transaction, 2015.

Gellman, Irwin F. *The Contender: Richard Nixon, the Congress Years, 1946–1952*. New York: Free Press, 1999.

——. *The President and the Apprentice: Eisenhower and Nixon, 1952–1961*. New Haven: Yale University Press, 2015.

Gieske, Millard. *Minnesota Farmer-Laborism: The Third Party Alternative*. Minneapolis: University of Minnesota Press, 1979.

Gillon, Steven M. *The Democrats' Dilemma: Walter F. Mondale and the Liberal Legacy*. New York: Columbia University Press, 1992.

——. *Politics and Vision: The ADA and American Liberalism, 1947–1985*. New York: Columbia University Press, 1987.

Goldish, Sidney. "The Minnesota Poll and the Election." *Public Opinion Quarterly* 12 (Winter 1948–49).

Goldman, Eric F. *The Tragedy of Lyndon Johnson*. New York: Alfred A. Knopf, 1969.

Goldstein, Gordon M. *Lessons in Disaster: McGeorge Bundy and the Path to War in Vietnam.* New York: Henry Holt, 2008.

Goodwin, Doris Kearns. *The Fitzgeralds and the Kennedys: An American Saga.* New York: Simon and Schuster, 1987.

Goodwin, Richard. *Remembering America: A Voice from the Sixties.* Boston: Little, Brown, 1988.

Gould, Lewis L. *1968: The Election That Changed America.* Chicago: Ivan Dee, 1993.

Grant, Phillip A. "The 1952 Minnesota Republican Primary and Eisenhower Landslide." *Presidential Studies Quarterly* 9 (Summer 1979).

Greenfield, Jeff. "What Makes Hubert Not Run?" *New York Times,* April 4, 1976.

Greenstein, Fred I. "Eisenhower as Activist." *Political Science Quarterly* 94 (Winter 1979–80).

——. *The Hidden-Hand Presidency: Eisenhower as Leader.* New York: Basic Books, 1982.

Griffith, Winthrop. *Humphrey: A Candid Biography.* New York: William Morrow, 1965.

Haldeman, H. R. *The Haldeman Diaries: Inside the Nixon White House.* New York: G. P. Putnam's, 1994.

Hamby, Alonzo L. *Beyond the New Deal: Harry S. Truman and American Liberalism.* New York: Columbia University Press, 1973.

——. *Man of the People: A Life of Harry S. Truman.* New York: Oxford University Press, 1995.

Hannaford, Peter, ed. *Washington Merry-Go-Round: The Drew Pearson Diaries, 1960–1969.* Lincoln: University of Nebraska Press, 2015.

Harrison, Hope M. *Driving the Soviets up the Wall: Soviet-East German Relations, 1953–1961.* Princeton, NJ: Princeton University Press, 2003.

Hatfield, Mark O., with the Senate Historical Office. "Hubert H. Humphrey." In *Vice Presidents of the United States, 1789–1993.* Washington, DC: US Government Printing Office, 1997.

Haynes, John Earl. *Dubious Alliance: The Making of Minnesota's DFL Party.* Minneapolis: University of Minnesota Press, 1984.

——. "Farm Coops and the Election of Hubert Humphrey to the Senate." *Agricultural History* 57 (April 1983).

Helsinki, Chester C. "Some Comments on the Revenue Act of 1950." *University of Pennsylvania Law Review* 99 (January 1951).

Herrera, Allison. "Humphrey Era Lacked Acrimony Prominent in Today's Politics." The Uptake, Aug. 30, 2012. http://theuptake.org/2012/08/30/humphrey-era-lacked-acrimony-prominent-in-todays-politics/.

Herring, George C. *America's Longest War: The United States and Vietnam, 1950–1975.* 4th ed. New York: McGraw-Hill, 2002.

——. *From Colony to Superpower: United States Foreign Relations since 1776.* New York: Oxford University Press, 2008.

Hess, Gary R. *Presidential Decisions for War: Korea, Vietnam, and the Persian Gulf.* 2nd ed. Baltimore: Johns Hopkins University Press, 2009.

Higgins, Trumbull. *The Perfect Failure: Kennedy, Eisenhower, and the CIA at the Bay of Pigs.* New York: W. W. Norton, 1988.

Hoffman, Elizabeth Cobbs. *All You Need Is Love: The Peace Corps and the Spirit of the 1960s.* Cambridge, MA: Harvard University Press, 1998.

Hoopes, Townsend. *The Devil and John Foster Dulles: The Diplomacy of the Eisenhower Years.* Boston: Little, Brown, 1973.

Hughes, Ken. *Chasing Shadows: The Nixon Tapes, the Chennault Affair, and the Origins of Watergate.* Charlottesville: University of Virginia Press, 2014.

Humphrey, Hubert H. *Beyond Civil Rights: A New Day of Equality.* New York: Random House, 1968.

——. *The Cause Is Mankind: A Liberal Program for Modern America.* New York: Praeger, 1964.

——. *The Education of a Public Man: My Life and Politics.* Minneapolis: University of Minnesota Press, 1991. Orig. publ. 1976.

——. "Government Organization for Arms Control." *Daedalus* 89 (Fall 1960).

——. "My Father." *Atlantic Monthly* 218 (November 1966).

——. "My Marathon Talk with Russia's Boss." *Life,* January 12, 1959.

——. *The Political Philosophy of the New Deal.* Baton Rouge: Louisiana State University Press, 1970.

——. "The Senate on Trial." *American Political Science Review* 44 (September 1950).

——. *War on Poverty.* New York: McGraw-Hill, 1964.

——. "What Hope for Disarmament?" *NYT Magazine,* January 5, 1958.

Hung, Nguyen Tien, and Jerold L. Schecter. *The Palace File.* New York: Harper and Row, 1986.

Isaacson, Walter. *Kissinger: A Biography.* New York: Simon and Schuster, 1992.

Isaacson, Walter H., and Evan Thomas. *The Wise Men: Six Friends and the World They Made.* New York: Simon and Schuster, 1986.

Izumi, Masumi. "American Concentration Camps: Repeal of the Emergency Detention Act and the Public Historical Memory of Japanese Internment." *Pacific Historical Review* 74 (May 2005).

Johnson, Lyndon Baines. *The Vantage Point: Perspectives of the Presidency, 1963–1969.* New York: Holt, Rinehart and Winston, 1971.

Kampelman, Max M. "Hubert Humphrey: Political Scientist." *PS* 11, no. 2 (Spring 1978).

Karabell, Zachary. *The Last Campaign: How Harry Truman Won the 1948 Election.* New York: Vintage Books, 2000.

Kaufman, Burton I. *Presidential Profiles: The Carter Years.* New York: Facts on File, 2006.

Kaufman, Burton I., and Scott Kaufman. *The Presidency of James Earl Carter, Jr.* Lawrence: University Press of Kansas, 2006.

Kearns, Doris. *Lyndon Johnson and the American Dream.* New York: St. Martin's, 1991.

Keillor, Stephen J. *Hjalmar Peterson of Minnesota: The Politics of Provincial Independence.* St. Paul: Minnesota Historical Society Press, 1987.

Kennedy, Edward M. *True Compass: A Memoir.* New York: Grand Central, 2009.

Klehr, Harvey, and John Earl Haynes. *The American Communist Movement: Storming Heaven Itself.* New York: Twayne, 1992.

Knock, Thomas J. *The Rise of a Prairie Statesman: The Life and Times of George McGovern.* Princeton, NJ: Princeton University Press, 2016.

Kutler, Stanley I. "Eisenhower, the Judiciary, and Desegregation: Some Reflections." In *Eisenhower: A Centenary Assessment*, edited by Gunter Bischof and Stephen E. Ambrose. Baton Rouge: Louisiana State University Press, 1995.

———. *The Wars of Watergate: The Last Crisis of Richard Nixon.* New York: W. W. Norton, 1990.

LaFeber, Walter. *The Deadly Bet: LBJ, Vietnam, and the 1968 Election.* Lanham, MD: Rowman and Littlefield, 2005.

Lash, Joseph P. *Eleanor: The Years Alone.* New York: W. W. Norton, 1972.

Lass, William E. *Minnesota: A History.* 2nd ed. New York: W. W. Norton, 1998.

Latham, Earl. "The Politics of Basing Point Legislation." *Law and Contemporary Problems* 15 (Spring 1950).

Lawn, Connie. *You Wake Me Each Morning.* Bloomington, IN: [Universe, self-published], 2010.

LeBow, Richard Ned, and Janice Gross Stein. *We All Lost the Cold War.* Princeton, NJ: Princeton University Press, 1994.

"Legends in the Law: A Conversation with Max Kampelman." *Washington Lawyer*, February 2006.

Leuchtenburg, William E. "FDR and the Kingfish." In *The FDR Years: On Roosevelt and His Legacy.* New York: Columbia University Press, 1997.

Light, Paul C. "Hubert Humphrey and Political Science." *Perspectives on Political Science* 21, no. 1 (Winter 1992).

Little, Douglas. *American Orientalism: The United States in the Middle East since 1945.* Chapel Hill, NC: University of North Carolina Press, 2002.

Logan, Frenise A. "Racism and Indian-US Relations, 1947–1953: Views in the Indian Press." *Pacific Historical Review* 54 (February 1985).

Lovegall, Frederik. *Choosing War: The Lost Chance for Peace and the Escalation of the War in Vietnam.* Berkeley: University of California Press, 1999.

Mackenzie, G. Calvin. "Hubert H. Humphrey: Reflections on a Twentieth Century Life." *Perspectives on Political Science* 21, no. 1 (Winter 1992).

Mailer, Norman. *Armies of the Night: History as Novel/The Novel as History.* New York: Penguin, 1968.

———. *Miami and the Siege of Chicago.* New York: Primus, 1968.

Manfred, Frederick. "Hubert Horatio Humphrey: A Memoir." *Minnesota History* 46 (Fall 1978).

Mann, James. "In Praise of Mild Reforms." *Boston Globe*, Aug. 21, 2007.

Mann, Robert. *A Grand Delusion: America's Descent into Vietnam.* New York: Basic Books, 2001.

———. *The Walls of Jericho: Lyndon Johnson, Hubert Humphrey, Richard Russell, and the Struggle for Civil Rights.* New York: Harcourt, 1996.

Martin, John Bartlow. *Adlai Stevenson and the World: The Life of Adlai E. Stevenson.* Garden City, NY: Doubleday, 1978.

——. *Adlai Stevenson of Illinois: The Life of Adlai E. Stevenson*. Garden City, NY: Doubleday, 1977.

Matson, Kevin. *When America Was Great: The Fighting Faith of Postwar Liberalism*. New York: Routledge, 2006.

McCarthy, Eugene. *The Year of the People*. New York: Doubleday, 1969.

McCauliffe, Mary S. "Liberals and the Communist Control Act of 1954." *Journal of American History* 63 (September 1976).

McDougall, Walter A. . . . *The Heavens and the Earth: A Political History of the Space Age*. Baltimore: Johns Hopkins University Press, 1997.

McWilliams, Carey. "Minneapolis: The Curious Twin." *Common Ground* (1946).

Meriwether, James H. "Worth a Lot of Negro Votes: Black Voters, Africa, and the 1960 Presidential Campaign." *Journal of American History* 95 (December 2008).

Miles, Darren. "The Art of the Possible: Everett Dirksen's Role in Civil Rights Legislation in the 1950s and 1960s." *Western Illinois Historical Review* 1 (Spring 2009).

Millikan, Eugene. *A Union against Unions: The Minneapolis Citizens Alliance and Its Fight against Organized Labor, 1903–1937*. St. Paul: Minnesota Historical Society Press, 2001.

Miroff, Bruce. *The Liberals' Moment: The McGovern Insurgency and the Identity Crisis of the Democratic Party*. Lawrence: University Press of Kansas, 2007.

Mitau, G. Theodore. "The Democratic-Labor Party Schism of 1948." In *The North Star State: A Minnesota Reader*, ed. Anne J. Aby. St. Paul: Minnesota Historical Society Press, 1997.

Mondale, Walter. *The Good Fight: A Life in Liberal Politics*. New York: Scribner, 2010.

Morgan, Ted. *Reds: McCarthyism in America*. New York: Random House, 2003.

Morison, Bradley L. "His Honor at Thirty-Seven." *Survey Graphic*, June 1948.

Myrdal, Gunnar. *An American Dilemma: The Negro Problem and Modern Democracy*. New York: Harper and Brothers, 1944.

Nash, Philip. *The Other Missiles of October: Eisenhower, Kennedy, and the Jupiters, 1957–1963*. Chapel Hill: University of North Carolina Press, 1997.

Nathanson, Eric. "Two Favorite Sons: The Humphrey-McCarthy Battle of 1968." *Minnesota Tribune*, May 25, 2011.

Nichols, David A. *A Matter of Justice: The Beginning of the Civil Rights Revolution*. New York: Simon and Schuster, 2007.

Offner, Arnold A. *Another Such Victory: President Truman and the Cold War, 1945–1953*. Stanford, CA: Stanford University Press, 2002.

Oren, Michael. *Six Days of War: June 1967 and the Making of the Modern Middle East*. New York: Ballantine Books, 2002.

Oshinsky, David M. *A Conspiracy So Immense: The World of Joe McCarthy*. New York: Oxford University Press, 2005.

——. *Polio: An American Story*. New York: Oxford University Press, 2005.

Pach, Chester J., and Elmo Richardson. *The Presidency of Dwight D. Eisenhower*. Rev. ed. Lawrence: University Press of Kansas, 1991.

Parry, Robert. "LBJ's 'X' File of Nixon's 'Treason.' " *Consortium News*, March 3, 2012. https://consortiumnews.com/2012/03/03/lbjs-x-file-on-nixons-treason/.

Paterson, Thomas G. "Foreign Aid under Wraps: The Point Four Program." *Wisconsin Magazine of History* 56 (Winter 1972).

Paterson, Thomas G., and William J. Brophy. "October Missiles and November Elections: The Cuban Missile Crisis and American Politics, 1962." *Journal of American History* 73 (June 1986).

Patterson, James T. *The Eve of Destruction: How 1965 Transformed America.* New York: Basic Books, 2012.

———. *Mr. Republican: A Biography of Robert Taft.* Boston: Houghton Mifflin, 1972.

———. *Restless Giant: The United States from Watergate to Bush v. Gore.* New York: Oxford University Press, 2005.

Paul, Randolph. *Taxation in the United States.* Boston: Little, Brown, 1954.

Paul, William B. "Excess Profits Tax." *Accounting Review* 27 (January 1952).

Pearson, Drew. "Freeman Is Too Young." *Lowell (MA) Sun,* July 14, 1960.

———. "Humphrey Delegates Vital." *Lowell (MA) Sun,* July 8, 1960.

———. "Humphrey Stomps Out of Briefing." *Lowell (MA) Sun,* Oct. 6, 1962.

Perlstein, Rick. *Before the Storm: Barry Goldwater and the Unmaking of the American Consensus.* New York: Hill and Wang, 2001.

———. *Nixonland: The Rise of a President and the Fracturing of America.* New York: Scribner, 2008.

Poen, Monte M. *Harry Truman versus the Medical Lobby: The Genesis of Medicare.* Columbia: University Press of Missouri, 1979.

Porter, Kirk H., and Donald Bruce Johnson. *National Party Platforms, 1840–1960.* Urbana: University Press of Illinois, 1961.

Powers, Thomas. *The Man Who Kept Secrets: Richard Helms and the CIA.* New York: Pocket Books, 1981.

Reichard, Gary W. "Mayor Hubert H. Humphrey." *Minnesota History* 56, no. 2 (Summer 1998).

———. *Politics as Usual: The Age of Truman and Eisenhower.* Rev. ed. Arlington Heights, IL: Harlan Davidson, 2004.

Reston, James. "Chicago: The Contrast between Humphrey and Nixon." *NYT,* August 28, 1968.

Reynolds, David. *Summits: Six Meetings That Shaped the World.* New York: Basic Books, 2007.

Risjord, Norman. *A Popular History of Minnesota.* St. Paul: Minnesota Historical Society Press, 2005.

Ross, Irwin. *The Loneliest Campaign: The Truman Victory of 1948.* New York: Signet Books, 1968.

Sandbrook, Dominic. *Eugene McCarthy and the Rise and Fall of Postwar American Liberalism.* New York: Alfred A. Knopf, 2004.

Scammon, Richard M., and Ben J. Wattenberg. *The Real Majority: An Extraordinary Examination of the American Electorate.* New York: Coward McCann and Geoghegan, 1970.

Schaff, Jon D. "A Clear Choice: George McGovern and the 1972 Presidential Race." In *George McGovern: A Political Life, a Political Legacy,* edited by Robert P. Watson. Pierre: South Dakota State Historical Society Press, 2004.

Schaffer, Howard B. *Chester Bowles: The New Dealer in the Cold War.* Cambridge, MA: Harvard University Press, 1993.

Schapsmeier, Edward L., and Frederick H. Schapsmeier. "Eisenhower and Agricultural Reform: Ike's Farm Policy Legacy Appraised." *American Journal of Economics and Sociology* 51 (April 1992).

Schell, Herbert S. *History of South Dakota.* 4th ed., rev. Pierre: South Dakota State Historical Society Press, 2004.

Schlesinger, Andrew, and Stephen Schlesinger, eds. *The Letters of Arthur Schlesinger, Jr.* New York: Random House, 2013.

Schlesinger, Arthur M., Jr. *Journals, 1952–2000.* New York: Penguin, 2007.

———. *A Thousand Days: John F. Kennedy in the White House.* Boston: Houghton Mifflin, 1965.

Schrecker, Ellen. *Many Are the Crimes: McCarthyism in America.* Boston: Little, Brown, 1998.

Schulman, Bruce J. *Lyndon B. Johnson and American Liberalism: A Brief Biography with Documents.* Boston: Bedford Books of St. Martin's, 1995.

Scott, Peter Dale. "The United States and the Overthrow of Sukarno, 1965–1967." *Pacific Affairs* 58 (Summer 1985).

Seshol, Jeff. *Mutual Contempt: Lyndon Johnson, Robert Kennedy, and the Feud That Defined a Decade.* New York: W. W. Norton, 1997.

Sherman, Norman. *From Somewhere to Nowhere: My Political Journey, a Memoir of Sorts.* Minneapolis: First Avenue Editions, 2016.

———. "The Political Style of Hubert H. Humphrey." *Perspectives on Political Science* 21, no. 1 (Winter 1992).

Shermer, Elizabeth Tandy. "Origins of the Conservative Ascendancy: Barry Goldwater's Early Senate Career and the De-Legitimization of Labor." *Journal of American History* 95 (December 2008).

Sitkoff, Harvard. *King: The Pilgrimage to the Mountaintop.* New York: Hill and Wang, 2008.

———. *The Struggle for Black Equality.* New York: Hill and Wang, 2008.

Small, Melvin. "The Election of 1968." *Diplomatic History* 28 (September 2004).

———. *Johnson, Nixon, and the Doves.* New Brunswick, NJ: Rutgers University Press, 1988.

Smith, Jean Edward. *Eisenhower in War and Peace.* New York: Random House, 2013.

Solberg, Carl. *Hubert Humphrey: A Biography.* New York: W. W. Norton, 1984.

Soper, Jean B., et al. "Basing Point Pricing and Production Concentration." *Economic Journal* 101 (May 1991).

Stern, Mark. "Lyndon Johnson and Richard Russell: Institutions, Ambitions, and Civil Rights." *Presidential Studies Quarterly* 21 (Fall 1991).

———. "Presidential Strategies and Civil Rights: Eisenhower, the Early Years, 1952–1954." *Presidential Studies Quarterly* 19 (Fall 1989).

Stern, Sheldon. *Averting "The Final Failure": John F. Kennedy and the Secret Cuban Missile Crisis Meetings.* Stanford, CA: Stanford University Press, 2003.

Stewart, John G. "Hubert Humphrey and Civil Rights: The Politics of Racial Progress." *Perspectives on Political Science* 21, no. 1 (Winter 1992).

Stone, I. F. "Everybody's Guide to Liberalism." *New York Review of Books,* Sept. 24, 1964.

Stuhler, Barbara. *Ten Men of Minnesota and American Foreign Policy, 1898–1968.* Minneapolis: University of Minnesota Press, 1972.

Summers, Anthony. *The Arrogance of Power: The Secret World of Richard Nixon.* New York: Viking, 2002.

Taubman, William. *Khrushchev: The Man and His Era.* New York. W. W. Norton, 2003.

Taylor, Jeff. *Where Did the Party Go? William Jennings Bryan, Hubert Humphrey and the Jeffersonian Legacy.* Columbia: University of Missouri Press, 2006.

Thomas, Evan. *Being Nixon: A Man Divided.* New York: Random House, 2015.

———. *Robert Kennedy.* New York: Simon and Schuster, 2007.

Thurber, Timothy N. *The Politics of Equality: Hubert H. Humphrey and the African-American Freedom Struggle.* New York: Columbia University Press, 1999.

Torres-Spelliscy, Ciara. "Got Corruption? Nixon's Milk Money." Brennan Center for Justice, Oct. 21, 2013. http://www.brennancenter.org/blog/got-corruption-nixon%E2%80%99s-milk-money.

Tucker, Nancy Bernkopf. *Taiwan, Hong Kong, and the United States, 1945–1992: Uncertain Friendships.* New York: Twayne, 1994.

Van Dyk, Ted. *Heroes, Hacks, and Fools: Memoirs from the Political Inside.* Seattle: University of Washington Press, 2007.

Wainstock, Dennis. *Election Year 1968: The Turning Point.* New York: Enigma Books, 2012.

Walton, Richard J. *Henry Wallace, Harry Truman, and the Cold War.* New York: Viking, 1976.

Watson, Robert P., ed. *George McGovern: A Political Life, a Political Legacy.* Pierre: South Dakota State Historical Society Press, 2004.

Webster, George D. "Taxpayer Relief: The Revenue Act of 1951." *Accounting Review* 27 (January 1957).

Weiner, Tim. *One Man against the World: The Tragedy of Richard Nixon.* New York: Henry Holt, 2015.

"The Welder." *Time*, Nov. 22, 1954.

Welsh, William B. "The Not So Imperial Vice-Presidency." *Perspectives on Political Science* 21, no. 1 (Winter 1992).

White, Theodore H. *The Making of the President, 1968.* New York: Atheneum, 1969.

Wicker, Tom. *JFK and LBJ: The Influence of Personality upon Politics.* New York: William Morrow, 1968.

Wilentz, Sean. *The Age of Reagan: A History, 1974–2008.* New York: HarperCollins, 2008.

Winquist, Thomas R. "The Civil Rights Act of 1957." *Michigan Law Review* 56 (February 1958).

Woodring, Carl. *Literature: Embattled Profession.* New York: Columbia University Press, 1999.

Woods, Randall Bennett. *Fulbright: A Biography.* New York: Cambridge University Press, 1995.

———. *LBJ: Architect of American Ambition.* New York: Free Press, 2006.

Zelizer, Julian E. *The Fierce Urgency of Now: Lyndon Johnson, Congress, and the Battle for the Great Society.* New York: Penguin, 2015.

Zhang, Shu Guang. *Deterrence and Strategic Culture: Chinese-American Confrontations, 1949–1958*. Ithaca, NY: Cornell University Press, 1992.

Zubok, Vladislav, and Constantine Pleshakov. *Inside the Kremlin's Cold War: From Stalin to Khrushchev*. Cambridge, MA: Harvard University Press, 1996.

THESES AND UNPUBLISHED PAPERS

Bovard, James. "How American Food Aid Keeps the Third World Hungry." A Heritage Foundation Paper. August 1, 1988 [in author's possession].

Humphrey, Hubert H. "The Middle East and Southern Europe." Report. Washington, DC, 1957.

Neustadt, Richard Mitchells. "Democrats, Delegates, and Democracy: Presidential Nominating Politics at the 1968 Democratic Convention." Honors thesis, Department of Government, Harvard University, 1969.

VIDEO

Caouette, Mick. *Hubert H. Humphrey: The Art of the Possible*. Stillwater, MN: South Hill Films, 2010.

INDEX

Abel, J. W., 355
abortion, 355
Abrams, Creighton, Jr., 296, 317, 324, 325
Acheson, Dean, 123, 126, 272, 444n15
Adams, Edie, 351
Adams, John, 278–79
Adams, Sherman, 131
Adenauer, Konrad, 167
Adjubei, Alexei, 166–67
affirmative action, 179–80
Agency for International Development
   (AID), 168, 223, 237
Agnew, Spiro, 310, 319, 320, 330–31, 337,
   371; antiwar movement attacked by, 341;
   as governor, 305; resignation of, 367; as
   vice president, 345
Agricultural Trade Development and
   Assistance Act (1954), 104
Aid to Families with Dependent
   Children, 221
Aiken, George, 125
Albert, Carl, 295, 296, 300
Alien and Sedition Acts, 77
Alien Registration Act (1940), 76
Alioto, Joseph, 299, 300
Allen, Barney, 27
Alliance for Progress, 169
Alperovitz, Gar, 259–60

Amalgamated Clothing Workers, 25
American Bowling Congress (ABC), 35
American Civil Liberties Union
   (ACLU), 107
American Federation of Labor (AFL), 19,
   22, 28, 41, 44, 47, 55, 86
American Federation of Labor–Congress
   of Industrial Organizations (AFL-CIO),
   150, 188, 242, 261, 265, 276, 312, 346, 359,
   385; HHH's award from, 370; HHH's
   presidential candidacy (1968) backed by,
   319; McGovern's presidential candidacy
   (1972) opposed by, 362; voter registration
   drive by, 328–29
American Federation of Teachers (AFT),
   32, 38
American Hospital Association, 66
American Legion, 43
American Medical Association (AMA),
   66, 71
American Red Cross, 32
Americans for Democratic Action (ADA),
   2, 94, 127, 269, 385; Democratic
   presidential nomination (1948) and, 48,
   61; divisions within, 107; Minnesota
   chapter of, 42, 43–47, 343; right-wing
   attacks on, 72, 77; Vietnam War and,
   231, 243

American Veterans Committee, 43
amnesty, for draft evaders, 355
Amoco, 275
Andersen, Elmer, 173
Anderson, C. Elmer, 112, 113
Anderson, Clinton, 123, 125
Anderson, Elmo, 94
Anderson, Eugenie, 47, 49, 128, 143, 195, 200, 211, 384; as ADA official, 40, 43; at Democratic National Convention (1948), 3, 4, 6; HHH's presidential campaign (1972) and, 340, 343, 352, 358; as Senate candidate, 132; as UDA official, 41, 42
Anderson, Wendell, 345
Andreas, Dwayne, 215, 252, 277, 333, 339, 356; Food for Peace backed by, 104; HHH's blind trust managed by, 103, 133; HHH's presidential candidacy (1968) backed by, 275, 307; HHH's Senate candidacy (1970) backed by, 344; Nixon contribution from, 368
Andreas, Inez, 215, 252, 339
And They Shall Walk (Kenny), 36
Anti-Ballistic Missile (ABM) system, 340, 347, 365
antitrust laws, 73–74
antiwar movement, 243, 247, 248, 259–60, 265, 271, 341
Apple, R. W., 380
Archer-Daniels-Midland (ADM) Company, 133
Armies of the Night (Mailer), 260
arms control, 121, 173–76, 211, 227, 252, 253, 361, 365; HHH's commitment to, 134–36, 161, 162–63, 165, 166, 173–75
Arms Control and Disarmament Agency (ACDA), x, 162–63, 225
Articles of Confederation, 63
Arvey, Jacob, 4
Associated Milk Producers, Inc. (AMPI), 368–69
Aswan Dam, 136
Atomic Energy Commission (AEC), 135

Auerbach, Carl, 126
Australia, 111
Austrian State Treaty (1955), 112

Bailey, John M., 316
Baker, Howard H., Jr., 391
Baker, Robert (Bobby), 96, 159
Baker, Russell, 142
Baker v. Carr (1962), 212
Balaguer, Joaquín, 245, 427n6
Ball, Charles H., 227
Ball, George, 226–27, 228, 238, 290, 315–16, 318, 321
Ball, Joseph, 38, 39, 45, 49, 52, 55, 60, 83; HHH's defeat of, 58; as internationalist, 1, 50, 54; Marshall Plan opposed by, 54, 56, 57; Senate appointment of, 25; Taft-Hartley Act backed by, 44, 50, 54, 56
Baltimore Sun, 67
Bao Dai, king of Vietnam, 80, 110
Barden, Graham, 67
Barker, Bernard, 366, 368
Barkley, Alben, 51–52, 83
Barnett, Ross, 177
Barr, Joseph, 276, 280
Barrie, Robert, 414n31
basing point system, 74
Bayh, Birch, 376
Baylor, Elgin, 299
Bay of Pigs invasion, 164–65, 173, 256
Beckington, Herbert, 218, 262, 266
Begin, Menachem, 385
Bell Telephone, 33
Ben Gurion, David, 138, 168
Benson, Elmer, 15, 26, 33
Benson, Ezra Taft, 104, 113
Benton, William, 58, 88, 93, 94, 133, 143, 159, 230, 430n16
Bentsen, Lloyd, 377
Beria, Lavrenti, 108
Berle, Adolf A., 73
Berlin, 242, 252, 253; crisis in (1961), 141–42, 165–68, 232

Berlin Wall, 163, 165, 166, 167, 168, 253

Berman, "Chickie," 30

Berman, Edgar, 289, 339, 350; as HHH's physician, 257–58, 369, 382, 384, 390, 394; as HHH's political adviser, 274, 297, 298, 300, 302, 379, 380, 381; HHH's shortcomings viewed by, 287, 293; LBJ's obstructionism viewed by, 286, 295

Bethe, Hans, 136

Beyond Civil Rights (Humphrey), 337

Biden, Joseph, 378

Biemiller, Andrew, 2, 3, 4

Biggs, W. R., 447n2

Biological Weapons Convention (1972), 163

Bjornson, Valdimar (Val), 113, 210

Black, Hugo, 87

Black Power movement, 220, 246

Blaik, Earl "Red," 180, 181

Blair, James M., Jr., 154

Blatnik, John, 41, 57

Blaustein, Jacob, 275

Blough, Roger, 197

Boggs, Hale, 275, 279, 295, 296, 297, 298

Boilermakers union, 44

Bond, Julian, 259, 294

Bork, Robert, 367

Bosch, Juan, 231

Bowles, Chester, 49, 53

Boynton v. Virginia (1960), 176

Braden, Thomas, 362

Bradley, Omar, 35

Brandt, Willy, 139, 141

Brannan, Charles, 103

Breathitt, Ned, 277

Brekke, Gerald, 382, 383

Bremer, Arthur, 355

Bricker, John, 27

Broder, David, 444n15

Brooks, Wayland, 58

Browder, Earl, 25

Brown, Clarence, 183

Brown, Edmund "Jerry," 377, 381

Brown, Edmund "Pat," 196, 197, 206, 305

Brown, Max, 417n27

Brownell, Herbert, 101, 124, 125, 129

Brown v. Board of Education (1954), 101, 118, 124, 152, 176

Bruce, David K. E., 218

Bryan, William Jennings, 5, 11, 27

Bulganin, Nikolai, 135

Bumpers, Dale, 379

Bundy, McGeorge, 170, 182, 206, 229, 234, 237, 239, 329; HHH constrained by, 225, 230, 231; Vietnam War viewed by, 226, 238, 265, 272, 322, 325

Bundy, William, 236, 306

Bunker, Ellsworth, 252, 262, 273, 325–26

Burns, Arthur, 384

Busby, Horace, 272

busing, 188, 353, 354, 355, 361

Butler, John Marshall, 105–6, 130

Butterfield, Alexander, 367

Byrd, Harry, 67, 68–70, 72, 93, 99, 194

Byrd, Robert, 147–48, 150, 191, 383–84, 387, 391

Byrd Committee (Joint Committee on Reduction of Nonessential Expenditures), 67, 68–69, 75

Byrnes, James, 93

Cahn, Julius, 139

Cairo Declaration (1943), 111

Calhoun, John C, 438n39

Califano, Joseph, 221, 258, 278

Cambodia, 109, 110, 342, 349, 374

Capehart, Homer, 72, 83

Cargill, Inc., 35, 103

Carleton College, 44

Caro, Robert, 124

Carter, James Earl (Jimmy), 7; HHH allied with, ix, 384; HHH honored by, 387–93; Humphrey-Hawkins bill signed by, 386; Middle East policies of, 385; as presidential candidate, 377–83

Carver, George, 272

Castro, Fidel, 157, 158, 164, 171, 172, 173

Cause Is Mankind, The (Humphrey), 194

Cavanaugh, James, 258
Celler, Emanuel, 191
Central Intelligence Agency (CIA), 164, 170, 223, 224, 225, 250, 260
Central Labor Union (CLU), 44, 55
Chamberlain, Neville, 41
Chamber of Commerce, 66
Chaney, James, 423n23
Channing, Carol, 206
Charles, prince of Wales, 339
Chatek, Smaile, 55
Chavez, Cesar, 356
Chennault, Anna, 306, 323, 325, 326, 327, 331, 333
Chennault, Claire, 306
Chestnut, Jack, 344, 351, 368–69, 376, 377
Chiang Kai-shek (Jiang Jieshi), 111, 112, 235
Chile, 168
China, x, 110, 122, 222, 347, 372; containment of, 111, 244, 254; Cultural Revolution in, 251; Khrushchev criticized by, 173; Khrushchev's skepticism toward, 140, 141; during Korean War, 80, 81, 82, 109; Nixon's visit to, 361; as nuclear threat, 173, 175; Quemoy and Matsu crisis and, 111–12; Soviet frictions with, 175; United Nations membership for, 149, 347; Vietnam War and, 226, 227, 228, 231, 232, 238, 240, 242, 245, 350; during World War II, 21, 306
Chisholm, Shirley, 351, 358
Church, Frank, 127, 228, 230, 377, 381
Churchill, Winston, 218, 363
Civil Rights Act (1957), 128, 130, 187, 328
Civil Rights Act (1964), x, 182–92, 194, 300, 337, 347, 372; as campaign issue, 193, 211, 212, 328
Civil Rights Act (1965), 337
Clark, Jim, 220
Clark, Joseph, 178, 188
Clark, Ramsey, 258
Clements, Earle, 153
Cleveland, Grover, 90

Clifford, Clark, 271, 272, 305, 309, 322, 328, 331–32, 333; bombing halt backed by, 273, 274, 310, 318, 321, 324, 326; LBJ viewed by, 288, 305; as Truman's aide, 45
Clifton, Chester "Ted," 224
Cold War, 53, 72
Collingwood, Charles, 254
Collins, Frank, 37
Colombia, 168
Combination (criminal group), 21, 29
Committee for the Marshall Plan to Aid European Recovery, 43
Committee on Civil Rights, 2
Committee to Defend America by Aiding the Allies, 20
Commodity Credit Corporation (CCC), 104
Communist Control Act (CCA), 105–7
Communist Information Bureau (Cominform), 43
Communist Party USA (CPUSA), 25, 53, 76, 105–6, 107
Community Relations Service, 185
Congressional Black Caucus, 372, 386
Congress of Industrial Organizations (CIO), 19, 25, 28, 44, 47, 55, 86
Congress of Racial Equality (CORE), 186, 260
Connally, John B., 212, 272, 277, 290, 367; at Democratic National Convention (1964), 198, 206; at Democratic National Convention (1968), 294, 297; HHH's presidential candidacy (1968) backed by, 279, 310; McCarthy's vice-presidential prospects (1964) and, 194, 198; Mississippi credentials fight (1964) and, 198; Nixon's reelection (1972) backed by, 362; as vice presidential prospect (1968), 282, 294; Yarborough vs., 181, 294
Connally, Thomas, 73
Connell, William (Bill), 216, 236, 351, 369; at Democratic National Convention (1964), 204; at Democratic National

Convention (1968), 294, 302; HHH's presidential candidacy (1968) and, 274, 275, 277–78; Senate viewed by, 132; as Vietnam hawk, 240, 287, 316
Connor, Eugene "Bull," 178
containment, 107; of China, 111, 244, 254; of Soviet Union, 42, 43, 45, 57, 79, 81, 90, 91, 109
Conyers, John, 286
Coolidge, Calvin, 10
Cooper, John Sherman, 106, 235
Corcoran, Thomas, 327
Cotton, Norris, 421n66
Cousins, Norman, 174
Couve de Murville, Maurice, 254
Covington and Burling (law firm), 126
Cowles, Gardner, 255, 275
Cowles, John, 29, 30, 35, 46, 54
Cox, Archibald, 366–67
Craig, Earl, 343–44, 378
Crangle, Joseph, 378
Cranston, Alan, 312, 348
Criswell, John, 250–51, 283, 292, 297, 307
Cronkite, Walter, 254, 270, 336
Cuba, 157, 158, 232; Bay of Pigs invasion of, 164–65, 173, 256; Soviet missiles in, 170–73, 174, 212, 227; Soviet troops in, 175
Cultural Revolution (China), 251
Currier, Stephen, 195
Curtis, Carl, 421n66
Cushing, Richard, 150
Czechoslovakia, 45, 108, 122, 290, 295, 296

Daily Worker, 77, 86, 94
Daley, Richard, 158, 195, 205, 276, 283, 290, 307, 333; Democratic National Convention (1968) and, 291, 292, 293, 294, 297, 299, 300, 304, 338; Democratic National Convention (1972) and, 360
Daniel, Margaret Truman, 274
Daniel, Price, 106
Daniel, W. Lee "Pappy," 407n48
Daspit, Alex, 17

Day, Vincent, 21, 22
Dayton family, 37
Dean, John, 366, 367
Declaration of Human Rights (1948), 372
de Gaulle, Charles, 218, 252, 254
DeLoach, Cartha "Deke," 325
Delton, Jennifer, 43–44, 54
Demetriou, George, 46, 49
Democratic Advisory Council (DAC), 123
Democratic-Farmer-Labor Party (DFL), 55, 97; agribusiness and, 115; congressional races won by, 27–28, 122; at Democratic National Convention (1948), 49; divisions within, 1, 38, 40, 43–48, 76; HHH nominated for Senate by, 48; in HHH's presidential campaign (1968), 283; origins of, 25–26; Vietnam policy of, 242
Democratic National Committee (DNC), 25, 307, 342–43, 359
Democratic Policy Committee, 340, 341, 348
DeSapio, Carmine, 144
desegregation, 4, 346; of armed forces, 2, 53, 73; of Democratic convention delegations, 200; of interstate commerce, 101, 176; of Minnesota National Guard, 50; as presidential campaign issue (1956), 117; of public accommodations, 178, 179, 187; of public housing, 65; of schools, 101, 102, 118, 123, 125, 129–30, 152, 176, 179, 188, 189, 305, 353, 354, 361
Dewey, John, 17
Dewey, Thomas E., 1, 27, 50, 54, 57–58, 312, 443n4
Díaz Ordaz, Gustavo, 273
Dickman, Ralph, 29
Didier, Calvin, 393
Diem, Bui, 306, 323, 331
Diem, Ngo Dinh, 110, 111, 222
Dies, Martin, 76
Dingell, John, 65

Dirksen, Everett, 175, 183, 184, 186–91, 318, 326, 331

DiSalle, Mike, 144, 293

Dixiecrats (States' Rights Party), 53, 71, 91, 92, 170

Dobrynin, Anatoly, 170, 172, 305, 308

Dodd, Thomas, 174, 197, 205, 206

Dogole, S. Harrison, 351, 352

Dole, Robert, ix, 383, 387, 388

Dominican Republic, 231, 245

Donovan, Joseph, 271

Douglas, Paul, 72, 86, 88, 160–61; civil rights backed by, 127, 128, 130, 177, 178; at Democratic National Convention (1948), 6; election to Senate of, 58, 60; filibuster reform backed by, 123; HHH viewed by, 4, 5, 104; in Senate minority leadership fight (1953), 94, 96, 97; tax reform efforts by, 74–75

Douglas, William O., 1, 49, 51, 87

draft evasion, 355

Drummond, Roscoe, 142

Dubinsky, David, 42

Dulles, Allen, 141

Dulles, John Foster, 109, 110, 112, 138, 139, 141; containment denounced by, 107; HHH's criticism of, 111, 113, 135, 136

Dungan, Ralph, 181

Eagleton, Thomas, 360–61, 445n66

East Germany (German Democratic Republic; GDR), 108, 138–39, 140, 165–66, 168, 238

Eastland, James, 102, 124, 179, 184

Economic Bill of Rights (1944), 372

Economic Opportunity Act (1964), 210

Economic Problems of Socialism (Stalin), 108

Ecuador, 168

Education of a Public Man (Humphrey), 380

Egypt, 136, 137, 168, 347, 389, 390

Ehrenburg, Ilya, 166–67

Ehrlichman, John, 366, 370

Eide, T. A., 22

Einstein, Albert, 42, 78

Eisele, Albert, 349

Eisenhower, Dwight D., 1, 49, 81–82, 103–4, 309; arms control and, 136, 163; Berlin crisis and, 141–42; civil rights policies of, 101–2, 125, 128, 129–30; Cuba invasion planned by, 164; declining popularity of, 131–32; Democratic criticisms of, 149, 152, 156, 157, 161, 176; farm bill vetoed by, 116; Indochina policy of, 109–10, 111, 225, 227, 318; Khrushchev's view of, 139; Korean armistice sought by, 108; Middle East policy of, 136; mutual security budget of, 134–35; nonalignment viewed by, 135; as presidential candidate (1952), 89–94, 336; as presidential candidate (1956), 120–22, 336; Quemoy and Matsu crisis and, 111–12

Eisenhower, Edgar, 121

Eisenhower, Mamie, 306

Eisenhower Doctrine, 136, 137

Elementary and Secondary Education Act (1965), 219

Ellender, Allen, 185

Eller, Jerome, 204

Ellis, Handy, 6

Ellsberg, Daniel, 349

Emancipation Proclamation, 6, 62, 178, 180, 185

Emergency Detention Act, 78

Employment Act (1946), 372

employment discrimination, 2, 4, 45

Engle, Clair, 190, 191

Equal Employment Opportunity Commission (EEOC), 181, 185, 186–87

Equal Opportunity and Full Employment Act (Humphrey-Hawkins; 1976), 372, 373, 378, 381, 383, 385–86

Erlander, Tage, 233

Ervin, Sam, 190

Ethiopia, 80

Ewald, Ray, 83, 132, 133

Ewing, Oscar, 26, 66
Export-Import Bank, 268

Fair Deal, 61, 63, 68, 89–90, 91, 93, 94, 98, 364
Fair Employment Practices Committee (FEPC), 2, 67, 71, 73, 101; federal proposals for, 24, 50, 64, 89, 100, 130, 152, 178, 179, 181; in Minneapolis, 29, 33–34, 35; state-level, 72, 92; Truman's support for, 61, 64
Fair Housing Act (1968), x
Family Assistance Plan, 340
Farmers Union Grain Terminal Association, 55
Faubus, Orval, 129, 212
Federal Bureau of Investigation (FBI), 31, 67
Federal Civilian Employee Loyalty Program, 76
Federal Election Campaign Act (1971), 368
Federal Highway Act (1956), 121
Federal Power Commission (FPC), 94–95
Federal Reserve, 372, 384, 386
Federal Security Agency (FSA), 66
Ferguson, Homer, 77
filibuster: of civil rights bills, 62–63, 64, 125, 127, 128, 177, 183, 185, 187, 188, 190; HHH's attacks on, 71, 72, 91, 101, 102, 131, 160, 177, 187, 346; LBJ's defense of, 123
Finch, Robert, 438n47
Flynn, Edward J., 4, 52
Food for Peace (PL 480), 137, 223, 268; Goldwater's opposition to, 213; HHH's support for, 113, 157, 194, 213, 313, 393; JFK's call to expand, 104–5; Republican cooptation of, 156, 157
Food Stamps, 116, 210
Force Act (1870), 125
Ford, Gerald, 382, 390, 392; economic policies of, 373–74; Nixon pardoned by, 371; as presidential candidate (1976), 376, 380, 383; vice presidential selection of, 367
Ford, Henry, II, 197, 275
Ford, Wendell, 379
Formosa (Taiwan), 80, 111–12, 242, 347
Forrestal, James, 50
Fortas, Abe, 182, 273, 427n61
Foster, William C., 163
Fourteenth Amendment, 186
France, 80, 82, 175; Berlin occupied by, 138; HHH's hostile reception in, 254; involvement in Indochina of, 109, 110–11, 243, 264; as nuclear power, 176
Francis of Assisi, Saint, 303
Frankel, Max, 322
Fraser, Donald M., 43, 173
Freedom Riders, 161, 176
Freedom Summer (1964), 198
Freeman, Fulton, 273
Freeman, Jane, 182, 215
Freeman, Orville, 15, 19, 116–17, 182, 234, 237, 269, 275, 298, 420n41; as agriculture secretary, 158, 160; at Democratic National Convention (1948), 3, 6; at Democratic National Convention (1952), 92; as Democratic Party official, 40; in DFL fight, 44, 45–46, 47; as gubernatorial candidate, 91, 94, 113, 122, 132, 156, 158; HHH praised by, 215; HHH's presidential candidacy (1960) backed by, 142, 143; HHH's presidential candidacy (1968) and, 307, 309, 310, 311, 320–21; LBJ viewed by, 216, 289–90; as mayoral aide, 43; as senatorial campaign manager, 53, 57; as vice presidential prospect (1960), 152, 153–54, 155; as vice presidential prospect (1964), 194
Fritchey, Clayton, 256, 257
Fulbright, J. William, 236, 239, 240, 244, 280
Full Employment and Balanced Growth Act (1978), x
Funston, Keith, 197

Gagarin, Yuri, 164, 218
Gaither, H. Rowan, Jr., 131
Galbraith, John Kenneth, 42, 235, 256, 257
Gale, Richard Pillsbury, 20–21, 28
Gallagher, William, 28
Gandhi, Indira, 238
Gartner, David G., 390, 391
Gates, Fred, 29, 59, 217, 334, 346
Gaza Strip, 136, 137
Gellman, Irwin F., 124
General Mills, 46, 103, 104
Geneva Accords (1954), 230, 272–73
George, Walter, 69, 75, 104, 113, 114, 118
German Democratic Republic (GDR; East Germany), 108, 138–39, 140, 165–66, 168, 238
Germany: postwar partition of, 112, 138; postwar reconstruction of, 41; US forces in, 253; during World War II, 17, 20, 81
Gibson, William, 388
Gilligan, John, 295
Ginsburg, David, 284, 286, 295, 296, 297
Glenn, John, 382
Goetz, Betty, 135, 163
Golda (play), 388
Goldberg, Arthur, 152, 244, 315, 316, 319
Goldman, Eric, 197, 208
Goldman Sachs, 275
Goldwater, Barry, 195, 199, 209, 345, 370, 384; arms control opposed by, 163, 175, 211; bellicosity of, 210, 211, 213, 214, 227; civil rights bill opposed by, 191; Democratic attacks on, 207–8, 210, 211, 212–13, 215, 349; extremism of, 197, 210, 214; presidential nomination secured by, 196; Senate election of, 94
Gomulka, Wladyslaw, 167
Goodman, Andrew, 423n23
Goodwin, Richard, 294, 295, 304
Gore, Albert, 118, 119–20, 123, 127
Graham, Billy, 310, 320
Graham, Frank, 72
Gravel, Mike, 384

Great Britain, 82, 110, 111; Berlin occupied by, 138; Middle East meddling by, 122, 137; postwar economy of, 42
Great Depression, 12, 13, 17, 33
Great Society, x, 214, 255, 286, 328, 364
Grechko, Andrei, 339
Greece, 42, 79, 89, 168, 252
Green, Francis, 91
Green, William, 55
Greene, Charles P., 146
Greenfield, Jeff, 378
Gruening, Ernest, 426n48
Guatemala, 164
Gulf of Tonkin Resolution (1964), 198, 224, 266, 268–69, 342

habeas corpus, 78, 87
Habib, Philip, 237
Hague, Frank, 4
Haldeman, H. R., 363, 366
Hamer, Fannie Lou, 200–201, 202
Hamill, Pete, 348
Hannegan, Robert, 27, 45
Harding, Warren G., 10
"Hard Lessons of War and Peace, The" (Humphrey), 349–50
Harriman, W. Averell, 237; arms control views of, 174; at Paris peace talks, 286, 287, 288, 309, 316, 318, 321, 324; as presidential candidate (1956), 119
Harrington, Stephanie, 348
Harris, Fred, 277, 278, 280, 301–2, 316, 342, 377
Harris, Herbert, 388
Harris, LaDonna, 434n40
Harris, Louis, 146
Harris, Robert, 35
Harris, Thomas, 105
Harrison, Gilbert, 256
Hart, Gary, 356, 373
Hart, Philip, 178, 180, 189, 258, 293
Hatcher, Richard, 286
Hatfield, Mark, 281, 342, 348
Hawkins, Augustus, 372

Hays, Brooks, 91, 118
Heaney, Gerald, 43, 44, 145, 198
Heath, Ted, 253
Heller, Walter, 75
Hellman, Lillian, 243
Helms, Richard, 272, 370
Henderson, Gerald, 48
Hennepin CIO Council, 28
Hennings, Thomas, 130
Henry, Aaron, 201
Henry V, king of England, 189
Hersey, John, 243
Herter, Christian, 141
Hickenlooper, Bourke, 189
Higher Education Act (1965), 219
Hill, Lister, 60, 66, 118
Hillman, Sidney, 25
Hitler, Adolf, 17, 45, 79, 80, 108, 236, 265
Ho Chi Minh, 109, 110, 222, 226, 231, 272
Hodges, Luther, 420n41
Hoey, Clyde, 408n51
Hoff, Philip, 285
Hoffa, Jimmy, 146, 147
Holland, Spressard, 72
Hollifield, Chet, 277
Honeywell Corporation, 32–33
Honolulu Declaration (1966), 236–37, 240, 243
Hoover, J. Edgar, 77, 78, 260
Hope, Clifford, 104
Hospital Construction Act (1946), 403n23
House Un-American Activities Committee (HUAC), 76
Howard, Frances Humphrey (sister), 10, 13, 14, 36, 387, 390
Howes, W. W., 26
Hoyt, Palmer, 369
Hruska, Roman, 421n66
Hughes, Emmet John, 207, 241
Hughes, Harold, 277, 300, 342
Hughes, Howard, 447n88
Hughes, Richard, 258, 276, 277, 301, 302, 316
Hughes, Thomas, 227, 228, 249, 266

Hugo, Victor, 188
Hubert H. Humphrey (Solberg), xi
Humphrey, Addie Register, 9
Humphrey, Christine Sannes (mother), 9, 10, 13, 14, 15, 59, 211
Humphrey, Douglas (son), 36, 59, 133, 337
Humphrey, Fern (sister), 10, 13
Humphrey, Frances (sister), 10, 13, 14, 36, 387, 390
Humphrey, Frances Estella (aunt), 9
Humphrey, Harry Barker (uncle), 9, 14, 17, 25
Humphrey, Hubert Horatio (HHH):
activist government espoused by, 55; adversaries' respect for, 104, 113, 203; Africa visited by, 268; agricultural policies of, 55, 56, 103–4, 113, 115, 213, 217; as anti-Communist, 40–47, 55, 76–81, 82, 85, 99, 103, 105–9, 111, 113, 134; approval ratings of, 255; arms control pursued by, 134–36, 161, 162–63, 165, 166, 173–75; awards to, 36–37; baptism of, 11; Berlin crisis and, 165–68; birth of, 9–10; bowling alleys desegregated by, 34–35; Byrd Committee opposed by, 67–70; charter reform backed by, 37–38; Chicago violence viewed by, 304–5; China visited by, 372; civil rights championed by, x, 1–7, 16, 18, 23, 24, 33–35, 49, 50, 61–64, 72–73, 101–2, 113, 123–31, 152–53, 176–92, 220, 329; civil rights plank backed by (1948), 1–7, 39, 51–52, 58, 152–53, 176, 269, 295, 298, 335, 387; in college, 12–13, 15; as college instructor, 24, 338–39; compromise embraced by, 71; as crimefighter, 30–31; Cuba invasion viewed by, 164–65, 173; Cuban missile crisis and, 170–73; "Daisy" ad disavowed by, 211; Democratic National Convention (1968) and, 292–305; détente backed by, x; DFL formation and, 25–26; Dixiecrats denounced by, 53, 71; domino theory

Humphrey, Hubert Horatio (HHH)
(*continued*)
accepted by, 109–10, 222; education aid
backed by, 163–64, 194; farm supports
backed by, 55, 56, 103–4, 113, 115, 213,
217; father's influence on, 12; as favorite
son presidential candidate (1952),
89–90, 91; FDR admired by, 18, 22, 99;
finances of, 337; foreign aid backed by,
x, 103–4, 168–69, 194; full employment
bill introduced by, 372, 373, 385–86;
gaffes by, 263, 278–79, 300, 343, 357; in
graduate school, 2, 15–19; Great Society
backed by, 218–19; gubernatorial
candidacy declined by, 27; health care
policies of, x, 55, 65–66, 71, 194, 346,
360; health problems of, 257–58, 369,
382–87; housing policies of, 31–32, 34,
64–65; immigration reform backed by,
x, 87, 88–89, 219; as internationalist, 41;
JFK advised by, 167, 169; JFK contrasted
with, 161; judicial appointment
engineered by, 83–84; jury trial dispute
and, 126–28; Korean War viewed by,
80–81; labor-management relations
brokered by, 32–33; LBJ admired by,
99–100, 132, 269–70, 347, 364; LBJ's
abuse of, 215–16, 249–50; LBJ's praise of,
254; LBJ's similarities with, 98–99;
liberalism embraced by, x–xi, 14, 23;
liberals displeased with, 255–57; literary
preferences of 251; as majority whip,
159–61, 249–50; as mayoral candidate
(1943), 21–23; as mayoral candidate
(1945), 25, 28–30; mayoralty relished by,
35–36, 335; Middle East viewed by,
136–38; military commission sought by,
27; monopolies opposed by, 73–74; in
Moscow, 138–41; Muriel courted by,
13–14; Nixon's resignation viewed by,
371; Peace Corps backed by, 161–62, 313;
posthumous tributes to, ix, 391–94; as
presidential candidate (1960), 27, 133,
142–51, 155; as presidential candidate

(1968), 273–88, 292–336; as presidential
candidate (1972), 350–59; as presidential
prospect (1976), 375–80; Quemoy and
Matsu crisis and, 111–12; segregation
witnessed by, 2, 16; as Senate candidate
(1948), 1, 45–48, 52–57, 58; as Senate
candidate (1954), 112–14; as Senate
candidate (1960), 156, 157, 158; as Senate
candidate (1970), 339–40, 343–45;
Senate majority leadership sought by,
383–84; in Senate minority leadership
fight (1953), 94–97; as senator (1971–78),
345–48, 369–70, 376, 387; as
senator-elect, 59–60; small business
championed by, 73; steel mill seizure
backed by, 86–87; as Stevenson's
campaign surrogate, 93; talkativeness
of, 4, 61, 69, 113, 301; tax policies of, x,
74–75; Truman's electability doubted
by, 48–49; urban riots (1967) and,
258–59; as vice president, 265–337; as
vice president–elect, 215–17; as vice
presidential candidate (1964), 193–215;
vice presidential nomination declined
by (1972), 361; as vice presidential
prospect (1956), 116–20; as vice
presidential prospect (1960), 155;
as vice presidential prospect (1968),
255; Vietnam War viewed by, 223–48,
250–57, 259–67, 271–73, 283–89, 292,
293, 298, 302–3, 307–9, 312, 315–18,
333, 340–41, 345, 349–50, 365, 374–75;
at War Manpower Commission, 20;
Watergate scandal viewed by, 366;
wealthy friends of, 132–33; wedding
of, 14; work ethic of, 250; as WPA
official, 19
Humphrey, Hubert Horatio, Sr. (father), 3,
6, 9, 10–11, 15, 29, 50; death of, 67;
declining health of, 59; HHH
influenced by, 12; as state legislator,
11, 14
Humphrey, Hubert Horatio "Skip," III
(son), 20, 24, 59, 133, 146, 271

Humphrey, John Wadsworth (grandfather), 9

Humphrey, John Wadsworth, Jr. (uncle), 9

Humphrey, Muriel Fay Buck (wife), 3, 23, 24, 26, 39, 118, 190, 217, 258, 339, 392; courtship of, 13–14; HHH's absences and, 36; during HHH's campaigns, 146, 151; during HHH's graduate school career, 15, 16, 17, 18–19; during HHH's last illness, 389, 390; HHH's presidential candidacy (1960) and, 142; HHH's presidential candidacy (1968) and, 275, 287, 289, 300, 304, 333–34; HHH's presidential candidacy (1972) encouraged by, 350, 352; HHH's presidential prospects (1976) and, 377, 379, 380; HHH's vice presidential candidacy (1964) and, 204, 206, 208, 211, 215; JFK assassination and, 181–82; Kennedys resented by, 151, 152; LBJ and, 218; remarriage of, 417n27; RFK assassination viewed by, 282; as Senate spouse, 59, 60; as senator, 386; as vice presidential spouse, 233, 235, 241, 248, 252, 268, 273, 274

Humphrey, Nancy (daughter), 15, 16, 18, 24, 59, 151, 158

Humphrey, Olive (aunt), 25

Humphrey, Ralph Wadsworth (brother), 3, 9, 10, 11, 13, 160, 208, 211, 258

Humphrey, Robert (son), 59, 133, 190, 192, 258

Humphrey, Robert Ford (uncle), 9

Hungary, 122

Hunt, E. Howard, 366

Hunt, Lester, 96

Hunter, Croil, 35

Hussein, king of Jordan 168

Hyneman, Charles S., 15, 17, 19, 20

immigration, x, 87–89, 108, 219

Independent Citizens Committee of the Arts, Sciences, and Professions, 42

India, 79–80, 81, 103, 104, 110, 176, 235

Indochina, 80, 82, 109–10

Indonesia, 81, 251, 256, 263, 264

inflation, 310, 372, 381, 383; in developing nations, 104; during Ford's presidency, 373; full employment linked to, 385, 386; during Nixon's presidency, 310, 347; during postwar years, 53; poverty aggravated by, 365, 369, 370, 371

Ingersoll, Robert G., 11

International Ladies' Garment Workers' Union (ILGWU), 42, 56, 275, 319

Interstate Commerce Commission (ICC), 176

Iran, 41

Iraq, 138

Israel, 50, 122, 136–38, 168, 176, 347, 356, 359, 387; Egyptian overtures to, 385, 390; Yom Kippur War against, 365

Istomin, Eugene, 393

Italy, 170, 171, 172, 253

Jackson, Andrew, 18

Jackson, Henry M. "Scoop," 351, 377, 378

Jackson, Jesse, 390

Japan, 21, 110, 306

Jarman, Dabney, 369

Javits, Jacob, 180

Jaworski, Leon, 367–68, 370

Jefferson, Thomas, 5, 10, 18, 27, 51

Jenkins, Walter, 194, 200, 201, 203, 204, 205, 238

Jenner, William, 130

Jiang Jieshi (Chiang Kai-shek), 111, 112, 235

Job Corps, x, 217

John Birch Society, 213

Johnson, Claudia Alta "Lady Bird" Taylor, 98, 182, 198, 203, 205, 273, 391–92; on campaign trail, 214; HHH admired by, 194; LBJ's mistreatment of, 216; Eugene McCarthy and, 204

Johnson, Luci Baines, 98, 205, 241, 273

Johnson, Lynda Bird, 98, 205

Johnson, Lyndon B. (LBJ), 113, 142, 170; abusiveness of, 215–16; as anti-Communist, 99; antiwar movement misunderstood by, 260, 296; approval ratings of, 255; civil rights backed by, 100, 124, 125, 130–31, 176, 182–83, 184, 187, 188, 189, 192, 280; civil rights retreat by, 220–22; Cronkite's outburst viewed by, 270; as dealmaker, 97; death of, 364; defense buildup proposed by, 134; at Democratic National Convention (1956), 119–20; at Democratic National Convention (1960), 153; Democratic National Convention (1968) and, 291, 292–93; FDR backed by, 99; filibuster reform opposed by, 123, 131, 177; Gulf of Tonkin episode misrepresented by, 224, 266, 268–69; HHH praised by, 116, 120, 254; HHH's admiration for, 99–100, 132, 269–70, 347, 364; HHH's emotional dependence on, 241, 289, 295; HHH's presidential candidacy (1960) promoted by, 149; HHH's presidential candidacy (1968) and, 275–76, 278, 287, 300, 307, 308, 309, 319–21, 324, 330, 334; HHH's similarities with, 98–99; HHH tormented by, 131, 258, 259, 283, 286, 289, 295, 305, 307, 309, 311, 313, 324, 326–28, 389; insecurities of, 203, 206, 207, 214, 218, 324; jealousy of, 203, 208; JFK assassination and, 182; JFK's presidential candidacy opposed by, 147–48; jury trial dispute and, 126–27; liberals disdained by, 182, 183; McCarthy's Vietnam policy differences with, 205; McGovern's candidacy viewed by, 361; Nixon's underhandedness viewed by, 325, 326, 331; North Korean attack viewed by, 81; oil and gas interests backed by, 94–95, 100; paranoid behavior of, 215, 218, 228, 249, 260, 267, 324; personal wealth of, 99, 133; philandering by, 197; presidential ambitions of, 98, 144, 146, 147, 150, 155; presidential library of, 347; reelection of (1964), 214; reelection campaign abandoned by (1968), 274, 284; reelection concerns of, 199; ruthlessness of, 96; as Senate majority leader, 114; as vice president, 204, 205, 219; as vice president–elect, 159–60; as vice presidential candidate (1960), 155, 158; vice presidential candidates considered by (1964), 193–200, 201, 203–5; as vice presidential prospect (1956), 118–19; Vietnam plank dispute (1968) and, 296–98; Vietnam policies of, x, 173, 205, 222–48, 250, 251–57, 261, 265, 272–74, 284–90, 295, 302–3, 309, 315, 316–17, 318, 321–28, 349; voting rights backed by, 220; vulgarity of, 195, 216, 221, 309

Johnson, Paul, 198

Johnson, Rebekah Baines, 98

Johnson, Sam, 98, 139

Joint Chiefs of Staff (JCS), 163, 174, 175, 223, 266, 273, 290; misjudgments of, 256; Vietnam escalation backed by, 270

Joint Committee on Reduction of Nonessential Expenditures (Byrd Committee), 67, 68–69, 75

Joint Economic Committee (JEC), 372, 373, 374

Jones, Jim, 329

Jordan, 168

Jordan, Hamilton, 384

Judd, Walter H., 21, 23, 43, 113, 173

Kampelman, Maggie, 182

Kampelman, Max, 91, 153, 182, 204, 351, 379, 414n31, 438n39; as anti-Communist, 85, 86, 105, 106; at Democratic National Convention (1956), 117–18, 119; as HHH's legislative director, 43, 85–86; HHH's presidential candidacy (1968) and, 275, 277; HHH's vice presidential candidacy (1964) and, 193, 195; HHH's work ethic viewed by, 250

Kasherman, Arthur, 30

Katzenbach, Nicholas, 178, 221, 269, 315

Kazin, Alfred, 243

Keating, Kenneth B., 177, 213

Kefauver, Estes, 60, 74, 78, 88, 96, 97, 106, 123; jury trial dispute and, 126, 127; as presidential candidate (1952), 89–90, 91, 92; as presidential candidate (1956), 117, 118; as vice presidential prospect (1956), 119, 120

Keith, A. M. "Sandy," 246–47

Kelly, Ed, 4, 6, 33

Kelm, Douglas, 43, 44

Kelm, Edgar, 26, 33

Kempton, Murray, 107, 313

Kennedy, Edward M. (Ted), 282, 311, 332, 343, 383; Chappaquiddick incident and, 339, 340; as presidential prospect (1968), 293, 294–95, 297, 299; as presidential prospect (1972), 350, 351; as presidential prospect (1976), 376; vice presidential nomination declined by (1968), 292, 301, 302; vice presidential nomination declined by (1972), 360, 361

Kennedy, Jacqueline Bouvier, 145, 169, 182

Kennedy, John F. (JFK), 104, 109, 118, 194, 203, 279, 303, 309, 391; arms control and, 163, 173, 174, 175; assassination of, 181–82, 195, 355; Berlin crisis and, 165; civil rights policies of, 176, 177, 178–79, 181, 185; Cuba invasion authorized by, 164; Cuban missile crisis and, 170–73; education aid backed by, 164; family wealth of, 133, 149, 150; HHH contrasted with, 161; HHH's foreign policy advice to, 167, 169; jury trial dispute and, 127; Peace Corps established by, 162; philandering by, 197; posthumous tributes to, 207, 282; as presidential candidate (1960), 143–55, 156, 157–58, 215, 284, 305; as Senate candidate (1952), 156; as vice presidential prospect (1956), 119–20, 145; Vietnam policies of, 222, 223, 225

Kennedy, Joseph P., 149, 150, 213

Kennedy, Robert F. (Bobby; RFK), 147, 149, 151, 155, 157, 208, 234, 303; assassination of, 281–82, 355; as attorney general, 160, 176, 177, 187, 188, 209; during Cuban missile crisis, 172; at Democratic National Convention (1964), 207; HHH's jibe at, 280; LBJ disdained by, 195; during midterm elections (1966), 247; as presidential candidate (1968), 271, 275–76, 278, 279, 281, 283, 287, 293, 295, 301, 312; as presidential prospect (1968), 240, 242, 246, 248; as Senate candidate, 205, 213, 214; vice presidential ambitions of (1964), 195, 196; as vice presidential prospect (1968), 241, 242, 246, 248, 255; Vietnam War viewed by, 238, 265

Kenny, Elizabeth "Sister," 36

Kent State shootings, 342

Kerr, Robert, 416n10

Khan, Mohammed Ayub, 238

Khmer Rouge, 342, 374

Khrushchev, Nikita, 108, 136, 211; arms control and, 173–74, 175; Berlin occupation viewed by, 138, 140–41; Berlin Wall authorized by, 165–66, 168; Cuba invasion and, 164; Cuban missile crisis and, 170–73, 175; on Soviet nuclear arsenal, 139–40; Stalin denounced by, 134; US visit sought by, 141–42

Kiesinger, Kurt Georg, 253

Kilgore, Harley, 77–78

Kim Il Sung, 80

King, A. D., 178

King, Coretta Scott, 157, 259, 356

King, Cyril E., 60

King, Edward, 201

King, Martin Luther, Jr., 282, 303, 390; antiwar efforts of, 255, 259; arrests of, 157, 178, 271; assassination of, 276–77; March on Washington led by, 180; Mississippi credentials fight (1964) and, 200, 201, 203; Selma-to-Montgomery march led by, 219–20; voter registration drive by, 128

King, Martin Luther, Sr., 157–58
Kirkpatrick, Evron, 15, 18, 21, 22, 24, 25, 29, 148, 275, 438n39
Kirkpatrick, Jeanne, 438n39
Kissinger, Henry, 323, 333, 340, 362, 365, 374, 382, 392
Kleindienst, Richard, 366
Kline, Marvin L., 21, 22–23, 29–30
Knowland, William, 87, 97, 125
Knutson, Harold, 57
Komer, Robert, 252
Kopechne, Mary Jo, 339
Korean War, 66, 73, 74, 75, 77, 80–82, 90, 108; public frustration with, 92, 222, 261; United Nations' backing of, 227
Kosygin, Alexei, 226, 228, 235, 251, 283, 339
Krim, Arthur, 307, 308
Krock, Arthur, 61, 138, 234
Kuchel, Thomas, 160, 179, 180, 184, 190, 192
Ku Klux Klan, 98, 180, 198, 213
Kupcinet, Irv, 390
Kuznetsov, Valery, 139
Ky, Nguyen Cao, 225, 236, 237, 239, 240, 252, 262–63, 264

Lacy, Virgil P., 192
Lafayette, Gilbert Du Motier, marquis de, 254
Lafever, Ernest, 142
La Follette, Robert, 56
Lance, Bert, 385
Landrum-Griffin Act (1959), 144
Lansdale, Edward, 222–23, 224, 237
Laos, 109, 110, 238, 326, 349, 375
Lawrence, David, 4, 199, 201, 280
League of Nations, 79
Lee, Rudolf, 67
Legislative Reorganization Act (1946), 68, 70
Lehman, Herbert, 72, 74–75, 88, 96, 97
Lehrer, Tom, 219
LeMay, Curtis, 319
Lemnitzer, Lyman, 163

Lennen & Newell (L&N; advertising agency), 368–69
Levin, Sander, 293
Lewis, Anthony, 131, 353, 377
Lewis, Fulton, Jr., 67
Liddy, G. Gordon, 366
Lie, Trygve, 337
Limited Test Ban Treaty (1963), x, 163, 175, 207–8, 212, 300
Lincoln, Abraham, 6, 18, 78, 87, 356, 391, 393
Lindsay, John, 351
line-item veto, 365
Linowitz, Sol, 274
Lippmann, Walter, 139, 285, 313
Lisagor, Peter, 219
literacy tests, 152, 177, 179, 217
Lodge, Henry Cabot, Jr., 66, 156, 157, 237
Loeb, James, Jr., 40, 42, 49
Loeb, John L., 368
Logan Act (1799), 442n55
Long, Huey, 14, 16
Long, Russell, 16, 63, 74, 83, 183, 275
Longshoremen's union, 144
Lon Nol, 374
Lord, Miles, 417n26
Loughery, Thomas, 195–96
Louisiana State University (LSU), 2, 15
Lowenstein, Allard K., 269, 320, 414n31
Lucas, Scott, 3, 4, 51, 60, 62, 69, 73, 78
Lucey, Patrick, 144
Lundeen, Ernest, 25
lynching, 2, 45, 50, 52, 64, 67, 100, 101, 102, 161

Macalester College, 24, 338
MacArthur, Douglas, 80, 81, 82, 99
MacGregor, Clark, 343, 344–45
Macmillan, Harold, 167, 174
Maddox, Lester, 255, 273, 294
Maeterlinck, Maurice, 123
Magnuson, Warren, 313

Maguire, Richard, 278

Mailer, Norman, 260, 304

Malaya, 82

Malaysia, 251, 263

Malenkov, Georgi, 108

Manchester Union-Leader, 353

Mann, Robert, 128

Mansfield, Mike, 96, 97, 159, 160, 322, 383, 427n61; Civil Rights Act (1964) and, 183, 184–85, 187, 188, 190, 191; NATO force reductions proposed by, 347; as vice presidential prospect (1964), 197, 199; Vietnam War opposed by, 223, 226, 228, 234, 236, 240, 345

Mao Zedong, 372

Marcos, Ferdinand, 234, 235

Marder, George, 52

marijuana, 355

Marshall, Fred, 57

Marshall, George C., 42–43, 93

Marshall, Thurgood, 260, 268

Marshall Plan, 42–43, 48, 49, 54, 56, 77, 254

Marshall Plan for the Cities, 336, 378

Martin, Joseph, 128

Mayo, Robert, 113

Mazey, Emil, 347

McCarran, Pat, 76, 87–88, 106

McCarran Internal Security Act (ISA; 1950), 76–78, 105–6

McCarran-Walter Immigration and Nationality Act (1952), 87–89, 108

McCarthy, Abigail, 194

McCarthy, Eugene, 122, 156, 206–7, 208, 210, 230, 278–79, 292, 302, 304, 307; as ADA official, 43, 44, 47; as congressional candidate (1948), 57; HHH endorsed by (1968), 322, 329, 332, 335, 336, 389; HHH's presidential candidacy (1960) backed by, 143; HHH's presidential candidacy (1968) snubbed by, 313; HHH's vice presidential efforts (1956) backed by, 91, 117, 118; JFK disliked by, 154, 279; LBJ vilified by, 205; as

presidential candidate (1968), 261, 268–70, 271–72, 275–76, 279–84, 289, 294–95, 297, 298, 300–301, 303, 312, 320, 362; as presidential candidate (1972), 351; as Senate candidate (1958), 132; Senate reelection of (1964), 214; Senate retirement announced by, 339, 344; as vice presidential prospect (1960), 153, 155; as vice presidential prospect (1964), 194–95, 197, 198, 203–5, 268; Vietnam War viewed by, 198, 205, 228, 239, 287, 295

McCarthy, Joseph R., 93, 94, 97, 119; censure of, 107; HHH's denunciation of, 77, 78; Red Scare ignited by, 76; RFK's work for, 195, 213

McClosky, Herbert, 20, 21, 22, 23

McCloy, John J., 162, 163

McCone, John, 141, 229

McConnell, John, 281

McCord, James W., 361

McCormack, John W., 6, 207, 217

McCulloch, William, 183, 191

McDivitt, James, 218

McFarland, Ernest, 94

McGovern, George: as Food for Peace director, 105, 173; HHH's presidential candidacy (1976) encouraged by, 376, 379; as HHH's protégé, 105, 122, 173, 312; as House candidate, 121; as nomination reform chairman, 342; as presidential candidate (1968), 287, 292, 295, 297, 298, 300, 303; as presidential candidate (1972), 351, 352–63, 389; as Senate candidate, 173, 312; vice presidential nomination declined by, 301; Vietnam War opposed by, 228, 230, 295, 297, 342, 348, 356, 362, 365

McGovern, Terry, 358, 361

McGrath, J. Howard, 2, 21, 51

McGrory, Mary, 241

McIntyre, Thomas, 269

McKinney, Frank, 91

McMahon, Brien, 72, 91

McNamara, Robert, 182, 206, 229, 251, 265; appointment of, 160; Cuba quarantine proposed by, 171; HHH allied with, 163, 247; Pentagon Papers commissioned by, 349; protestors vs., 250; vice presidential ambitions disclaimed by, 194; Vietnam skepticism of, 241, 245, 261

McPherson, Harry, 309

McWilliams, Carey, 33

Means, Gardner C., 73

Meany, George, 152, 153, 196, 275, 296, 346, 362, 380

Medicaid, 214, 217

Medicare, 214, 217, 313, 328, 346, 347, 364, 365

Mein Kampf (Hitler), 108

Meir, Golda, 138, 168, 387, 388

Menshikov, Mikhail, 139

Meredith, James, 177

Merrill, Robert, 392–93

Michel, Robert, 421n65

Mikoyan, Anastas, 140

Miller, William E., 196, 212, 213

Milliken, Eugene, 75

minimum wage, 121, 152, 163, 369

Minneapolis: anti-Semitism in, 33; crime and corruption in, 21–22, 23, 29, 30–31; housing shortage in, 32; milling industry in, 21; polio epidemic in, 36; racial discrimination in, 33

Minneapolis and St. Louis Railroad, 29

Minneapolis Morning Tribune, 29, 36, 37, 58

Minneapolis Railroad Brotherhoods, 28

Minneapolis Star-Journal, 22, 29, 37, 49, 67

Minneapolis Times, 29, 37, 49

Minneapolis Veterans' Trailer Housing 31–32

Minnesota Formula, 33

Minnesota Jewish Council, 24

Mintener, J. Bradshaw, 29, 30, 37, 38

Mississippi Freedom Democratic Party (MFDP), 198–203, 204, 205

Mitchell, Clarence, 186, 188, 190

Mitchell, John, 306, 323, 366, 370

Model Cities Program, 246, 347

Modern Corporation and Private Property, The (Berle and Means), 73

Mondale, Walter F. (Fritz), ix, 206, 379, 387, 388, 389, 391; HHH eulogized by, 392, 393; as HHH's campaign comanager (1968), 277, 280; as Minnesota attorney general, 158; Mississippi credentials fight (1964) and, 200, 201, 202; as presidential prospect (1976), 376; as senator, 216, 247; as student activist, 44; as vice presidential candidate (1976), 381–82, 383; vice presidential nomination declined by (1972), 360; Vietnam War opposed by, 350

Monroe Doctrine, 170–71

Monroney, Allmer Stillwell "Mike," 275

Moos, Malcolm, 338

Morgan, Charles P., 181

Morgan, Edmund, 245

Morgan, Edward P., 181

Morrison, John, 351

Morse, Wayne, 164, 184–85, 274; anti-Communist efforts backed by, 86, 105; antilynching bill sponsored by, 63–64; Vietnam War opposed by, 232, 239, 240, 281, 298, 426n48

Morton, Thruston, 270

Mothers against the War, 260

Moursond, A. W., 203

Moyers, William (Bill), 192, 204, 228, 231, 283, 316

Moynihan, Daniel Patrick, 220–21

Mudd, Roger, 304

Multiple Independently Targetable Re-Entry Vehicles (MIRVs), 340, 347, 365

Mundt, Karl, 182, 421n66

Murk, George E., 22

Murphy, Charles, 296, 309

Murray, James, 60, 65, 72, 88, 96, 97, 103

Murray, Philip, 44, 85

Muskie, Edmund, 295, 298, 382, 391; as presidential candidate (1972), 348, 350, 351, 352–54; as vice presidential candidate (1968), 301–2, 310, 319, 330, 332, 333, 337; vice presidential nomination declined by (1972), 361

Muskie, Jane, 337, 353

Mussolini, Benito, 80

Mutual Security Act (1951), 103, 108

Mutual Security Act (1954), 136

Myers, Francis, 4, 51, 72

Myrdal, Gunnar, 62

Naftalin, Arthur, 15, 21–22, 24, 29, 41, 42, 46, 85

Nagy, Imre, 122

Najarian, John, 386

Napolitan, Joseph, 320

Nasser, Gamal Abdul, 122, 137, 168

National Association for the Advancement of Colored People (NAACP), 24, 34, 102, 127–28, 192, 385, 390

National Citizens Political Action Committee, 42

National Committee for a Sane Nuclear Policy (SANE), 135, 260

National Committee on Fair Play in Bowling Alleys, 35

National Defense Authorization Act (NDEA), 134, 164

National Emergency Civil Rights Mobilization, 71

National Housing Act (1949), 64–65

National Labor Relations Board, 113

National Liberation Front (NLF; Viet Cong), 223, 236, 263, 264, 265, 285, 287, 295, 296, 318, 323–24, 327; HHH's denunciations of, 238, 239, 242, 243, 252, 253; popular support for, 262, 266; Tet offensive by, 270; US barracks attacked by, 225–26

National Mobilization to End the War in Vietnam, 291, 299

National Security Council (NSC), 171, 218, 224, 225, 226, 229, 235, 296

National Student Association, 250

National Youth Administration, 98

Nazism, 17

Nazi-Soviet Pact (1939), 76, 79

Negro Family, The (Moynihan), 220–21

Nehru, Jawaharlal, 79

Nelson, Gaylord, 117, 144, 230, 360, 376

Nestingen, Ivan, 145

Netherlands, 253

New Deal, x, 5, 28, 35, 67, 68, 90, 91, 93, 98, 219, 328; HHH's thesis on, 17–18; opposition to, 94; Republican support for, 50

New Democratic Coalition, 343

New Republic, 240

Newspaper Guild, 54

Newsweek, 287

New York City, 374

New York Post, 46

New York Times, 61, 134, 142, 192, 219, 243–44, 283–84, 310, 354; civil rights coverage by, 178; HHH endorsed by (1968), 319; Pentagon Papers published by, 349

New Zealand, 110

Niles, David K., 3

Nitze, Paul, 142

Nixon, Richard M., x, 90, 110, 121, 123, 288, 300, 382, 389, 392; busing moratorium urged by, 354; "Checkers" speech by, 93; executive privilege claimed by, 365; inauguration of, 337; law-and-order rhetoric of, 299, 322; minimum income proposed by, 340; nonalignment viewed by, 135; political prophecies by, 247; as president-elect, 337; as presidential candidate (1960), 146, 149, 156, 156, 157, 158, 305, 307; as presidential candidate (1968), 287, 288, 289, 290, 292, 302, 305–6, 308, 310–13, 316–31, 333–36; as presidential candidate (1972), 358, 361–63; resignation of, 370–71; as vice president,

Nixon, Richard M. (*continued*)
  219; Vietnam negotiations undermined
  by, 322, 323, 325, 328, 333; Vietnam
  policies of, 340–41, 348, 350, 363; wage
  and price controls imposed by, 347; War
  Powers Act vetoed by, 366; Watergate
  scandal enveloping, 366–68, 370
nonalignment, 79, 135
North Atlantic Treaty Organization
  (NATO), 81, 168, 172, 347; conservative
  opposition to, 77; Eisenhower's
  command of, 89, 90, 92; HHH's support
  for, 79, 108, 112; West German
  membership in, 112, 167
North Korea, 176, 270
Northwest Airlines, 35
Novak, Robert, 445n66
Nuclear Non-Proliferation Treaty (1968),
  163, 175, 312, 347
Nugent, Patrick, 273

O'Brien, Lawrence: as DNC chairman,
  307, 342–43, 359; as HHH's campaign
  manager (1968), 283, 286, 293, 295, 297,
  302–3, 307, 308, 311, 314, 316, 320; as
  JFK's aide, 149, 277
Ochab, Edward, 167
O'Connor, Patrick, 153, 274
O'Donnell, Kenneth, 195, 199–200, 279,
  295
O'Dwyer, Paul, 319, 329
O'Dwyer, William, 49
Office of Economic Opportunity, 301,
  365
Office of Strategic Services (OSS), 222
oil and gas depletion allowance, 75, 100,
  149, 194, 212, 360
Olds, Leland, 94–95
O'Mahoney, Joseph C., 126
O'Neill, Thomas P. "Tip," ix, 388, 393
One World (Willkie), 23
Operation Chaos, 260
Operation Mongoose, 173
Operation Rolling Thunder, 226, 245

Organization of American States (OAS),
  231
Oswald, Lee Harvey, 181

Paine, Thomas, 10
Pakistan, 104, 111, 176
Panama Canal Treaty (1977), 384, 389–90
Park Chung Hee, 258
Pathet Lao, 375
Paul VI, Pope, 253, 256
Peace Corps, x, 161–62, 217, 233, 301,
  313, 393
Pearson, Drew, 285, 288, 334
Pentagon Papers, 349
People's Republic of China. *See China*
Perpich, Rudy, 376, 386, 388, 393
Peru, 168
Pescadores (Penghu) Islands, 111, 112
Peterson, Hjalmar, 117
Peterson, P. Kenneth, 156, 157
Philippines, 111, 235, 251
Philipps, Rufus, 223, 224
Phillips, George, 22, 28
Phouma, Souvanna, 238
Pillsbury, John, 29
Pillsbury Company, 103, 104
Pioneer Women, 387
Poland, 41, 108
poll taxes, 2, 50, 67, 100, 101, 102, 124, 152,
  161, 177
Pompidou, Georges, 254
Popular Front, 28, 40, 44, 45, 46, 47, 53
Porter, Jack, 98
Porter, Paul, 59
Porter, Sylvia F., 216
Potter, Philip, 349
Prague Spring, 290
Presidential Council on Equal
  Opportunity (PCEO), 216, 221
Profiles in Courage (Kennedy), 145
Progressive (magazine), 240
Progressive Citizens of America (PCA),
  42, 43
Progressive Party, 3, 53, 76

Prohibition, 11
public housing, 61, 65, 72, 152, 280
Public Press, 30
Pulliam, Eugene, 250, 277
Purtell, William A., 94

Quie, Albert, 388

Railroad Union Brotherhood, 47
Randolph, Jennings, 296
Rauh, Joseph, Jr., 146, 152, 153, 177, 186,
    190, 414n31; as ADA cofounder, 42, 49;
    as anti-Communist, 107; antiwar efforts
    of, 259; at Democratic National
    Convention (1948), 2, 3; at Democratic
    National Convention (1956), 118; as
    HHH's liaison to liberals, 255–56, 257;
    Mississippi credentials fight (1964) and,
    199–202
Rayburn, Sam, 3, 6, 98, 114, 118, 123; at
    Democratic National Convention
    (1956), 119; at Democratic National
    Convention (1960), 154, 155
Read, Benjamin, 315, 339
Reagan, Ronald, 305, 376–77, 380
Reconstruction, 125, 186
Reconstruction Finance Corporation, 72
Reddy, Helen, 389
Red Scare, 76
Reedy, George, 99, 131, 203, 204, 217–18
Rehnquist, William, 347
Reive, Emile, 55
Republican Party: African American
    support for, 124; HHH courted by, 23;
    HHH's overtures to, 29; HHH's split
    with, 38–39; Minnesota dominated by,
    1, 21, 25, 41, 50; New Deal support
    within, 50; party platform of (1952),
    90–91
Reston, James, 165, 191, 203, 359, 383;
    HHH praised by, 277, 336, 347–48, 376,
    380; HHH's electability doubted by,
    283; HHH's troubles viewed by, 243–44,
    246, 247–48, 280–81

Reuther, Walter, 44, 123, 221; as ADA
    cofounder, 42; HHH's vice presidential
    candidacy (1960) backed by, 152, 153;
    Kefauver's vice presidential candidacy
    (1956) backed by, 118, 119; Mississippi
    credentials fight (1964) and, 199, 200,
    201, 204
Ribicoff, Abraham, 160, 300
Richardson, Elliot, 366, 367
Rielly, John E., 223, 225, 227, 236, 240, 241,
    274
right-to-work laws, 64, 131, 152, 329
Robertson, A. Willis, 63, 184
Robinson, Jackie, 299
Rockefeller, Nelson, 177, 301, 305, 323, 371,
    382, 392
Rolvaag, Karl, 143, 145, 173, 216, 246–47
Romania, 41
Romney, George, 259, 305
Roosevelt, Eleanor, 42, 49, 78, 119, 123,
    142, 143
Roosevelt, Franklin D. (FDR), 1, 5, 11, 14,
    16, 97, 142, 303, 372; death of, 28; as
    governor, 95; HHH's admiration for, 18,
    22; LBJ's admiration for, 203; leftist
    support for, 40; as presidential candidate
    (1940), 25; as presidential candidate
    (1944), 27, 50, 54
Roosevelt, Franklin D., Jr., 149, 151
Roosevelt, Theodore, 56
Rosenberg, Ethel, 76
Rosenberg, Julius, 76
Rosenberg, Marvin, 147, 193
Rostow, Eugene, 325
Rostow, Walt, 265, 317, 318, 324, 327;
    Nixon's Vietnam meddling and, 325,
    328, 331; Vietnam plank dispute (1968)
    and, 296, 297
Round Table of Christians and Jews, 34
Rowe, James (Jim), 61, 159, 316, 327–28,
    379, 427n61; as HHH's campaign
    manager, 142–43, 146, 151, 153, 277, 319,
    332; HHH's vice presidential ambitions
    (1964) and, 193–94, 196–97, 201, 204, 205

Royall, Kenneth, 180, 181
Ruckelshaus, William, 367
Rural Electrification Agency, 213, 365
Rusk, Dean, 166, 174–75, 206, 218, 229, 234, 235, 236, 239, 251, 265, 272, 275, 309, 318, 420n41; appointment of, 160; arms control housed under, 163; bombing halt opposed by, 310, 326; Committee of Principals led by, 225; HHH sidelined by, 225, 331; as Nixon apologist, 321, 332; Schlesinger's criticism of, 257; Vietnam negotiations urged by, 324, 326; Vietnam plank dispute (1968) and, 296, 297, 308
Russell, Richard, 118, 131, 160, 324; arms control opposed by, 163, 174; civil rights bills opposed by, 52, 62, 64, 72, 102, 183, 187–92; filibuster reform opposed by, 123; HHH disparaged by, 60, 99; jury trial dispute and, 126–27; LBJ allied with, 94, 95
Ryan, Edwin, 30–31, 32

Sachs, Alexander, 325
Sadat, Anwar, 385
St. Lawrence Seaway Project, 121
St. Olaf's College, 44
Salinger, Pierre, 281
Sanders, Carl, 379
Sanford, Terry, 301, 302, 319, 342
Saudi Arabia, 136
Scaife, Richard, 448n18
Schlesinger, Arthur, Jr., 42, 107, 146, 147, 197, 217, 293, 313, 318; antiwar views of, 259, 284–85, 301; HHH confronted by, 256, 257; HHH endorsed by (1968), 329
Schultze, Charles, 385
Schwartz, Harry, 134
Schwerner, Michael, 423n23
Scott, Hugh, 446n87
Selective Service Act (1948), 73
Selective Service Act (1950), 86
Semple, Robert, 313
Sevareid, Eric, 243

Seymour, Gideon, 21, 23
Shannon, William V., 136, 245, 350
Shastri, Lal Bahadur, 235
Sheehan, Neil, 439n70
Shelley v. Kramer (1948), 213
Sherman, Norman, 274, 304, 330, 344, 351, 368
Sherman, William T., 213
Shields, James, 46, 48, 53
Shipstead, Henrik, 25
Shivers, Allen, 93
Short, Robert (Bob), 118, 119, 278, 307, 308, 378–79
Shriver, Sargent, 157, 162, 301, 361
Siegenthaler, John, 176
Simms, William (Bill), 59
Simon, Paul, 376
Simon, William, 374
Sirhan, Sirhan B., 434n56
Smathers, George, 119, 127, 280, 321, 331
Smith, Alfred E., 11
Smith, Betty, 390
Smith, Howard, 76, 181, 183, 192
Smith, Margaret Chase, 76
Smith, Stephen, 293, 294
Smith Act (1940), 105–6
Social Security, 180, 361; Eisenhower's view of, 93, 121; health insurance decoupled from, 65; HHH's support for, 55, 65, 72, 148, 152, 160, 328, 365, 373; Truman's support for, 61
Soil Bank Program, 115–16, 121
Solberg, Carl, xi
Solomonson, Bruce (son-in-law), 151, 158, 271, 293
Solomonson, Victoria (granddaughter), 158–59, 332
Sorensen, Theodore, 295
Southeast Asia Treaty Organization (SEATO), 111
Southern Christian Leadership Conference, 128
Southern Manifesto, 123–24, 364
South Korea, 109

Soviet Union, 53, 82, 99, 103, 104, 110, 238, 365; Austrian State Treaty signed by, 112; containment of, 42, 43, 45, 57, 79, 81, 90, 91, 109; during Cuban missile crisis, 170–73, 175; Czechoslovakia invaded by, 290, 295; Eastern Europe policies of, 41; economy of, 175; food crisis in, 165; Hungarian uprising crushed by, 122; Middle East meddling by, 347; Nazi pact with, 76, 79; North Korean aggression linked to, 80, 82, 108; nuclear arsenal of 135, 139–40, 162–63, 173, 174, 252, 253; space program of, 164; *Sputnik* launched by, 131, 134, 135, 142; US hot line with, 174, 212; Vietnam War and, 226, 227, 228, 232, 240, 242, 244–45, 321, 350; during World War II, 20

Space Council, 225

Spain, 104

Spannaus, Warren, 271

Sparkman, John, 91, 92

Spivak, Lawrence, 61

Spock, Benjamin, 259

Sprague, Lucien, 29

SST (supersonic transport), 346

stagflation, 371

Stalin, Joseph, 45, 80, 81, 108, 134

Starkey, Frank, 28

Stassen, Harold E., 15, 21, 23, 25, 27, 54, 135; as presidential candidate (1948), 50; as presidential candidate (1952), 90

states' rights, 2, 3, 4, 188, 191

States' Rights Party (Dixiecrats), 53, 71, 91, 92, 170

Stennis, John, 128–29, 155, 185, 367

Stern, Isaac, 392–93

Stettinius, Edward R., Jr., 28

Stevenson, Adlai, 58, 107, 123, 139, 159, 182, 303; death of, 218; Nixon viewed by, 156; as presidential candidate (1952), 90–94, 336; as presidential candidate (1956), 116–19, 120–21, 194, 336; as presidential prospect (1960), 142, 143, 144, 146, 147, 150, 153, 154–55; as vice presidential prospect (1964), 196

Stevenson, Coke, 98

Stewart, Milton, 3–4

Stokes, Carl, 300

Stokes, Thomas L., 405n20

Strategic Arms Limitation Treaty (SALT), 175, 339, 340, 347, 361, 365

Strauss, Robert, 379, 380

Student Nonviolent Coordinating Committee (SNCC), 198, 259

Students for a Democratic Society (SDS), 291

Students for Democratic Action (SDA), 44

Subversive Activities Control Board (SACB), 76, 77, 105

Suez Crisis, 122, 136

Suharto, 256, 263

Sukarno, 256, 263

Sullivan, Gael, 45

Symington, Stuart, 118, 146, 147, 150, 154, 155

Syndicate (criminal group), 21, 29, 30

Syria, 138, 168, 347

Taft, Robert, 60, 64, 66, 81, 90, 92; filibuster reform opposed by, 101; as Foreign Relations chairman, 97; as Senate majority leader, 94

Taft, William Howard, 401n52

Taft-Hartley Labor Management Act (1947), 44, 50, 54, 85, 113; HHH's opposition to, 56, 64; right-to-work laws authorized by, 131; Truman's veto of, 48, 49

Taiwan (Formosa), 80, 111–12, 242, 347

Talmadge, Herman E., 187

Taylor, Glen, 53

Taylor, Maxwell, 223, 224, 229, 272, 324

Teamsters union, 22, 31, 44, 144

Teller, Edward, 175

Tennessee Valley Authority (TVA), 212, 214

Tet Offensive (1968), 270, 272

Textile Workers, 55

Thailand, 81, 111

Theory of the Leisure Class, The (Veblen), 73

Thi, Nguyen Chanh, 225

Thieu, Nguyen Van, 239, 252, 264, 272, 306, 323, 325, 327, 350, 374; accession of, 236, 262; HHH rebuffed by, 262, 266; Ky vs., 263; peace efforts resisted by, 323, 325, 328, 331

Thomas, Elbert, 66

Thompson, Anton (Tony), 340

Thompson, Llewellyn, 226–27, 228

Thomson, James (Jim), 237, 238, 240

Thousand Days, The (film), 207

Thurmond, J. Strom, 53, 128, 186, 190, 213, 305, 387

Thye, Edward, 27, 50, 60, 83, 90, 94, 132

Till, Emmett, 411n41

Time, 57, 69, 107, 113–14, 279, 336

Tito, Joseph, 61

To Secure These Rights, 2, 4, 45, 51

Trade Expansion Act (1962), 252

Treaty of Tlatelolco (1967), 273

Trotsky, Leon, 405n18

Troyanowsky, Oleg, 139

Trujillo, Rafael, 427n6

Truman, Harry S., 1, 28, 103, 142, 170, 212, 219, 271, 277, 303, 372; antitrust exemption vetoed by, 74; appointments by, 83–94, 94–95; armed forces desegregated by, 53; Byrd Committee opposed by, 70; civil rights advocates dismissed by, 6; civil rights report backed by, 2, 4, 5, 45, 48, 176; death of, 364; Fair Deal proposed by, 61; foreign policy of, 41, 42, 43, 44, 46, 97, 309; HHH and, 143, 312; Indochina policy of, 109; Korean War conducted by, 80, 81, 89, 222; loyalty program established by, 76; MacArthur dismissed by, 82; McCarran Act vetoed by, 78; McCarran-Walter Act vetoed by, 89; military buildup backed by, 74; presidential campaign ended by (1952),

90; as presidential candidate (1948), 7, 48, 50, 51–52, 54, 56, 57–58, 61, 295; steel mills seized by, 86–87; Taft-Hartley Act opposed by, 64; as vice presidential candidate (1944), 27

Truman Doctrine, 42, 49

Trust Agricultural Political Education (TAPE) fund, 368–69

Turkey, 42, 79, 89, 104, 168, 252; US missiles in, 170, 171, 172

Twain, Mark, 251

Tydings, Millard, 70

Tyler, Gus, 275

Udall, Morris (Mo), 377, 378

Ulbricht, Walter, 165

unemployment, 72, 73, 210, 346, 347, 371, 373, 385; among blacks, 101, 211, 220

Union for Democratic Action (UDA), 40, 41–42

United Arab Republic, 168

United Auto Workers (UAW), 42, 319

United Democrats for Humphrey (UDH), 277

United Electrical Workers, 25, 86

United Farm Workers, 356

United Labor Committee for Political Action (ULC), 28, 32

United Mine Workers (UMW), 144

United Nations, 140, 149, 174, 226, 231, 232, 244, 372; during Cuban missile crisis, 171–72; Goldwater's opposition to, 214; HHH's support for, 22, 28, 56, 79, 278, 312, 342; during Korean War, 80, 81, 227; Republican support for, 50; Taiwan expelled from, 347

U.S. Steel, 74

United Steelworkers, 87

University of Minnesota, 32, 338, 342, 387

Unruh, Jesse, 195, 293, 312, 332, 336

Untermeyer, Louis, 243

Urban League, 34, 386

urban renewal, 61, 65, 72, 214, 246, 347

Valenti, Jack, 205, 233, 234, 237, 240, 245, 249, 302

Vance, Cyrus, 316, 318, 324, 333

Vandenberg, Arthur, Jr., 212

Van Dyk, Ted, 193, 274, 277, 282, 286, 287, 316, 358, 368

Veblen, Thorstein, 73

Veterans Administration (VA), 35

Vietnam, x, 171, 219; China and, 226, 227, 228, 231, 232, 238, 240, 242, 245, 350; Democratic National Convention (1968) debate over, 295–97; Eisenhower's policy toward, 111, 222; France stymied in, 109–10; France's warnings on, 218; Goldwater's views on, 210, 214; Gulf of Tonkin Resolution and, 198, 224, 266, 268–69, 342; HHH's views on, 223–48, 250–57, 259–67, 271–73, 283–89, 292, 293, 298, 302–3, 307–9, 312, 315–18, 333, 340–41, 345, 349–50, 365, 374–75; LBJ's views on, x, 173, 205, 222–48, 250, 251–57, 261, 265, 272–74, 284–90, 295, 302–3, 309, 315, 316–17, 318, 321–28, 349; McCarthy's views on, 198, 205, 228, 239, 287, 295; public opposition to war in, 243, 247, 248, 259–60, 265, 271, 341

Vinson, Fred, 86

Voice of America, 108

voting rights, 2, 45, 101, 123, 124, 125–28, 178, 202

Voting Rights Act (1965), x, 214, 220, 347

Wage Stabilization Board (WSB), 86, 87

Wagner, Robert, 63–64, 65

Wagner, Robert, Jr., 119, 197

Wagner Act (1935), 64, 105

Walker, Daniel, 427n29

Walker, Frank, 25–26

Wallace, DeWitt, 338

Wallace, George, 178, 213, 220; as presidential candidate (1964), 186, 188; as presidential candidate (1968), 305, 308, 310, 311, 312, 313, 319, 320, 329, 333,
334–35; as presidential candidate (1972), 351, 353, 354, 355, 358; as presidential candidate (1976), 377

Wallace, Henry A., 3, 26, 27, 28, 41; Communist influence imputed to, 46, 47, 51; Marshall Plan denounced by, 43; as presidential candidate (1948), 45, 48, 49, 51, 53, 55, 57–58; Truman Doctrine denounced by, 42

Wallace, Lurleen, 273

Wallgren, Monrad (Mon), 407n38

Walter, Francis, 87–88

War Manpower Commission, 20

War on Poverty (Humphrey), 194

War Powers Act (1973), 365–66

Warren, Earl, 50, 101, 217, 218

Warsaw Pact, 122

Watergate scandal, 361–62, 366–69, 370

Waters, Herbert, 103, 149

Watson, Marvin, 218, 274, 282, 297

Wattenberg, Ben, 344

Watts riots (1965), 220

Weaver, Robert, 260

Weaver, Warren, 246

Wechsler, James, 46, 49, 245, 256

Weinberg, Sydney, 275

Welch, Ronald, 21

Wells, Samuel G., 37

Welsh, Matthew, 343

Welsh, William, 275, 295, 296, 297, 315, 438n39

Westmoreland, William C., 236, 237, 239, 252, 262, 265, 266, 270

Wheeler, Earle, 229, 265–66, 272, 308, 324

Wherry, Kenneth S., 67

White, Edward, 2nd, 218

White, Kevin, 360

White, William Allen, 20

White, William S., 431n33

White Citizen's Councils, 102, 124

Whitman, Ann, 411n36

Whitmore, Willet, 382

Wicker, Tom, 242–43, 261, 285, 297, 358, 380

Wildavsky, Aaron, 439n71
Wilkins, Roy, 127, 192, 199
Williams, G. Mennen, 118
Williams, John T., 190
Willkie, Wendell, 23, 25
Wilson, Fred, 37
Wilson, Harold, 251–52, 253
Wilson, Woodrow, 10, 11, 18, 401n52
Wilson and Company (meatpackers), 156
Wirtz, Willard, 275, 278, 316
Wishart, Robert, 25, 28, 30, 32, 38, 40, 55
Wofford, Harris, 157, 176
Woodrow Wilson International Center for Scholars, 339
Works Progress Administration (WPA), 18, 19
World Bank, 346
World War II, 20, 254, 306

Wright, J. Fielding, 53
Wylie, Alexander, 404n37
Wyman, Eugene, 195, 352

Yarborough, Ralph, 127, 181, 294
yellow-dog contracts, 64
Yom Kippur War, 365
Yorty, Sam, 277, 312, 358
Young, Stephen, 211, 230
Youngdahl, Luther K., 1, 34, 45, 50, 57, 83–84, 112
Youngdahl, Oscar, 21
Youngdahl, Reuben K., 34
Young Democratic Farmer-Labor (YDFL) clubs, 44
Youth International Party ("Yippies"), 291
Yugoslavia, 61, 104

Ziegler, Ronald, 361